AF709308

Contributions to Economics

The series *Contributions to Economics* provides an outlet for innovative research in all areas of economics. Books published in the series are primarily monographs and multiple author works that present new research results on a clearly defined topic, but contributed volumes and conference proceedings are also considered. All books are published in print and ebook and disseminated and promoted globally. The series and the volumes published in it are indexed by Scopus and ISI (selected volumes).

Georgios I. Zekos

Artificial Intelligence and Competition

Economic and Legal Perspectives in the Digital Age

Springer

Georgios I. Zekos
International Hellenic University
Serres, Greece

ISSN 1431-1933 ISSN 2197-7178 (electronic)
Contributions to Economics
ISBN 978-3-031-48082-9 ISBN 978-3-031-48083-6 (eBook)
https://doi.org/10.1007/978-3-031-48083-6

© The Editor(s) (if applicable) and The Author(s), under exclusive license to Springer Nature Switzerland AG 2023
This work is subject to copyright. All rights are solely and exclusively licensed by the Publisher, whether the whole or part of the material is concerned, specifically the rights of translation, reprinting, reuse of illustrations, recitation, broadcasting, reproduction on microfilms or in any other physical way, and transmission or information storage and retrieval, electronic adaptation, computer software, or by similar or dissimilar methodology now known or hereafter developed.
The use of general descriptive names, registered names, trademarks, service marks, etc. in this publication does not imply, even in the absence of a specific statement, that such names are exempt from the relevant protective laws and regulations and therefore free for general use.
The publisher, the authors, and the editors are safe to assume that the advice and information in this book are believed to be true and accurate at the date of publication. Neither the publisher nor the authors or the editors give a warranty, expressed or implied, with respect to the material contained herein or for any errors or omissions that may have been made. The publisher remains neutral with regard to jurisdictional claims in published maps and institutional affiliations.

This Springer imprint is published by the registered company Springer Nature Switzerland AG
The registered company address is: Gewerbestrasse 11, 6330 Cham, Switzerland

Paper in this product is recyclable.

To my lovely wife
ΣΟΦΙΑ ΠΡΟΔΡΟΜΟΥ ΓΡΗΓΟΡΙΑΔΟΥ
& to my son
ΙΩΑΝΝΗΣ-ΜΑΡΙΝΟΣ ΖΕΚΟΣ

Contents

1 Introduction 1
References 8

2 Defining Competition and AI Developments 9
2.1 Introduction 9
2.2 The Role of Algorithms 13
2.3 Capitalism and Competitiveness 15
2.4 Antitrust/Competition Law 16
2.5 Competition and MNEs 21
2.6 Competition and IPRs 28
2.7 Competition Law, Competition, and Democracy 32
2.8 AAI and Legal Liability 38
2.9 Algorithms Versus Human Decision-Making 47
2.10 Dynamic Pricing Algorithms 48
2.11 E-Platforms Power 55
2.12 Digitalization and Digital Entrepreneurship 56
2.13 AI in Transportation and Competition 58
2.14 AI, Competition, and Torts 59
2.15 Humans Versus AAI Humanoids 62
References 64

3 Competition and Governance 67
3.1 Introduction 67
3.2 Technology and Governance 69
3.3 Algorithmic Governance 70
3.4 Cyberspace and AAI 73
3.5 Supply Chains and AAI 75
3.6 Governance and Public Administration 77
3.7 Knowledge Management 78
3.8 MNEs and Knowledge 80
3.9 AI Monetary Policy, Banks, and Competition 81
3.10 Cyber-Currencies and MNEs 83

3.11 Autonomous Private Money and Competition . . . 85
3.12 AI and Securities . . . 89
3.13 Regulating Cryptocurrencies . . . 91
3.14 Crypto Assets, Cryptocurrencies, and Monetary Policy . . . 94
3.15 Digitalization, DMA, MiCA, and Competition . . . 96
References . . . 100

4 Competition, Market Power, and Politics . . . 101
4.1 Identifying Market Power . . . 101
4.2 Antitrust and Politics . . . 106
4.3 AI Technologies and Labor . . . 112
4.4 Labor and Antitrust . . . 114
4.5 Lobbying and Competition . . . 120
4.6 Bank Antitrust . . . 125
4.7 Algorithmic Management and Labor Competition . . . 129
Bibliography . . . 132

5 Antitrust and AAI . . . 135
5.1 Introduction . . . 135
5.2 The Rule of Reason Competition Approach . . . 136
5.3 Competition and the Regulatory Authority of the Actors . . . 139
5.4 Cartels and Competition . . . 141
5.5 False Advertising and Competition . . . 142
5.6 Platforms and Competition . . . 145
5.7 EU's Artificial Intelligence Act . . . 155
5.8 Digital Monopolies . . . 158
5.9 Competition in the Digital Era . . . 163
5.10 Antitrust Complexities . . . 166
5.11 Mergers and Competition . . . 170
5.12 Deficiencies of Modern Antitrust Enforcement . . . 179
5.13 AI and Market Self-Correcting . . . 181
5.14 Predatory Pricing . . . 182
5.15 Antitrust in the AAI Era . . . 185
5.16 Defining Competitive Process . . . 188
References . . . 199

6 USA Versus EU Competition . . . 201
6.1 Introduction . . . 201
6.2 Chicago Versus Harvard . . . 201
6.3 EU Versus USA . . . 203
6.4 Developments on Competition Law . . . 217
References . . . 222

7 **Chicago School, Harvard School, and New Brandeis Movement** . . . 223
7.1 Introduction . . . 223
7.2 Chicago School Versus Harvard School . . . 224
7.3 Post-Chicago School . . . 249
7.4 Populists and Competition . . . 249
7.5 New Brandeis Movement . . . 250
Bibliography . . . 255

8 **Formalism in Competition** . . . 257
8.1 Introduction . . . 257
8.2 Formalism and the Rule of Reason . . . 259
8.3 Formalism and Anticompetitive Effects . . . 261
8.4 The Effects-Based Approach and Legal Formalism . . . 261
References . . . 266

9 **Digital Transformation of EU and Competition** . . . 267
9.1 Introduction . . . 267
9.2 EU Materialization . . . 268
9.3 EU Functioning . . . 269
9.4 Federalism in EU Via ECJ . . . 272
9.5 AI Advancement and Competition . . . 275
9.6 Political Integration of EU . . . 277
9.7 Digitizing EU . . . 281
9.8 AI Networking . . . 285
9.9 The European Court of Justice is Rejected as the Single EU Supreme Court . . . 286
9.10 AAI Transforms EU and Competition . . . 288
9.11 Conclusions . . . 290
Bibliography . . . 291

10 **Digital Economy and Competition** . . . 293
10.1 Introduction . . . 293
10.2 AI and HRM . . . 294
10.3 Legal Personality of Corporations . . . 295
10.4 Knowledge and Development in Digital Economy . . . 298
10.5 Competition in China . . . 301
10.6 Digital Providers . . . 302
10.7 E-Commerce and Competition . . . 305
10.8 Market Concentration in the Platform Economy . . . 307
10.9 Competition in Digital Platforms . . . 309
10.10 Standardization and Competition . . . 313
10.11 Digital Providers and Competition . . . 314
10.12 DMA and Competition . . . 321
10.13 Data and Competition . . . 331
10.14 Regulating Platforms . . . 336
10.15 Data, Information, and IPRs . . . 339

10.16 Market Power and Platforms . . . 343
10.17 Digital Power of Platforms in Digital Sovereignty and Data Ruling . . . 345
10.17.1 Introduction . . . 345
10.17.2 Digital Sovereignty . . . 347
10.17.3 Digital Power of Platforms . . . 350
10.17.4 Data Ruling . . . 351
10.18 *Ex Ante* Competition Rules and Platforms . . . 353
10.19 Competition and Platform Work . . . 357
References . . . 359

11 AAI and FDI . . . 361
11.1 Introduction . . . 361
11.2 Outlining FDI . . . 362
11.3 FDI Developments . . . 364
11.4 Digital FDI . . . 369
11.5 AI and MNEs . . . 371
11.6 Venture Capital and AI . . . 374
11.7 E-MNEs . . . 375
References . . . 378

12 Econometric Analysis of Digital Economy and Competition . . . 379
12.1 Introduction . . . 379
12.2 Property Rights and Competition . . . 382
12.3 Liability and AI . . . 384
12.4 Authorship Under AI and AAI Technology . . . 387
12.5 Copyright and AAI . . . 390
12.6 Patents and AAI . . . 396
12.7 Trademarks and AAI . . . 403
12.8 Methodology and Data . . . 408
12.9 Empirical Results . . . 409
12.9.1 FDI Inflows/GDP OLS Model 1/Model 1a Beta Coefficients . . . 409
12.9.2 Linear Results Model 2/Model 3 Regarding FDI Inflows . . . 410
12.9.3 FDI Outflows OLS Model 4/ Model 5 Beta Coefficients . . . 411
12.9.4 FDI Inflows Model 6 OLS Standardized Variables . . . 411
12.10 Conclusions . . . 414
Bibliography . . . 415

13 Conclusions . . . 417
References . . . 426

Chapter 1
Introduction

Artificial intelligence (AI) is used to handle big data for calculations, forecasts, and predictions and so AI performs high-speed precise calculations and predictions for critical decisions. Moreover, developments in technology are leading to the production of machines with the intellectual capacity to produce and invent, just like humans. Currently, AI robot technology cannot carry out complex thinking and application of principles which will be implemented by the forthcoming advanced artificial intelligence (AAI) technology producing AAI humanoids.

It is argued that since AI can simulate the activities of the human brain and interact autonomously with human beings, many fields where AI is implicated need to be regulated, so as to balance the demand for progress with ethical issues and human rights. Moreover, it is worth noting that AI is distinguished by autonomously generated inventions and is self-assembling which means automating duties that normally require human intelligence. [1] AI is applied to a variety of business models such as business-to-business (B2B), business to-consumer (B2C), back-office infrastructure, and business applications, for example, web search engines, e-mail Spam detectors, or any business application where forecasting is a central task in decision-making or enhances the value of data.

Cyberspace and new technology generate software attaching innovation, functionality, and inventiveness of new utilities, which are more electronic than mechanical with traditional understanding, and so the intangibility of expression of software should not be an obstacle in patentability, as long as there is an invention expressed electronically in a virtual world with real-world expressions and effects. Thus, a software invention can be a new physical or electronic and virtual object, which performs a new function, either electronic/virtual or physical, with virtual effects felt in the real world. If the invention is a process that generates electricity, then we

[1] Clark D. Asay, Artificial Stupidity, 61 WM. & Mary L. Rev. 1187, 1190 (2020) (defining AI as computing systems that perform tasks that normally would require human intelligence).

© The Author(s), under exclusive license to Springer Nature Switzerland AG 2023
G. I. Zekos, *Artificial Intelligence and Competition*, Contributions to Economics,
https://doi.org/10.1007/978-3-031-48083-6_1

define the invention as a new function that is identifiable by a new physical or physically understandable virtual object.

AI technology extends human competencies and so current AI-powered technologies collaborate with humans towards improved decision-making and improving the quality of life. It seems that AI technology is much better than the human brain when carrying out certain tasks. To that extent, AAI will bring forward AAI humanoid robots digitizing human's behavior and, in the distant future, even replacing humans and so generating an AAI society living in an electronic configuration. Will AAI creatures have the capability to appear in a material mode and alongside to be transformed into a spiritual one transferred into a parallel universe like Gods in Greek mythology? It could be said that from the time that AAI creatures depart from any human control, their capabilities will be further higher than humans and, of course, humans will have a big problem of survival. Of course, the capabilities of any AAI world will not be more advanced than God's capacity due to the fact that humans generate any new developments such as AI technology based on their brain capacity designed by God for human's material life. On the other hand, the AAI brain might function even at unthinkable levels which will generate another electronic world spiritually at another level than the current material humans' world. [2]

AI inventions generated by AAI systems will produce virtual results transferable into the human world as well via AI tools. Technological innovation is altering private markets around the globe and new developments in digital technology have generated new opportunities for subtle and evasive forms of anticompetitive behavior by private corporations.

Seeing that AI programs become more complex, the capacity to understand a given output shrinks. AI decision-making technology automates many undertakings involving learning and devising solutions in a number of business processes and virtually every industrial setting. [3] Moreover, AAI will generate the autonomous AAI society which will function out of any humans control and so shaking the foundations of the conventional human world. Additionally, AAI society is supposed to operate in a more objective way for the good of AAI society and not for any AAI elite and so not substantiating that AAI technology will be merely a new instrument of expression outspreading the existing misgivings of human society rather than being a new device for the emergence of a new unprejudiced global society.

---

[2]See Georgios I. Zekos, Advanced Artificial Intelligence and Robo-Justice, 2022 https://link.springer.com/book/10.1007/978-3-030-98206-5, Georgios I. Zekos, Political, Economic and Legal Effects of Artificial Intelligence: Governance, Digital Economy and Society, 2022 https://link.springer.com/book/10.1007/978-3-030-94736-1 , Georgios I. Zekos Economics and Law of Artificial Intelligence : Finance, Economic Impacts, Risk Management and Governance, 2021 https://link.springer.com/book/10.1007/978-3-030-64254-9

[3]Roberto Verganti, Luca Vendraminelli & Marco Iansiti, Innovation and Design in the Age of Artificial Intelligence, 37 J. Prod. Mgmt. 212, 215–19 (2020).

Software increases speed and accuracy and so speedy digitalization has altered the manner international players interact, advancing new opportunities for international and bilateral cooperation and underlining the role of the emergent players within global governance. Hence, the use of algorithmic devices by international public authorities is altering the manner in which norms are made and enacted because the digital turn not only empowers specific players and corporate forms of expertise but also machine-learning modules and data analysis are imported into the domain of global governance. Thus, the introduction of AI systems and the emergence of the AAI society will instigate the advancement of AAI global governance managed by AAI humanoids.

It is argued that an algorithm can be efficiency-enhancing and pro-competitive [4] being a "sequence" of operations transforming an input into an output. Algorithmic tasks are those for which the path to the solution is clear and straightforward tasks for which an algorithm occurs. Moreover, due to algorithmic opacity, there is a need for information disclosures of AI algorithms. Algorithms play a noteworthy role in the business model of platforms such as Facebook and TikTok, sharing economy including Uber, Airbnb, video games, and many others. Also, algorithms support corporations in their monitoring, prevention, and detection efforts benefiting from widely available know–how on screening for anticompetitive behaviors.

Computational intelligence techniques and algorithms empower a computational analysis of big data sets making known patterns used to inform and advance decision-making and so building smart computational intelligence techniques.

Intellectual property (IP) is information springing from the human mind covering any intelligence, skills, code, writing, or data. In addition, IP outlines a corporation's structures and strategies in knowledge and information management. It has to be taken into account that a company's capacity to preserve and protect its IP is vital to the corporation success for the reason that proprietary technology is a pro, a corporation can have. Hence, corporations are extending IP strategies by protecting information about their products and services from the outside world. The existence of IPRs has an impact on competition and so if the rationale of a patent is exclusively to block the development of other companies, the acquisition of such a patent is abusive. It is worth mentioning here that the discovery of natural matters using a new technique cannot be considered an invention and so the invention should bring forward a new practical usage of the new substance or a new product either material or intangible. [5]

It has to be taken into account that technology neutrality signifies a central principle of law-making and regulation in areas that touch on emerging technology and so neutrality necessitates that law-makers consider which activities to regulate,

---

[4]OECD (2023), Algorithmic Competition, OECD Competition Policy Roundtable Background Note, www.oecd.org/daf/competition/algorithmic-competition-2023.pdf.

[5]Zekos, 'Patenting Biotechnology', 2004 (1) The Journal of Information, Law and Technology (JILT). http://elj.warwick.ac.uk/jilt/04-1/zekos.html . New citation as at 15/07/04: http://www2.warwick.ac.uk/fac/soc/law/elj/jilt/2004_1/zekos/ Georgios I. Zekos, Patent Law in the Cyberspace Era, Electronic Communication Law Review 9: 281–309, 2002.

notwithstanding whether the regulated person or entity uses a particular technology to undertake those activities. It is worth noting that a regulation regulates people's behavior and the behavior of machines is regulated to the extent that machine behavior affects people's behavior. Moreover, the point of regulation is the effect of behavior on society or on other people that is the focus of regulation. [6]

Copyright and other IP rights incentivize creativity and innovation by granting the author a monopoly to exploit the work for a certain period of time but in the existing copyright system. Presently, AI is not taken into consideration as a possible creator of a literary, artistic, and musical work.

The most traditional form of IP protection for new technologies is a patent by conferring the exclusive right to discoveries to its inventors. Patent law is built upon a fundamental assertion that only substantial inventions receive patent protection while minor improvements remain in the public domain. There is a need for a balance between the necessity to promote innovation and the recognition that imitation and advancement through imitation are both crucial to invention itself and for a competitive economy. [7] Patent protection is granted for the reason that the social benefits derived from such protection outweigh the social costs of patents' limited monopoly.

Trademark law is an understanding that trademarks offer social value and so should be legally protected. Trademarks permit consumers to reward the brands they like and deny patronage to the ones they do not and so producers are incentivized to preserve consistent, high standards for their merchandises. Thus, trademark law prevents others from using deceptively similar marks on their merchandises and so those producers do not have to worry that their investment will be unproductive.

It is worth mentioning here that the antitrust laws were accepted against the economic concentration and the escalation of industrial trusts such as the railroad's control. [8]

Competition does not only take part in product markets but also in capital markets. The competition encompasses an effort to lower costs per unit of output with the goal to get more profit and market share by enhancing the rate of return of the capital invested. Furthermore, competition has to be a device for diffusing economic power and dispersing power in the market sphere which means that complete competition must be protected and so competition law-based judgments should build a unified internal market governed by the rules of free and undistorted competition. Antitrust should concentrate on protecting and stimulating competition, which is finally about economic outcomes.

First of all, the antitrust objective is to promote competition and a competitive market maximizes "consumer welfare" which means that antitrust law pursues

[6] Bert-Jaap Koops, Should ICT Regulation Be Technology-Neutral?, in 9 Starting Points For Ict regulation: Deconstructing Prevalent Policy One-Liners 77 (Bert-Jaap Koops et al. eds., 2006).

[7] Bonito Boats, Inc v Thunder Craft Boats, Inc, 489 US 141, 146 (1989).

[8] Lina Khan, The Ideological Roots of America's Market Power Problem, 127 Yale L.J.F. 960, 965 (2018).

conduct diminishing competition and damaging consumer welfare by increasing price, plummeting output, or offering consumers inferior options. [9] Thus, antitrust averts those same subordinates from coordinating among themselves to strengthen their own hand in negotiations.

It has to be taken into account that the passage of the antitrust laws reflected a constitutional adoption in industrial and national policy indicating that lawmakers passed antitrust laws so as to codify a set of foundational principles. On the other hand, the loss of antitrust is a threat not just to open markets and fair competition, but to the core of democratic governance. [10]

Antitrust law stipulates the rules for market capitalism. Moreover, antitrust law is the "residual regulator" of market power and so the body of law that governs unless it is superseded by more tailored competition rules. Antitrust law advances the free market, while privacy laws unsettle the free market to protect consumers. Increasingly global and digital economy portrays a new antitrust landscape. Furthermore, antitrust law does not specify ex ante exactly what a company is permitted or prevented to do and so it is opting instead to evaluate, ex post, a company's compliance with a general directive to keep away from restraining market output. Moreover, antitrust law is "standards-based" and the outlines of its standards are specified by politically insulated courts. Furthermore, antitrust law treats the complaints triggering adverse market consequences such as a lack of competition and does not simply handle the symptoms of diminished competition via increased prices and downgraded quality. It is worth noting that regulation causes a lessened role for the antitrust laws and so when the government makes rules about price or output, market forces no longer govern and so antitrust is put aside. Hence, as an industry experiences deregulation or removal from the regulatory process, antitrust emerges as the residual regulator.

It has to be taken into account that laws are not fast and flexible enough to manage systems that are continually changing and whose uses are multiplying. Moreover, regulation encompasses political efforts under which different interest groups compete to gain the most from a specific government policy and so regulation is procured by the industry and is intended and managed mainly for its benefit. [11] Antitrust law was generated out of political instability that arose from the industrialization of national economies. [12] Moreover, antitrust has grounded on political decisions

---

[9] Herbert Hovenkamp, Is Antitrust's Consumer Welfare Principle Imperilled?, 45 J. Corp. L. 65, 67 (2019).

[10] Harlan M. Blake & William K. Jones, In Defense of Antitrust, 65 Colum. L. Rev. 377, 381 (1965) (describing antitrust as "an integral part of the economic constitution of the United States"); William N. Eskridge, Jr. & John Ferejohn, Super-Statutes, 50 Duke L.J. 1215, 1217, 1231 (2001) (stating that "[t]he Sherman Act of 1890 . . . is a classic super-statute . . . or a law that can be considered "quasi-constitutional"); Thomas B. Nachbar, The Antitrust Constitution, 99 Iowa L. Rev. 57, 88–93 (2013) (describing antitrust as "a rule against private regulation . . . that is akin to private nondelegation, a constitutional doctrine").

[11] George J. Stigler, The Theory of Economic Regulation, 2 Bell J. Econ. & Mgmt. Sci. 3, 6 (1971).

[12] Hans B. Thorelli, The Federal Antitrust Policy: Origination of An American Tradition (1955).

embracing broad legal commands dealing with how governments and private individuals tackle various kinds of market activities. [13] It could be said that antitrust is a device for policing and managing private markets.

Additionally, Jonathan Kanter [14] said that "Antitrust promotes material progress, quality, and innovation, at the same time that it supports our democracy and preserves a society of choice and opportunity. Antitrust helps make us both prosperous and free." To that extent, the Sherman Act is enforced forcefully to prevent the illegitimate acquisition, maintenance, and extension of monopoly power by judging conduct on its merits, and based on the total course of conduct involved which means recognizing that the rationale of antitrust law is to protect competition.

The digital economy has revolutionized business patterns, products, services, communications, and social interactions. To that extent, the digital economy has become a priority for government policy and acceleration of measures for the digital development furthers competitiveness in all sectors of the national economy. Modern investment policy generates competitive advantages for attracting investments from digital MNEs offering strategic opportunities for digital development for a country by employing digital technologies into the global value chains. Digital technologies alter the competitive advantages of numerous countries by reforming the global economic pattern. AI is reforming production mode, organization mode, service mode, and innovation mode which means upgrading the industry and so advancing global value chain to expand digitally. Hence, digital technologies have a profound impact on manufacturing global value chain. [15] To that extent, Foreign direct investment plays a central role in accelerating digital development.

Digital platforms are multi-sided platforms establishing market presence and achieving scale at considerably lower costs which allows resourceful interactions between producers, developers, and consumers; superior to the traditional market structures. [16]

Governance denotes mechanisms of steerage that are institutionalized, regularized, and systematized by summarizing power rising to a specific level of reappearance. Besides, algorithmic governance implies the direction of human behavior by sequential computational procedures executed in a wide range of settings. [17] Likewise, platform governance is encompassing technical protocols,

---

[13] Axel Berger and Karl P. Sauvant, eds., Investment Facilitation for Development: A Toolkit for Policymakers (Geneva: ITC, 2021), https://www.intracen.org/publication/investment-facilitation-for-development-toolkitpolicymakers

[14] Jonathan Kanter, Antitrust Enforcement: The Road to Recovery https://www.justice.gov/opa/speech/assistant-attorney-general-jonathan-kanter-delivers-keynote-university-chicago-stigler Standard Oil Co. v. FTC, 340 U.S. 231, 248 (1951).

[15] Fu Q (2022) How does digital technology affect manufacturing upgrading? Theory and evidence from China. PLoS One 17(5): e0267299. https://doi.org/10.1371/journal.pone.0267299

[16] Parker, G., G. Petropoulos and M. Van Alstyne (2020) 'Digital platforms and antitrust', Working Paper 06/2020, Bruegel. https://www.bruegel.org/sites/default/files/wp_attachments/WP-2020-06-1.pdf

[17] Yeung K, Lodge M, eds. 2019. Algorithmic Regulation. Oxford, UK: Oxford Univ. Press.

ownership structures, laws, valuation practices, and other mechanisms of control reinforcing the need of digital intermediation, and exchange. The economic power of digital platforms is rising globally and they are accused of rising economic inequality and correlated negative social phenomena.

Digital technology has intensified a central matter of consumer protection such as privacy due to the fact that technology has augmented the amount and the ease by which personal data is collected, stored, and shared, leaving consumers in a weak position. Data has become a new element of production in manufacturing, a new engine to release the perspective of economic growth, accelerate the diffusion of knowledge, and boost the allocation of resources. It has to be taken into account that knowledge is the basis of new innovations that produce effectiveness and prolong competitive advantages.

Algorithms automate tasks that formerly had been performed by humans and the speed and accuracy of these digital algorithms have made them central to developing automated systems augmenting or replacing humans in a range of assignments. Moreover, courts are turning to various digital algorithms in an effort to investigate or even predict crime, along with making decisions concerning pretrial detention, parole, etc. Also, governments are beginning to use digital algorithms to govern social services programs, adjudicate claims for government benefits, and support regulatory functions. [18]

Price-setting algorithms from competing retailers collude and so causing costs for customers. [19] "Oligopsony" pricing happens when buyers agree to engage in joint purchasing negotiations and to propose a common purchase price to their suppliers and so preventing competition among buyers on input prices for the reason that the prices of raw materials and finished goods purchased for resale are a central element of buyers' overall costs. [20]

The aim of the current work is to give answers to the following questions by presenting the current understanding of competition and competition law and practice influencing the status of an economy. There is a detailed investigation of the matter of competition and AI with reference to the United States and EU and so identifying divergences and convergences regarding the principles upon which competition law and enforcement is grounded on. Also, there will be an economic

[18] Cary Coglianese & Lavi M. Ben Dor, AI in Adjudication and Administration, 86 Brook. L. Rev. 791 (2021); David Freeman Engstrom, Daniel E. Ho, Catherine M. Sharkey & Mariano-Florentino Cuéllar, Government By Algorithm: Artificial Intelligence In Federal Administrative Agencies 22–29 (2020), https://www-cdn.law.stanford.edu/wp-content/uploads/2020/02/ACUSAI-Report.pdf (examining the deployment of AI by federal agencies).

[19] Greg Rosalsky, When Computers Collude, NPR: Planet Money (Apr. 2, 2019, 7:30 AM), https://www.npr.org/sections/money/2019/04/02/708876202/when-computers-collude

[20] *In re* Beef Indus. Antitrust Litig., 907 F.2d 510, 515 (5th Cir. 1990) (stating that an oligopsonist "could form an alliance with other oligopsonists in the relevant market and attempt to depress prices and increase profits"). Peter J. Hammer and William M. Sage, *Monopsony as an Agency and Regulatory Problem in Health Care*, 71 Antitrust L.J. 949, 967 (2004) ("[L]ower input prices do not lead to lower consumer output prices.").

and a legal analysis of the topics taking into account the new developments in AI technology. Should the consumer welfare standard be abandoned? Should more stringent rules and regulations become the norm concerning competition? Does antitrust authorize large, powerful corporations as the primary mechanisms of economic and market coordination? Was the economics approach of the Chicago School a marketing mastermind degrading competition law role? Has competition enforcement become more "technocratic"? Will AI endorse current competition approaches by merely implementing competition practice or an objective competition will be imposed for the good of trade? Will AI generate first of all an objectively central understanding of competition? Will AI apply objectively to all cases of competition regardless of any political policy? Will AI utilize big data and apply competition to all cases regardless of any subjective consideration?

References

1. Asay, C. D. (2020). Artificial stupidity. *William & Mary Law Review, 61*, 1187, 1190.
2. Hovenkamp, H. (2019). Is antitrust's consumer welfare principle imperiled? *Journal of Corporation Law, 45*, 65, 67.
3. Khan, L. (2018). The ideological roots of America's market power problem. *Yale Law Journal Forum, 127*(960), 965.
4. Parker, G., Petropoulos, G., & Van Alstyne, M. (2020). *Digital platforms and antitrust* (Working Paper 06/2020). Bruegel. https://www.bruegel.org/sites/default/files/wp_attachments/WP-2020-06-1.pdf
5. Yeung, K., & Lodge, M. (Eds.). (2019). *Algorithmic regulation*. Oxford University Press.
6. Zekos, G. I. (2021). *Economics and law of artificial intelligence: Finance, economic impacts, risk management and governance*. Springer. https://link.springer.com/book/10.1007/978-3-030-64254-9
7. Zekos, G. I. (2022). *Advanced artificial intelligence and robo-justice*. Springer. https://link.springer.com/book/10.1007/978-3-030-98206-5
8. Zekos, G. I. (2022). *Political, economic and legal effects of artificial intelligence: Governance, digital economy and society*. Springer. https://link.springer.com/book/10.1007/978-3-030-94736-1

Chapter 2
Defining Competition and AI Developments

2.1 Introduction

Technological innovation produces new products and services providing new value to consumers. Thus, AI is an intangible capital asset that corporations may invest into and use to make output through a production function and so AI's applications such as autonomous vehicles, voice-recognition and speech-/text-generating systems, or trained neural networks to enhance business energy consumption, would depict AI's prospective to upsurge company productivity. The operative use of AI technologies brings about extra intangible assets such as datasets, company-specific human skills, and establishing new company processes. [1] Moreover, the governance of AI must advance the cooperation of the multiple stakeholders involved, expressly their interests, resources, and decision-making logics.

It has to be taken into consideration that technologies vary in their design, their markets, their implications, and the directness with which they engage with the law. Thus, the implementation of a new legal technology is the possibility that it modifies the substance of the law and taking place the technology in question affects the form of some legal rule, norm, principle, etc.

Furthermore, specific legal technologies such as AI and AAI are more possible to raise issues related to access to justice by reducing the cost of legal services, thereby improving access to justice, or consecutively offer devices only available to those who can afford them which means making access to justice less equal. As a consequence of the functional implications that are in their character, particularly

---

[1] Nordhaus, W.D. (2021). Are we approaching an economic singularity? Information technology and the future of economic growth. American Economic Journal: Macroeconomics 13(1), 299–332 Rammer, C., Czarnitzki, D., Fernández, G.P. (2021). Artificial Intelligence and Industrial Innovation: Evidence from Firm-Level Data. ZEW Discussion Paper No. 21-036.

© The Author(s), under exclusive license to Springer Nature Switzerland AG 2023
G. I. Zekos, *Artificial Intelligence and Competition*, Contributions to Economics,
https://doi.org/10.1007/978-3-031-48083-6_2

legal technologies are more likely to raise professional ethics-related design considerations [2] at least at the beginning of their employment in legal services.

It is worth mentioning here that the digital realm crosses the entire globe and so the source of power varies which means that the swing in power relationships is effectuated by the digital transformation of big data, blockchain technology, and AI. AI developments and algorithms are mainly advanced and employed by private players and so technologies offered by private companies, and the data bought from large data collectors, are being progressively replied upon by sectors such as intelligence agencies, the public and private banking system, and political parties. Essentially, the legal, economic, political, criminal, and military domains have undergone transformation as a result of the digitalization of the globe. Anyway, public–private partnerships, policy networks, and private governance all reflect the nature of a world in which the state is arguably no longer the central governing authority.

Present AI systems are software programs interacting with physical or digital environments and, which, by getting, collecting, and interpreting data; decide the best actions to take with the purpose of achieving a given objective. On the other hand, the forthcoming AAI systems will encompass humanoid robots acting like humans even with more capacities and abilities. Furthermore, the fast-growing improvements in the performance of AI in combination with the digital age have steered a range of new and exciting technologies expanding and enhancing access to creative works for the public.

New technological developments such as big data, blockchain technology, and algorithms raise questions concerning the regulation of such technologies. It is worth noting that innovation has to make certain productivity growth, augmented employment rate, and extensive consumer choice. To that extent, AI-based systems have outperformed medical specialists in diagnosing certain diseases.

Corporations have gradually embraced automated systems to set prices and track business transactions which means that market conduct has become more and more complex and swiftly varying, and markets have become gradually more networked and collaborative. [3]

In order to keep pace with the altering technologically advanced market background, antitrust authorities should augment their internal capabilities both to monitor and analyze markets with speed and accuracy and to identify prospective regulatory violations in demand of investigatory scrutiny.

It is worth noting that innovations in the digital domain are affecting the daily processes and interactions of people, educational institutions, corporations, and governmental organizations. Improvements in the digital domain such as in blockchain technology, big data, and machine learning are modeling the lives of

[2] William Lucy, 'Access to Justice and the Rule of Law' (2020) 40 Oxf J Leg Stud 377 (arguing for a more nuanced appreciation of the relationship between access to justice and the rule of law.).

[3] Herbert Hovenkamp, Monopolizing and the Sherman Act (2021), https://papers.ssrn.com Herbert Hovenkamp, The Looming Crisis in Antitrust Economics, 101 B.U. L. Rev. 489, 544 (2021)

people, organizations, and societies and so calling for operative governance to protect the basic interests and desires of these players. Instantaneously, the character of governance is also transforming which means that policy-making is moving away from top-down governance by the state toward more horizontal modes of governance. Thus, policy-making relies on interactions and societies and becoming increasingly governed by networks encompassing a diverse set of public and private players. It has also been recognized that the digital era is gradually fragmenting the playing field between governance actors.

AI-based technologies gradually substitute and complement humans in managerial tasks such as decision-making. AI enables machines to accomplish cognitive functions formerly linked with human minds and so AI alters the sources of competitive advantage. Hence, AI substitutes humans' cognitive capabilities when AI systems replace bankers in equity investment and take over from physicians in medical treatment. It could be said that current AI complements rather than substitutes humans' cognitive capabilities.

AI shifts the sources of competitive advantage and generates new persistent sources of competitive advantage which means that the adoption of AI in a competitive domain initiates substitution. Now, AI is used extensively to automate predictions concerning strategic decision-making and problem-solving tasks. AI systems have quasi-unlimited information processing capability offering better predictions than humans do. Presently, humans remain sources of sustainable advantage by combining and assimilating their capabilities with AI capabilities into uniquely complementary bundles. Krakowski et al. [4] argue that "people still matter, which confirms the RBV's traditional focus on human cognitive capabilities' continued relevance. Another key insight is that AI substantially changes the ways in which people make a difference."

Perfect competition is a market situation, which as a result of the free entry of a large number of previously competing corporations has evolved to the point of equilibrium where no further competition within the industry is probable.[5] G.I. Zekos thinks that competition is a situation where the market's environment allows businesses to enter, to compete and leave the market on equal footing and so the unbalance between the equality of footing of the corporations in a market shows the workable level of competition. Consequently, the workable level of competition varies rolling on a scale which reaches to the point not to cross the borderline drawn by the established principles of competition law to get into the uncompetitive field. It has to be taken into account that ease of entry defeats monopolization claims.[6] It has to be taken into consideration that competition law should prevent relocation

[4]Krakowski, S., Luger, J., & Raisch, S. (2022). Artificial intelligence and the changing sources of competitive advantage. Strategic Management Journal, 1–28. https://doi.org/10.1002/smj.3387 p. 24.

[5]Fama, E. and Laffer, A. (1972) The Number of firms and Competition, American Economic Review, 62(4), pp. 670–674.

[6]United States v. Syufy Enters., 903 F.2d 659, 666–669 (9th Cir. 1990).

through market power. Acceptance of welfare maximization and economic efficiency as the reference points for competition policy is still not unanimously accepted.[7]

It has to be taken into account that perfect competition is based on an absolute norm against inter-firm coordination while justifying a position to corporate consolidation and vertical restraints. Domination via vertical contracting became a viable business strategy. Moreover, the rule against horizontal coordination is an instrument of antitrust enforcement. On the other hand, relaxing antitrust enforcement against vertical restraints was a key goal of the Chicago School.

Effective competition is a vital driver of the growth and jobs strategy by removing restrictions and unwarranted market power and dynamically by promoting innovation and so increasing international division of labor and comparative advantage.

The established view of competition looks at competition as a course of allocating resources to their best possible use and through the instrument of price mechanism leads to an equilibrium where prices equal to marginal social costs of production.[8] On the one hand, competition can produce both positive and negative welfare effects in a local level by altering the *level* of incentives on offer and in state level by causing an increase in the quality and volume of FDI inflow through more effective and cost-efficient incentives. On the other hand, competition may aggravate poor incentive policies leading officials to employ ineffective motivation mechanisms or to recommend incentives that are greater than the net payback of the investment project to the host state.

It is worth noting that competition is based on the freedom to have allowance of rivalry in order to have a free trade in a free market and not a manipulated trade suitable for the sizable capital. It seems that Gerla [9] explains the business rivalry sense of "competition" as to the Sherman Act for the reason that legislators were also willing to accommodate various limits upon business rivalry. By the way, the Sherman Act did not prohibit corporations from merging into conglomerates.

It has to be taken into account that incentive competition inspires the establishment of business-friendly environments making probable the effective allocation of investment but there is concern about the transfer of resources from governments to

[7]Hamburg. J. Basedow, *Konsumentenwohlfahrt und Effizienz—Neue Leitbilder der Wettbewerbspolitik?*, 57 Wirtschaft Und Wettbewerb 712 (2007) (concluding that welfare and efficiency cannot be exclusive goals of competition policy and that "free competition" is a key policy goal in itself).

[8]McNulty, P.J. (1968) Economic Theory and The Meaning of Competition, Quarterly Journal of Economics, 82(4), pp. 639–656. Richardson, G.B.(1975) Adam Smith on Competition and Increasing Returns in A. Skinner and T. Wilson ed. Essays in Smith, A. Skinner and T. Wilson. Clarendon Press: Oxford, pp. 350–360. Schumpeter, J. (1934) The Theory of Economic Development, Cambridge, Mass: Harvard University Press. Schumpeter, J. (1942) Capitalism, Socialism and Democracy. New York: Harper and Row.

[9]Harry S. Gerla, Restoring Rivalry as a Central Concept in Antitrust Law, 75 Neb. L. Rev. 209, 211–22 (1996) (arguing that the ordinary language sense of "competition," supported by pre-Chicago judicial precedent and legislative history, denotes moment-to-moment business rivalry and not economic efficiency).

corporations through incentives.[10] Also, incentive competition leads to disproportionate business turnover and so businesses may moderate the "depth" of their investment in any one location, letting them to move and capitalize any incentive offers. In addition, incentive competition has been commended for inspiring the making of business-friendly environments and facilitating the competent allocation of investment.[11]

Likewise, freedom of competition covers the freedom of corporations to choose their action parameters besides market power might impede both freedom of choice between different suppliers and freedom to decide on corporations' action parameters in competition with other corporations.

It is worth noting that monopoly is perceived as an antithesis of competition.[12] On the other hand, competition apart from equating demands and supplies within the context of a given industrial structure and a given technology has to adjust both structure and technology to the new prospect created by global markets.[13] It could be argued that competition is interrelated with monopoly power and so the level of competition is balanced with the level of monopoly power. Moreover, competition promotes effectiveness. Can a corporation compete without monopolizing? A corporation cannot compete without monopolizing and so much of the global business is a mixture of competition and monopoly. Every act of competition on the part of a businessman encloses some degree of monopoly power in economic theory.[14]

2.2 The Role of Algorithms

Algorithms have become increasingly commonly utilized in many ways such as approximating human speech, assisting planes in flying, cars in driving, and predominantly those of the self-driving variety. Despite the fact that algorithms have become a part of daily life in many manners, their operation is behind the scenes.

---

[10] Williamson, J.G. (1997) *Globalization and inequality, past and present.* World Bank Research Observer 12, 117–35. Fisher, P., and Peters, A., (1996) "Taxes, Incentives and Competition for Investment", *The Region*, June 96. Wilson, J. (2001), "Welfare-Improving Competition for Mobile Capital." Department of Economics, Michigan State University, *Mimeo.*

[11] Charlton, A. (2003), "Incentive Bidding for Mobile Investment: Economic Consequences and Potential Responses", Technical Paper no. 203, OECD Development Centre, Paris.

[12] Smith, A. (1976) The Wealth of Nations. Oxford: Clarendon. Vickers, (1995) Concepts of competition, Oxford Economic Papers, 47(1), pp. 1–23. Waterson, M. (1984) Economic Theory of Industry. Cambridge: Cambridge University Press. Winter, S. G. (1984) Schumpetarian competition in Alternative Technological regimes, Journal of Economic Behaviour and Organisation, 5(4), pp. 287–320.

[13] Hayek, F.A. (1948) Individualism and Economic Order, Chicago: University of Chicago Press. Hawtrey, R.G. (1943) Competition from Newcomers, Economica, 10(new series: 37–40), pp. 219–222.

[14] Bresnahan, T.F., and Reiss, P.C. (1991) Entry and Competition in Concentrated markets, Journal of Political Economy, 99(5), pp. 977–1009.

Should algorithmically generated content be considered speech? Are the controllers of algorithms content providers or intermediaries? Should interferences be validated under which settings? Do the implications of the freedom of expression framework apply to algorithmically generated speech? It could be said that when liability is enforced for infringing algorithmic speech, the algorithmically generated content is given freedom of expression protection.

Information is central for social coordination and for governance due to the fact that digital data are the modern embodiment of information which means that the settings of the digital domain influence governance substantially. It has to be taken into account that there are a number of ways that algorithms interact with freedom of expression. Moreover, the usage of algorithms in how news and information is communicated to users has an effect on the right to receive information.

In the United States, courts have generally stated that search engine results constitute speech, despite the fact that search engine results simply present content provided by others. [15] Moreover, it is argued that algorithmic yield does not constitute speech as a result of it containing a low degree of expressiveness, or because it should be categorized as a communicative device under the First Amendment's functionality doctrine. On the other hand, a search engine's autocomplete utility along with a search engine's outcomes is forms of speech.

The Universal Declaration of Human Rights (UDHR) has formed the foundation of many human rights instruments safeguarding freedom of opinion and expression. Moreover, the Charter of Fundamental Rights of the European Union provides protection for the right to freedom of expression being exceptionally vital for the survival of a democratic society. [16]

It is worth noting that the capacity to "receive and impart information and ideas" through any media, "regardless of frontiers" denotes the application to all speech that crosses borders which means that speech that is transmitted over the cyberspace and via AI technology should be given the same freedom of expression protection as domestic speech, irrespective of the place of origination. Thus, many current forms of algorithmic speech originating from servers located in other countries are considered as speech.

Transparency and due process considerations are emerging in any case challenging antitrust by algorithm. The Wisconsin Supreme Court [17] rejected the challenge on the ground that the results from the algorithm were not determinative of the

[15] Zhang v. Baidu.com, Inc., 10 F. Supp. 3d 433, 435 (S.D.N.Y. 2014); Langdon v. Google, Inc., 474 F. Supp. 2d 622, 629–30 (D. Del. 2007); Search King, Inc. v. Google Tech., Inc., No. 02-1457, 2003 WL 21464568, at *3 (W.D. Okla. May 27, 2003).

[16] The Foundation of International Human Rights Law, U.N., https://www.un.org/en/sections/universal-declaration/foundation-international-humanrights-law/index.html Charter of Fundamental Rights of the European Union art. 11, Dec. 7, 2000, 2000 O.J. (C 364).

[17] State v. Loomis, 881 N.W.2d 749 (Wis. 2016) Nicole Gillespie, Steve Lockey & Caitlin Curtis, Trust in Artificial Intelligence: A Five Country Study (2021), https://assets.kpmg/content/dam/kpmg/au/pdf/2021/trust-in-ai-multiple-countries.pdf (reporting that in five countries, including the U.S., only 28 percent of survey respondents overall are willing to trust artificial intelligence and no

governmental judgment but simply an aid to a human decision. European General Data Protection Regulation regulates that businesses that are subjected to algorithmic tools deployed by antitrust authorities will enjoy at least some right to an explanation of how these algorithms work. [18] The GDPR stipulates for a right to a human decision, which will limit European antitrust authorities' ability to implement fully automated, "human-out of-the-loop systems" in the future. [19]

2.3 Capitalism and Competitiveness

Capitalistic market systems have shown an unparalleled competence to advance the growth of technological knowledge and its transformation into new, better, and more valuable products and more effective production processes. Capitalism has reached this target principally by combining decentralization with strong inducements for producing innovation, as innovators are rewarded by significant profit in ways in principal independent of the legal protection of monopoly rights. Is perfect competition the most efficient market structure? Profit is the key inspiration for technological innovation and competition works evenly well with respect to static efficiency and to advancing the invention of new technologies and products.[20]

Competitiveness is the aptitude of a country to operate resourcefully and productively in relation to other countries while maintaining living standards for its citizens high. First, from a macroeconomic perspective, competitiveness is the scale to which a country produces goods and services that meet the test of international markets while concurrently growing the real incomes of its people over the long term under free trade and fair market conditions in globalization. Second, at the microeconomic level, competitiveness is the competence to sell commodities gainfully and so a company in order to be competitive has to have lower prices offering products of better quality with better service than its competitors. Third, the international competitiveness of a country is the sum of the export performance of all national corporations.

The foreign activities of corporations moderate their dependence on the resources and factors of production available in their home country, and their competitiveness may move independently from the resources shaping the competitiveness of their home country. On the one hand, the competitiveness of countries rests on the

more than about 60% have confidence that business and government can "use and regulate antitrust and govern AI in the best interest of the public").

[18]Regulation 2016/679, OJ 2016 L 119/, Art. 13.

[19]Art. 22 ("The data subject shall have the right not to be subject to a decision based solely on automated processing, including profiling, which produces legal effects concerning him or her or similarly significantly affects him or her.").

[20]Karl Marx, 1 Capital: A Critique of Political Economy (Penguin Books 1976) (1867); Adam Smith, The Wealth of Nations (Prometheus Books 1991) (1776); Joseph A. Schumpeter, Capitalism, Socialism & Democracy (Harper & Bros., 2d ed. 1947).

quantity and quality of the immobile resources such as climate, land, and other natural resources, and most kinds of labor located within them implicating the knowledge level. On the other hand, the competitiveness of corporations is based on the kind of assets that are transferable by the corporations from country to country within them. In a world that is becoming more and more globalized and integrated, and in which the advantages of corporations derive from intangible assets such as technological level and knowledge involving AI that are evidently not tied to any specific location, home countries continue to exercise a strong influence on the advantages that corporations develop.

It has to be taken into consideration that there is a direct relationship between the competitive activities of the corporations that comprise a country's industrial force and the country's national competitiveness.[21]

2.4 Antitrust/Competition Law

Taking into account that law integrates the values of the society, it means that among the conflicted values the law legitimizes the amalgam which is considered to express in the best way the regulated matter. Any type of law involves interpretation when its content is unstipulated in an individual case of its application in order the general wording to apply in the specific events of an action. [22] To that extent, taking into consideration that competition is a complex essence involving the amalgamation and combination of many economic matters, competition law needs interpretation which means judgment of encompassed values and their contribution in avoiding anticompetitive process. Hence, competition law is a form of a normative system encompassing rules outlawing unjustified restraints of trade. Thus, competition law deals with value disagreements encompassing different interpretive attitudes towards the concept of competition and the values, purposes, interests, and principles captured in competition rules. [23]

It is well known that law is a normatively inflexible set of rules which enforcers have to apply and adjudicators particularize without lapsing their role. Due to neutrality and generality of law, law has to adjust to new knowledge and different market circumstances in order to acclimate different values which means that competition law has to tackle competition within new technological environments

[21] Francis, A., 1992. The process of national industrial regeneration and competitiveness. Strat Manage J 13 (Special Issue), 61–78.

[22] See A Marmor, Philosophy of Law , Princeton University Press, 2014. R Dworkin, Justice for Hedgehogs, Harvard University Press, 2011.

[23] R Dworkin, A Matter of Principle (Harvard University Press, 1985. R Dworkin, Law's Empire , Harvard University Press, 1986, pp. 45–53 (law invites a certain "interpretive attitude" according to which its users consider that it has a certain value, serves a certain interest or purpose or enforces some principle).

influencing values and trade. [24] Judges interpret the law not entering the policy domain which means that they state "what the law is" because they will lose their legitimacy and will be discredited as "doing politics and judicial activism" [25]. Judges' interpretation of competition law should lie in the true intention of the lawmakers. [26] On the other hand, it could be said that judges of Supreme Courts do and should rest their judgments on controversial cases on arguments of political principle generating presented. [27]

Antitrust laws stimulate fair competition. To that extent, antitrust laws also referred to as competition laws are statutes developed by the US government to protect consumers from predatory business practices. Moreover, antitrust and competition laws around the globe are rapidly advancing and corporations face new risks and challenges in keeping up with the complicated and transforming rules.

Is antitrust legislation a device to keep big enterprises from muscling out smaller competitors? Antitrust laws are applied to a wide range of business activities, embracing but not restricted to market allocation, bid rigging, price fixing, and monopolies. Antitrust legislation could be a device to keep big corporations from muscling out smaller competitors. To that extent, a global platform is needed to manage antitrust and competition law risks. It could be said that antitrust is concerning "accommodating capital and policing labor." [28]

The federal antitrust laws such as the Sherman, Clayton, and Federal Trade Commission Acts define competition status. [29] The Sherman Antitrust Act of 1890 made monopolies and trusts illegal. More than two decades later, the Clayton Antitrust Act of 1914 expanded the Sherman Act by prohibiting business activities, such as price discrimination, that corporations could use to lay the groundwork for monopolistic practices.

Indeed, competition laws make certain that fair competition occurs in an open-market economy and progressing along with the market, attentively guarding against would-be monopolies and disruptions to the productive course of competition. Moreover, effective competition aids consumers by assisting businesses to offer goods and services on the most favorable terms. Also, antitrust rules disallow

[24] T-Mobile Netherlands BV et al v Raad van bestuur van de Nederlandse Mededingingsautoriteit, C-8/08, ECLI:EU:C:2009:343, para 38 (competition rules laid down in the Treaty "aim to protect not only the interests of competitors or of consumers, but also the structure of the market and, in doing so, competition as such").

[25] J T Lang, 'Has the European Court of Justice Been Involved in "Judicial Legislation"?' (2011) 96 Svensk Juristtidning 299.

[26] N Fennelly, 'Legal Interpretation at the European Court of Justice' (1996) 20(3) Fordham International Law Journal 656.

[27] G Zekos, Political, Economic and Legal Effects of Artificial Intelligence, 2022, https://link.springer.com/book/10.1007/978-3-030-94736-1#toc

[28] Sandeep Vaheesan, Accommodating Capital and Policing Labor: Antitrust in the Two Gilded Ages, 78 Md.L. Rev. 766 (2019).

[29] Sherman Act, 15 U.S.C. §§ 1–7. Clayton Act, 15 U.S.C. §§ 12–27. Federal Trade Commission Act, 15 U.S.C. §§ 41–58.

agreements between market operators impeding competition, and the abuse of dominance. Furthermore, competition inspires efficiency and innovation decreasing prices which means that in order to be effective, competition necessitates businesses to act independently of each other, but subject to the competitive pressure exerted by the others. Competition on the merits indicates the departure from the market or the marginalization of competitors that are less competent and so less attractive to consumers. It is argued that competition was defined as a challenge between companies for customers. [30] G.I. Zekos argues that competition policy should lead to the deconcentrating of national and global commerce based on fair principles of equal opportunity and the rule of law and so denoting equal position to antagonize for innovation and economic development.

Likewise, antitrust law is supporting fair economic competition as a real-world process rather than a theoretical ideal, reducing vertical control as a means of economic and market organization and replacing it with more horizontal forms of cooperation. Moreover, antitrust law guarantees substantively unrestricted economic outcomes, eliminating the immense influence of the economically powerful and government and so imposing consumer protection. It is worth noting that currently the enforcement of antitrust law has caused inequality as a consequence, in part, of the current antitrust regime. [31] Nachbar [32] argues that antitrust law seeks to avert first "market harm," portrayed and assessed as "a harm to efficiency," and second "regulatory harm," a "harm to the freedom of choice felt by those participating in the market." Moreover, Crane [33] says that antitrust law should exist principally to achieve allocative efficiency and to advance consumer welfare.

Concerning consumers, competition offers the highest quality products at the lowest possible prices, and society's resources are distributed most competently when businesses are subject to the objectivities of a competitive market. Antitrust and competition laws seek to prevent the benefits of a competitive market from being undermined by anticompetitive practices. On the other hand, the erosion of antitrust in the direction of allowing vertical price and nonprice restraints has essentially legalized labor outsourcing, misclassification, and the gig economy which means that dominant corporations having access to a wider range of profitable business models utilize greater power and control over workers than they once performed. Hence, antitrust allows expanding the power of the economy's most powerful players instead of prohibiting monopolies.

---

[30] Harry S. Gerla, Restoring Rivalry as a Central Concept in Antitrust Law, 75 NEB. L. REV. 209, 211–222 (1996).

[31] Marshall Steinbaum & Maurice E. Stucke, The Effective Competition Standard: A New Standard for Antitrust, 87 U. Chi. L. Rev. 595, 595 (2020). Jonathan B. Baker & Steven C. Salop, Antitrust, Competition Policy, and Inequality, 104 Geo. L.J. Online 1, 10–13 (2015) (discussing the connection between antitrust and inequality).

[32] Thomas B. Nachbar, The Antitrust Constitution, 99 Iowa L Rev 57, 85 (2013).

[33] Daniel A. Crane, The Economics of Antitrust Enforcement, in 4 Antitrust Law And Economics 1, 2 (Keith N. Hylton ed., 2010).

Also, in enacting antitrust laws, governments want to restrain the power of large-scale capital and protect concerted labor action from intrusions. Legislators of the antitrust laws comprehended corporate power broadly and passed the antitrust laws to protect consumers and producers from influential corporate sellers and buyers, preserving markets open to all comers and so shielding the political system against corporate capture. It is argued that a "neo-Chicago" [34] approach "accepts the Chicago tenet that legal rules" should be evaluated "in terms of efficiency" combined with the utilization of "post-Chicago insights in designing these rules".

It has to be taken into account that the Supreme Court has restricted the scope of anti-monopoly law and constricted the capacity of plaintiffs to challenge predatory pricing [35] and refusals to deal. [36] To that extent, the Supreme Court and the federal antitrust agencies have changed antitrust by deactivating the aptitude of these laws to control corporate power. Thus, the federal antitrust agencies have become the key policymakers and published merger guidelines that have become increasingly lenient of corporate consolidation in order to advance the consumer welfare. [37] It seems that the Supreme Court and lower courts have rewritten precedent on monopolization to favor large corporations.

At times, the antitrust laws have been applied to control corporate consolidation and even break up durable monopolies not advancing the consumer welfare. The erosion of antitrust has authorized the advancement of the gig economy and dominant corporations have access to a wider range of profitable business models employing greater power and control over workers than they once did. Essentially, this trend within antitrust is expanding the power of the economy's most powerful players. Antitrust law has never been a major player in supporting worker welfare and antitrust enforcement has focused on anticompetitive conduct directed against downstream purchasers, not workers. To that extent, the Supreme Court made clear that a buyer cartel directed at farmers was a per se violation of the Sherman Act [38] clarifying that "a market wide agreement among employers setting wages at levels that would not prevail in a free market may violate the Sherman Act." [39] Moreover, matters concerning anticompetitive conduct directed at workers have been increasing. [40] It is argued that antitrust should be formed in manners that will eventually make consumers, and workers too, better off overall with regard to their buying and

[34] David S. Evans and A. Jorge Padilla, Designing Antitrust Rules for Assessing Unilateral Practices: A Neo-Chicago Approach, 72 U Chi L Rev 73, 75 (2005).

[35] Brooke Group Ltd. v. Brown & Williamson Tobacco Corp., 509 U.S. 209, 222, 224 (1993).

[36] Verizon Commc'ns. Inc. v. Law Offices of Curtis V. Trinko, LLP, 540 U.S. 398, 408 (2004).

[37] Mandeville Island Farms, Inc. v. Am. Crystal Sugar Co., 334 U.S. 219, 235–36 (1948); Weyerhaeuser Co. v. Ross-Simmons Hardwood Lumber Co., 549 U.S. 312, 320 (2007).

[38] Mandeville Island Farms v. Am. Crystal Sugar Co., 334 U.S. 219 (1948).

[39] Brown v Pro Football, Inc., 518 U.S. 231, 252 (1996) (citing Anderson v. Shipowners Ass'n of Pac. Coast, 272 U.S. 359 (1926)).

[40] Carl Shapiro, Antitrust in a Time of Populism, 61 INT'L J. INDUS. ORG. 714, 733 (2018).

selling undertakings, by advancing the efficiency of markets which is known as the promotion of "consumer welfare." [41]

It could be said that the existing antitrust background considers economic coordination as a kind of trespass against the public good, where the public good is outlined by the competitive order and the supplementary conception of efficiency. Undeniably, antitrust's present allocation of coordination rights has counted on two varying claims concerning the company utilized in law and economics thinking. On the one hand, vertically organized companies are considered top quality in their contributions to society, compared with other economic arrangements. On the other hand, antitrust's company exemption necessitates moderating and quashing the importance of the preferential antitrust treatment the company receives by describing it as a simple collection of contracts constrained by the market. Are these claims inconsistent? It could be said that the Bork approach, at its foundation, specifies that economic coordination should be structured by command rather than by cooperation, whether that command is endorsed via customary employment relationships or via contracts that personify and amplify preexisting "polarities of power." To that extent, Sanjukta Paul [42] argues that "competition law—frequently understood as simply maintaining so-called free markets, and institutionally a site of one of law and economics' most complete victories—allocates economic coordination rights in idiosyncratic and autonomous ways that cannot be derived from independent principles."

It seems that law assigns economic coordination rights in order to establish a competitive order which is based on political decisions which are implemented via law grounded on economics rather than political devices and so directing the law and economics focus on competition via an economic road. It has to be taken into account that coordination rights are assigned to the corporation by antitrust law rather than by corporate law by extending the business corporation's public nature and public duties.

It is worth mentioning here that the incorporation of economics into antitrust law has been the extensive rejection of broad rules of per se illegality. Thus, in the United States, the Supreme Court abandoned most per se rules, leaving only naked horizontal price fixing and market division. [43] In addition, the Court established higher

[41] Siva v. Am. Bd. of Radiology, 38 F.4th 569 (7th Cir. 2022) (noting "antitrust's goal of promoting consumer welfare"); City of Oakland v. Oakland Raiders, 20 F.4th 441, 457 (9th Cir. 2021) ("The principal objective of antitrust policy is to maximize consumer welfare by encouraging firms to behave competitively...") United States v. Anthem, Inc., 855 F.3d 345, 366 (D.C. Cir. 2017) ("The principal objective of antitrust policy is to maximize consumer welfare by encouraging firms to behave competitively.") Olympia Equipment Leasing Co. v. Western Union Telegraph Co., 797 F.2d 370, 375 (7th Cir. 1986) (noting shift "from the protection of competition as a process of rivalry to the protection of competition as a means of promoting economic efficiency").

[42] Sanjukta Paul Antitrust as Allocator of Coordination Rights 67 UCLA L. Rev . 378 (2020) at 431.

[43] Leegin Creative Leather Prods., Inc. v PSKS, Inc., 551 U.S. 877, 900 (2007) (minimum resale price maintenance subject to the rule of reason); Illinois Tool Works Inc. v. Indep. Ink, Inc., 547 U.S. 28, 42–43 (2006) (no presumption of market power or rule of per se illegality for patent tieins); State Oil Co. v. Kahn, 522 U.S. 3, 17 (1997) (maximum resale price maintenance subject not

evidentiary standards in resale price maintenance cases [44] and a hard to satisfy two-part test for plaintiffs in predatory pricing cases overturning the per se rule against retail price maintenance in its entirety. [45] Furthermore, the Court developed analysis under which even practices that resemble per se offenses are tested for possible efficiencies that are summarized in the FTC's 2003 PolyGram opinion. [46]

It could be said that the goal of antitrust law should be to protect and promote competition and so antitrust has to deliver the broader social and economic transformation by ascertaining lower prices that result from competition, increasing the wages of workers and the quality of consumer products. Thus, the goal of antitrust is to protect and promote competition and so there is a need of finding the criteria for achieving it.

2.5 Competition and MNEs

MNE activity generates positive spillovers to national economies, upgrading the productivity of local companies via the transfer of advanced production technologies, managerial knowledge, and working practices.

First of all, the competitiveness of the MNE depends on its capacity to make better use of the competencies located in the numerous subsidiaries and the subsidiaries that are essential to the MNE employing numerous methods for developing competence. Knowledge, capabilities, and resources have become the central point of behavior and development in corporations and differences between corporations are attributable to their changing capability to generate, exploit, and combine knowledge, skills, and resources. Moreover, the subsidiary's competence and the utilization of that competence have been shown to have an effect on the corporate role of the subsidiary. The competitiveness of the local market environment is a substantial characteristic of the subsidiary's corporate role. Why MNEs choose one mode of servicing the foreign market versus the other? Sustainable competitive advantage (SCA)[47] has an affirmative effect on the cycle time of the worldwide sourcing process and the organization's overall business performance. Hence, MNEs establish their activities abroad in technological areas where they are strong at

per se illegal and subject to the rule of reason); Cont'l T.V., Inc. v. GTE Sylvania Inc., 433 U.S. 36, 58 (1977) (territorial restrictions subject to the rule of reason).

[44] Bus. Elecs. Corp. v. Sharp Elecs. Corp., 485 U.S. 717 (1988), Monsanto Co. v. Spray-Rite Serv. Corp., 465 U.S. 752 (1984).

[45] Brooke Grp. Ltd. v. Brown & Williamson Tobacco Corp., 509 U.S. 209, 222–23 (1993); Matsushita Elec. Indus. Co. v. Zenith Radio Corp., 475 U.S. 574, 586–87 (1986).

[46] PolyGram Holding, Inc., FTC Dkt. No. 9298, 2003 WL 21770765 (July 28, 2003) (Commission Opinion), petition for review denied, PolyGram Holding Inc. v. FTC, 416 F.3d 29 (2005).

[47] Hult, G. T. M., Hurley, R. F., Giunipero, L. C., and Nichols, E. L. Jr.: Organizational Learning in Global Purchasing: A Model and Test of Internal Users and Corporate Buyers. *Decision Sciences* 31(2), (2000).

home.[48] Moreover, MNEs choose different entry modes in order to accomplish their international marketing ambitions. Besides, countries are seeking to advance their competitive position by encouraging the flow of inward investment, while corporations are pursuing gradually global strategies resulting in integrated production and marketing activities globally.

Many MNEs are gaining a competitive advantage by acquiring resources and capabilities such as technological know–how by utilizing AI, superior organizational and managerial assets, and access to foreign distribution channels and marketing information. FDI is a vibrant process in which past investment experience functions as a predictor of future investment channels. It is worth mentioning here that there is a positive direct effect of FDI for host locations in terms of building up financial capital, advantages from the transfer of technology, innovation, and so improving the structure of the economy along with the local firms. Moreover, FDI drives the involvement in global value chains of local firms and so boosting value-added trade which means attracting FDI creating value in the economy by energizing the local commercial environment. [49] Alexandra Horobeţ [50] et al. argue that "that the highest predictive power in attracting FDI is given by each country's particularities, followed by the market size, the digitalization of the economy and labour market."

The emergence of global value chains (GVCs) has permitted emerging economies to integrate into the global economy faster than in the past. Participation in GVCs is regarded by governments as a fast track to industrialization and so strategies to augment the participation within GVCs are part of economic development policies. Moreover, the growing digitalization of production is expected to be the biggest game-changer in this process, reversing the significance and length of GVCs and reorienting global production and trade. Thus, GVCs generate significant results for participating corporations. Taking into account that GVCs endure central transformation and so remaking the global trade and investment landscape, James X. Zhan [51] argues that "We are entering a decade of de-globalization and the mainstreaming of sustainability... All this implies a change in investment policy thinking from the international production networks..."

---

[48] Patel, P., Vega, M.,1999. Patterns of internationalisation of corporate technology: location versus home country advantages. Research Policy 28 (2/3), 145–155. Kuemmerle, W.,1999. The drivers of foreign direct investment into research and development: an empirical investigation 30 (1), Research Policy 1–24.

[49] Adarov, A., & Stehrer, R. (2020). Capital dynamics, global value chains, competitiveness and barriers to FDI and capital accumulation in the EU (No. 446). Wiiw Research Report.

[50] Alexandra Horobeţ, Oana Cristina Popovici, Lucian Belascu, Shaping Competitiveness for Driving FDI in CEE Countries, December 2021 Romanian Journal of European Affairs Vol. 21, No. 2, p. 64.

[51] James X. Zhan, GVC transformation and a new investment landscape in the 2020s: Driving forces, directions, and a forward-looking research and policy agenda, Journal of International Business Policy (2021) 4, 206–220 p219.

FDI has been influential in the expansion of GVCs, with MNEs coordinating GVCs through their networks of foreign affiliates and non-equity mode partners. [52] Moreover, country-level macroeconomic issues inspire FDI inflows, such as market size, openness, taxes, labor costs, trade costs, and exchange rate, among others. To that extent, FDI is above all motivated by the availability of lower-cost resources and new markets and so the rational response of the MNE is to retain its technological capacity at home and concentrate foreign production on relatively low value-added activities.

It has to be taken into account that the risk of operating in a relatively unsophisticated market is high and such risks can be minimized if production is restricted to assembly operations. The majority of product innovation takes place in the central or prosperous regions as opposed to the peripheral or less-prosperous regions which means that the full benefits of indirect and dynamic effects are only likely to be forthcoming when MNEs set up subsidiaries with more strategic autonomy and so allowing subsidiaries to develop linkages through local procurement activities as they take part in more value-added activities. Only when this autonomy from the parent organization is highly developed, the effect of technology and other asset transfer is likely to improve the competitive position of the local economy. Even if linkages are allowed to develop as MNE subsidiaries become more embedded into the host economy, the precise effect on regional development is difficult to calculate. Also, the role of MNE subsidiaries in the process of regional development is also ambiguous.[53] It is only those subsidiaries, which have extensive levels of strategic autonomy, performing a range of value-added activities that have the potential to influence local economic development to any great extent.[54] Additionally, inward investment is likely to stimulate the production of global competitors in the recipient country.[55]

FDI flows have significant momentum principally because of booming merger and acquisition (M&A) markets and rapid growth in international project finance due to loss in financing conditions and key infrastructure stimulus packages. Cross-border M&As in infrastructure sectors stipulate global FDI. It is characteristic that the war in Ukraine is having impacts well beyond its immediate vicinity, triggering a triple food, fuel, and finance crisis, with rising prices for energy and basic commodities driving inflation and worsening debt spirals which means that investor uncertainty and risk adversity influence downward global FDI. [56] Moreover, the direct

[52] Giroud, A., and Mirza, H. (2015). Refining of FDI motivations by integrating global value chains' considerations. The Multinational Business Review, 23(1), 67–76.

[53] Young, S., Hood, N. and Peters E., "Multinational enterprises and regional economic development", Regional Studies, Vol. 28 No. 7, 1994, pp. 657–77.

[54] Williams, D.A., "Entry mode decisions of multinational enterprises and their impact on the regional economy: a framework for analysis", British Review of Economic Issues, Vol. 17 No. 43, 1995, pp. 27–52.

[55] https://unctad.org/publication/world-investment-report-2022

[56] Global Investment Trends and Prospects https://unctad.org/system/files/official-document/wir2022_ch01_en.pdf

consequences of the war on investment flows embrace the halting of existing investment projects, a departure of MNEs from the Russian Federation, widespread loss of asset values and sanctions essentially impeding outflows.

Vertical FDI is made by corporations that geographically break their production into stages, normally on the basis of factor intensities, utilizing lower factor prices overseas or reducing transactions costs by internalizing upstream or downstream activities.[57] It has to be taken into account that capital denotes anything used to produce goods by encompassing money, machinery, equipment, buildings, know–how, etc. which means that physical capital, human capital, natural wealth, technological level, and innovation are providing corporations' competitiveness on the global market and the augmentation of economies' competitiveness within the global economic system. If various stages of the production process are distinguished by several levels of labor amount, there is an allocation of the stages with high labor intensity to countries with low levels of labor costs and the stages needing lots of skills or capital to high-income countries. Consequently, there is a complementarity between a corporation's foreign and home operations, since both are involved to produce the good. In the short run, substitution between the employment's levels at home and abroad take place if an activity beforehand conducted at home is relocated overseas.[58] To that extent, MNEs using the vertical FDI model diminish employment at home, relative to production, by allocating labor-intensive stages of their production to their affiliates in developing countries.[59] The possibility to invest in a low-cost host country augments the corporation's competitiveness, advance its use of economies of scale, and reduce its costs leading to an increase in home-country employment. It has to be taken into consideration that activities transferred by MNEs to low-cost countries are unskilled-labor intensive from the point of view of the home economy, but skilled-labor intensive from the point of view of the host country. On the other hand, corporations following the horizontal FDI model open out and increase their existing advantages by moving their activities overseas. Horizontal MNEs are multi-plant enterprises that look for utilizing their existing advantages and replicate roughly the same activities in many locations. Thus, the strategic reason for moving outward is the intention to reap benefits of the market opportunities in a foreign country and use the economies of scale result and

---

[57] Kokko, A. (2006), "The Home Country Effects of FDI in Developed Economies", The European Institute of Japanese Studies, *EIJS Working Paper* No. 225.

[58] Braconier, H. and K. Ekholm (1999), "Swedish Multinationals and Competition from High and Low-Wage Countries", *CEPR Discussion Paper* No. 2323. Braconier, H. and K. Ekholm (2001), "Foreign Direct Investment in Central and Eastern Europe: Employment Effects in the EU", *CEPR Working Paper* No. 3052.

[59] Faggio, G. and J. Konings (2003), "Job creation, job destruction and employment growth in transition countries in the 90s", *Economic Systems*, Vol. 27, pp. 129–154. Hansson, P. (2005), "Skill Upgrading and Production Transfer within Swedish Multinationals in the 1990s", *Scandinavian Journal of Economics*, Vol. 107, Issue 4, pp. 673–692. Helpman, E., Melitz, M. J. and S. R. Yeaple (2004), "Export versus FDI with Heterogeneous Firms", *The American Economic Review*, Vol. 94, Issue 1, pp. 300–316.

so the corporation either exports the good produced at home to other locations or produces it in its foreign affiliates.

Regardless of their soft law character, the OECD Guidelines for Multinational Enterprises [60] are recommendations from governments to multinational enterprises on responsible business conduct having a clear prospective to generate impactful outcomes for victims of corporate misconduct. The Guidelines have been used to assist national legislators to close gaps in existing domestic law and so in FNV vs. NUON Energy, [61] the NCP recommended that the government close the gap of paying foreign workers less than Dutch workers performing the same duties and the Dutch parliament did so soon thereafter. Thus, the soft law Guidelines are a useful device not only in assisting greater corporate responsibility to abide by human rights and the environment but also in improving the legal framework on corporate accountability.

MNEs examine their various options and determinants in multinational market competition in order to achieve maximum performance on a global basis. Multinational market competition is a unique case of multipoint competition and so competitive moves in attack and response are the most basic units in any competitive rivalry. Which are the determinants of the particular tactical options for dealing with competitive attack in multiple national markets? The decisive success of any competitive action depends vitally on whether that action goes unchallenged or whether the response is delayed.

It has to be taken into consideration that high visibility, high perceived potential, and high strategic threat provoke rapid responses from incumbent corporations. The greater the dependence on a market under attack, the more the respondent will react mainly to a price action than other types of competitive moves.[62] It could be said that a combination of high visibility and low difficulty is particularly possible to stir up a large number of responses. Also, multipoint competition refers to situations where corporations compete synchronously against the same rivals in multiple product markets, or multiple national markets.[63] Hence, a corporation's action and reaction across a host of markets are based not only on its market overlap with rivals but also

---

[60] https://www.oecdwatch.org/oecd-ncps/the-oecd-guidelines-for-mnes/

[61] http://mneguidelines.oecd.org/database/instances/nl0021.htm Gary Marchant, Lucille Tournas, and Carlos Ignacio Gutierrez, Governing Emerging Technologies Through Soft Law: Lessons for Artificial Intelligence—An Introduction, 61 Jurimetrics J. 1–18 (2020).

[62] Chen, M.-J., MacMillan, I.C., 1992. Non-response and delayed response to competitive moves: the roles of competitor dependence and action irreversibility. Acad Manage J 35, 539–570. Chen, M.-J., Miller, D., 1994. Competitive attack, retaliation and performance: an expectancy-valence framework. Strat Manage J 15, 85–102.

[63] Gimeno, J., Chen, M.-J., 1998. The dynamics of competitive positioning: a pair-wise perspective. Acad Manage Proc BPS: O1-O8. Gimeno, J., Woo, C.Y., 1996. Hyper-competition in a multimarket environment: the role of strategic similarity and multimarket contact on competitive de-escalation. Organ Sci 7, 322–341.

on the resemblance between the resource profiles of these multi-market rivals.[64] It could be argued that the significance of business resource and capability in influencing a corporation's behavior in multipoint competition together with a corporation's resource allocation in multipoint competition can redirect competitors' resource allocation pattern, augmenting the corporation's own sphere of influence without triggering an all-out war.[65] Additionally, competition among MNEs derives to cross-border coordination of competitive moves by MNEs which means that global competitive moves demand sacrificing revenues, profits, or competitive position in specific national markets. MNEs design their global strategy in such a manner as to maximize its overall global performance. Globally coordinated competitive moves strengthen the competitive advantages of specific national markets and augment the MNE's global position.

While there is variation in the definitions of national competitiveness, most have certain core aspects embracing a nation's capability to raise the wealth and welfare of its inhabitants and the capacity of its corporations to discover and then profit from technologies and products in world markets.[66] The main concept in the national competitiveness definitions untaken seems to be the ability of the corporations within a country to increase their productivity leading to the boost of economic benefits by the residents of the country. Moreover, efforts toward further holistic improvements of the investment climate of the nation will better serve a country's industrial base than will initiatives directed at aiding any particular industry.[67] To that extent, with increased industrial globalization, subsidiaries of foreign corporations also play a role in determining a nation's competitiveness, as well as its development. In Dunning's [68]eclectic paradigm and, generally, in theories of foreign direct investment, nations are considered to hold varying capabilities that lead to country-specific or location advantages and that let firms within those countries attain competitive advantages based on the resources that are contained in that nation. Thus, amplified integration of the global economy has transformed incomes around the globe and competition from imports of low-skill intensive goods has a

[64]Baum, J.A.C., Korn, H.J., 1996. Competitive dynamics of interfirm rivalry. Acad Manage J 39 (2), 255–291.

[65]McGrath, R.G., Chen, M.-J., MacMillan, I.C., 1998. Multimarket manoeuvring in uncertain spheres of influence: resource diversion strategies. Acad Manage Rev 23 (4), 724–740.

[66]Porter defines a nation's competitiveness as depending upon the "capacity of its industry to innovate and upgrade" Porter, M.E., 1990. The competitive advantage of nations. Free Press, New York. p. 73. Scott and Lodge define it as "a country's ability to create, produce, distribute, and/or service products in international trade while earning rising returns on its resources" Blaine, M., 1993. Profitability and competitiveness: lessons from Japanese and American firms in the 1980s. Cal Manage Rev 36(1), 48–74. p. 63 According to Blaine, "a nation's competitiveness refers to its ability to produce and distribute goods and services that can compete in international markets, and which simultaneously increase the real incomes and living standards of its citizens".

[67]Brewer, T.L., 1993. Government policies, market imperfections, and foreign direct investment. J Int Bus Studies 24(1), 101–120.

[68]Dunning, J.H., 1988. The eclectic paradigm of international production: a restatement and some possible extensions. J Int Bus 19, 1–31.

descending force on wages for unskilled workers in wealthy nations supplying the widening of income disparities.

The world consists of information just as it contains material and energy. Businesses base their competitive advantages to a considerable degree on the resources and characteristics of their home countries and these resources play a crucial role in forming their advantages than resources elsewhere for the reason that the capacity of corporations to access resources in foreign countries by way of foreign investment is limited. Furthermore, perfect competition itself is not at all suitable to provide adequate reasons for a sufficient production level of technological innovation in society. Competition slows down innovation since the competitive advantage attained by an innovation erodes rapidly as its price declines relative to the industry's marginal cost and its profit decreases to its "normal" level. Moreover, innovation and technological change is a prime driving force behind economic growth and development conducted by domestic businesses and/or foreign MNEs resident there. New technology is not always offered on the market via licensing arrangements and so joint ventures with innovating multinationals are the best means of learning new technology. Alliance with foreign innovating corporations is the best basis for certain forms of managerial human capital formation, with potential spillovers into the national economy. To that extent, spillovers are a fundamental mode of technology transfer and diffusion for developing countries and it is a way that these countries are insisting to encourage.

Since the meaning and the content of competition are not absolute and monolithic, it could be said that competition and innovation are not related in a linear correlation.[69] To that extent, Chicago scholars have been influenced by the Schumpeterian understanding of innovation and their key apprehension is that the ex-post rewards to innovators should not be weaken by the application of antitrust law for the reason that there is a risk of destabilizing the ex-ante enticement to innovate.[70] Thus, in order to preserve the incentive to innovate, the possession of monopoly power will not be considered illegitimate except it goes along with an element of anticompetitive conduct. For instance, in cases such as *Microsoft*[71] referring *to* interoperability information or *Intel*, the Commission analysis and remedies focus on boosting competition and allowing innovation to be developed within the existing network of the market in question. To that extent it could be said that article 102 TFEU is an instrument to make certain that markets remain open for all prospective innovators.

Is there an interaction between FDI and competition policy? It seems that competition for investment delivers nation-wide efficiency, guaranteeing that

[69] Aghion, P. et al. (2005), "Competition and Innovation: An Inverted-U Relationship" 120 QJEcon 701. Goettler, R.L. and Gordon, B.R. (2011), "Does AMD Spur Intel to Innovate More?" 119 J Pol Econ 1141.

[70] Ginsburg, D.H. and J.D. Wright (2012), "Dynamic Analysis and the Limits of Antitrust Institutions" 78 Antitrust LJ 1.

[71] *Microsoft (Tying)* [2010] OJ C 36/7.

investment projects are matched to the locations in which their value is greatest. Government competition polices hamper incumbent's capability to implement anti-competitive strategies and those practices influence FDI.[72]

2.6 Competition and IPRs

Is there any involvement of IPRs in new economy and in attracting FDI inflows? Intellectual property is at the center of the e-economy known as "knowledge-based economy" picturing the new economic environment in which the creation and the management of knowledge play a prevalent part in wealth creation, as compared with the traditional factors of production, explicitly land, labor, and capital. [73] The new industries that developed are characterized by: negligible marginal costs, consumer lock-in effects, value-based pricing, a concentration on intellectual property protection, moderate capital requirements, very high rates of innovation, swift and repeated entry and exit, and network effects imparting economies of scale in consumption.

It has to be taken into account that intellectual property rights[74] do not exist in a vacuum but they are closely linked and affected by competition policies and foreign direct investment laws. Adoption of an adequate competition law is necessary in order to protect the market from anticompetitive practices by IPRs rights' holders.[75] Intellectual property rights holders have expanded the boundaries of their claims, bringing those rights into ever-greater conflict with the primary principles and assumptions of the antitrust laws.[76]

It is worth mentioning here that digital technologies such as artificial intelligence, big data, and cloud computing are flourishing and so AI technologies transform the global economy and initiate new growth openings for startups and businesses galvanizing people and communities in all regions of the globe. AI innovations are technologies executing commands and advance their performance based on feedback and learning processes, without human intervention. Digital platforms, technology-enabled devices assisting transactions between people, offer infrastructure to build new products or services or initiate institutional infrastructure such as

[72] Noland, M., (1999). "Competition Policy and FDI: A Solution in Search of a Problem", Institute for International Economics Working Paper http://www.iie.com/publications/wp/1999/99-3.htm

[73] https://www.wipo.int/edocs/pubdocs/en/wipo_pub_450_2020.pdf . World Intellectual Property Report 2022: Executive Summary https://www.wipo.int/publications/en/series/index.jsp?id=38

[74] G Zekos, IPRs protection and their impact upon FDI, GDP Growth & Trade, 2013 www.scholars-press.com Germany.

[75] United Nations Conference on Trade and Development, 2001, Competition Policy and The Exercise of Intellectual Property Rights, TD/B/COM.2/CLP22, 3 (July 2, 2001).

[76] Reza Dibadj, Saving Antitrust, 75 U. Colo. L. Rev. 745, 779–80 (2003).

database blockchains. [77] Currently, AI technologies are leveraging the large data collected with their huge data processing resources to self-improve.

As a result of the vertically integrated platforms of big tech companies, the information these companies gather from users is leveraged to augment downstream products and services generating economic development. Moreover, it is generated in the interoperability between apps and payment methods. Additionally, from an antitrust perspective, a few companies running a large share of the economic system are harmful to further innovation and future economic growth and so raising competitive matters about whether leveraging market power in an upstream vertical segment might restrain competition and innovation downstream. Hence, by using data collected from past user buying patterns on the digital platform, comparable but competing products are delivered from the parent company of the digital platform. On the other hand, taking into account that there is no barrier to entry in the traditional anticompetition sense, there are economic arguments to counter suggestions of an antitrust threat from the digital platforms because e-platforms are uninterruptedly innovating and competing with one another. [78]

Policymakers should embrace strategies for upholding IPRs protection as well as management and development of IPRs resources classified into four fundamental categories: developing national IPRs strategy, formulating and enforcing needed laws, providing good infrastructures, and launching appropriate educational and training programs.

How competition in the product market affects the rate of innovation? Innovation advocates interplay between organizational structure and technological change involving imitation or anticipated repositioning by rival companies. There are various technical innovations that implicate evidently modest changes to the existing technology but that have rather striking competitive effect.[79]

Developing countries tend to have IPRs systems that support information diffusion through low-cost imitation of foreign products and technologies suggesting that scenarios for domestic invention and innovation are unsatisfactorily developed to justify protection. Nonetheless, malfunctioning IPRs could restrain technical change even at low levels of economic development because many inventions and product innovations are designed at local markets gaining from domestic protection of patents, utility models, and trade secrets. Also, the most advantageous level of IPR protection should assess between the social profit of enhanced innovation and the social costs of monopolistic distortions and income inequality. Conclusively, in an open economy, accomplishing the globally most advantageous level of protection

[77] https://www.wipo.int/edocs/pubdocs/en/wipo-pub-944-2022-en-world-intellectual-property-report-2022-the-direction-of-innovation.pdf

[78] Varian, H.R. (2021). Seven deadly sins of tech? Information Economics and Policy: Antitrust in the Digital Economy, 54, 100893. DOI: https://doi.org/10/ghc4t6 Gilbert, R.J. (2021). Separation: A cure for abuse of platform dominance? Information Economics & Policy: Antitrust in the Digital Economy, 54, 100876. DOI: https://doi.org/10/ghpcvk

[79] Rebecca M. Henderson & Kim B. Clark, (1990) Architectural Innovation: The Reconfiguration of Existing Product Technologies and the Failure of Established Firms, 35 Admin. Sci. Q. 9, 10.

needs an international coordination of IPR protection. The object of any legal protection is to maximize the investment of time, energy, and capital in innovative activities while minimizing any restriction on the public's freedom to utilize goods resulting from such inventiveness.[80] Is there a need for a mere convergence or a total harmonization of IPR protection? Nordhaus[81] argues that the most advantageous patent length should be evaluated between the static distortion consequence of patent protection and the dynamic return from enhanced innovation.

Do IPRs award a monopolistic market power to right holders? Society acquires four kinds of benefits from granting short-term monopoly rights to innovators such as first, the incentive of private innovation as the primary economic gain of IPRs; second, the utilization of the new knowledge in productive activity leading to higher incomes, employment, and competitiveness for the economy as a whole; third, the spreading of new knowledge to other agents due to IPRs and contractual agreements (procurement, licensing or sales) or diffusion[82]; and fourth, the legal framework increases the cost of technology to the buyer. The simple incidence of an intellectual property right does not assume the existence of market power and so IPRs do not grant automatically a monopolistic market power to right holders.

It has to be taken into account that increased dominance by a single corporation must not be interpreted as a lack of competition but it may suggest that the technological leader has the most motivation to innovate for the reason that competitive pressure is sound. Moreover, competition policy could augment the pace of technological advancement in the economy by making a distinction between innovative industries. Thus, competition for the market is expected to strengthen the incentive to rapidly achieve considerable size and market share, perhaps in order to have one's standard adopted by the industry. Likewise, the significance of intellectual property rights depends on the capacity of rights holder to exercise a certain degree of market power.[83] Similarly, Scherer considers that competition promotes innovation than intellectual property[84] which means that intellectual property protection has to be constructed in a way of permitting entrance of competitors.

[80] Labcorp v. Metabolite Laboratories, Inc., 548 U.S. 124 (2006).

[81] Nordhaus, William D. (1969), Invention, Growth and Welfare: A Theoretical Treatment of Technological Change, Cambridge MA: The M.I.T. Press.

[82] Anderson, R.D. (1998) The interface between competition policy and intellectual property in the context of the international trading system, Journal of International Economic Law, 1(1), pp. 655–678. Mirit Eyal-Cohen, Innovation Agents, 76 Wash. & Lee L. Rev. 163, 205–06 (2019) (explaining how an enterprise can reduce its overall cost-per-unit when it produces two or more interrelated products, compared to firms producing each product separately and in similar quantities).

[83] Ramello, G.B. (2003) Copyright and antitrust issues, in: W.J. Gordon and R. Watt (Eds), The Economics of Copyright: Developments in Research and Analysis, pp. 118–147 (Cheltenham, UK and Northampton, MA, USA: Edward Elgar).

[84] Scherer, F.M. (2005), Patents. Economics, Policy and Measurement (Cheltenham, UK and Northampton, MA, USA: Edward Elgar).

As mentioned earlier, MNEs deal concurrently with location and governance decisions and MNE's success is grounded on "advantageous" technological assets. Also, MNEs make changes in their portfolio of invention activities along geographic and organizational boundaries. Institutional deficiencies force MNEs to internalize the production and exchange of value-creating resources. Thus, MNEs innovative performance is boosted when the corporation's R&D activities are based in locations where IPR protection is strong. [85] Hence, MNEs with innovation activities in locations of high IPR protection display higher innovation performance than those in the middle and especially the lower, category. Consequently, MNEs use their inventive capacities to generate patents bringing advantages underlying their internationalization. [86] MNEs exploit internal organization to counter the appropriability hazards in the external environment when implementing innovation activities in weak institutions.

It has to be taken into account that the digitalization of the global economy has enabled MNEs to exploit digital technologies to appropriately circumvent paying corporate income taxes by shifting their profits from high-tax rate states to low-tax rate states. Hence, if an MNE's permanent establishments producing digital products or services are located in a country with low corporate tax rates just for tax-planning reasons. To that extent, it is examined that MNEs have to pay at least 15% of corporate income taxes at the global level and so making ineffective tax-planning strategies involving transfer pricing and royalty payments, which take advantage of the tax rate variances and the tax treaties among different countries. [87] By the way, if global investments of MNEs are executed as a part of tax-planning strategies, MNEs will react to a new international tax system by altering their investment patterns to minimize their tax burdens and so maximizing their profits.

Which is the scope of Protection for Intellectual Property Rights? Employing compulsory licensing to restrict IPR for the rationale of promoting competition can have the contrary effect, deterring innovation and competition by persuading those who gain from the compulsory license to imitate existing products rather than innovating new products themselves. It has to be taken into consideration that the inventor–patentee has a legal right to prevent others from using that invention and the possibility of potentially high profit is a major incentive for undertaking risky and costly innovative activities, and so the whole thrust of the IPR laws is to use that incentive to promote innovation. For that reason, there is no violation under US antitrust law for unilaterally pricing an IPR license "too high." Moreover, there should not be a presupposition that a patent or other IPR creates market power which

[85] Randolph Luca Bruno, Riccardo Crescenzi , Saul Estrin and Sergio Petralia, Multinationals, innovation, and institutional context: IPR protection and distance effect, Journal of International Business Studies (2022) 53, 1945–1970.

[86] Mario Kafouros , Niron Hashai , Janja Annabel Tardios and Elizabeth Yi Wang, How do MNEs invent? An invention-based perspective of MNE profitability, Journal of International Business Studies (2022) 53, 1420–1448.

[87] Sangjun Yea, Impacts of New International Tax System on Multinational Firms' FDI, World Economy Brief April 28, 2022 Vol. 12 No. 17 at: https://ssrn.com/abstract=4122482

means that a thorough market analysis is needed to ascertain the scope of the relevant market and whether the patented invention has market power.[88] The existence of monopoly rents in a product market is the focal motivation for competitors to enter the market by imitating the dominant company. Nevertheless, imitation-producing destruction may vary from one market to another, in accordance with the level of expected rents, the ambiguity over the return of the investments, and the legal protection of intellectual rights.

It has to be taken into account that pre-competitive effects may result from integrating complementary technologies, reducing transaction costs, clearing blocking positions, and circumventing expensive infringement litigation. Anticompetitive effects may occur when the arrangements embrace collective price or output limit, or grant back requirements that may restrain R&D by parties. Taking into account that antitrust examination and intervention are taking place ex post and IPRs protection has been strengthened, a broader competition policy approach is constructive in making certain a pro-competitive use of IPRs. [89]

It is worth noting that open trade increases access to services and goods, advances quality and variety of goods and services, and diminishes costs. Nevertheless, excessive concentration of production, restrictive trade policies, supply chain disruptions, and regulatory divergence endanger the capability of responding to global demands in occasions such as pandemics. [90] Thus, by harmonizing regulation and establishing international standards for needed goods and production processes enhance the efficiency of markets. Finally, the concise presentation reveals an important role of IPRs and competitiveness in attracting FDI inflows.

2.7 Competition Law, Competition, and Democracy

It is worth mentioning here that the legal rules of competition law outlaw:

1. Anticompetitive agreements (Section 1 of the Sherman Act in the USA or Article 101 TFEU in the EU).
2. The abuse of substantial market power (Section 2 of the Sherman Act and Sections 2–3 of the Clayton Act in the USA, or Article 102 TFEU in the EU).
3. Anticompetitive mergers (Section 7 of the Clayton Act in the USA and Regulation 139/2004 EC in the EU).

Is there disagreement on the proper or actual goal of competition law? Should the mission of competition law be the safeguarding of competitive process in restoring

[88] Daryl Lim, 2009 “Innovation and Access: Legal Strategies at the Intellectual Property Rights and Competition Law Interface”; Legal Strategies, Published by Springer Berlin Heidelberg, pp. 403–437.

[89] World Trade Organization. (2022).

[90] https://www.wto.org/english/res_e/publications_e/trade_therapy2022_e.htm

efficient markets via ex-ante legal rules? Would competition law be transformed into multi-dimensional device on the hands of governments and politics beyond the principle of being a branch of law? Should competition law promote efficiency, growth, and innovation, but also the long-term interests of consumers?

G. I. Zekos [91] has written that "European competition law moved from a norm of presumption of illegality to a default assumption of legality, where the responsibility of proof rests with either the party alleging a breach or government antitrust authorities... It could be argued that political interests have influenced the concept of competition... Increased globalization has opened markets to anticompetitive conduct by foreign companies... the internationalization of antitrust enforcement is the answer to this globalization of anticompetitive conduct... Consequently, economics and law in tandem contribute to the competitiveness of any economy in the 21st century globalization." Competition policy encompasses both economic measures and the endorsement of competition law. Hence, there is a need of distinguishing competition as an economics function and competition law which offers the neutral legal rules in order to have a well-functioning competitive process in the market contributing to the safeguard of competition in an economy. Thus, the role of competition law has to be that of presenting the legal principles letting the run of the competitive process and clearly specifying the disallowed activities and actions which means that principles, elements, aspects, and results of applied economics cannot be considered as the principles of competition law.

It is worth mentioning here that the following views of scholars concerning the goal of competition law will show the divergence or convergence about it:

1. Amato [92] regards consumer welfare as a synonym for efficiency and competition law and attempts to strike a balance between economic freedom, on the one hand, and constraining market power, on the other hand.
2. Ahdar [93] receives efficiency as a goal competition law not only promoting efficiency, growth, and innovation but also the long-term interests of consumers.
3. Odudu [94] considers that the goal of competition policy is consumer welfare.
4. Heyer [95] has interpreted Bork's thesis as arguing for total welfare.

[91] See G I Zekos, Economics and Law on Competition in 21st Century Globalization, 2014, Nova Science Publishers, Inc. p311,312.

[92] G Amato Antitrust and the Bounds of Power: The Dilemma of Liberal Democracy in the History of the Market, Oxford: Hart Publishing, 1997.

[93] R Ahdar 'Consumers, redistribution of income and the purpose of competition law' (2002) 23 European Competition Law Review 341.

[94] O Odudu 'The wider concerns of competition law' (2010) 30 Oxford Journal of Legal Studies 559.

[95] K Heyer 'Consumer welfare and the legacy of Robert Bork' (2014) 57 Journal of Law & Economics 19.

5. Bork [96] specified that "the ultimate goal of antitrust law is not to maximize the total wealth of society, but to protect consumers from behavior that deprives them of the benefits of competition."
6. Neven et al. [97] are of the view that EU competition law is about consumer protection and the reaching of the best possible circumstances for EU consumers.
7. Fels and Edwards [98] regard that legitimacy, appeal, and acceptance of EU competition law are grounded on objectives with a clear political and social dimension which means taking into consideration broader objectives.
8. Gerber [99] argues that EU competition's targets can be understood accurately only in light of Europe's "ordoliberalism tradition and the goal of achieving the common market."
9. Motta [100] thinks that the proper goal of competition law should be total welfare.
10. Townley [101] rejects a total welfare purpose for EU competition law by welcoming that consumer welfare is the proper goal because competition law should try to promote broader public policy goals.
11. Nazzini [102] considers that the goal of Article 102 TFEU is the maximization of total social welfare via productivity growth.
12. Akman [103] equates that term "fairness" with "anticompetitive" concerning Article 102 TFEU.
13. Kaplow [104] regards welfare as the right goal of competition law and competition law rules are in fact more in harmony with total welfare maximization.
14. Melamed and Petit [105] argue that the consumer welfare standard should be preserved in EU competition law.

---

[96] RH Bork 'Legislative intent and the policy of the Sherman Act' (1966) 9 The Journal of Law and Economics 7; J Kirkwood and RH Lande 'The fundamental goal of antitrust: protecting consumers, not increasing efficiency' (2008) 84 Notre Dame Law Review 191.

[97] D Neven et al Trawling for Minnows: European Competition Policy and Agreements Between Firms (London: Centre for Economic Policy Research, 1998).

[98] A Fels and G Edwards 'Working paper III—competition policy objectives' in C-D Ehlermann and LL Laudati (eds) European Competition Law Annual 1997: Objectives of Competition Policy Oxford: Hart Publishing, 1998.

[99] DJ Gerber Law and Competition in Twentieth Century Europe: Protecting Prometheus (Oxford: Oxford University Press, 1998).

[100] M Motta Competition Policy: Theory and Practice , Cambridge: Cambridge University Press, 2004.

[101] C Townley Article 81 EC and Public Policy Oxford: Hart Publishing, 2009.

[102] R Nazzini The Foundations of European Union Competition Law: The Objective and Principles of Article 102 , Oxford: Oxford University Press, 2011.

[103] P Akman The Concept of Abuse in EU Competition Law: Law and Economic Approaches (Oxford: Hart Publishing, 2012) pp. 49–106.

[104] L Kaplow 'On the choice of welfare standards in competition law' in D Zimmer (ed) The Goals of Competition Law Cheltenham: Edward Elgar, 2012.

[105] AD Melamed and N Petit 'The misguided assault on the consumer welfare standard in the age of platform markets' (2019) 54 Review of Industrial Organization 741.

15. Waked [106] recognizes the welfare goal of antitrust law complemented by goals that are more oriented towards equity and redistribution.
16. Lianos [107] sees the targets of EU competition law as being about the redistribution of wealth.
17. Monti [108] says that consumer welfare and economic efficiency are the goals of EU competition law.
18. Geradin et al. [109] ascertain key objectives of EU competition law, embracing economic freedom and plurality, market integration, along with consumer welfare, economic efficiency, and consumer choice and fairness.
19. Ayal [110] argues that competition law should protect a broader notion of fairness that takes into consideration the interests of all players involved, involving those of monopolists or undertakings with market power.
20. Parret [111] considers that EU competition law has multiple aims, embracing market integration, but also economic freedom, economic efficiency, industrial policy, justice, fairness, and protecting the interests of consumers.
21. Hovenkamp [112] argues that the Chicago School of antitrust, with its emphasis on a more economic approach and efficiency, fails to capture the reality of how corporations make short-term choices and so concluding that antitrust will inevitably always have a noneconomic, or political, content.
22. Fox [113] considers that competition law can be used to preserve the competitive process by preserving productive, dynamic, and market efficiency.
23. Andriychuk [114] gives emphasis on consumer welfare.
24. Van den Bergh and Camesasca [115] argue that only efficiency and consumer welfare are proper normative ends of competition law.

[106] D Waked 'Antitrust as public interest law: redistribution, equity, and social justice' (2020) 65 The Antitrust Bulletin 87.

[107] I Lianos 'The poverty of competition law: the long story' CLES Research Paper Series No 2/2018, www.ucl.ac.uk/cles/sites/cles/files/cles_2-2018.pdf

[108] G Monti EC Competition Law, Cambridge: Cambridge University Press, 2007.

[109] D Geradin et al EU Competition Law and Economics, Oxford: Oxford University Press, 2012.

[110] A Ayal Fairness in Antitrust ,Oxford: Hart Publishing, 2016.

[111] L Parret 'Shouldn't we know what we are protecting? Yes we should! A plea for a solid and comprehensive debate about the objectives of EU competition law and policy' (2010) 6(2) European Competition Journal 339.

[112] H Hovenkamp 'Antitrust policy after Chicago' (1985) 84 Michigan Law Review 213.

[113] E Fox 'The efficiency paradox' in R Pitofsky (ed) How the Chicago School Overshot the Mark: The Effect of Conservative Economic Analysis on US Antitrust , Oxford: Oxford University Press, 2008.

[114] O Andriychuk 'Rediscovering the spirit of competition: on the normative value of the competitive process' (2010) 6(3) European Competition Journal 575.

[115] R van den Bergh and PD Camesasca European Competition Law and Economics: A Comparative Perspective (Sweet & Maxwell, 2nd edn, 2006) p. 18.

25. Foer and Durst [116] consider that the consumer welfare goal for antitrust is confusing and incomplete and so competition policy actually has multiple economic, political, cultural, and historic targets.
26. Stylianou K. and Iacovides M. [117] argue that "EU competition law shows the likely relevance of broader goals for other EU law policies, not least state aid, the internal market, consumer protection, external trade, and the EU's current industrial policy of digital transformation and the European Green Deal. Forming part of EU law that applies to companies, competition law also shows the extent to which EU private law might become constitutionalised, requiring that companies not only do not contravene, but also promote, through their market conduct, human and labour rights, and other public policy goals."

It is apparent that there are both great variety and wide disagreement of views on the proper or actual goal of competition law. All the elements referred by scholars are elements of development due to taking part freely in the market which means allowing all players to compete in the market with no advantages allocated to firms with market power by endorsing ex ante legal rules governing competitive process and so denoting anticompetitive actions. A specific law such as competition law cannot regulate all aspects of law concerning different category activities such as civil law matters, labor law, consumer law, and even political economy rationales and so the central rationale has to be a single one encompassing all elements influencing the central principle; for example, concerning competition law, the rationale is the protection of competition via keeping open entrance in the market for all possible players. G. I. Zekos considers that competition law via its legal principles protects a competitive process by leaving open the door of entrance in a market which means that the freedom of all actors to run in a market will generate growth, innovation, and efficiency by applying the principles of economy in tandem with effective management. To that extent, Wu [118] regards that the consumer welfare standard of competition law should be discarded in favor of protecting competition and so the protection of competition standard is easier to apply since prospective threats to the competitive process are far more noticeable than reductions in consumer welfare. Taking into consideration that digital markets generate harms that are not captured by the welfare criterion but can be clarified on the grounds of harm to the process of competition, Marty [119] considers that welfare undoubtedly best captures the priorities of competition law, but that it required to be complemented by a consideration for the protection of the process of competition as well.

---

[116] A Foer and A Durst 'The multiple goals of antitrust' (2018) 63(4) The Antitrust Bulletin 494 at 498 and 501–506.

[117] Stylianou K, Iacovides M (2022). The goals of EU competition law: a comprehensive empirical investigation. Legal Studies 42, 620–648. https://doi.org/10.1017/lst.2022.8 p648.

[118] T Wu 'After consumer welfare, now what? The "protection of competition" standard in practice' (2018) Competition Policy International at 4–9.

[119] F Marty 'Is the consumer welfare obsolete? A European Union competition law perspective' GREDEG Working Paper No 2020-13, https://ideas.repec.org/s/gre/wpaper.html.

The European Commission has declared that competition policy should ensure that abusive use of market power by a few does not undermine the rights of the many. [120] Taking account that concerns over the economic power of big tech firms have gained even further momentum, competition law cannot solve the matter of many other branches of law such as Labor law and Consumer law because it abolishes its effectiveness by engaging further in matters of political economy, politics, constitution law, etc. Of course, a well-functioning competition law contributes to democracy but competition law cannot regulate the well-functioning of democracy. To that extent, Elias Deutscher [121] writes that "Prophets of a new 'anti-monopoly movement' increasingly see competition law as a suitable tool to rein in and impose democratic checks on private economic power...The proposition that competition law... promotes democracy is anything but obvious." Concerning the role of competition law, Richard Bunworth [122] argues for the development of the socially conscious consumer standard by saying that "the use of legal certainty as a form of trump card to defeat any proposal for change prevents us exploring what could be offered through subtle or more major redirections. This status quo bias in antitrust is merely serving prevailing corporate interests and undermines efforts to tackle broader societal problems that could come within its purview... If we are serious about promoting the aims of the Treaties then bold steps should be taken in competition law now." On the other hand, competition law should deal with advancing competition in a market and not becoming a treaty promoter or something else outside the role of being a specific law tackling anticompetitive activities via its per se rules. To that extent, anticompetitive are actions damaging the competitive process. [123]

It is argued that innovation plays a central role in defining competitive dynamics and market boundaries. [124] To that extent, Thibault Schrepel [125] argues that "EU courts assign a fragmented role to innovation in competition law cases."

---

[120] European Commission, XVth Report on competition policy (1985) 11.

[121] Elias Deutscher, The Competition-Democracy Nexus Unpacked—Competition Law, Republican Liberty, and Democracy, Yearbook of European Law, Vol. 00, No. 0 (2022), pp. 1–74 https://doi.org/10.1093/yel/yeac003 p. 2,4.

[122] Richard Bunworth, It's Time to Acknowledge the Socially Conscious Consumer in the Room: Antitrust and the Need for a Shift Away from the Consumer Welfare Standard, UCD Working Papers in Law, Criminology & Socio-Legal Studies Research Paper No. 06 / 2023 P8.

[123] Interface Group v. Mass. Port Auth., 816 F.2d 9, 10 (1st Cir. 1987) (Breyer, J.) ("'Anticompetitive' also has a special meaning: it refers not to actions that merely injure individual competitors, but rather to actions that harm the competitive process, a process that aims to bring consumers the benefits of lower prices, better products, and more efficient production methods." (citing Brown Shoe, 370 U.S. at 320)).

[124] Yang, Li, and Li, "Mechanism of Innovation and Standardization Driving Company Competitiveness in the Digital Economy" Journal of Business Economics and Management, Vol. 24, No. 1 (2023), 54–73 (the level of innovation and standardization of a company drives its competitiveness).

[125] Thibault Schrepel, A Systematic Content Analysis of Innovation in European Competition Law, Amsterdam Law & Technology Institute (ALTI) Working Paper 2-2023 p1.

It could be said that mergers contribute and boost national and international competitiveness [126] and so European merger policy presented a structural concern about the excessive concentration of economic power via the maintenance of an essentially competitive market structure by relying on legal presumptions of anticompetitiveness against certain types of business conduct expressed by the distinction between by-object and by-effect restrictions of competition under Articles 101 (1)-102 TFEU stressing the need for conduct in line with competition on the merits rather than promoting economic principles of political economy or politics as the role of competition law. [127] Elias Deutscher [128] says that "a reinterpretation of the role of competition law as 'anti-concentration law' would demand a general agreement about the fact that even otherwise efficient markets fail to 'price in' all the economic, societal, and political costs of the excessive concentration of private economic power."

Also, G. I. Zekos considers that allocating many targets in a branch of law via vague terminology generates a legal uncertainty which allows companies to escape and, therefore, a failure of the law, such as competition law, to tackle effectively a single rationale of the particular branch that is allowing all players in the market to act freely and be able to enter equally in an open entrance sphere of economic activity. Hence, in a free entrance market, antagonism has to be grounded on following strictly economic principles and effective management which means that principles and factors of political economy cannot be deemed to be the context/goal/rationale of competition law.

2.8 AAI and Legal Liability

Taking into account that a simple software automation is abolishing some particularly repetitive jobs, such as basic data entry, algorithms will replace shortly many existing jobs. Moreover, automation generates new jobs and so the workforce is becoming progressively digital which means that people work alongside algorithms occasionally independently, sometimes overseeing them, sometimes overseen by them. There is accelerating demand for a variety of wholly new specialist roles linked with the latest emerging technologies. Additionally, corporate algorithms

[126] European Commission, 'Le problème de la concentration dans le marché commun: The problem of concentration in the Common Market' (1966). Information Memo P-1/66 5,7,8 www.aei.pitt.edu/40303/

[127] Case 56/65 Société Technique Minière v Maschinenbau Ulm ECLI:EU:C:1966:38 p. 249. Case T-203/01 Michelin v Commission (Michelin II) ECLI:EU:T:2003:250 paras 241–44. Case 85/76 Hoffmann-La Roche v Commission (n 187) para 90.

[128] Elias Deutscher, The Competition-Democracy Nexus Unpacked—Competition Law, Republican Liberty, and Democracy, Yearbook of European Law, Vol. 00, No. 0 (2022), pp. 1–74 https://doi.org/10.1093/yel/yeac003 p. 74.

comprise a rising digital workforce generating a public threat because corporations will become increasingly immune from liability for harms, they trigger. [129]

The global total corporate investment in AI reached a very high volume [130] and AI is deemed to be a device for increasing the efficiency of problem solving. Taking into account that even the law gives minimum guidance on the role and tasks of managers, AI present and future managing role grounded on independent decision-making should be based on an administrative and judgement role generating the concern about the understanding and interacting with human beings due to the fact that AI is characterized by augmented intelligence. In other words, standardization and algorithmizing are successfully developed by AI.

Furthermore, the amplified AI innovative level puts pressure which develops steadily and consistently leading to a challenge of legal risks, ethics, and AI uncontrollable progress. Due to the forthcoming decision-making process, there is a need of dropping risks and increasing certainty and avoiding the punishments via the delegation of liability to AI owing to AI participation in current decision-making not mentioning the forthcoming autonomous decision-making of AAI entities running AI companies and corporations due to global digitalization in until now human-centered society.

It is worth noting here that the imperative legal point of the AI effect is that AI has become a legal entity in practice and it has to be recognized legally by governments in order to have a certainty contributing to innovation as well. Hence, AI entities exist irrespective of the existence of their legal personhood. Moreover, the example of this legal feasibility is the availability of the corporate legal personhood analogy. Taking into account that autonomy, intelligence, and awareness are the elements to receive the legal personhood, AAI has to incorporate those factors in order to be effectively run in the forthcoming AAI society and AAI economy. In other words, AAI technology will build an AAI society run by AAI humanoids generating AAI economy in an AAI globalized world.

The law needs to depend on its own systems nature to appropriately provide the appropriate structure for the interaction of technology and society that will continue to uphold important societal values. Hence, it is worth noting that the law itself, being a product of human decision-making, is riddled with incoherencies in its substance and implementation and so AI law has to achieve coherency in its substance and implementation due to the objective functioning of AI technology.

It is worth mentioning here that when the law acknowledges an AI entity as subject of rights, it also regulates such AI entity's duties and potential liabilities in order to achieve legal certainty in AI society. Authors do not have only their exclusive rights, but they also owe duties to others and bear liabilities for their

[129] Mihailis E. Diamantis, Employed Algorithms: A Labor Model Of Corporate Liability For AI, 2023 Duke Law Journal [Vol. 72:797].

[130] Nyenno, I., Truba, V. & Tokarchuk, L. (2023). Managerial Future of the Artificial Intelligence. Virtual Economics, 6(2), 72–88. https://doi.org/10.34021/ve.2023.06.02(5)

own conducts. [131] Consequently, even though contemporary AI technologies can produce certain kinds of literary and artistic works, they are still not capable of complete autonomy with perceiving their independent existence what would permit them to have their rights and bare liabilities for their activities. On the other hand, AAI humanoid robots having all the abilities and capabilities of humans will have duties and liabilities in a fully functioning AAI society. Accordingly, AAI technologies can contribute to the making of cultural goods and so substituting humans in creative endeavors and it is up to humans to utilize AI systems logically avoiding the self-elimination of humans via AAI creatures generated originally by humans. Otherwise, humans are at risk of misplacing control in the distant future allowing the emergence of an AAI life against a human life.

It is argued that there is a higher possibility of using AI technologies as devices for producing cultural goods than employing them for independently generating new things. Also, the works produced by contemporary technologies depend upon data used for machine learning and so entrusting room for human involvement in the generation of such works. It has to be taken into account that the granting of copyright or sui generis protection to the works created by AI technologies will alter contemporary copyright law and policy in all jurisdictions by attributing the role of authors to AAI creatures and their central significance in the creative process. Data limitations are an impediment to the use of machine-learning algorithms in many contexts but the AAI technology will eliminate this problem due to the interoperability of AAI systems which means elimination of any bias or outdated data.

It is worth mentioning here that replacing human-made law with AI will occur soon. Also, the lower cost of legal services via AI and AAI technology will improve access to justice. [132] Nevertheless, the wave of digital transformation is touching not only the European courts very unevenly but also courts all over the globe.

First of all, until now the human legal community plays a role in shaping the law and so a human judge can possibly be persuaded through reasoned legal argument which means that the same has to happen with an AI judge in a more objective way via the capability of an AAI judge to evaluate more data in every case due to the AAI capacity. Second, the legal community and the public play a role in shaping the law through argument, such that the law is a collective societal construction.

AI judiciary will be less biased as long as bias could not be inserted into the AI systems. Will AI judges underappreciate and undervalue the human aspects of law? The answer is no as long as AAI robo-judges will act objectively by implementing a well-structured AI law providing solutions to all problems of AI society where humans have to survive. AAI robo-judges will have the ability to dynamically

---

[131] European Declaration on Digital Rights and Principles 2022. https://digitalstrategy.ec.europa.eu/en/library/european-declaration-digital-rights-and-principles .

[132] For a detailed analysis see Georgios I. Zekos, Advanced Artificial Intelligence and Robo-Justice, 2022 https://link.springer.com/book/10.1007/978-3-030-98206-5

adapt over time to changing circumstances because will have the brain to function even better than humans.

Will AAI robo-people become the new creatures in a new AAI world? Amanda Levendowski [133] argues that "AI systems are biased because humans are biased. Indeed, AI systems learn to be all too human from reading, viewing, and listening to human created works." On the other hand, fair use can promote the making of fairer AI systems, not mentioning the prospect of AAI technology to function objectively and independently by any human bias. It has to be taken into account that AAI humanoid robots will function like humans with better capacities and even developing capabilities concerning their soul, fillings, etc. higher than humans.

Will AI bring more monopolization to the market? The centrality of rehiring the current AI indicates the development of monopolies concerning various markets taking into consideration the interoperability needed in order for AI to function autonomously and automatically. Anyway, in an AAI society, a single AAI system will be able to function successfully all the digital activities which means that AAI will bring concentration of activities but competition for a better functioning on both legal and economic aspects of an AAI society will occur.

It seems that many companies are building algorithmic models to automate all management spectrums, including hiring and firing. [134] Moreover, technology platforms are utilizing processes to resolve disputes. [135] Besides, it is argued that machine decision-making can be technically inexplicable and difficult to contest. [136]

It is worth noting that the Algorithm Accountability Act establishes "algorithmic accountability reports" [137] and the GDPR determines a complex set of regulations for algorithmic decision-making covering multiple contexts and sectors. Moreover, the US Act increases transparency over how algorithms and automated systems are used in decision-making contexts with the purpose of diminishing discriminatory, biased, or harmful outcomes [138] and so holding organizations accountable for their

[133] Amanda Levendowski, How Copyright Law Can Fix Artificial Intelligence's Implicit Bias Problem, 93 Wash. L. Rev. 579 (2018). https://digitalcommons.law.uw.edu/wlr/vol93/iss2/2 at 630.

[134] Ifeoma Ajunwa, An Auditing Imperative for Automated Hiring Systems, 34 Harv. J.L. & Tech. 621, 631–33 (2021).

[135] Rory Van Loo, Federal Rules of Platform Procedure, 88 U. Chi. L. Rev. 829, 836–37 (2021).

[136] Isak Mendoza & Lee A. Bygrave, The Right Not to Be Subject to Automated Decisions Based on Profiling, in EU Internet Law 77, 83 (Tatiani-Eleni Synodinou, Philippe Jougleux, Christiana Markou & Thalia Prastitou eds., 2017) ("The Commission . . . expressed a fear that such processes will cause humans to take for granted the validity of the decisions reached and thereby reduce their own responsibilities to investigate and determine the matters involved.").

[137] Algorithm Accountability Act of 2019, S. 1108, 116th Cong. (2019); H.R. 1655, 66th Leg., 2019 Reg. Sess. (Wash. 2019) (explaining that the act, "[r]elating to establishing guidelines for government procurement and use of automated decision systems," attempts to establish "algorithmic accountability report[s]").

[138] Algorithmic Accountability Act of 2022. On 3 January 2023, the Algorithmic Accountability Act of 2022 was rejected after failing to pass before the 117th Congress adjourned. https://www.gibsondunn.com/federal-policymakers-recent-actions-seek-to-regulate-ai/ See Koen Vranckaert, How Cautious is too Cautious? The US and EU Artificial Intelligence Roadmap (Part 3: the

use of algorithms and other automated systems that are implicated in making critical decisions which influence the lives of individuals in the United States. Also, algorithmic decision-making brings to light causal connections between inputs and outcomes. In addition, GDPR integrates both systemic governance measures and numerous individual rights for data subjects concerning transparency, notice, access, a right to object to processing, and, for those subject to automated decision-making, the right to contest certain decisions. [139] Also, the Organisation for Economic Co-operation and Development (OECD) converged on stimulating world trade by incorporating a right to contest in its recommendations on AI. [140] To that extent, Canada has the Directive on Automated Decision-Making demanding an algorithmic impact assessment for each automated decision-making system deployed by a federal institution but its impact is limited to corporations offering technology that embrace elements of automated decision-making to the federal government. [141]

The European Commission approved the Digital Markets Act (DMA) governing the obligations of digital gatekeepers toward the businesses that depend on them forbidding certain practices "that limit contestability or are unfair [142]" and the Council of Europe adopted recommendations on AI, clarifying that individuals should be provided "effective means to contest relevant determinations and decisions." Moreover, the UNCITRAL has involved in a process of global model law drafting and there is a growing effort in global law-making at both the vertical and horizontal levels with the aim of strengthening democratic legitimacy through more effective participation which could be utilized in making progress in AI law.

It is worth mentioning here that soft law has been regarded as a residual category constituting aspirational norms. [143] Will AI law follow the soft law process globally?

Algorithmic Accountability Act 2022), https://www.law.kuleuven.be/citip/blog/how-cautious-is-too-cautious-the-us-and-eu-artificial-intelligence-roadmap-part-3-the-algorithmic-accountability-act-2022/

[139] Commission Regulation 2016/679, 2016 O.J. (L 119/1).

[140] OECD, Recommendation of the Council on Artificial Intelligence, § 1.3.iv, OECD Legal Instruments (May 5, 2019), https://legalinstruments.oecd.org/en/instruments/OECD-LEGAL-0449

[141] https://www.tbs-sct.canada.ca/pol/doc-eng.aspx?id=32592

[142] Proposal for a Regulation of the European Parliament and of the Council on contestable and fair markets in the digital sector (Digital Markets Act), COM (2020) 842 final (Dec. 15, 2020). Proposal for a Regulation of the European Parliament and of the Council on a Single Market for Digital Services (Digital Services Act) and amending Directive 2000/31/EC, COM (2020) 825 final (Dec. 15, 2020). Regulation (EU) 2022/1925 of the European Parliament and of the Council of 14 September 2022 on contestable and fair markets in the digital sector and amending Directives (EU) 2019/1937 and (EU) 2020/1828 (Digital Markets Act) OJ L 265, 12.10.2022, pp. 1–66. https://eur-lex.europa.eu/legal-content/EN/TXT/?uri=CELEX%3A32022R1925

[143] Ali, Shahla F. (2021) Forming Transnational Dispute Settlement Norms: Soft Law and the Role of UNCITRAL's Regional Centre for Asia and the Pacific (Edward Elgar). Nolan, A. (2020). Artificial intelligence, digital technology and advanced production. In OECD (ed.). The Digitalisation of Science, Technology and Innovation: Key Developments and Policies. OECD Publishing, 119–142. Adam Thierer, Soft Law in U.S. ICT Sectors: Four Case Studies, 61 Jurimetrics J. 79 (2020).

The nature of AI law based on virtual jurisdiction is a sui generis law demanding a different road of implementation. The introduction of AI law will mean standardization and simplicity defining in clear words all occasions of the applicability of the law with a clear enforcement way which means avoiding the complications requiring a lot of interpretation and so avoidance of enforcement. The conventional legal world has endorsed complicated legal wording and so allowing judges and enforcers to implement the law most of the time according to the interests of the capitalist' elite and the society leading to a further complicated situation where many matters remain unenforced regardless of the existence of legal rules. The objectivity of AI law is needed and so the endorsement of an AI law more biased and unimplemented is not desirable because the emergence of an AAI society functioning in an identical way to that of the conventional society will not mean progress but merely a shift in the materiality of the globe.

It is argued that lawmakers in the near future might use technologies such as AI to personalize legal rules to the individual histories and characteristics of individuals. On the other hand, AI will generalize the law to particular conditions and not generating every time a personalized law in order to function in an electronic globe run by AAI humanoid robots.

Likewise, existing forms of legislation and adjudication make and apply rules being general propositions that associate with generically described actions, events, and other facts about the world specified legal consequences. The algorithms issue its dictates in the form of commands, not rules but the commands echo and denote rules and not merely mathematical symbols. The rule of law presupposes a law comprised of rules and the algorithmic commands have to express and encompass this. Algorithmically driven law merely automatically refers to the rule of law already established and it does not generate a personal law out of individual interests against the implied general interests in order to generate the established rules of law. Of course, in an AAI society, the AAI rule of law will be implemented because in any other case, the automation cannot function.

Algorithmic law-making and adjudication presupposes that the law's goals and values are known in advance with exact precision so that algorithms would know what to maximize by an objective interpretation. In the AAI era, the AAI technology will decide the laws needed in order to maximize justice for the interests of the AAI society since AAI tools will generate the needed AAI laws.

Personalized law-making necessitates lawmakers to come to an agreement on a law's objectives and so AAI will ascertain the means that best achieve those objectives in proportion to the magnitude of each which signifies the possibility of AAI law being applied to personal cases. Thus, in order to have the rule of algorithms, lawmakers must express the ends they seek to achieve and their relative weights enabling AAI technology to be implied. On the other hand, in the AAI era, AAI technology will generate the law-making according to the best data concerning AAI society. In other words, the AAI will generate and improve the needed rules and laws applicable to the AAI society by the established robo-justice.

In AAI society, AAI mechanisms will decide the whole life of the AAI society via the AAI constitution and the relevant agencies functioning automatically according to the decisions of AAI governance and implementing the AAI rule of law and governance.

The utilization of means manipulating the functioning of the economy for the good of an elite leads to a revolution of the mass against the elite, and the power moves to other hands which means that a logical use of resources for the development of an economy is the best way for an elite to keep its leadership in the society.

Will AI alter the approach of utilizing power for personal interest rather than for the good of the whole society? On the one hand, as long as AI is utilized by humans as their newest tool of functioning, the old doctrines will prevail. On the other hand, it is supposed that the introduction of AAI autonomous and objective technology will lead to the prevailing of the doctrines that all actions have to be taken for the good of the whole society. If AAI humanoids mimic human nature in acting first for personal good, then the objectivity of the functioning of AAI technology and AAI humanoids is put in doubt. It seems that the future will reveal the reality of AAI humanoids, etc.

Can AI be regulated by using traditional governmental regulatory approaches? It could be said that "soft law" mechanisms not directly enforceable by the government will be utilized such as private standards, codes of conduct, and best practices in order to control AI systems. AI presents a range of issues and concerns that go beyond traditional regulatory means and so many risks produced by AI are not within any being regulatory agency's jurisdiction, such as technological unemployment, human–machine relationships, biased algorithms, and existential risks from AAI humanoids. It has to be taken into account that the pace of advancement of AI outstrips the competence of any traditional regulatory system to keep pace with. Hence, soft law has become a needed and inevitable element of the governance framework for nearly all new technologies such as AI.

Will AI systems have legal personhood? It has to be taken into account that there is no obvious human to hold accountable for many of the injuries that algorithms trigger today. Moreover, legal responsibility is promoted concerning algorithms' liability which means that algorithms will be responsible and so liable for the harms they inflict. [144] Also, the widespread perception that corporations are not morally responsible entities in tandem with the fact that algorithms own nothing, subsequently, they cannot pay for harms they cause. Hence, under the current AI technology, humans will be liable for the damages caused by the utilized AI technology which was guided by them and which has caused the specific injury.

Modern algorithms are enormously complex and expensive which means that many are beyond the capability of any individual human being to own, code, or manage and so individual businesses do design, own, or manage today's most important algorithms. Moreover, many algorithms are developed by private,

[144] Christina Mulligan, Revenge Against Robots, 69 S.C. L. Rev. 579, 579–80 (2018) (discussing holding robots themselves accountable for harm); Nicholas Diakopoulos & Sorelle Friedler, How To Hold Algorithms Accountable IT Tech. Rev. (Nov. 17, 2016), https://www.technologyreview.com/s/602933/how-to-holdalgorithms-accountable/

closely-held, "unicorn" businesses run by wealthy individuals and so, in such situations, vicarious corporate liability is needless or even suboptimal as compared to individual liability. Thus, the liability is personal that of the human guiding the particular AI technology that has caused the particular damage.

It is worth mentioning here that "vicarious" liability appears throughout US law. [145] To that extent, M. E. Diamantis [146] argues that "If algorithms cannot pay for themselves, any money for algorithmic harms—that is to say, legally cognizable harms that algorithms cause—must come from third parties. Transferring legal responsibility from the direct source of a harm to a different otherwise innocent entity is called 'vicarious liability'." It is argued that companies should pay for the injuries of "their" algorithms. [147]

It has to be taken into account that harmful defects in algorithms whether anticipated or not occur at any link in the chain of development and deployment, or even from interactions between links. In that case, all corporations are responsible due to the fact that they have agreed in producing and utilizing the particular AI technology. Of course, corporation law will define the liability of all parties liable for the utilized AI technology. Transfers of ownership and licensing agreements can be used by corporations in order to deal with their liability for the damages caused by AI technology.

Corporate algorithms hurt people and algorithms have also manipulated stock markets, colluded over prices, and caused traffic deaths. Thus, while algorithms become more hi-tech occupying even larger economic and social responsibilities, the scope and severity of algorithmic misconduct will continue to increase. To that extent, corporate law cannot deal with the advancing sources of corporate harm due to the fact that corporate liability applies only to humans acting on behalf of corporations. It is worth noting here that for a corporation to be liable, the law requires that a corporate employee cause harm while intending to benefit the corporation and while acting within the scope of their employment. Current algorithms are not employees nor do current algorithms have intentions or scopes of employment which means that current law falls short when corporate algorithms, rather than employees, trigger harm and so corporations can escape accountability for harmful algorithmic conduct such as traffic accidents and discriminatory lending for which they would ordinarily be liable. [148] Hence, currently the law does not hold algorithms themselves liable and so the law does not recognize algorithms as potential defendants. Besides, AAI algorithms with autonomy, intelligence, and awareness can be considered as employees alike humans which means that current

[145] Pinkerton v. United States, 328 U.S. 640, 647 (1946). 9 See, e.g., Conn. Gen. Stat. § 52–572 (2021); Kan. Stat. Ann. § 38–120 (2021); Or. Rev. Stat. § 30.765(1); 4 Modern Tort Law: Liability and Litigation § 28:40 (2d ed. 2020).

[146] Mihailis E. Diamantis, Vicarious Liability for AI, at: https://ssrn.com/abstract=3850418 P3.

[147] Marta Infantino & Weiwei Wang, Algorithmic Torts: A Prospective Comparative Overview, 2019, 29 Transnat'l L. & Contemp. Probs. 309, 346–53.

[148] Mihailis E. Diamantis, The Extended Corporate Mind: When Corporations Use AI To Break the Law, 91 N.C. L. Rev. 893, 910–11 (2020).

law does not fall short when AAI corporate algorithms employees trigger harm and so corporations cannot escape accountability for harmful algorithmic conduct such as traffic accidents and discriminatory lending for which they will be liable. Thus, the utilized AI technology accomplishing various tasks could be considered to be alike humans and so applying the rules of corporate law to AI technology as well.

It has to be taken into consideration that while algorithms become more intelligent and autonomous, the link between algorithmic harm and any identifiable human deficiency will become gradually questionable. Nonetheless, the remarkable prospective of today's most advanced algorithms is their unpredictability. [149] On the other hand, humans know the capacities of the current AI technology accepting their malfunctioning and so becoming liable as well.

It is worth noting here that decades before corporations started replacing employees with algorithms, they turned to contract workers. [150] Taking into account that algorithms are gradually capable of performing tasks that corporations assigned to employees just a decade ago and so because algorithms are not employees, doctrines for holding corporations liable when people get hurt cannot apply easily. [151] Even today, corporate algorithms discriminate against loan applicants, manipulate stock markets, collude over prices, and trigger traffic deaths. M.E. Diamantis [152] argues that "If a corporation employs an algorithm that causes criminal or civil harm, the corporation should be liable just as if the algorithm were a human employee."

Finally, the law must assist society in taking advantage of the rewards of algorithms, while minimizing the harms by handling the problem of AI personhood. The solution is giving legal personality to autonomous AAI systems and considering the value of their products/services as their ownership from where damages to third parties can be paid. In the case of the current AI technology managed by humans, the value of their products/services should be utilized as the outcome from where damages to third parties can be paid as well.

---

[149] ACM Code of Ethics and Professional Conduct § 1.2, https://www.acm.org/code-of-ethics (stating that computing professionals have a duty to "avoid harm" stemming from their work).

[150] Heather Huston, Beware of Tort Exceptions to Limited Liability, Wolters Kluwer (Jan. 24, 2022), https://www.wolterskluwer.com/en/expert-insights/beware-of-tort-exceptions-tolimited-liability ("An employer also may be able to avoid liability for its agents or employees through the use of independent contractors."). Dynamex Operations W., Inc. v. Superior Ct., 416 P.3d 1, 35, 37 (Cal. 2018) (adopting a standard that presumes all workers are employees instead of independent contractors and shifts the burden on the entities to establish that independent contractor is the proper classification for the individual, and, noting that, in some circumstances, "the workers' role within the hiring entity's usual business operations is more like that of an employee than that of an independent contractor").

[151] Kevin Alden, Strict Liability for the Information Age, 46 B.Y.U. L. Rev. 1619, 1620 (2021) ("[Amazon] has been able to avoid liability for the ten deaths and sixty other 'serious injuries' caused by their vehicles by placing a legal firewall between itself and the drivers . . . .").

[152] Mihailis E. Diamantis, Employed Algorithms: A Labor Model of Corporate Liability for AI, Vol. 72/2023 Duke Law Journal797 P797.

2.9 Algorithms Versus Human Decision-Making

It has to be taken into account that moving toward algorithmic decision-making systems risks eroding the communal moral and cultural foundation upon which democracy and individual freedom rest which means challenging the social foundations of liberal democratic political orders. [153] To that extent, Coglianese, Cary and Lai, Alicia [154] argue that "the choice is one of digital algorithms versus human algorithms, each with their own advantages and disadvantages. And to the extent that automated systems based on digital algorithms would make improvements over human algorithms for specific tasks, they should be adopted."

It is worth noting that human decision-making is inclined to errors and biases causing several governing failures both large and small. In reality, in some situations, human decision-making is more susceptible to incomprehensibility, bias, and error than are digital algorithms which means that when evaluating the use of AI systems in governmental settings, any projected shortcomings of AI systems must be placed in proper perspective and, to that extent, the US Supreme Court has recognized that, "[i]t is an unalterable fact that our judicial system, like the human beings who administer it, is fallible." [155] Also, the human misjudgments in reply to the COVID-19 crisis [156] are an example of fallibility in public administration. [157] Besides, algorithms help advancing government's performance. [158] Furthermore, algorithms accomplish specific tasks better than humans and so, concerning fairness

[153] Samuel Gibbs, Elon Musk: Artificial Intelligence Is Our Biggest Existential Threat, Guardian (Oct. 27, 2014), https://www.theguardian.com/technology/2014/oct/27/elon-musk-artificial-intelligence-ai-biggest-existential-threat ("Elon Musk has . . . declared artificial intelligence the most serious threat to the survival of the human race."); Rory Cellan-Jones, Stephen Hawking Warns Artificial Intelligence Could End Mankind, BBC News (Dec. 2, 2014), http://www.bbc.com/news/technology-30290540 ("The development of full artificial intelligence could spell the end of the human race.").

[154] Coglianese, Cary and Lai, Alicia, "Algorithm vs. Algorithm" (2022). Faculty Scholarship at Penn Law. 2795. 2022 Duke Law Journal [Vol. 72:1281] https://scholarship.law.upenn.edu/faculty_scholarship/2795 p. 1287

[155] Herrera v. Collins, 506 U.S. 390, 415 (1993).

[156] Hamsa Bastani, Kimon Drakopoulos, Vishal Gupta, Jon Vlachogiannis, Christos Hadjicristodoulou, Pagona Lagiou, Gkikas Magiorkinis, Dimitrios Paraskevis & Sotirios Tsiodras, Efficient and Targeted COVID-19 Border Testing Via Reinforcement Learning, 599 Nature 108, 108 (2021).

[157] Michael Lewis, The Premonition: A Pandemic Story 85, 160–85, 295 (2021) (chronicling misperceptions and missteps that impeded successful public health responses).

[158] Kevin C. Desouza, Artificial Intelligence In The Public Sector: A Maturity Model 7–8 (2021), https://www.businessofgovernment.org/sites/default/files/Artificial%20Intelligence%20in%20the%20Public%20Sector_0.pdf

in government decision-making, algorithms are fairer and more consistent than humans. [159]

Algorithms encompass increased accuracy, more consistent outcomes, faster computational speeds, and greater productivity. In addition, algorithms are performing a variety of tasks better than humans can. Likewise, a single digital system can substitute many different human decision-makers, permitting greater consistency over a series of repeated decisions and so avoiding discrepancies and inconsistencies arising between governmental judgments which means that algorithms will produce consistent outputs. [160]

Generally, algorithms outpace human algorithms, displaying qualities such as accuracy, consistency, speed, and productivity. Also, concerning the negatives such as opacity and bias, current algorithms are much better than humans, even if they are not altogether perfect or error-free due to the fact that present AI algorithms are designed and operated by humans and so AAI technology algorithms will have much more accuracy, consistency, speed, and productivity abolishing most of the negatives. Hence, governance supported by current algorithms obviously gives rise to concerns about how these new digital devices will influence the effectiveness, fairness, and openness of governmental decision-making. Thus, In State v. Loomis, [161] the Wisconsin Supreme Court supported the state's use of a risk assessment algorithm in the sentencing process in large part for the reason that it was simply one input into the sentencing decision.

It is necessary to achieve the compatibility of algorithmic decision-making and governance with due process and other constitutional and societal values. [162]

2.10 Dynamic Pricing Algorithms

Platforms play a fundamental role in the AI economy and algorithms are becoming more widely used for pricing and other business functions. Moreover, using algorithms instead of humans to make decisions is becoming more widespread in commerce. Thus, digital companies rely on algorithms to set prices, among other

[159] Michael Kearns & Aaron Roth, The Ethical Algorithm: The Science Of Socially Aware Algorithm Design (2019) (discussing ways that digital science can incorporate adherence to ethical principles into machine-learning technologies).

[160] Daniel Kahneman, Olivier Sibony & Cass R. Sunstein, Noise: A Flaw In Human Judgment 336 (2021) ("A great deal of evidence suggests that algorithms can outperform human beings on whatever combination of criteria we select.").

[161] State v. Loomis, 881 N.W.2d 749 (Wis. 2016).

[162] Cary Coglianese & David Lehr, Transparency and Algorithmic Governance, 71 Admin. L. Rev. 1 (2019) (asserting that machine-learning algorithms are understandable to the public and that algorithmic governance need not necessarily pose a threat to fair and transparent government). Rory Van Loo, Rise of the Digital Regulator, 66 Duke L.J. 1267, 1281–82 (2017) (reviewing the use of algorithms to facilitate comparison among the offerings on travel websites and other platforms).

tasks. Algorithmic pricing is noteworthy in the context of platforms for the reason that digital platforms have become high-flying in the economy.

Which is the association between algorithmic pricing and competition? Do algorithms enable tacit collusion? Even though corporations have made use of pricing software for decades, technological spreads have generated a swing from mechanically set prices to AI-powered algorithms handling enormous quantities of data and interacting, learning, and making decisions with unparalleled speed and sophistication. To that extent, the advancement of algorithmic-pricing software has raised fears concerning the prospective influence on corporation behavior and competition. Above all, the prospective for the use of algorithms as a method to facilitate collusion, either tacit or explicit, has arisen.

Taking into account that an algorithm can better uncover underlying fluctuations in wholesale prices or better predict demand, a result of the rapid expansion of big data and AI-driven market analysis by corporations is that personalized pricing strategies become gradually feasible and hi-tech. Hence, AI advances are utilized to learn more about consumer tastes along with more accurately price products as a function of these tastes. Thus, big data accelerate price discrimination practically implemented in markets which means that accurate determination of ideal personalized pricing increases corporation profits. Furthermore, taking into consideration that there is mass adoption of algorithmic pricing software in markets, pricing software adoption influences competition in the market due to the qualities of the algorithmic pricing and so there is a need of investigating compliance with competition law. Stephanie Assad et al. [163] argue "that the adoption of algorithmic pricing has affected competition and facilitated tacit-collusion in the German retail gas market."

Dynamic pricing denotes a set of pricing strategies that increase profits by adjusting the set price in line with changing variables in supply and demand. Platform pricing poses an extra challenge for algorithms because they must learn to set an optimal price level and structure. Algorithmic pricing is a method of automatically setting prices using pre-programmed instructions to maximize sellers' profits offering several benefits, such as low cost of setting prices and better forecasts. To that extent, algorithms may also reduce prices and increase consumer surplus leading to better service and better product availability. It is worth noting that algorithmic pricing under asymmetric conditions leads some sellers to respond faster to a price drop by competitors than others which means that the slower competitors miss the rationale to cut prices for the reason that they will not gain bigger demand, which increases prices for all sellers in a quasi-collusive equilibrium. [164]

---

[163] Stephanie Assad, Robert Clark, Daniel Ershov, Lei Xu , Algorithmic Pricing and Competition: Empirical Evidence from the German Retail Gasoline Market, CESifo Working Paper No. 8521 p43.

[164] Brown, Zach Y., and Alexander MacKay. 2023. "Competition in Pricing Algorithms." *American Economic Journal: Microeconomics*, 15 (2): 109–56.

Even if algorithmic systems can adjust prices for legitimate reasons, they also permit new possibilities for anticompetitive behavior. Antitrust implications are caused by the growing reliance on corporations' dynamic pricing algorithms. To that extent, when a product has limited capacity and an expiration date, technology now lets a company, with relative ease, to make larger swings in prices while still being assured of the sale. [165]

With the spread of e-commerce and AI technology, a wider array of corporations utilize dynamic pricing strategies in real time and so perfect price discrimination is now increasingly possible to approximate. [166] A pricing algorithm is a sequence of computational actions by using data inputs to set prices for a product or service and so algorithms can be programmed to maximize any variable by utilizing the inputted data and decision tools. [167] Dynamic pricing algorithms extend beyond e-commerce retailers and so Uber utilizes a price-surging algorithm to set the price of a ride share according to real-time factors such as available drivers and demand for rides. [168] Uber's standard driver's agreement plainly asserts that drivers are required to charge the rider the price "recommended" by Uber. [169]

Algorithms learn to set supra-competitive prices abiding by some view of equilibrium. Even though setting supra-competitive prices may not be illegal in most jurisdictions, it might harm consumers due to the objective of pricing algorithms in maximizing expected profits. Hence, algorithmic price-setting causes a series of both intentional and unintentional market distortions and so leads to possible cases of algorithmic collusion. [170] Moreover, algorithmically facilitated anticompetitive conduct in multi-company interactions is not detectable through traditional ways. [171] Also, algorithmically fostered anticompetitive behavior may be entirely unconscious.

Pricing algorithms autonomously learn to coordinate prices and set them at supra-competitive levels. [172] Companies in the United States and EU use pricing

[165] Cristian Santesteban & Shayne Longpre, How Big Data Confers Market Power to Big Tech: Leveraging the Perspective of Data Science, 65 Antitrust Bull. 459 (2020).

[166] Axel Gautier, Ashwin Ittoo & Pieter Van Cleynenbreugel, AI Algorithms, Price Discrimination and Collusion: A Technological, Economic and Legal Perspective, European J.L. & Econ. (2020).

[167] Thomas H. Cormen, Charles E. Leiserson, Ronald L. Rivest & Clifford Stein, Introduction To Algorithms 5, 192–93, 843–49 (3rd ed. 2009).

[168] UBER, How Surge Pricing Works, https://www.uber.com/us/en/drive/driver-app/how-surge-works/

[169] Complaint, Gill v. Uber Techs., Inc., CGC-22-600284, Dkt. No. BL-9, at 6 (Cal. Super. Ct. June 21, 2022). United States v. Colgate & Co., 250 U.S. 300, 307 (1919) (holding that a private business did not violate the Sherman Act by announcing in advance the price at which its goods could be resold and terminating a contract with a vendor that had sold at a lower price).

[170] Stephanie Assad et al., Autonomous Algorithmic Collusion: Economic Research and Policy Implications, 37 Oxford Rev. Of Econ. Pol'y 459 (2021).

[171] Meyer v. Uber Technologies, Inc., No. 16-2750, 16-2752 (2d Cir. 2017). Salil K. Mehra, Algorithmic Competition, Collusion, and Price Discrimination, in The Cambridge Handbook Of The Law Of Algorithms 205 (Woodrow Barfield, ed., 2021).

[172] Tuwe Löfström, Hilda Ralsmark & Ulf Johansson, Collusion In Algorithmic Pricing 8 (2021).

algorithms and track their competitors on a daily basis. It has to be taken into account that automating pricing lets corporations cut costs and save resources by taking the human decision-maker out of the loop. Additionally, by exploiting predictive and strategic analytics, pricing algorithms empower corporations to respond to shifting market conditions in a speedier and more advanced manner. [173]

It is worth noting that algorithms revolutionize pricing behavior by enabling corporations to update prices more frequently and automate pricing decisions which means that asymmetric pricing technology augments price levels, intensifies the price effects of mergers, and generates price dispersion. To that extent, Zach Y. Brown and Alexander MacKay [174] argue that "High-frequency pricing algorithms can soften competition and increase profits in equilibrium, even if the firms are otherwise identical. . .simple pricing algorithms can increase prices in competitive equilibrium and may even obtain the fully collusive outcome... pricing algorithms can make punishment less severe, reducing the likelihood of collusion."

It is worth mentioning here that pricing algorithms can help foster collusion [175] and so algorithmic tacit collusion may form a business strategy. Moreover, without evidence of an agreement, it is difficult, if not impossible, to contest algorithmic tacit collusion under US and EU antitrust laws even if the widespread use of algorithms leads to higher prices. [176]

Algorithms present noteworthy advantages in decision-making by speeding the collection, organization, and analysis of data, empowering quicker decisions and reactions and so enabling the formulation of new strategies for reaching an objective. To that extent, the Danish Competition Council discovered that a digital platform for professional services formed an illegal cartel when its algorithm recommended minimum prices that service providers should charge clients on the platform. [177]

Markets are filled by new generations of pricing algorithms, powered by AI and so such algorithms reach a given objective, such as maximizing profits, without human intervention which means that algorithms are autonomously discovering a

---

[173] Zach Y. Brown & Alexander MacKay, Competition in Pricing Algorithms 1 (Harv. Bus. Sch. Working Paper No. 20-067, 2020).

[174] Zach Y. Brown & Alexander MacKay, Competition in Pricing Algorithms, American Economic Journal: Microeconomics Vol. 15 No. 2 May 2023 pp. 41–42.

[175] Ariel Ezrachi & Maurice E. Stucke, Sustainable and unchallenged algorithmic tacit collusion, 17 Nw. J. Tech. & Intell. Prop. 217 (2020).

[176] OECD 'Algorithmic Competition' (2023) www.oecd.org/daf/competition/algorithmic-competition-2023.pdf Luc Rocher, Arnaud J. Tournier, & Yves-Alexandre de Montjoye, 'Adversarial competition and collusion in algorithmic markets' Nature Machine Intelligence, Volume 5,May 2023, 497–504 497. Ariel Ezrachi and Maurice E. Stucke, The Role of Secondary Algorithmic Tacit Collusion in Achieving Market Alignment, Working paper CCLP(L)54 at: https://ssrn.com/abstract=4546889

[177] Ageras case. Press Release, Danish Competition and Consumer Auth., Danish Competition Council: Ageras has infringed competition law (June 30, 2020), https://www.en.kfst.dk/nyheder/kfst/english/decisions/20200630-danishcompetition-council-ageras-has-infringed-competition-l

profit-maximizing price scheme. [178] Thus, algorithms make it easier for competitors to harmonize prices, leading to increased prices in markets where such harmonization was previously much more difficult. On the other hand, AAI technology will discover easily and correct automatically any anticompetitive actions.

It is worth noting that autonomous price coordination by algorithms is not captured under antitrust laws owing to the fact that the application of antitrust is conditioned on the existence of an agreement between corporations to coordinate trade terms by cartelistic conduct. Consequently, utilization of an algorithm to reinforce a cartelistic agreement falls under the law. [179] It has to be taken into account that presuming complete knowledge of market conditions, AAI algorithms make prices more competitive, not less.

It has to be taken into consideration that the sophistication of algorithms augments their capacity to extract information from big data, empowering better prediction along with the expected reactions of rivals to alterations in market conditions and so settling the optimal price equilibrium in a dynamic background. Hence, algorithms' capacity, accompanied by the prospective removal of human decision-making biases, diminishes the risk of making pricing mistakes. Furthermore, algorithms steer corporations in market complexity by clarifying prospective focal points or collusive strategies in markets whose joint-profit maximizing equilibria cannot be revealed by human capacity. [180] AI-powered pricing algorithm improves market players' capacity along with their incentive to coordinate. It could be said that algorithms limit the capacity of markets to otherwise generate low, competitive prices and so AI-powered pricing algorithms can make it easier for competitors to synchronize and uphold increased prices in markets where such coordination was formerly much more difficult. [181]Thus, when all corporations utilize pricing algorithms, simple linear strategies will verify supra-competitive prices not mentioning the case of AAI technology where all transactions will take part via AAI systems enabling the achievement of perfect competition and so accurate pricing.

"Collusion" refers to a joint profit maximization strategy put in place by competing corporations, focusing on the final coordinated outcome and so it includes both illegal cartelization and legal oligopolistic coordination. [182] Algorithmic

[178]Apoorva Ganapathy, Quantum Computing in High Frequency Trading and Fraud Detection, 9 Eng'g Int'l 61 (2021).

[179]US v. Topkins, No. CR 15 201 (N.D.C.A., 6 April 2015). Joseph E. Harrington Jr, The Effect of Outsourcing Pricing Algorithms on Market Competition (2021), SSRN: https://ssrn.com/abstract=3798847.

[180]Ibrahim Abada & Xavier Lambin, Artificial Intelligence: Can Seemingly Collusive Outcomes Be Avoided? (2020), https://ssrn.com/abstract=3559308 (finding such a result when rivals observe only market prices rather than the direct actions of rivals).

[181]Peter Seele et al., Mapping the Ethicality of Algorithmic Pricing: A Review of Dynamic and Personalized Pricing, 170 J Bus. Ethics 697 (2021).

[182]Alexander Stewart-Moreno, EU Competition Policy: Algorithmic Collusion in the Digital Single Market, 1 York L. Rev. 49, 67 (2020). Elena Donini, Collusion and Antitrust: The Dark Side of

collusion can cope with more multifaceted economic environments with imperfect information and imperfect monitoring. [183]

Antitrust prohibitions of coordinated conduct are conditioned on the existence of "an agreement in restraint of trade" which means the offer and acceptance of an agreement not to compete. Consequently, oligopolistic coordination is not captured under the law, even though its consequences on consumers are similar to those of an illegal cartel which means that the simple existence of an oligopolistic market structure in which a small group of producers take part in parallel pricing of an identical product does not violate the antitrust laws. [184]

Antitrust laws limit some actions that modify market conditions in a manner that makes possible algorithmic coordination. [185] On the other hand, algorithmic coordination can be considered as a joint monopoly which means that companies running the algorithms are subject to the legal restrictions imposed on monopolies. By the way, monopoly power is the capacity of a seller to control all or a substantial part of the market and so dictating the terms of trade, involving charging prices in excess of its marginal cost and forcing unfavorable non-price provisions on its customers.

Nonetheless, even if a joint monopoly is proven, there is a need to show that the algorithms monopolized their power. Yet algorithms do not engage in exclusionary conduct, and high prices are not prohibited, as such. [186] Therefore, the accumulative entrustment of price-setting to algorithms has the prospective for "opening a back door" via which corporations could collude lawfully which means that as the use of algorithms becomes more commonplace, more markets will move from collusion to coordination and so while both lead to supra-competitive prices, only the former is prohibited by laws. [187] Hence, the programming of the coordination of algorithms leading to uncompetitive prices rather than competitive prices must be considered as containing exclusionary conduct.

Pricing Algorithms 51 (2019), https://www.associazioneantitrustitaliana.it/wpcontent/uploads/2020/10/Tesi-Elena-Donini.pdf

[183] Emilio Calvano et al., Algorithmic Collusion with Imperfect Monitoring, 79 Int'l J. Indus. Org. 79 (2021). Jeschonneck Malte, Collusion among autonomous pricing algorithms utilizing function approximation methods (DICE Discussion Paper, No. 370, Heinrich Heine Univ. Düsseldorf, 2021). Karsten T. Hansen, Misra Kanishka & Mallesh M. Pai, Frontiers: Algorithmic Collusion: Supra-Competitive Prices via Independent Algorithms, 40 Mktg. Sci. 1 (2021). 115.

[184] E.I. Dupont de Nemours & Co. v. FTC, 729 F.2d 128, 139 (2nd Cir. 1984) Theatre Enterprises Inc. v. Paramount Film Distrib. Corp., 346 U.S. 537, 541 (1954)("this Court has never held that proof of parallel business behavior conclusively establishes agreement or, phrased differently, that such behavior itself constitutes a Sherman Act offense").

[185] Axel Gautier, Ashwin Ittoo & Pieter Van Cleynenbreugel, AI Algorithms, Price Discrimination and Collusion: A Technological, Economic and Legal Perspective, 50 Eur. J. of L. & Econ. 405, 429–430 (2020).

[186] Verizon Communications Inc. v Law Offices of Curtis V Trinko, LLP, 540 U.S. 398 (2004).

[187] Thibault Schrepel, The Fundamental Unimportance of Algorithmic Collusion for Antitrust Law, notes, Harv. J. of L. & Tech. (Feb. 07, 2020) https://jolt.law.harvard.edu/digest/the-fundamental-unimportance-ofalgorithmic-collusion-for-antitrust-law .

It could be said that algorithmic coordination disputes assumptions about the capacity of competitors to coordinate without an agreement. On the other hand, deep down, the decision of firms to employ pricing algorithms encompasses an agreement because they know that the programming of the algorithm engrosses an uncompetitive result. Effective regulation is required to guide the design, development, and use of such algorithms, so as to minimize the prospective risks and maximize the prospective benefits for society. [188] Algorithmic transparency and explainability make it easier to investigate coordination and RegTech companies already present a multitude of services intended to build compliance into algorithms. [189] Moreover, companies should employ mechanisms facilitating audits of AI systems, such as logging all the system's processes and outcomes to make certain traceability. [190]

Corporations can use AI to monitor corporation communication for suspicious signs, such as keywords in competitor communication leading to an early flagging of possibly problematic behavior, structural, price, or performance-based screens. [191]

It has to be taken into account that pricing decisions are being automated or partly delegated to algorithms optimizing outcomes with limited or no human intervention. Moreover, EU and US law prohibit as illegal per se, or as a restriction by object, agreements as to price or related competitive factors, and existing prosecutions grounded on algorithmic pricing have implicated express collusion between human actors using pricing algorithms to execute the collusive scheme. [192] In fact, simple utilization of an algorithm, leading to coordinated results through tacit collusion, would involve the de facto immunity from prosecution under rules governing anticompetitive agreements; despite the fact that algorithms are more effective than tacitly colluding humans in producing coordinated prices. [193] On the other hand, jurisdictions must tolerate consideration of efficiencies rather than to

---

[188] Michal S. Gal, Limiting Algorithmic Cartels, 38(1) Berkeley Journal of Law and Technology (2023).

[189] Vinicius Klein & Eduardo Molan Gaban, A New Language for AI and the Legal Discourse, 18, 19 (2021), https://bit.ly/3EoKTaz

[190] Eur. Comm'n, High-Level Expert Group on Artificial Intelligence, Assessment List for Trustworthy Artificial Intelligence (ALTAI) for Self-assessment, (July 17, 2020), https://digital-strategy.ec.europa.eu/en/library/assessment-list-trustworthy-artificial-intelligence-altaiself-assessment

[191] Org. for Econ. Co-operation & Dev., Competition Compliance Programmes 40 (2021), https://www.oecd.org/daf/competition/competition-complianceprogrammes2021.pdf Asker, J., Fershtman, C., & Pakes., A. (2021). Artificial intelligence and pricing: The impact of algorithm design. Technical report, National Bureau of Economic Research. Courthoud, M. (2021). Algorithmic collusion on online marketplaces. The Asian-Pacific Industrial Organization Conference. Singapore. Klein, T. (2021). Autonomous algorithmic collusion: Q-learning under sequential pricing. The RAND Journal of Economics.

[192] United States v. David Topkins, Plea Agreement, Crim. No. 15-201 (N.D. Cal. Apr. 30, 2015); Online sales of posters and frames, Case No. 50223 (CMA 12 Aug. 2016).

[193] In re Text Messaging Antitrust Litig., 782 F.3d 867, 874 (7thCir. 2015); Cases C-40 to 48, 50, 54 to 56, 111, 113 and 114–73 Suiker Unie; Case 172/80 Zünchner v Bayerische Vereinsbank; Case T-442/08 Cisac v Commission [2013].

resort to per se condemnation and so the EU approach under Article 101(3) is better suited to achieve than is the US per se standard. [194]

2.11 E-Platforms Power

It is characteristic that worldwide the public is recognizing the extreme concentration of wealth and power in the hands of a few e-platforms that contact exploitative and often unauthorized surveillance, harvesting, processing, and disclosure of personal data. [195]

Oligopolistic platforms such as social networks and search engines use free content to draw individuals onto their platforms and take advantage of influential network outcomes which means that such platforms then use data harvesting and surveillance not only in amplifying the time that users spend on the platform but also in selling advertising and personal data and so allowing third parties secretly to utilize them in order to control individuals' opinions, spending, and political position. [196]

Moreover, the advancement of fair use doctrine must take into consideration the circumstances in which dominant platforms use the free circulation of works to reap user attention by advancing their communicative power both with regard to copyright owners and to users.

AI technology has amplified individuals' opportunities to generate and share works which coincides with a remarkable increase in the concentration of ownership of platforms for disseminating content, and a striking concentration of cyberspace users' attention. On the other hand, cyberspace does not shift the role of commercial media organizations in choosing and filtering content. Moreover, media sources that were central before cyberspace also dominate in cyberspace which means that the same ownership merely utilizes AI technology. To that extent, cyberspace filtration algorithms functioning on search engines and social networks produce a hierarchy of visibility in cyberspace. Hence, platforms exploit their users' base, and their capabilities in selling advertisements and worthy data which means that the commercial misuse of cyberspace users' personal data embraces a new public e-territory. Also, platforms epitomize both horizontal and vertical strategies for obtaining the surplus value of user data and so the platform provider's target is to become and stay on the central point of intermediation for parties in their target markets.

It has to be taken into consideration that platforms like Google and Amazon want to be able to copy works and to deliver links to works, without paying the copyright

---

[194] EU General Court in Case T-342/99, Airtours v. Commission.

[195] Henry Fraser PhD, The Disappointments of Networks, 19 Chi. -Kent J. Intell. Prop. 1 (2020). Available at: https://scholarship.kentlaw.iit.edu/ckjip/vol19/iss1/10

[196] Julie Cohen, Internet Utopianism and the Practical Inevitability of Law, 18 Duke L. & Tech. Rev. 85–96 (2019).

owners of those works, and so permitting them to run a profitable data analysis and ad-selling business. On the other hand, bolstering copyright owners' formal exclusive rights with regard to platforms may fail to profoundly alter the power dynamics as between copyright owners and platforms. It could be said that AI copyrights generate the same problems concerning the exploitive power of platforms as long as humans control AI systems because in the case of AAI, copyrights generated automatically by AAI systems will objectively be distributed to the AAI public under the doctrine of AAI creativity imposed by the rationale of the AAI society.

2.12 Digitalization and Digital Entrepreneurship

Digitalization is determined by the computerization of the economy, robotization, and the automation of production processes. It is worth noting that a decline in the price of digital technology is one of the key factors adding to the increase in digital capital investment and so an increase in digital capital is opening a broader adoption of digital technologies which means accelerating the diffusion of innovations from the frontier to non-frontier businesses and boosting convergence in firm-level productivity. Hence, it is a digital investment that augments the average firm's TFP growth. [197] To that extent, Robert Anderton et al. [198] show that "digitalisation tends to have on average a positive impact on firm-level TFP growth. However, the impact of digitalisation on productivity is very heterogenous across firms. First, there is an important component associated with sectoral heterogeneity, with the average firm in most sectors not being able to reap the productivity benefits from digital investment. Second, only the 30% most productive laggard firms benefit from digitalisation." Nevertheless, an increase in digital investment by itself is not enough for firms to turn into frontier firms.

Is digitalization a massive game-changer that brings huge advances in productivity? Of course, digitalization alters firms' productivity growth and is productivity game-changer for firms able to utilize on a full scale all devices of digital technology including AI. On the other hand, if digitalization embraces only general-purpose technology, then its productivity gains will be normally slow to materialize. [199] Thus, digitalization is a productivity game-changer only for a minority of firms that are the most capable of obtaining the productivity gains of digital technologies by utilizing specific digitalization devices fitting not only to their production mechanism but also to their governance strategy and plans.

[197] Tambe, Prasanna, Lorin Hitt, Daniel Rock, and Erik Brynjolfsson. 2020. Digital Capital and Superstar Firms. Technical report. National Bureau of Economic Research.

[198] Robert Anderton, Vasco Botelho, Paul Reimers, Digitalisation and productivity: gamechanger or sideshow? ECB Working Paper Series No 2794 / March 2023 p41

[199] Brynjolfsson, Erik, Daniel Rock, and Chad Syverson. 2021. "The Productivity J-Curve: How Intangibles Complement General Purpose Technologies." American Economic Journal: Macroeconomics 13, no. 1 (January): 333–72.

It has to be taken into account the significance of social events in modeling organizations' early structures and influencing their modifications and so digitalization has not only stimulated the digital transformation of different industries but also accelerated the course of digital entrepreneurship. Hence, digitalization confirmed a revolutionary alteration in the ways of delivering and consuming financial services, above all payment services.

Digital entrepreneurship has been described as an entrepreneurial process in which information technology steps up the expansion of digital enterprises. Hence, digital technology, social media, and other evolving information and communication technologies enable the identification, evaluation, and enhancement of entrepreneurial opportunities. [200] Furthermore, compared with traditional entrepreneurship, a significant characteristic of digital entrepreneurship lies in the ultimate alterations in the pace of integrating elements in the entrepreneurial procedure and how entrepreneurs handle risk and uncertainty.

Digital technology motivates entrepreneurial aims and the openness of digital technology can diminish the risk and social pressure sensed by entrepreneurs. Moreover, digital technology advances cognitive capability and perceived feasibility enhancing entrepreneurial intentions. Also, digital technology boosts the opportunities that entrepreneurs can find by facilitating discovering entrepreneurial opportunities, by identifying the connections between seemingly unrelated events or trends and so highlighting the significance of digital technology in opportunity discovery and lessens the role of entrepreneurs.

Furthermore, digital technology empowers entrepreneurs in getting resources for survival and growth and so as a result of its openness, entrepreneurs can utilize digital technology to match their demands with the resources available to them. Consequently, resource invocation has become a resource utilization method for digital entrepreneurs [201] enabling value co-creation in the business model concerning start-ups and stakeholders. Start-ups go beyond the value proposition of a trader and play the role of value integrator, and collaborator.

It has to be taken into consideration that digital technology intensifies the complexity and uncertainty of the entrepreneurial environment and advances the capacity of start-ups to interact with multiple parties to energetically develop into a platform-based ecosystem. Provided that digital technology diminishes the cost of tie-building by growing its breadth and depth in traditional social networks, digital technology is shifting the discovery and creation mechanisms of opportunities in traditional entrepreneurship. Also, digital technology stimulates the entrepreneurial process by energizing entrepreneurial willingness, entrepreneurial opportunities, and business models. Moreover, digital opportunities are large scale and borderless by

[200] Autio, E., Nambisan, S., Thomas, L. D., & Wright, M. (2018). Digital affordances, spatial affordances, and the genesis of entrepreneurial ecosystems. Strategic Entrepreneurship Journal, 12(1), 72–95.

[201] Liu, Z., & Qiu, Z. (2020). Digital intelligence entrepreneurship: From "Half wisdom era " to "All Wisdom Era". Exploration and Free Views, 11, 141–149.

accelerating the flow and dispersion of resources on social entrepreneurship platforms.

It is characteristic that AI technology has been utilized recently by Lockheed Martin in order to fly a Variable In-flight Simulation Test Aircraft showing the steady expansion of the use of AI in armed forces and relevant activities. Moreover, Microsoft presented its new Edge research engine incorporating the system Bing which is an advanced AI application concerning cyberspace search. [202] Also, Alibaba has developed its own AI engine named "Tongyi Qianwen" in order to antagonize ChatGPT. It seems that the Bing's new AI chatbot illustrates the forthcoming developments towards the emergence of an army of AAI humanoid robots having self-consciousness which initially has to be filled with information and the needed inputs in order to function as entities or their consciousness will be controlled accordingly by a very advanced AAI center. Will the producers of AAI humanoid robots become new gods on earth?

2.13 AI in Transportation and Competition

Cyberspace has eroded the significance of physical location, and online activities take part anywhere in cyberspace. The merger of the physical world with the virtual world has brought with it a broad range of novel, complex, and valuable transactions regarding transportation. [203] Bills of lading [204] have existed for centuries and are one of the oldest forms of contract under both the common law and the civil law. [205] Lincoln, Spencer F. [206] says that "As a contract, the bill of lading is subject to the same general rules which govern written contracts, and hence cannot be varied by parol evidence." Also, F. Potamianos [207] argues that the bill of lading is a contract with the carrier.

---

[202] See ChatGPT application and chatbot AI.

[203] G Zekos, Economics and Law of Digital Economy, 2020 Nova Science Publications New York USA. www.novapublishers.com

[204] Γ. Ζέκος, Ηλεκτρονική Φορτωτική: Τυποποιημένη σύμβαση μεταφοράς ή ένα απλό αποδεικτικό προφορικής σύμβασης μεταφοράς , 2018 Δίκαιο Επιχειρήσεων & Εταιριών 294 Τεύχος 3/2018, Μάρτιος 2018 http://www.nbonline.gr/journals/3/volumes/916/issues/1580 Γ Ζέκος "Συμβάσεις Μεταφοράς, Ευθύνη των Μεταφορέων & Διαδίκτυο" 2017 Εκδόσεις Π. Σάκκουλα https://www.sakkoulas.gr/el/editions/g-zekos-symvaseis-metaforas-evthyni-ton-metaforeon-diadiktyo-2i-ekd-2017/

[205] W.P. Bennett, The Bill of Lading as a Document of Title to Goods, Cambridge, 1914 at p. 4. The Delaware 20 Led 779. The Roseline [1987] 1 Lloyd's Rep 18 p. 20 "I have come to the conclusion that this distinction seems somewhat metaphysical".

[206] Lincoln, Spencer F., "Bills of Lading" (1892). *Historical Theses and Dissertations Collection.* Paper 248. *Cornell Law School* at: http://scholarship.law.cornell.edu/historical_theses P3.

[207] F Potamianos "*The Contract of Carriage by Sea,*" Vol. 1, 1962, Athens pp. 40–44.

G.I. Zekos [208] supports the view that a bill of lading accepted by the shipper, without any complaint and in the absence of a clause within its content that the bill of lading is not the contract, is the original contract of carriage transferred by the endorsement of a negotiable bill of lading. Thus, a bill of lading has to be the original contract of carriage which is transferred as such via endorsement. Otherwise, a merely evidence of the original contract of carriage bill of lading has to be endorsed as such being merely evidence of the original contract of carriage for every third-party holder.

AI technology employed in transportation means that all papers will be issued by an AI system covering the whole process of transportation without any human involvement and so the legal functioning of all issued papers has to be standardized which means that the function of the AI bill of lading as a contract of carriage has to be clear and not like English law where a bill of lading is merely evidence of the contract demanding the discovery of the contract of carriage by considering if and which oral discussions and negotiations are contractual terms. Hence, Goddard's view in the Ardennes case cannot be accepted as the precedent of the contractual role of bills of lading in the AI era. [209] In other words, oral evidence cannot be applicable in the case of transportation facilitated by AI systems founded on electronic communications and so the bill of lading has to be the contract of carriage which will be endorsed as such to any third-party holder of the bill of lading not mentioning the case where the whole transportation will be supported by AAI humanoid robots dealing with all the paperwork which will be entirely electronically standardized. Thus, an AAI system can easily accommodate the functionality of bills of lading and not mentioning the capacity of AAI technology that will automatically issue the needed documents such as an e-bill of lading contract.

2.14 AI, Competition, and Torts

The globe is encompassing various forms of AI including algorithms aimed to mimic different aspects of human intelligence. Another AI tool is a neural network which is capable of managing more complex problems imitating the manner brains make decisions. [210] Tort law has long worked as a remedy for those injured by negligent

[208] G Zekos "Judicial analysis of the contractual role of bills of lading Under Greek, English and United States law" 1998 PhD Thesis, University of Hull. https://hydra.hull.ac.uk/resources/hull:829 . G Zekos, The Law of Air, Road & Sea Transportation, 2016 Nova Science Publications New York USA. www.novapublishers.com

[209] G. Zekos, Artificial Intelligence And E-Bills of Lading Contracts, Journal of Internet Law April 2021 Vol. 24 N8 pp. 3–10 Wolters Kluwer.

[210] Joshua Yeung, Three Major Fields of Artificial Intelligence and Their Industrial Applications, Towards Data SCI. (Feb. 22, 2020), https://towardsdatascience.com/threemajor-fields-of-artificial-intelligence-and-their-industrial-applications-8f67bf0

actions or poorly designed products, and so injuries instigated by AI are no exception. [211] Also, tort law faces regarding human-operated AI systems. [212]

Negligence claims are comprised of four required elements: (1) duty, (2) breach, (3) causation, and (4) damages. Moreover, the assumption of risk defense is available to parties defending against not only negligence claims but also products and strict liability and misrepresentation claims. The field of "AI torts" will embrace not only injuries triggered by autonomous vehicles but also robots powered by machine learning, software algorithms programmed with AI components, and humans counting on AI to assist them in a variety of tasks. [213]

It has to be taken into account that embedded AI-driven algorithms, ever-present in your daily tasks, are hidden from view and often do not instigate the types of injuries typically remedied through torts. Nonetheless, physical manifestations of AI in robot or vehicle forms engaged in human contact are expected to result in tort injuries. AI is not the first new technology that triggers injuries that may be remedied by tort doctrine. Moreover, as a new technology or knowledge of its risks becomes more commonplace, courts are permitting the assumption of risk defense not extending to product defects. Also, injuries produced by product defects will be litigated under a strict product liability regime holding manufacturers of AI to a much higher standard of care. Similarly, courts often expect defendants to show that plaintiffs had actual knowledge of the defect before permitting the assumption of risk defense to block recovery. [214] The subjective knowledge needed for the assumption of risk makes it difficult for defendants to prove that plaintiffs injured by AI technologies fully realized the risks they undertook, since AI is often created a "black box" strictly as a result of its lack of explainability. [215] Until the use of AI

[211] Umeda v. Tesla, Inc., No. 5:20-cv-02926 (N.D. Cal. Apr. 28, 2020) (PACER) (bringing wrongful death, negligence, and strict products liability claims where Tesla in autopilot mode killed pedestrian); Banner v. Tesla, Inc., No. 50:19-cv-09962 (Fla. Palm Beach County Ct. Aug. 1, 2019) (PlainSite) (bringing products liability and negligence claims where decedent's car crashed while in autonomous pilot mode); Nilsson v. Gen. Motors LLC, No. 4:18-cv-00471 (N.D. Cal. Jan. 22, 2018) (PACER) (bringing negligence claim where motorcyclist was injured by self-driving car); Cruz v. Talmadge, 244 F. Supp. 3d 231, 232–33 (D. Mass. 2017) (considering tort claims against semiautonomous GPS company for directing twelve-foot-tall bus to drive under ten-foot bridge).

[212] Andrew D. Selbst, Negligence and AI's Human Users, 100 B.U. L. Rev. 1315, 1321 (2020) (discussing challenges including issues with foreseeability, duty to investigate AI compromises, and the reasonable person standard).

[213] Rural Cmty. Workers All. v. Smithfield Foods, Inc., 459 F. Supp. 3d 1228, 1238-40 (W.D. Mo. 2020) (finding that meat processing plant owner did not fail to adequately protect workers at plant from COVID-19).

[214] Tillman v. C.R. Bard, Inc., 96 F. Supp. 3d 1307, 1354 (M.D. Fla. 2015) (holding that plaintiff's consent to risks inherent to implant of vascular filter did not mean that she assumed risk of unreasonably dangerous device) Ashmen v. Big Boulder Corp., 322 F. Supp. 3d 593, 597 (M.D. Pa. 2018) (finding genuine issue of material fact regarding whether snowboarder who collided with snowmaking equipment knew of this potential danger).

[215] Aaron Chou, Note, What's in the "Black Box"? Balancing Financial Inclusion and Privacy in Digital Consumer Lending, 69 Duke L.J. 1183, 1187–88 (2020) ("Many key players have criticized

grows, juries will explore the subjective understanding of individual plaintiffs to evaluate the risks of each AI-driven technology and so tort claims will arise. [216] Workplace robot injury cases are the most common right now. [217]

Courts have held that recreational activities satisfy the voluntary requirement but they have distinguished the voluntariness present in such activities from employment or transportation needs. Nevertheless, a selection to engage with AI in and of itself cannot probably lead to a voluntary assumption of all risks linked with the technology. [218] Tesla manufacturers require all purchasers to sign a contract that attempts to nullify tort liability through an exculpatory clause in the company's new warranty contract. [219] Of course, AI and its interrelated technologies will have a drastic influence on all aspects of the insurance industry, from distribution to underwriting and pricing to claims [220] not mentioning the emergence of the AAI humanoids world.

Commercial use of AI-driven technologies has already begun and Courts in agricultural/farm settings outline the use of robots as a "condition" of the property under landowner duties. [221] Workplace injuries today are governed by state workers' compensation laws and employees are banned from making torts claims, such as negligence, against their employers and so workers injured by AI in the workplace will not have a viable negligence claim. [222] Likewise, even though AI tort claims by employees against employers may fail under worker compensation laws, such

algorithms for being 'black boxes,' a term used to describe the opacity of their processes." Gabriel Nicholas, Explaining Algorithmic Decisions, 4 Geo. L. Tech. Rev. 711, 717, 726–27, 729–30 (2020).

[216] Cruz v. Talmadge, 244 F. Supp. 3d 231, 232 (D. Mass. 2017).

[217] Holbrook v. Prodomax Automation Ltd., No. 1:17-cv-00219, 2017 WL 6498908, at *1 (W.D. Mich. Nov. 5, 2020).

[218] Nalwa v. Cedar Fair, L.P., 290 P.3d 1158, 1163 (Cal. 2012) ("And participation in recreational activity, however valuable to one's health and spirit, is voluntary in a manner employment and daily transportation are not.").

[219] Terms of Use, EZ-Robot, https://www.ez-robot.com/terms-of-use.html ("EZ-Robot (and manufacturers and distributors) assumes no responsibility or liability for any errors or inaccuracies that may appear in any documentation or files or any software that may be provided.").

[220] Ramnath Balasubramanian, Ari Libarikian & Doug McElhaney, Insurance 2030—The Impact of AI on the Future of Insurance, McKinsey & Co. (Mar. 12, 2021), https://www.mckinsey.com/industries/financial-services/our-insights/insurance-2030-the-impact-of-ai-on-the-future-of-insurance

[221] Bishop v. DeLaval Inc., 466 F. Supp. 3d 1016, 1021 (W.D. Mo. 2020). Hunter v. Durr Sys., Inc., No. 2:06-cv-00411, 2007 WL 1215075, at *2–3 (M.D. Ala. Apr. 24, 2007) (treating robotic paint booths as condition on property).

[222] Delawder, 178 F. App'x at 202; W. VA. Code Ann. § 23-4-2(d)(1) (2021) (stating that establishment of workers' compensation system was intended to remove employee-employer disputes from tort system) Tracy Hresko Pearl, Compensation at the Crossroads: Autonomous Vehicles & Alternative Victim Compensation Schemes, 60 WM. & Mary L. Rev. 1827, 1828 (2019) (arguing that autonomous vehicle accidents should be governed by no-fault victim compensation fund financed by tax on sale of all fully autonomous vehicles).

employees and their families may sue the manufacturer under negligence, and products liability. [223]

It is worth mentioning here that courts today portray the lack of informed consent as a negligent act. [224] Anyway, the risks associated with AI-driven technologies are not only more intricate but also more pervasive.

2.15 Humans Versus AAI Humanoids

It is argued that the human brain continues to massively outperform AI technology in a range of tasks and so there is an effort to produce biocomputers powered by organoid intelligence systems as future advances for AI technology. Cortical Labs work with brain organoids and biocomputing suggests unprecedented advances in computing speed, processing power, data efficiency, and storage capabilities. To that extent, brain organoids are developed from skin or small blood samples of patients suffering from neural disorders. [225]

Cinema has already produced fictions with the interaction of humans versus AAI humanoids. It is characteristic of the film concerning a humanoid endeavor to become human as he gradually acquires emotions. [226] Will AAI humanoids have the capacity of reproducing as humans? Will humans and AAI humanoids get married and produce a new type of humanoids? Will AAI humanoid robots need material goods and services or their existence will be based on the electronic consumption of electronic goods and services?

It is worth mentioning here that Yuval Harari [227] forewarned that "artificial intelligence can already hack humans. He also believes it will soon create a new religion with its own Bible written by artificial intelligence." On the other hand, current AI runs under humans programming and not any autonomous objective AAI humanoids having earned their independence from any humans' control which means that the whole AI can be manipulated accordingly and be presented as an objective creation of AI.

It is a big mistake to use the human brain in order to develop AI because there is no AI but the regeneration of humans in order to produce anti-humans. AI has to be a totally new mechanical/electronic technology and not an effort to manipulate

[223] Holbrook v. Prodomax Automation Ltd., No. 1:17-cv-00219, 2020 WL 6498908, at *1 (W.D. Mich. Nov. 5, 2020).

[224] Cobbs v. Grant, 502 P.2d 1, 8 (Cal. 1972) (noting that courts have historically split on whether informed consent falls under a negligence or battery theory and adopting a negligence theory).

[225] Real AI Will Need Biology: Computers Powered by Human Brain Cells https://neurosciencenews.com/organoid-intelligence-ai-22714/

[226] Bicentennial Man (film) https://en.wikipedia.org/wiki/Bicentennial_Man_(film)

[227] https://www.jiosaavn.com/shows/yuval-harari%3A-ai-can-hack-humans%E2%80%A6.new-ai-written-bible-is-possible-soon/0G9VWO3p48Y_ https://www.firstpost.com/world/ai-bots-capable-of-starting-new-religions-warns-yuval-noah-harari-12540282.html

humanity. It is not only unethical but also very dangerous to re-engineer humans in order to create anti-humans controlled by humans.

Will a war of humanity against AAI humanoid robots show the inhumanity of humans? As long as humans release AAI humanoid robots expressing feelings, emotions, and all humans' characteristics, then the extinction of such a creature will illustrate the bad side of humans which means that there is a need for a deep thought concerning the creation of AAI humanoid robots on the first place. The thought of utilizing AAI humanoid robots as slaves of humans needs a deep thought because it has examine the occasions of replicating slavery upon creatures that merely are created by a different material but encompassing the same spiritual rationales that have caused human slavery.

It is currently accepted that in exceptional circumstances or specific contexts, AIs are treated as-if they are humans when performing certain tasks for particular purposes. [228] The emergence of AAI humanoids functioning in their AAI world in combination with their functioning in a human world will generate their legal status in both humans and AAI worlds and, at the same time, the big question is how humans will treat AAI humanoids when AAI humanoids will have more advanced thinking and their civilization will be even out of the reach of humans' brain. On the other hand, the elite might have under control a society of AAI humanoids in order to serve their needs of conquering earth and so even exterminating the vast of human population and keeping a number of them as their slaves.

It is worth mentioning here that, in the United States, FDA has approved the human study of brain implants.[229] There is an effort to convert information taken from neurons into an understandable binary code so as to accomplish a greater grasp of brain function and the capability to stimulate these neurons back and so the whole work is grounded on the idea of transforming humans into AAI humanoids. In other words, humans want to transfer their soul and life into another body made of a long-lasting material in order to stay alive not waiting for the spiritual life after death. Will humans be able to transfer their human soul into an AAI entity? Will the human soul continue autonomously functioning on the eternity or merely the transferred brain will function as a recorded program via an AAI robot? Will humans transform the human soul into AAI soul? It has to be taken into account that the integrated brain–machine interface platform [230] seems to be advanced in order to develop AAI technology which will be exploited by humans to achieve the development of

---

[228]Jack M Balkin, The Path of Robotics Law 6 Cal L Rev 45, 55 (2015) (describing the "substitution effect" that occurs when, for particular limited purposes, we treat AIs as special-purpose human beings). Carys J. Craig, The Relational Robot: A Normative Lens for AI Legal Neutrality—Commentary on Ryan Abbott, The Reasonable Robot, Jerusalem Review of Legal Studies, Vol. 25, No. 1 (2022), pp. 24–39. Ryan Abbott, Rational Robots: A Response to Interesting, Renegotiated, and Relational Robots, Jerusalem Review of Legal Studies, Vol. 25, No. 1 (2022), pp. 40–53.

[229]https://en.wikipedia.org/wiki/Neuralink https://www.reuters.com/science/elon-musks-neuralink-gets-us-fda-approval-human-clinical-study-brain-implants-2023-05-25/

[230]https://www.biorxiv.org/content/10.1101/703801v4

programmed AAI humanoid robots and not autonomous AAI entities. Moreover, there is an effort to produce humanly controlled AAI robots probably be exploited as the new AAI slavery. How competition will function in a world of AAI robots controlled by humans? It could be said that probably the same competition principles of the conventional world will apply to an AAI world controlled by humans.

Which will be the spirit of life under AAI technology? Will the eternity of life in an AAI body be the ultimate target of living? It is obvious that the scale of life and spirituality under the new material of existence of AAI humanoids will be different and so the spiritual achievements of AAI humanoids might be higher than the current humans have managed. Of course, the AAI environment will generate different outcomes and life concerning the AAI society, unless even the supposed autonomous life under AAI technology will be controlled by an elite. The mystery of unknown lies ahead.

References

1. Adarov, A., & Stehrer, R. (2020). Capital dynamics, global value chains, competitiveness and barriers to FDI and capital accumulation in the EU (No. 446). Wiiw Research Report.
2. Horobeț, A., Popovici, O. C., & Belascu, L. (2021). Shaping competitiveness for driving FDI in CEE countries. *Romanian Journal of European Affairs, 21*(2), 64.
3. Shapiro, C. (2018). Antitrust in a time of populism. *International Journal of Industrial Organization, 61*, 714, 733.
4. Ginsburg, D. H., & Wright, J. D. (2012). Dynamic analysis and the limits of antitrust institutions. *Antitrust Law Journal, 78*, 1.
5. Krakowski, S., Luger, J., & Raisch, S. (2022). Artificial intelligence and the changing sources of competitive advantage. *Strategic Management Journal, 1*, 1–28.
6. Lapatinas, A., Kyriakou, A., & Garas, A. (2019). Taxation and economic sophistication: Evidence from OECD countries. *PLoS One, 14*(3), e0213498.
7. Kafouros, M., Hashai, N., Tardios, J. A., & Wang, E. Y. (2022). How do MNEs invent? An invention-based perspective of MNE profitability. *Journal of International Business Studies, 53*, 1420–1448.
8. Steinbaum, M., & Stucke, M. E. (2020). The effective competition standard: A new standard for antitrust. *University of Chicago Law Review, 87*, 595.
9. Gal, M. S. (2023). Limiting algorithmic cartels. *Berkeley Journal of Law and Technology, 38*(1).
10. Diamantis, M. E. (2023). Employed algorithms: a labor model of corporate liability for AI. *Duke Law Journal, 72*, 797.
11. Diamantis, M. E. (2020). The extended corporate mind: When corporations use AI to break the law. *North Carolina Law Review, 91*, 893, 910–893, 911.
12. Mihailis, E. Diamantis, vicarious liability for AI. https://ssrn.com/abstract=3850418
13. Nordhaus, W. D. (2021). Are we approaching an economic singularity? Information technology and the future of economic growth. *American Economic Journal: Macroeconomics, 13*(1), 299–332.
14. Seele, P., Dierksmeier, C., Hofstetter, R., & Schultz, M. D. (2021). Mapping the ethicality of algorithmic pricing: A review of dynamic and personalized pricing. *Journal of Business Ethics, 170*, 697.
15. Rammer, C., Czarnitzki, D., & Fernández, G. P. (2021). *Artificial intelligence and industrial innovation: Evidence from firm-level data* (ZEW Discussion Paper No. 21-036).

16. Vaheesan, S. (2019). Accommodating capital and policing labor: Antitrust in the two gilded ages. *Maryland Law Review, 78*, 766.
17. Paul, S. (2020). Antitrust as allocator of coordination rights. *UCLA Law Review, 67*, 378.
18. Zekos, G. (1998). *Judicial analysis of the contractual role of bills of lading Under Greek, English and United States law*. PhD Thesis, University of Hull. https://hydra.hull.ac.uk/resources/hull:829
19. Zekos, G. (2020). *Economics and law of digital economy*. Nova Science. www.novapublishers.com
20. Zekos, G. (2014). *Economics and law on competition in 21st century globalization* (p. 311, 312). Nova Science.
21. Zekos, G. (2022). *Political, economic and legal effects of artificial intelligence*. Springer. https://link.springer.com/book/10.1007/978-3-030-94736-1#toc
22. Zekos, G. (2016). *The law of air, road & sea transportation*. Nova Science. www.novapublishers.com
23. Zekos, G. (2021). Artificial intelligence and E-bills of lading contracts. *Journal of Internet Law, 24*(8), 3–10. Wolters Kluwer.
24. Zekos, G. (2022). *Advanced artificial intelligence and robo-justice*. Springer. https://link.springer.com/book/10.1007/978-3-030-98206-5

Chapter 3
Competition and Governance

3.1 Introduction

Globalization refers primarily to the progressive elimination of barriers to trade and investment and unprecedented international mobility of capital. Moreover, globalization is a complex, forceful legal, and social process that takes place within an integrated whole without regard to geographical boundaries. Globalization of the world economy boosts the flow of capital investment among countries.

Economic globalization denotes the intensifying flow of trade, goods, and services among countries via FDI. Effective public policies must improve the regulatory environment in view of attracting international capital flows and improving the financial viability of the industrial sector. [1] Political globalization signifies cumulative interactions between states in their common interest and so there is regional and international cooperation in different pursuits. Ultimately, social globalization indicates the development of a common culture and a decrease in the differences between people. Economic and political globalization inspires governments to adopt e-governance technology in order to handle the constant demands for efficiency and speed in an ever-changing environment.

It is worth noting that globalization is an imperative part of both the internal and the external environment. To that extent, public administration does not exist in a vacuum dealing with the environment, both internal and external, to perform the duties of the government. Public organizations are inspired by global phenomena and so globalization instigates the leadership challenges and responsibilities. Moreover, leadership scrutinizes the transformations happening in the world in order to take suitable decisions touching the public. Leadership no longer possesses the monopoly in the control of public life and so several players have a stimulus on the events in any country in which the leaders become reactive rather than the active

[1] Lapatinas, A., Kyriakou, A and Garas, A., 2019. Taxation and economic sophistication: Evidence from OECD countries. PLoS One 14(3): e0213498.

© The Author(s), under exclusive license to Springer Nature Switzerland AG 2023

G. I. Zekos, *Artificial Intelligence and Competition*, Contributions to Economics,
https://doi.org/10.1007/978-3-031-48083-6_3

policymaker. Furthermore, globalization has presented new contests of ethics and accountability by confronting organizations with complex and interdependent matters. Globalization has caused revolutionary alterations in information and communication technologies that have altered the globe's political and economic landscape.

The transmission of modern technology in the globalization course is fundamental in developing technological and research capabilities via technology transfer. Also, technological advancement helps to accumulate physical capital which is a precondition for developing and exporting more sophisticated products. Stéphane Nguea and Hervé Fotio [2] argue that "a higher level of the overall globalization index significantly enhances economic sophistication. Besides, economic and political globalization, and de facto measures of social globalization have a positive and significant effect on economic sophistication."

Increased globalization has led to a "borderless world," in which an ever-increasing percentage of a nation's workforce is employed by foreign-owned enterprises, foreign subsidiaries have thus become more and more important contributors to a nation's competitiveness by providing product and process technology and technical and managerial skills. It is characteristic that privatization as part of the globalization procedure often leads to the modernization of productive infrastructures for bringing forth resource-complementarity in the economy.

Globalization entails an increase in the spillovers reinforcing a global financial cycle. While globalization has expedited global risk-sharing and diversification, national financial conditions are driven by a "global financial cycle," distinguished by large common movements in asset prices, gross capital flows, and leverage. Moreover, globalization has been an imperative factor influencing the properties of business cycle dynamics, the sensitivity of activity, inflation, and financial settings to external circumstances. Hence, globalization plays a role in letting a better understanding of the monetary policy transmission mechanism, the reaction role of the central bank, and the monetary policy advancements. [3] It could be said that globalization has transformed the interrelationships between economies and between sectors within economies and so commercial globalization has had a positive influence on global productivity by enhancing allocative competence and external competition. Nonetheless, the support to productivity growth is declining, as trade integration slows, and the contestability of global markets swings towards winner-takes-all dynamics.

Digital technologies boost globalization as they make it easier to trade services across borders upsetting the employment and wages of some workers. Hence, digitalization touches the relative shares of employment along the skill and wage distribution, directly widening the distribution of labor income. Digitalization enables automation of various tasks and while digitalization does not automatically

---

[2] Stéphane Mbiankeu Nguea, Hervé Kaffo Fotio, Does globalization enhances product sophistication? https://ssrn.com/abstract=3997981 at 11.

[3] Occasional Paper Series, The implications of globalization for the ECB monetary policy strategy, No 263 / September 2021.

lead to an overall loss in employment, it not only leads to a replacement of existing jobs but also generates new jobs through reinstatement and through employment gains stemming from higher productivity. Also, automation and digitalization amplify wealth inequality and so there are per se changes in earnings inequality but automation boosts the return to capital, which in turn leads to an increase in wealth inequality. [4] It could be said that current AI run according to the human decisions that structured them in the first place. Even though current AI cannot eventually reach the depth and breadth as humans, it enables automation by replacing traditional labor to perform routine and non-routine tasks and so to some extent, such development brings numerous benefits to corporations, as augmenting productivity and efficiency due to the fact that AI permits the capturing, consolidation, and processing of large amounts of information on clients, suppliers, and competitors. Moreover, corporate capability to replace workers with AI technology touches managerial investment decisions. Also, corporations with the capability to replace labor with AI automation embrace more aggressive financial policies. [5]

Digital technologies do not only present cost and/or efficiency advantages but also have many applications due to the fact that they are combined with many other more specific technologies, for the benefit of further innovation which means that digital technologies are prospective catalysts for technological advancement and far-reaching growth in the medium to long term. Of course, the value added by AI is not endless but it adds to the previous technology and so, with the capability of AAI technology utilized by humanoids and working on their limits of capability in an objective way, AAI will add something more.

3.2 Technology and Governance

Governance [6] roles encompass the capacity to take part in policy-making at any stage. Power relationships refer to the relative power that a player, or a certain role, has over other players within policy-making and its enforcement and so within various modes of governance, different aspects of power relationships are regarded relevant.

[4]Hubmer, Krusell and Smith, 2020 Hubmer, J., Krusell, P. and Smith Jr, A. A. (2021). Sources of US wealth inequality: Past, present, and future. NBER Macroeconomics Annual 35(1), 391–455. Moll, Rachel and Restrepo, 2022 Moll, B., Rachel, L., and Restrepo, P. (2021). Uneven growth: automation's impact on income and wealth inequality, NBER Working Papers, No 28440, National Bureau of Economic Research.

[5]Bates, T.W., Du, F., Wang, J.J., 2020. Workplace automation and corporate financial policy. SSRN 3556935.

[6]G Zekos, Risk management, corporate governance in 21st century digital economy, 2014 Nova Science Publications New York USA. https://novapublishers.com/shop/risk-management-and-corporate-governance-in-21st-century-digital-economy/

It has to be taken into consideration that governance mechanisms have been modified as a result of globalization, augmented technical specialization, and functional differentiation. Nonetheless, governance adapts to the technical innovations of the digital domain in general, and to the increasing use of blockchain and AI technology.

AI technologies impose their own governance norms and so the altering functions of governance players and so governance mechanisms compel reconceptualization due to the fact that legal norms are lagging behind regarding the pace of technical innovations, but also for the reason that the prospective illegitimate uses of big data cause a great threat to fundamental rights demanding some form of regulation.

It is worth noting that public players, customarily regarded as protectors of public interest, lack the means to successfully govern the spaces generated by many technological innovations. Additionally, public players have been subject to critique for the extensive collection of the data of people, and the leaks of such data as well.

It has to be taken into account that the digital domain needs regulation and governance so as to establish a more legitimate and constructive balance of power. Thus, alterations in policy-making and governance initiate new concepts signifying a change in policy-making as subject to nonstop change of patterns of interaction and relations among players. Horizontal modes of policy-making have emerged due to the demands of globalization and the operational differentiation of sectors of society.

It is worth noting that digital power is flexible, as different actors perform different governance roles within different contexts and so there are times when the networks through which roles are issued function as governance actors themselves. Zwitter and Hazenberg [7] argue that "The integration of actors into governance mechanisms, based on their ability to achieve policy outcomes, runs the risk of privatizing oversight into the hands of those with the most power."

3.3 Algorithmic Governance

Algorithmic governance reveals central questions about the role of participation in a democratic society as well as companies are converting into noteworthy sites of democratic contestation. [8] Moreover, the emerging forms of power and control appearing from AI technologies are privatization, informality, and flexibility in government service provision and so generating concerns of transparency, accountability, and fairness grounds.

---

[7]Zwitter A and Hazenberg J (2020) Decentralized Network Governance: Blockchain Technology and the Future of Regulation. Front. Blockchain 3:12. doi: 10.3389/fbloc.2020.00012 p 7.

[8]Jocelyn Simonson, Police Reform through a Power Lens, 130 Yale L.J. 778, 787 (2021) (arguing that a key goal of police reforms is often to "shift power away from the police and toward policed communities").

Additionally, algorithmic governance [9] makes government more effective, more accurate, and fairer. Moreover, the advent of automation in governance rests on public–private collaborations, intensifying both public and private power and augmenting transparency and accountability gaps. AI technologies are shaping law enforcement giving rise to algorithmic justice via robo-courts and consequently the emergence of robo-justice. To that extent, competition enforcement has become more "technocratic," entrusted to industrial-policy specialists, and compartmentalized as a regulatory discipline. [10]

As mentioned earlier, transparency [11] is central to a legitimate government and a fair society by offering a basis for more expressive public participation in all facets of governmental decision-making. Hence, the decision maker should state the reasons for his/her determination denoting the evidence he/she relied on and so in the case of AAI decision-making, the same principle has to be applied going along with the objectivity of AAI technology. [12] Thus, algorithmic governance poses real concerns about transparency grounded on matters of algorithm's source code and its objective function. [13] In other words, algorithmic governance has to follow the law's demands for transparency while still augmenting efficacy, efficiency, and even legitimacy in government.

Also, algorithmic governance advances [14] without the approval of those whom it most profoundly influences which means that algorithmic mechanisms support existing hierarchies [15] but the emergence of AAI systems has to bring objectivity to the functioning of the market. To that extent, artificial objectivity generates opportunities for more competent and reliable government. It could be said that the growth of algorithmic governance is a logical outgrowth [16] of policy appraising efficiency, markets, and privatization due to the fact that AI decision-making

---

[9] Christian Katzenbach & Lena Ulbricht, Algorithmic Governance, 8 Internet Pol'y Rev. 2 (Nov. 2019) (defining algorithmic governance as "a form of social ordering that relies on coordination between actors, is based on rules and incorporates particularly complex computer-based epistemic procedures.").

[10] Daniel A. Crane, Technocracy and Antitrust, 86 Tex. L. Rev. 1159, 1160 (2008).

[11] Michael Luca, Jon Kleinberg & Sendhil Mullainathan, Algorithms Need Managers, Too, Harv. Bus. Rev. (2016) ("Algorithms are black boxes . . . . [They] often can predict the future with great accuracy but tell you neither what will cause an event nor why.").

[12] Goldberg v. Kelly 397 U.S. 254 (1970).

[13] Hous. Fed'n of Teachers, Local 2415 v. Hous. Indep. Sch. Dist., 251 F. Supp. 3d 1168, 1180–83 (S.D. Tex. 2017) (rejecting plaintiffs' arguments that school district's reliance on secret algorithm violated their right to substantive due process and granting defendant's motion for summary judgment).

[14] Ryan Calo & Danielle Keats Citron, The Automated Administrative State: A Crisis of Legitimacy, 70 Emory L.J. 797 (2021).

[15] Hannah Bloch-Wehba, Global Platform Governance: Private Power in the Shadow of the State, 72 S.M.U. L. Rev. 27, 34 (2019) ("At critical junctures, governments supported the emergence of online self-governance and self-regulation in the belief that it would stimulate innovation.").

[16] Julie E. Cohen, Between Truth And Power: The Legal Constructions Of Informational Capitalism 189–90 (2019) (describing the role of compliance monitoring, reporting, and standard-setting).

systems are encompassing social and political rationales and so prioritizing freedom and competence. AAI technology is expected to gather all wisdom in governing fairly and objectively for the best interests of people in an AAI society rather than any AAI elite.

Algorithmic governance [17] is "democratic" as long as it embraces an administrative system that is eventually accountable to the public through political and legal channels. Moreover, algorithmic governance based on current AI technology algorithmic mechanisms might reinforce existing hierarchies and justify continuing disparities. [18] On the other hand, AAI technologies will have to impose objectivity which means the elimination of any human-made disparities but it is questionable to the generation of AAI disparities due to their emergence in AAI society via AAI humanoids or any other AAI entity.

Has equality been achieved via democracy after centuries of implementation? Is there real democracy behind the curtains of a democracy in practice? Have capitalists earned their wealth via democratic entrepreneurship or democracy is the road to uncontrolled imposition? Taking into account that some countries function democratically [19] to a certain degree, in general, G.I. Zekos considers that an elite sells democracy in order to have its hands free to act according to its own interests and simultaneously have people grounded by the fabrication of democratic proceedings. The failure of globalization via technology guided by humans to establish a wealthy and healthy globe reveals the undemocratic way of governance prevailing on the planet earth.

It is worth noting that the rise of automation is shifting the power and capacity of the public sector across diverse domains and so objective automation leads to equality and standardization. It is argued that algorithms are more "efficient" than human decision-makers or human bureaucracies and so governments have backed the emergence of online self-governance and self-regulation in order to accelerate innovation. [20] It is argued that technology can restrict, model, and regulate behavior as efficiently as law and regulation itself and so generating the law of technology which achieves the same rationales as written law. Will AI law achieve the objective rationales of conventional law via its technological basis? Taking into consideration that the data that algorithms operate on are objectively accurate, algorithmic governance can rationalize the government's delivery of services more effectively than via conventional means and so the "objectivity" and "efficiency" of AI decision-making

[17] See Christian Katzenbach & Lena Ulbricht, Algorithmic Governance, 8 Internet Pol'y Rev. 2 (2019) (defining algorithmic governance as "a form of social ordering that relies on coordination between actors, is based on rules and incorporates particularly complex computer-based epistemic procedures[]").

[18] Ifeoma Ajunwa, The Paradox of Automation as Anti-Bias Intervention, 41 Cardozo L. Rev. 1671, 1673–75 (2020) (exploring the role of algorithms in "perpetuating inequality in the labor market").

[19] Nikolas Bowie, Antidemocracy, 135 Harv. L. Rev. 160, 167 (2021) ("[W]hat has historically distinguished democracy as a unique form of government is its pursuit of political equality.").

[20] Hannah Bloch-Wehba, Global Platform Governance: Private Power in the Shadow of the State, 72 S.M.U. L. REV. 27, 34 (2019).

procedures justify cost-cutting measures, etc. It is worth noting that algorithmic decision-making can both rely upon and reproduce existing bias and so functioning not objectively. Also, it has to be taken into account that objectivity is based upon the political approach of what is rightful for a society which in the AI era has to be globally rightful for humanity and not only for a global elite. Hence, algorithmic governance has to be objectively objective and so neutral and fair.

3.4 Cyberspace and AAI

Cyberspace contributes to enhancing the development of global markets for products, services, information, and capital. The creation of new products and the development of new technologies also contribute to the globalization of markets. It is worth noting that digital services penetrate virtually every aspect of modern life, and the digital economy contributes more than $2 trillion to the annual GDP of the United States. [21] ICT devices and their development have presented diverse and extended routes for information diffusion through cyberspace. Globalization is enhanced as a result of ICT adoption which in turn augments economic growth as a result of improvements in economies of scale. Likewise, ICT could rather be harmful to economic growth particularly in the absence of economic transformation. [22]

As a result of cyberspace running, digital platforms generate markets and so they offer infrastructure and act as umpires to develop and enforce governing norms by which platform users must abide. On the other hand, Amazon, Google, Apple, and Facebook also utilize their platforms to deliver their own services to end-users and in direct competition with third-party sellers. Moreover, Amazon sells products in its own name on Amazon Marketplace competing with third-party traders on the platform. Also, Google and Apple both run app stores presenting applications from countless independent developers along with Google's and Apple's own applications, such as the G-Mail or Apple Music apps. [23] Likewise, Amazon is holding a position of "super dominance" in the Italian market for marketplace intermediation services, as confirmed on the basis of different indicators [24] and so online platforms generate extreme forms of economic power.

---

[21] Kevin Barefoot et al., Measuring the Digital Economy, 99 J. U.S. Bureau Econ. Analysis 1, 6–7 (2019).

[22] Kurniawati, M.A. (2020), "The role of ICT infrastructure, innovation and globalization on economic growth in OECD countries, 1996–2017", *Journal of Science and Technology Policy Management*, Vol. 11 No. 2, pp. 193–215.https://doi.org/10.1108/JSTPM-06-2019-0065 Jayaprakash, P., & Pillai, R. R. (2021). The Role of ICT for Sustainable Development: A Cross-Country Analysis. The European Journal of Development Research, 1–23.

[23] Rory Van Loo, The New Gatekeepers: Private Firms as Public Enforcers, 106 VA. L. Rev. 467, 474–80 (2020).

[24] FBA Amazon, Provvedimento n. 29925, 9 December 2021.

Furthermore, digital platforms have become central marketplaces bringing together the demand and supply of goods and services online which means that platforms outline the functionality of cyberspace and platforms have secured systemic relevance by modeling the global economy. [25] To that extent, algorithms might be used by platform corporations to participate in subtle forms of self-preferencing behavior, which could well in some cases constitute unlawful anticompetitive conduct. Moreover, new non-price types of anticompetitive behavior may arise, such as the prospect of companies using automated natural language processing devices to manipulate and fake online consumer reviews in an effort to gain competitive advantage. [26] Enforcement agencies must develop increased technical competence to understand new kinds of algorithmic competition.

It has to be taken into account that the digital era has transformed communication, consumption of information, and participation in politics. Moreover, big data has surfaced as an instrumental resource for decision-making in different fields, including politics and so politicians and parties use the information collected about voters to better comprehend their demands, interests, and preferences in order to cultivate more valuable campaign strategies. To that extent, there is a need for transparency and accountability in how data is collected and used. Nevertheless, the use and management of Big Data in politics has stimulated new challenges for democratic governance, justice, and the rule of law which means that big data turns out to be a gradually valuable resource. It is worth noting that using Big Data presents considerable challenges for democratic governance, such as privacy protection and data security. Consequently, strong regulatory and ethical frameworks need to be put in place to make certain that the use of Big Data in democratic governance is transparent, accountable, and respecting individual rights and freedoms. [27] Democratic governance is advanced by utilizing e-government enabling greater citizen participation in decision-making and management of public services via digital platforms and online communication devices. Moreover, e-government promotes greater access to public information via networks expanding government transparency and accountability. Hence, Big Data, E-government, and democratic governance work together to advance government efficiency providing citizens' privacy rights are recognized. [28]

It is characteristic that there is a rise of techno-nationalism down to the uneven developments of globalization and e-globalization fueled by algorithms and data. Largely, in an economy more and more driven by data analysis, access to and control

---

https://www.agcm.it/dotcmsdoc/allegati-news/A528_chiusura%20istruttoria.pdf (in Italian).

[25] Nikolas Guggenberger Essential Platforms 24 stan. Tech. L. Rev. 237 (2021).

[26] Helena Quinn, Kate Brand & Stephan Hunt, Algorithms: Helping Competition Authorities Be Cognisant of the Harms, Build Their Capabilities and Act, 3 Concurrences 5, 6 (2021).

[27] Christodoulidis, E. The myth of democratic governance. In The Law of Political Economy: Transformation in the Function of Law; Cambridge University Press: Cambridge, UK, 2019.

[28] Tejedo-Romero, F.; Araujo, J.F.F.E.; Tejada, Á.; Ramírez, Y. E-government mechanisms to enhance the participation of citizens and society: Exploratory analysis through the dimension of municipalities. Technol. Soc. 2022, 70, 101978.

over data congruently becomes an increasing potential source of market power for corporations functioning in a globalized AI environment which will become soon a globalized AAI environment.

3.5 Supply Chains and AAI

Globalization homogenizes economies diminishing the country specificity of shocks fostering FDI and so the current FDI promotes future FDI. It has to be taken into consideration that economic and political globalization boosts economic sophistication. Moreover, financial globalization, trade openness, and FDI enhance economic sophistication.

Global supply chains (GSCs) have become a tool for development and so corporations have increased resilience in GSCs by making them more domestic, shorter supply chains through regionalized production, more diversified by cutting dependence on one or a few countries, and more electronic by using digital technology to track the supply chain better. It is characteristic that the central product in GSCs often is not the finished product, but rather key components or raw materials such as semiconductor shortages being critical inputs for many end-product industries, from advanced electronics to automobiles and home appliances or pharmaceutical ingredients being essential for medicines. Moreover, contemporary GSCs can be remarkably complex, necessitating cross-border trade and investment collaboration. To that extent, supply chains augment strategic competitiveness and so creating a workforce with the needed skills for the AI era is the best path for effective international and public–private partnerships.

The digital economy is globalizing and FinTech is being developed in line with the global trends in digital transformations, thus becoming a new foundation for economic globalization. FinTech is exemplified by a high level of internationalization and globalization offering the needed context for its development. [29] The digital economy advances new avenues not only for innovation but also for monopolization and so companies leverage data to reduce or exclude competition which means that by accumulating and analyzing user data, corporations can predict consumer behavior, recognize loyal and profitable customers, start customized marketing campaigns, and foresee their competitors' business strategies getting the upper hand in negotiating with suppliers and business partners. Thus, firms successfully eliminate competition and exert anticompetitive impact long before their dominance is echoed in market share or price control.

It is worth noting that the consumer generates data largely unconsciously, through every observable activity. To that extent, as data analytics devices become more

[29] Bollaert, H., Lopez-de-Silanes, F., & Schwienbacher, A. (2021). FinTech and access to finance. Journal of Corporate Finance, 68, Article 101941. DOI: https://doi.org/10.1016/j.jcorpfin.2021.101941

advanced, companies that control data [30] will have the capability to exert enormous impact and extract excessive profits from consumers. It could be said that antitrust enforcement should consider a company's "data share" to ascertain its monopoly power. The FTC has also begun to take notice of the link between data ownership and monopoly power.

It could be argued that control over data in a given market is equivalent to monopoly power and so storing and utilizing data might undermine competition which means that direct ownership of data generates difficulties for competitors to get or use and which can be utilized to create barriers to competition. On the other hand, GDPR is a device against anticompetitive behavior.

It could be said that the augmenting complexity of business behavior and its dependence on high-level digital technology is expected to make the antitrust regulator's task respectively complex, such that the government would benefit from the use of digital technology too.

It is worth noting that COVID-19 [31] has distorted globalization, and the threat of additional pandemics may cause further changes in international trade and travel. Moreover, the global pandemic has reformed the importance of global supply chains due to the fact that manufacturing and shipping and material shortages are fueling inflation. Besides, the global economy will persist, and its technologies will continue to advance. To that extent, AI has introduced new ways of globalization leading to AI globalization. Will AAI technology and AAI humanoid robots generate AAI globalization due to the automation and the nature of AAI technology and consequently the materialized AAI society? The connectivity and applicability of AAI technology globally will unavoidably produce AAI globalization. It seems that the forthcoming AAI technology will overtake any national policies against globalization due to the nature of AAI systems. In addition, it is expected that the forthcoming AAI globalization will bring forward objectivity considering the needs of the inhabitants of AAI society. It is uncertain that humans can survive in an AAI society governed by AAI systems and ruled by autonomous AAI humanoid robots which will be transformed into AAI humanoids due to advancements in AI technology. Will AAI life exterminate human life? Let us hope that humans will not lose control of technology and that AAI technology will remain a device for improving and not eliminating human life.

[30] Liang Guo et al., Automated Competitor Analysis Using Big Data Analytics, 23 Bus. Proc. Mgmt. J. 735, 735–36 (2017).

[31] Pol Antràs et al., Globalization and Pandemics, NBER Working Paper 27840, (September 2020). http://www.nber.org/papers/w27840

3.6 Governance and Public Administration

First of all, globalization has raised the concern of government effectiveness resulting from an increased level of competition in the world. To that extent, governance refers to the strategies of governments and non-governmental organizations intended at initiating, facilitating, and mediating network processes and so it could be said that network management is regarded to be a "meta-governance." Accountability and openness are fundamental for the promotion of good governance and accountability. The technological revolution has enabled the people to deal with many matters. Both public and private organizations are compelled to advance performance to stay competitive. Besides, the government is responsible for providing improved services to the people. The rise of the global society has brought about the revolutionary trades in the world.

Furthermore, governance is a way to reposition public administration as a pre-eminent discipline grounded on the new global realities and so the fundamental mission of public administration is to implement policies. In a globalized world, no state should live in isolation because of opened-up opportunities for the public concerning the affairs of government and greater openness and accountability. The increasing demand for preserving sustainability and dropping income inequality has added new pressures to the government and so the stakeholders are not limited to the territorial boundaries of a country. [32]

Globalization has expedited greater openness and transparency of the affairs of government and so intensifying competition among the territories of the globe to achieve an advantage in the international marketplace. Thus, the non-stop demand for free trade, assisted by the open borders policy, strengthens the levels of competition. Additionally, globalization has tolerated the easy movement of capital, which has permitted MNEs to invest and transfer their capital anywhere in the globe. Simultaneously, it has opened up opportunities for people to buy and sell products and services stimulating market liberalization as a device of capitalism which means that no country can operate in isolation in a global economy. Hence, globalization has made public services more transparent, which is a stage toward greater accountability. Also, accountability and openness are fundamental for the promotion of good governance and accountability. On the other hand, corruption triggers inefficiencies by dropping competition and favoring insiders with information and so bringing about additional transaction costs. G.I. Zekos [33] says that in many societies, economic growth embraces a significant amount of corruption. When political power

[32] Denise Hearn, Cynthia Hanawalt, and Lisa Sachs, "Antitrust and Sustainability: A Landscape Analysis," Columbia Center on Sustainable Investment and Sabin Center for Climate Change Law (July 2023).

[33] Zekos, G. I. (2004). Ethics Versus Corruption in Globalization. The Journal of Management Development, 23(7–8), 631–647. p. 631 "Globalization brings forward the immense need for common ethical norms. A norm has to be established as legitimate before it may become binding for members of the norm-generating community".

is utilized for economic return, it reallocates resources from the poor to the rich. Consequently, corruption can have an upsetting effect on the running of nations by lowering the competence of economic and political systems. [34]

The availability of technology has led to a growing demand for e-governance regarding the delivery of services. E-governance is used for recruitment of the employees and the provision of services to clients allowing access to government services from remote places. Moreover, e-governance has eliminated time and location barriers for the clients and the government employees. Hence, e-governance stipulates a continuous route for the participation of the people in government services. Also, e-governance has become part of modern public administration depending upon information and communication technology and the privatization movement has placed greater needs on the public sector to advance effectiveness. There is an increasing drift toward the AI automation of routine tasks.

Transparent and trusted data governance for regulatory compliance and reporting is of excessive significance for financial institutions. The EU [35] has a wide definition of sustainability which encompasses "activities that support economic, environmental and social (including labour and human rights) development." The European Financial Reporting Advisory Group (EFRAG) has the license to deliver sustainability-reporting standards in line with the Corporate Sustainability Reporting Directive (CSRD). [36] It has to be taken into consideration that in order to objectively fulfill reporting duties, to assess risks linked to funding decisions taken, and to make possible a feasible impact assessment of investments and operative efforts, there is a need of collecting and analyzing data along the complete value chain of corporates. Moreover, feasible data governance mechanisms via AI and AAI can control data and avert any inefficiency. Moreover, decentralization of data management boosts data monitoring, resulting in better reporting.

3.7 Knowledge Management

Currently, the process of globalization and the application of new technologies have instigated key modifications linked to the recording, organization, and management of knowledge. Hence, the use of intelligent techniques in the process of knowledge

[34] G. Zekos, Do Ethics And Corruption Shape The Rule Of Law Or Vice Versa? International Journal of Ethics, 2020 Volume 16, Number 1 https://novapublishers.com/shop/volume-16-issue-1-international-journal-of-ethics/

[35] European Commission. "Guidelines on the applicability of Article 101 of the Treaty on the Functioning of the European Union to horizontal cooperation agreements", European Commission, June 1, 2023. https://competition-policy.ec.europa.eu/system/files/2023-06/2023_revised_horizontal_guidelines_en_0.pdf

[36] EU Sustainable Finance Package, (2021). https://finance.ec.europa.eu/publications/sustainable-finance-package_en

seizing, structuring, sharing, representation, and strategic planning enhances an organizational asset.

First of all, knowledge is produced and amplified through constant transformations of forms of knowledge. Knowledge management has become more and more vital as a source of value for companies. AI is one of the technical advancements included in Industry 4.0 simplifying many activities, predominantly in the managerial role. A knowledge-based economy is a source of competitiveness for businesses and countries displaying their capability to innovate along with the development of new methods and procedures. Hence, knowledge management embraces the processes that are utilized to identify, collect, and reinforce knowledge and so knowledge management controls the course of information and making certain that the right people receive the fitting information at the right time.

Human knowledge is very dynamic since existing knowledge is constantly being improved by new ones. [37] To that extent, AAI humanoid robots will bring forward the AAI knowledge generated by AAI technology and the development of the AAI society.

AI has been launched as a basis for AI knowledge management progressing knowledge gaining, developing, and sharing on top of effective utilization within corporations. AI technologies have been exploited to raise the performance of knowledge management systems in corporations to further their overall performance. Moreover, AI is becoming more and more central in corporate knowledge management, facilitating the acquisition and reprocessing of expert information. Likewise, AI is a multi-purpose technology when it comes to machine-learning tools. Corporations are handling massive amounts of data using AI and so they use the results in entering new markets, developing new goods, and providing new services.

Due to the intense competition that businesses face today, along with massive amounts of data, limited resources, and the following demand for speed in decision-making, corporations employ AI tools, mainly because of the expected implications exhibited by leading digital businesses. To that extent, the process of modification demands a re-examination of business strategy and so there is an integration of AI capabilities in corporations' functioning. Taking into account that the target of corporations is to achieve long-term performance and competitive advantage, they incorporate technology into the decision-making process following their corporate strategies. Thus, by utilizing AI, corporations uphold their competitive edge outperforming their competitors in the long run.

It has to be taken into consideration that knowing how to manage knowledge is essential in modern companies because it allows the development of an effective organizational structure and assists in the performance of various organizational

[37] Farnese, M. L., Barbieri, B., Chirumbolo, A. & Patriotta, G. (2019). Managing knowledge in organizations: A Nonaka's SECI model operationalization. Frontiers in psychology, 10(2730), p. 1–15. https://www.frontiersin.org/articles/10.3389/fpsyg.2019.02730/full

tasks and processes that have the potential to lead to the discovery of new information.

First of all, information is being exploited as a resource in today's business world. A knowledge management system embraces the integration of information technology to portray, organize, transfer, and distribute information. To that extent, knowledge management processes are becoming more automated, permitting AI systems to gather information and draw inferences from knowledge in a manner readable by machines. Knowledge platforms should be attached to AI in order to have an instantaneous collection and examination of data improving at any moment the Knowledge Management (KM). The integration of information technology and AI concepts into knowledge management methods empowers companies to get the information they want for a more competent decision-making process. [38]

AAI will generate new knowledge and automatically will be known and implemented by the AAI humanoid robots having the capacity to simultaneously adapt the system to the demands of the AAI society which means that the manifestation of AAI KM is expected.

KM system permits corporations employees to access, update, share business data, information, and knowledge and so creating and maintaining competitive advantage, minimizing risk, enhancing productivity, abridging work, and assisting businesses make faster and better decisions. Adding AI to KM substantially diminishes the extent of supervision demanded for program management. Furthermore, AAI technology will generate the AAI KM needed for AAI functions in AAI society.

3.8 MNEs and Knowledge

MNEs capability to source knowledge is crucial to the success of subsidiaries due to the fact that knowledge is the basis of new innovations generating efficiencies and sustaining competitive advantages. Moreover, MNEs' selection of whether to internally or externally source knowledge is formed by the decision to focus on managing knowledge through global value chains or promoting knowledge development in the host region by supporting new ventures and R&D activities. Thus, as MNEs become gradually centralized and headquarters get more monitoring and control competencies, knowledge-sourcing decisions are progressively centralized, degrading the capacity of subsidiaries to independently source knowledge in their host environments. It has to be taken into consideration that subsidiaries amalgamate the international competencies of the MNE with host region-exclusive advantages due to the fact that subsidiaries have embeddedness being in and of the MNE and the host

[38] Vadari, S. & Desik, P. H. A. (2021). The role of AI/ML in enhancing knowledge management systems. IUP Journal of Knowledge Management, 19(2), 7–31.

district. [39] To that extent, MNE subsidiaries obtain knowledge internally though intra-MNE networks and externally from the host region owing to the fact that MNE subsidiaries are local knowledge architects by advancing development of local corporations which means that MNE innovation deeds are globally dispersed with their results shared internally. [40]

It is worth mentioning here that the transfer of knowledge through different distant or local sourcing activities is based on trust. Moreover, trust models the knowledge environment vital to MNE subsidiaries' technology sourcing and innovation. Nonetheless, trust also interacts with external characteristics embracing host region government support for the knowledge economy to shape innovation performance demanding different knowledge acquisition by MNE subsidiaries.

It has to be taken into account that upon investment in a country, an MNE becomes exposed to a prospective degradation of the host country institutional quality and probable confiscation of local host-market assets. Thus, in countries with weak property rights, economic policy uncertainty produces uncertainty not only about policy alterations but also taking risks owing to prospective changes in investor protection laws, regulatory regimes, and monetary and fiscal policies. [41] In addition, foreign investors have limited protection from host countries' legal and political institutions. To that extent, subsidiaries in high EPU settings undergo slower asset and employment advancement and so EPU shocks in one market are linked with the reallocation of resources to subsidiaries in other countries. Finally, direct and indirect spillover effects from rising EPU in host countries initiate a noteworthy drop in firm-level investment and growth. Lin et al. [42] argue that "rising EPU in host countries leads to significant declines in MNC value. The effect is more pronounced for intangible capital-intensive and financially constrained firms."

3.9 AI Monetary Policy, Banks, and Competition

The Federal Reserve sets monetary policy to accelerate economic activity during downturns and avert overheating during expansions. Also, the Federal Reserve does not control the money supply directly relying on private banks to transfer its wanted monetary conditions to the broader economy.

---

[39] Abubakar, Y. A., Hand, C., Smallbone, D., and Saridakis, G. 2019. What specific modes of internationalization influence SME innovation in Sub-Saharan least developed countries (LDCs)?. Technovation, 79, 56–70.

[40] Lorenzen, M., Mudambi, R., and Schotter, A. 2020. International connectedness and local disconnectedness: MNE strategy, city-regions and disruption. Journal of International Business Studies, 51(8), 1199–1222.

[41] Julio, B. and Yook, Y. (2016). Policy uncertainty, irreversibility, and cross-border flows of capital. Journal of International Economics, 103:13–26.

[42] Leming Lin, Atanas Mihov, Leandro Sanz, Economic Policy Uncertainty and Multinational Companies, March 18, 2022 at: https://ssrn.com/abstract=4060441 p29.

The Federal Reserve motivates banks' behavior by adapting the interest rate it pays on banks' reserve balances and by purchasing and selling securities in the open market. [43] In addition, intensifying concentration in the banking sector unsettles the transmission of monetary policy because in uncompetitive markets, banks do not adjust their behavior in reaction to Federal Reserve policy alterations which means that monetary policy does not have its wanted outcome. Moreover, when the Federal Reserve loosens monetary policy to inspire economic activity, lenders in concentrated areas utilize their market power by keeping high interest rates rather than passing on cheaper rates to borrowers. Consequently, banks capture bigger profits but, in the process, they hinder the Federal Reserve's objective of spurring borrowing and economic activity. [44] Additionally, when the Federal Reserve tightens monetary policy to avert overheating, banks in concentrated areas utilize their market power by keeping their deposit rates rather than passing on higher interest rates to depositors. Furthermore, bank consolidation endangers competition by escalating risks to financial stability and so large bank mergers augment financial instability. [45] While the Dodd-Frank Act guided the banking agencies to think about financial stability in connection with merger applications, the agencies' appraisals to date have been primary. Additionally, the DOJ's bank merger framework disregards financial instability regardless of the threat that financial crises cause to competition. Speeding up bank concentration inhibits monetary policy transmission reducing the Federal Reserve's capacity to accelerate economic activity when conditions warrant.

It is worth noting that online-only financial corporations have occurred as competitors to traditional banks and so the expansion of these new financial corporations has stimulated endeavors to reduce the bank antitrust framework. To that extent, innovative financial technologies have altered the competitive dynamics of the banking sector and so digital financial service providers exhibit greater convenience and faster loan approvals. Hence, fintech corporations now command more than one-third of the personal loan market exceeding traditional banks. [46]

Fintech is doubtful to contest the anticompetitive outcomes of bank consolidation for the reason that digital financial services do not substitute for locally rooted banks.

---

[43] Lida R. Weinstock, Cong. Rsch. Serv., If11020, Introduction to U.S. Economy: Business Investment (2021), https://crsreports.congress.gov/product/pdf/IF/IF11020 (analyzing how strong macro economy promotes business investment).

[44] Nimrod Segev & Matthew Schaffer, Monetary Policy, Bank Competition, and Regional Credit Cycles: Evidence from a Quasi-Natural Experiment, 64 J. Corp. Fin. 101494 (2020); Yifei Wang et al., Bank Market Power and Monetary Policy Transmission: Evidence From a Structural Estimation 29 (Nat'l Bureau of Econ. Rsch., Working Paper No. 27258, 2020); Youngju Kim et al., Bank Competition and Transmission of Monetary Policy, 28 Applied Econ. Letters 421, 421 (2020) ("GDP and credit respond less strongly to monetary policy shocks in economies where the bank market is more concentrated.").

[45] Amy G. Lorenc & Jeffrey Y. Zhang, How Bank Size Relates to the Impact of Bank Stress on the Real Economy, 62 J. Corp. Fin. 101592 (2020) (concluding that financial stress at large banks has a significantly stronger, negative impact on the real economy compared to smaller banks).

[46] Christopher K. Odinet, Predatory Fintech and the Politics of Banking, 106 Iowa L. Rev. 1739, 1753–58 (2021). Julie Andersen Hill, Covid-19, Banks, and Fintechs, 74 Q. Rep. 346, 350 (2021).

Regardless of the appearance of fintech, consumers and businesses still choose banks locally [47] and so fintech does not counterweight the anticompetitive outcomes of bank consolidation. [48] Apart from fintech's growth, reinforcing bank antitrust continues to be fundamental for stimulating competition in the financial sector. [49]

3.10 Cyber-Currencies and MNEs

MNEs make up a significant part of international trade constituting a central channel for the cross-border transfer of technology and capital flows. Cyberspace and electronic technology force transparency in MNEs' behavior, more and more of NGOs' activities [50] are directed against MNEs whose business practices are scrutinized apprehensively and who are confronted with growing demands and new rules.

The growth in the use of cyberspace has been one of the most interesting technological and political developments of the late twentieth century. Thus, the emergence of e-MNEs [51] and the development of e-commerce, e-business, e-logistics, and e-marketing augment the powers of MNEs. Also, the network structures of MNEs allow an operational elasticity that makes the realization of arbitrage advantages possibly created by the utilization of differences in the law and cost structures in various countries.

Blockchain technology is reforming digital currency, in order to improve logistics and help manage digital identity in a decentralized and trustless way. Decentralization, privacy, and anonymity have been the advancements of the cryptocurrency movement since its initiation. Cryptocurrencies [52] and decentralized finance potentially stimulate financial inclusion, reduce transaction costs, increase security, and provide new capital for startups.

[47] Neil Bhutta et al., Changes in U.S. Family Finances from 2016 to 2019: Evidence from the Survey of Consumer Finances, 106 Fed. Rsrv. Bull. 1, 17 (2020) (reporting that 79% of families used online banking had visited a local bank branch in the preceding 12 months, compared to 85% of families that did not use online banking).

[48] Terri Friedline, Banking On A Revolution: Why Financial Technology Won't Save A Broken System 141 (2021).

[49] United States v. Marine Bancorporation, Inc., 418 U.S. 602, 632 (1974) ("[I]t [is] difficult to establish that the [potential competition doctrine] invalidates a particular geographic market extension merger.").

[50] G Zekos, MNEs and Human Rights in International Law in Globalization, 2006 The ICFAI Journal of International Business Law, issue October p7 www.icfaipress.org

[51] G Zekos, Economics, Finance and Law on MNEs, 2007 Nova Science Publishers, NY www.novapublishers.com G Zekos, MNE's in 21st Century, 2016 Nova Science Publications New York USA. www.novapublishers.com

[52] G. Zekos, Economics and Legal Understanding of Virtual Currencies, Banking & Financial Services Policy Report, Volume 38 Number 8 August 2019 Wolters Kluwer.

AI technologies challenge the financial institutions dominating the world of stocks and bonds [53] and so fintech innovations due to high-speed connectivity and an explosion of collected data alter commercial characteristics and behaviors. Moreover, new forms of money have sprung up attracting vast amounts of economic activity. [54] Well-functioning trading markets for stocks are decisive to any economy since they stimulate the productive allocation of capital by ascertaining precise prices for the shares of publicly traded corporations and so assisting investors to competently enter and exit their investments.

The emergence of bitcoin and other crypto assets pressures the present perception of reference currencies, in which the public confidence gradually fades away as monetary policies standing behind them strive to excuse their "own low performance by euphemisms of non-conventional interference." Also, the financial and banking sector is an area where AI applications are present and expanding.

New technologies and the globalization of the economy have facilitated tax avoidance through the shifting of profits by MNEs to low-tax jurisdictions. Hence, MNEs artificially transfer profits across borders and internalize these profit-shifting opportunities in their decision-making. In other words, the digitalization of world economies has empowered MNEs to utilize digital technologies to conveniently evade paying corporate income taxes by moving their profits from high-tax rate countries to low-tax rate countries. [55]

The emergence of cryptocurrency poses new and growing tax law challenges. To that extent, Jean Hindriks and Yukihiro Nishimura [56] argue that "low-tax countries may have a greater incentive to abandon enforcement cooperation in response to minimum tax. . .for intermediate tax differentials, the minimum tax can break down the enforcement cooperation making the high-tax countries (but not the low-tax countries) worse off."

Strategic financial management is utilized in escalating profitability and market value of MNE via the implementation of long-term effective management of its assets and liabilities and so the role of strategic financial management is concentrating on augmenting the financial capacity of MNE which means its capability to use successfully its own financial resources and to attract debt capital. Consequently, the expansion and implementation of factors of financial strategy is grounded on the usage of methods of financial market forecasting. Thus, the central priorities in strategic financial management for MNE remain the globalization of its activities through foreign direct investment and international production encompassing AI technologies and networking.

---

[53]Howell E. Jackson, The Nature of the Fintech Firm, 61 Wash. U. J.L. & Pol'y 9, 10–11 (2020). Hilary J. Allen, Driverless Finance, 10 Harv. Bus. L. Rev. 157 (2020).

[54]Michael Klausner, Michael Ohlrogge & Emily Ruan, A Sober Look at SPACs, Yale Journal on Regulation Vol. 39:228 2022

[55]Sangjun Yea, Impacts of New International Tax System on Multinational Firms' FDI, at: https://ssrn.com/abstract=4122482

[56]Jean Hindriks and Yukihiro Nishimura, The Compliance Dilemma of the Global Minimum Tax, at: https://ssrn.com/abstract=4065252 p17.

3.11 Autonomous Private Money and Competition

Bitcoin is a private, decentralized digital currency, for which transactions are authenticated using cryptographic technologies. Unlike CBDC, private, centralized money produces income that stays in private hands and not the fiscal authorities. [57] It has to be taken into account that privately owned payment systems such as PayPal, M-Pesa, Alipay, and Square have acquired extensive popularity. Lately, cryptocurrencies, stablecoins, and decentralized finance have shown prospectively to broaden and disrupt the financial or monetary system. Moreover, countries and central banks around the globe develop their own digital currencies, markedly, Central Bank Digital Currencies (CBDCs). CBDC is any widely held electronically recorded central bank liability available for transfer, whether recorded on a distributed ledger or a more conventional database. Moreover, CBDC is just one of many recent developments in payment technologies.

How do the emergence of cryptocurrencies and the development of CBDCs shape international currency competition? Does the quantity of private money represent an increase in the offered value by the economy? Does autonomous private money increase the quantity of money without any extra value produced in an economy? Is the issue of cryptocurrencies covered by value production? The cryptocurrency comprises an imperfect substitute for national currencies as a store of value or medium of exchange, yet it is not linked with a centralized government and undergoes fast advances in its technology comparative to other currencies. It has to be taken into account that the lack of strong national fiat currencies denotes a vacuum in the currency space which private cryptocurrencies fill. Prominently, the growth rate of cryptocurrency usage and convenience generates endogenously increase with adoption, giving rise to dynamic feedback and network effects. The cryptocurrency market has achieved extensive acceptance and so the digitization of money, via CBDC implementation, becomes manifest. The question is whether cryptocurrencies must be covered by a produced value in an economy because otherwise there will be a problem with value of the money.

It is characteristic that countries face competition from cryptocurrencies and other fiat currencies and their decisions to employ CBDCs are strategic. Thus, the United States and the US dollar benefit from regulation involving dollar stablecoins to be backed by US dollar reserves. The recent collapse of cryptocurrencies market denotes that cryptocurrencies cannot alter the role of money in an economy and the equitation of money and value of economy survives.

It has to be taken into consideration that government's objectives for the digitization of money have to do with an effort to boost the digital economy. Moreover, the digitization of money and cryptocurrencies are not parallel and the circulation of cryptocurrencies in parallel with fiat money has to follow the rules of monetary policy, etc. The economic implications of the issue of cryptocurrencies have to be examined.

[57] Maxi Guennewig, Currency Competition with Firms, Discussion Paper No. 378.

It is specified that "we are witnessing the birth of Bretton Woods III—a new world (monetary) order centered around commodity-based currencies in the East that will likely weaken the Eurodollar system and also contribute to inflationary forces in the West." [58] Does money represent real value? The answer is no due to cryptocurrencies plus uncontrolled printing of money and there is an imbalance concerning the quantity of money on the market versus the value of economy. [59] Moreover, Zoltan Pozsar [60] argued that "commodities are collateral, and collateral is money, and this crisis is about the rising allure of outside money over inside money." Thus, central banks have to cope with the inflationary shocks of the "commodities basis."

Does the public currency lose its role as a medium of exchange due to cryptocurrencies and firms forming digital currency? The issue of electronic money by the central banks of different states following the monetary policy rules is different from the issue of cryptocurrencies regardless of any monetary policy rules and so producing a huge quantity of money regardless of any economic development and growth.

It has to be taken into account that in an economy with integrated international financial markets, monetary policymakers have the capacity to control their monetary tools to accomplish their objective. Also, having a global currency restricts central banks in pursuing their objectives by limiting the effect of their monetary policy instruments and so under competition with cryptocurrencies, the central bank can face some restrictions on interest rates and inflation if the government currency has to retain a role as a medium of exchange. [61] In addition, the role of money as a medium of exchange is altered by the uncontrolled issue of cryptocurrencies and CBDCs. There is a need to investigate the effects of cryptocurrency competition with the international monetary system. To that extent, Pierpaolo Benigno et al. [62] argue that "the introduction of a globally used currency may substantially change the landscape of international monetary policy." Furthermore, it has to be taken into consideration that even if a cryptocurrency token has no inherent or fundamental value, it may still attain a value role in an equilibrium as the unique token for permitting payments between agents. [63]

[58] https://www.credit-suisse.com/about-us-news/en/articles/news-and-expertise/we-are-witnessing-the-birth-of-a-new-world-monetary-order-202203.html

[59] See for more: G Zekos, Monetary policy and risk management in financial globalization, 2015 Nova Science Publications New York USA. https://novapublishers.com/shop/monetary-policy-and-risk-management-in-financial-globalization/

[60] https://bitcoinmagazine.com/markets/zoltan-pozsar-on-bitcoin-financial-system

[61] Pierpaolo Benigno. Monetary policy in a world of cryptocurrencies. CEPR Discussion Paper No. DP13517, 2019.

[62] Pierpaolo Benigno, Linda M. Schilling, and Harald Uhlig, Cryptocurrencies, Currency Competition, and the Impossible Trinity Working Paper · No. 2019-108 p44.

[63] Alexandre Olbrecht , Gina Pieters, Crypto-Currencies and Crypto-Assets: An Introduction, Eastern Economic Journal (2023) 49:201–205 https://doi.org/10.1057/s41302-023-00246-1

Cryptocurrency is a form of digital money intended to be used over cyberspace and transfer value online, all without the necessity of a middleman like a bank or a payment processor. Moreover, cryptocurrencies are decentralized and so they are not issued or controlled by any government or other central authority which means that cryptocurrencies are managed by peer-to-peer networks running free, open-source software, known as the blockchain technology. In general, a central factor underlying cryptocurrencies is the mechanism of validating transactions in a decentralized way, with no central or trusted authority implicated. Furthermore, cryptocurrency is a digital representation of value that is widely used now to denominate the prices of goods or services and so operating as a "unit of account." Hence, cryptocurrency is used to make payments and is subjectively recognized by the parties to a transaction as an alternative to legal tender and objectively treated as a "medium of exchange." Thus, Bitcoin was envisioned from its outset to be used as a medium of exchange for financial transactions outside the domain of traditional institutions and government control. Nowadays, Bitcoin and other major cryptocurrencies are recognized as a payment method by a large number of different businesses and entities in the United States and worldwide. Also, cryptocurrencies can also work as a "store of value" and so it is admitted that Bitcoin can successfully serve as a store of value, particularly in an inflationary macroeconomic environment. Likewise, Bitcoin is seen as a store of value as people put their savings in it and investors bet on its price, not mentioning that there are even financial products and derivatives that are connected to its price. 64

US courts have addressed the classification of crypto as either money or a type of property outside the tax context and have generally considered it as money. In United States v. Faiella, [65] the court ascertained that Bitcoin is money for purposes of anti-money-laundering law for the reason that it is used as a medium of exchange and is in wide circulation. Moreover, in Shavers, [66] the court stated that "Bitcoin has a measure of value, can be used as a form of payment, and is used as a method of exchange. As such, the Bitcoin investments in this case can satisfy the 'investment of money' prong set out by the Supreme Court in Howey." Also, in United States v. Ulbricht, [67] the court stated that a "money laundering statute is broad enough to encompass use of Bitcoins in financial transactions." Hence, Bitcoin is considered to be used as a medium of exchange and a means of payment [68] but in Florida v Espinoza [69] held that "Bitcoin is not a normally used means of exchange" and so not

[64] Arvind Sabu, Realization's Vexations: Taxing Cryptocurrency Hard Forks, Jurimetrics Vol. 61 Issue No. 3, p. 16 (2021).

[65] 39 F. Supp. 3d 544, 545 (S.D.N.Y. 2014).

[66] SEC v. Trendon T. Shavers & Bitcoin Sav. & Tr., No. 4:13-CV-416, 2014 U.S. Dist. LEXIS 194382, at 17 (E.D. Tex. Aug. 26, 2014).

[67] 31 F. Supp. 3d 540, 570 (S.D.N.Y. 2014).

[68] United States v Murgio, 15-cr-769 (AJN) (S.D.N.Y., Jan. 12, 2017).

[69] F14-2923 (Fla 11th Cir, 22 July 2016).

money. It is characteristic that Judge Breyer in Wisc. Cent. Ltd. v. United States [70] stated that ""money" might 1 day include crypto currency" which means that the door is open for cryptocurrencies to be used as money. Furthermore, in the Hedqvist case, [71] the Court of Justice of the European Union tackled the tax treatment of cryptocurrencies for VAT purposes by expressing the view that the exchange of traditional currencies for units of Bitcoin and other "non-traditional currencies" is a financial transaction and so VAT exempt under Article 135(1)(e) of the EU VAT Directive, notwithstanding the explicit reference in that provision to "currency, bank notes and coins used as legal tender" which means that the court ruling applies to "non-traditional currencies, that is to say, currencies other than those that are legal tender in one or more countries, in so far as those currencies have been accepted by the parties to a transaction as an alternative to legal tender and have no purpose other than to be a means of payment."

It has to be taken into account that cryptocurrency is the latest form of private money. Cryptocurrencies with fluctuating prices are usually called fiat cryptocurrencies, as the value of each coin is not backed by any collateral. Cryptocurrencies with stable prices are usually called stablecoins as the value of each coin is pegged to the value of a non-crypto asset such as the US dollar. To that extent, cryptocurrency was launched as an alternative form of money that could "decentralize" finance away from central governmental control generating problems to the monetary policy of countries.

A 'new world' with real-time payments at both domestic and global levels based on central bank digital currency is possible. What about payments in an AAI world? Of course, payments will be made by AAI humanoids in an electronic form and probably via a centralized system run by AAI technology.

It is worth noting that Crypto-friendly Swiss regulation permits SwissQuote to be one of the few banks worldwide offering both brokerage accounts on traditional securities and cryptocurrency wallets by monitoring transactions in cryptocurrencies, not in a vacuum but as part of the retail investors' overall portfolio decisions. [72]

It seems that cryptocurrencies are both a monetary happening and a new class of financial security. To that extent, crypto-oriented retail investors participate in cross-assets buying or selling sprees, consequently generating cross-asset uninformed trading flows. Antoine Didisheim and Luciano Somoza [73] present that "The fast rise of cryptocurrencies from an obscure technology to a multi-trillion-dollar market has been followed by a fast legitimization. We now see cryptocurrencies being

[70] 138 S. Ct. 2067, 2076 (2018).

[71] The judgement of the Court of Justice of the European Union (CJEU) in Skatterverket v. David Hedqvist Case C264/14 ("Hedqvist").

[72] Siegel Bernard, T., Fidelity's New 401(k) Offering Will Invest in Bitcoin, The New York Times, April 26th, 2022.

[73] Antoine Didisheim , Luciano Somoza, The End of the Crypto-Diversification Myth, Swiss Finance Institute Research Paper Series N°22–53 p28.

included in the portfolios of long-established hedge funds, well-known investors, and households' 401(K)s."

It has to be taken into consideration that Bitcoin was intended to function as a "peer-to-peer electronic cash system" that is, a reliable means of payment outside the control of centralized monetary authorities. While Bitcoin has grown hugely in value, but still sees comparatively little use as a means of payment. On the other hand, the lightning network (LN) is a secondary transaction layer that runs outside the blockchain and is a net settlement system, which means that the off-chain netting benefits of the LN can assist Bitcoin to scale and function better as a means of payment. To that extent, Anantha Divakaruni and Peter Zimmerman [74] argue that "adoption of the Lightning Network has led to a reduction in Bitcoin blockchain congestion and lower mining fees... the Lightning Network can help Bitcoin achieve greater scalability, allowing it to operate better as a payments system. According to our results, if the LN had existed in 2017, congestion could have been 93 percent lower." Hence, as Bitcoin becomes a more competent payments system, users are better off.

It is characteristic that the presence of multiple currencies endangers the key function of central banking in controlling prices and inflation or eventually limits their operational tools and the interest rate.

3.12 AI and Securities

Bitcoin is an electronic form of currency unbacked by any real asset and without specie, such as coin or precious metal [75] which means that massive utilization of cryptocurrencies will generate big problems concerning monetary policy.

The effective regulation of securities markets has a significant effect on capital formation, economic security, and growth of the global economy but cyberspace has generated novel regulatory challenges for all SECs. AI technology has introduced a new method for trading corporate equities and tracking their ownership.

It is worth noting the use of cyber currencies along with the difficulty in tracing virtual currencies facilitating payments for illegal activities such as illicit drugs, etc. illustrates the new environment of contacting business. [76]

---

[74] Divakaruni, Anantha, and Peter Zimmerman. 2022. "The Lightning Network: Turning Bitcoin into Money." Working Paper No. 22-19. Federal Reserve Bank of Cleveland. https://doi.org/10.26509/frbc-wp-202219. p1.

[75] Derek A. Dion, *I'll Glady Trade You Two Bits on Tuesday for a Byte Today: Bitcoin, Regulating Fraud in the E-Conomy of Hacker-Cash*, 2013 U. Ill. J.L. Tech & Pol'y 165, 167 (2013). "It is not regulated by a central bank or any other form of governmental authority; instead, the supply of Bitcoins is based on an algorithm which structures a decentralized peer-to-peer transaction system."

[76] Carol R. Goforth, Regulation of Crypto: Who Is the Securities and Exchange Commission Protecting?, 58 AM. BUS. L.J. 643, 648 (2021). Shaanan Cohney, David A. Hoffman, Jeremy Sklaroff & David Wishnick, CoinOperated Capitalism, 119 Colum. L. Rev. 591 (2019); Lawrence

It is essential to define if and when the sale of digital assets is a security. To that extent, when ascertaining whether the sale of digital assets is a security, the most vital class of the definition is whether the sale qualifies as an investment contract. Therefore, it is worth noting that a broad definition of the term "security" was analyzed in the case of SEC v. W.J. Howey [77] and in case all four features of the Howey test are not met, an instrument will not be an investment contract, and consequently will not be a security.

Nevertheless, the Howey test was developed well before the invention of digital assets, and technology has enhanced in this area more quickly than regulation. To that extent, in SEC v. Shavers, [78] the Shavers founded and operated Bitcoin Savings and Trust (BTCST) which was an online investment format where all investments were admitted, and returns were paid in the cyber-currency Bitcoin. The court decided that for the reason that Bitcoin would be used to purchase goods and services, it was "clear that Bitcoin can be used as money." Once the court concluded that Bitcoin was money, the court held that BCST was engaging in investment contracts, subject to SEC regulations.

Bitcoin is used as money to purchase items online or pay for individual living expenses [79] but Bitcoin is limited to those places that accept it as currency. Nonetheless, it is exchanged for conventional currencies, such as the US dollar, Euro, Yen, and Yuan. Consequently, Bitcoin is a currency or form of money, and investors wishing to invest in BTCST provided an investment of money. The Court clarifies that the BTCST investments meet the definition of investment contract, and, as such, are securities.

The DAO Report specified that digital tokens themselves may be securities. A digital token is a security both in its initial offering and when it is exchanged on a secondary market. [80] It is worth mentioning here that DAO is a decentralized autonomous organization (DAO Entity), which is a virtual organization that is "embodied in computer code and executed on a distributed ledger or blockchain." [81]

The holders of DAO tokens, through smart contracts, are having voting rights on corporate governance issues through an automated system and so supplanting conventional mechanisms of corporate governance and management with AI systems which means that contractual terms are formalized, automated, and enforced

---

J. Trautman, Virtual Currencies: Bitcoin & What Now After Liberty Reserve, Silk Road, and Mt. Gox?, 20 Rich. J. L. & Tech. 13 (2014), http://www.ssrn.com/abstract=2393537.

[77] 328 U.S. 293 (1946).

[78] SEC v. Shavers, No. 4:13-CV-416, 2014 WL 4028182, at *1 (E.D. Tex. Aug. 6, 2013). https://law.justia.com/cases/federal/district-courts/texas/txedce/4:2013cv00416/146063/23/

[79] https://casetext.com/case/sec-exch-commn-v-shavers-1

[80] Michael Mendelson, From Initial Coin Offerings to Security Tokens: A U.S. Federal Securities Law Analysis, 22 Stan. Tech. L. Rev. 52, 54 (2019). Ori Oren, Ico's, Dao's, and the Sec: A Partnership Solution, 2018 Colum. Bus. L. Rev. 617, 621 (2018).

[81] U.S. Securities and Exchange Commission, Report of Investigation Pursuant to Section 21(a) of the Securities Exchange Act of 1934: The DAO (July 25, 2017), http://www.sec.gov/litigation/investreport/34-81207.pdf

using software. [82] In addition, the SEC concluded that and the moreover alter it DAO tokens are classified as securities subject to SEC registration. [83] Moreover, the Commodities Futures Trading Commission (CFTC) regards virtual currencies as commodities, and subject to CFTC jurisdiction. [84] It could be said that since a digital asset is sold, directly or indirectly, then it is an investment. [85]

It has to be taken into account that federal agencies have to review policies associated with cryptocurrencies and other digital assets embracing consumer protection in the procurement of the digital assets. [86]

3.13 Regulating Cryptocurrencies

Financial regulation has concentrated on efficiency, fairness, and stability and so cryptocurrency is a disruptive financial innovation remaking the global financial system by attempting to replace money itself. [87] It is worth mentioning here that after the failure of the Continental Congress to issue paper money not backed by gold or silver, the United States Constitution expressly in Article 1 §8 gave only the Federal Government the power to coin money. The States in Article I §10 were clearly prohibited from "making anything but gold and silver coin a tender in payment of debts." [88] Gold has an indispensable role in the monetary system for the reason that it is used as a foreign exchange reserve having a role in the face of inflation.

Bitcoin has been surrounded by marketing and product integrity problems as well as severe environmental problems and so Bitcoin was first just a payout system plagued by slower transaction times and high transaction costs. Crypto has been utilized in illegal transactions such as money laundering, tax evasion, or to trade illegal goods. Moreover, crypto remains subject to price volatility affected by many crypto thefts. [89]

[82] Justin Henning, The Howey Test: Are Crypto-Assets Investment Contracts?, 27 U. Miami Bus. L. Rev. 51, 64 (2018).

[83] Uselton v. Comm. Lovelace Motor Freight, Inc. 940 F.2d 564, 574. Revak v. SEC Realty Corp., 18 F.3d 81, 87 (2d Cir. 1994).

[84] CFTC v. McDonell, 287 F. Supp. 3d 213, 226 (E.D.N.Y. 2018).

[85] SEC Strategic Hub for Innovation & Fin. Tech., Framework for "Investment Contract" Analysis of Digital Assets (2019), https://www.sec.gov/files/dlt-framework.pdf

[86] Biden's Executive Order on Cryptocurrency, CoinDesk (March 9, 2022), https://www.coindesk.com/policy/2022/03/09/heres-the-full-text-of-bidens-executive-order-oncryptocurrency/

[87] Paul Sullivan, As Bitcoin's Price Surges, Affluent Investors Start to Take a Look, N.Y. Times, Jan. 29, 2021.

[88] Joel Seligman, Misalignment: The New Financial Order and the Failure of Financial Regulation 1–2 (Wolters Kluwer 2020).

[89] Werner Vermaak, Where Are the World's Crypto Tax Havens in 2021?, www.coinmarketcap.com; Paul Krugman, How Crypto Became the New Subprime, N.Y. Times (Jan. 28, 2022): Paul Vigua & Sarah E. Needelman, Crypto Theft One of Largest, Wall St. J. (Mar. 30, 2022).

New market structures and technologies have developed to abolish barriers to trade and compete with institutional incumbents. Taking into account the dangers of cryptocurrency and its financial and environmental risks, the Chinese government has tightened its grip on the crypto-industry. [90] It seems that while China banned all digital currencies, ruling that all virtual currency transactions are illegal focusing solely on cryptocurrency, finally it is decided that Nonfungible Tokens could continue to be traded in China as long as they were linked to blockchains such as Ethereum or Bitcoin. [91] Hence, it is deemed that ban on cryptocurrencies is grounded on curtailing financial crime and preventing economic instability. [92] William Magnuson [93] argues that “regulators, courts and scholars alike need to adopt a more comprehensive understanding of the proper ends of market regulation, one that emphasizes the purpose and spirit of finance over the false promise of efficiency.”

The SEC has brought cases against the issuers of cryptocurrencies in the so-called “initial coin offerings,” contending either that they failed to properly register the cryptocurrencies with the SEC or that they offered false or misleading information to investors. Also, the Commodity Futures Trading Commission has bought charges against crypto exchanges for running swaps facilities without proper registration. [94]

It is worth noting that information-rich markets are free of outright monopolies and other transaction costs achieving efficiency [95] and so “economic efficiency” means that economic resources are utilized in such a manner that value is maximized. [96] AI Big tech firms achieve better information due to data collection via their platforms.

---

[90] Coco Feng, China Puts Cryptocurrency Mining on Industrial Blacklist in Final Step to Eliminate the Activity, South China Morning Post, Oct. 22, 2021.

[91] Anne Stevenson-Yang, Crypto vs. China’s Digital Currency: Never the Twain Shall Meet, www.forbes.com (Jan. 12, 2022) (“China dislikes the energy consumption and greenhouse gasses associated with crypto-currency mining”). Hiroke Tabuchi, Ban from China Made Bitcoin Less Friendly to Climate, Study Says, N.Y. Times (Feb. 26, 2022). Colsen News, China Bans Cryptocurrencies But Preserves NFT (Jan. 18, 2022).

[92] https://www.weforum.org/agenda/2022/01/what-s-behind-china-s-cryptocurrency-ban/

[93] William Magnuson, The Failure of Market Efficiency, 48 BYU L. Rev. 827 (2023). https://digitalcommons.law.byu.edu/lawreview/vol48/iss3/7 p1.

[94] SEC v. Ripple Labs, Inc., S.D.N.Y., CA 20-cv-10832, Dec. 22, 2020 (alleging that Ripple Labs sold digital assets worth over $1.4 billion without registering the assets with the SEC as required by the securities laws). CFTV v. HDR Global Trading Ltd., SDNY, CA 20-cv-08132 at 2, Oct. 1, 2020 (alleging that the defendant was “operating as an unregistered futures commission merchant . . . and operating a facility for the trading of swaps without being registered as a swap execution facility . . . or as a designated contract market”).

[95] Cass R. Sunstein, Information Regulation and Informational Standing: Akins and Beyond, 147 U. PA. L. Rev. 613, 625 (1999) (“From the standpoint of efficiency, information remedies can be better than either command-and-control regulation or reliance on unregulated markets alone.”).

[96] SEC Chairman Gary Gensler, Testimony before Senate Committee on Banking, Housing, and Urban Affairs, Sept. 14, 2021 (“We keep our markets the best in the world through efficiency, transparency, and competition.”).

It is worth noting that Crypto mania had succeeded by the Great Crypto Crash of 2022. [97] Moreover, US Administration issued an Executive Order ordering a comprehensive review of Digital Assets [98] encompassing not only cryptocurrencies but also a wide range of derivative products such as stable coins and competitive products such as Central Bank Digital Currencies, popularly known as CBDCs, and tokens, including nonfungible tokens.

It could be said that cryptocurrencies are facilitating capital flight from markets, bypassing conventional restrictions. It is argued that crypto does not threaten the financial system as long as the numbers are not big enough to do that. [99] Unlike traditional stablecoins, several stablecoins were algorithmic stablecoins not backed by specific assets but rely on an algorithmic program to retain a relationship to the US dollar.

Cryptocurrency exchanges, comparable to exchanges for stocks, bonds, and other financial assets, permit customers to exchange fiat currencies for cryptocurrencies and so cryptocurrency exchanges are financial intermediaries letting customers to trade crypto assets, against either fiat currencies or other crypto assets. To that extent, Junyi Hu and Anthony Lee Zhang [100] specify that "The ability to deposit and withdraw implies that an important function of crypto exchanges is also to serve as "on/off-ramps" for crypto: allowing users to deposit fiat, exchange fiat for crypto, and withdraw crypto, or vice versa" which means that the value of cryptocurrencies is linked with fiat currencies in order to circulate in the market and not vice versa.

Sales of cryptocurrency held by investors can be taxed as property and subject to ordinary income taxation. When a crypto coin or digital asset fulfills the Howey test, [101] the Commission and the courts have determined that a crypto platform or coin is an investment contract, a type of security as defined in the Federal Securities laws. Moreover, the SEC Report settled that DAO tokens were securities for the reason that investor profits were derived from the managerial efforts of "Slock." [102]

[97] Caitlin Ostroff, Crypto-Market Turbulence Intensifies as Prices Gyrate, Wall St. J. (May 13, 2022).

[98] Executive Order on Ensuring Responsible Development of Digital Assets (Mar. 9, 2022).

[99] Kristin Johnson, Regulating Decentralized Finance: Cryptocurrency Exchanges, 62 Wm. & Mary L. Rev. 1911, 1953 (2021).

[100] Junyi Hu, Anthony Lee Zhang, Competition in the Cryptocurrency Exchange Market, at: https://ssrn.com/abstract=4472475 p6.

[101] SEC v. W.J. Howey, Co., 328 U.S. 293 (1946).

[102] The DAO, Sec. Ex. Act Rel. 81,207 (2017).

3.14 Crypto Assets, Cryptocurrencies, and Monetary Policy

As mentioned earlier, Bitcoin is a peer-to-peer electronic cash system enabling money in this cryptocurrency to be sent online, pseudonymously, and directly to a recipient without using a centralized intermediary, such as a bank. Currently, Bitcoin has transformed into an alternative hedge and safe haven for investors because of its speed in recovering from high volatilities which means that there is an allocation of investments in Bitcoin. [103] Moreover, Bitcoin's extreme rise has crushed investments in capital markets and commodity goods through altering investment decisions and managing investors' risks and so the explosive movement of Bitcoin has instigated instability in the capital market. [104] It is argued that placing Bitcoin as safe heaven is very risky as a result of its speculative and zero fundamental nature and so possibly initiating an economic bubble in the future.

It has to be taken into account that cryptocurrencies are comprehended as an unambiguous challenge to perceived shortcomings in monetary policy and the existing monetary system due to Bitcoin price behavior underlining its large volatility and low connectivity to in actual fact any other traditional asset or macroeconomic activity. Cryptocurrencies have no inherent value and their perceived value is based largely on supply and demand in the market. Thus, monetary policy innovations by both the Fed and the ECB have a sizable influence on Bitcoin prices. Sören Karau [105] argues that "disinflationary euro area monetary policy shocks lead to a persistent fall in Bitcoin valuations, whereas inflationary central bank information shocks lead to a price increase. Conversely, I find a mirror image for US shocks: Bitcoin prices increase after the monetary contraction but fall following the expansionary central bank information shock."

Crypto assets are a store of value which can be transferred or exchanged digitally and so they are intended to give individuals greater control over their finances, serving as a decentralized kind of electronic currency enabling peer-to-peer global transactions, without the input of a centralized authority such as a country or a bank. Moreover, crypto assets are a digital representation of value or contractual rights that

---

[103] Fang F, Ventre C, Basios M, Kanthan L, Martinez-Rego D, Wu F, Li L (2022) Cryptocurrency trading: a comprehensive survey. Financ Innov 8:13. https://doi.org/10.1186/s40854-021-00321-6 Voshmgir S (2021) Token Economy: How Blockchains and Smart Contracts Revolutionize the Economy https://www.oreilly.com/library/view/what-is-the/9781492072973/ch01.htm

[104] Paule-Vianez, J., Prado-Román, C., & Gómez-Martínez, R. (2020). Economic policy uncertainty and Bitcoin. Is Bitcoin a safe-haven asset? European Journal of Management and Business Economics, 29(3), 347–363. https://doi.org/10.1108/EJMBE-07-2019-0116 . López-Cabarcos, M. Á., Pérez-Pico, A. M., Piñeiro-Chousa, J., & Šević, A. (2021). Bitcoin volatility, stock market and investor sentiment. Are they connected? Finance Research Letters, 38(December), 101399. Antonakakis, N., Chatziantoniou, I., & Gabauer, D. (2019). Cryptocurrency market contagion: Market uncertainty, market complexity, and dynamic portfolios. Journal of International Financial Markets, Institutions and Money, 61, 37–51. https://doi.org/10.1016/j.intfin.2019.02.003, https://doi.org/10.1016/j.frl.2019.101399

[105] Sören Karau, Monetary policy and Bitcoin , Deutsche Bundesbank No 41/2021 P25.

can be transferred, stored, or traded electronically, and which stereotypically use cryptography, distributed ledger technology (DLT), or similar technology. It is argued that crypto-assets probably cannot be categorized as money in any of them and they are not tied to any good with a market value and they are not issued by a national state. Crypto-asset technology is producing new financial assets and new means of intermediation. Also, the new technology has the prospective to restructure activity presently taking place in the traditional financial sector. Crypto-assets transformed the prospective of decentralized systems in the financial sector. Furthermore, investments related to crypto assets are integrated into the portfolios of institutional investors. The FPC continues to judge that direct risks to the stability of the UK financial system from crypto assets and DeFi are presently limited. On the other hand, the pace of growth and prospective for interconnections with the wider financial system indicate that they will cause a number of financial stability risks in the future. [106] To that extent, the transformation of Bitcoin as a digital asset and commodity has been grounded on its escalating value and widespread utilization of Blockchain technology. [107]

Augmenting popularity and high levels of market volatility have fostered the stakes of the digital asset experimentation. The crypto-asset world is not very connected to the real economy and crypto-asset markets are not (yet) regulated exhaustively, which means that there are hardly any reliable reporting systems. [108] Cryptocurrencies were first advanced as a digital currency to use as money. DNB does not consider unbacked cryptos to be money. [109] Nevertheless, crypto is not legal tender in Australia and is not extensively accepted as payment. [110]

Prices of crypto-assets have been open to macroeconomic fundamentals such as monetary policy shocks and so they are exposed to liquidity risk. Moreover, liquidity in the crypto-asset system is unambiguously based on a few stable coins pegged to the US dollar. Presently, the crypto-asset system is not highly connected to the financial system. Also, given that crypto-asset entities do not have the needed licenses themselves, they depend on banks as a bridge between central bank

---

[106] Financial Stability in Focus: Financial Policy Committee, Cryptoassets and decentralized finance March 2022. https://www.bankofengland.co.uk/-/media/boe/files/financial-stability-in-focus/2022/cryptoassets-and-decentralised-finance.pdf

[107] VanEck. (2021). TDigital Assets: The Investment Case for Bitcoin. https://www.vaneck.com/insights/blogs/investment-outlook/the-investment-case-for-bitcoin. Poongodi, M., Vijayakumar, V., & Chilamkurti, N. (2020). Bitcoin price prediction using ARIMA model. International Journal of Internet Technology and Secured Transactions, 10(4), 396. https://doi.org/10.1504/IJITST.2020.108130

[108] Directive 2014/65/EU of the European Parliament and of the Council of 15 May 2014 on markets in financial instruments and amending Directive 2002/92/EC and Directive 2011/61/EU (OJ L 173, 12.6.2014, p. 349).

[109] https://www.dnb.nl/en/general-news/dnbulletin-2022/unbacked-crypto-assets-not-suitable-as-money/ Cunha, P. R., Melo, P., & Sebastião, H. (2021). From Bitcoin to Central Bank Digital Currencies: Making Sense of the Digital Money Revolution. Future Internet, 13(7), 165. https://doi.org/10.3390/fi13070165

[110] Crypto-assets. https://asic.gov.au/regulatory-resources/digital-transformation/crypto-assets/

currencies and the crypto-asset world to receive funding. Claudia Buch [111] argues that "Crypto-assets promise more innovative ways of providing financial services than the traditional financial system, but they also entail risks that are strikingly similar: high market concentration, complexity, common exposures, and high operational risk. And, in the end, it is not technologies that manage risks but people. The history of finance is ripe with examples of risks that have been shifted to uninformed parties—willingly or unwillingly."

It has to be taken into account that creating a harmonized legal framework for crypto-assets results in greater legal certainty and so accelerating the adoption of crypto-assets in the EU financial services sector. To that extent, MiCA protects consumers against risks connected with the investment in crypto-assets and helps them avoid fraudulent schemes. With the new rules, crypto-asset service providers must follow strong obligations to protect consumers' wallets and become liable in case they lose investors' crypto-assets. Also, MiCA protects investors by augmenting transparency and putting in place a comprehensive framework for issuers and service providers embracing compliance with the anti-money laundering rules which means that this regulation safeguards financial stability, while tolerating innovation and promoting the attractiveness of the crypto-asset sector. [112] It is characteristic that MiCA backs innovation and fair competition, while safeguarding a high level of protection of retail holders and the integrity of markets in crypto-assets which means that crypto-asset service providers expand their businesses on a cross-border basis, expediate their access to banking services by empowering them to run their activities efficiently. Likewise, the act disallows insider dealing practices or use of inside information about crypto-assets to acquire, or dispose of, those crypto-assets, directly or indirectly, whether for that person's own account or for the account of a third party.

3.15 Digitalization, DMA, MiCA, and Competition

It is worth mentioning here that the ongoing digitalization is leading to rapid transformations in the whole structure of the global economy. Two driving forces are obvious: first, digital platforms as the dominant business model, and second, an expanding role for intangible inputs such as data and software. Despite the fact that both pledge major productivity gains, warnings are growing that they also give rise to market power and enable anticompetitive practices.

---

[111] Claudia Buch, Are crypto-assets a threat to financial stability? https://www.bundesbank.de/en/press/speeches/are-crypto-assets-a-threat-to-financial-stability%2D%2D908084

[112] Regulation (EU) 2023/1114 of the European Parliament and of the Council of 31 May 2023 on markets in crypto-assets, and amending Regulations (EU) No 1093/2010 and (EU) No 1095/2010 and Directives 2013/36/EU and (EU) 2019/1937 L 150/40 Official Journal of the European Union OJ L 150, 9.6.2023, pp. 40–205.

It is argued that unregulated adoption of automation and AI leads to social, economic, and political harms by damaging competition, consumer privacy, and consumer choice, generating unduly automating work, accelerating inequality by pushing down wages, and deteriorating worker productivity. Thus, policies are required to tackle the side effects of digitalization by forwarding competition and market contestability building productivity against the background of increased market concentration. To that extent, the free entry of competitors is not only crucial to diminish monopoly rents but also to accelerate future technological advancement. Nevertheless, promoting competition in a world with fast-evolving technologies is demanding for regulators, principally since a coordinated cross-border regulation is required.

It has to be taken into account that a stable and sound regulatory framework promotes development and investment in AI technologies due to the fact that digital services are distinguished by a first-mover advantage and massive economies of scale magnetizing new entrants being a criterion for the creation of high-value-added jobs. Hence, the EU Digital Services Act is an essential step in this direction by simplifying the "start-up and scale-up" of digital services in Europe and so generating legal certainty, which offers security of investment against regulatory risks, and a common regulation effective throughout the EU, as only then the size advantages of the EU market are fully unleashed. It is worth noting that Microsoft is pushing ChatGPT to a new level by amalgamating it into its Copilot software, generating a "Chatpilot" being a software device for offering personalized assistance as part of various Microsoft applications. [113] Chatpilot might become a vital driver of innovation and efficiency, but it should also become a monitoring object for competition law enforcers and digital regulators because AI technologies might be used for anticompetitive activities allowing the controlling of the EU's new Digital Markets Act (DMA) and general competition law in order to avoid being caught in contacting anticompetitive actions.

Digital markets are systemically well established by not many of the largest online platforms, which, as a result of a perfect mixture of their competence and luck, have monopolized most of the markets, transforming themselves into unescapable intermediaries, gatekeepers, contributing to consequently commissioning, shaping, charging, and handling each of the endless storms of digital transactions. It has to be taken into account that the strengthening of gatekeepers' dominance [114] happens without a violation of ex post competition rules which means that once reaching their status as incumbents, these undertakings methodically control and outline the issues of competition without essentially engaging in any conduct prohibited by ex post competition law.

---

[113] Peter Georg Picht, ChatGPT, Microsoft and Competition Law—Nemesis or Fresh Chance for Digital Markets Enforcement?, at: https://ssrn.com/abstract=4514311

[114] Regulation (EU) 2022/1925 of the European Parliament and of the Council of 14 September 2022 on contestable and fair markets in the digital sector and amending Directives (EU) 2019/1937 and (EU) 2020/1828, OJ L 265/1, 12 October 2022.

It has to be taken into consideration that DMA forwards the entrenched market positions of a small number of large digital 'gatekeeper' platforms by imposing a set of particular obligations that are planned to support both 'market contestability' and the 'fair treatment of business users' by these platforms. While large digital platforms have produced significant innovations and consumer benefits in the past, the existing concentration of market power is estimated to harm end users and business users, now and in the future. [115]

Does not competition law apply to big digital players? The gap between the entrenched systemically monopolized digital markets, on the one hand, and the available antitrust toolkits, on the other, indicates the obvious: the rules either must be fundamentally redesigned, or there is little sense in all the anticipation regarding the "new era" of digital competition policy at all. Of course, digital players have become big via AI technology which is supposed to function in an objective way adding to competition. On the other hand, an AAI technology has to function objectively in order to be applicable in AAI society run by AAI humanoids which means that in case the functioning of AI and AAI technologies is subjective, then the elite will have a new technology to implement its plans more effectively and decisively upon humans and their plans might include the elimination of people and their replacement with AAI workers obeying and fulfilling the plans of a small elite on earth.

MiCA regulation sets rules for dealing with crypto assets in the EU and it is binding for all crypto assets that do not qualify as financial instruments, deposits, or structured deposits under the EU financial services legislation and that will be offered to EU consumers and investors or traded on an EU trading platform for crypto assets. [116] Moreover, the regulation is broad and covers the offerings and marketing of all crypto assets embracing utility tokens, asset-referenced tokens, e-money tokens, and the authorization and operation of crypto assets service providers. Furthermore, the central objectives of the regulation are to: offer legal certainty, maintain innovation, protect consumers and investors, and guarantee financial stability.

MiCA excludes new paradigms such as the DeFi (Decentralized Finance) industry and non-fungible tokens (NFT) and so MiCA leaves several components of the digital asset world outside its scope. Central bank digital currencies (CBDCs) also fall outside the scope of MiCA. Moreover, MiCA also sets conditions for crypto-asset issuers and crypto-asset service providers (CASPs). Crypto-asset issuers must offer complete and transparent information about the crypto-assets they issue, and fulfil disclosure and transparency rules. Crypto-asset service providers must be registered and employ security ratios and anti-money laundering compliance.

---

[115] A. Fletcher, 'Digital competition policy: Are ecosystems different?', OECD, 2020, https://one.oecd.org/document/DAF/COMP/WD(2020)96/en/pdf

[116] Regulation (EU) 2023/1114 of the European Parliament and of the Council of 31 May 2023 on markets in crypto-assets, and amending Regulations (EU) No 1093/2010 and (EU) No 1095/2010 and Directives 2013/36/EU and (EU) 2019/1937 *J L 150, 9.6.2023, pp. 40–205.* https://www.esma.europa.eu/esmas-activities/digital-finance-and-innovation/markets-crypto-assets-regulation-mica

Does MiCA regulation violate the principle of "technological neutrality"? It seems that MiCA regulation violates the principle of "technological neutrality" that establishes the core of the current e-money legislation, presenting doubts about whether a technically specific legislation for e-money tokens (EMTs) is required. Hence, departing from technologically neutral legislation initiates unnecessary complexity and so diminishing adaptability to future technological innovations by generating inconsistencies harming the businesses and customers that count on it. Furthermore, MiCA's objective is to further innovation and makes certain fair competition. Fair competition denotes a condition where various companies compete on equal terms, without any unfair advantages or disadvantages. On the other hand, granting exclusive access to central bank deposit facilities to banks generates an uneven playing ground for other market participants competing with banks. Thus, banks' privileged access to central banks' deposit facilities grants a substantial competitive advantage and establishes unfair discrimination among market players which means that competitors not only have unequal access to the public resource of central bank deposit facilities, consequently infringing the equal access principle, but this also furthers augmented financial instability. Additionally, the market will shift away from e-money tokens toward tokenized [117] commercial bank deposits as the preferred form of on-chain money as a result of banks' access to central bank facilities. Likewise, banks will use their privileged access to central banks to engage in cartel-like behavior and crush external competition. [118]

It is worth noting that MiCA will make it highly difficult for small players to enter the crypto-asset market which means influencing competition in the market. Concerning MiCA, the regulation failed to realize the fact that the digital market is principally cross-boundary, meaning that a CASP in another jurisdiction who does not essentially intend to issue his tokens within the EU might have EU investors willing to invest. It could be said that MiCA prioritizes the protection of banks' interests rather than advancing innovation and development in Europe and so its fragmentation undermines the current e-money legislation, setting antitrust concerns and escalating the prospective for financial instability. In other words, MiCA undermines its own objectives by backing particular market players rather than prioritizing the broader societal advantages of innovation and development in the European e-money token market.

[117] Sibert, A., Tollenaar, N., & Buiter, W. (2022). E-money tokens, tokenised money-market shares, and tokenised bank deposits. https://cepr.org/voxeu/columns/

[118] German Banking Industry Committee's proposal for achieving fungibility among deposit tokens. Oliver Wyman, JP Morgan Chase and Co. (2022). Deposit tokens. https://www.jpmorgan.com/onyx/documents/deposit-tokens.pdf

References

1. Bates, T. W., Du, F., & Wang, J. J. (2020). Workplace automation and corporate financial policy. SSRN 3556935.
2. Christodoulidis, E. (2019). The myth of democratic governance. In P. F. Kjaer (Ed.), *The law of political economy: Transformation in the function of law*. Cambridge University Press.
3. Ajunwa, I. (2020). The paradox of automation as anti-bias intervention. *Cardozo Law Review, 41*, 1671, 1673–1675 (exploring the role of algorithms in "perpetuating inequality in the labor market").
4. Lapatinas, A., Kyriakou, A., & Garas, A. (2019). Taxation and economic sophistication: Evidence from OECD countries. *PLoS One, 14*(3), e0213498.
5. Moll, B., Rachel, L., & Restrepo, P. (2021). *Uneven growth: automation's impact on income and wealth inequality* (NBER Working Papers, No 28440). National Bureau of Economic Research.
6. Guggenberger, N. (2021). Essential platforms. *Stanford Technology Law Review, 24*, 237.
7. Van Loo, R. (2020). The new gatekeepers: Private firms as public enforcers. *Virginia Law Review, 106*, 467, 474–480.
8. Zekos, G. (2014). *Risk management, corporate governance In 21st century digital economy*. Nova Science.
9. Zekos, G. (2020). Do ethics and corruption shape the rule of law or vice versa? *International Journal of Ethics, 16*(1).
10. Zekos, G. (2006). MNEs and human rights in international law in globalization. *The ICFAI Journal of International Business Law,* Issue October, p. 7. www.icfaipress.org
11. Zekos, G. (2007). *Economics, finance and law on MNEs*. Nova Science. www.novapublishers.com
12. Zekos, G. (2016). *MNE's in 21st century*. Nova Science. www.novapublishers.com

Chapter 4
Competition, Market Power, and Politics

4.1 Identifying Market Power

Market power is the capacity of a corporation facing little competition to boost its profits by cutting back on its output, either quantitatively or qualitatively. Moreover, while companies earn higher profits when they exercise market power, consumers undergo harm in the way of higher prices and/or diminished quality and so market power allows raising prices profitably by restricting output. On the other hand, market power occurs on the buyer side of the market, denoted as monopsony power, where a buyer exerting monopsony power holds back demand to drive down price and so augmenting its profits. [1] By the way, monopsony is the capability of buyers to dictate prices, working conditions and terms of employment that transfer some of the values generated by the employer–employee relationship to the employer. It could be said that monopsony power could diminish both consumer and aggregate welfare and so courts have denied holding monopsonists liable under Section 2 of the Sherman Act for harm to upstream sellers without convincing proof of consumer harm. The Supreme Court [2] found no violation when a plaintiff did not show a dangerous probability that monopsonist Weyerhaeuser could recoup from alleged predatory bidding on a key input by raising prices downstream and so the Court disallowed the premise that exercising monopsony power automatically harms downstream consumers as well as monopsonist suppliers.

It has to be taken into consideration that when economic power is concentrated, it damages not only economic freedom but also political freedom due to the fact that the rich and powerful utilize their resources to capture the government and swindle it in their favor which means that economic wealth shapes politics and politics

[1]Roger D. Blair & Jeffrey E. Harrison, Monopsony: Antitrust Law And Economics (1993).

[2]Weyerhaeuser Co v Ross-Simmons Hardwood Lumber Co 549 US 312 (2007) Leegin Creative Leather Prods., Inc. v. PSKS, Inc., 551 U.S. 877, 897 (2007) (observing that market power is necessary for anticompetitive harm, and thus liability, from RPM).

© The Author(s), under exclusive license to Springer Nature Switzerland AG 2023
G. I. Zekos, *Artificial Intelligence and Competition*, Contributions to Economics,
https://doi.org/10.1007/978-3-031-48083-6_4

influence or form the law accordingly. [3] There was an effort of solving problems linked with the excessive power of large corporations [4] but regulations incorporate political imperfections permitting interest groups to control markets for their own advantage.

It could be said that regulators may advance immediately effective rules prohibiting dominant corporations from exercising their market power. Moreover, the principal limitation of ex ante conduct rules is that they often produce costly errors for the reason that the planners endorsing generally applicable, resource-allocating directives outside a specific, examinable factual context lack the information required to ascertain in advance which precise behaviors will diminish market output and which will augment it.

It is worth noting that markets may steadily fail to allocate resources in a manner that produces as much value as possible for the members of the society. To that extent, government interventions to correct instances of market failure might not take place as well. Thomas A. Lambert [5] argues that "Ex ante conduct rules are faster and more determinate, but they are more likely to generate high error costs because planners lack the information they need to determine, in advance and for a wide variety of actors, what behaviors will enhance or reduce social welfare."

Again, digital markets currently feature a dominant provider such as Google for Internet search, YouTube for hosting user-generated videos, Amazon for online retailing, Google's suite of advertising technology services for buying and selling digital advertisements, Facebook for social networking, and Apple's and Google's proprietary app stores for their particular mobile operating systems (iOS and Android) which means that the lack of competition in these markets has resulted in predictable market-power damages embracing higher prices and decreased quality. Presently, monopoly has generated supra-competitive prices for mobile-app distribution and digital-advertising services.

It is argued that monopolies drive evolution for the reason that the monopoly profits stipulate a powerful motivation to innovate which means that monopolies are innovating since profits empower them to make the long-term plans and to finance research projects that companies locked in competition cannot consider.

Customarily, governments have employed means to address market power concerns such as antitrust law remedying the circumstances in which market competition breaks down by collusion and monopoly. [6] Nowadays, Sherman Antitrust Act § 1 forbids agreements that "unreasonably" restrain trade, and § 2 prevents unreasonably exclusionary conduct generating market power. To that extent, in all cases, the reasonableness of a challenged act turns on its apparent impact on market output

[3] G Zekos, Political, Economic and Legal Effects of Artificial Intelligence, 2022, https://link.springer.com/book/10.1007/978-3-030-94736-1#toc

[4] Carl Shapiro, Antitrust in a Time of Populism, 61 Int'l J. Indus. Org. 714, 715 (2018).

[5] Thomas A. Lambert, Addressing Big Tech's Market Power: A Comparative Institutional Approach, 75 SMU L. Rev. 73 (2022) https://scholar.smu.edu/smulr/vol75/iss1/8 p 115.

[6] Sherman Antitrust Act of 1890, ch. 647, 26 Stat. 209 codified 15 U.S.C. §§ 1–7.

which means that if the act boosts market output for the benefit of consumers, it is reasonable; if output reduction and consumer damage are expected, the act is unreasonable and consequently illegal. [7] There are agreements or practices which as a consequence of their destructive consequence on competition are categorically presumed to be unreasonable and consequently illegal without detailed inquiry as to the precise damage, they have triggered. [8]

It has to be taken into account that horizontal inter-firm coordination is a device that is used by influential corporations, and not only by smaller actors and so horizontal coordination is a device available to smaller, independent actors in the market maintaining their status. To that extent, investment banks and venture capitalists via the companies they control pursue horizontal consolidation and vertical control of smaller actors in their scopes as alternate strategies for securing a grip or for stabilizing their markets like taking place in oligopolistic markets containing powerful corporations.

Antitrust law has played an essential part in the making of the workplace [9] in which dominant corporations utilize control over smaller actors in their orbits while renouncing responsibility for their activities. Justice Stevens [10] supported the Chicago School analysis condemning horizontal coordination among small actors as a distortion of ideal market outcomes. It could be said that a corporation's ability to exclude competition is linked to its number of customers.

Digital technologies are a critical determinant of economic growth, national security, and international competitiveness. To that extent, the effect of digitalization is that via technological developments in information collection, storage, and exchange, digitalization influences the interface of corporations with their customers, with momentous outcomes on e-commerce and fintech and so large technology corporations and digital platforms are extending market share in both financial and goods retailing which means that these two markets become increasingly interlinked. Thus, digitalization makes it possible to generate and process information in a fully automated way and so by analyzing data AI permits for a fully automated data exchange between market participants or members of the value chain. In other words, network effects and efficiency gains are economic consequences of these process innovations for both e-commerce and fintech generating problems of competition in the market. Luca Dedola et al. [11] argue that "Digital

[7] United States v. Grinnell Corp., 384 U.S. 563, 570–71 (1966); Thomas A. Lambert, Defining Unreasonably Exclusionary Conduct: The "Exclusion of a Competitive Rival" Approach, 92 N.C. L. Rev. 1175, 1178 (2014). Herbert Hovenkamp, The Antitrust Enterprise: Principle And Execution 2–5, 8 (2005) (describing an output-focused understanding of competition).

[8] N. Pac. Ry. Co. v. United States, 356 U.S. 1, 5 (1958).

[9] Continental T.V., Inc. v. GTE Sylvania Inc., 433 U.S.36 (1977) (expanding the permission of geographical market allocation restraints placed by franchisors upon franchisees, and heralding the contemporary permissive attitude toward vertical restraints more generally).

[10] Fed. Trade Comm'n v. Super. Ct. Trial Lawyers Ass'n, 493 U.S. 411 (1990).

[11] Luca Dedola, Michael Ehrmann, Peter Hoffmann, Ana Lamo, Gonzalo Paz Pardo, Jiri Slacalek, Georg Strasser, Digitalisation and the economy, ECB Working Paper Series No 2809 P34.

technologies open up great opportunities but also pose substantive challenges, and their ultimate effects will largely depend on the adoption of appropriate public policies at the national and international level. While the potential benefits of digitalisation for growth and consumer welfare may be often apparent, their drawbacks and challenges, and how to address them, may appear less obvious."

It has to be taken into consideration that the market competition equilibrium is overwhelmed by matters such as inadequate data sharing, excessive computing power investment, and insufficient allocation of computing power to innovation departments denoting that there is a need of planning strategies to foster efficient resource allocation and sustainable growth in the digital age. To that extent, Danxia Xie et al. [12] argue that " in a socially optimal equilibrium, consumers should share their data with firms until the marginal benefits equal the marginal costs. The marginal benefits arise from two sources: the utilization of data in the production sector, which enhances output, and the utilization of data in the innovation sector, which expands product variety."

The digital platform economy has revolutionized the manner consumers interact with each other, work, shop, and practically all aspects of everyday life reaping the full advantages of the digital era. The rise of cyberspace has not eliminated market imperfections. To that extent, it is decisive that digital markets stay healthy and competitive tolerating the materialization of new and innovative products and services. On the contrary, the digital platform economy has seen the rise of high-technology enterprises wielding unprecedented market power (Google, Apple, Facebook, and Amazon). Digital markets display a series of economic characteristics which are liable to give rise to positions of lasting and extensive market power. It could be said that the persistent market power of large digital platforms, coupled with a perceived failure of antitrust investigations to secure the contestability of digital markets, brings forward the need to update antitrust rules so that they are fit for the digital age. [13]

Are digital markets unique? Digital markets are not naturally monopolistic [14] because platforms frequently compete with non-platforms not mentioning that network effects of digital markets arise with regard to specific inputs and services, and not to entire corporations. A digital firm is naturally monopolistic as long as deals with new goods and services offered only by the specific digital firm and not be able to be copied.

German Competition Act [15] disallows self-preferencing by dominant corporations imposing on them affirmative obligations of interoperability and data

[12] Danxia Xie, Wenshi Wei, Yao Li, A General Theory of Digital Economy The World after Turing, https://ssrn.com/abstract=4531884 p 26.

[13] Jullien, B., & Sand-Zantman., W. (2021). The economics of platforms: A theory guide for competition policy. Information Economics and Policy Vol. 54.

[14] Herbert Hovenkamp, Antitrust and Platform Monopoly, 130 Yale L.J. 1901, 1933, 1950 (2021).

[15] German Competition Act, https://www.gesetze-im-internet.de/englisch_gwb/; Gibson Dunn, "Digitalization Act": Significant Changes to German Antitrust Rules (Jan. 28, 2021), https://www.gibsondunn.com/digitalization-act-significant-changes-to-german-antitrust-rules/

portability and so advancing a new category of market power by corporations with vital substance for competition across markets embracing digital actors that have considerable impact on certain markets without having substantial market shares in those markets. Moreover, dominant corporations with financial strength and access to data related to competition are prohibited from conduct generating self-favoring and so impeding competitors by leveraging market power. Data collected in a market in which a company is dominant cannot be utilized to generate or increase barriers to entry in other markets and so hindering interoperability and data portability which means offering insufficient information to other corporations to evaluate its services.

Antitrust laws are meant to protect sellers and workers. Also, antitrust laws are intended to prevent harmful accumulations of market power implied from the seller's possession of a predominant share of the market but under current merger policy, the burden is on enforcers to make the case that merging corporations will possibly lessen competition and so resulting in lax merger review and uncontested large-scale acquisitions. To that extent, the Supreme Court has rationalized that underlying market power is the capacity to compel a purchaser to do something that he would not do in a competitive market. [16] Thus, the offense of monopoly under 15 U.S.C. § 2 has two components: first, the possession of monopoly power in the relevant market; and second, the willful acquisition or maintenance of that power as distinguished from growth or development as a consequence of a superior product.

Moreover, labor-market concentration utilizes downward pressure on wages and stimulates employers to shift the costs of training onto workers which means that greater inequality [17] among corporations hiring in a labor market arises. [18]

[16] Eastman Kodak Co v Image Technical Services, Inc, 504 US 451, 464 (1992). Jefferson Parish Hospital District No 2 v Hyde, 466 US 2, 14 (1984).

[17] Jonathan B. Baker& Steven C. Salop, Antitrust, Competition Policy, and Inequality, 104 Geo. L. Online 1, 14 (2015) ("Concerns with inequality can implicate antitrust and competition policy in two general ways. First, in that market power contributes to inequality, more aggressive antitrust enforcement might play a remedial role. Second, antitrust enforcers and regulatory agencies such as the Federal Communications Commission (FCC) might make reducing the effects of inequality a high priority in developing enforcement and regulatory initiatives.").

[18] David Berger, Kyle Herkenhoff, and Simon Mongey, Labor Market Power, Institute of Labor Economics Discussion Paper No 12276, Apr 2019.

4.2 Antitrust and Politics

It is argued that, in enacting the antitrust laws, Congress made a political pick regarding the desirability of market competition and the undesirability of particular conduct harmful to it. Zingales [19] observes that concentration [20] levels in most industries have increased and so augmenting the capacity to collect supra-competitive rents which makes it easier to organize and lobby for laws and policies that will safeguard this rent collection capacity. Moreover, Ariel Katz [21] argues "that unchecked private economic power may be as injurious to individual freedom and other liberal values as unchecked political power, and that the two may be mutually constitutive." It is characteristic that the Chicago School insisted that antitrust law could only be legitimately concerned with maximizing economic efficiency. It seems that antitrust law was always concerned not only with the economic aspects of competition but also with the connection between market competition and politics via the implementation of demands of the law.

The increasing power of computational technology has intertwined antitrust policy with international politics and national security. Electronic technology has augmented the ways of attack and altered traditional weapons of war. Thus, innovations in hardware and software have launched new techniques of espionage and cyberwarfare such as cyber propaganda, trolling, and sophisticated hacking and so technological acceleration has led to an international battle for technological supremacy generating a "technology cold war." [22]

Risks of devious applications of AI for influencing public opinion and electoral interference need attention. When AI is in the hands of oppressive governments or unethically operating corporations, AI can be utilized for political gain, exploitation, and weakening of political freedom.

Antitrust regulation of technology is central to the economy because it is altering the future of the tech industry and having domino effects on sectors from healthcare and manufacturing to transportation and energy. It could be said that the undermining of antitrust as a check on concentrated private power has caused economic inequality. [23] Besides, boosting efficiency is not the single objective of

---

[19] Luigi Zingales, Towards a Political Theory of the Firm, 31 J Econ Perspectives 113 (2017).

[20] Gustavo Grullon, Yelena Larkin & Roni Michaely, Are US Industries Becoming More Concentrated?, 23 Rev. Fin. 697, 700 (2019) ("industry concentration over the last two decades has markedly increased.").

[21] Ariel Katz ,The Chicago School and the Forgotten Political Dimension of Antitrust Law , The University of Chicago Law Review 87:413 P457 Barak Orbach, The Present New Antitrust Era, 60 Wm & Mary L Rev 1439, 1439 (2019) ("[t]he present new antitrust era is a product of growing tensions and contradictions among policy prescriptions").

[22] Jon Harper, U.S., Allies Bolstering Electronic Warfare Systems, Nat'l def. Mag. (Feb. 27, 2020), https://perma.cc/75JW-Y94B ("The U.S. is expected to lead the way in electronic warfare spending [over the next several years.]").

[23] Lina Khan & Sandeep Vaheesan, Market Power and Inequality: The Antitrust Counterrevolution and Its Discontents, 11 Harv. L. & Pol'y Rev. 235 (2017).

antitrust and identifying economic freedom but fairness is an additional desirable purpose. In addition, exercises of power by large companies operate as structures of private governance which means that antitrust law and policy must be a key means of democracy reforming.

It seems that antitrust has become much more technical, predominantly in subjects such as merger enforcement and exclusionary behavior, but also in more collateral matters such as judging causation and calculating damages. [24] Thus, due to the fact that its technical competence has amplified, its "movement" quality has declined and becomes a political matter and so technical antitrust has become less stimulating to politicians, who cannot win elections by talking about Indexes or average variable cost.

It has to be taken into consideration that laws organizing the economy, involving antitrust, should be concentrated on preventing economic domination. It seems that antitrust law is at its best a device for verifying the power of dominant corporations. On the one hand, competition cannot be reduced to its result such as allocative efficiency. On the other hand, competition has to be an instrument of dispersion of economic and political power which means that there can be no efficiency without free competition.

It is worth mentioning here that the Chicago School transferred the analytical emphasis away from the process required for competition [25] and towards an outcome such as consumer welfare. On the other hand, a valuable process concerning competition implementation results in competitive outcomes for the whole economy and subsequently to players of the markets such as consumers and customers.

It is worth noting that competition law's purpose ought to be to stimulate and protect a political economy offering a society's best amalgam of competition and cooperation, in view of its culture, history, technology, and political situation at a given period of time. [26]

Fox [27] advocates that antitrust law preserves the competitive process by maintaining the incentives generating productive, dynamic, and market efficiency which means that welfare, in the form of total welfare rather than just consumer welfare, encapsulates the priorities of competition law via the protection of the process of competition due to the fact that digital markets involve harms that are not portrayed by the welfare criterion but are clarified on the grounds of harm to the process of competition.

---

[24] Herbert Hovenkamp, Whatever Did Happen to the Antitrust Movement?, 94 Notre Dame L. Rev. 583, 585 (2018).

[25] Eleanor M. Fox, Against Goals, 81 Fordham L. Rev. 2157, 2160 (2013) ("The big choice is between outcome orientation, on the one hand, and concern for process as well as outcome, on the other".).

[26] A Foer and A Durst 'The multiple goals of antitrust' (2018) 63(4) The Antitrust Bulletin 494 at 498 and 501–506.

[27] E Fox 'The efficiency paradox' in R Pitofsky (ed) How the Chicago School Overshot the Mark: The Effect of Conservative Economic Analysis on US Antitrust (Oxford: Oxford University Press, 2008) pp 79–88.

To that extent, antitrust statutes underline the importance of competition by declaring the safeguarding of competition as their purpose. Again, the preservation of competition in commerce has always served as the most perceptive and apparent objective of competition laws. Hence, the objective of upholding competition is concentrated on the protection of a procedure, while advancing consumer welfare arranges "the maximization of a value" which means that there is a need for redeploying antitrust on protecting the competitive procedure and so generating enforcement more in line with real business existences and implementing the legal intent.

It is worth noting that corporations with market power can damage competition over a significant period for the reason that the marketplace finally will undercut the success of any anticompetitive restraints as consumers change to substitutes or new companies enter the market. [28] On the other hand, markets do not always respond as quickly as scholars assume because of market inactivity and information failures, a business can hamper competition over some period of time. Thus, characteristically suspect conduct is expected to harm competition in most cases and so there is no need for dispensing with a market power analysis of conduct. [29]

Vertical integration enhances innovation through the sharing of technological information common to separate stages of an industry. Moreover, vertical mergers encompass the integration of two ventures up or down operating in different markets and not engaging in direct competition and so merger approval typically occurs because under current DOJ merger guidelines, non-horizontal mergers implicate companies not operating in the same market, their combination would result in no immediate change in the level of market concentration. [30] It has to be taken into account that vertical integration may result in downstream companies being cut off from suppliers. [31] By contrast, horizontal mergers activate closer scrutiny for the

---

[28] Thomas M. Jorde and David J. Teece, *Rule of Reason Analysis of Horizontal Arrangements: Agreements Designed to Advance Innovation and Commercialize Technology*, 61 Antitrust L.J. 579, 602–03 (1993) (stating that the marketplace will discipline firms that attempt to restrain trade if they lack substantial market power); M. Laurence Popofsky and David B. Goodwin, *The "Hard-Boiled" Rule of Reason Revisited*, 56 Antitrust L.J. 195, 203 (1987) (indicating that two firms that agree to a horizontal restraint are unlikely to injure competition if they lack market power). FTC v. Superior Court Trial Lawyers Ass'n, 493 U.S. 411, 434–35 (1990). Dennis A. Yao and Thomas N. Dahdouh, *Information Problems in Merger Decision Making and Their Impact on Development of an Efficiencies Defense*, 62 Antitrust L.J. 23, 27 (1993) ("Efficiency considerations and general principles of law suggest that the party with access to the relevant information should bear the burden of proving an issue dependent on that information.").

[29] Phillip Areeda, *The Changing Contours of the Per Se Rule*, 54 Antitrust L.J. 27, 28 (1985). "Once we decide that a class of practice is in the vast generality of cases detrimental and unjustified, why bother with the complicated and expensive inquiry into power?".

[30] Brent Skorup & Adam Thierer, Uncreative Destruction: The Misguided War on Vertical Integration in the Information Economy, 65 fed. Comm. L.J. 157, 173 (2013).

[31] Janusz A. Ordover et al., Equilibrium Vertical Foreclosure, 80 am. Econ. Rev. 127, 131–40 (1990).

reason that the proposed transaction entangles two companies whose combination concentrates a single market by dropping the number of standalone competitors.

It has to be taken into account that a merger may be designed to kill a future or 'potential' competitor is often overlooked as too speculative and that is why American and European agencies permitted Facebook and Google to buy many of their major prospective competitors which means that innovation and dynamic consequences, being harder to evaluate, do not get due consideration. Also, antitrust enforcement agencies are unable or unwilling to judge instances where a merger or acquisition has multidimensional effects with instantaneous effects on vertical, horizontal, core, and adjacent markets such as in the case of multifaceted market diversification of Amazon which is vertically and horizontally integrated by creating, packaging, selling, and storing all sorts of content.

An original objective of federal antimonopoly legislation was to promote fair competition and business practices, and to furnish a check on emerging consolidations of economic power in both inter- and intra-company arrangements. [32] There is a positive correlation between concentration and profits but concentration may mark superior efficiency rather than a lack of competition. It could be said that commercial decisions are inspired either by attempts to multiply monopoly power or by efforts to advance efficiency which means that horizontal market power is not the immediate objective but the operation is intended to boost efficiency. To that extent, antitrust laws are enforced with the objective of promoting efficiency. Reiter v. Sonotone Corp [33] specified that Congress constructed "the Sherman Act as a 'consumer welfare prescription'." It could be said that consumer welfare stipulates a legitimate criterion insofar as it does not carry underlying values or political choices. In other words, consumer welfare has to be improved via rightful competition due to the fact that this criterion has to be the protection of the competitive process which means that competition policy should sanction all practices worsening the competitive process. In addition, consumer welfare cannot be the only criterion, as it does not capture all the damage to competition.

It is argued that that the dominant technology companies hurt consumers, laborers, and small businesses by contributing to wealth inequality by earning monopoly profits for their shareholders and so excessive political power that undermines democracy. [34] To that extent, governments have used several different methods restricting welfare losses from market power such as antitrust law aiming at averting the creation or enhancement of market power by means other than competition on the merits. Moreover, direct regulation is another way of banning

[32] Neil W. Averitt, The Meaning of "Unfair Methods of Competition" in Section 5 of the Federal Trade Commission Act, 21 B.C. L. REV. 227, 234–35 (1980) (describing the legislative history of the FTC Act, highlighting legislators' central concern with the concepts of fair and unfair competition).

[33] 442 U.S. 330, 343 (1979).

[34] Lina M. Khan, Amazon's Antitrust Paradox, 126 Yale L.J. 710, 739–40 (2017); Marshall Steinbaum & Maurice E. Stucke, The Effective Competition Standard: A New Standard for Antitrust, 87 U. Chi. L. Rev. 595, 595 (2020).

certain exercises of market power and promoting market competition. The state possesses the right to use means such as antitrust law in order to achieve its objectives translated into implementation of competition. [35]

It is worth noting that under the effective-competition standard, antitrust policy would protect individuals, consumers, workers, and others throughout the supply chain, but would also concentrate on upholding opportunities for competitors, stimulating individual autonomy and well-being, and de-concentrating private power. Hence, the protection-of-competition test examines consumer welfare harms, [36] but the ultimate concern would be "distortion or suppression of the competitive process."

Again, antitrust does not prohibit the creation, maintenance, or improvement of market power by procompetitive means such as innovation or gains in productive efficiency and so it does not forbid a company that has acquired market power legitimately from exercising that power by charging supra-competitive prices. In other words, the simple possession of monopoly power, and the parallel charging of monopoly prices, is not only legal but also it is an imperative part of the free-market system. To that extent, in order to safeguard the motivation to innovate, the possession of monopoly power is not unlawful except if it is accompanied by an element of anticompetitive conduct. [37]

It has to be taken into consideration that the accumulative concentration of market power has both a conceivable impact on efficiency by preventing prospective competitors from investing and from innovating but also on the vigor of democracy due to the fact that the higher the financial risks connected with adverse political choices, the higher the capability and the incentives to invest for utilizing an effect on political power.

Antitrust policy is a device in a complex global economy and political landscape being utilized in the context of a state's overall international policies and goals. National security is entangled with antitrust policy. In addition, antitrust law has always marked foreign policy being evident in the various international antitrust organizations and agreements in existence. Enforcement decisions have political and economic consequences for countries globally. Nonetheless, antitrust law plays a vital role in international politics nowadays as a result of the rise of technology not mentioning the emergence of AI and AAI. Thus, technology has transformed foreign intelligence and espionage and so countries have struggled for control of the technology industry instigating "the technology cold war." Many countries such as the United States, Russia, and China have used antitrust regulation to advance their status in this technology war. Consequently, technological advancement necessitates

[35] Max Weber, Politics as Vocation, in From Max Weber: Essays In Sociology 78 (H.H. Gerth & C. Wright Mills eds. & trans., 1958) (observing that government possesses a "monopoly of the legitimate use of physical force within a given territory".

[36] Le v Zuffa, LLC, 216 F Supp 3d 1154, 1163 (D Nev 2016) ("[R]eduction of competition does not invoke the Sherman Act until it harms consumer welfare."), quoting Rebel Oil Co v Atlantic Richfield Co, 51 F3d 1421, 1433 (9th Cir 1995).

[37] Verizon Commc'ns Inc. v. L. Offs. of Curtis V. Trinko, LLP, 540 U.S. 398, 407 (2004).

that antitrust enforcement be carefully harmonized with foreign policy. [38] In 2020, the DOJ indicted Huawei for intellectual property theft and conspiring to steal trade secrets. [39]

There is a global war concerning 5G technologies demanding the isolation of Huawei provider of 5G, not mentioning that the United Kingdom is pursuing an alliance of democratic nations seeking to generate an alternative pool of 5G technology and equipment. [40] It is argued that by compelling an expansive compulsory licensing remedy has the prospective to negatively influence innovation in 5G technologies and compromise national security. [41] In 2018, Chinese antitrust regulators blocked Qualcomm from acquiring rival chipmaker NXP ordering Chinese public institutions to replace foreign software and computer equipment with local suppliers within a few years. Thus, both China and the United States have leveraged antitrust regulation to give national corporations a strategic international competitive advantage. Notwithstanding, the clash over the future of technology exposes how antitrust regulation plays a central part in an effort for technological, economic, and political power.

It seems that antitrust in the United States has resisted the effort to politicize it and so despite being embedded in vague and expansive statutory language, the US antitrust is economically grounded, evolutionary, and limited to a set of achievable social welfare goals. It has to be taken into account that the EU has endorsed an aggressive pursuit of technology platforms under its antitrust laws. Moreover, bringing high-profile cases against large Internet platforms should not prioritize political expediency over the rule of law. Otherwise, it would open facilitating damaging tendencies, such as non-economic decision-making, rent-seeking, regulatory capture, and politically motivated enforcement which means that once antitrust is extended beyond its economic constraints and infused with political content, it ceases to be an exceptionally precious device for addressing real economic harms to consumers and becomes a device for routing around legislative and judicial constraints.

Competition law has to remain law regulating the equality of companies in looking for customers and not becoming a tool in the hands of politics. It could be said that the excessive concentration of markets leads to economic power directing to political power [42] which means that protecting competitive markets and averting

[38]FTC v. Qualcomm, Inc., 969 F.3d 974 (9th Cir. 2020) (No. 19-16122) (arguing that an antitrust enforcement decision against Qualcomm, a domestic company, will shift the United States' dominance in 5G technologies and harm national security).

[39]Chinese Telecommunications Conglomerate Huawei and Subsidiaries Charged in Racketeering Conspiracy and Conspiracy to Steal Trade Secrets, U.S. Dep't Just. (Feb. 13, 2020), https://perma.cc/B8LX-6QQH

[40]Srijan Shukla, UK Wants 5G Alliance of 10 Countries, Including India, to Avoid Reliance on Chinese Huawei, Print (May 29, 2020, 4:34 PM), https://perma.cc/9WWW-69W4

[41]FTC v. Qualcomm, Inc., 969 F.3d 974 (9th Cir. 2020) (No. 19-16122).

[42]Matt Stoller, How Democrats Killed Their Populist Soul, The Atlantic (Oct. 24, 2016), https://www.theatlantic.com/politics/archive/2016/10/how-democrats-killed-their-populist-soul/504710/

concentrations of immense power are indispensable components of democratic development. A noteworthy and costly result of the augmented politicization of antitrust is the expansion of antitrust exemptions and so the growth of the sphere of economic activity to which antitrust does not apply at all.

It could be said that US antitrust law has proved a much weaker tool for policymakers to attack the conduct of large tech companies and so US antitrust law has been ineffective at preventing the consolidation of industries. It seems that politics is hiding behind vague economic approaches concerning the impact upon competition.

It is clear that politics by promoting the Chicago School thoughts have utilized economics in the competition area in order to pass capital interests against the real need of consumers and not the ones imposed via marketing upon them. Will the Chicago School approach be imposed upon AI society via controlled AI technology? Will the advancement of AAI technology impose a singularity in all aspects of life and even eliminate competition by imposing standardization of technology for every aspect of employment of AAI systems in a global AAI society inhabited by AAI humanoid robots running under a single brand? It seems that as long as AI is a tool in the hands of humans, the Chicago School approach concerning antitrust law will apply in many jurisdictions. On the other hand, the advancement of an AAI society based on objective AAI functioning will impose certain criteria of advancing competition rather than corporations' interests regarding antitrust law and policy allowing a free entrance market for all participants. In other words, the game of the Big Tech companies will end in favor of a free online commerce rather than the currently nearly monopolized one.

In the World Government Summit 2023, Klaus Schwab underlined the necessity to develop new mechanisms that strengthen international cooperation in today's multipower world. On the other hand, the holder of the better AI technology will govern the globe accordingly as G.I. Zekos [43] has written that "advanced electronic technology can be used in order to paralyze an inferior technology of a state and therefore threatening practically its sovereignty."

4.3 AI Technologies and Labor

It has to be taken into account that greater globalization lets successful entrepreneurs grow their profits more rapidly and so putting further upward pressure on income inequality which means that when economies of scale are present, the integration of global markets results in a growing concentration of the market power among a few

[43] Zekos G, 'Internet or Electronic Technology: A Threat to State Sovereignty', Commentary 1999 (3) The Journal of Information, Law and Technology (JILT). http://elj.warwick.ac.uk/jilt/99-3/zekos.html . New citation as at 1/1/04: http://www2.warwick.ac.uk/fac/soc/law/elj/jilt/1999_3/zekos/

worldwide leaders. To that extent, concentration is very salient in the case of IT enterprises such as Amazon or Alphabet, but also in other zones in which digital innovation is crucial, embracing pharmaceuticals or automobiles. Even though sometimes rental fees from innovation are shared with the workers, the labor share has lessened more in states with more digital innovation and innovative sectors with more market concentration.

Likewise, AI is a general-purpose technology influencing work in almost every occupation. Automation, involving AI-enabled automation, influences overall aggregate employment and aggregate wages, along with the wage and employment distribution. Moreover, new technology developments abolish jobs by automating tasks (displacement effect) or by complementing human labor which means permitting for a more flexible allocation of tasks and intensifying productivity (productivity effect) and so, in turn, contributing to amplified demand for labor in non-automated tasks. Also, some tasks and jobs are being replaced but new tasks and jobs are generated either owing to innovation or due to old technologies becoming so cheap that their demand starts rising and so facing the well-known "reinstatement effect." Furthermore, there are several indirect means that act across industries such as the spillover effects, either by increases in productivity transmitted across businesses through the intermediate inputs or by upturns in incomes that generate higher aggregate demand. In other words, upsurges of automation and new technology have been convoyed with concern regarding the future of jobs and with fears about labor becoming redundant.

It has to be taken into consideration that there is an urgent need to improve the productivity outcomes from the digital economy, particularly through the completion of the Single Digital Market in EU. [44] AI coupled with analytics presents greater focus and contextual insights, permitting both technical and non-technical workers to function more competently. To that extent, G.I. Zekos considers that the current AI forces workers to become more skillful but not eliminating human work but the forthcoming AAI technology implemented by humanoids will put humanity in danger/jeopardy of its existence as a type of entity on earth because any autonomy of humanoids acting in a better way than humans mean no need of humans to exist according to the material concept of existence.

It is worth noting here that automation diminishes the labor share of value added as capital and so replacing labor. Simultaneously, automation augments a corporation's productivity and demand for labor expressed as a productivity effect. AI technologies generate new duties in which labor has a comparative advantage, altering the task content of workers, and escalating labor share and demand and so there is a disparity between technological prospective and its actual implementation for the reason that some technologies take time to circulate in industries. Moreover, workers do not stay inactive, but they learn new skills and adapt their set of duties in reply to automation showing worker flexibility which means that the introduction of

[44] Stefania Albanesi, António Dias da Silva, Juan F. Jimeno, Ana Lamo, Alena Wabitsch, New technologies and jobs in Europe, ECB Working Paper Series No 2831.

new technology augments the necessity for labor because of complementarity to the new tasks and improvement in corporation productivity. Thus, digital transformation fosters the requirement for highly cognitive and non-routine tasks, benefitting high-wage workers, and intensifying polarization and inequality. AI software and robots have displaced low- and medium-skilled workers. In this manner, while investment in digital technologies produces new economic opportunities, digital transformation stimulates reshoring. Will AAI technology and AAI humanoid robots eliminate human workers? Of course, in an AAI society, human labor will be replaced by AAI humanoid robots' labor.

It has to be taken into account that AI is a prediction technology, and predictions are at the heart of decision-making under uncertainty, making AI applicable to resolve a range of business problems with opposing prospective consequences on labor. On the one hand, corporations employ AI to automate certain duties by relocating labor and contributing to the ongoing trends of deskilling. On the other hand, investments in AI have been linked with product innovation demanding complementary investments which means that investments in AI are correlated with key alterations in corporations' labor composition and organization. Also, AI investments accumulate increasingly over time causing impacts that are not immediate, making the long-differences strategy well-suited for company venues in the AI era. [45] Nonetheless, failures of AI technologies causing harm undermine trust in such technologies impeding their development and use which means that AAI systems have to solve problems of malfunction of AI.

4.4 Labor and Antitrust

Antitrust enforcement has focused on anticompetitive conduct directed against downstream purchasers, not workers. It is representative that competition authorities have supposed that labor markets are rather competitive and that labor monopsony power is a comparatively infrequent phenomenon.

It seems that the Sherman Act was intended to treat combinations of capital and combinations of labor in the same manner. Hence, the Sherman Act's more general coverage and Section 7 of the Clayton Act, which applies to mergers, already ban the relevant anticompetitive outcomes in all markets by applying equally to sellers and purchasers, embracing purchasers of labor. [46] It could be said that the question is not about antitrust immunity for antitrust violations committed by labor, but rather about labor protection from antitrust violations committed by employers. Moreover, the

[45] Agrawal, Ajay K., Joshua S. Gans, and Avi Goldfarb, "AI Adoption and System-Wide Change," Working Paper 28811, National Bureau of Economic Research May 2021. Series: Working Paper Series.

[46] Todd v. Exxon Corp., 275 F.3d 191, 195 (2d Cir. 2001). State by Raoul v. Elite Staffing, Inc., No. 1-21-0840, 2022 WL 1819541, at *1 (Ill. App. Jun. 3, 2022) (applying an Illinois antitrust act to condemn a horizontal anti-poaching agreement under the per se rule).

anticompetitive behaviors embrace horizontal wage-fixing and anti-poaching agreements, along with vertical noncompeting agreements restraining employee mobility and mergers that have output-limiting results in both product and labor markets. [47]

In both North America and Europe, competition policy has focused on safeguarding well-functioning product markets and on capturing conduct on the supply side of the market. [48] Regardless that the EU and the US Horizontal Merger Guidelines stipulate for the application of competition law to both sides of the market, the basis of application is given on how the analysis should be performed in downstream markets. It is worth mentioning here that in the European Union, the EU competition rules are grounded on Article 3(3) of the Treaty on European Union, which stimulates "a highly competitive social market economy, aiming at full employment and social progress." Also, in the European Union, no formal obstacle exists to recognize harm to workers as a standalone anticompetitive harm.

It could be said that anticompetitive conduct by employers colluding qualifies as "by object" under EU competition law embracing wage fixing, no-poach, no-solicitation agreements, as well as exchange of commercially sensitive information. Article 101 of the TFEU does not currently capture non-competes for the reason that they are concluded by the workers and the employers. The Court of Justice of the European Union has embraced that collective bargaining agreements between employers and workers adjusting salaries and other working conditions do not infringe EU competition law. [49] The European Commission has published guidelines to address this issue, noting that collective negotiation and bargaining between certain categories of "solo self-employed" and their counterparties is explicitly permitted. [50]

It has to be taken into account that the EU courts have never explicitly adopted the enhancement of consumer welfare as the main aim of EU competition law but the EU plainly stated that, in buyer power cases, it intervenes when the merger notably impedes competition, including by protecting the competitive process, "even if it cannot be demonstrated that such reduction of competition affects consumer welfare. [51]"

[47] Jien v. Perdue Farms, Inc., 2020 WL 5544183, at *7 (D. Md. Sep. 16, 2020) (involving a class action suit alleging a large, industry-wide wage-fixing conspiracy for low-wage chicken processors).

[48] Organisation For Economic Co-Operation And Development, Purchasing Power And Buyers' Cartels 6 (2022).

[49] Case C-309/99, J.C.J. Wouters, J.W. Savelbergh & Price Waterhouse Belastingadviseurs BV v. Algemene Raad van de Nederlandse Orde van Advocaten, intervener: Raad van de Balies van de Europese Gemeenschap, 2022 E.C.R. I-1690. Case C-519/04 P, Meca-Medina and Majcen v. Commission of the European Communities, 2006 E.C.R. I Case C-413/13, FNV Kunsten Informatie en Media v. Staat der Nederlanden, ECLI:EU:C:2014:2411, ¶ 23 (Dec. 14, 2014); Case C-67/96, Albany International BV v. Stichting Bedrijfspensioenfonds Textielindustrie, 1999 E.C.R., I-5882.

[50] Commission Regulation 2022/374, 2022 O.J. (C 374) 11.

[51] Case M.9409, Aurubis/Metallo Group Holding ¶ 376 (July 1, 2020).

Anyway, labor market concentration has a negative average influence on employment. [52] Also, notwithstanding growing evidence of concentration in labor markets in both the United States and European countries, competition enforcement has been distinguished by a noteworthy asymmetry. Thus, competitive product markets have been the almost exclusive concentration of competition authorities in both continents.

It has to be taken into account that managers need to be informed of the prospective of AI for boosting productivity and so increasing labor productivity by complementing human labor and automating specific tasks. Dirk Czarnitzki et al. [53] found that "employing AI technologies has a positive and significant impact on firm productivity. In particular, we showed that both the use of AI and the intensity with which firms exploit the potentials of AI significantly increases both sales and valued-added. This effect remains robust after controlling for several technological features of the firm."

Does antitrust accommodate capital and control labor? It is worth mentioning here that antitrust has contributed to the increasing imbalance of power between employers and workers due to the fact that antitrust has legalized vertical restraints, permitting the economy's most powerful players to closely direct and supervise the behavior of less-powerful players and, second, antitrust has been used by those same powerful players to prevent less-powerful players from organizing and managing on their own behalf against such concentrations of power. Taking into account that antitrust harm in labor markets is independently actionable means that proving an unlawful restraint in a labor market does not necessitate independent proof of harm in the related product market. Clayton Act outlaws tying and exclusive dealing and explicitly applies only to sellers or lessors. [54] Nonetheless, tying and exclusive dealing are condemned under both provisions of the Sherman Act, which apply to buyers and sellers alike. [55]

Although most workers remain statutory employees of some employers, they are gradually remote from the decision-making entity that exerts power over their day-to-day lives and terms of work. [56] Moreover, progressively, employers categorize their workers as exempt contractors rather than employees due to court rulings,

[52] Martin Popp, Minimum Wages in Concentrated Labor Markets (Bavarian Graduate Program Econ., Discussion Paper No. 214, 2021).

[53] Dirk Czarnitzki, Gastón P. Fernández , and Christian Rammer Artificial Intelligence and Firm-level Productivity ZEW – Leibniz Centre for European Economic Research NO.22-005 | 02/2022 at: https://ssrn.com/abstract=4049824 p 23

[54] 15 U.S.C. § 14 ("It shall be unlawful for any person . . . to lease or make a sale . . . .").

[55] Nat'l Collegiate Athletic Ass'n v. Alston, 141 S. Ct. 2141, 2154 (2021) ("Nor does the NCAA suggest that, to prevail, the plaintiff student-athletes must show that its restraints harm competition in the seller-side (or consumer facing) market as well as in its buyer-side (or labor) market." Mandeville Island Farms, 334 U.S. at 235 (condemning a buyer-side cartel without inquiring into harm on the output side of the market).

[56] David Weil, The Fissured Workplace: Why Work Became So Bad For So Many And What Can Be Done To Improve It (2014) Harvard University Press.

technologies that empower employers to manage workers from afar, and industry deregulation that legalizes new, vertically dis-integrated business models. [57]

Likewise, the court ruled that it cannot be exercised de facto control over "independent business men," in contravention of the antitrust laws generating a sharp distinction and a comprehensive delineation between the realm of labor and antitrust: if subordinate entities are "independent business men" and not employees, it is illegal to exercise control. [58] Thus, the deployment of independent contractor status for workers, not just for the independent businesses who employ them, makes each individual worker an independent business, and so discarding of any protections under labor law.

The antitrust separation of workers from lead corporations is the erosion in the jurisprudence of the Sherman Act's prohibitions on vertical restraints. It has to be taken into account that a vertical restraint is a contractual provision of operation inhibiting the autonomy of the counterparty in the case where each party activates at a distinct segment of the supply chain. Hence, if a contract imposes that the final retail price is vertical price-fixing and so other vertical restraints embrace the varieties of exclusive practices that suppliers might impose on their affiliated dealers or distributors, like compulsory purchase contracts—known as full-line forcing or requirements contracts. [59] It is worth mentioning here that calming [60] the law of vertical restraints is part of an overall allocation of coordination rights in which domination is preferred over cooperation as long as consumers are reaping the gains by the domination.

It could be said that the erosion of antitrust in the direction of tolerating vertical price- and non-price restraints has actually legalized labor outsourcing, misclassification, and the gig economy resulting in dominant corporations having access to a wider range of profitable business models that exert greater power and control over workers than they once did. Essentially, antitrust is increasing the power of the economy's most powerful players instead of imposing fair competition. Besides, G.I. Zekos considers that high-quality goods and services at the lower possible price in the market should be the basis of competition regardless of the number of corporations in a free entrance market. The employment of AI and the forthcoming AAI should lead to an objective fair competition in trade against the current preference of the legally imposed competition in implementing the interests of capital via big corporations.

---

[57] Lawson v. Grubhub, Inc., 2017 U.S. Dist. Lexis 106291.

[58] United States v. Richfield Oil Corp., 99 F. Supp. 280 (S. D. Cal., 1951), aff'd, 343 U.S. 922 (1952). Simpson v. Union Oil Co. of California, 377 U.S. 13 (1964).

[59] Charlotte Slaiman, Decoding Antitrust Law: A Primer For Advocates (2019), https://www.publicknowledge.org/documents/decoding-antitrust-law-a-primer-for-advocates

[60] George L. Priest, Bork's Strategy and the Influence of the Chicago School on Modern Antitrust Law, 57 J.L. & Econ. S1, S10–S13 (2014) (arguing that Bork was distinctive in leveraging the prohibition of price-fixing in order to undermine other antitrust regulation, particularly the regulation of vertical restraints, and that this strategy was central to his influence upon the law and legal institutions).

Flexibility is acknowledged as one of the major shifts in the future of work and is driven by the different qualities of the platform work due to the rise of freelancing and uses of platform ecosystems. Moreover, flexibility refers to the hours worked and workplace location, to freedom for the workers to adjust their resources, and to decide when to work. It has to be taken into consideration that digital technologies have led to the development of new forms of flexible work, such as information and communication technology-enabled mobile work, high flexibility in hours, and place of work. Moreover, online platforms design features and algorithmic management is exploited by digital labor platforms to assign, monitor, and evaluate work. [61]

Concerning the effects of mergers in labor markets, merger guidelines should effectively assess whether mergers may lessen competition in labor markets, thereby harming workers. To that extent, the present horizontal merger guidelines apply equally to labor markets. On the other hand, the likelihood of challenging employee misclassification as an unfair method of competition under Section 5 of the FTC Act echoes a momentous shift in the law and an unprecedented expansion of the scope of the FTC Act. [62] Explicitly, the FTC indicated that it deems an employer's intentional misclassification of its employees as independent contractors to be an unfair method of competition since misclassification gives non-compliant employers a cost advantage over employers which follow labor guidelines. [63] Thus, misclassification can lead to competitive harm in part for the reason that workers cannot "resist" unfavorable terms and conditions.

While the Chicago School elevated economic analysis and the consumer welfare standard in antitrust policy and doctrine, it also launched a strict separation between labor and product market regulation, focusing exclusively on worker combinations' anticompetitive effects on consumer prices.

Antitrust policy should generate incentives empowering markets to achieve their highest realistically sustainable output and so when a practice harms consumers by raising prices and reducing output, it harms labor as well. Due to the fact that labor is production input, antitrust restraints in product markets have vital and harmful effects on labor without raising actionable antitrust questions. [64] To that extent, merger law does not make a distinction between product markets and labor markets, or even between seller restraints and buyer restraints by purely outlawing acquisitions of the shares or assets of another company where "the effect of such acquisition

[61] Salomé Viljoen, A Relational Theory of Data Governance, Yale Law Journal 131:573 2021.

[62] Federal Trade Commission, Remarks of Chair Lina M. Khan Regarding the Request for Information on Merger Enforcement (Jan. 18, 2022).

[63] Castellanos v. State, 2021 WL 3730951, at *2–5 (Cal. Super. Ct. Aug. 20, 2021) (holding that an act passed by public referendum to categorize app-based drivers as independent contractors is "an unconstitutional continuing limitation on the Legislature's . . . plenary power to determine what workers must be covered or not covered by the worker's compensation system").

[64] Hiba Hafiz, Labor Antitrust's Paradox, 87 U. Chi. L. Rev. 381, 388–91 (2020).

may be substantially to lessen competition, or to tend to create a monopoly. [65]" In some markets, the source of merger profits is expected to be wage suppression rather than increases in product prices which means that a merger of two corporations may be harmless on the selling side but anticompetitive on the hiring side. [66] It seems that court has ever condemned a merger because of its anticompetitive effects in labor markets. [67]

A merger between competitors for labor input gives rise to unilateral horizontal effects, dropping employment and wages below competitive levels. Moreover, coordinated effects, such as explicit or tacit collusion, would lead to similar outcomes. To that extent, Satoshi Araki [68] et al. argue that "Well-functioning labor markets require competition authorities to ensure that employers' monopsonies or oligopsonies are not formed or abused... The existing EU legislative framework, as it stands, can address many forms of anticompetitive creation or exploitation of employer's power under the consumer welfare standard."

Mergers should not reduce labor market competition. Courts find that when labor market restraints benefit workers and not consumers, the consumer welfare standard trumps and the restraint violates the antitrust laws. [69] Moreover, the Supreme Court held a more searching rule-of-reason inquiry that was needed to establish whether the restriction harmed consumers. [70]

Labor market power is not a consequence of barriers to entry or excessive concentration and so antitrust tools of merger review and the prohibition of collusion present a partial role in tackling the problems of labor market power. To that extent, Naidu and Posner have recognized that antitrust policy tenders only a partial remedy to labor market power. [71] In addition, Matthew Dimick [72] argues that "Antitrust

[65] Abhay Aneja & Prasad Krishnamurthy, Merger Deregulation, Wages, and Inequality: Evidence from the U.S. Banking Industry (July 2022) (https://perma.cc/38PV-L5H9) (finding that looser enforcement of bank merger laws led to lower wages in that market).

[66] Weyerhaeuser Company v. Ross-Simmons Hardwood Lumber Company, 549 U.S. 312 (2007) United States v. Anthem, Inc., 855 F.3d 345, 381 (D.C. Cir. 2017) (Kavanaugh, J., dissenting) (arguing that the court should have remanded for consideration of the effect of a merger on employees).

[67] Ioana Marinescu & Herbert J. Hovenkamp, Anticompetitive Mergers in Labor Markets, 94 Ind. L.J. 1031 (2019).

[68] Satoshi Araki, Andrea Bassanini, Andrew Green, Luca Marcolin, and Cristina Volpin, Labor Market Concentration and Competition Policy Across the Atlantic, 2023] The University of Chicago Law Review 90:2/ 339, pp 378–379.

[69] National Society of Professional Engineers v United States435 US 679 (1978).

[70] California Dental Association v Federal Trade Commission, 526 US 756, 759, 781 (1999). Benefits Laura Alexander & Steven C. Salop, Antitrust Worker Protections: The Rule of Reason Does Not Allow Counting of Out-of-Market, 2023 The University of Chicago Law Review 90:2/ 273.

[71] Suresh Naidu & Eric A. Posner, Labor Monopsony and the Limits of the Law, 57 J. Hum. Resources 284 (2022).

[72] Matthew Dimick, Conflict of Laws? Tensions Between Antitrust and Labor Law, 2023 The University of Chicago Law Review [90:2/379, P 418.

seeks to counter inequality and employer monopsony power by reducing product or labor market concentration or explicitly banning collusive wagesetting practices... if antitrust law only offers a partial remedy to labor market monopsony, then this reduces the substitution effect of antitrust with collective bargaining."

In NCAA v. Alston, [73] the Supreme Court treated monopsony in a comparable fashion to monopoly—equating monopsony's suppressed input costs and lower input supply to monopoly's suppressed prices and loss of output. It has to be taken into consideration that monopsony power is just as harmful to competition as monopoly is in product markets. Hence, even when the product market is competitive, monopsony power still downgrades productive efficiency by twisting how the output is distributed between corporations and so harming workers by manipulating the absence of outside options for those workers which means cutting wages and worsening working conditions. [74]

4.5 Lobbying and Competition

It could be said that lobbying can be a mechanism for powerful corporations to influence laws and regulations at the expense of the public interest and so causing unjustified influence, unfair competition, and policy capture, to the impairment of effective policymaking. [75] Also, lobbying is each movement taking place with the objective of directly or indirectly inspiring the construction or employment of the policy and decision-making activity concerning legislative or regulatory movements. Moreover, lobbying has become more and more multifaceted, embracing new devices for influencing such as social media. [76] It seems that lobbying targets

[73] NCAA v. Alston, 141 S.Ct. 2141 (2021). at 2155 (declining to decide whether a court should sacrifice "a legally cognizable interest in competition in one market to better promote competition in a different one."). Ioana Marinescu & Herbert Hovenkamp, Anticompetitive Mergers in Labor Markets, 94 Indiana L. J. 1031, 1063 (2019) (concluding that the consumer welfare standard focused on monopolistic reductions in output is well suited to address buyer power abuses); Roger G. Noll, "Buyer Power" and Economic Policy, 72 Antitrust L. J. 589 (2005) (concluding that buyer power abuses would also harm consumers).

[74] Anna Sokolova & Todd Sorensen, Monopsony in Labor Markets: A Meta-Analysis, 74 Indus. & Lab. Rels. Rev. 27, 51 (2021); Arindrajit Dube, Jeff Jacobs, Suresh Naidu & Siddharth Suri, Monopsony in Online Labor Markets, 2 Am. Econ. Rev.: Insights 33, 44–45 (2020).

[75] The existing regulatory framework in EU outlines lobbying as 'all activities (...) carried out with the objective of directly or indirectly influencing the formulation or implementation of policy and the decision-making processes of the EU institutions, irrespective of where they are undertaken and of the channel or medium of communication used, for example via outsourcing, media, contracts with professional intermediaries, think tanks, platforms, forums, campaigns and grassroots initiatives'. https://eur-lex.europa.eu/legal-content/EN/TXT/PDF/?uri=CELEX:32014Q0919(01)&from=EN

[76] https://www.oecd.org/corruption-integrity/reports/lobbying-in-the-21st-century-c6d8eff8-en.html

regulation, which affects everyone. It is argued that lobbying is opposed to bribery but it seems that corrupt practices are linked with lobbying work. [77]

It could be said that regulatory clarification is required to settle ambiguities and mostly tackle the allegations that legal lobbying inflates in terms of clear and legitimate law-making processes. Attention has to be paid to the difficulty of piercing the veil of any unfitting actions taking place during a supposed legal lobbying.

Congressional modifications are offering amplified opportunities for lobby groups to use political influence as a way to generate new legislation. [78] Moreover, the Lobbying Disclosure Act stipulates the legality of political lobbying and so the right to lobby is protected by both the 1st Amendment and the Lobbying Disclosure Act of 1995. It is argued that lobbyists model laws, legislation, and public policy promoting the interests of the group or entity that pays them. [79] Also, the power of lobbying is immense in influencing the policy endorsed by policymakers. In Canada, the rationale of the Lobbying Act [80] is to safeguard transparency and accountability in the lobbying of federal public office holders in contributing to the integrity of the government decision-making process. Lobbyists are working in areas such as competition law, intellectual property, and financial policy by influencing both the formulation and the implementation of policy at many levels of government, from legislators to regulatory agencies. [81]

It has to be taken into consideration that competition is not just about the number of corporations in a market but also about permitting new entrants to confront incumbent corporations. Consequently, since competition is the best manner to advance the functioning of a market for the well-being of consumers, any barriers to entry should be seen as an anticompetitive act. Corporations innovate and expand their practices to gain market shares which could lead a few corporations to dominate some markets by becoming more efficient and lowering prices for consumers but their dominant status could lead them to abuse their position given the lack of options for consumers. It is argued that lobbying efforts [82] and new regulations established barriers to entry and so increases in regulatory burdens are correlated with amplified profit margins for incumbent corporations which means that the power of entrants to grow is adversely disturbed and so albeit new corporations

[77] United States v. Harriss, 347 U.S. 612 (1954) https://www.lobbyists4good.org/why-is-lobbying-legal

[78] Lobbying Disclosure Act of 1995.

[79] https://www.investopedia.com/financial-edge/0912/the-differences-between-bribery-and-lobbying.aspx

[80] Lobbying Act (R.S.C., 1985, c. 44 (4th Supp.)).

[81] Korkea-aho E (2021). Legal Lobbying: The Evolving (But Hidden) Role of Lawyers and Law Firms in the EU Public Affairs Market. German Law Journal 22, 65–84. https://doi.org/10.1017/glj.2020.97

[82] Germán Gutiérrez Thomas Philippon Declining Competition And Investment In The U.S. Working Paper 23583 http://www.nber.org/papers/w23583

manage to enter the market, they cannot grow easily. [83] In other words, regulation is partly responsible for rising concentration and industry concentration leads to increased market power. Thus, barriers to entry mean less competition concealing an anticompetitive activity.

It is worth noting that industrial concentration not only directly touches consumers through market power and so possibly raising higher prices and dropping quantities but also indirectly via politics [84] which means that incumbent corporations lobby politicians to erect barriers to entry in order to guard their market power. [85] It could be said that the more market power a corporation secures, the more it will lobby in order to retain, and even enhance, its monopoly. Also, a corporation's power and the prospective anticompetitive quality of that power are uncovered by the structural role it plays in markets.

There is a link between competition and innovation and competition reduces the level of profits, but it also makes them more elastic to innovation. Richard Gilbert [86] argues that "differences in market structure, the characteristics of innovations, and the dynamics of discovery lead to seemingly endless variations in the theoretical relationship between competition and [innovation]." Moreover, the risk of entry drives innovation incentives in sectors close to the technology frontier and so advanced incumbents innovate in order to avoid competition. [87] Corporations that do not face the threat of entry do not have a strong need to invest and innovate.

The COVID-19 pandemic has underlined how globalization and digitalization are reforming the globe and so revealing the demand for preserving lobbying rules adapted to new realities involving rapid technological transformation, global competition for influence, and people who plead for higher standards of integrity and inclusiveness in policy making.

Is lobbying a necessity or a trojan horse since the authorities responsible for any policy have the duty to bring forward the best rules for the whole society rather than for the elite? Lobbying remains too open to abuse because guidelines do not cover all branches of government. To that extent, rules on conflict of interest exist in most settings, but specific integrity standards have to be established for interactions between policymakers and lobbyists. [88] It seems that lobbying expenditures and product market strategic variables are inter-reliant and so there is a need of appraising the degree of corporations' coordination in their political activities based on

[83] https://www.fraserinstitute.org/blogs/lobbying-can-lead-to-monopolies-which-can-lead-to-higher-prices-and-or-lower-quality

[84] Cowgill, B, A Prat, and T Valletti (2022), "Political power and market power", CEPR Discussion Paper 17178.

[85] https://cepr.org/voxeu/columns/political-power-and-market-power-evidence-mergers

[86] Gilbert, R. (2006). Looking for Mr. Schumpeter: Where Are We in the Competition-Innovation Debate? In Innovation Policy and the Economy, Volume 6, NBER Chapters, pp. 159–215. National Bureau of Economic Research, Inc.

[87] Aghion, P., R. Blundell, R. Griffith, P. Howitt, and S. Prantl (2009, Feb). The effects of entry on incumbent innovation and productivity. Review of Economics and Statistics 91 (1), 20–32.

[88] https://www.opensecrets.org/federal-lobbying

lobbying data. Moreover, corporations lobby for political decisions dropping their costs and so altering their competitiveness.

Digitalization has made coordinating lobbying campaigns cheap and simple, then again social media often conceal public debate in the era of misinformation and disinformation permitting the spreading of deceitful information and so controlling public opinion. To that extent, globalization and the internationalization of legislative and regulatory topics remind all lobbyists that it is needed to converge their energies on affecting decision-makers at all relevant levels. [89]

Is AI a device utilized in lobbying? Of course, AI is utilized by humans in any effort of contacting lobbying in the current electronic era. On the other hand, AAI systems used by AAI entities have not to be used for lobbying since AAI technology is destined to bring objectivity in an AAI society and not transfer all wrongs of present society into AAI society by merely altering the level of technology or even merely a transformation of the material made of the inhabitants of the referred societies of humans and that of AAI humanoid robots.

It is characteristic that spending on lobbying in many industries remains decidedly concentrated on only a few big actors in the market. Furthermore, the digital zone where spending on lobbying has augmented considerably echoes its increasing significance in the economy.

It is essential to advance the integrity of all players via tougher integrity rules and so governments must do more to guarantee that public officials cooperate with lobbyists with impartiality and in the public interest which could be achieved by certifying that influence is not assembled in the hands of the powerful. To that extent, it is worth noting that Big Tech companies are EU's lobby spenders by delivering allegedly neutral reports to influence the EU's competition policy and so smoothing the course for Big Tech monopolies and mergers. Furthermore, Big Tech monopolies are backing their interests in the forming and implementation of the EU's competition policy with the assistance of lobbyists and their behind-the-scenes impact on behalf of their Big Tech customers is substantial when it comes to EU merger control. [90] Also, Big Tech is the biggest lobby zone in the EU by spending and a noteworthy amount of lobbying "firepower" in EU is employed by Google, Amazon, Meta (formerly Facebook), Apple, and Microsoft.

Big Tech's political weight has been cultivated in conjunction with its ever-increasing market power and so generating the risk that it has grown "too big to regulate." Additionally, digital corporations have exploited their economic power and monopoly position to methodically violate laws and their enforcement by imposing unfair terms on users and small businesses. Moreover, it seems that lobbying works for favorable legislation legitimizing illegal business models.

---

[89] Recommendation CM/Rec(2017)2 adopted by the Committee of Ministers of the Council of Europe on 22 March 2017 and explanatory memorandum https://rm.coe.int/legal-regulation-of-lobbying-activities/168073ed69

[90] https://corporateeurope.org/en/2023/01/spamming-regulator#

Furthermore, Big Tech corporations are running a "copy-acquire-kill" strategy with their competitors, resulting in ever-more market concentration due to the fact that EU has not interfered to block any of these mergers. [91] To that extent, the Big Tech industry has achieved monopoly power due to the fact that a few corporations have taken over cyberspace concerning online advertisements, e-commerce, social networks, online apps, search, e-mail, the cloud, etc. Thus, Big Tech corporations have used mergers and acquisitions to "gain market power, acquire data, and snuff out any threats from would-be competitors." [92] It seems that mergers and acquisitions by Amazon, Apple, Meta, and Google are multiplied over the years. [93]

It is worth mentioning here that lobbyists play an imperative role in the field of EU competition policy performing on behalf of Big Tech corporations by delivering reports to DG competition when it comes to mergers. In other words, lobbyists are influencing legislation on competition policy by articulating how competition policy enforcement has to look in practice. On the other hand, lobbyists do not register in the EU's Transparency Register, they do not respond to invitations, and the reports they deliver to DG competition in the interest of their customers are not released to the public. To that extent, there is a need for more transparency concerning the role of lobbying in materializing EU competition policy. [94] Big Tech corporations rely on lobbyists offering favorable economic arguments to legitimize mergers to regulators by proving that merges do not harm consumers and their business behavior is not abusive. Mergers are almost never blocked. It has to be taken into account that the arena of competition economics is controlled by a few lobbying consultancies and there are no data on economic consultancies available in the EU Transparency Register.

Merger investigations by competition authorities are not getting any input from civil society but economic consultancies have confidential access to these proceedings by delivering economic submissions on behalf of their clients and so embracing a novel lobbying strategy: spamming the regulator. It seems that Brussels is full of lobbyists who never disclose that they are working for the companies. [95] It is characteristic that instead of a legal advice, legal lobbying is progressively common both at the EU level and so lobbying services offered by law companies are a new incident due to that fact that the job of a lawyer is obviously incompatible with that of a lobbyist. On the other hand, it seems that law companies engage in actions/

[91] https://corporateeurope.org/en/2023/01/spamming-regulator#

[92] https://www.economicliberties.us/press-release/economic-liberties-releases-big-tech-abuse-merger-trackers/#

[93] https://www.economicliberties.us/big-tech-merger-tracker/

[94] https://www.lobbycontrol.de/wp-content/uploads/open-letter_transparency-in-EU-merger-control.pdf

[95] https://braveneweurope.com/the-counterbalance-the-european-system-of-monopoly

services that can be categorized as having the objective of persuading legislators and regulators. [96]

Is there lobbying behind-the-scenes? It seems that economic consultancies are not only representing clients in merger cases or advise the Commission in expert groups but also they are publishing reports on behalf of corporate clients by organizing key events on competition policy in the EU. Up to now Big Tech companies have taken advantage of economic consultancies' undercover lobbying and the secrecy in competition policy and so the ultimate step to fight Big Tech's monopoly is to open up the antitrust establishment to more public scrutiny rather than merely insisting on the legitimacy of lobbying. [97]

4.6 Bank Antitrust

There are increasing levels of AI technology implementation and financial investment. [98] AI in banking is maturing, bringing the prospective for higher-complexity solutions and so as AI gets popularity in banking, financial institutions (FIs) are building on their existing solutions to solve gradually multifaceted challenges. Certain AI use cases have acquired prominence across banks' operations, with chatbots in the front office and anti-payments fraud in the middle office as the most mature.

It is worth mentioning here that AI could be both useful and dangerous due to the fact that AI works by absorbing and analyzing data, picking up on patterns, and then predicting what comes next. To that extent, AI can be utilized in creating letters to require taxpayers to take certain actions like handing over personally identifying data or paying over assets and so there are AI-generated scams such as phishing and other fraud techniques. [99]

Banks use AI to change the customer experience but AI in banking applications is not just limited to retail banking services. Hence, the back and middle offices of investment banking and all other financial services for that matter are promoted from AI. AI is also being employed by banks within middle-office functions to evaluate risks, detect and prevent payment fraud, and advance processes for anti-money

[96] For an analysis see Korkea-aho E (2021). Legal Lobbying: The Evolving (But Hidden) Role of Lawyers and Law Firms in the EU Public Affairs Market. German Law Journal 22, 65–84. https://doi.org/10.1017/glj.2020.97

[97] https://www.thegoodlobby.eu/2021/12/14/democracy-for-sale/

[98] Eleni Digalaki, The Impact of Artificial Intelligence in the Banking Sector & How AI Is Being Used in 2022, Bus. Insider (Feb. 2, 2022, 2:04 PM), https://www.businessinsider.com/ai-inbanking-report

[99] Kelly Phillips Erb, AI-Generated Tax Scams Can Look A Lot Like They Came From The IRS https://www.forbes.com/sites/kellyphillipserb/2023/05/17/ai-generated-tax-scams-can-look-a-lot-like-they-came-from-the-irs/?sh=35153db41ead

laundering (AML). [100] There is a need for a holistic AI strategy spreading across banks' business lines, usable data, and partnerships with external partners.

It is argued that the current approach to bank antitrust, based on consumer welfare, has failed in two critical respects due to the fact that as bank mergers have amplified the cost and diminished the availability of basic financial services and since its narrow concentration on consumer prices, the prevailing standard has disregarded numerous non-price harms stemming from bank consolidation, involving diminished product quality, enhanced entry barriers, and greater macroeconomic instability.

Hence, it is decisive to boost competition in the financial sector and throughout the US economy. To that extent, the New Brandeisians regenerated worries concerning industrial consolidation and corporate "bigness" embracing aggressive merger enforcement and de-concentration strategies in technology, pharmaceuticals, transportation, and healthcare. [101] An executive order was issued directing the administration to "combat the excessive concentration of industry" and "promote competition" throughout the US economy. [102]

There is a spectacular and sustained consolidation of the US banking sector and so bank consolidation has fueled conglomeration throughout the US economy. [103] As the US Supreme Court [104] put it, "concentration in banking accelerates concentration generally," which means that in order to boost competition in the US economy, policymakers must prevent harmful consolidation in the banking sector. [105]

It is argued that corporate conduct harms competition only if it results in higher prices or lower output and markets are "self-correcting" which means that there is no need for government intervention in the form of antitrust enforcement. [106] To that extent, the Chicago School's consumer welfare approach dominates bank merger oversight and so the DOJ and the federal banking agencies have ceased challenging

---

[100] G Zekos, Finance Crimes: Insider Trading and Money Laundering, 2020 Nova Science Publications New York USA. www.novapublishers.com

[101] Herbert Hovenkamp, Is Antitrust's Consumer Welfare Principle Imperiled?, 45 J. Corp. L. 65, 81–92 (2019).

[102] Promoting Competition in the American Economy, Exec. Order No. 14,036, 86 Fed. Reg. 36,987, 36,988–89 (July 14, 2021).

[103] Quarterly Banking Profile: Third Quarter 2021, 15 FDIC Q., no. 4, 2021, at 5.

[104] United States v. Phila. Nat'l Bank, 374 U.S. 321, 370 (1963).

[105] Jeremy C. Kress, Modernizing Bank Merger Review, 37 YALE J. ON REGUL. 435, 446–47 (2020). A bank's primary federal regulator is either the Federal Reserve, the Office of the Comptroller of the Currency (OCC), or the Federal Deposit Insurance Corporation (FDIC), depending on its charter type.

[106] William E. Kovacic, The Chicago Obsession in the Interpretation of US Antitrust History, 87 U. CHI. L. REV. 459, 471–78 (2020); Herbert Hovenkamp & Fiona Scott Morton, Framing the Chicago School of Antitrust Analysis, 168 U.PA. L. Rev. 1843, 1848 (2020).

bank mergers, even as bank consolidation reaches a historic peak. [107] Following the consumer welfare standard, numerous non-price harms from bank consolidation have disregarded. Also, bank mergers have fueled the cost and diminished the availability of credit, inflated the fees that banks charge for basic financial services. [108] Additionally, large bank mergers have not delivered pledged efficiency gains and so the consumer welfare approach to bank antitrust has not reduced prices or increased economic efficiency. [109]

It has to be taken into account that merging banks utilize their market power by paying lower interest rates on deposit accounts. The US antitrust laws were intended to protect not only a broad range of consumer interests such as product quality and privacy but also societal objectives involving the preservation of open markets and system stability. On the other hand, bank consolidation has undermined these objectives and so bank mergers have led to extensive branch closures, inconveniencing customers who previously gained from proximity to bank offices. Also, megamergers have generated "too big to fail" banks that enjoy unfair funding advantages over smaller companies and so distorting competition and discouraging new entrants. [110]

It is worth mentioning here that bank consolidation has jeopardized macroeconomic stability, since larger banks aggravate systemic risk and impair monetary policy transmission. Under the consumer welfare approach, bank antitrust enforcers and courts have ignored these harmful outcomes and so high concentration in mortgage lending diminishes the sensitivity of mortgage markets to monetary policy. [111] Likewise, bank consolidation is boosted by relaxing financial regulations and expediting mergers approvals [112] which means that rising bank concentration is stimulating further industrial consolidation and counteract policymakers' efforts to

---

[107] Mark Glick, How Chicago Economics Distorts "Consumer Welfare" in Antitrust, 64 Antitrust Bull. 495, 509–10 (2019) (discussing the consumer welfare standard as applied to bank mergers).

[108] Bernadette A. Minton et al., Bank Mergers, Acquirer Choice and Small Business Lending: Implications for Community Investment 29 (Nat'l Bureau of Econ. Rsch., Working Paper No. 29284, 2021), https://www.nber.org/papers/w29284 (bank mergers involving acquirers with more than $10 billion in assets are associated with a decline in small business loans).

[109] Erik Devos et al., Efficiency and Market Power Gains in Bank Megamergers: Evidence from Value Line Forecasts, 45 Fin. Mgmt. 1011, 1029 (2016) (mergers resulting in banks with more than $150 billion in assets do not produce efficiency gains).

[110] Hoai-Luu Q. Nguyen, Are Credit Markets Still Local? Evidence from Bank Branch Closings, 11 AM. Econ. J.: Applied Econ. 1, 15–17 (2019) (finding evidence of significant branch closures by merging banks).

[111] Gregor N.F. Weiss et al., Systemic Risk and Bank Consolidation: International Evidence, 40 J. Banking & Fin. 165, 174–77 (2014) (finding a significant increase in the post-merger systemic risk of consolidating banks and their competitors); Emily Flitter, How Bank Regulators Are Trying to Oust a Trump Holdover, N.Y. Times (Dec. 10, 2021), https://www.nytimes.com/2021/12/10/business/jelenamcwilliams-fdic-bank-regulation-trump.html

[112] Orla McCaffrey, Bank Mergers Are on Track to Hit Their Highest Level Since the Financial Crisis, Wall St.J. (Sept. 28, 2021), https://www.wsj.com/articles/bank-mergersare-on-track-to-hit-their-highest-level-since-the-financial-crisi

boost competition throughout the economy. [113] Bank mergers are linked with less competitive labor markets throughout the economy. [114]

The US's once-powerful bank antitrust movement stemmed from the country's longstanding distrust of concentrated economic and political power. On the other hand, the anti-interventionist Chicago School ideology that now governs bank antitrust has harmed consumers, businesses, and the broader economy because when banks merge, they utilize their market power by raising the cost of loans, increasing transaction fees, and paying less interest to depositors. Thus, the con sumer welfare standard has not safeguarded consumers from these harmful consequences and so under the existing bank merger framework, consolidation has augmented the cost and diminished the availability of consumer loans which means that it has failed to generate efficiency advances. [115] Furthermore, competition between banks is often non-price in nature and so there is competition concerning the speed of approval of a loan being vital to the borrower than a slight difference in the interest rate. Also, there is competition focusing on location, quality of customer service, alternative delivery channels, and the set of products being offered which means that price effects alone do not offer a complete picture of market dynamics.

It has to be taken into account that banks compete with one another not only on pricing but also on many other aspects. As the Supreme Court stated in Philadelphia National Bank, [116] "competition among banks exists at every level—price, variety of credit arrangements, convenience of location, attractiveness of physical surroundings, credit information, investment advice, service charges, personal accommodations, advertising, and miscellaneous special and extra services."

By contrast, antitrust enforcers have overlooked impairments in product quality when assessing bank mergers and so the DOJ and the banking agencies have ignored the modes in which bank consolidation limits branch access, diminishes customer service, and endangers consumer privacy. Hence, under the consumer welfare standard, antitrust enforcers have not considered reductions in branch access as an element of their bank merger evaluations and so the existing bank merger framework overlooks harm to consumer privacy. Besides, the post-Chicago School resurgence of bank consolidation has generated merger-related branch closures throughout the

---

[113] Arthur E. Wilmarth, Taming The Megabanks 335–56 (2021) (urging the reinstatement of the Glass-Steagall Act); Jeremy C. Kress, Solving Banking's "Too Big To Manage" Problem, 104 Minn. L. Rev. 171, 212–30 (2019) (proposing to break up "too big to manage" banks).

[114] Suresh Naidu et al., Antitrust Remedies for Labor Market Power, 132 Harv. L. Rev. 536, 572–95 (2018) (urging antitrust enforcers to review labor-market effects of proposed mergers).

[115] Telis Demos, So Your Bank is Buying Another: Don't Panic, Wall St. J. (Oct. 6, 2021), https://www.wsj.com/articles/so-your-bank-is-buying-another-dont-panic-11633519800 ("A recent McKinsey & Co. study found that among 58 midcap bank mergers from 2010 to 2021, only 17 merged institutions' returns outperformed peers over the two years postdeal.").

[116] United States v. Phila. Nat'l Bank, 374 U.S. 321, 368 (1963).

country and so while merging banks consolidate operations and slash overhead costs, they close branches in neighboring locations. [117]

Financial institutions manipulate consumers and get competitive advantages by harvesting and monetizing customer data. Mergers permit banks to collect and link customer data in new manners, making it simpler for them to price discriminate and take advantage of customers' biases. Also, banks sell transaction-level data to retailers pursuing particular promotions to consumers founded on their distinctive purchasing habits. It has to be taken into account that consolidation of customer data not only undercuts consumers' privacy but also subjects them to augmented risks that their personal information could be compromised via data breaches. [118] Also, the existing bank merger framework ignores product quality.

It has to be taken into consideration that big banks have been able to borrow at favorable rates compared to smaller competitors and so the enlargement of the "too-big-to-fail" subsidy via bank consolidation alters the competitive dynamics of the financial sector leading to unfair competition. As well, megabanks' artificial funding advantages possibly discourage new banks from forming. Hence, due to the consumer welfare standard, antitrust enforcers do not take into consideration how bank consolidation harms competition by preserving the "too-big-to fail" subsidy.

4.7 Algorithmic Management and Labor Competition

First of all, the direct effect of digital transformation concerns the data that digital technologies generate, collect, store, process, transfer, and communicate. Hence, taking into account that digital technologies permit to collection and processing of data for the coordination of work, algorithmic management is deployed in manners that will considerably influence work organization and job quality.

Algorithmic management [119] is applied to areas such as Just-in-Time production or manufacturing and so the use of digital technologies across all economic activities and the availability of massive amounts of data makes algorithmic management possibly disruptive for the future of work. Furthermore, while algorithmic management depends on digital technologies and data, it involves organizational and

[117] Mary Wisniewski, Survey: While Checking Fees Vary Wildly By Race and Age, Americans Stay Loyal to Their Banks, Bankrate (Jan. 15, 2020), https://www.bankrate.com/banking/best-banks-consumer-survey-2020/

[118] Gregory Day & Abbey Stemler, Infracompetitive Privacy, 105 Iowa L. Rev. 61, 61 (2019) ("[B] ecause antitrust's framework typically uses consumer prices to measure welfare . . . privacy injuries have largely avoided antitrust scrutiny."). Frederic Boissay et al., Big Techs in Finance: On the New Nexus Between Data Privacy and Competition 10–13 (Bank for Int'l Settlements, Working Paper No. 970, 2021) (discussing anticompetitive uses of customer data in finance).

[119] Sara Baiocco, Enrique Fernandez-Macías, Uma Rani, Annarosa Pesole, The Algorithmic Management of work and its implications in different contexts, Background paper n°9 June 2022 www.ilo.org International Labour Organization.

institutional selections on the particular use of AI technologies for work coordination reasons which means that algorithmic management is molded by socio-institutional [120] and organizational features contributing to its development and outcomes. Also, the intensifying digitization of the economy has led to the expansion of algorithmic management practices in more conventional working environments, such as factories, offices, hotels, retail, and wholesale warehouses.

The digital revolution is steered by the increase in the capacity to store, process, and communicate information by means of electronic devices, cloud services, and cloud infrastructure which means that algorithmic management combines new technologies such as big data analytics, machine learning, and geolocation in advancing economic practices. Algorithmic management uses AI technologies in automating the functions previously carried out by human management for the coordination of work. [121]

It has to be taken into account that in algorithmic management, the rules have to be so encoded as to be implemented in an automatic manner. The rules of algorithmic management have not to be biased and unfair which means that AI technologies maximize some parameters stipulated currently by humans and so possibly AI systems permit to shift human intervention to a higher level of abstraction, denoting broad objectives and strategies which the AI will transform into objective rules for decision-making which will be algorithmically implemented affecting the workers. Hence, an effective algorithmic management necessitates a degree of standardization and rationalization of tasks by the reorganization of work procedures, handling digital devices to arrange and standardize tasks, and centralizing control and decision-making. [122]

It has to be taken into consideration that the power of the data ecosystem has never been greater but the system itself is becoming more difficult to navigate as a result of growing complexity [123] and so algorithmic management is essential.

As mentioned earlier, algorithmic management is widespread and developed in digital labor platforms and so the platform integrates a series of algorithms for matching suppliers and consumers of those labor services, and for synchronizing the provision of those labor services which means that digital labor platforms incorporate algorithmic management implementing the key functions of conventional management. On the other hand, regardless that the function of planning is supported by algorithms in digital labor platforms, strategic decisions remain under the control of the human managers of the actual corporations behind digital labor

---

[120] ILO 2021. World Employment and Social Outlook 2021: The Role of Digital Labour Platforms in Transforming the World of Work, Geneva: ILO.

[121] Jarrahi, M. H., Newlands, G., Lee, M. K., Wolf, C. T., Kinder, E., and Sutherland, W. 2021. "Algorithmic management in a work context", in Big Data & Society, vol. 8 (2): 1–14.

[122] Gautié, J., Jaehrling, K., and Perez, C. 2020. "Neo-Taylorism in the Digital Age: Workplace Transformations in French and German Retail Warehouses", in Industrial Relations, vol. 75(4): 774–795.

[123] World Economic Forum, Anne Josephine Flanagan, Advancing towards Digital Agency: The Role of Trusted Data Intermediaries, February 2022 www.weforum.org

platforms because entirely AAI platforms administered by AAI humanoids have not been formed yet.

Furthermore, digital labor platforms display that the degree of automation of the management of work can become very high using algorithms due to the fact that the increasing digitization of everything is a feature facilitating the rising use of algorithms for the management of labor. In reality, digitization does not only accelerate but also promote the growing use of algorithmic management and so the persistent digitization of all kinds of economic processes, embracing labor transactions that take place within and across economic organizations, augments algorithmic management. Online platforms are not held responsible for content on their forums, like newspapers. [124]

The availability of data on an unprecedented scale, combined with heightened AI capacities and cloud infrastructure to store the data, has led to the advancement of AI. Hence, the vast amount of data collected plays an imperative part in algorithmic management practices exploited by platforms. Thus, data and algorithms are employed in digital labor platforms [125] to run the numerous functions of management such as planning and organizing of work, controlling and organizing, which involves the allocation of work and direction of workers along with disciplining and rewarding workers. [126]

It is worth noting that antitrust enforcement guarantees a balance of power between workers and employers which has to be applied in the case of digital labor platforms. Antitrust law ascertains that particular actions by employers against their workers, such as hiring cartels, are simply illegal. [127] Moreover, labor laws create and protect the rights of workers to organize and build power against employers in labor markets. Hence, restrictions on competition should not be broader than addressing legitimate subjects of regulation, such as safety and consumer protection, minimizing any prospective anticompetitive effect. [128]

It is specified that local labor markets in the United States are highly concentrated and have become more concentrated since the late 1970s which means that concentration touches workers further up the supply chain because powerful buyers

[124] Inyoung Cheong, Freedom of Algorithmic Expression, 91 U. Cin. L. Rev. 680 (2023) https://scholarship.law.uc.edu/uclr/vol91/iss3/2

[125] Rani, U., and Furrer, M. 2021. "Digital Labour Platforms and New Forms of Flexible Work in Developing Countries: Algorithmic Management of Work and Workers", in Competition & Change, vol. 25 (2): 212–236.

[126] Wood, A. 2021. Algorithmic Management: Consequences for Work Organisation and Working Conditions, JRC Working Papers Series on Labour, Education and Technology 2021-07, Seville: European Commission.

[127] Mandeville Island Farms, Inc. v. Am. Crystal Sugar Co., 334 U.S. 219, 235–36 (1948).

[128] Letter from Andrew I. Gavil, Deborah L. Feinstein & Martin S. Gaynor, Fed. Trade Comm'n, to Brendan Reilly, Chicago City Council 4 (Apr. 15, 2014), https://www.ftc.gov/system/files/documents/advocacy_documents/ftc-staff-comment-honorable-brendan-reillyconcerning-chicago-proposed-ordinance-o2014-1367/140421chicagoridesharing.pdf

pressurize suppliers who in sequence seek to cut costs by holding down wages. [129] It is characteristic that while the Supreme Court [130] held that the antitrust laws apply to buyers of goods and services, such as employers, the antitrust response to the problem of employer power has been ignored and so when reviewing corporate mergers, the antitrust agencies have presumed that the affected labor markets are competitive which means that the labor market consequences of mergers and arguably enabled the consolidation of labor markets have not scrutinized. [131]

Are labor markets normally competitive? US courts have always recognized that the antitrust laws apply to input markets, involving labor markets. [132] Antitrust principles apply to labor markets in the same manner they apply to product markets. Labor markets are overwhelmed by frictions, involving those resulting from employer concentration, search costs, and job differentiation. To that extent, mergers instigate harms in labor markets by escalating labor market power enabling corporations to suppress wages and so workers leave the labor markets and others are misallocated. [133] To that extent, Eric A. Posner [134] argues that "antitrust enforcement should be at least as strict in labor markets as in product markets".

Bibliography

1. Shapiro, C. (2018). Antitrust in a time of populism. *International Journal of Industrial Organization, 61*, 714, 715.
2. Cowgill, B., Prat, A., & Valletti, T. (2022). *Political power and market power* (CEPR Discussion Paper 17178).
3. Hovenkamp, H. (2021). Antitrust and platform monopoly. *Yale Law Journal, 130*, 1901, 1933, 1950.
4. Hovenkamp, H. (2018). Whatever did happen to the antitrust movement? *Notre Dame Law Review, 94*, 583, 585.
5. Jullien, B., & Sand-Zantman, W. (2021). The economics of platforms: A theory guide for competition policy. *Information Economics and Policy, 54*.
6. Khan, L., & Vaheesan, S. (2017). Market power and inequality: The antitrust counterrevolution and its discontents. *Harvard Law & Policy Review, 11*, 235.

[129] Efraim Benmelech, Nittai Bergman & Hyunseob Kim, Strong Employers and Weak Employees: How Does Employer Concentration Affect Wages? 16 (2018). José Azar, Ioana Marinescu & Marshall I. Steinbaum, Labor Market Concentration 10 (2017), http://www.marinescu.eu/AzarMarinescuSteinbaum.pdf .

[130] Am. Tobacco Co. v. United States, 328 U.S. 781 (1946).

[131] Suresh Naidu, Eric Posner & E. Glen Weyl, "Antitrust Remedies for Labor Market Power," 132 Harvard Law Review 537 (2018).

[132] Anderson v Shipowners Ass'n of Pacific Coast 272 US 359 (1926). NCAA v O'Bannon 580 US 815 (2016); NCAA v Alston 141 S Ct 2141 (2021).

[133] David Berger, Kyle Herkenhoff and Simon Mongey, 'Labor Market Power' (2022) 112 American Economic Review 1147.

[134] Eric A. Posner, Enforcement of US antitrust law in labour markets, Journal of Antitrust Enforcement, 2023, 00, 1–6 https://doi.org/10.1093/jaenfo/jnad020 p6.

7. Khan, L. M. (2017). Amazon's antitrust paradox. *Yale Law Journal, 126*, 710, 739, 740.
8. Zingales, L. (2017). Towards a political theory of the firm. *Journal of Economic Perspectives, 31*, 113.
9. Steinbaum, M., & Stucke, M. E. (2020). The effective competition standard: A new standard for antitrust. *University of Chicago Law Review, 87*, 595.
10. Dimick, M. (2023). Conflict of laws? Tensions between antitrust and labor law. *The University of Chicago Law Review, 90*(2), 379.
11. Naidu, S., & Posner, E. A. (2022). Labor monopsony and the limits of the law. *Journal of Human Resources, 57*, 284.
12. Zekos, G. (2022). *Political, economic and legal effects of artificial intelligence*. Springer. https://link.springer.com/book/10.1007/978-3-030-94736-1#toc

Chapter 5
Antitrust and AAI

5.1 Introduction

Antitrust is involved with corporate behaviors generating market power by encompassing coordinated conduct leading to collusion and exclusionary actions that produce monopoly power. [1] It is worth mentioning here that there is an increase worrying about industry concentration over the last years.[2]

On the one hand, many acts of coordination among companies augment market output by creating benefits for consumers regardless that business practices grab business from the actor's rivals and so exclude them from the market. On the other hand, excluding companies from the market means not free entrance and so indicates absence of competition which will allow better outcomes for trading requiring antitrust enforcement.

There is the risk that the antitrust rules allow large corporations to exploit their market power to such a great extent and so lose the support of the consumer coalition. Moreover, the reduced vigor of implementing antitrust rules has led to amplified market concentration across the economy being accountable for recent declines in the share of GDP going to labor. [3] In addition, there is a decline in labor's

[1]Section 1 of the Sherman Act, 15 U.S.C. § 1 (2018) (forbidding agreements that unreasonably restrain trade), and Section 7 of the Clayton Act, 15 U.S.C. § 18 (2018) (forbidding anticompetitive mergers). 19. Such actions are policed by Section 2 of the Sherman Act, 15 U.S.C. § 2 (2018) (forbidding monopolization, attempts to monopolize, and conspiracies to monopolize), and Section 3 of the Clayton Act, 15 U.S.C. § 14 (2018) (forbidding exclusive dealing and tying arrangements that reduce market competition).

[2]Gustavo Grullon, Yelena Larkin & Roni Michaely, Are US Industries Becoming More Concentrated?, 23 Rev. Fin. 697, 700 (2019).

[3]Jonathan B. Baker, Economics and Politics: Perspectives on the Goals and Future of Antitrust, 81 Fordham L. Rev. 2175, 2186–89 (2013).

© The Author(s), under exclusive license to Springer Nature Switzerland AG 2023
G. I. Zekos, *Artificial Intelligence and Competition*, Contributions to Economics,
https://doi.org/10.1007/978-3-031-48083-6_5

share of GDP owing to the rise of "superstar" companies. [4] Noting here that it is vital the role of states in antitrust enforcement. [5]

5.2 The Rule of Reason Competition Approach

It is worth noting that a rule-of-reason case is so costly to try which means that it is expected that fewer antitrust violations will be challenged. Is there a need to subject virtually all antitrust-relevant conduct to what antitrust calls the rule of reason? It has to be taken into consideration that the rule impedes a court from condemning conduct violating the antitrust laws until the court is convinced that the challenged conduct damages consumers in the specific case at issue. Hence, it could be said that the rule of reason is a license to engage in case-by-case adjudication. [6] In other words, whether a transaction unduly restrains trade is decided by the courts, on a case-by-case basis, using a rule of reason that judges all relevant elements in assessing a defendant's purpose in fulfilling the restraint and the restraint's upshot on competition. [7]

It has to be taken into account that courts cannot apply the rule of reason without a precise definition of the relevant market because without a definition of the market, there is no way to determine the party's capacity to diminish or abolish competition. [8] Consequently, the relevant market is defined as "the area of effective competition" and so identifying the ground within which noteworthy substitution in consumption or production happens which means that the relevant market corresponds to the commercial realities of the business. [9]

To that extent, the adoption of the rule of reason has led to the policy of diminished enforcement advocated by the Chicago School approach and so every time the Court judges some practice that would ordinarily violate the antitrust laws in itself, and rulings affecting consumers must be considered in every case before liability can attach which means that the Court has not advanced the correctness of

---

[4] David Autor, David Dorn, Lawrence F. Katz, Christina Patterson & John Van Reenen, The Fall of the Labor Share and the Rise of Superstar Firms, 135 Q.J. Econ. 645, 648–49 (2020).

[5] California v. Am. Stores Co., 495 U.S. 271, 284 (1990).

[6] Cal. Dental Ass'n v. FTC, 526 U.S. 756, 779 (1999) (describing rule of reason analysis as requiring "plenary market examination").

[7] Orson, Inc. v. Miramax Film Corp., 79 F.3d 1358, 1367 (3d Cir. 1996) Nat'l Soc'y of Prof'l Eng'rs v. United States, 435 U.S. 679, 696 (1978) ("Ethical norms may serve to regulate and promote this competition [within the learned professions] and thus fall within the Rule of Reason.").

[8] *Walker Process Equipment, Inc.* v. *Food Machinery & Chemical Corp.*, 382 U. S. 172, 177 (1965).

[9] *Brown Shoe Co.* v. *United States*, 370 U. S. 294, 336–337 (1962).

adjudication but rather essentially revoked the rule of illegality for that practice. [10] Hence, the Court started to draw the rule of reason's veil across the antitrust landscape. Furthermore, after the Court added the recoupment requirement to predatory pricing claims demanding courts to take into consideration the long-term effects for consumers of below-cost pricing, enforcers all but stopped bringing cases. In addition, owing to the complexity of winning a case, the US government seldom brings predatory pricing claims. [11] It is worth noting that a criterion in holding a competitor liable under the antitrust laws for charging low prices is a manifestation that the competitor had a reasonable prospect, or, under § 2 of the Sherman Act, a critical probability, of recouping its investment in below-cost prices. In addition, the Supreme Court held that Brooke had failed to prove competitive injury as a matter of law and so stating that the evidence did not prove that Brown and Williamson had a reasonable possibility of recovering its losses from its alleged below-cost pricing scheme in decelerating the growth of the generic market. [12]

It is worth noting here that the per se rule states that an agreement is assumed to be illegal and anticompetitive if it falls within the broad parameters of the statute such as price-fixing agreements between the competitors which are regarded to be illegal [13] and so corporations and the market know from the beginning which acts are illegal leading to anticompetitive outcomes and consequently competition is preserved in advance in a way. On the other hand, rule of reason means investigating whether the said agreement is legal or not and so placing emphasis on the necessity for inquiry before regarding the said act to be illegal [14] and so corporations firstly act and afterward authorities are investigating the results of their activities which means having an impact on competition which afterward has to be corrected in case of anticompetitive results. It is distinctive that the per se Rule finds its roots in the Harvard school of thought and the Rule of Reason finds its roots in the Chicago School of thought. [15]

It could be said that the rule of reason presumption means that the Court will force a per se rule of illegality only when the conduct is so apparently harmful to

---

[10] Herbert Hovenkamp, Federal Antitrust Policy: The Law of Competition and Its Practice (5th ed. 2016) ("Many Progressive Era liberals believed that the rule of reason would greatly weaken the Sherman Act . . . .".

[11] C. Scott Hemphill, The Role of Recoupment in Predatory Pricing Analyses, 53 Stan. L. Rev. 1581, 1585 (2001).

[12] Brooke Grp. Ltd. v. Brown & Williamson Tobacco Corp., 509 U.S. 209, 243 (1993); "There is no per se rule of nonliability under Robinson-Patman Act for predatory price discrimination when recoupment is alleged to take place through supra competitive oligopoly pricing, but Competitor's alleged below-cost sales of generic cigarettes through discriminatory volume rebates did not create competitive injury in violation of Robinson-Patman Act".

[13] Broadcast Music Inc vs. Columbia Broadcasting System Inc, 441 US 1, 8 (1979).

[14] Gellhorn E and Tatham T, 'Making Sense Out of the Rule of Reason' (1984) 35 Case Western Reserve Law Review 155.

[15] Piraino T, 'Reconciling the Harvard and Chicago Schools: A New Antitrust Approach for the 21st Century' (2007) 82 Indiana Law Journal 345 (2007).

consumers that the rule of reason's case-by-case analysis would end in the proscription of all, or nearly all, of the conduct anyway. [16] Moreover, "per se rules [17]" are used when settings make the probability of anticompetitive conduct so great as to render unjustified further examination of the challenged conduct, but in case the ultimate finding is the product of a presumption or actual market analysis then the principal investigation remains the same by illustrating whether or not the challenged restraint boosts competition. When conduct is explicitly harmful, the rule of reason necessitates that the conduct be rebuked without further inquiry, and so creating the notion that the conduct is subject to a per se rule of illegality. Correspondingly, when conduct is unequivocally good for consumers, the rule of reason necessitates that the Court abstain from condemning the conduct, without further inquiry, and so generating the notion that the conduct is per se legal.

Additionally, it could be argued that the rule of reason is the root of "antitrust's 40-year enforcement winter" and so the Court has to embrace burden-shifting frameworks compelling defendants to prove the absence of harm to consumers which means that enforcers have the burden of proving the presence of harm themselves. [18] In other words, the Court must either accept the Chicago view that competition is the enemy of growth, or reject it, and begin ruling conduct per se illegal again. To that extent, Chicago School assumes that situations of overwhelming dominance are no longer deemed a problem, and the implementation of antitrust rules must be based on efficiency, irrespective of any concerns linked to the competitive structure on the relevant market.

Judge Learned Hand [19] had stated that antitrust law seeks to "put an end to great aggregations of capital because of the hopelessness of the individual before them". Likewise, Robert Bork [20] recommends the maximization of consumer welfare as the only principle for competitive decision-making which is endorsed by the Schor v Abbott Labs judgment of the 7th Cir. in 2007 [21]: "If a manufacturer cannot make itself better off by injuring consumers through lower output and higher prices, there is no role for antitrust law to play."

It has to be taken into consideration that the use of an economic approach is projected to augment legal certainty for the authority in charge of enforcing competition rules and so the effects-based approach was seen as the only way to enforce

[16] Nat'l Collegiate Athletic Ass'n v. Bd. of Regents of Univ. of Okla., 468 U.S. 85, 103–04 (1984).

[17] . Bus. Elecs. Corp. v. Sharp Elecs. Corp., 485 U.S. 717, 726 (1988) ("[T]here is a presumption in favor of a rule-of-reason standard . . . .").

[18] Jonathan B. Baker, Evaluating Appropriability Defenses for the Exclusionary Conduct of Dominant Firms in Innovative Industries, 80 Antitrust L.J. 431, 435 (2016) (arguing that failing to promote competition may harm innovation).

[19] The United States v Alcoa, 148 F.2d 416 (2d Cir. 1945).

[20] Bork, R. H. (1966). Legislative Intent and the Policy of the Sherman Act. Journal of Law and Economics, 9, 7–48. https://doi.org/10.1086/466617 Bork, R. H. (1978). The Antitrust Paradox—A Policy at War with Itself. The Free Press.

[21] Schor v Abbott Labs, 457 F.3d 608, 611, 7th Cir., 2007.

competition laws efficiently.[22] Moreover, the consumer welfare test embraces issues of welfare distribution, while the total welfare[23] test concentrates only on efficiency, disregarding any consideration of the distribution of welfare. To that extent, the Chicago approach focuses on 'consumer welfare' supposing to promote "efficiency", resulting in low prices for consumers.

Additionally, it has to be taken into account that while the Chicago School debates for the robustness of markets and the requirement for minimal regulatory interventions, the Harvard School focuses on the institutional limitations concerning adjusting even real market failures.[24] Thus, the two schools cultivate comparable noninterventionist results.

It is characteristic that applying the 'consumer welfare' standard denotes that a merger is anticompetitive if it upsets the competitive procedure harming free trading which means that the consumer welfare standard lets regulators and courts to concentrate on long-term transformations requiring economic analysis in order to prove the likelihood of market power at some later date.

5.3 Competition and the Regulatory Authority of the Actors

Can per se unlawful conduct exempt from antitrust law based on the regulatory authority of the actors? If per se unlawful conduct exempt from antitrust law based on the regulatory authority of the actors, then there is preemption of antitrust law.[25] It is characteristic that when the damaging effects of a restraint are obvious, there is no need to inquire into market power and so if a restraint is evidently anticompetitive on its face, the burden should move to the defendant to come forward with evidence of some procompetitive advantage that justifies the restraint.[26]

The state action doctrine does not protect Oregon physicians from federal antitrust liability for their activities on hospital peer review committees. It is argued that competition, as a government-protected social policy, must be weighed against other

[22] Gerber, D. (2010). Global Competition—Law, Markets and Globalization, Oxford University Press.

[23] Kronman, A. T. (1980). Wealth Maximization as a Normative Principle. Journal of Legal Studies, 9(2), 227–242. https://doi.org/10.1086/467637

[24] Daniel A. Crane, Chicago, Post-Chicago, and Neo-Chicago, 76 U. Chi. L. Rev. 1911, 1919 (2009).

[25] Patrick v. Burget, 486 U.S. 94, 102–03 (1988).

[26] The Supreme Court recognized in *NCAA v. Board of Regents* 468 U.S. 85, 109 (1984) that "[a]s a matter of law, the absence of proof of market power does not justify a naked restriction on price or output." Polygram Holding, Inc. v. FTC, 416 F.3d 29, 36 (D.C. Cir. 2005) ("If, based upon economic learning and the experience of the market, it is obvious that a restraint of trade likely impairs competition, then the restraint is presumed unlawful and, in order to avoid liability, the defendant must either identify some reason the restraint is unlikely to harm consumers or identify some competitive benefit that plausibly offsets the apparent or anticipated harm.").

protected values and so anticompetitive activity receives comparable immunity covered by the Noerr-Pennington doctrine. [27] Congress enacted the Sherman Act pursuant to its power under the commerce clause, and the Supreme Court has approved the significance of the Act's procompetitive policy and so the federal antitrust laws preempt state laws authorizing or compelling private parties to engage in anticompetitive behavior. [28] The Supreme Court [29] treats the Sherman Act as "a common-law statute" that is customized by the Court to "meet the dynamics of present economic conditions." To that extent, the NCAA restrains competition among colleges for the services of "student-athletes," and standard setting organizations by entailing a variety of restraints in the form of standardization. [30] Moreover, the Supreme Court upheld a district court ruling that the National Collegiate Athletic Association rules limiting education-related compensation violated Section 1 of the Sherman Act and so shortly after the Court's decision, the NCAA voted of its own accord to permit a student athlete to receive compensation in exchange for use of their name, image, and likeness (NIL). [31]

It has to be taken into account that state law, federal law, constitutional law, or some generally admitted public interest aim must authorize the organization to regulate some aspect of the market, the regulation at issue must be within the scope of that authorization, and the process used to embrace and apply the regulation must be suitable under the circumstances. [32]

The NCAA has long limited the compensation and benefits that student athletes may receive safeguarding its compensation rules from ordinary antitrust scrutiny but the supreme court decided that the National Collegiate Athletic Association ("NCAA") is not above the normal operation of antitrust law holding that the NCAA has infringed the antitrust laws. [33]

---

[27] California Motor Transp. Co. v. Trucking Unlimited, 404 U.S. 508 (1972).

[28] 324 Liquor Corp. v. Duffy, 479 U.S. 335 n.8 (1987).

[29] Leegin Creative Leather Prods., Inc. v. PSKS, Inc., 551 U.S. 877, 899 (2007).

[30] O'Bannon v. NCAA, 802 F.3d 1049 (9th Cir. 2015) (upholding the right of the NCAA to regulate payments to college athletes).

[31] Comment On, *NCAA v. Alston141 S. Ct. 2141 (2021), 135 Harv. L. Rev. 471.*

[32] N.C. Dental Bd. of Exam'rs v. FTC, 574 U.S. 494, 494–95 (2015) (finding collusive suppression of competition from non-dentists subject to antitrust and forbidden because it is not shielded by state action immunity).

[33] Nat'l Collegiate Athletic Ass'n v. Alston, 141 S.Ct. 2141, 2169 (2021) (the National Collegiate Athletic Association's ("NCAA") limits on student-athlete compensation violates the Sherman Antitrust Act of 1890). The NCAA still restricts the compensation that schools can offer directly to their athletes unrelated to education.

5.4 Cartels and Competition

Is it acceptable a degree of diminishing of "competition"? It has to be taken into account that the antitrust laws speak of the conduct they prohibit in unmistakably economic terms, such as "restraint of trade," "monopoly," and diminishing of "competition." To that extent, Hovenkamp [34] considers that the Chicago School movement attractiveness was not the belief of less enforcement notwithstanding of the facts, but rather the idea of handling economics to analyze business conduct in an effort to capitalize on social welfare which in fact might nullify the rationale of competition in many occasions in favor of fulfilling the interests of capital.

US antitrust law rests on a central distinction between restraints that are ancillary to legitimate productive business ventures or transactions, and those that are the result of a naked, [35] cartelistic restraint on competition that generates, allocates, and/or manipulates market power. It has to be taken into consideration that most cartels are per se illegal, but courts have refused to condemn some. Moreover, cartels are generally illegal regardless of their effect on consumer welfare, and this still dominates much of antitrust but this is resulting in a lack of consistency in the subsequent antitrust standards. Most of cases implicate a cartel that is subject to oversight by a public agency and so applying some form of preemption based on state or federal law or constitutional provisions. [36]

Are competition exceptions an innovation to bypass real competition and fulfilling the interest of some elite? The question to be answered is what factors explain why some cartels can be legal, but the vast majority is not. Most cases encompass express exemptions from antitrust law found in federal statutes, [37] constitutional protections, and state action immunities. On the other hand, state action immunity did not apply to hospital authorities making acquisitions that substantially lessen

[34] Herbert Hovenkamp The Looming Crisis in Antitrust Economics 2021 Boston University Law Review Vol. 101:489.

[35] United States v. Kemp & Assocs., 907 F.3d 1264 (10th Cir. 2018) (rejecting the trial court's use of rule of reason to decide a cartel case where defendants asserted significant efficiencies resulted from the naked restraint).

[36] S. Motor Carriers Rate Conf. v. United States, 471 U.S. 48, 52 (1985) (allowing trucking companies to collude on prices based on state supervision); Cal. Retail Liquor Dealers Ass'n v. Midcal Aluminum, Inc., 445 U.S. 97, 105 (1980) (lack of active supervision resulted in rejection of state effort to authorize minimum prices). Credit Suisse Secs. (USA) LLC v. Billing, 551 U.S. 264, 267 (2007) (considering whether the antitrust claims conflicted with federal securities law).

[37] Parker v. Brown, 317 U.S. 341, 346 (1943) (upholding California state law permitting agricultural commodity price regulation); N.C. State Bd. of Dental Exam'rs v. FTC, 574 U.S. 494, 503 (2015) (showing a dental regulatory agency required disinterested oversight of its decisions to qualify for state action immunity); Allied Tube & Conduit Corp., 486 U.S. at 497–98 (affirming the right of a trade association to create standards that excluded products from the market to ensure reasonable fire safety, but rejecting specific decisions based on bad and unreviewable process).

competition, [38] not mentioning that sham litigation can violate antitrust law. [39] Accordingly, the constitutional rights to petition the government and to litigate have boundaries such that abuse of those rights can cause antitrust liability for the reason that the conduct falls outside the scope of the preemption. [40] Antitrust law application of exclusionary monopolistic conduct is rejected due to the fact that state and federal regulators were better able to control the conduct. [41]

States have the authority to authorize some kinds of anticompetitive conduct but for the state action exemption to apply, the courts must decide whether the statute does not oust competition with regulation. The Court has discarded the claim that general authorization for ordinary corporate rights, such as a buying property, constitutes an implied right to monopolize the market. [42] Also, Peter C. Carstensen [43] argues that "naked restraints of competition are always per se illegal unless exempt."

5.5 False Advertising and Competition

Antitrust law analyses single-corporation conduct taking place when a corporation unilaterally employs false advertising. The Supreme Court has documented the role of truthful advertising in a free enterprise system. [44] Moreover, limitations on truthful advertising impair competition by restricting consumers' capacity to discover information about the price and quality of goods or services, thereby decreasing competitors' motivations to compete with each other. [45] It has to be taken into

[38] FTC v. Phoebe Putney Health Sys., Inc., 568 U.S. 216, 224–25 (2013).

[39] Cal. Motor Transp. Co. v. Trucking Unlimited, 404 U.S. 508, 511 (1972) (holding that it is immaterial how an antitrust violation is demonstrated if the facts establish massive, concerted, and purposeful group activity to deter individuals from accessing the courts).

[40] Credit Suisse Secs. (USA) LLC v. Billing, 551 U.S. 264, 282 (2007) (giving an expansive interpretation of the scope of preemption which some find troubling); Oneok v. Learjet, 135 S. Ct. 1591, 1603 (2015) (rejecting claim that antitrust exemption for wholesale prices of natural gas preempts state antitrust claims on behalf of retail customers where the prices were fixed through the wholesale market).

[41] Verizon Commc'ns, Inc. v. Law Offices of Curtis V. Trinko, LLP, 540 U.S. 398, 416 (2004).

[42] FTC. v. Phoebe Putney Health Sys., Inc., 568 U.S. 216, 233–35 (2013).

[43] Peter C. Carstensen, The Incoherent Justification for Naked Restraints of Competition: What the Dental Self-Regulation Cases Tell Us About the Cavities in Antitrust Law , 2020 Loyola University Chicago Law Journal [Vol. 51, 680].

[44] Bates v. State Bar of Ariz., 433 U.S. 350, 364 (1977).

[45] Polygram Holding, Inc., 136 F.T.C. 310, 355 (2003) at 354 (finding agreement among rivals not to advertise products was "presumptively anticompetitive"). Brief of the Federal Trade Commission at 1, 1-800 Contacts, Inc. v. FTC, No. 18-3848 (2d Cir. Oct. 7, 2019) ("Without timely information about competing products and sellers, . . . consumers cannot make informed choices and markets cannot function properly.").

account that there is a higher barrier to the application of antitrust law due to that fact that harm is needed to the market as a whole.

It is worth noting that there are difficulties demonstrating a monopolization claim because revealing monopoly power encompasses the challenges of defining a market and presenting power within that market. Nonetheless, courts and regulatory bodies continue to focus on market share and price as the primary devices to diagnose monopolization. The Supreme Court generally defines monopoly power as "the power to control prices or exclude competition." [46] Even though monopolization claims often are brought by competitors, consumers can sue for damage triggered by exclusionary conduct. [47] In monopolization case law courts found violations when the defendant's conduct does not bear any legitimate justification and where there are destructions to the market as a whole. [48] A market consists of a group of goods or services that are close substitutes for each other and traditionally, courts have determined market power "indirectly," implying from a company's market share in a "relevant market" and so that methodology overshadowed antitrust analysis through the twentieth century, but economists have gradually backed more "direct" measures counting on empirical measurement of output responses to price variations. The Supreme Court argues that the antitrust merger provision Section 7 of the Clayton Act necessitates a market definition. [49] Furthermore, Section 7 of the Clayton Act necessitates courts to "judge the likelihood of anticompetitive effects in the context of the 'structure, history, and probable future' of the particular markets that the merger will affect" [50] which means that only an examination of the real-world evidence involving ordinary course documents, bidding data, and testimony from market participants evidences a truthful portrait of the industry and competitive dynamics. [51]

[46] 15 U.S.C. § 2; Verizon Commc'ns, Inc. v. Law Offices of Curtis V. Trinko, LLP, 540 U.S. 398, 407 (2004).

[47] Aspen Skiing Co. v. Aspen Highlands Skiing Corp., 472 U.S. 585, 608–11 (1985) (discussing the two elements of the offense of monopolization as defined by the Sherman Act). 15 U.S.C. § 2 ("Every person who shall monopolize, or attempt to monopolize, or combine or conspire with any other person or persons, to monopolize any part of the trade or commerce among the several States, or with foreign nations, shall be deemed guilty of a felony . . . ."); Energy Conversion Devices Liquidation Tr. v. Trina Solar Ltd., 833 F.3d 680, 685 (6th Cir. 2016) ("It does not suffice for a plaintiff to allege only that 'the defendant has tried to knock out other businesses'; the plaintiff must show that 'the means it has employed to that end are likely to . . . injure consumers.'").

[48] In re Aggrenox Antitrust Litig., 94 F. Supp. 3d 224, 246 (D. Conn. 2015) ("[W]hen direct evidence is available that a party profitably charges supracompetitive prices, the existence of market power can be established from that fact alone.").

[49] Brown Shoe Co. v. United States, 370 U.S. 294, 324 (1962) (interpreting the Clayton Act's "section of the country" and "line of commerce" language as requiring a geographic market and a product market, respectively).

[50] *New York v. Deutsche Telekom AG Deutsche Telekom,* 439 F. Supp. 3d at 199, 206–07 *New York v. Deutsche Telekom AG*, 439 F. Supp. 3d 179 (S.D.N.Y. 2020).

[51] *FTC v. RAG-Stiftung RAG-Stiftung*, 436 F. Supp. 3d at 287, 312. *FTC v. RAG-Stiftung*, 436 F. Supp. 3d 278 (D.D.C. 2020).

Courts have never condemned monopolization without first defining a market and in the digital-monopoly case United States v. Microsoft Corp, [52] the government used indirect evidence of market share to reveal market power in a relevant market. Moreover, if the defendant is a natural monopoly, then driving rivals out of the market cannot be unlawful under the antitrust laws. In addition, the features of a natural monopoly make it unfitting to apply the usual rule that success in driving competitors from the market is evidence of illegal monopolization [53] and so natural-monopoly status designates a necessity for "utility" form regulation instead of antitrust enforcement. Regulation generalizes and applies the same rules to several companies in an area, while antitrust necessitates a fact-specific inquiry for each company.

Hence, the measurement of market power, as price changes can engender responsive effects on both sides and so viewed in isolation, a price rise on one side of the platform may look like an exercise of power, but it may be offset by a cost rise or an upsurge in services on the other side being mostly significant for measurements of price–cost relationships. To that extent, in Colorado v Google [54] asserted a relevant market of "general search text advertising," exclusive of other forms of online and offline advertising and so the data should be available to measure directly the residual elasticity of demand for such advertising. It could be said that concerning the reasons of a competitive assessment there is little profound distinction between defining a two-sided market and defining two interrelated markets, providing the effect of the cross-platform network is recognized and analyzed which means that cross-platform network results augment the competitive constraints that exist, while also raising a barrier to entry by prospective rivals and impeding the emergence of new competitive constraints. [55]

It is worth noting here that in order to safeguard the motivation to innovate, the possession of monopoly power will not be found unlawful unless it is supplemented by an element of anticompetitive conduct. [56]

False advertising occurs even if just an individual competitor is injured. Federal law presumes that false advertising impairs competition. Moreover, anticompetitive conduct, the center of antitrust law, raises price and diminishes quality. In addition, false advertising, the core of much consumer protection law, misleads consumers and distorts markets. Thus, both kinds of conduct harm consumers. To that extent, the Supreme Court has determined that "false or misleading advertising has an

[52] United States v. Microsoft Corp., 253 F.3d 34, 51, 56–57 (D.C. Cir. 2001).

[53] Greenville Publ'g Co. v. Daily Reflector, Inc., 496 F.2d 391, 397 (4th Cir. 1974).

[54] Colorado v. Google LLC, No. 1:20- cv-03715 (D.D.C. Dec. 17, 2020).

[55] SC Innovations, Inc. v. Uber Techs., Inc., No. 18-cv-07440-JCS, 2020 WL 2097611, at *3 (N.D. Cal. May 1, 2020) (refusing to dismiss a complaint alleging that Uber surge pricing constituted unlawful monopolistic price discrimination); Meyer v. Kalanick, 477 F. Supp. 3d 52, 57 (S.D.N.Y. 2020) (sustaining the arbitrator's conclusion that Uber's surge pricing did not violate the antitrust laws).

[56] Verizon Commc'ns Inc. v. Law Offs. of Curtis V. Trinko, 540 U.S. 398, 407 (2004).

anticompetitive effect." [57] It has to be taken into consideration that antitrust liability will dis-incentivize corporations from engaging in advertising that is dubious. Harms from false advertising are economic when deceived consumers are deprived of the advantages of their bargains. [58]

AT&T used deceptive behavior to extend its competitive lead over other firms and so the court decided that the law's neglect of the injuries instigated by false advertising endangers structural harm to competitive markets. [59] On the other hand, the use of adhesion contracts to avert consumers from getting restitution for false advertising is one noteworthy distortion in the existing competitive environment. [60]

It is characteristic that Facebook and other Big Tech corporations preserve their market dominance by exploiting the network outcomes that strengthen user value in the consumer-facing market and advertiser benefits in digital advertising markets.

5.6 Platforms and Competition

A digital platform is a website, app, or other digital setting networking commercially with one or more groups of users. [61] Platforms that sell solely digital content do not characteristically have serious capacity constraints on their products. Regardless that a platform is digital, not all of its output is inevitably digital, but platforms such as Facebook, Google Search, Spotify, and Netflix produce digital content almost exclusively.

Antitrust law has proved to be an adaptive device and the great challenge for antitrust in the twenty-first century is to develop remedies to oversee digital platforms. Ross Levine et al. [62] argue that competition enforcement does indeed promote innovation. Platforms' monopolies build on not on a single IP right but on a package of exclusive rights ranging from patents on software to network infrastructure, supply infrastructure, and from trade contractual relationship. Moreover, any monopoly must be restricted in scope and duration to safeguard competition.

The activities of big corporations in the digital economy today raise noteworthy competition concerns but it is not proven that they directly harm end-users or result

[57] Cal. Dental Ass'n v. FTC, 526 U.S. 756, 771 n.9 (1999) (citing FTC v. Algoma Lumber Co., 291 U.S. 67, 79–80 (1934)).

[58] Boltex Mfg. Co. v. Ulma Piping USA Corp., No. 4:17-CV-01400, 2020 WL 598284, at *6 (S.D. Tex. Feb. 7, 2020).

[59] AT&T Mobility LLC v. Concepcion, 563 U.S. 333, 350–52 (2011).

[60] FTC v. AT&T Mobility LLC, 87 F. Supp. 3d 1087 (N.D. Cal. 2015) (No. C-14-4785 EMC), rev'd and remanded, 835 F.3d 993 (9th Cir. 2016), reh'g en banc granted, 864 F.3d 995 (9th Cir. 2017).

[61] Herbert Hovenkamp, Platforms and the Rule of Reason: The American Express Case, 2019 Colum. Bus. L. Rev. 35, 47.

[62] Ross Levine, Chen Lin, Lai Wei and Wensi Xie, Competition Laws and Corporate Innovation, NBER Working Paper No. w27253 (May 2020) at 30, available at https://papers.ssrn.com/sol3/papers.cfm?abstract_id=3615449

in allocative inefficiencies. Moreover, business platforms are distinguished by zero price models supporting specific equipment and services and very high rates of innovation which means that customers do not lose out in the short term and perhaps, even in the long term, providing market positions keep on contestable because competitive and technological instability makes the apparently monopolistic positions of the moment instable. [63]

It has to be taken into account that in digital markets, barriers to entry are required as a result of the investments, the accumulated data and the controlled data flows, the algorithms created, and the data processing capabilities, but also the gained position of a market gatekeeper or keystone player in a digital industrial platform. To that extent, the dependency of complementors generate a certain number of competitive damages that cannot be fully reflected in consumer welfare embracing discriminatory access to a platform with vital infrastructure characteristics involving unfair access not only concerning competitors in a downstream or related market but also in transactional terms.

Online platforms operate in a consumer-facing market for digital services and a market for online advertising and so in order for a platform to keep its position in both the digital services and the online advertising markets, it must uphold the most desirable platform for users averting users from switching to other platforms. [64] Hence, user traffic is central to both markets for the reason that they each unveil strong network outcomes. The platforms encompass constant trade-offs between the transfer of personal data and the provision of services.

It is vital to make certain that upstarts have a fair opportunity to compete and challenge incumbent corporations due to the fact that the threat of being overtaken by rivals stipulates corporations to innovate and produce new products that consumers want. [65] It is worth noting that where a platform has acquired a large market share by being steadily better than its competitors and where it must respond to constant competitive demands to uphold that position, it functions within a competitive market even with a large market share.

Big Tech companies trade in online platform markets where they offer vital facilitation services between buyers and sellers, users and content providers, and advertisers and consumers and so their deals embrace search engines, social networks, e-commerce, digital advertising, and operating systems, where platforms connect parties online to enable transactions. Moreover, the amplified functionality and speed of cyberspace have made platforms extremely effective in connecting end-users. In addition, the profits earned by these companies generate strong

[63] Marty, F. & Warin, T. (2020). Innovation in Digital Ecosystems: Challenges and Questions for Competition Policy. Cahier Scientifique du CIRAN.

[64] Fiona Scott Morton Et Al., Stigler Ctr. for the Study Of Econ. & the State, Stigler Committee on Digital Platforms 34 (2019), https://research.chicagobooth.edu/-/media/research/stigler/pdfs/digital-platforms%2D%2D-committee-report%2D%2D-stigler-center.pdf

[65] Competition & Mkts. Auth., Online Platforms And Digital Advertising: Market Study Interim Report 8 (2019), https://assets.publishing.service.gov.uk/media/5dfa0580ed915d0933009761/Interim_report.pdf

motivations for others to enter these markets. To that extent, fewer Big Tech companies have dominated many online markets for years and the Big Tech large-scale acquisition programs have weakened the natural process of competitive entry, with companies entering the market with the exclusive objective of being acquired, as there would be no other conceivable endgame.

Will competition law choose to protect consumer choice over privacy and equality rights in a world of AI-processed client data? It seems that given the many uses of AI systems, there is no indispensable causal link between AI and market super-dominance leading alone into an abuse of power. The utilization of advanced AI becomes the fourth synergistic component that will make big tech companies' position unshakable and superdominant due to the fact that big tech companies' position will become unattainable for other competitors as the scale of big data collected will make possible these largest online platforms to both gradually accurately profile customers via their AI systems making certain even more sophisticated collection and mining of client data. It seems that online platforms of big tech firms have managed to persuade investors of the extraordinary prospective of their business to such an extent that they can afford to select growth over profitability in the long run. [66]

It has to be taken into account that Facebook has faced noteworthy scrutiny due to its enormous user base, as well as its dominance holding a virtual monopoly over online speech with limited recognition that cyberspace even exists outside of the platform. It is argued that Facebook's internal content moderation decisions essentially govern online speech in countries like Myanmar and Indonesia. Moreover, online platforms have been the subject of extensive direct regulatory attention with reference to the content they host, predominantly in the European Union. [67]

Furthermore, once a dominant company establishes itself in an online platform market, the network consequences and data-driven efficiencies in digital markets strengthen dominance even when new rivals improve or create novel goods. Hence, while strong network consequences instigate markets to produce a dominant company, they permit small nascent competitors with a desirable alternative platform to climb quickly disputing such dominance. To that extent, innovating startup companies stipulate competitive pressure in such markets when they present rapid user growth and the prospective to enter the dominant company's main market.

Antitrust law should treat digital platform markets for what they are: markets that have some distinctive qualities, but markets nonetheless susceptible to fact-specific antitrust analysis. [68] Herbert Hovenkamp [69] argues that "the less intrusive and more

[66] European Commission: Commission Staff Working Document Preliminary Report—Sector Inquiry into Consumer Internet of Things. Brussels, 9.6.2021 SWD(2021) 144 final.

[67] Michael Karanicolas, Too Long; Didn't Read: Finding Meaning In Platforms' Terms Of Service Agreements, Spring 2021 University Of Toledo Law Review Vol. 52.

[68] Ohio v. American Express Co. (Amex), 138 S. Ct. 2274, 2294–97 (2018) (Breyer, J., dissenting).

[69] Herbert Hovenkamp, Antitrust and Platform Monopoly, 2021 Yale Law Journal 130:1952 P 1956.

individualized approach of the antitrust laws is better for consumers, input suppliers, and most other affected interest groups than broad-brush regulation."

It is worth mentioning here that there is antitrust precedent for recognizing "cluster" market definitions, which are markets for noncompeting products or services sold from a common plant or platform. [70] Thus, "cluster" markets permit things that are not substitutes for each other to be clustered together in one antitrust market regardless that clustering confers competitive advantages to multiproduct companies in terms of economies of scope and transactional complementarities.

Does the winner in digital platforms take all? Even some platforms are winner take all, the policy effects are unclear, but in the case of natural monopolies is needed amplified antitrust enforcement for the reason that the market itself will not discipline dominant platforms. [71] It could be said that few platforms are natural monopolies. Even if a digital platform dictates a winner-take-all, or natural monopoly, it is vital to individualize the specific assets and operations that are in fact natural monopolies from those that are not. Hence, no matter whether the Amazon platform is a natural monopoly, most of the things that it sells are not which means that a well-designed policy will restrict the monopoly characterization to those particular inputs to which it applies, leaving other parts of production to competition. To that extent, if a platform is not a natural monopoly, competition should be both feasible and required.

It has to be taken into consideration that natural monopolies are outlined as activities in which entry by another company raises total costs which means that the presence of such monopolies rationalizes a government reversing its presumption in favor of market competition. Moreover, such a reversal is the anticipation that total economic costs from an activity will be lower as a consequence of production by a single company, with society gaining from evading duplicative costs. It is worth noting that businesses classified as containing natural monopoly activities form 10% or more of economic activity embracing electricity and gas, public transport, ports, post, telecommunications, rail, water, and waste and are politically significant. To that extent, Sean F. Ennis [72] argues that "even when standard conditions of a natural monopoly are met, entry may at times reduce total production costs, holding quantity constant," which means that not always natural monopoly triggers competitiveness.

It is worth noting that most digital platforms have competitors in at least some of the markets in which they function and online sellers of all magnitudes become visible everywhere, extending from single customers to big companies, to online sellers and to numerous newspapers, magazines, and other periodicals. Moreover, competitive markets adjust all the time, and the market shares of individual

[70] FTC v. Staples, Inc., 190 F. Supp. 3d 100, 117 (D.D.C. 2016).

[71] Daniel A. Hanley, A Topology of Multisided Digital Platforms, 19 Conn. Pub. Int. L.J. 271, 289–91 (2020).

[72] Sean F. Ennis, The natural monopoly paradox: incumbent inefficiency and entry, at: https://ssrn.com/abstract=4364914 p33.

companies vary. [73] Further, markets for new technologies and artificial intelligence go through lengthy periods in which multiple technologies compete with one another until a single winner materializes and so some markets go from less to more competitive as a result of technological transformation. It is worth noting that market shares and structural presumptions are not capable of predicting competitive consequences and, accordingly, of specifying optimal policy choices.

The fact that the platforms are not natural monopolies rationalizes amplified alarm for platform acquisitions of "nascent" companies. In addition, new entry should be making these markets more competitive, but systematic acquisition of recent entrants diminishes competitive density. Besides, if a platform is a natural monopoly, it will be able to uphold its position merely by charging a price that is not disproportionately above its costs. To that extent, competition to be the natural monopolist might exist, and antitrust policy fosters such competition. In addition, natural-monopoly status is not automatically permanent but its extent depends on technology and market size, both of which can alter. Thus, concerning "Utilities," even if only one business is ultimately the seller, companies can bid against one another for that privilege, driving prices to the competitive level. [74]

Furthermore, markets generating a single winner are generally ones where economies of scale, network results, or the demand for interoperability back a single format managed by a single private company. Moreover, qualities that make the appearance or upholding of a single technology winner less likely to embrace interoperability or pooling of indispensable information or data. Hence, Androids, iPhones, and other cellular phones interconnect, facilitating users to engage in a full range of communications with one another.

The Supreme Court [75] states that only platforms compete against other platforms and so American Express did not compete with alternatives such as cash or debit cards for the reason that its anti-steering rule did not apply to these products. In fact, the court held that the two companies do not compete, as a matter of law, because two-sided platforms can only compete with other two-sided platforms. [76] Also, it is argued that normally only horizontal restraints qualify as unreasonable per se and so restraints that are not unreasonable per se are assessed under the rule of reason, which necessitates courts to conduct a fact-specific assessment of market power and market structure in judging the restraint's actual impact on competition which means that the objective is to extricate between restraints with anticompetitive outcome that

[73] In re IBM Peripheral EDP Devices Antitrust Litig., 481 F. Supp. 965, 981 (N.D. Cal. 1979) (calculating the average IBM market share at more than 57% between 1969 and 1975); Lawrence A. Sullivan, Monopolization: Corporate Strategy, the IBM Cases, and the Transformation of the Law, 60 Tex. L. Rev. 587, 599 (1982) (noting that IBM's market share was 75% in 1964 and 70% in 1971).

[74] Harold Demsetz, Why Regulate Utilities?, 11 J.L. & Econ. 55, 57–60 (1968).

[75] Ohio v. Am. Express Co., 138 S. Ct. 2274, 2287 (2018)). At 2283.

[76] American Express Co., 138 S. Ct. 2274 (2018), The Court held that Amex's anti-steering provisions did not violate §1 of the Sherman Antitrust Act.

are detrimental to the consumer and restraints encouraging competition that are in the consumer's best interest.

Uber was prevented from charging a price significantly higher than its costs due to competition from taxicab companies. Will Uber and Lyf drive traditional taxis out of the market? It is not clear due to the fact that taxicab companies will adopt technologies that make them more competitive with multi-homing customers. Nonetheless, antitrust policy unavoidably looks at shorter or middle runs, so what counts is the extent of substitution now and whether a particular two-sided platform competes with a more traditional market is one of fact, not of law. Thus, DOJ has to prove that a proposed transaction would harm competition in a properly defined relevant antitrust market. [77]

It has to be taken into consideration that even if costs drop constantly as output increases or network consequences are large, a digital platform is still not automatically a natural monopoly. Product differentiation is an element of competition and so even though a natural monopolist can eliminate a rival with an identical product merely by charging a competitive price, the differentiated entrant faces a different demand permitting new entry even against a much larger incumbent. Hence, railroads faced noteworthy competition from trucking, and AT&T's competition for its traditional landlines came from wireless technology providers. Moreover, concerning digital platforms, Facebook displaced MySpace, not by merely going head-to-head with a noticeably identical product, but rather by presenting a set of inter-member communication services that MySpace lacked. It could be said that the most substantial competitive pressures to Facebook Blue will come from differentiated products that offer users a distinctive way of interacting with friends and family for which Facebook Blue is not adjusted. Thus, Facebook is pushing the technology to do anything users want.

To that extent, the capacity of corporations to differentiate their goods or services at least partly rationalizes the dominant platform strategy of buying up nascent digital companies. Moreover, these acquisitions are not simply horizontal but rather fall into the category of "product extension" mergers, which are acquisitions expanding the variety of products or services that the acquiring company offers. Hence, there is an attempt either to gain product differentiation or to cut off efforts by others to develop differentiated alternatives. Therefore, antitrust policy regarding startup acquisitions becomes relevant.

Large platforms such as Facebook, Amazon, or Google preserve their positions by buying up all of the prospective challengers before they develop into more formidable rivals. Thus, the systematic platform acquisitions of tech startups prevent the eventual emergence of substantial rivals and not producing price increases or innovation reductions in the short run by facilitating collusion in the post-merger

[77] *United States v. Sabre Corp.*, 452 F. Supp. 3d 97 (D. Del. 2020), *vacated*, No. 20-1767, 2020 WL 4915824 (3d Cir. July 20, 2020).

market. [78] Additionally, the court held that the significant capacity benefits enabled by the merger will stimulate competition with AT&T and Verizon and so the Proposed Merger was not expected to considerably lessen competition in the RMWTS Markets. There is a need of evidencing a probability of substantially lessened competition. [79] It is worth noting here that the court specified [80] that the competitor integration policy limits only how canvas apps on Facebook operate, and leaves app developers entirely free to develop applications for Facebook's competitors. Moreover, the States' exclusive dealing theory fails as a matter of law and an exclusive dealing claim to survive a motion to dismiss the plaintiffs must effectively assert that the exclusive contract "caused substantial market foreclosure." [81] Here, the States proclaimed only that the competitor integration policy "discouraged developers from creating apps that bridged" but not that this policy substantially foreclosed Facebook's competitors.

Competition problems in digital platforms present some novel encounters and antitrust law can handle them which means that courts and other antitrust policy makers should treat digital platforms as corporations that have unique qualities, but not so unique needing the abandonment of what we know about competition in high-technology and product-differentiated markets.

On the one hand, competition is being impaired by restricting consumers' freedom of choice. On the other, harm to competition takes the form of harm to innovation which means that access to technological channels can be closed off by the platform and so causing damage to dynamic effectiveness. To that extent, once a platform "controls" the innovation dynamics of its complementors, it can diminish the reasons and capacities to develop disruptive innovations which mean that the impairment to innovation damages the velocity of innovation and composition. Assumed the market power that platforms possess and their potentially irreversible character means that the criterion of consumer welfare concerning competition has to remain by affixing particular considerations regarding labor tradition. Consequently, it is no matter of talking merely damage to consumer welfare but tackling prospective harm to effective competition. Hence, the lawfulness of dominant corporations' practices must be evaluated not by their net influence on consumer welfare but upon the substance of fair competition which influences consumer affairs.

In fact, the scale of damages is considerably broader by reducing the prospective for the development of startups, amplified inequalities, privacy problems, growing fake news, among others. Therefore, it is more a matter of regulating the economic power of specific companies than an issue of defending competition. Furthermore, it

---

[78] United States v. Baker Hughes, Inc., 908 F.2d 981 (D.C. Cir. 1990) (refusing to condemn a merger in a concentrated market); New York v. Deutsche Telekom AG, 439 F. Supp. 3d 179 (S.D.N.Y. 2020) (same).

[79] *United States v. AT&T, Inc.*, 310 F. Supp. 3d 161 (D.D.C. 2018), *aff'd*, 916 F.3d 1029 (D.C. Cir. 2019).

[80] New York v. Meta Platforms, Inc., 66 F.4th 288, 295 (D.C. Cir. 2023).

[81] Vazquez-Ramos v. Triple-S Salud, Inc., 55 F.4th 286, 301 (1st Cir. 2022).

is argued that competition laws must protect the competition procedure itself and not its result being efficiency in the market. [82] G.I.Zekos argues that competition law has to protect competition not only as a process but also leading to a fair competition outcome based on equal opportunities of all firms to develop innovation and having the best results distributed to customers.

Again, the advancement of digital markets itself lawfully augments the scope of competitive concerns and so the growth of the platform economy amalgamates the competitive reasoning concerns under other branches of law such as consumer law since the users of the platforms are private individuals, which is also the case of contract law. Thus, platforms involve numerous vertical contractual restrictions regarding, restrictive practices and competition law enforcement. In addition, contractual imbalances raise points not only for the parties concerned but also for competition owing to the rise of exclusionary abuses, exploitative abuses, and abuses of economic dependence that competition law must tackle. [83]

It is worth noting that barriers to accessing the market harm the consumer relating to freedom of choice and the diversity of options available. Additionally, if the principal player controls the technological course of its complementors, it can delay any disruptive innovation and lock its complementors into innovations that reinforce their dependence on it.

Nowadays, digital platforms serve as indispensable facilities for the digital economy. Moreover, platforms leverage their exclusive control over search engines, e-commerce platforms, and app stores to bar rivals from markets for digital content, goods, and services by this means harming consumers and suppressing innovation. Also, forming and protecting monopolies, via exclusive rights or otherwise, can incentivize innovation. Conversely, any monopoly must be controlled in scope and duration to safeguard competition.

It is argued that platforms abuse their power by disregarding and discerning against third parties on their platforms. Moreover, Amazon exploits consumer and third-party merchant data to copy goods of independent sellers by prioritizing its own products in search results on its site. Also, Google and Apple app stores favor their own applications in search listings and drive purchasers away from independent developers. [84] The court decided that Apple's intentionally closed system averts competition in the aftermarket for iPhone apps empowering the App Store to collect a higher price per app than if Apple were forced to entice app seekers in a

[82] Wu, T. (2018). The Curse of Bigness: Antitrust in the New Gilded Age. Columbia Global Reports. Steinbaum, M. & Stucke, M. E. (2018). The Effective Competition Standard: A New Standard for Antitrust. WP Roosevelt Institute.

[83] Bougette, P., Budzinski, O., & Marty F. (2019). Exploitative Abuse and Abuse of Economic Dependence: What Can We Learn from an Industrial Organization Approach? Revue d'Economie Politique, 129(2), 261–286. https://doi.org/10.3917/redp.292.0261

[84] Jack Nicas & Keith Collins, How Apple's Apps Topped Rivals in the App Store It Controls, N.Y. TIMES (Sept. 9, 2019), https://perma.cc/K6DH-UCCS

competitive market. [85] Law enforcement efforts and regulations influencing the mobile app sector already has proven effective in altering business practices considered to be anticompetitive. [86] Manuel Wörsdörfer [87] says "Apple's closed ecosystem comes with several advantages, such as enhanced quality (control), user experience, security, privacy, and reliability/trustworthiness. Yet, it also leads to multiple antitrust issues, including high transfer costs for customers—i.e., prevented or restricted multihoming, switching, and interoperability—and significant market entry barriers for competitors, e.g., via network effects, tying and bundling, and other forms of discriminatory platform access." Hence, Apple is engaged in multiple forms of anticompetitive behavior. [88]

It has to be taken into account that barriers to entry for emerging competitors protect incumbent platforms from competitive forces that normally limit market power which means that freed from such restraints, incumbent platforms can participate in exclusionary behavior in the market for goods and services offered on the platform. Thus, digital platforms developed in an era of unregulated expansion into unmarked territory and so the platforms' activities in the digital economy suppresses competition, excludes markets, restrains innovation, and, eventually, harms consumers. [89]

There is a necessity to grant competitors equal and fair access to needed infrastructure for commerce. Likewise, markets on the platform do not resemble level playing fields, in which the quality and price of products and services ascertain their success in the marketplace. On the other hand, empowering platforms to exercise "gatekeeper power" over noteworthy parts of the industry is a reality against any form of competition allowing "capital" to build an advantage against any other entrants. To that extent, digital platforms have become the leading force in digital commerce by allowing them to utilize their power to discriminate against third-party firms, foreclose markets and extract monopoly rents.

Products and services on platforms are integrated into the platforms and the open cyberspace is becoming a network of platforms. Markets for digital platforms are highly concentrated in many sectors and both the supply and demand sides of the

[85] Apple v. Pepper, No. 17-204, slip. op. at 6 (U.S. Sep. 24, 2018) Department of Commerce. (2023). Competition in the Mobile Application Ecosystem. www.ntia.gov/sites/default/files/publications/mobileappecosystemreport.pdf

[86] ACM: Apple Changes Unfair Conditions, Allows Alternative Payments Methods in Dating Apps, Authority for Consumers and Markets (Netherlands) (June 11, 2022), https://www.acm.nl/en/publications/acm-apple-changesunfair-conditions-allows-alternative-payments-methods-dating-apps ; Distributing Dating Apps in the Netherlands, Apple Developer, https://developer.apple.com/support/storekit-external-entitlement/

[87] Manuel Wörsdörfer, Apple's Antitrust Paradox, https://ssrn.com/abstract=4487386 p6.

[88] Kotapati, B., Mutungi, S., Newham, M., Schroeder, J., Shao, S., & Wang, M. (2020). The Antitrust Case Against Apple. https://papers.ssrn.com/sol3/papers.cfm?abstract_id=3606073. Wörsdörfer, M. (2022). What Happened to 'Big Tech' and Antitrust? And How to Fix Them! Philosophy of Management 21(3). 345–369. Wörsdörfer, M. (2022). Big Tech and Antitrust: An Ordoliberal Analysis. Philosophy & Technology 35(3).

[89] United States v. Google, LLC, No. 1:20-cv-03010-APM (D.D.C. Oct. 20, 2020).

market are based on platforms to access the digital economy. Moreover, many platforms have vertically integrated concluding the function as impartial umpires in downstream markets and taking into account that the absence of alternatives empowers them to discriminate and extract monopoly rents from an ever-larger section of the digital economy. It could be said that the supremacy of the largest online platforms, based on a self-reinforcing cycle of big data collection and AI processing, has already led competition authorities, or legislators on both sides of the Atlantic, to propose new ex ante regulation for internet gatekeepers. Here, competition law has to generate new AI tools to be applied in parallel with traditional ex post-enforced prohibitions.

Do dominant technology platforms like Google, Amazon, Facebook, and Apple threaten innovation? First of all, technological developments under free of regulatory oversight have worsened innovation problems by allowing corporations like Google, Facebook, and Amazon to achieve market dominance by accumulating data and acting as an all-knowing middleman between customers and upstream suppliers. Concerning the regulation of digital platforms Nikolas Guggenberger [90] argues for "a two-tiered remedy: At its first level, regulators and courts must bar platforms from discriminating and self preferencing. At its second level, after an appropriate amortization period, antitrust enforcers must upend platform-monopolies entirely, by forcing interoperability between platforms."

Small companies' businesses are more inventive and producing more patents per employee. On the other hand, instead of generating innovative products, corporations have counted on lax merger regulation to buy out competitors, or by employing anticompetitive practices to prevent them from entering markets in the first place. [91] It has to be taken into account that functioning in highly concentrated markets, these dominant corporations do not innovate in order to escape losing business to rivals but simply either grab others' innovations or buy out the innovators at paltry prices.

Since corporations like Facebook and Google, which let consumers access their services for free, proving consumer harm poses a challenge. Do consumers pay for free services by offering corporations with valuable data? It has to be taken into account that dominant tech platforms utilize user data made available only to them by monitoring what their users do both on and off their platforms and so taking the best-performing ideas, functionality, and non-patentable products initiated by independent providers.

Big tech firms either discriminate against innovative independent content providers [92] or vertically amalgamate with. It is worth noting that as soon as a new company enters the technology market, it is hard to survive due to the fact that big

[90] Nikolas Guggenberger, Essential Platforms, 24 Stan. Tech. L. Rev. 237 (2021) At 237.

[91] Lina M. Kahn, Amazon's Antitrust Paradox, 126 Yale L. J. 710,737(2017).

[92] Lina M. Kahn, The Separation of Platforms and Commerce, 119 Colum. L. Rev. 973, 992 (2019) ("There are numerous means by which Amazon can disfavor any particular merchant: It can suspend or shut down accounts overnight, withhold merchant funds, change page displays, and throttle or block favorable reviews.").

tech companies either squeeze startups by copying them or they pay to buy them early eliminating a threat. In other words, big companies eliminate less efficient smaller rivals offering employment opportunities and so by producing massive profits for their managers and largest stockholders, big companies worsen wealth inequality.

It has to be taken into consideration that antitrust cases encompassing monopolization and abuse of dominance in digital markets look like traditional vertical restriction cases where a dominant corporation in a specific market uses its market power to limit competition in adjacent markets. Anne C. Witt [93] argues that "The existing competition rules, at least as currently interpreted, are insufficient to protect competition in digital platform markets that are prone to tipping... even where the dominant digital platform has grown by means of acquisitions or has engaged in exclusionary conduct, competition law enforcement has proved ineffective."

Platforms use tying strategies so as to deprive rival companies of appropriate economies of scope in the tied product market at an earlier stage, so preventing it from entering the primary tying market later. [94] To that extent, in digital platforms, if the tying product and the tied product markets are subject to fierce competition from prospective challengers with disruptive innovations, the anticompetitive outcomes of tying are less serious. [95] Tying has become a common practice in digital platforms causing both procompetitive consequences and anticompetitive results and so tying practices fall within competition law scrutiny because when a platform has already reached a decisive mass engenders anticompetitive concerns through tying during the process of platform expansion. Mandrescu [96] detects that platforms choose between "on platform expansion" or "cross platform expansion" through tying.

5.7 EU's Artificial Intelligence Act

The accelerating digitalization of society and the economy has shaped a situation where a few large platforms control imperative ecosystems in the digital economy. Digital services embrace a large category of online services, from simple websites to

[93] Anne C. Witt, Platform Regulation In Europe—Per Se Rules To The Rescue?, Journal of Competition Law & Economics, 18(3), 670–708 https://doi.org/10.1093/joclec/nhac001 P681.

[94] Qian Wu and Niels J. Philipsen, The Law and Economics of Tying in Digital Platforms: Comparing Tencent and Android, Journal of Competition Law & Economics, 2023, 19, 103–122 https://doi.org/10.1093/joclec/nhac011

[95] Pina Akman, A Web of Paradoxes: Empirical Evidence on Online Platform Users and Implications for Competition and Regulation in Digital Markets, 16 Virginia Law and Business Review 217 (2022).

[96] Daniel Mandrescu, Tying and Bundling by Online Platforms—Distinguishing between Lawful Expansion Strategies and Anticompetitive Practices, 40 Computer Law & Security Review: The International Journal of Technology Law and Practice, 8 (2021).

internet infrastructure services and online platforms and so the rules stated in the DSA principally concern online intermediaries and platforms. [97]

The Digital Services Act and Digital Markets Act generate a safer digital space where the fundamental rights of users are protected founding a level playing field for corporations. While the DMA safeguards a contestable and fair digital market by compelling a list of obligations on large platforms (gatekeepers), the DSA encompasses general rules on the liability of providers of online intermediary services and preserves their diligence by approving a layered approach and inflicting more extensive obligations on online platforms and large online platforms. Hence, the former is generally linked with competition law and market access, whereas the latter is commonly related to consumer protection and liability matters.

The European Union's Digital Markets Act (DMA) [98] initiative, which is set to introduce ex ante regulatory rules for "gatekeepers" in online platform markets, is one of the most important pieces of legislation to emanate from Brussels in recent decades. The DMA complements the EU and Member State competition rules facilitating the harmonization of rules at the EU level under Article 114 TFEU so as to circumvent fragmentation that could otherwise undermine the functioning of the Internal Market. Furthermore, DMA complements competition rules by tackling unfair practices by gatekeepers that either fall outside the existing EU competition rules or antitrust enforcement involving the situation in specific markets by intervening after the restrictive or abusive practice takes place engaging investigative procedures that take time. In addition, DMA diminishes the detrimental structural consequences of unfair practices ex ante by leaving open the prospect of further ex post intervention by EU or national competition law enforcement. It has to be taken into account that ex ante interventions prevent corporations from getting too much market power and ex post enforcement measures tackle abuses of dominance when they take place.

Also, DMA offers the Commission the power to impose fines and periodic penalty payments alike those available for violations of EU competition rules. According to the DMA, [99] the difference in market power could lead to an entrenchment of the powerful position of the gatekeepers and to unfavorable trading conditions for the non-gatekeepers. [100] Moreover, fairness in the DMA means that corporations receive different entitlements in line with their market power and so

[97] Regulation (EU) 2022/2065 of the European Parliament and of the Council of 19 October 2022 on a Single Market For Digital Services and amending Directive 2000/31/EC (Digital Services Act) *OJ L 277, 27.10.2022, p. 1–102.*

[98] Regulation (EU) 2022/1925 of the European Parliament and of the Council of 14 September 2022 on contestable and fair markets in the digital sector and amending Directives (EU) 2019/1937 and (EU) 2020/1828 (Digital Markets Act) *OJ L 265, 12.10.2022, p. 1–66.*

[99] Regulation (EU) 2022/1925 of the European Parliament and of the Council of 14 September 2022 on contestable and fair markets in the digital sector and amending Directives (EU) 2019/1937 and (EU) 2020/1828 (Digital Markets Act).

[100] Recital 33 Regulation 2022/1925 cit.

those with more market power receive fewer entitlements and see their economic freedom restricted, and those with less market power receive more entitlements.

The DMA is grounded on the understanding that unfair practices in the digital sector are predominantly common in core platform services as a result of certain features, embracing extreme scale economies, strong network consequences, data-driven advantages, and vertical integration. Moreover, the DMA presents a targeted set of harmonized rules that applies only to those undertakings that meet these criteria, which are illustrated in detailed quantitative thresholds in Article 3 of the DMA.

AI has become a resource of interactive, autonomous, and self-learning agencies performing tasks that would otherwise necessitate human intelligence and intervention to be successfully executed. The EU's Artificial Intelligence Act (AIA) has been drafted as a set of harmonized rules to aid organizations in designing trustworthy AI systems. Thus, delegating tasks to AI systems augments consistency, advances efficiency, and boosts access to a service or product. Moreover, AI is used to adjust the quality of community services through more accurate forecasting. To that extent, as a result of AI's ability to draw inferences from large and even less-structured data, AI is a valuable device for facilitating new solutions to complex problems. Furthermore, AI systems reduce human control and so remove human responsibility.

EU priority is to make certain that AI systems used in the EU are safe, transparent, traceable, and non-discriminatory which means that AI systems should be supervised by people in order to avoid destructive results [101] rather than encompassing autonomous compliance but, on the other hand, the forthcoming AAI technology will force EU to comply with the rules of dealing with AAI systems. Currently, the key objective of the AIA is to make certain that AI systems within the EU are safe, and comply with existing laws on fundamental rights, norms, and values. Moreover, the AIA describes AI systems mostly by including logic- or rule-based information processing, along with probabilistic algorithms. Like the GDPR, it applies to all corporations desiring to run AI systems within the EU, irrespective of whether they are based in the EU or not. The AIA embraces a *risk-based approach* to regulating AI systems demanding providers of high-risk AI systems to conduct conformity assessments before placing their product or service on the European market. Nevertheless, while the AIA specifies a wide range of procedural prerequisites for conformity assessments grounded on internal control, it does not offer any detailed guidance on how these rations should be implemented in practice. Basically, the AIA seeks to make certain that AI systems conform with existing EU laws, rights, and values to avert harm to its citizens. The AI rulebook bans the use of the technology for exploiting vulnerabilities.

[101] On 14 June 2023, MEPs adopted Parliaments negotiating position on the AI Act. The talks will now begin with EU countries in the Council on the final form of the law. Dragos Tudorache said: "The AI Act will set the tone worldwide in the development and governance of artificial intelligence, ensuring that this technology, set to radically transform our societies through the massive benefits it can offer, evolves and is used in accordance with the European values of democracy, fundamental rights, and the rule of law."

It is also imperative to say that the AIA has extra-territorial reach applying to any corporation running an AI system within the EU and corporations located outside the EU. The Artificially Intelligent Act [102] distinguishes the difference between "AI" and "AI systems" forbidding AIA practices, embracing subliminal manipulation under Article 5(1)(a) and (b), social scoring under Article 5(1)(c), remote biometric identification and classification under Article 5(1)(d), and mistreatment of vulnerabilities. [103] Moreover, AIA does not encompass any provision for liability to pay damages incurred by AI systems. Also, the AIA does not consider harmonizing itself with EU Data Protection Law. To that extent, the AIA has acknowledged a wide array of challenges, but the AIA has not referred to any individual rights but merely appreciated the fears posed by AI to fundamental rights without the provision of any legislative framework through which individuals can pursue their rights. The AIA draft does not foresee any robust machinery against AI-driven decision-making. Moreover, it does not confer any power on the European AI board to make certain strict compliance with the rules engrafted under AIA. Also, the AIA does not describe when, how, and at what stage human oversight is necessitated. It could be said that the law should adopt AI and robotics as a device wherever required to back the structural values of the legislative contribution delivering valuable, vibrant, constructive, and progressive administration of justice.

5.8 Digital Monopolies

It is characteristic that the FTC stimulates antitrust and regulatory efforts by tackling the power of big tech corporations. [104] As it is mentioned earlier, it is witnessed that principal Internet platforms exploit their power to prevent market entrants, to extract monopoly profits, and to gather intimate personal information that they can utilize for their own benefit. To that extent, there is a need to enforce the Clayton Act and in general the antitrust laws fairly and energetically.

Vertical restraints often pose no risk to competition unless the entity imposing them has market power, which cannot be evaluated. [105] The US Supreme Court supported that not all vertical restraints should be condemned. [106] The Advocate General argued that in order to ascertain whether an agreement restricted competition one had to carry out "a comprehensive examination of their economic

[102] Veale, M.; Borgesius, F.Z. Demystifying the Draft EU Artificial Intelligence Act—Analysing the good, the bad, and the unclear elements of the proposed approach. Comput. Law Rev. Int. 2021, 22, 97–112.

[103] Explanatory Memorandum of the AIA, COM (2021) 206 Final. Available online: https://eur-lex.europa.eu/legal-content/EN/ALL/?uri=celex:52021PC0206

[104] Executive Order 14036 of July 9, 2021, Promoting Competition in the American Economy 86 FR 36987.

[105] Daniel A. Crane, Market Power Without Market Definition, 90 Notre Dame L. Rev. 31 (2014).

[106] White Motor Co. v. United States, 372 U.S. 253 (1963).

repercussions." [107] Nonetheless, the ECJ found that a vertical restraint imposing absolute territorial protection infringed competition law generating the first "cleavage" between EU and US antitrust laws: the former involved agreements that divided national markets, the latter more involved the economic consequences of company conduct. [108]

While the US Supreme Court has not accepted "margin squeeze" as a stand-alone offense, the EU recognizes margin squeeze as a discrete example of abuse of dominance. In TeliaSonera, [109] the Court approved the application of an equally efficient competitor test that takes into consideration the dominant operator's costs and revenues holding that while an anticompetitive effect is "probable" where the wholesale product at issue is "indispensable" for the supply of the end product, still an anticompetitive effect can be generated when the wholesale product is not indispensable which means that indispensability is an issue for appraisal but not a necessary condition. Moreover, the Court held that it is required to ascertain the levels of "margin squeeze of competitors at least as efficient as the dominant undertaking." The TeliaSonera case settled that margin squeeze must have an anticompetitive effect on the market. Unlike the EU which acknowledges a broad perception of margin squeeze, the USA does not acknowledge margin squeeze as a stand-alone abuse. The Supreme Court [110] ruled that "if there is no [antitrust] duty to deal at the wholesale level and no predatory pricing at the retail level, then a firm is not required to price both of these services in a manner that preserves its rival's profit margin" and so recognizing that absent an antitrust duty to deal or predatory pricing, a "margin squeeze" cannot establish a valid antitrust claim on its own. Moreover, the linkLine judgment was similar to the TeliaSonera judgment as they both concerned ADSL services.

It is argued that a company with no antitrust duty to take care of its rivals at all is under no obligation to provide those rivals with a "sufficient" level of service. [111] Section 2 of the Sherman Act makes it illegal to "monopolize, or attempt to monopolize, or combine or conspire with any other person or persons, to monopolize any part of the trade or commerce among the several States, or with foreign nations." [112] Hence, merely retaining monopoly power and charging monopoly prices does

---

[107] Joined Cases 56 and 58–64, Établissements Consten S.à.R.L. and Grundig-Verkaufs-GmbH v Commission of the European Economic Community (1966) ECR 299 p. 358.

[108] Anu Bradford, Adam Chilton, & Filippo Lancieri, The Chicago School's Limited Influence on International Antitrust, 87 U. Chi. L. Rev. 2 (2020), https://scholarship.law.columbia.edu/faculty_scholarship/2512/, Anu Bradford, Adam Chilton, Katerina Linos, & Alexander Weaver, The Global Dominance of European Competition Law Over American Antitrust Law, 16(4) J. Empir. Leg. Stud. 731 (2019), https://scholarship.law.columbia.edu/faculty_scholarship/2513/

[109] Konkurrensverket v TeliaSonera Sverige AB Case C-52/09, EU:C:2011:83.

[110] Pacific Bell Telephone Company, dba AT&T California, et al., v. linkLine Communications, Inc., et al., 555 U.S. 438 (2009).

[111] In Verizon Communications Inc. v. Law Offices of Curtis V. Trinko, LLP, 540 U. S. 398, 410 (2004).

[112] 15 U. S. C. §2.

not violate §2 which means that the statute aims at "the willful acquisition or maintenance of that power" as differentiated from growth or development by means of a superior product, etc. [113] Businesses are free to decide the parties with whom they will trade, as well as the prices, terms, and conditions of that trading. [114] Any duty to deal has to come from the statute alone and so the only way that the antitrust agencies and courts could not apply Section 2 in regulated sectors at all is if the US Congress specifically says in the statute regulating the sector that the statute supersedes the antitrust laws.

Taking into account that conduct that is "per se illegal," encompassing violations of the antitrust laws, like outright price-fixing agreements and Section 2 allegations of monopolization, attempted monopolization, and conspiracy to monopolize were brought only civilly, DOJ obtained a guilty plea to a criminal violation of Section 2 for the first time in decades, launching an effort to revive criminal enforcement of monopolization law. [115] To that extent, Section 2 is applicable only when an attempt to collude would have resulted in a party securing or preserving monopoly power in a defined market and so the automatic per se condemnation reserved for specific categories of "manifestly anticompetitive" horizontal agreements, like price fixing, bid-rigging, and market allocation. [116] DOJ's criminal enforcement endeavors have been restricted to the so-called "hardcore," or per se, offenses under Section 1 of the Sherman Act such as price-fixing, bid-rigging, and market allocation schemes between competitors. [117]

The EU competition rules are horizontal in nature applying to all economic sectors. It is characteristic that excessive pricing has become a central category of EU competition law infringement cases concerning pharmaceuticals alongside pay for delay. [118] Excessive prices are considered unfair prices in Article 102a TFEU and are a form of abuse of dominance. [119]

It is worth noting that there is a distinctive application of competition rules in EU and US concerning the same pricing policy approved by an undertaking. In the USA, an antitrust claim can arise in a "price squeeze" situation only if some other antitrust violation is being performed. Again, there is no excessive pricing in the USA and so high pricing composes an infringement only if it amounts to a de facto refusal to deal and if refusing to deal would be an antitrust infringement in the occurrences of dominance, lack of business justification, etc. Besides, low pricing can be an infringement only if constituting below-cost predatory pricing. Thus, without the

---

[113] *United States* v. *Grinnell Corp.*, 384 U. S. 563, 570–571 (1966).

[114] *United States* v. *Colgate & Co.*, 250 U. S. 300, 307 (1919).

[115] *United States v. Zito*, No. CR 22-113 (D. Mont. Sep. 19, 2022).

[116] *Bus. Elecs. Corp. v. Sharp Elecs. Corp.*, 485 U.S. 717, 723 (1988).

[117] Daniel A. Crane, Criminal Enforcement of Section 2 of the Sherman Act: An Empirical Assessment, 84 Antitrust Law Journal No. 3 (2022).

[118] Aspen EU (Case AT.40394) Commission Decision [2021] 724 final.

[119] André den Exter, 'Fighting excessive pharmaceutical prices: Evaluating the options' (2020) 27 European Journal of Health Law 1.

occurrence of either of those independent infringements, there can be no margin squeeze and so it is not a "stand alone" infringement.

It has to be taken into account that a detailed regulatory scheme such as that generated by the 1996 Act normally induces the question of whether the regulated entities are not shielded from antitrust scrutiny altogether by the doctrine of implied immunity. [120] Thus, the Supreme Court assumes that it is less expected to find a refusal to deal infringement in a regulated commerce when the regulations enact various provisions designed at preventing anticompetitive behavior and so in those cases, the Court considers the regulation for the economic "context" in which the conduct is taking place to ascertain if it is expected to have an anticompetitive effect which means founding a legitimate justification for the refusal.

The Court of Justice [121] specified that the margin squeeze test is grounded on the costs and the strategy of the dominant undertaking itself, instead of on the specific condition of its actual or prospective competitors. Moreover, the "as-efficient-operator test" permits dominant corporations to evaluate the lawfulness of their activities and is consistent with the general principle of legal certainty. [122] Again, behavior resembling a price squeeze may be undertaken for efficiency or procompetitive reasons such as to abolish a double marginalization or to meet competition from another technology. [123] Furthermore, it is needed to establish that the practice generates an anticompetitive outcome on the retail market and that the practice is not in any way economically justified. Consequently, the Court approved that margin squeeze is not a per se abuse and so there is a need to prove the prospective for anticompetitive effects on the specific facts. [124]

The dominant undertakings' pricing practices are abusive when they have possibly an exclusionary effect "capable of making market entry more difficult or impossible" and so in the lack of any consequence on the competitive situation of competitors, a pricing practice cannot be classified as exclusionary which means that actual exclusionary results must be shown so as to ascertain the abusive nature of a particular practice. [125]

The Directorate General for Competition at the European Commission enforces competition law in the areas of antitrust, merger control, and State aid. The Treaty of the Functioning of the European Union (TFEU) does not define the core elements of Article 102 and the law under Article 102 protects competitors, but only if they are as efficient as the dominant undertaking. The Court of Justice found that a pricing practice constitutes and abuse under Article 102 if it has an exclusionary effect on

[120]In Verizon Communications, Inc. v. Law Offices of Curtis V. Trinko, LLP, 540 U.S. 398 (2004).

[121]Case T-5/97 Industrie des Poudres Sphériques v Commission [2000] ECR II-3755, ¶ 180. Deutsche Telekom v Commission https://curia.europa.eu/juris/liste.jsf?language=en&num=C-280/08

[122]Case COMP/38.784 - Wanadoo España v Telefónica, recital 310.

[123]OECD policy roundtable paper of 2009, http://snipurl.com/1xypj6

[124]Deutsche Telekom v Commission.

[125]Case T57/01 Solvay v Commission [2009] ECR II-4621.

competitors who are at least as efficient as the dominant undertaking. [126] There is a difference in the way Article 102 and Sherman Act Section 2 function, for the reason that the economic circumstances are very different in the two jurisdictions. In the EU, there are still countries where you will find big firms, which used to be former state monopolies. Besides, it is problematic to ascertain whether any liability for margin squeeze remains in the USA under Section 2 of the Sherman Act following the case in Linkline. [127]

Again, the "*indispensability*" criterion is element of the legal test under Article 102 TFEU when a dominant company denies an input available because to order such a company to share its input interferes with central rights such as the right to property and the right to contract along with the reasons to invest. Where these rights and incentives are not at play, for the reason that the dominant company has already given access to the input but tries to limit competition by requiring unfair terms for such access, the *indispensability* criterion is not an element of the legal test.

First of all, in *Telia Sonera* and in *Telefónica* the CJEU had already explained that the indispensability criterion is not vital for price predation cases. Besides, in *Slovak Telecom* [128] the CJEU has explained that the indispensability criterion is not required in non-price predation cases and so after *Slovak Telecom* it will be easier to prove a breach of Article 102 TFEU in cases where a dominant corporation supplies an input to its competitors but degrades such supply by any means.

To that extent, the CJEU has refined that in cases of "constructive" or "implicit" refusal to supply to a competitor of an infrastructure, facility, or service, the prerequisite of the *indispensability* of such input is not needed for an abuse of dominance in breach of Article 102 TFEU to take place. Rather, the *indispensability* of the input is demanded for the application of Article 102 TFEU only in the narrow situation of outright refusal to supply an input to a competitor.

The Court of Justice confirmed that *Slovak Telekom* had abused its dominant position in the Slovak market for broadband internet services by limiting the access of alternative operators to its local circle. In addition, i*n Slovak Telekom, the court* maintains the relevance of the essential facilities doctrine and of *Bronner* criteria explaining that they only apply to refusal to deal cases. Hence, if a dominant corporation decides to deal with rivals, it could violate Article 102 TFEU by deteriorating the terms offered to such rivals, even if the relevant input is not objectively required to compete in the downstream market. Moreover, denial to deal infringes Article 102 TFEU only if it is "*able to give rise to at least potentially anticompetitive effects, or exclusionary effects, on the markets concerned.*" [129]

---

[126] Case C-280/08 P Deutsche Telekom v Commission [2010] ECR I-955. Case T-336/07 Telefonica and Telefonica de Espana v Commission ECLI:EU:T:2012:172.

[127] Pacific Bell Telephone Co. v Linkline Communications INC., 129 S. Ct. 1109 (2009).

[128] C-165/19 P - Slovak Telekom v Commission Judgment of 25 March 2021 in Case C-165/19 P. Deutsche Telekom AG, Case C-152/19 P.

[129] C-165/19 P - Slovak Telekom v Commission Judgment of 25 March 2021(para 51).

The EU has introduced specific legislation with a view to creating a fair and transparent business environment for smaller businesses and traders on online platforms. [130]

There is no duty to aid competitors. It could be said that the regulatory framework that exists in Verizon [131] case reveals that regulation drastically reduces the possibility of major antitrust harm. Section 2 of the Sherman Act, being the symbol for free enterprise, prevents unlawful monopolization but it does not give judges "carte blanche" to uphold that a monopolist changes its manner of doing business whenever some other approach might yield greater competition. [132] In addition, Justice Antonin Scalia delivered the Court's opinion that the alleging breach of Verizon's Telecommunication Act duties to share its network with competitors did not state a claim under the Sherman Act due to the fact that the 1996 act did not modify antitrust law or add new claims and so Verizon did not violate preexisting antitrust standards.

5.9 Competition in the Digital Era

Taking into account that the digital revolution continues to transform competition among corporations, antitrust enforcement strives to remain efficient. It is worth mentioning here that the USA has long depended on a system of dual antitrust enforcement through both the Federal Trade Commission (FTC) and the Department of Justice (DOJ) which means that both have jurisdiction to enforce antitrust laws. Is there confusion due to retaining two antitrust enforcement agencies? It seems that by retaining two antitrust enforcement agencies generates contemporary confusion. [133] It has to be taken into account that certainty is central for investors, and possible and actual conflicts between DOJ and the FTC reduce certainty. To that extent, antitrust issues influencing technology are particularly complex generating concerns how best to apply antitrust law to emerging technologies and so in case the DOJ and the FTC will proceed on different theories augment uncertainty. Furthermore, the court finds that the FTC assumed that Qualcomm's conduct violated antitrust laws, despite the DOJ's approval of Qualcomm's conduct. [134] It could be said that Congress will

[130] Regulation (EU) 2019/1150 of the European Parliament and of the Council of 20 June 2019 on promoting fairness and transparency for business users of online intermediation services, OJ L 186, 11.7.2019, pp. 57–79 (known as the "Platform-to-Business-Regulation").

[131] Verizon Communications v. Law Offices of Curtis V. Trinko, LLP, 540 U.S. 398 (2004).

[132] United States v. Topco Associates, Inc., 405 U. S. 596, 610 (1972).

[133] Federal Trade Commission v. Qualcomm, Inc. 411 F. Supp. 3d 658 (N.D. Cal. 2019). John D. McKinnon & Brent Kendall, U.S. Antitrust Enforcers Signal Discord over Probes of Big Tech, Wall St. J. (Sept. 16, 2019, 10:11 PM), https://perma.cc/R8AV-2NKL

[134] FTC v. Qualcomm, Inc., 411 F. Supp. 3d 658, 683 (N.D. Cal. 2019).

improve enforcement efficiency and efficacy by harmonizing the agencies' procedures and by plainly articulating their respective responsibilities. [135]

It has to be taken into consideration that antitrust decisions, particularly in technology, directly influence geopolitical competition and international relations. To that extent, tech giants like Apple and Google might employ outsized market power and harm competition. [136]

Besides, technology enhances so quickly that seemingly entrenched monopolists are in fact easily replaced by competition which means that increased competition regulation for the technology is not effective. Moreover, network outcomes do not entail entrenchment leading to quicker destabilization of a market leader position. [137]

It is worth noting that competition law will apply to emerging technology and conventional antitrust tests will be adapted to new markets, products, and methods of competition introduced by the digital revolution and AI. On the other hand, Google, Facebook, and Amazon have monopolized markets, uncontrolled by traditional antitrust laws, regulators around the globe are thinking and not acting in order to establish fair competition. It seems that big firms technologically overtake the application of many laws due to politics and at some stage, the legal society comes out to regulate the market, while big firms have secured profits out of anticompetitive actions.

New technologies and AI research and development have moved from the public sector to the private sector and so private corporations are affected more directly by antitrust policies. Moreover, a tech startup receives funding from investors according to its acquisition prospective and so merger and acquisition policies play a noteworthy part.

While dominant platform businesses [138] have been accused of levying monopoly power, platform giants and their house brands actually keep prices low. It is characteristic that House brands tolerate customers to avoid paying high prices for the trademarks of other large firms and so forcing name brands to cut their own

[135] Joint Submission of Antitrust Economists, Legal Scholars, And Practitioners To The House Judiciary Committee on the State of Antitrust Law and Implications for Protecting Competition in Digital Markets 13 (May 15, 2020), https://perma.cc/2QN4-JJP3 (PDF).

[136] Rachel Martin, Have Tech Companies Become Too Powerful? Congress Will Investigate, Nat'l Pub. Radio (June 4, 2019, 5:00 AM), https://perma.cc/KU7Y-LA2X ("Some [members of] Congress think that [Facebook, Google, Apple, and Amazon] have gotten way too big and have way too much power to the point that they are snuffing out competition and actually harming consumers.").

[137] Catherine Tucker, Network Effects and Market Power: What Have We Learned in the Last Decade?, 32 Antitrust 72, 73 (2018).

[138] Dana Mattioli, Amazon Scooped Up Data from Its Own Sellers to Launch Competing Products, Wall St. J. (Apr. 23, 2020, 9:51 PM), https://perma.cc/B5VV-U8C6 ("Amazon.com Inc. employees have used data about independent sellers on the company's platform to develop competing products, a practice at odds with the company's stated policies."); Kim Hyun-bin, Naver Under Fire for Unfair Marketing Practices, Korea Times (May 27, 2020, 7:12 PM), https://perma.cc/M3MD-9K5Z ("Naver, the country's leading internet portal, is once again drawing negative attention for trying to sneak in advertisements to enhance benefits for its paid members, which many critics claim is an abuse of its dominant market power.").

prices. [139] It could be said that improving the effectiveness of competition rules in digital markets is a valuable objective and so competition authorities should focus their efforts on reinjecting competition in the market through the imposition of restorative remedies.

Mergers between platforms and nascent technologies generate new enquiries. First of all, mergers and acquisitions will establish the monopoly power of the platform. Besides, by averting such mergers supports nascent technologies to develop into strong competitors, differentiating the landscape and augmenting consumer choice. On the other hand, the likelihood of profitable acquisitions augments innovation by incentivizing a larger number of startups. Moreover, in order to reach a large market and grow quickly, startups characteristically demand funding from external investors which in fact the big firms are looking for advancement in their competitiveness via new technologies offered by startups. It is worth mentioning here that tech firms, such as Intel, Apple, Google, and Netflix, had their beginnings as small startups.

Undoubtedly, the acquisition of a prospective or nascent competitor can cause harm to customers and innovation, yet it can also result in an outcome revealing a great deal of consumer value. Besides, acquisitions of nascent competitors in platform industries are prone to tipping, and with tipping comes the prospective for durable market power and substantial barriers to entry which means that competition has to be implemented on this occasion. [140]

Startups are risky enterprises but the vision of acquisition drives investment and as mentioned earlier startup funding is based on the acquisition prospective of the startup and so it is likely that the startup will be purchased by a Big Tech incumbent and result in a payday for investors. Hence, antitrust regulation of mergers and acquisitions governs investment behavior that is central to the tech economy.

Large technology platform firms rely heavily on R&D and advance consumer choice which means that by prohibiting their advance via acquisitions diminishes those benefits. Furthermore, acquisitions actually tolerate businesses to offer more options in the marketplace. To that extent, Facebook offers an ad-free service in its acquired texting service WhatsApp as a result of ad revenue that Facebook receives from its other offerings which means that otherwise, consumers might not have an ad-free option.

On the other hand, it could be said that antitrust concern about monopoly has to be taken into account in order not to have anticompetitive conditions preventing any free entrance. Again, as mentioned earlier, the rapid pace of transformation in high-tech makes antitrust enforcement counterproductive due to the fact that while a business may own a monopoly in one technology, that technology may be quickly abolished.

---

[139] Herbert Hovenkamp, The Warren Campaign's Antitrust Proposals, Regul. Rev. (Mar. 25, 2019), https://perma.cc/SX4B-5PWP

[140] Megan Browdie et al., United States: Technology Mergers, Glob. Competition Rev. (Sept. 20, 2019), https://perma.cc/6ZN7-6QWJ

By the time the application of the antitrust law is determined as it touches current technologies, they may well have moved on to be different in kind. It could be said that during the interim, a high range of anticompetitive behavior allows uncertainty to reign discouraging economic investment which means that a low level of anti-competitive behavior motivates all investors to get in the race for advancement. G.I. Zekos argues that the difficulty is piercing the veil of high-tech companies in order to find out any anticompetitive agreements.

5.10 Antitrust Complexities

Antitrust policy is related to applications of market power, which is the power to profit by dropping output below the competitive level and moving up prices unreasonably above cost. Moreover, antitrust doctrine does not condemn companies merely for the reason that they are very large and so discarding imposing liability based on size since size and market power do not always go hand in hand. [141]

Section 2 of the Sherman Act expressly prohibits both monopolization and attempts. It is obvious that the presence and degree of any anticompetitive consequence vary and so anticompetitive complexities mean that the FTC must prove its case as in other rule-of-reason cases. [142] The Supreme Court [143] refused to force a per se rule of illegality for the reason that doing so would prevent a "significant amount of procompetitive conduct" and stating that per se rules of illegality "can be counterproductive. They can increase the total cost of the antitrust system by prohibiting procompetitive conduct the antitrust laws should encourage." To that extent, the Chicago School regards erroneous over-enforcement of the antitrust laws as a key threat to the economy, and the post-Chicago School considers erroneous under-enforcement as a greater threat to the economy.

Decisions that are based on an in-depth economic assessment of the investigated conduct's actual effects are highly case-specific and are consequently doubtful to result in administrative precedent and clear guidance for the wider business community. Besides, per se rules are generally applicable conduct rules that are not conditional on an analysis of consequences but ascertain legal presumptions of illegality for certain kinds of conduct that is expected to have detrimental results which means that such rules lessen the enforcement cost, diminish the length of proceedings, and so confirming clear boundaries for all undertakings that fall within their latitude.

[141] FTC v. Qualcomm Inc., 969 F.3d 974, 990 (9th Cir. 2020) (quoting United States v. Microsof Corp., 253 F.3d 34, 58 (D.C. Cir. 2001)); Viamedia, Inc. v. Comcast Corp., 951 F.3d 429, 453 (7th Cir. 2020) (same).

[142] Fed. Trade Comm'n v. Actavis, Inc., 570 U.S. 136, 159 (2013).

[143] Leegin Creative Leather Prods. v. PSKS, Inc., 551 U.S. 877, 894–95, 907 (2007).

It is worth mentioning here that Chicago School approach thinks that over-enforcement of the antitrust laws is risky since innovative behavior looks like anticompetitive behavior and erroneous condemnation of innovative behavior could damage economic growth. [144] According to Chicago, innovation can deceptively appear to be anticompetitive for the reason that innovation destroys competitors who fail to carry on. Furthermore, innovation is beneficial for consumers, delivering them better goods at lower prices which means that they should not be an object of the antitrust laws. On the other hand, the innovator who succeeds at diminishing costs, and drops prices as a result, to the advantage of consumers, looks like a predatory pricer. [145] In addition, for Chicago, the daunting thing about the apparent resemblance between innovation and anticompetitive behavior is that innovation is not just good for consumers, but is in fact the most essential driver of consumer welfare and economic growth. It is worth mentioning here that innovation is the driver of development and so an elastic implementation of antitrust law to a certain degree is a pro, but, on a higher scale of no implementation of antitrust law, the better innovation is prohibited to the detriment of society and environment. It has to be taken into account that antitrust enforcement stimulates innovation and so competitive markets generate greater motivations for innovation. Additionally, according to Chicago, letting a few bad players get away with monopolizing markets likely would instigate much less damage to consumers, for the reason that history has revealed that even the most entrenched monopoly [146] position ultimately erodes under the force of new technologies, such as AI, and shifting tastes. In other words, antitrust has to allow the market to do its work.

The Post-Chicago School has disputed that failing to convict a bad corporation takes an even greater toll on innovation, by initiating an economy of large corporations with little motivation to destabilize their market positions by innovating. There is need of comparing the resulting costs with the social benefits of antitrust enforcement. [147] Moreover, monopolies like Google and Facebook can hold back the competitive threat of new technologies by buying up nascent innovative competitors like Nest and WhatsApp which leads to excluding the incentive of these enterprises

[144] Geoffrey A. Manne & Joshua D. Wright, Innovation and the Limits of Antitrust, 6 J. Competition L. & Econ. 153, 167 (2010).

[145] Jonathan B. Baker, Exclusionary Conduct of Dominant Firms, R&D Competition, and Innovation, 48 Rev. Indus. Org. 269, 270 (2016).

[146] Frank H. Easterbrook, The Limits of Antitrust, 63 Tex. L. Rev. 1, 15 (1984). Novell, Inc. v. Microsoft Corp., 731 F.3d 1064, 1076 (10th Cir. 2013) (Gorsuch, J.) ("If the [monopolization] doctrine [of no duty to deal] fails to capture every nuance, if it must err still to some slight degree, perhaps it is better that it should err on the side of firm independence—given its demonstrated value to the competitive process and consumer welfare—than on the other side where we face the risk of inducing collusion and inviting judicial central planning.").

[147] Jonathan B. Baker & Steven C. Salop, Antitrust, Competition Policy, and Inequality, 104 Geo. L. J. Online 1, 21 (2015) ("While raising concerns about false positives, the Court has not analyzed the incidence and consequences of false positives, nor compared the resulting costs with the social benefits of antitrust enforcement or the incidence and consequences of false negatives and under-deterrence.").

to continue to innovate and so shielding their new parents from any threat to their dominance. On the other hand, the possibility of new start-ups continually to emerge and so generating new advances in technology relies on competition in the market. Besides, by mistakably condemning good corporations of course has a cost, but so long as markets stay competitive, markets will continue to create innovative companies, and not all of these innovative companies will fall to antitrust "scythe."

The Supreme Court in the Marine Bancorporation case required an extravagant evidentiary burden for a violation of § 7 of the Clayton Act based on the elimination of prospective competition. [148] According to the Court, two preconditions must exist before an actual potential competition theory "establishes a violation of § 7. Firstly, the prospective competitor could enter the market at issue absent the merger. Secondly, such entry would generate deconcentration or other noteworthy procompetitive effects". Moreover, one common fact pattern that can encompass a loss of future competition takes place when a large incumbent company purchases a highly capable business running in an adjacent space such as in the technology sector. To that extent, well-known examples involve Google's acquisition of YouTube in 2006, DoubleClick in 2007, and Facebook's acquisition of Instagram in 2012. [149]

Facebook operated in a rapidly changing competitive environment where the basic technological undergirding of the social network was advancing, embracing the growing significance of mobile technology to connect users online. On the other hand, new companies can arise on the market by utilizing the latest AI technology and overtaking any established company indicating the existence and workability of competition.

It could be said that Facebook's 60% market share certainly is enough to support a claim of an attempt to monopolize, even though neither the FTC nor the states' complaints allege attempted monopolization which means that if Facebook continues to buy additional young companies and enforce its restrictions on app developers and other parties, then there will have an impact upon competition, not mentioning that already Facebook users are subject to high switching costs for the reason that they would have to transfer their accumulated personal data. [150]

It has to be taken into account that if a market is not a natural monopoly, then the appearance of a dominant company involves exclusionary practices, and superior management. The Supreme Court [151] stated that "monopoly would be inevitably prevented if no extraneous or sovereign power imposed it and no right to make unlawful contracts having a monopolistic tendency were permitted." Thus, US antitrust law refuses to condemn a dominant company apart from proof of one or more anticompetitive practices which means that a dominant company ought to do

[148] United States v. Marine Bancorporation, Inc., 418 U.S. 602, 604 (1974).

[149] Carl Shapiro, Antitrust in a Time of Populism, 61 Int'l J. Indus. Org. 714, 740 (2018).

[150] FTC v. Facebook, Inc., 1:20-cv03590-JEB (D.D.C. Dec. 9, 2020) § 65.

[151] Standard Oil Co. v. United States221 U.S. 1, 62 (1911).

no more than charging a competitive price with the purpose of eliminating rivals or sporadically defend itself against an attack from someone else.[152]

Also, it has to be taken into consideration that the natural-monopoly question for networks is distinctive for the reason that it implicates two specific questions such as if the network is a natural monopoly and if the network is controlled by a single company. For instance, the global telephone system is a natural-monopoly network for the reason that the extent of network externalities is global and a larger network always has advantages over a smaller one. Nonetheless, the telephone system is competitively structured for the reason that it is controlled by many corporations, denoting that no single company dominates it. It is worth noting that the high degree of interoperability is an important factor cutting against natural monopolies facilitating competition inside the network. However, Section 1 of the Sherman Act outlaws only "*unreasonable* restraints."[153] Moreover, restraints are unreasonable per se for the reason that they always or almost always restrict competition and decrease output.[154] To that extent, only "horizontal" restraints being restraints imposed by agreement between competitors qualify as unreasonable per se which means that restraints that are not unreasonable per se are assessed under the "rule of reason" demanding courts to perform a fact-specific evaluation of "market power and market structure" in order to evaluate the restraint's actual outcome on competition.[155] In other words, there is a need of distinguishing between restraints with anticompetitive result that are damaging to the consumer and restraints inspiring competition that are in the consumer's best concern.[156]

It has to be taken into account that the concentration of economic power in the USA and its after-effects on competition have led to a re-examination of the place of consumer welfare as the single benchmark for evaluating competitive practices. Hence, there is a need of determining between a competition policy securing the result of competition such as allocative efficiency and a competition policy protecting the competition process for its own sake. Competition law has to achieve both elements.

[152]Union Leader Corp. v. Newspapers of New Eng., Inc., 284 F.2d 582, 587 (1st Cir. 1960) ("We do not think the fact that competition is in a natural monopoly climate can limit a defendant's right to defend itself.").

[153]*State Oil Co.* v. *Khan*, 522 U. S. 3, 10 (1997).

[154]*Business Electronics Corp.* v. *Sharp Electronics Corp.*, 485 U. S. 717, 723 (1988).

[155]*Copperweld Corp.* v. *Independence Tube Corp.*, 467 U. S. 752, 768 (1984).

[156]*Leegin Creative Leather Products, Inc.* v. *PSKS, Inc.*, 551 U. S. 877, 886 (2007).

5.11 Mergers and Competition

Clayton Act prevents mergers and acquisitions which significantly lessen competition or tend to create monopolies and so under the Clayton Act, as modernized by the HSR Act, if a deal meets certain criteria linked to transaction size, and size of the parties to the transaction, premerger notification is needed and the FTC or the Department of Justice will review the merger. [157] The current approach to antitrust review of mergers fails to avert "killer acquisitions," in which dominant companies acquire nascent competitors with the principal goal of lessening competition. [158] Facebook's acquisition of Instagram can be viewed as one example of a monopolistic practice. [159]

To that extent, killer acquisitions aim toward terminating the development of the target's innovative product to obstruct future competition which means that killer acquisitions will result in a reduction in the development of substitutes. Motta and Peitz [160] dispute that such acquisitions harm consumer welfare because of anticompetitive amalgamations of data, increased prices, and reduced opportunities for entrants. It seems that killer acquisitions assemble in certain activities like pharmaceuticals [161] and their competitive suppression consequences necessitate specific norms. [162] Lemley and McCreary [163] contemplate that adverse consequences on competition arise from venture capitalists' and startups' obsession with "exit strategy" as being purchased by a dominant competitor. Hence, the appreciation that large technology corporations acquire startups to suppress competitive threats generates changes in merger policy. By the way, Marc Ivaldi [164] et al. argue that "one could not observe a disappearance of the target's products, a weakening of competing firms, and/or a post-merger lowering or absence of entry and innovation. . .that

[157] 15 U.S.C. § 18. Premerger Notification and the Merger Review Process, Fed. Trade Comm'n, 27, https://www.ftc.gov/tipsadvice/competition-guidance/guide-antitrust-laws/mergers/premerger-notification-merger-review

[158] Colleen Cunningham et al., Killer Acquisition, 129 J. Pol. Econ. 649, 685–87 (2021).

[159] FTC Sues Facebook for Illegal Monopolization, Fed. Trade Comm'n. (Dec. 9, 2020), https://www.ftc.gov/news-events/press-releases/2020/12/ftc-sues-facebook-illegal-monopolization (asserting that Facebook's acquisition of Instagram was part of a "systematic strategy" to "eliminate threats to its monopoly").

[160] Massimo Motta & Martin Peitz, 'Big Tech Mergers' (2021) 54 Information Economics and Policy 100868.

[161] Daniel Sokol, 'Merger Law for Biotech and Killer Acquisitions' (2021) 72 Florida Law Review Forum 1.

[162] Donald Bowen III, Laurent Fresard, & Gerard Hoberg, 'Rapidly Evolving Technologies and Startup Exits' (2021) Swiss Finance Institute Research Paper No. 19–22. Colleen Cunningham, Song Ma, & Florian Ederer, 'Killer Acquisitions' (2021) 129 (3) Journal of Political Economy 649.

[163] Mark A. Lemley & Andrew McCreary, 'Exit Strategy' (2021) (101) Boston University Law Review 1.

[164] Marc Ivaldi, Nicolas Petit, and Selçukhan Ünekbaş Killer Acquisitions Evidence From EC Merger Cases In Digital Industries , at: https://ssrn.com/abstract=4407333 P1,21. Axel Gautier & Joe Lamesch, 'Mergers in the Digital Economy' (2021) 54 Information Economics and Policy 1.

current merger policy shifts in digital markets might be more based on belief, than evidence."

Are the existing legal instruments appropriate to sanction the competitively negative outcomes of vertical integration, both by way of new downstream online platform acquisitions and by way of so-called "killer" acquisitions? Article 101(1) TFEU forbids any form of coordination that deliberately substitutes practical cooperation between enterprises for the risks of competition.

It is worth noting that courts are able to afford a presumption of legality or illegality to most competitive conduct and so the structure of most transactions discloses whether it is right to apply a presumption of legality or illegality.[165] On the one hand, courts and antitrust enforcement agencies have determined that vertical mergers and joint ventures between non-competitors and vertical resale restraints imposed by suppliers on their distributors almost always have a net positive result on consumers and so courts categorize such vertical transactions at the end of the antitrust analysis as legal. On the other hand, horizontal agreements among competitors to fix prices, restrict competition, or assign territories almost always restrict competition without any offsetting efficiency advantage for consumers and so such horizontal agreements are categorized at the end of the antitrust analysis as illegal. Also, motive and intent play leading roles in anticompetitive conduct, specific competitive behavior reveals its impact and so courts should distinguish good from bad intention.[166]

On the one hand, inter-brand competition refers to the competition that exists among corporations at a given level of the value chain. On the other hand, intra-brand competition is the rivalry that exists among the distributors or retailers of a specific brand of a given product/service.

Vertical resale restraints only involve "intra-brand competition," but they do not negatively affect inter-brand competition and so their only impact on inter-brand competition is beneficial.[167] Thus, vertical resale restraints given that have the beneficial effect of encouraging dealers to provide quality-related services that make a manufacturer's products more competitive against other brands should be

[165] *Polygram Holding,* 416 F.3d at 37 ("[A]s economic learning and market experience evolve, so too will the class of restraints subject to summary adjudication.").

[166] *Poller v. CBS.*, 368 U.S. 464, 473 (1962)., *Broadcast Music, Inc. v. CBS* 441 U.S. 1, 19 (1979)., *Business Electronics Corp. v. Sharp Electronics Corp* 485 U.S. 717 (1988). Aspen Skiing Co. v. Aspen Highlands Skiing Corp., 472 U.S. 585, 610–11 (1985); McLain v. Real Estate Bd. of New Orleans, Inc., 444 U.S. 232, 243 (1980).

[167] Cont'l T.V., Inc. v. GTE Sylvania, Inc., 433 U.S. 36 (1977) (applying rule of reason rather than per se approach to Sylvania's territorial restrictions on its television dealers on grounds that restrictions only adversely affected intrabrand competition among Sylvania dealers and benefitted interbrand competition between Sylvania and other television manufacturers). Jathon Sapsford, Norihiko Shirouzu and Joseph B. White, *Toyota Maps Plan to Displace GM as Top Car Maker*, Wall St. J., Nov. 19, 2005, at A1 (describing Toyota's plans to overtake General Motors as "the world's biggest maker of cars").

legal.[168] Besides, a plaintiff can negate the presumption of legality for vertical resale restraints by demonstrating that the reason for the restraint was not to augment the supplier's effectiveness but purely to calm down dealers attempting to limit competition from their rivals.[169] Internal growth or vertical mergers by manufacturers into the resale level are treated not rigorously under the antitrust laws for the reason that the integration of productive activities is apparent and so vertical restrictions should be per se legal as long as they are beneficial to consumers.[170]

Also, vertical mergers and joint ventures are between corporations that are not real or prospective competitors raising a presumption of legality for vertical mergers and joint ventures simply by proving their existence for the reason that such transactions do not restrict any definite or impending competition between the parties. Likewise, most courts and agencies have upheld mergers and joint ventures among companies that are not real or possible competitors.[171]

It is worth noting here that joint ventures are formed to achieve precise objectives enabling their partners to compete in areas outside the narrow range of the venture and so competitors may enter into joint ventures that are limited to areas in which they are not presently competing.[172] Hereafter, if the function of the venture is to let the corporations enter new markets from which they would have been independently foreclosed, the venture will not restrict competition in any manner. For instance, joint venture among pharmaceutical companies that allow partners access to patents needed to produce a multivalent childhood vaccine that could be effective against several diseases at once, this category of joint venture promotes competition by enabling the introduction of a new competitor that otherwise might never have come

[168] Sports Center, Inc. v. Riddell, Inc., 673 F.2d 786 (5th Cir. 1982); Del Rio Distrib., Inc. v. Adolph Coors Co., 589 F.2d 176 (5th Cir. 1979); Donald B. Rice Tire Co. v. Michelin Tire Corp., 483 F. Supp. 750 (D. Md. 1980).

[169] *United States v. General Motors Corp.*, 384 U.S. 127 (1966) (applying per se rule when a group of automobile dealers induced General Motors not to sell to automobile discount houses). Nynex Corp. v. Discon, Inc., 525 U.S. 128 (1998) (declining to apply a per se analysis to a decision by a local telephone company to switch from one supplier to another); Bus. Elecs. Corp. v. Sharp Elecs. Corp., 485 U.S. 717 (1988) (refusing to apply per se rule when a single dealer induced manufacturer of electronic calculators to terminate rival dealer).

[170] Ernest Gellhorn and Teresa Tatham, *Making Sense Out of the Rule of Reason*, 35 Case W. Res. L. Rev. 155, 178 (1984); Richard A. Posner, *The Rule of Reason and the Economic Approach: Reflections on the* Sylvania *Decision*, 45 U. Chi. L. Rev. 1, 13 (1977).

[171] *United States v. FCC*, 652 F.2d 72, 96–101 (D.C. Cir. 1980) (en banc) (holding joint venture to construct a communications satellite network does not violate antitrust laws if parents were not actual or potential competitors in the relevant market). Robert Pitofsky, *A Framework for Antitrust Analysis of Joint Ventures*, 74 Geo. L.J. 1605, 1608–09 (1986) (asserting that joint ventures among non-competitors in unconcentrated markets should be legal per se).

[172] Thomas A. Piraino, Jr, *Beyond Per Se, Rule of Reason or Merger Analysis: A New Antitrust Standard for Joint Ventures,* 76 Minn. L. Rev. 1, 7 (1991) ("While mergers eliminate all competition between the parties, joint ventures, by virtue of their limited scope, leave the parties free to compete in areas not covered by the joint venture.").

into existence.[173] Besides, a joint venture designed to exclude competitors of the parties from one of the markets affected by the merger is illegal.

Vertical mergers or joint ventures should be disallowed when the transaction allows the corporations control over a supply needed for competition in one of the markets affected by the transaction and so a plaintiff should only rebut the presumption of legality for a vertical merger or joint venture by displaying that, in order to compete successfully in the market affected by the transaction, it must access the products or services of one of the parties. Consequently, the businesses in the merger or joint venture would have the authority to eliminate their rivals from the related market.[174]

It is worth noting that the US Supreme Court established strict rules against price fixing and limited the power of the government to challenge corporate mergers. [175] However, the antitrust laws accelerated the rise of monopolies and oligopolies due to the fact that states proved economically ineffective against the new, giant corporations operating in national markets and global ones.

Mergers evaluation is based on their impact on customers and the depth of market shares and market concentration is not an end in itself, but is constructive by illustrating the merger's competitive consequences. [176] Horizontal mergers in highly concentrated markets are questioned in an effort to remedy the foreseen harms of horizontal mergers in concentrated markets and so both the FTC and the DOJ often allow these consolidations to proceed on the condition that the merging parties agree to divest assets in the market in which they compete head-to-head or agree to behavioral duties and restrictions. [177]

Horizontal agreements among sellers or buyers to fix prices, restrict output, or assign territories almost always damage consumers and so courts assume the illegality of such conduct and move the burden to defendants to demonstrate that their

---

[173]United States v. FCC, 652 F.2d 72, 94 (D.C. Cir. 1980) (upholding joint venture for the production of communications satellites based on fact that, because of high start-up costs, the joint venture partners "were unlikely both to enter the field separately"). In *United States v. Penn-Olin Chemical Co.*, 389 U.S. 308 (1967) (per curiam), "the Court upheld a joint venture after the district court found that neither party was likely to have entered the relevant market in the absence of the joint venture."

[174]United States v. AT&T Corp., 59 Fed. Reg. 44,158, 44,162–63 (Aug. 26, 1994) (allowing merger between long-distance telephone company and cellular telephone company, on condition that telephone company provide cellular phones to its rivals upon equal terms); Agreement Containing Consent Order, *In re* Time Warner Inc., No. 961-0004, 1996 FTC LEXIS 389 (allowing merger between Time Warner and Turner Broadcasting, on condition that merged company give its rivals nondiscriminatory access to its cable operations).

[175]United States v. Addyston Pipe & Steel Co., 175 U.S. 211 (1899); United States v. Joint Traffic Ass'n, 171 U.S. 505 (1898); United States v. Trans-Mo. Freight Ass'n, 166 U.S. 290 (1897). United States v. E.C. Knight Co., 156 U.S. 1 (1895).

[176]U.S. Dep't of Justice & Fed. Trade Comm'n, Horizontal Merger Guidelines § 1 (2010).

[177]Pac Bell. Tel. Co. v. Linkline Commuc'ns, Inc., 555 U.S. 438, 451 (2009) ("To avoid chilling aggressive price competition, we have carefully limited the circumstances under which plaintiffs can state a Sherman Act claim by alleging that prices are too low.").

rationale in collaborating was not to control competition but to augment the effectiveness of a legitimate joint venture advantageous to consumers. Moreover, courts have applied the per se rule to horizontal cartels among sellers to fix prices, restrict output, or allocate territories and such arrangements have an apparent anticompetitive effect and lack any effective rationalization.[178] To that extent, horizontal cartels raise prices, reduce output, and limit customer's range of choices and so such direct restrictions on inter-company competition strike at the heart of the open competitive system that the antitrust laws were intended to protect.[179] Furthermore, indirect price-fixing methods, such as restrictions on output, have the same anticompetitive effect, and horizontal territorial allocations are no less destructive for the reason that horizontal territorial allocation often has a more undesirable result on competition than horizontal price fixing.[180]

Big Tech dominates the technology sector in many economies and technology corporations such as Google, Amazon, Apple, Facebook, and Microsoft get the top five spots on the NASDAQ by market capitalization. To this extent, startup companies stipulate competitive pressure since they are able to siphon off or "cream skim" customers and collect valuable data. Thus, Big Tech buys other firms in order to solidify and protect their dominance. Also, Big Tech acquisition of startup firms gains the incumbent by diminishing competitive pressure of prospective entrants on the periphery of the market or by averting future entry and expansion by such firms that could destabilize the incumbent's dominance. As long as new startups can emerge competition is still alive. Competition is a constant mobility of efforts for new development in order to achieve better earnings.

It has to be taken into consideration that the acquisition of startup firms aids the dominant firm by dropping the disciplining competitive pressure of prospective entrants on the periphery of the market or by precluding future entry and expansion by such firms undermining the incumbent's dominance. Mergers encompass economies of scale making likely the elimination of the duplicate efforts in comparable research projects. Mergers augment the suitability of inventions by dropping technological spillovers to competitors. Furthermore, an augment in market power by

---

[178] United States v. Addyston Pipe and Steel Co., 85 F. 271, 293 (6th Cir. 1898), *aff'd*, 175 U.S. 211 (1899) (refusing to consider possible justifications for horizontal price fixing); Verizon Commc'ns, Inc. v. Trinko, 540 U.S. 398, 408 (2004).

[179] Joseph F. Brodley, *The Economic Goals of Antitrust: Efficiency, Consumer Welfare, and Technological Progress,* 62 N.Y.U. L. Rev. 1020, 1023 (1987) (stating that "the economic goal of antitrust policy is to increase the material welfare of society through the instrument of interfirm rivalry"). United States v. Socony-Vacuum Oil Co., 310 U.S. 150, 221 (1940) (approving per se illegality of any conspiracy among competitors designed to raise, lower, fix, or stabilize prices on the grounds that such conspiracies directly interfere with "the free play of market forces").

[180] FTC v. Ind. Fed'n of Dentists, 476 U.S. 447, 464–66 (1986) (holding illegal a refusal by dentists to provide patients' X-rays to insurers); Nat'l Soc'y of Prof'l Eng'rs v. United States, 435 U.S. 679, 692–96 (1978) (holding illegal a ban on competitive bidding); United States v. Container Corp. of America, 393 U.S. 333, 337–38 (1969) (holding illegal the exchange of price information); Chicago Prof'l Sports Ltd. P'ship v. NBA, 754 F. Supp. 1336, 1364 (N.D. Ill. 1991) (holding illegal the reduction by a sports league of the number of games broadcast).

reason of a merger could feed back onto the innovation strategy of the merging corporations. It has to be taken into account that competition is threatened when a dominant information technology platform or other large company gains a prospective rival and then the prospective rival is anticipated to innovate were it to enter, conceivably leading the dominant incumbent to upgrade its goods or services in response, the competitive destructions from merger encompasses diminished innovation incentives, not just lessened future price competition. Facebook's example reveals how acquisitions can play a crucial role in the rise to dominance and the preservation of dominance by a Big Tech incumbent. [181]

It is worth noting that increasing concentration has augmented market power but there are problems concerning measurement, inference, and identification. [182] On the other hand, deconcentration measures and antitrust policies are inspired by a need to check concentrated private power and promote fair treatment. Any measures, actions, and provisions must stifle competition in the market in order to be anticompetitive. [183]

The laissez-faire was considered the best approach in terms of economic policy but the inter-war period was characterized by the defense of the cartel as an efficient way of organizing the economy and escaping destructive competition. It is worth mentioning here that a merger would bring noteworthy efficiency gains in businesses distinguished by high levels of fixed costs.

The EU expanded the reach of its competition laws [184] and extra-territorial jurisdiction arises when a violator makes another party change its course of conduct with a view to foreclosing competition triggering harm in the EU. European competition authorities have gradually adopted consumer welfare as the sole criterion for competition rules enforcement. Additionally, in EU competition law, the consumer welfare criterion is being contested at the very moment when it seems to be gaining ground. It is worth noting that the EU seeks to review mergers ex ante that is before they are concluded, so as to prevent creation or strengthening of dominant positions in the EU market.

As Jan Kregl [185] refers, competition law regulation is having a largely ex post character, meaning that regulatory steps are taken and restrictive measures are implemented as a reaction to the assumed anticompetitive conduct. On the other hand, the EU merger control procedure is built on the opposite principle, having an ex ante effect, and so while it is relatively feasible to undo the damage instigated by cartel agreements or by abuse of dominance, restoring the premerger market

---

[181] Chris Hughes, It's Time to Break Up Facebook, N.Y. Times (May 9, 2019), https://www.nytimes.com/2019/05/09/opinion/sunday/chris-hughes-facebook-zuckerberg.html

[182] Joshua D. Wright, Towards a Better Understanding of Concentration: Measuring Merger Policy Effectiveness, at 9, OECD Doc. DAF/COMP/WD(2018)69 (June 6, 2018) https://one.oecd.org/document/DAF/COMP/WD(2018)69/en/pdf

[183] Ohio v. Am. Express Co., 138 S. Ct. 2274 (2018).

[184] Case C-413/14 P, Intel v Commission. Case T-286/09, Intel Corp v Commission.

[185] Jan Kregl, Gun-Jumping and Eu Merger Control Selected Issues and Types of Problematic Conduct, Prague Law Working Papers Series No. 2023/II/2.

situation once the concentration has already been implemented is much more complicated which means that there is a need for ex ante controlling measures letting a prospective concentration assessment arose because the ex post regulation does not serve an effective and working competition.

It seems that the most fundamental root of European competition law lies in judging its failure to overcome the market power of large corporations. The goal of EU merger control is to prevent concentrations from causing lasting harm to competition [186] in the EU and remedies are by far the most common device by which the European Commission seeks to accomplish this and so constituting the Commission's most commonly used form of intervention. Are remedies valuable in averting price increases from mergers? Kwoka [187] argues that "many challenged mergers are subject to remedies that fail to prevent post-merger price increases." Moreover, the Commission in order to avert harm to competition is to prohibit a concentration. Apart from formal interventions, merger control also blocks harm to competition by deterring anticompetitive mergers from being planned and some mergers are discarded by the parties for the reason that competition authorities raise competition concerns. Besides, in the USA, most problematic mergers are not blocked by the courts but cleared with remedies, through "consent orders" (FTC) and "consent decrees" entered by a court at the request of the Department of Justice. Nonetheless, apart from the deterrent outcome of prohibitions, effective remedies are central in guaranteeing that merger control fulfils its undertaking of keeping markets competitive. Furthermore, the prevalence of structural remedies in EU merger control leads to the risk of forcing European actors to abandon activities or discard strategic assets in favor of competitors from outside Europe.

It is worth noting here that under the EU merger control regime, the term "gun-jumping" stands for an early implementation of a concentration in advance of its notification or before receiving an approval of the transaction which amounts to infringements of Articles 4 (1) and 7(1) of the Council Regulation No 139/2004 of 20 January 2004 (EUMR). [188]

It seems that the Commission's line to merger remedies is not essentially different from the one of the Department of Justice and the FTC due to the fact that all these authorities use remedies, not prohibitions, as the principal device to tackle anticompetitive consequences from mergers. It is worth noting that the internal competition

---

[186] Council Regulation (EC) No 139/2004 of 20 January 2004 on the control of concentrations between undertakings [2004] OJ L24/1 (EU Merger Regulation), rec 5: '[I]t should be ensured that the process of reorganisation does not result in lasting damage to competition (...)'.

[187] John Kwoka, Mergers, Merger Control and Remedies: A Retrospective Analysis of U.S. Policy (MIT Press 2015) 159 John Kwoka, 'Mergers, Merger Control, and Remedies: A Response to the FTC Critique' (2017).

[188] Power, Vincent, 2020. Gun-Jumping in European Union Merger Control: The Law and Practice. Irish Journal of European Law. 22, p. 66–82. The General Court upheld the Commission's tough decision in the Altice/PT Portugal case and confirmed the highest fine for gun-jumping offence up to date under the EU merger control regime. Altice Europe NV v Commission, Case T-425/18, ECLI:EU:T:2021:607, para. 369.

laws of the EU Member States have approved extensive objectives that go beyond the criterion of consumer welfare, which is never mentioned in Regulation 17/62 and encompasses both restrictive practices law and antitrust law. Thus, the undertaking of restoring the balance of economic power is never absent from competition law, as is the protection of the consumer and broader "non-economic" values. Moreover, competition law is settling the different objectives delegated to market competition, which are by nature conflicting. [189] The effects-based approach stipulates a case-by-case estimation of the lawfulness of market practices merely based on net effect on consumer welfare. To that extent, the 2012 Post Danmark judgment preserved the primacy of the objective of efficiency over choice, quality, or innovation considering that competition on the merits leads to the departure from the market or the marginalization of competitors that are less competent and so less attractive to consumers from the point of view of "price, choice, quality or innovation." [190] The Intel judgment handed down in September 2017 marks the Court's endorsement of the effects-based approach and the Court of Justice has been gradually moving toward an effects-based approach. [191] The EU Court of Justice and the EU Commission hold on to a plurality of objectives among which efficiency is a fundamental but not exclusive component and so on these objectives pursue the protection of free, undistorted competition on the merits.

It is worth noting that the EU scrutinized the social networking market and again found no competitive concerns. [192] The European Commission's report documents the lack of suitable measures, despite its own reliance on user numbers as a proxy for market shares. Second, the perceived ease of entry and broad consideration of prospective competitors disregard the data barrier that reinforces company dominance in online platform markets and makes it difficult for the government to isolate the impact of eliminating individual rival businesses. Besides, according to the US Horizontal Merger Guidelines, a 5% market share would demonstrate the prospective for WhatsApp to have noteworthy procompetitive effects in markets for social networking or digital advertising. In addition, the EU cites conflicting views on the distinct boundaries of social networking markets, but even if these boundaries were clear, proof of deconcentration still necessitates proper measures of market share and current participation in the market and so harm to prospective future competition was

[189] Council: Regulation No 17: First Regulation implementing Articles 85 and 86 of the Treaty, 21 February 1962. Roda, J.-C. (2018). Réflexion sur les objectifs du droit français de la concurrence, Recueil Dalloz, 1504.

[190] Judgment of the Court of Justice (Grand Chamber), 27 March 2012, Post Danmark A/S v Konkurrencerådet, C-209/10.

[191] General Court, 12 June 2014, Intel Corporation v Commission, case T-286/09. Judgment of the Court (Grand Chamber) of 6 September 2017, Intel Corp. v European Commission, case C-413/14P.

[192] Commission Decision of Mar. 10, 2014 Declaring a Concentration to be Compatible with the Common Market (Case No. COMP/M.7217—Facebook/WhatsApp) According to Council Regulation (EC) No. 139/2004, 2014 O.J. (C 7239), https://ec.europa.eu/competition/mergers/cases/decisions/m7217_20141003_20310_3962132_EN.pdf

alone inadequate to challenge the merger. The Supreme Court [193] supported that the "intense congressional concern" about increasing concentration "warrants dispensing, in certain cases, with elaborate proof of market structure, market behavior, or probable anticompetitive effects." Thus, the Philadelphia National Bank structural presumption remains intact today and so the plaintiff, typically the government, bears the initial burden in a § 7 horizontal merger case of proving that the challenged merger should be presumed to significantly harm competition which is done by displaying that the transaction will lead to undue concentration. [194] Additionally, the Supreme Court considered the application of antitrust laws to the commercial banking industry by holding the statute applicable to bank mergers and so the Court established a presumption that mergers that covered at least 30% of the relevant market were presumptively unlawful. In *United States v. Baker Hughes Inc.* [195] the court considered a § 7 challenge by saying that the later Supreme Court decisions changed § 7 jurisprudence: "Without overruling Philadelphia Bank, then, the Supreme Court has at the very least lightened the evidentiary burden on a section 7 defendant." Moreover, after the *Heinz* case, [196] the agencies are pressing courts to demand too high a level of proof as to rebuttal evidence. It seems that the full burden of demonstrating a merger will harm competition is placed on the government itself and inspired by the Chicago School supposition that most mergers are efficiency producing. [197] To that extent, the Chicago School proclaimed that only mergers to monopoly were a legitimate antitrust concern, and that mergers that do not result in monopoly are usually efficiency expanding and undertaken for that purpose which means that the Chicago School advocates discarded the structural approach to mergers by trading it with a results analysis and so enhancing the burden to merger challenges. [198]

In USA v AT&T Inc, [199] the district court denied the Government's request for an injunction under Section 7 of the Clayton Act, since the Government had not confirmed that the merger was expected to substantially lessen competition and so the merger would result in substantial benefits to customers of the merged company, explicitly, the merger would trigger AT&T to lower the price of DirecTV. The court also held that the evidence denoted that the industry had become dynamic in recent years with the appearance of distributors of only on-demand content, such as Netflix

[193] United States v. Philadelphia Nat'l Bank, 374 U.S. 321, 363 (1963).

[194] Herbert J. Hovenkamp & Carl Shapiro, Horizontal Mergers, Market Structure, and Burdens of Proof, 127 Yale L.J. 1996, 2008–14 (2018). Carl Shapiro, Protecting Competition in the American Economy: Merger Control, Tech Titans, Labor Markets, 33 J. Econ. Persps. 69, 74 (2019).

[195] 908 F.2d 981 (D.C. Cir. 1990).

[196] 246 F.3d 708, 720 (D.C. Cir. 2001).

[197] John Kwoka, The Structural Presumption and the Safe Harbor in Merger Review: False Positives or Unwarranted Concerns?, 81 Antitrust L.J. 837 (2017).

[198] Frank H. Easterbrook, The Limits of Antitrust, 63 Tex. L. Rev. 1, 3 (1984); see Robert H. Bork, The Antitrust Paradox: A Policy At War With Itself 221 (1978).

[199] United States v AT&T Inc, 310 F Supp 3d 161, 253–54 (DDC 2018), affd 916 F3d 1029 (DC Cir 2019).

and Hulu which means that the allowance of fewer players on the market upsurges competition against the Harvard School approach regarding competition.

The European Commission has approved, under the EU Merger Regulation, the acquisition of Fitbit by Google and the approval is conditional on full compliance with a commitments package offered by Google. [200] On the other hand, the European Commission's decision to fine Google for its self-preferencing maneuvers in Google Search is restricted to specific vertical shopping services. [201]

It is worth noting that the implementation of AI tools is becoming essential to support and improve antitrust agencies' capacity to detect, analyze, and remedy anticompetitive practices which means that advances in information technology and data analytics makes possible considerable improvements to real time, dynamic analyses of mergers.

It seems that the existing law of mergers is ill-equipped to tackle the tech firms' acquisition of startups as a consequence of a rule called the "potential competition" doctrine addressing the consequences of an acquisition where one firm is in the market and the other is "waiting in the wings" or on the periphery of the market.

5.12 Deficiencies of Modern Antitrust Enforcement

It has to be taken into consideration that antitrust law is advanced entirely through adjudication facilitating fact-specific analysis of liability and remedies. First of all, competitive markets are a foundation of economic liberty and so absence of competition empowers dominant corporations to exercise their market power with harmful tactics. Thus, in uncompetitive markets, corporations with market power raise prices for consumers, reduce salaries for workers, and choke off new entrants and other upstarts and so undercutting innovation and business vitality. Taking into account that antitrust law is matured entirely through adjudication means that antitrust adjudication bears shortcomings because courts analyze most forms of conduct under the "rule of reason" standard. Rohit Chopra & Lina Khan [202] argue that a rule of reason approach is nothing more than "a broad and open-ended inquiry into the overall competitive effects of particular conduct [which] asks judges to weigh the circumstances to decide whether the practice at issue violates the antitrust laws." It could be said that the FTC has to step into the competition breach by promulgating ex ante rules to enforce better the prohibition against "unfair methods

[200] Mergers: Commission Clears Acquisition of Fitbit by Google, Subject to Conditions, Eur. Comm'n (Dec. 17, 2020), https://ec.europa.eu/commission/presscorner/detail/en/ip_20_2484

[201] Margrethe Vestager, Speech at the Forum Europe Conference on the Digital Services Act, 3 July 2020, https://ec.europa.eu/commission/commissioners/2019-2024/vestager/announcements/speech-forum-europe-conference-digital-services-act_en

[202] Rohit Chopra & Lina Khan, The Case for "Unfair Methods of Competition" Rulemaking, 87 U. Chi. L. Rev. 357 (2020).

of competition" outlined in Section 5 of the Federal Trade Commission Act. [203] Also, taking into consideration that the "rule of reason" entangles a broad and open-ended inquiry into the overall competitive consequences of certain conduct demanding judges to weigh the surroundings in investigating whether the practice at issue infringes antitrust laws implicates judges in a struggle to categorize anticompetitive behavior and to apply complex economic criteria in consistent manners which is unaffordable instigating uncertainty. To that extent, judges themselves have appraised antitrust standards as being highly difficult to manage which means that if a standard is not administrable, it won't generate predictable outcomes. Thus, the absence of clear standards and rules in antitrust denotes that market players face uncertainty in not adopting legal norms into their business decisions. Likewise, uncertainty deprives market members and the public of notice concerning what the law is, undercutting due process being a central norm in legal systems.

It is worth noting that judges and juries in complex cases apply economic criteria and so making considerable mistakes inflicting serious costs. [204] Thomas A. Piraino [205] considers that the rule of reason has become unclear and so preventing antitrust practitioners from advising their customers regarding the legality of certain behavior. Due to the fact that fines issued were invalidated as "unconstitutionally vague" under the Due Process Clause, the Court declined to address the First Amendment implications of the FCC's indecency regulations. [206] It has to be taken into consideration that laws which regulate persons or entities must give fair notice of conduct that is forbidden or needed. [207] In other words, absence of fair notice causes constitutional due process matters. Thus, clarity in regulation is fundamental in protections stipulated by the *Due Process Clause of the Fifth Amendment* and a regulation is vague when it is unclear as to what fact must be proved. According to Marshall Steinbaum & Maurice E. Stucke, [208] evidence points to less competition, higher markups, bigger concentration, and increasing wealth and income inequality which means that the existing state of competition law advances the interests of MNEs. On the

[203] 15 U.S.C. § 45 ("Unfair methods of competition in or affecting commerce, and unfair or deceptive acts or practices in or affecting commerce, are hereby declared unlawful.").

[204] Leegin Creative Leather Products, Inc v PSKS, Inc, 551 US 877, 917 (2007) (Breyer dissenting) FTC v Actavis, 570 US 136, 173 (2013) (Roberts dissenting) ("[T]he majority declares that such questions should henceforth be scrutinized by antitrust law's unruly rule of reason. Good luck to the district courts that must, when faced with a patent settlement, weigh the 'likely anticompetitive effects, redeeming virtues, market power, and potentially offsetting legal considerations present in the circumstances.'").

[205] Thomas A. Piraino Jr, A New Approach to the Antitrust Analysis of Mergers, 83 BU L Rev 785, 807 (2003).

[206] FCC v Fox Television Stations, Inc, 567 US 239, 253 (2012) FCC v. Pacifica, 438 U.S. 726 (1978) Case 3:17-cv-01930-B Document 110 Filed 12/31/19 OFAC's enforcement action against Exxon Corporation.

[207] Universal Health Servs., Inc. v. United States, 579 U.S. 176, 136 S. Ct. 1989, 2001, 195 L. Ed. 2d 348 (2016) ("Escobar") Safeco Ins. Co. of Am. v. Burr, 551 U.S. 47 (2007).

[208] Marshall Steinbaum & Maurice E. Stucke, The Effective Competition Standard: A New Standard for Antitrust, 2019 The University of Chicago Law Review 86:595.

other hand, antitrust laws are intended to handle concentrated economic power which is the essence of antitrust from tackling a variety of goals to focusing merely on the concept of consumer welfare. Moreover, the legal meaning of the antitrust laws involving exclusively harm to consumers and their welfare, as assessed almost exclusively by price and quantity outcomes in output markets, destroys the rationale of competition.

The rule of reason necessitates a case-by-case adjudication [209] and so courts verify the existence of harm. Courts have elevated the burden of proof on the government and other antitrust plaintiffs to such an extent that the Sherman and Clayton Antitrust Acts have become unenforceable for many anticompetitive practices, other than cartels.

5.13 AI and Market Self-Correcting

It is worth noting that antitrust has been vital for structuring the economy now and in the past, either in favor of concentrating economic power or against it. Additionally, strong antitrust enforcement is central to preserving a competitive market structure. The Chicago School thought that markets are self-correcting and that free entry is a "natural" condition that erodes incumbent market power and so there was no necessity for robust antitrust enforcement to generate or uphold the settings required to make competition effective. In other words, contemporary antitrust consensus stems from the belief that market forces could naturally correct the occasional occurrences of market power and could do to this point better and quicker than government intervention.

On the one hand, which is the need for the occurrence of antitrust given that the market naturally hinders the emergence of any market power. On the other hand, antitrust plays a decisive role in stimulating open and competitive markets. Hence, antitrust policy is a required device to restore the market power problem, but in practice has been ascertained not sufficient due to political matters and in fact the overruling of politics above antitrust law.

Will AAI technology eliminate any thought of competition in AAI market by imposing a single objective advancement of automated fulfilment of society by plenty of available electronic sources for the AAI humanoid robots requiring merely plenty of e-energy to function? Will scarcity of e-energy generate problems in AAI market requiring competition rules as well? The current AI market controlled by humans requires the application of competition rules and policies to function properly.

Competition policy advances an economy by stimulating important values, including autonomy and overall well-being via valuing buyer power. It has to be

---

[209] Cal. Dental Ass'n v. FTC, 526 U.S. 756, 779 (1999) Orson, Inc. v. Miramax Film Corp., 79 F.3d 1358, 1367 (3d Cir. 1996).

taken into account that antitrust was never about stimulating either allocative efficiency or consumer welfare. To that extent, antitrust planned to deconcentrate private power by protecting the competitive procedure. Likewise, the objective of promoting an effective competitive procedure generates some setbacks such as outlining an effective competitive process. AI might bring forward a standard effective competitive process via a certain AI algorithm applying to all cases of competition law and anticompetitive behavior. The mathematical transformation of law into AI algorithms will necessitate standardization and not vague interpretations. Thus, without standardization antitrust becomes a reiteration since the objective of competition law is upholding competition by baring anticompetitive behavior and not merely discussing anticompetitive behavior.

Antitrust laws are considered vital attributing right for the personal commercial freedom of people and so [210] minimizing competition at the retail level is a horizontal restraint encompassing a per se violation of § 1 of the Sherman Act.

It is worth noting that if anticompetitive conduct is wrongly permitted to live on, the result will be the sort of monopoly pricing that invites entry and may thereby self-correct. Also, monopolistic behavior may not always be removed by the market in an apt way, mainly where powerful network upshots are present. Thus, AI technology human control will not self-correct competition since powerful private network upshots will be present continuously.

5.14 Predatory Pricing

Taking into consideration the principle of Sherman Act, Section 2 assertion is that a corporation is not competing on the merits and so pursuing conduct is not permissible such as pricing intended to hamper or suppress legitimate competition. Thus, monopolists do not attempt to suppress competition on the merits and so Sherman violations arise from the view that "[a] business rival has priced its products in an unfair manner with an object to eliminate or retard competition and thereby gain and exercise control over prices in the relevant market." [211] The US Supreme Court upheld a finding of harm to competition when Continental Baking entered a market and underpriced Utah Pie, a smaller but locally dominant rival. [212] Thus, when a company uses unreasonably exclusionary conduct driving its rivals from the market or somehow raises their costs in order to make them fewer challenging competitors, its market power grows. On the other hand, the US Supreme Court considers that the simple possession of monopoly power, and the concurrent charging of monopoly

[210] United States v Topco Associates, Inc, 405 US 596, 610 (1972).

[211] Brooke Group Ltd. v. Brown & Williamson Tobacco Corp., 509 U.S. 209, 222 (1993).

[212] Utah Pie Co. v. Cont'l Baking Co., 386 U.S. 685, 687–89 (1967).

prices, is not illegal [213] which means that solely possessing monopoly power and charging monopoly prices does not violate § 2 of the Sherman Act. [214]

The absence of competition stems from systemic failures in the market and so corporations' triumph by brute force, using questionable methods to prevent the formation of any competition and so antitrust law was invented to address situations like these. Moreover, antitrust laws seek to discipline anticompetitive behavior resulting in higher prices and reduced output. [215] Also, corporations take advantage of their market power and so distort competition and trigger long-term consumer harm.

Predatory pricing transpires when a company charges less for its product or service than it costs to produce. Below-cost pricing [216] is performed by corporations with monopoly power in order to drive rival competitors, principally more efficient competitors, from the market and so once the company eliminates its rivals, it raises prices and takes up again receiving monopoly profits. It could be said that the rationale of predatory pricing is to exclude competition so a corporation afterward recoup its short-term losses by charging supra-competitive prices. [217] Hence, predatory pricing harms consumers by restraining competition, increasing prices over the long term, reducing choices between providers, and dropping enticements to innovate and advance efficiency.

It is worth noting that predatory pricing claims necessitate a probability analysis since the plaintiff must prove that when the defendant was charging a price below cost, it possessed a likelihood of later recouping that investment in below-cost pricing by charging a monopoly price. Moreover, predatory pricing is one form of anticompetitive conduct offering the basis for either a monopolization or attempted monopolization claim, nonetheless, the latter is more common. [218] Courts generate

---

[213] Verizon Commc'ns Inc. v. Law Offices of Curtis V. Trinko, LLP, 540 U.S. 398, 407 (2004).

[214] Pac. Bell Tel. Co. v. Linkline Commc'ns, Inc., 555 U.S. 438, 447–48 (2009).

[215] Jonathan B. Baker, The Case for Antitrust Enforcement, 17 J. Econ. Persp., Autumn 2003, at 27, 27 (describing the "central role" of antitrust as "protecting consumers against anticompetitive conduct that raises prices, reduces output, and hinders innovation and economic growth").

[216] Thomas F. Cotter, Note, Cargill, Inc v. Monfort of Colorado, Inc.: The Supreme Court Restricts Private Antitrust Challenges to Horizontal Mergers, 1987 Wis. L. Rev. 503, 522 (1987) ("To engage successfully in . . . predatory activity, however, a firm must possess . . . 'market power,' which is to say that the firm enjoys some degree of control over the price that prevails on the market . . . .").

[217] Frank X. Schoen, Note, Exclusionary Conduct After Trinko, 80 N.Y.U. L. Rev. 1625, 1628 (2005) (describing the harm to consumers from a failure to address predatory pricing).

[218] Transamerica Comput. Co. v. IBM Corp., 698 F.2d 1377, 1384 (9th Cir. 1983) ("Predatory pricing occurs when a company that controls a substantial market share lowers its prices to drive out competition so that it can charge monopoly prices, and reap monopoly profits, at a later time."). Christopher R. Leslie, Predatory Pricing and Recoupment, 113 Colum. L. Rev. 1695, 1746–51 (2013) (explaining the difference between a dangerous probability of monopolization and a dangerous probability of recoupment).

the risk of "hindsight" bias [219] through antitrust opinions because judges evaluating predatory pricing claims should "explore not only whether recoupment was possible but also whether it in fact occurred." Taking into account that Section 2 of the Sherman Act denounces both actual monopolization and attempted monopolization, [220] actual monopolization is illegal when a corporation uses anticompetitive conduct to gain or maintain a monopoly. [221] It is characteristic that the Supreme Court designed a three-element test for attempted monopolization [222]: "(1) ... the defendant has engaged in predatory or anticompetitive conduct with (2) a specific intent to monopolize and (3) a dangerous probability of achieving monopoly power." Hence, there is a need to prove that plaintiffs have suffered antitrust injury triggered by the defendant's illegal anticompetitive conduct.

In Brooke [223] case, the Supreme Court set a high threshold for predatory pricing claims and concluded that a predatory pricing claim under Section 2 of the Sherman Act necessitates: " (1) the plaintiff establishes the alleged predator priced below its costs; and (2) the alleged predator had the prospect of recouping losses sustained during the predation period" and so the Brooke Group standard has proven difficult to satisfy. [224] It has to be examined whether the alleged predator engaged in anticompetitive conduct, for the reason that there are "circumstances in which a price cut will make consumers worse off, not better off." [225] Moreover, an "objective

[219] Beck v. Ohio, 379 U.S. 89, 96 (1964) Andrew E. Taslitz, Foreword: The Death of Probable Cause, 73 L. & Contemp. Probs. i, viii (2010) ("[W]arrants require judges to gauge probable cause before knowing what, if anything, will be found. Warrants thus avoid the problem of 'hindsight bias.' ").

[220] SmileCare Dental Grp. v. Delta Dental Plan of Cal., Inc., 88 F.3d 780, 783 (9th Cir. 1996) (including "causal antitrust injury" as an element of attempted monopolization). Savory Pie Guy, LLC v. Comtec Indus., Ltd., No. 14 CV 7527 (VB), 2016 WL 7471340, at *11 (S.D.N.Y. Dec. 28, 2016) (finding no dangerous probability of monopolization and granting summary judgment to Defendant-in part because Plaintiff remained in business after Defendant's allegedly anticompetitive conduct took place).

[221] United States v. Grinnell Corp., 384 U.S. 563, 570–71 (1966) (reciting the legal definition of the offense of monopoly under the Sherman Act).

[222] In Spectrum Sports, Inc. v. McQuillan,67 506 U.S. 447, 456 (1993).

[223] Brooke Group Ltd. v. Brown & Williamson Tobacco Corp., 509 U.S. 209, 222– 24 (1993). Cargill, Inc. v. Monfort of Colo., Inc., 479 U.S. 104, 121 (1986) ("While firms may engage in the practice [of predatory pricing] only infrequently, there is ample evidence suggesting that the practice does occur.").

[224] Aaron S. Edlin, Stopping Above-Cost Predatory Pricing, 111 Yale L. J. 941, 941 (2002) ("Since 1993, when the Supreme Court decided Brooke Group Ltd. v. Brown & Williamson Tobacco Corp., no predatory pricing plaintiff has prevailed in a final determination in the federal courts.").

[225] Barry Wright Corp. v. ITT Grinnell Corp., 724 F.2d 227, 230 (1st Cir. 1983).

standard" is advanced under which "non-objective evidence will not transform above-cost pricing into illegal predatory conduct." [226]

It is characteristic that under the existing consumer welfare standard, [227] monopolies have little to fear because courts have limited their prospective liability for their anticompetitive actions and so cases regarding predatory pricing have all disappeared which means that monopolies have no duty to deal. It is argued that without a dangerous probability of recoupment, competition remains unharmed even if individual competitors suffer based on the rationale that antitrust laws were passed for the protection of competition, not competitors. [228] On the other hand, in AKZO [229] case decided that it is illegal if a dominant company prices below average variable cost to exclude a competitor and so if the dominant company prices between total cost and average variable cost, then this could be abusive with evidence of anticompetitive intent.

Is antitrust's sole end consumer welfare, a view known as the "consumer welfare standard [230]"? Congress passed antitrust laws to stimulate a host of political and economic ends by encompassing the interests of workers, producers, entrepreneurs, and citizens. Likewise, the consumer welfare standard does not identify "welfare" and disregards adverse consequences on workers, suppliers, quality, and innovation. Also, consumer welfare doctrine is not endorsed in competition throughout the supply chain, in the labor market, and in the economy as a whole.

5.15 Antitrust in the AAI Era

As discussed earlier, industries are gradually ascertaining and utilizing AI in developing or delivering goods and services. AI is infiltrating virtually all business areas and accomplishing several functions. [231]

[226] AMR Corp., 140 F. Supp. 2d at 1195 ("The rationale for cost-based analysis rests in the limited ability of courts to accurately separate real-world predation from vigorous but lawful competition, and the inherent threat to competition that a failure to make such a recognition creates.").

[227] Fred S. McChesney, Talking 'Bout My Antitrust Generation: Competition for and in the Field of Competition Law, 52 Emory L.J. 1401, 1407 (2003) ("[T]he debate over whether antitrust is to pursue economic or social goals is finished: economics has won.").

[228] United States v AMR Corp, 335 F3d 1109, 1121 (10th Cir 2003).

[229] AKZO Chemie BV v Commission of the European Communities, ECR I-3359, 3454–56 (EU Just 1991).

[230] Reiter v. Sonotone Corp., 442 U.S. 330, 343 (1979).

[231] AlphaGo, Deepmind, https://bit.ly/3gq26Wx ("AlphaGo is the first computer program to defeat a professional human Go player, the first to defeat a Go world champion, and is arguably the strongest Go player in history.").

Competition law has seen questionably the protection of trademarks as directly opposed to the objectives of competition law. [232] Even though competition law is stimulating the freedom of competition in the market and, with some exceptions in particular markets, deregulation, the purpose of intellectual property law is to protect the IP right holders and limit competition against them whenever they fulfill particular criteria. [233]

Today, economists use both direct and indirect methodologies for evaluating power in digital markets but conventional market definition and market share measurements are unreliable in cases concerning digital platforms due to the fact that the procedure is driven mainly by data, case-specific facts, and expert economic testimony. [234]

Has the basis of antitrust been altered due to the transformation of the market or competition has to be applied in a different way for e-markets? The role of antitrust has to be the same regardless of the type of market but expressed by the updated measures in order to emphasize the role of competition in commercial life. It has to be taken into account that direct measurement of power in antitrust litigation is technical and somewhat novel and the Supreme Court has supported more direct measures in some cases concerning horizontal restraints. Besides, the Supreme Court in Amex [235] held that a relevant market must be defined in a vertical restraints case even where the plaintiffs had presented direct proof of market power.

Also, it has to be taken into consideration that AI is having a large influence on the economy by expanding productivity and economic growth and so lowering the cost of doing business which means that AI modifies the economy and techniques of conducting business where it is applied by, enhancing human aptitudes in commercial applications, and shifting competition and entry barriers for startups. Furthermore, AAI technology will alter competition due to the autonomous reaction of AAI systems based on big data and overcoming any human intervention and so generating an objective competition that has to be defined in abstract terms understandable by AAI entities and implemented objectively in AAI society.

The digitalized legal ecosystem's technological substructures certify prompt facilitation of access to justice. Moreover, the legal ecosystem encompasses an all-inclusive body of interconnected systems certifying the appropriate running of revitalizing administration of justice. The intervention of AAI is adding a more significant technology-driven responsibility in the legal system due to the fact that technology is turning the status quo on its head, from AAI robot lawyers to AAI

---

[232] Ioannis Kokkoris, Can Competition Considerations Trump Trademarks Rights?, 20 Chi.-Kent J. Intell. Prop. 91 (2021). https://scholarship.kentlaw.iit.edu/ckjip/vol20/iss1/8

[233] Ioannis Lianos, Competition Law and Intellectual Property Rights: Is the Property Rights' Approach Right?, in Cambridge Yearbook of European Legal Studies 153 (2006).

[234] Chris Pike, Rethinking Antitrust Tools for Multi-Sided Platforms: 2018, OECD (Apr. 6, 2018), http://www.oecd.org/daf/competition/Rethinking-antitrust-tools -for-multi-sided-platforms-2018.pdf

[235] Ohio v. Am. Express Co., 138 S. Ct. 2274, 2286 (2018). FTC v. Actavis, Inc., 570 U.S. 136, 157 (2013); FTC v. Ind. Fed'n of Dentists, 476 U.S. 447, 460–61 (1986).

robot judges to automated intelligent system analysis. Contemporary AI technology still delivers technological inability to match human-level reasoning for specific categories of legal tasks and so the AAI has to solve all present inabilities owing to advanced capabilities and capacities of AAI humanoid robots comprising the forthcoming AAI society. Also, the incorporation of AI instruments stands the test of objectivity in making certain excellent protection of the rights of the parties.

It has to be taken into consideration that granting legal personhood is vital followed by imposing liabilities in the legal sense of the actions of AAI robots. Also, the present AI-backed system controlled by humans is transforming how the justice delivery system will work in the near future. AI-driven robotic innovations have the prospective to behave like watch guards and robot eyewitnesses generating concerns about data collection undertaken by the robots and the ways and measures to regulate the same to evade any data leakages.

AI competition law is forthcoming by utilizing the development of AI law in tandem with AI enforcement via robo-justice. Administrators must also have relevant and up-to-date data available to support thorough algorithmic analysis. [236] AAI technology utilized by AAI humanoid robots brings another dimension to competition law and enforcement leaving the level of AI tool used by humans. Michael David Coutts [237] specifies that "the speed of technological development can be rapid, and competition authorities may suddenly find themselves in a world where algorithmic coordination is a known risk but without the tools or expertise to combat it." Hence, there is a need for AAI technology to detect any anticompetitive process via AI systems because humans will not be able to detect biased pricing algorithms causing harm to the competition process.

Robo-justice will eliminate all divisions of law and enforcement by having the central AAI robo-judge to send directly the case to various AAI divisions and the AAI humanoid robo-judges will examine the received cases by having even AAI court day with AAI humanoid applicants and AAI lawyers taking part in the process in order to solve the case and so the decision will be handed electronically with electronic enforcement on the spot. [238]

In the first place, the whole process of transforming the law into AAI law will be made by human programmers and be handed over to AI machines from where the AAI humanoid robots made by humans will move forward the whole process. On the other hand, the emergence of AAI humanoid robots without any humans involvement will mean the implant of another type of creation by creators from another dimension.

---

[236] Ai Deng, An Antitrust Lawyer's Guide to Machine Learning, 32 Antitrust 82, 82 (2017) ("The antitrust community is largely playing catch-up on technical aspects of AI and ML.").

[237] Michael David Coutts, Mergers, Acquisitions And Merger Control In An Algorithmic Pricing World, Journal of Competition Law & Economics, 2023, 19, 1–59 https://doi.org/10.1093/joclec/nhac008 P56.

[238] See for a detailed analysis G Zekos, Advanced Artificial Intelligence and Robo-Justice, 2022, www.springer.com

5.16 Defining Competitive Process

Digitalization has accelerated a modification in market dynamics, elevating the emergence of key platforms, networks and so the growth and evolution of the digital economy lifting competition enforcement challenges. Hence, competition enforcers must confront the intricacy of running their assessments in a digital environment and so generating uncertainty as to the character of competitive pressures and the aptitude of markets to self-correct. To that extent, new market actualities cause uncertainties as to the use of competition law, its effectiveness, and its objectives. On the other hand, the functioning of companies in an electronic environment via electronic means and AI technologies does not mean that companies will not compete for a market and clients denoting that competition will take place among companies merely with electronic means instead of the conventional ones. Thus, competition law is required along with the emergence of new tools for enforcement but the role of competition concerning the defense of fair competition and equality in the market are principles applied in any environment.

The exclusive orientation of antitrust on economics focusing exclusively on consumer welfare has produced excessive concentration as it takes place with platform companies [239] as well. It seems that platforms have produced loss of privacy, corporate censorship, foreign influence, and uneven wealth distribution. It is obvious that there is no need to penalize monopolies that are a consequence of a superior product, business management which means that it is legitimate for per se/ex ante rules allowing the generation of monopolies via advanced management and entrepreneurship.

It has to be taken into account that the Commission has distinguished that market shares offer a "useful first indication" of the existence of market power and in AKZO, [240] the Court of Justice substantiated the earlier position in Hoffmann-La Roche [241] that "very large shares are in themselves and save in exceptional circumstances, evidence of the existence of a dominant position" and clarified that "that is the situation where there is a market share of 50%." Moreover, the Commission and the EU Courts took additional features into consideration to substantiate the existence of a dominant position [242] by mentioning that high market shares are not inevitably indicative of market power. [243]

[239] https://www.axios.com/2018/09/12/ftc-hearings-competition-tech-industry-innovation Philip Verveer, Platform Accountability and Contemporary Competition Law, 2018, The Shorenstein Center on Media, Politics and Public Policy https://shorensteincenter.org/

[240] Case 62/86 AKZO v. Commission, ECLI:EU:C:1991:286.

[241] Case 85/76 Hoffmann-La Roche v. Commission, ECLI:EU:C:1979:36.

[242] Case T-30/89 Hilti v. Commission, ECLI:EU:T:1991:70, Case T321/05 AstraZeneca v. Commission, ECLI:EU:T:2010:266, Case T-228/97 Irish Sugar v. Commission, ECLI:EU:T:1999:246.

[243] Case T-79/12 Cisco Systems and Messagenet v. Commission, ECLI:EU:T:2013:635.

It is worth noting that even the aims that competition law should chase have been extensively disputed and firstly the concepts of efficiency and of consumer welfare have no universal meaning, secondly the political and societal setting within which the competition rules are applied diverges from place to place and from time to time. Thus, divergence concerning the role of competition law in the market and in society has occurred and in Post Danmark [244] I the Court of Justice explained that Article 102 TFEU is concerned only with the exclusion of rivals that are as efficient as the dominant company and that "not every exclusionary effect is necessarily detrimental to competition."

It seems that even AI technology being an instrument in the hands of humans has not advanced competition due an objective applicability which means that AI has to get autonomous and independent applicability in order to achieve objectivity in fulfilling its purposes. G. I. Zekos considers that objectivity encompasses objective value judgments based on data accepted as conclusive by the whole society and concerning the perception of a particular matter. Max Weber [245] held that the social sciences can achieve some degree of objectivity which means that the data utilized in order to have an outcome does not represent the whole society and so utilizing AI will be able to calculate all the possibly available data in order to achieve nearly the absolute objectivity according to humans' understanding. AAI humanoid objectivity might have a different context of understanding in an AAI society which will be achieved/formulated via the collected data by their latest AAI technology. According to Bessa Whitmore [246] "Objectivity refers to the idea that knowledge in the sciences and social sciences can be produced without bias—devoid of a researcher's values, assumptions, and influence." Moreover, objectivity is seen as faithfulness to facts made available to us by science. [247]

[244] Case C-209/10 Post Danmark (Post Danmark I), ECLI:EU:C:2012:172.

[245] Weber, Max, 1949, The Methodology of the Social Sciences, Edward A. Shils and Henry A. Finch (trans/eds), New York, NY: Free Press. Reiss, J. and Sprenger, J. (2020, Winter Edition). Scientific objectivity. In E.N. Zalta (Ed.) The Stanford Encyclopedia of Philosophy. https://plato.stanford.edu/archives/win2020/entries/scientific-objectivity/ Hoyningen-Huene, P. Objectivity, value-free science, and inductive risk. Euro Jnl Phil Sci 13, 14 (2023). https://doi.org/10.1007/s13194-023-00518-9

[246] https://ecampusontario.pressbooks.pub/showingtheory/chapter/objectivity/ Levitt, H. M., Surace, F. I., Wu, M. B., Chapin, B., Hargrove, J. G., Herbitter, C., Lu, E. C., Maroney, M. R., & Hochman, A. L. (2022). The meaning of scientific objectivity and subjectivity: From the perspective of methodologists. Psychological Methods, 27(4), 589–605. https://doi.org/10.1037/met0000363

[247] Philippe Stamenkovic, Facts and objectivity in science, Interdisciplinary Science Reviews 23 Dec 2022 https://www.tandfonline.com/doi/full/10.1080/03080188.2022.2150807 Inkeri Koskinen Defending a Risk Account of Scientific Objectivity, The British Journal for the Philosophy of Science Volume 71, Number 4 https://www.journals.uchicago.edu/doi/full/10.1093/bjps/axy053

It is worth noting that, in the USA, the HJC Report [248] concluded that the four "Big Tech" firms had gained and solidified dominant positions through anticompetitive conduct. The Congressional Research Service report [249] specified that "The antitrust laws aim to protect economic competition by prohibiting unreasonable restraints of trade, exclusionary conduct by dominant firms, and mergers and acquisitions that may "substantially" lessen competition or "tend to create a monopoly."" It is argued that "Bigness" was no longer automatically a curse, but often the product of superior efficiency. [250] Moreover, the Court came to adopt the economic efficiency/consumer welfare model as the exclusive or near-exclusive goal of antitrust law [251] and so declaring that "Congress designed the Sherman Act as a 'consumer welfare prescription. [252]'" Posner argued [253] that "the proper purpose of the antitrust laws is to promote competition, as that term is understood in economics." Of course, since trade encompasses economics, competition law embraces economic measures but competition law imposes the legal rules regulating the operation of the market and by determining the economic factors taken into account for the determination of procompetitive and anticompetitive actions. In other words, the rules of justice regulate the operation of the market by specifying the economic factors that are taken into account for the determination of anticompetitive process.

It is argued that antitrust law is not up to the task of dealing with dominance issues today, especially those implicating the largest digital platforms. [254] It has to be taken into account that in digital markets entry barriers emerge from network consequences and noteworthy switching costs which add to anticompetitive environment. [255]

[248] Investigation Of Competition In Digital Markets, Majority Staff Report And Recommendations, Subcomm. On Antitrust, Commercial and Admin. L. of the H. Comm. on the Judiciary 12–17 (2020).

[249] Congressional Research Service, Antitrust Reform and Big Tech Firms March 22, 2023 https://crsreports.congress.gov R46875 p2.

[250] Robert H. Bork, The Antitrust Paradox: A Policy At War With Itself xxx (1978).

[251] Crane, Chicago, Post-Chicago, and Neo-Chicago, 76 U. Chi. L. Rev. 1911 (2009).

[252] Reiter v. Sonotone Corp., 442 U.S. 330, 343 (1979). Brooke Group Ltd. v. Brown & Williamson Tobacco Corp., 509 U.S. 209, 225 (1993) ("It is axiomatic that the antitrust laws were passed for 'the protection of competition, not competitors.'") (citing Brown Shoe Co. v. United States, 370 U.S. 294, 320 (1962)).

[253] Richard A. Posner, Antitrust Law: An Economic Perspective ix (1976).

[254] FTC v. Shire ViroPharma, Inc., 917 F.3d 147, 149 (3d Cir. 2019) (alleging that the branded drug manufacturer was delaying generic competition by constantly making objectively baseless filings to the Food & Drug Administration); and FTC v. Qualcomm Inc., No. 17-CV-00220- LHK, 2019 WL 2206013, at *1 (N.D. Cal. May 21, 2019) (charging Qualcomm with refusing to license its standard-essential patents to rival chipmakers in order to protect its monopoly over processors used in cell phones).

[255] FTC v. Facebook, Inc., 581 F. Supp. 3d 34, 51 (D.D.C. 2022). FTC v. Facebook, Inc., No. 1:20-cv-03590 (D.D.C. Mar. 10, 2021).

How will we distinguish exclusionary conduct from legitimate competition on the merits? It is characteristic that Section 2 makes it unlawful to "monopolize" commerce by firstly the possession of monopoly power; and secondly "the willful acquisition or maintenance of that power as distinguished from growth or development as a consequence of a superior product, business acumen, or historical accident" [256] referred to as "exclusionary" or "anticompetitive" conduct which is differentiated from growth or development as a result of a superior product and business management. In case the incentive for a monopolist's refusal to deal is a wish to drive its competitor out of business affirms Section 2 liability. [257] Like tying, exclusive-dealing arrangements are vertical restraints that can be challenged under both Section 1 and Section 2 of the Sherman Act judging the extent of foreclosure, the duration of the restrictions, and any business justifications for the restrictions. [258]

It is distinctive that Devlin [259] says that the protection of consumers cannot be the rationale of antitrust law for the reason that consumer interests validate almost any government intervention in a market. It is argued that maximizing competition is self-destructive because companies cannot recover their fixed cost investments in R&D and so not improving their productivity which means that it should not be the sole rationale of antitrust law. On the other hand, the road toward maximizing competition is passing through the investment plans and management of all of the companies functioning in the same competitive environment where per se/ ex ante rules define the allowed conducts and actions equally to all competitors.

It is argued that Brandeis was determined to shrink concentrated financial and federal power, which he regarded as a danger to liberty and democracy. [260] It has to be taken into account that economic power has been utilized as a means of further exploitation of the globe against the interests of the people and more on furthering the wealth of an elite driving the world in the wrong direction instead of using all resources logically. Concentration to a certain degree of achieving economies of scale is fine but furthering the concentration to an uncontrolled degree is against any improvement for the good of the society and merely there is a holding to the dominance of the conglomerate. Moreover, it has to be taken into consideration that a robustly mercantile society grounded on powerful financial and economic institutions has failed to act properly in achieving innovation for the good of the society under all well-known political schemes and ideologies and so the digression of the globe has initiated due to the endless demands of the mercantile society for an illogical utilization of resources on earth and even moving toward a substitution of

[256] United States v. Grinnell Corp., 384 U.S. 563, 570–71 (1966).

[257] Aspen Skiing Co. v. Aspen Highlands Skiing Corp., 472 U.S. 585, 608–11 (1985). Viamedia Inc. v. Comcast Corp., 951 F.3d 429, 462 (7th Cir. 2020) (concluding that profit sacrifice is relevant but not always dispositive for refusal-to-deal liability).

[258] United States v. Dentsply Int'l, Inc., 399 F.3d 181, 197 (3d Cir. 2005) Barry Wright Corp. v. ITT Grinnell Corp., 724 F.2d 227, 236 (1st Cir. 1983).

[259] Alan J. Devlin, Reforming Antitrust 265 (2021). at 254–68 (contending that the consumer-welfare standard is descriptively inaccurate in several respects).

[260] Jeffrey Rosen, Louis D. Brandeis: American Prophet 1 , Yale Univ. Press 2016.

humans by AAI humanoids based on the expectation to use them as their slaves in accomplishing the accumulation of more material goods instead of attaining their spiritual elevation.

Courts utilize a case-by-case approach to assess claims of anticompetitive behavior rather than per se/ ex ante rules needing only interpretation and so antitrust investigations and litigation are time consuming, expensive, and very often contradictory judgments. [261] Due to the fact that it is difficult to predict whether specific conduct violates the law, antitrust enforcement is emasculated by permitting large corporations and digital platforms to profit from anticompetitive conduct. On the other hand, per se/ ex ante rules, interpreted determinedly by courts, generate an environment of competition for digital companies since technology can be controlled via technology and so the dominant position is changing according to the competencies of the newest technology. Werden [262] argues that the rule of reason indirectly examines the competitive process which is protected via the protection of consumers.

It is specified that the monopolization offense entails monopoly power plus a conduct element which denotes the existence of monopoly power and not development as a consequence of, but every monopolization defendant argues that its conduct accelerates "superior" operation. Daniel Francis [263] argues that "while the Sherman Act has prohibited monopolization (and attempts and conspiracies to monopolize) for more than 130 years, the core idea of "monopolization" remains maddeningly elusive." It has to be taken into account that the current monopolization doctrine in the USA involves proof of a corporation's monopoly power in a relevant market, and its use of improper ("exclusionary") conduct to produce, protect, or augment its monopoly and so the conduct has to incorporate an "anticompetitive effect." [264]

It is obvious that the enforcement of competition law will allow any prospective competitor to be able to invest on innovation and so forcing all other companies on the field to invest on innovation as well. To that extent, Jonathan B. Baker [265] argues

---

[261] William P. Rogerson & Howard Shelanski, Antitrust Enforcement, Regulation, and Digital Platforms, 168 U. Pa. L. Rev. 1911, 1917–18 (2020). Rohit Chopra & Lina M. Khan, The Case for "Unfair Methods of Competition" Rulemaking, 87 U. Chi. L. Rev. 357, 360–62 (2020).

[262] Gregory J. Werden, Antitrust's Rule of Reason: Only Competition Matters, 79 Antitrust L.J. 713, 713, 743 (2014) (arguing that "the rule of reason focuses solely on how a challenged restraint affects the competitive process," and that antitrust protects consumer welfare by protecting the "competitive process").

[263] Daniel Francis, Making Sense of Monopolization, 2022 Antitrust Law Journal Vol. 84/779. p 784.

[264] United States v. Grinnell Corp., 384 U.S. 563, 570–71 (1966) ; United States v. Microsoft Corp., 253 F.3d 34, 58 (D.C. Cir. 2001) ("A firm violates § 2 only when it acquires or maintains, or attempts to acquire or maintain, a monopoly by engaging in exclusionary conduct 'as distinguished from growth or development as a consequence of a superior product, business acumen, or historic accident.'"

[265] Jonathan B. Baker, Exclusionary Conduct of Dominant Firms, R&D Competition, and Innovation, Rev Ind Organ (2016) 48:269–287 p285.

that "a competition policy intervention that prevents dominant firms from excluding innovation rivals by raising their R&D costs will necessarily increase rival investment, and will increase dominant firm investment if and only if the dominant firm regards rival investment as a strategic complement."

The digital revolution has brought forward protests that Big Tech companies gained monopolization not via a superior product and good management but merely prohibiting the entrance of other competitors. problem and should do something about it. [266] Taking into account that Big Tech companies face "fierce" competition from one another and from new rivals, tech platforms maintain their dominant positions by their roles as gatekeepers for key digital ecosystems, as mobile operating systems, app stores, online marketplaces, and social networks [267] and so they are controlling access to these ecosystems and setting the rules within them which it encompasses anticompetitive process. In other words, antitrust adjudication is slow to effectively police markets portrayed by these winner-take-all dynamics and so remedies for anticompetitive conduct may be unable to restore meaningful competition on time. [268]

Can competition in the digital economy be addressed by existing conventional competition law? It could be said that competition law can effectively apply to digital markets and to harmful anticompetitive behaviors in the digital economy. New initiatives concerning competition have as their common objective to tackle growing fears over the progressively entrenched economic power that a handful of powerful digital platforms have accumulated over the last decade. [269]

It could be argued that focusing only on consumer welfare has led to sloppy competition enforcement, which has produced rising economic concentration, growing wealth inequality, and a political system seized by corporate interests. [270] Besides, the role of competition law is to allow free competition for all possible competitors to antagonize for a market share based on better goods via management utilization and not employing anticompetitive measures. It is worth noting that the consumer welfare standard is described in broad terms so it can be applied flexibly which means that it cannot be enforced in a consistent way in digital economy cases.

Does the market power mean anticompetitive effects? Market power has anticompetitive effects as long as excludes competition which means no free entrance

---

[266] Peter J. Hasson, The Manipulators: Facebook, Google, Twitter, and Big Tech's War on Conservatives (2020)

[267] How Tech's Defiance of Economic Gravity Came to an Abrupt End, The Economist (Dec. 24, 2022), https://www.economist.com/business/2022/12/24/how-techs-defiance-of-economic-gravity-came-to-an-abrupt-end

[268] Marco Cappai & Giuseppe Colangelo, Taming Digital Gatekeepers: The More Regulatory Approach to Antitrust Law, Stanford-Vienna TTLF Working Paper 9 (Stanford-Vienna TTLF, Working Paper No. 55, 2020).

[269] Elias Deutscher Reshaping Digital Competition: The New Platform Regulations and the Future of Modern Antitrust, The Antitrust Bulletin 2022, Vol. 67(2) 302–340.

[270] Sandeep Vaheesan, The Profound Nonsense of the Consumer Welfare Standard, 64 Antitrust Bull. 479 (2019).

into the market for every prospective competitor. It is characteristic that if a conduct in question is not anticompetitive under § 1, there is no need to separately examine the conduct under § 2 and so it is required restrictions to be anticompetitive along with a company's conduct to be anticompetitive. [271]

It is characteristic that platforms add value by suggesting suitable offers of sellers to buyers, enabling offer discovery and in so doing dropping search costs which means that these suggestions intensely affect competition and give platform providers noteworthy power. Does unfair competition through recommendations take place on platforms? Digital platforms influence the competition between players on their platforms mainly by how they advocate offers, what information they reveal, and how they charge platform players. [272] Moreover, unfair competition takes place if platforms use suggestions to steer competition toward individual sellers. Also, platform providers recommend firstly their own offers more blatantly than comparable third-party offers. Besides, Lukas Jürgensmeier and Bernd Skiera [273] observe "almost no evidence of unfair competition through organic search engine visibility on the Amazon Marketplace, we cannot conclude that competition through recommendations is fair on the entire platform. Amazon has several other opportunities to recommend offers unfairly, which are harder to evaluate as an outside researcher—one example being that Amazon could solely recommend their own products through other recommendations beyond the search engine." Thus, it seems that platforms utilize tactics not so observable in order to favor its own commerciality against a fair competition approach.

It has to be taken into account that dominant corporations are not entirely unconstrained to run, but economic power and the legitimate exercise thereof is an integral part of market functioning which means that all companies have to follow per se/ ex ante rules defining the "competitive process" in order to have a competitive market free from unfair competition and so courts have merely to interpret the per se/ex ante rules generating a precedent causing a legal certainty on the market and contributing to competition on merits. It could be said that there is no need to sell legal "complexity" via case-to-case interpretation and so not having a certain precedent permitting anticompetitive actions to pass undetected but, on the other hand, "simplicity" via a formalistic way of interpreting per se/ ex ante rules generates a precedent well known in the market and so producing certainty and fair competition. It has to be taken into account that in general European competition law, fairness has been interpreted as a reference to broad assurances of equal economic chances and equal procedural treatment. [274] Moreover, it has to be taken into

[271] Epic Games, Inc. V. Apple, Inc., No. 21-16506 (9th Cir. 2023) https://law.justia.com/cases/federal/appellate-courts/ca9/21-16506/21-16506-2023-04-24.html

[272] Cicilline, David N. (2021), "American Innovation and Choice Online Act," H.R.3816, 117th Congress, https://www.congress.gov/117/bills/hr3816/BILLS117hr3

[273] Lukas Jürgensmeier and Bernd Skiera, Measuring Fair Competition on Digital Platforms, at: https://ssrn.com/abstract=4393726 p33.

[274] A Pera, 'Fairness, Competition on the Merits and Article 102' (2022) European Competition Journal 229.

consideration that the DMA [275] addresses the valid issues regarding competition law by introducing a list of obligations for gatekeepers. It is worth noting that platform regulations encompass a broad set of ex ante rules and obligations and these rules are self-executing which means that they are invented in a manner that diminishes the demand for any further specification to a minimum. Hence, the ex ante rules are directly applicable and binding on the designated platforms incorporating a preventative approach in so far as they prohibit designated platforms from participating in certain forms of conduct by proscribing them ex ante. It could be said that an ex ante approach to building competition in digital markets is vital.

Data [276] represents a core economic asset with the prospective to generate noteworthy competitive advantage for corporations. To that extent, Roberto Augusto Castellanos Pfeiffer [277] argues that "that it is important to harmonies the enforcement of competition, consumer and data protection polices in order to choose the proper way to protect the users of dominant platforms, maximizing the benefits of the data-driven economy."

It has to be taken into account that EU competition law has been held to protect the structure of the market and, in so doing, competition as such along with promoting European market integration. Moreover, European jurisprudence has underlined the objective of maintaining an effective competitive structure. [278] Also, in T-Mobile, the Court of Justice explained that European competition law "is designed to protect not only the immediate interests of individual competitors or consumers but also to protect the structure of the market and thus competition as such." [279] Likewise, in GlaxoSmithKline, [280] the Court of Justice regarded that Article 101 TFEU "aims to protect not only the interests of competitors or of consumers, but also the structure of the market and, in so doing, competition as such." It could be said that the protection of an "effective competition structure" defines the objective of competition law rather than that indicated by the consumer welfare that results from an effective competition structure and so the competitive process as such defines the condemnation of conducts that harm undistorted

---

[275] Regulation (EU) 2022/1925 of the European Parliament and of the Council of 14 September 2022 on contestable and fair markets in the digital sector and amending Directives (EU) 2019/1937 and (EU) 2020/1828 (Digital Markets Act). https://eurlex.europa.eu/eli/reg/2022/1925

[276] D. Daniel Sokol and Roisin E. Comerford, "Antitrust and regulating big data", George Mason Law Review 23, no. 5 (2016): 1129–1162.

[277] Roberto Augusto Castellanos Pfeiffer, Digital Economy, Big Data and Competition Law, Market and Competition Law Review / volume iii / no. 1 / April 2019 p54.

[278] Case 6-72 Europemballage Corporation and Continental Can Company Inc. v Commission [1973] ECR-215, Case C-95/04 British Airways Plc v Commission Court of Justice, [2007] ECR I-2331, Case T-340/03 France Telecom SA v Commission [2007] ECR II-107, Joined Cases C-468 to 478/06 Sot. Lélos kai Sia and Others [2008] ECR I7139 Case C-280/08 P Deutsche Telekom v Commission [2010] ECR I-9555.

[279] C-8/08 - T-Mobile Netherlands and Others ECLI:EU:C:2009:343 , para 38 https://curia.europa.eu/juris/liste.jsf?language=en&num=C-8/08

[280] C-501/06 P - GlaxoSmithKline Services and Others v Commission and Others ECLI:EU:C:2009:610 https://curia.europa.eu/juris/liste.jsf?num=C-501/06&language=en

competition. [281] In the context of Article 102 TFEU, the protection of the effective competition structure has resulted in the imposition of a special responsibility on dominant companies not to distort competition in the market. [282] Hence, competition law enforcement guarantees that markets run appropriately and so consumers benefit from the efficiency and productivity stemming from effective competition between undertakings which means that competition law is promoting competition in a free-market system leading to efficiency maximization and competition on the merits. Article 101(3) TFEU explicitly denotes "fair share" as part of the individual exemption mechanism available to otherwise anticompetitive agreements. To that extent, it could be said that in both the USA and EU the rationale of keeping a competition structure is the basis of competition law because via a certain competition structure equality of players in the market is achieved which in the end leads to satisfying the needs of consumers in the best way.

Competition law must encompass a predictable and reliable normative prescription for the objective of prohibiting any anticompetitive process. Hence, judges interpret competition law in a way of apprehending the meaning of law in the light of its purpose which is to establish a competitive process enabling the openness of the market to all prospective competitors. [283] Antitrust enforcement is grounded on economically oriented rules applied by technocratic administrative agencies. [284] Moreover, EU competition law encompasses a set of rules and its enforcement seeks at improving market performance via total or consumer welfare maximization. [285] Also, EU competition law is grounded on certain values and its application takes part without reference to any non-legal normative facts.

Competition law is not part of economics which means that consumer welfare cannot be "the one and only disciplined and objective framework for courts and enforcers to assess a challenged conduct's likelihood to harm competition" and so fully relying on economic technocracy. On the other hand, competition law has to balance multiple non-economic factors as well. EU competition law integrates principles restricting any anticompetitive commercial practice affecting competition and harming sustainability concerning the market which is inductively affecting consumers on the market as well. Due to neutrality of law, EU competition law would adapt to changing intellectual and factual circumstances such as new technologies and AI.

Does EU competition law encompass many values and objectives or different values denote the safeguarding of competition in the market? As mentioned earlier,

[281] Case C-202/07 P France Télécom v Commission [2009] ECR I2369.

[282] Case C-322/81 Nederlandsche Banden-Industrie Michelin NV v Commission [1983] ECR 3461.

[283] C N Kakouris, 'Use of the Comparative Method by the Court of Justice of the European Community' (1994) 6 Pace International Law Review 273.

[284] Adi Ayal, Fairness in Antitrust , Hart Publishing, 2014. Richard Posner, Antitrust Law, University of Chicago Press, 2001.

[285] Daniel Crane, 'The Tempting of Antitrust: Robert Bork and the Goals of Antitrust' (2014) 79(3) Antitrust Law Journal 835. J Yan and S Sacher, 'Some Reactions to "Reactionary Antitrust"' (2020) Concurrences Competition Law Review 20.

on the one hand, Gerber [286] argues that competition law's aim is to remove distortions of competition, Schweitzer [287] upholds that competition law protects the competitive process, Kaman [288] argues that rationale of EU competition law increases efficiency, Nazzini [289] says that the goal of Competition law is to maximize total social welfare via productivity growth, Townley and Odudu support the view that the proper objective of EU competition law is consumer welfare, [290] Lianos [291] argues that EU competition law follows a plurality of values, Monti [292] says that competition law endorses unconnected objectives such as efficiency, consumer welfare, economic freedom, market integration, and rivalry, and Ezrachi [293] contends that the goals of EU competition law embrace consumer well-being, effective competition structures, efficiency and innovation, fairness, economic freedom, plurality, democracy, and market integration, but then again, on the other hand, all views grounded on various factors are converging on the openness of the market equally to any prospective competitor promoting fair competition on the economy. Thus, competition law has to put forward the legal principles in prohibiting any actions leading to affecting the openness of the market for any prospective competitor which means that any act prohibiting the entrance of any prospective competitor is encompassed in the anticompetitive process and so it is unlawful.

It could be said that the Commission has casted EU competition law as a consumer welfare prescription and so the Commission designates more value to welfare [294] and to the protection of competitors and commercial freedom but less value to efficiency. On the other hand, the openness of the market which is warranted by competition law is the basis and framework for achieving efficiency because efficiency is not ordered but it is gained in an open market via effective management. Moreover, the ECJ stated that the objective of competition law is "to protect not only the interests of competitors or of consumers, but also the structure of the market and,

---

[286] D J Gerber, Law and Competition in Twentieth-Century Europe: Protecting Prometheus, Oxford University Press, 2010.

[287] H Schweitzer, 'The History, Interpretation and Underlying Principles of Section 2 Sherman Act and Article 82 EC' in C-D Ehlermann and M Marquis (eds), European Competition Law Annual 2007: A Reformed Approach to Article 82 EC (Hart Publishing, 2008).

[288] P Akman, 'Searching for the Long-Lost Soul of Article 82 EC' (2009) 29 Oxford Journal of Legal Studies 267

[289] R Nazzini, The Foundations of European Union Competition Law: The Objective and Principles of Article 102 , Oxford University Press, 2011.

[290] C Townley, Article 81 EC and Public Policy (Hart Publishing, 2009), pp 13–43. O Odudu, 'The Wider Concerns of Competition Law' (2010) 30(3) Oxford Journal of Legal Studies 559

[291] I Lianos, 'Polycentric Competition Law' (2018) 71(1) Current Legal Problems 169.

[292] G Monti, EC Competition Law , Cambridge University Press, 2007.

[293] A Ezrachi, EU Competition Law Goals and the Digital Economy (Oxford Legal Studies, 2018), Research Paper 17.

[294] K Stylianou and M Iacovides, 'The Goals of EU Competition Law—A Comprehensive Empirical Investigation', https://ssrn.com/abstract=3735795 A Witt, 'Technocrats, Populists, Hipsters, and Romantics—Who Else Is Lurking in the Corners of the Bar?' (2019) Antitrust Chronicles 4.

in so doing, competition as such" [295] which means that an open market allows fair competition benefiting all actors in the markets which are both competitors and consumers. Thus, competition law forward an effective process of competition which is achieved by having various results caused by different factors and inputs. Finally, the role of law is to put forward cannons allowing the effective functioning of society in its various spheres such as its economy which means that competition law has to regulate the effective running of competition of the economy for the benefit of both producers and consumers. Therefore, it could be argued that any philosophizing/ theorizing about the role of law on competition with the purpose of merely philosophizing is not enhancing the contribution of competition law in a changing economic and social environment caused by new technologies and AI altering the whole life and activities of humans, since, in practice, there is a need for neutral ex ante rules prohibiting any anticompetitive process which means letting courts to generate a precedent and so bringing legal certainty on the market.

It is argued that competition encompasses the protection of the competitive process without illustrating the context of it and so an "effective competition" standard will allow the safeguarding of competitive market structures that protect individuals, purchasers, consumers, and producers based on equal opportunity basis which means upholding opportunities for competitors, advancing individual autonomy and well-being and so diffusing private power as the principal objective of antitrust laws. First of all, any obstacle to the entrance of a conventional or digital market is prohibited and corporations implying any such measure contact an anticompetitive process by disallowing the entrance of any prospective competitor in the particular market. In particular, the anticompetitive process encompasses the following: (1) Any vertical agreement covering over 50% of the particular market is ex ante and prima facie anticompetitive except if there is an open access prospective to the market for any possible competitor. (2) The existence of a monopoly does not mean anticompetitive environment as long as monopolization is based on investment, innovation, and good management provided that that the entrance into the market is totally open. The need for capital, the quality of production, and the hard antagonism in order to survive in the market does not indicate anticompetitive environment. (3) Any action putting obstacles to the free entrance of competitors in a market denotes anticompetitiveness. (4) The holding of a market share above 50% indicates the existence of prima facie anticompetitive environment, but if, at the same time, there is free entry into the market implies the absence of anticompetitive environment. (5) It has to be taken into account that data processing results in entry barriers when new entrants are unable either to collect data or to buy the same kind of data which means that data collection should not generate entrance problems in a digital market in order not to have an anticompetitive setting. The occasion of corporations having the capacity to collect and process data more effectively than

[295] GlaxoSmithKline v Commission and Commission v GlaxoSmithKline, C-501/06 P, C-513/06 P, C-515/06 P, C-519/06 P, ECLI:EU:C:2009:610. GlaxoSmithKline v Commission, T-168/01, ECLI:EU:T:2006:265.

their competitors being as one of their competitive differentials does not generate an anticompetitive setting regardless that these corporations quickly gain a dominant position. The utilization of data to advance the performance of corporations, to differentiate themselves from competition, and to develop new products and services obtained by a competitive process denotes competition on merits, regardless of producing economic power.

References

1. Crane, D. A. (2009). Chicago, post-Chicago, and neo-Chicago. *University of Chicago Law Review, 76*, 1911, 1919.
2. Autor, D., Dorn, D., Katz, L. F., Patterson, C., & Van Reenen, J. (2020). The fall of the labor share and the rise of superstar firms. *Quarterly Journal of Economics, 135*, 645, 648–645, 649.
3. Deutscher, E. (2022). Reshaping digital competition: The new platform regulations and the future of modern antitrust. *The Antitrust Bulletin, 67*(2), 302–340.
4. Grullon, G., Larkin, Y., & Michaely, R. (2019). Are US industries becoming more concentrated? *Review of Finance, 23*, 697, 700.
5. Hovenkamp, H. (2021). The looming crisis in antitrust economics. *Boston University Law Review, 101*, 489.
6. Hovenkamp, H. (2021). Antitrust and platform monopoly. *Yale Law Journal, 130*, 1952–1956.
7. Hovenkamp, H. J., & Morton, F. S. (2020). Framing the Chicago School of Antitrust Analysis. *University of Pennsylvania Law Review, 168*, 1843.
8. Lemley, M. A., & McCreary, A. (2021). Exit strategy. *Boston University Law Review, 101*, 1.
9. Marty, F., & Warin, T. (2020). *Innovation in digital ecosystems: Challenges and questions for competition policy*. Cahier Scientifique du CIRAN.
10. Karanicolas, M. (2021). Too long; Didn't read: Finding meaning in platforms' terms of service agreements. *University of Toledo Law Review, 52*.
11. Carstensen, P. C. (2020). The incoherent justification for naked restraints of competition: What the dental self-regulation cases tell us about the cavities in antitrust law. *Loyola University Chicago Law Journal, 51*, 680.
12. Akman, P. (2022). A web of paradoxes: Empirical evidence on online platform users and implications for competition and regulation in digital markets. *Virginia Law and Business Review, 16*, 217.
13. Chopra, R., & Khan, L. (2020). The case for "unfair methods of competition" rulemaking. *University of Chicago Law Review, 87*, 357.

Chapter 6
USA Versus EU Competition

6.1 Introduction

Antitrust laws in the USA, and competition rules in the EU, are set out in statutes of general applicability, written in broad, almost constitutional form. US antitrust is economically founded, evolutionary, and limited to a set of achievable social welfare purposes. It has to be taken into account that transparency of antitrust law's central function should lead to transparency in performing it.

The US and the EU antitrust agencies have concluded several bilateral cooperation agreements with their foreign counterparts enabling greater diffusion of basic economic theories triggering antitrust enforcement in the USA and the EU. The OECD and the International Competition Network have offered central settings for voluntary cooperation and diffusion of best practices, involving economic analysis of antitrust law. Nonetheless, these networks have not fully adopted the Chicago School's approach to antitrust law by endorsing a more expansive notion of antitrust enforcement while stressing the benefits of economic principles as a basis of antitrust policy.

6.2 Chicago Versus Harvard

The "Chicago School of Antitrust Analysis" utilized rigorous microeconometric analysis to transform antitrust enforcers' focus from economic power to economic incentives such as market power, entry, and efficiency.[1] Thus, the Chicago School's

[1] Herbert J. Hovenkamp & Fiona Scott Morton, Framing the Chicago School of Antitrust Analysis, 168 U. PA. L. REV. 1843 (2020).Andrew I. Gavil, William E. Kovacic, and Jonathan B. Baker, Antitrust Law in Perspective: Cases, Concepts, and Problems in Competition Policy 66–67 (West 2d ed 2008).

© The Author(s), under exclusive license to Springer Nature Switzerland AG 2023
G. I. Zekos, *Artificial Intelligence and Competition*, Contributions to Economics,
https://doi.org/10.1007/978-3-031-48083-6_6

ideas are comprehended as a commitment to a certain method of antitrust enforcement rather than an agreement on specific policy outcomes. In addition, the Chicago School supported to focus on the incentives of economic agents and not on the structure of the market to ascertain the competitive effects of mergers and corporation conduct altering the Harvard School approach which was concerned with market concentration. Therefore, the Chicago School advanced a less antitrust intervention grounded on a belief that markets would largely self-correct while governmental intervention could entrench monopolies. Hence, according to the Chicago School,[2] the key aim of antitrust was the promotion of consumer welfare and total welfare[3] and so considering that vertical mergers are generally efficient and rarely lead to foreclosure concerns. Equally, conglomerate mergers were seen as typically efficient, demanding little antitrust intervention.

It is worth noting that the Chicago School formed law of vertical restraints renounced an older precedent that had rejected coordination comparatively on the basis that it concerned a "kind of feudal dominion" that should not survive beyond company boundaries. The Supreme Court in Simpson[4] specified that vertically imposed price fixing by an oil company on gas station resellers is illegal and in State Oil[5] decided that maximum price restraints by powerful corporations upon small resellers are legal. To that extent, precedents are rationalized on the basis of economic arguments that vertical restraints generate efficiencies that eventually redound to the benefit of consumers, paralleling the economic reasons that were employed to validate corporate mergers allowing powerful corporations to dominate markets.[6]

While the USA has promoted the "development of sound antitrust laws" abroad, the EU system has had a more direct impact on states implementing competition policies for the first time.[7] It is worth noting that antitrust enforcement gradually

[2]Mel Marquis, Idea Merchants and Paradigm Peddlers in Global Antitrust, 28 Pac McGeorge Global Bus & Dev L J 155, 203 (2015) "the Chicago model has in general been studied more for its pitfalls than for its accuracy and appropriateness."

[3]Robert H. Bork, The Antitrust Paradox: A Policy at War with Itself 133 (Basic Books 1978) ("[T]he only legitimate goal of antitrust is the maximization of consumer welfare.").

[4]Simpson v. Union Oil Co. of California, 377 U.S. 13 (1964).

[5]State Oil Co. v. Khan, 522 U.S. 3 (1997).

[6]United States v. Richfield Oil Corp., 99 F. Supp. 280 (S.D.Cal. 1951)(holding vertical restrictions on gas station operators by oil company impermissible, reasoning that gas station operators were tenants, not employees, and thus principles of subordination in hierarchical vertical coordination were inappropriate outside the basically feudal subordination inherent in the employment relationship).

[7]Anu Bradford, et al., The Global Dominance of European Competition Law over American Antitrust Law, 16 J Empirical Legal Stud 731, 739–40, 745 (2019) (examining 126 countries' first competition law adopted and finding that more countries have implemented laws similar to the EU than to the US). William E. Kovacic, The United States and Its Future Influence on Global Competition Policy, 22 Geo Mason L Rev 1157, 1157 (2015) Dina I. Waked, Adoption of Antitrust Laws in Developing Countries: Reasons and Challenges, 12 J L Econ & Pol 193, 202 (2016) ("EC competition law is the dominant model of competition law in the world").

began to rely on economic experts and econometrics that are now all but mandatory in antitrust litigation. US antitrust enforcement changed considerably, echoing many of the teachings of the Chicago School.

It is worth mentioning here that courts, particularly those adhering to the then-Chicago and Harvard School economic theories, imposed their economic ideologies into the law and the Supreme Court began quoting them. It is expressed by the court the view that "federal courts are not economists, and we should avoid an unnecessary 'ramble through the wilds of economic theory.'"[8] There is a need to apply legal principles which will incorporate an economic substance but not entire economic theories to be taken as legal principles. To that extent, Maurice E. Stucke and Ariel Ezrachi[9] argue that "Economics, of course, can inform antitrust law and serve to ensure its measured application. But it should not be used to displace the law. An economics-based rule of reason, as it is implemented by the courts, offers little certainty once theory and modeling are stretched and manipulated to suit one's agenda."

6.3 EU Versus USA

It seems that EU and US antitrust policies differ in a number of vital matters. First of all, the structure of and approach to antitrust law in the EU assigns the Commission much greater discretion to deviate from established economic principles and procedural best practices in its antitrust enforcement and decision-making. Thus, antitrust enforcement at the EU level is driven almost entirely by the European Commission and unreviewed and unchecked by EU courts which means that EU antitrust is distinctly less economically founded, and unavoidably more politicized, than in the USA.

In actual fact, Article 102 TFEU more closely aligns with the original, pre-Chicago School understanding of Section 2 of the Sherman Act due to the fact that Article 102 TFEU rests on a perception of special responsibility for competition as a function of market power. Also, the EU statute goes beyond forwarding further monopolization and directly limits monopoly rent extraction. To that extent, a dominant firm has "a special responsibility not to allow its conduct to impair genuine undistorted competition" and so it is notable, as it compels a positive duty upon the dominant company to uphold competition, instead of a purely negative prohibition

[8] Host Int'l, Inc. v. MarketPlace, PHL, LLC, 32 F.4th 242, 253 (3d Cir. 2022).

[9] Maurice E. Stucke & Ariel Ezrachi, Innovation Misunderstood, https://ssrn.com/abstract=4547201 p 13. Ariel Ezrachi and Maurice E. Stucke, The Darker Sides of Digital Platform Innovation, Network Law Rev., Aug. 11, 2022.

of anticompetitive conduct.[10] Finally, Article 102 TFEU directly restricts the extraction of monopoly rents.

While the US centers on protecting the process of competition for the economic welfare of consumers, the EU upholds its competition laws to affect a wider range of political/economic/social objectives. Undeniably, the Commission has specified that European competition law chases multiple purposes. Concerning competition itself, the EU tracks objectives that are far more ambiguous than those chased under US antitrust law. While it is comparatively uncontroversial that antitrust law in the USA presently pursues a single goal, such as the maximization of consumer welfare, the issue is less settled in the EU. Moreover, the European Union has been reluctant to commit to a well-defined competition objective for its antitrust law.

Additionally, the US and European antitrust regimes diverge considerably with regard to the objectives they engage in, and the extent to which these are, or are not, based on mainstream economics. Although the USA is guided by the consumer welfare standard, the objectives of European competition enforcers are both diverse and often unchained from economic thinking. Furthermore, the EU courts have eventually exposed EU competition law to augmented politicization.

In many matters, EU merger law is fairly similar to US merger law, being guided by something resembling a consumer welfare model.[11] The Commission is compelled to set out clearly and concisely the decisive facts and legal and economic considerations, and the pleas in law and evidence having decisive value in the context of a merger decision.[12] The General Court of the European Union annulled the European Commission's 2016 decision to block the proposed merger between Hutchison 3G UK with its brand "Three" and Telefónica UK with its brand "O2" by clarifying the legal test for non-coordinated effects in oligopoly cases. The Court noted that the new merger regulation has to achieve an extension of the scope of the review, but also to preserve and strengthen the concept of a dominant position and to increase legal certainty. The new regulation should permit the Commission to catch mergers in oligopolistic markets that, without generating or strengthening an individual or collective dominant position, have led to a condition where firms could establish the parameters of competition by becoming a price maker rather than remaining a price taker post-merger. The Court decides that while the revised regulation now permits the Commission to catch cases without finding dominance,

[10]Case C-552/03, Unilever Bestfoods v. Comm'n, 2006 E.C.R. I-9091 §22. See Case C52/09, Konkurrensverket v. TeliaSonera Sverige AB, 2011 E.C.R. I-527 §§2, 3, 8, 24; Case C-202/07, Fr. Télécom SA v Comm'n, 2009 E.C.R. I-2369 §105.

[11]CK Telecoms ruling offers a fitting example. See Case T-399/16 CK Telecoms UK Investments Ltd v European Commission https://curia.europa.eu/juris/liste.jsf?num=T-399/16 Judgment of the General Court (First Chamber, Extended Composition) 28 May 2020 ECLI:EU:T:2020:217 Annuls Commission Decision C(2016) 2796 final of 11 May 2016 declaring incompatible with the internal market the concentration resulting from the acquisition of Telefónica Europe Plc by Hutchison 3G UK Investments Ltd.

[12]Bertelsmann and Sony Corporation of America v Impala, C-413/06 P, EU:C:2008:392, paragraph 169. Evropaïki Dynamiki v EMSA, C-252/10 P.

the circumstance that a merger takes place in a tight oligopoly situation is not enough for a prohibition decision which means that the test for non-coordinated consequences in oligopolistic markets unavoidably necessitates the elimination of vital competitive constraints that the merging parties had exerted upon each other. Hence, the reduction of competitive pressure on the market was not enough to demonstrate a prohibition of a merger which means that such an interpretation would lead to the Commission being able to outlaw any merger in an oligopoly at its own discretion. The Court sets the standard for the Commission to establish with a "strong probability" the existence of noteworthy impediment following the concentration.

The Commission found that the merger would have a negative effect on prices and the quality of services for consumers. According to the Commission's horizontal merger guidelines, a merger generates negative competitive outcomes if it excludes an "important competitive force." Again, some companies have more of an impact on the competitive process than their market shares and so a merger encompassing such a company alters the competitive dynamics in a noteworthy anticompetitive manner, predominantly when the market is already concentrated. In addition, the Commission has relied on this concept to rationalize competitive concerns in oligopoly situations. Nonetheless, according to the Court the general approach pursued by the Commission regarding the concept of the important competitive force was inaccurate and pointing out that the Commission confined itself to finding that the undertaking in question had attributed to competition on the market and so de facto giving power to the Commission to disallow any horizontal merger in an oligopolistic market infringing the principle of legal certainty. To that extent, the perception of an important competitive force must be interpreted in such a manner that the removal of such a firm from the market eliminates an imperative competitive constraint and so fulfilling the significant impediment to the effective competition test. Thus, in order to qualify as an important competitive force, the firm in question needs to stand out from its competitors in terms of influence on competition.

The Commission's horizontal guidelines clarify that products may be differentiated within a relevant market such that some products are closer substitutes than others and so rivalry between the parties has been an imperative source of competition on the market being a key factor in the analysis of the competitive effects of a merger. Furthermore, analogous to the "important competitive force" concept, "closeness of competition" is an argument that the Commission employs to raise competition points in oligopoly markets. The Court sets out that the horizontal merger guidelines must be read in light of recital 25 of the merger control regulation, which demands the removal of key competitive constraints the merging parties had exerted upon each other. While in oligopolistic markets everyone is close to some degree, closeness is relevant if it causes a competitive constraint and so the parties must be "particularly close" competitors. The Court found that the Commission had failed to provide evidence that the merging parties met this requirement by disputing whether the products on the mobile telephone market are sufficiently differentiated to generate relevant effects through "closeness of competition." If firms on the market are somehow "close" is not enough since any four-to-three mergers could be outlawed.

The Commission further supported its decision with a quantitative economic analysis reminding that "the transaction is likely to generate an incentive for the merged entity to significantly increase prices." The Commission had applied a GUPPI (Gross Upward Pricing Pressure Index) analysis assessing the upward pricing pressure following a merger based on diversion ratios and margins of the parties, taking into account (unlike the basic UPP-test) the likely reactions of competitors. The Court specified that the analysis applied by the Commission was sophisticated and generally a suitable tool for the analysis but it identified that the Commission did not consider the quantitative analysis as decisive evidence not illustrating that a quantified price increase would be substantial which means that the Commission must prove any increase with a high degree of probability. Consequently, when the Commission uses quantitative analyses, it must take into consideration all the relevant factors influencing the price level, involving standard efficiencies that could arise from the merger. Hence, the Court explained that these standard efficiencies as a part of a quantitative model must be separated from specific efficiencies, which are taken into consideration in the overall competitive evaluation of the concentration, so as to determine whether they are expected to counteract the restrictive consequences of the concentration. To that extent, the Commission did not stipulate whether the non-coordinated consequences identified would be "significant" or would result in a significant impediment to effective competition in the present case.

The Court made clear that the reasoning of the Commission was too speculative not assessing the influence on competition and competitors by re-stating that EU competition rules are principally intended to protect the competitive process as such, and not competitors. Moreover, the Court states that the EU Merger Regulation permits the Commission to catch anticompetitive mergers in non-dominant cases, but that in such cases the Commission must deliver convincing evidence that the merger will lead to the removal of vital competitive constraints resulting in a noteworthy impediment to effective competition. Furthermore, the Court refined that the Commission must produce convincing evidence to demonstrate with a strong possibility the existence of noteworthy impediments to competition following the concentration.

Also, the Court found that the Commission failed to show that the consequences of the merger on the UK's network-sharing agreements and on the mobile network infrastructure in the UK would establish a noteworthy impediment to effective competition. The Commission had failed to ascertain that the acquisition would have harmed competition or that prices would have increased.[13]

[13] Judgment of the General Court (First Chamber, Extended Composition) 28 May 2020 ECLI:EU:T:2020:217. Council Regulation (EC) No. 139/2004 of 20 January 2004 on the control of concentration between undertakings, OJ L 24, 29.1.2004.

Finally, the ECJ[14] recently decided that in order to block a merger or require remedies, the European Commission needs to show based on a "cogent and consistent body of evidence" that a merger "more likely than not" will result in a significant impediment to effective competition (SIEC).

The EUMR enables an efficient allocation of resources and a consistent merger review.[15] It is worth noting that the Court explained that Article 2(3) EUMR must be interpreted narrowly permitting the Commission to outlaw mergers in oligopolistic markets only in situations where the merger is influencing competitive conditions to an extent identical to the effect of individual or collective dominance. Thus, a significant impediment to effective competition must have a noteworthy influence on competition, similar to the impact that would take place if a dominant position were to arise which means that a prohibition as a result of a significant impediment to effective competition is only possible if the concentration would result in the elimination of a firm which extensively impedes the scope of action of the other participants in the market. Because of the higher requirements for proof involved, complex concentration proceedings in such markets will lead to even greater procedural expense and so the Commission has to collect and assess even more data than it already does now.

Undoubtedly, like US law, there is discretion in enforcement, and even within sensible constraints the EU is more suspicious of large mergers. Obviously, the political objectives of competition enforcement embrace concerns for unifying the single market, involving the consequences that markets have on labor broadly speaking. Besides, US competition law depends on demanding economic analysis. Moreover, the US Supreme Court has distinguished the limitations that courts face in differentiating between pro- and anticompetitive conduct in antitrust cases, and predominantly the risk this generates of reaching false positive decisions in monopolization cases.[16]

The EU's more "precautionary" approach to antitrust policy is embedded in a belief that markets do not or are unlikely to function well in general, and definitely not appropriate to self-correct in the face of monopolization. The precautionary principle comes at the expense of short-term growth which means that by approving a precautionary approach, a costly public policy in those instances is not clearly warranted by underlying risk and uncertainty.[17] The precautionary principles denote

[14]Case-376/20 P, Commission v CK Telecoms Investments Ltd, EU:C:2023:561. Giorgio Monti, EU Merger Control After the Grand Chamber's Judgment in Commission v CK Telecoms Investments, https://ssrn.com/abstract=4537510

[15]Carugati, C., Reforming Merger Control Notification Thresholds, Concurrences N° 2-2019, ART. N° 89868 (2019).

[16]Pac. Bell Tel. Co. v. linkLine Commc'ns, Inc., 555 U.S. 438 (2009); Credit Suisse Sec. (USA) LLC v. Billing, 551 U.S. 264, 265 (2007); Verizon Comm. v. Law Offices of Trinko, 540 U.S. 398 (2004).

[17]Nassim Nicholas Taleb, Rupert Read, Raphael Douady, Joseph Norman & Yaneer Bar-Yam, The precautionary principle (with application to the genetic modification of organisms), Arxiv Preprint Arxiv:1410.5787, 2 (2014). ("The purpose of the PP is to avoid a certain class of what, in

that policymakers should exclude certain mutually advantageous transactions on account of the social costs that they might inflict further down the line. Additionally, the precautionary principle has been correlated with anti-growth positions.[18] The Google Shopping decision reveals evidence that removing existing barriers to competition enforcement in the digital economy leads to harm to consumers.[19]

It has to be taken into consideration that the nonexistence of consumer harm so as to find antitrust injury is not incidental, but signifies a central alteration of antitrust enforcement, mainly when it comes to big tech firms and so together with the lack of clear knowledge, a modification in the burden of proof, and the lack of a consumer harm requirement with the intention of finding abuse of dominance all reveal the precautionary approach that the European Commission has now accepted.[20] European competition law is much more reliant on structural presumptions and precautionary reasoning. To that extent, the German competition authority attempted to use its antitrust authority to impose on consumers its distinctive political preferences.[21]

Of course, no one believes that markets are perfect, or that antitrust enforcement can never be appropriate. What is the function of the market in the modern economy, and particularly in high-growth, emerging economies? While US antitrust law involves a full-blown, effects-based analysis of challenged behavior in the context of monopolization or abuse of dominance and vertical restraints, the EU relies heavily upon presumptions of harm or extremely shortened analysis. Also, while US monopolization law bans only predatory or exclusionary conduct resulting in both the unlawful acquisition or maintenance of monopoly power and the making of net harm to consumers, the EU punishes the simple exercise of monopoly power such as the charging of "excessive" prices by dominant corporations or the use of "exploitative" business terms which means that the EU is punishing the simple

---

probability and insurance, is called "ruin" problems. A ruin problem is one where outcomes of risks have a non-zero probability of resulting in unrecoverable losses.").

[18] Jaap C Hanekamp, Guillaume Vera-Navas & SW Verstegen, The historical roots of precautionary thinking: the cultural ecological critique and 'The Limits to Growth', 8 Journal Of Risk Research, 299 (2005).

[19] Case AT.39740 Google Search (Shopping), Commission Decision of 27 June 2017, http://ec.europa.eu/competition/antitrust/cases/dec_docs/39740/39740_14996_3.pdf

[20] Aurelien Portuese, The Rise of Precautionary Antitrust: An Illustration with the EU Google Android Decision, CPI EU News November 2019, 4 (2019) ("The absence of demonstrated consumer harm in order to find antitrust injury is not fortuitous, but represents a fundamental alteration of antitrust enforcement, predominantly when it comes to big tech companies. Coupled with the lack of clear knowledge, a shift in the burden of proof, and the lack of a consumer harm requirement in order to find abuse of dominance all reveal the precautionary approach that the European Commission has now embraced.").

[21] OLG Düsseldorf, August 26, 2019, Case VI-Kart 1/19 (V). German Federal Court of Justice, June 23, 2020, KVR 69/19. Natasha Lomas, Facebook succeeds in blocking German FCO's privacy-minded order against combining user data, Techcrunch (Aug. 26, 2019), https://techcrunch.com/2019/08/26/facebook-succeeds-in-blocking-german-fcos-privacyminded-order-against-combining-user-data/

extraction of rents by a lawfully obtained dominant firm, while the US punishes only the unlawful extension of market power. Even the EU's highest court has acknowledged the paucity of the Commission's analysis in this area in its Intel decision.[22]

The GC in Michelin II (Case T-203/01) dealt with the anticompetitive effect of loyalty rebates considered sufficient to show that the abusive conduct of the dominant company "tends to" restrict competition or the conduct "is capable of" having that effect. Thus, for the purposes of applying Article 102, "establishing the anticompetitive object and the anticompetitive effect are one and the same thing." On January 26, 2022, the European General Court (GC) partially annulled a 2009 European Commission (Commission) decision, in which the Commission noticed that Intel had abused its dominant position by implementing a strategy of eliminating its competitors from the market. Thus, the Commission should have analyzed the consequences of Intel's conduct when evaluating whether it had infringed Article 102 of the Treaty on the TFEU.[23] Moreover, the GC noticed that the Commission's decision concerning the exclusivity rebates at issue was based on an error of law since it had considered Intel's rebates as automatically anticompetitive, and so had concluded that no effects analysis was needed to establish an abuse. In addition, the GC noticed that the Commission had failed to take into account all the relevant criteria required for an effects analysis such as the criterion relating to the share of the market covered by the rebates.[24] Hence, the European Courts will not uphold Commission decisions where the needed legal and evidentiary analysis is lacking.

The judgment demonstrates that the European Courts look in detail at evidence and economic analysis in antitrust cases, and will annul EC decisions if they do not undertake an effects-based analysis or if their economic analysis has errors. Thus, the analysis must establish legal standards concerning anticompetitive effects which means that the EC must support its infringement decisions with rigorous effects-based assessment, and not count on a formalistic approach grounded on "presumptions" of competitive harm. In other words, exclusivity rebates cannot be assumed to be an abuse of dominance once evidence is put to the EC of the absence of anticompetitive foreclosure. Furthermore, firms can count on economic analysis to evaluate the antitrust compliance of their rebate schemes, while the EC must endorse rigorous and careful analysis of anticompetitive foreclosure consequences. It could be said that there is a massive financial risk for European Union regulators when they lose challenges to antitrust fines.

It is characteristic that there is pressure in competition law between the wish for legal certainty as to the categories of behavior that will give rise to infringements,

---

[22]The General Court Judgement in Case T-286 / 09 RENV Intel Corporation v Commission.

[23]Case C-413/14 P—Intel Corporation Inc. v European Commission, judgment of September 06, 2017. In the leading case of Hoffmann-La Roche (Case 85/76), the ECJ ruled that loyalty rebates are intrinsically unlawful that may have a loyalty-inducing effect.

[24]Case C-413/14 P—Intel Corporation Inc. v European Commission, judgment of September 06, 2017. Case T-286/09 RENV Intel Corporation v Commission, judgment of 26 January 2022.

and the demand to evaluate the influence of such behavior in context to settle whether it has anticompetitive effects.

Is there a difference between the USA and the EU with regard to antitrust? As mentioned earlier, the difference between the USA and the EU with regard to the reliance on presumptions in antitrust cases is the relative adherence of the US regime to economic principles and their relative disregard for the EU. [25] There is a divergence concerning the quantification of anticompetitive harm, where European competition law compels a much less vigorous burden on authorities than does US law and so it seems that there is a failure of the EU's "competitive process" standard to separate competitive from anticompetitive exclusionary conduct in line with established economic principles. Moreover, compared to the USA, European competition law has recognized a wider set of per se prohibitions and sets a lower bar for plaintiffs to establish the existence of anticompetitive conduct.

Where US case law is steered by maximizing consumer welfare, EU competition law favors structural presumptions and places a much heavier weight on distributional considerations. Hence, US antitrust is undisturbed with firms that charge what some might consider "excessive" prices and so the plain possession of monopoly power, and the simultaneous charging of monopoly prices, is not only not unlawful; it is an imperative part of the free market system.[26] To that extent, charging monopoly prices is what magnetizes "business acumen" in the first place, encouraging risk taking generating innovation and economic growth. Besides, companies infringe EU competition law for the reason that they charge "excessive" prices[27] and so the ECJ held that charging a price which is excessive since it has no reasonable relation to the economic value of the product supplied is an abuse.

US antitrust law instructs allegations of predatory pricing to two strict conditions: (a) Monopolists must charge prices that are below some measure of their incremental costs and (b) there must be a realistic possibility that they will able to regain these first-period losses.[28] In the EU, the competition rules are in the Treaty on the Functioning of the European Union and the Merger Regulation offering a broad framework of general applicability, binding on the member states, their citizens through the doctrine of direct effect, the member states of the EEA, and other preferred trading partners of the EU. The EU has crafted block exemptions, de minimis limitations to the normal competition rules.[29] It has to be taken into account that European competition enforcement is accountable to political forces pursuing to

[25] Steven Berry, Martin Gaynor & Fiona Scott Morton, Do Increasing Markups Matter? Lessons from Empirical Industrial Organization, NBER Working Paper No. 26007 (Jun. 2019) at 5-6, http://www.nber.org/papers/w26007 ("In short, there is no well-defined 'causal effect of concentration on price,' but rather a set of hypotheses that can explain observed correlations of the joint outcomes of price, measured markups, market share, and concentration.").

[26] Verizon Communications v. Law Offices of Curtis Trinko, LLP, 540 U.S. 398, 407 (2004).

[27] Case C-27/76, United Brands v Commission, ECR 207, February 17, 1978, ¶ 250. Case C-52/09, Konkurrensverket v TeliaSonera Sverige AB, EU:C:2011:83, ¶ 30.

[28] Brooke Group Ltd. v. Brown & Williamson Tobacco Corp., 509 U.S. 209, 222-27 (1993).

[29] C.S. Kerse & Nicholas Khan, EU Antitrust Procedure 6th ed. (2012).

preserve the overall political legitimacy of the European Union. Moreover, competition policy is one of the topics where the Commission has exclusive competence and action in this field is crucial to the success of the growth agenda steering innovation and delivering clear benefits to consumers, businesses, and society as a whole.[30] The EU enforcement agencies are not constrained because of their clearly political function and the EU courts have eventually exposed EU competition law to amplified politicization.

The US structure, although molded by the political process through the election of Congress and the president confirmed the senior-most antitrust enforcement officials, is nonetheless largely insulated from direct political concerns. Moreover, the roles of the Department of Justice and the FTC are to impartially manage the laws written by Congress, as interpreted over time and a great number of cases by the courts. Undeniably there is policy-oriented decision-making taking place by US enforcement officials and the US administration's evident politicization of antitrust enforcement is brought to light by the testimony of a whistle blower.[31] Also, politicization of antitrust enforcement in the United States is limited in the first instance by the structure of the US system via the judiciary's strong check on political influences.

As mentioned earlier, Congress designed the antitrust laws to favor enforcement by catching certain anticompetitive practices. The Sherman Act involves a delegation of lawmaking power by Congress to the courts covering the field of antitrust. Sections 1 and 2 of the Sherman Act prohibit broad but definable categories of anticompetitive agreements and monopolization. In contrast, Sections 3 and 7 of the Clayton Act and Section 5 of the FTC Act are more elastic. Section 7 of the Clayton Act broadly forbids mergers and acquisitions where the outcome "may" tend to significantly lessen competition. Likewise, Section 3 of the Clayton Act disallows tying and exclusive dealing agreements where their effect also "may" tend to significantly lessen competition. Section 5 of the FTC Act takes a different line, outlawing unfair methods of competition and filling certain gaps in those statutes. Congress also has customized antitrust through statutory exemptions and immunities, granted for a variety of industries, from medical schools to soft drink bottlers to newspaper publishers.[32]

It has to be taken into account that the Sherman Act is taking affirmative steps to contain domination, to accommodate and promote democratic coordination, and to set rules of fair competition. Thus, the Sherman Act authorizes courts to generate

[30] Jean-Claude Juncker, President of the European Commission, Mission Letter to Margrethe Vestager, Commissioner for Competition 4 (Nov. 1, 2014), http://ec.europa.eu/archives/juncker-commission/docs/vestager_en.pdf

[31] "Oversight of the Department of Justice: Political Interference and Threats to Prosecutorial Independence."

[32] ABA Section of Antitrust Law, Federal Statutory Exemptions from Antitrust Law (2007). United States v. Booker, 543 U.S. 220 (2005) (making Sentencing Guidelines advisory, not mandatory, but requiring courts to take them into account).

new lines of law[33] and so the Sherman Act invites the federal courts to articulate a set of rules that will make them work in socially resourceful manners. Sanjukta Paul[34] states that "judges have arrogated to themselves the power to invent the criteria by which antitrust law will govern the economy, claiming all the while that Congress delegated this power of reinvention to them through the Sherman Act itself." It could be said that the Sherman Act is planned to stop unfair business methods so as to promote competitive markets.

The content of competition law concerning competition itself in the EU encompasses objectives that are far more ambiguous than those pursued under US antitrust law. While antitrust law in the US currently pursues the maximization of consumer welfare, the European Union has been reluctant to commit to a well-defined competition objective for its antitrust law. Furthermore, whereas the USA is steered by the consumer welfare standard, the objectives of European competition enforcers are both diverse and often freed from economic thinking. To that extent, the US Supreme Court has developed jurisprudence limiting provisions to certain practices that restrict consumer welfare.[35] Moreover, the courts have allowed defendants to argue that the competitive outcomes of a specific arrangement are not harmful to competition for the reason that the special characteristics of the product, the industry, or the corporations in question.[36] In Microsoft's decision, the court adopted a rule of reason for tying, but only for the software industry.[37]

Recently, FTC has communicated its wish to move toward some custom tailoring to deal with problems that might lie beyond the bounds of the Sherman and Clayton Acts. FTC was restricted to whether Qualcomm's licensing practices violated Section 1 and Section 2 of the Sherman Act; court did not consider whether there was a "standalone" Section 5 violation.[38] It seems that the Commission intends to go beyond conduct that violates the antitrust laws.[39] In addition, FTC has the power to engage in antitrust rulemaking but has done so only once.[40] The Executive Order advises the Commission to adopt rules dealing with a number of practices in which the key tech platforms engage but which might be hard to attack via antitrust

[33] Bus. Elec. Corp. v. Sharp Elec. Corp., 485 U.S. 717, 732 (1988).

[34] Sanjukta Paul, Recovering the Moral Economy Foundations of the Sherman Act, 2021 The Yale Law Journal 131:175 p. 254.

[35] 15 U.S.C. §§ 1, 2.

[36] National Soc. of Prof. Engineers v. United States, 435 U.S. 678 (1978).

[37] United States v. Microsoft, 253 F.3d 34 (D.C. Cir. 2001) (en banc).

[38] FTC v. Qualcomm, Inc., 969 F. 3d 974, 986 n.11 (9th Cir. 2020). FTC v. Sperry & Hutchison Co., 405 U.S. 233, 244 (1972).

[39] Statement of the Commission On the Withdrawal of the Statement of Enforcement Principles Regarding "Unfair Methods of Competition" Under Section 5 of the FTC Act, https://www.ftc.gov/system/files/documents/public_statements/1591706/p210100commnstmtwithdrawalsec5enforcement.pdf (July 9, 2021).

[40] Discriminatory Practices in Men's and Boy's Tailored Clothing Industry, 16 CFR Part 412 (1968). Rohit Chopra & Lina M. Khan, The Case for "Unfair Methods of Competition" Rulemaking, 87 U. Chi. L. Rev 357 (2020).

litigation, such as unfair data collection and "unfair competition in major Internet marketplaces."[41] While public attention in the USA has focused on increased market concentration, lessening competition, and rising economic inequality, the US Congress and enforcement agencies are facing escalating calls to strengthen the antitrust laws and their enforcement and so need to reconsider its approach to antitrust policy.[42]

It seems that EU competition law has been focused on "an increased role of economics in competition law," with emphasis placed on the promotion of economic efficiency and consumer welfare and so the goal of EU antitrust law has concentrated on consumer welfare emphasizing the effects-based analysis and the central role of the efficiency defense but market integration stays important.[43] On mergers, the European Commission's approach is similar to the USA' favoring of a more effects-based analysis of anticompetitive behavior but considering per se illegal certain types of conduct that are per se legal in the USA. Moreover, UNCTAD documents the shift in EU antitrust policy from a form-based to a more effects-based approach relying on economic analysis.[44]

Digital conglomerates are shaped owing to market power formed via predatory pricing and high levels of diversification.[45] Anyway, the EU disputes vertical and conglomerate mergers contrary to the Chicago School's principles that emphasize these types of mergers' pro-competitive effects and so vertical agreements that contain territorial restrictions or restrict the resale price of goods or services often lead to per se antitrust liability in the EU. Also, the EU treats exclusionary conduct by dominant corporations with suspicion of pursuing these companies' tying, discounting, exclusive dealing, along with predatory, discriminatory, or unfair pricing practices. Anu Bradford[46] et al. argue that "the EU shows it has not relinquished its rather 'maximalist' approach to antitrust, which is antithetical to the Chicago School's antitrust minimalism."

There are high-level differences between the EU and US approaches to competition policy. To that extent, the whole structure of an approach to antitrust law in the EU vests the Commission with much greater discretion to diverge from established economic principles and procedural best practices in its antitrust enforcement and

[41] Executive Order 14036 of July 9, 2021, Promoting Competition in the American Economy, 86 F.R. 36987, 36992.

[42] Suresh Naidu, Eric A. Posner, and Glen Weyl, Antitrust Remedies for Labor Market Power, 132 Harv L Rev 536, 547–49 (2018) (arguing that FTC and DOJ should enforce antitrust laws more often in labor market concentration cases).

[43] Jacques Crémer, Yves-Alexandre de Montjoye, and Heike Schweitzer, Competition Policy for the Digital Era *40 (EU 2019), https://perma.cc/8K4J-Q6BB

[44] United Nations Conference on Trade and Development Board, The Use of Economic Analysis in Competition Cases *8 (Apr 28, 2009), https://perma.cc/YX8M-C6VN

[45] M. Bourreau & A. de Streel, Conglomerates and EU Competition Policy (CERRE/CRIDS, March 2019), http://www.crid.be/pdf/public/8377.pdf

[46] Anu Bradford, Adam S. Chilton, & Filippo Maria Lancieri, The Chicago School's Limited Influence on International Antitrust, 2020 The University of Chicago Law Review 87:297 P312.

decision-making. Thus, antitrust enforcement at the EU level is driven almost entirely by the European Commission, a political body, and largely unreviewed and unchecked by EU courts[47] and so EU antitrust is less economically grounded, and unavoidably more politicized, than in the USA. Even though the EU's approach to competition policy appears close to that of the USA, it is diverging in the economic reasoning that underpins US antitrust law and divergences between EU and US law point to a number of key matters where the EU approach undermines consumers and constrain the region's economic growth. While the US concentrates on protecting the process of competition for the economic welfare of consumers, the EU has built and maintains its competition laws to affect a wider range of political/ economic/social objectives. Undeniably, the Commission has usually stated that European competition law pursues multiple objectives. To that extent, the European Commission[48] found that Google's online search services favor its own shopping service over competing shopping services and so Google had infringed Article 102 TFEU in relation to the national markets for specialized search services in 13 countries.

Which is the approach concerning Hub-and-Spoke Arrangements under EU Competition Rules and the USA? Online gig platforms are data-driven business models that utilize and develop algorithms and AI tools that learn from user behavior and adapt to make interactions more and more efficient enabling users to sell their labor or services to other users via the platforms.[49] The pricing algorithms play an imperative role in generating the efficiencies that platforms offer but competition issues occur once the platform steps in and coordinate prices, either by suggesting prices or by fixing prices centrally. Article 101 (1) TFEU distinguishes between by-object and by-effect restrictions of competition. Under EU competition law, hub-and-spoke arrangements facilitating price fixing between competitors are as illegal as entirely horizontal cartels.[50] Moreover, the coordination of transaction parameters by the platform is likely to have procompetitive effects.[51]

Algorithms examine pricing and quantities of products and services in a given market through data analysis and so by scrutinizing data identify patterns designating anticompetitive conduct such as market segmentation or price fixing.

EU competition law still considers certain vertical restraints with suspicion and apart from the general rule of Article 101 (1) TFEU, the Vertical Block Exemption Regulation (VBER) specifies which categories of vertical restraints are expected to be found contrary to Article 101 (1) TFEU, and which categories of vertical

---

[47] Ian S. Forrester, Due process in EC competition cases: A distinguished institution with flawed procedures, 34 Eur. L. Rev. 817 (2009).

[48] Case T-612/17—Judgment of the General Court Google v Commission.

[49] Airbnb (2021). "How do I turn Smart Pricing on or off?" https://www.airbnb.com/help/article/1168/how-doi-turn-smart-pricing-on-or-off . Uber (2021). "How Uber's dynamic pricing model works." https://www.uber.com/en-GB/blog/uber-dynamicpricing/

[50]. Case C-194/14 P AC Treuhand v Commission price-fixing, market-sharing. Case C-74/14 ETURAS.

[51] Case C-228/18 Budapest Bank.

restraints fulfill the criteria of Article 101 (3) TFEU and so do not violate competition rules.[52] The CECED decision indicated the fact that an agreement that advances public policy objectives more than it damages competition could be exempted under Article 101 (3) TFEU and the Guidelines on the application of Article 101 (3) TFEU exclude any broader, noneconomic considerations from its analysis, involving environmental and sustainability considerations.[53] The current situation under EU Competition law creates considerable legal uncertainty for any gig platform setting the prices for individual transactions through the use of algorithms.

Under the present state of US law, such a vertical price fix is illegal only if it leads to harm to consumers, signalled in price increases or quality reduction.[54] Also, a horizontal conspiracy among book publishers, orchestrated by Apple in fixing the price of e-books distributed through e-readers implicates competition law due to pricing influences.[55]

It is worth noting that e-commerce together with AI systems instantly and continuously identifies the behavior of other market participants, mainly the alteration in their supply, depriving competitive uncertainty. Wherever data on competitors' behavior and their prices is available for processing by AI in competitor's service, market transparency and familiarity with how competitors are acting in the market will be the normal state of affairs. It is worth noting that transparency of online markets, the availability of data on the behavior of competitors in them, and at the same time the capabilities of algorithms in the service of enterprises are elements contributing to the influence of AI on competition. It is worth mentioning here that the non-negotiated price collusion via algorithmic price parallelism generates the ability of a company to rapidly follow every move of its competitors and so non-contact behavior is not covered by the prohibitions of Section 1 of the Sherman Act and Article 101(1) TFEU.[56] Also, algorithms are used to monitor prices agreed

---

[52] Regulation 330/2010 on the application of Article 101(3) of the Treaty.

[53] Case IV.F.1/36.718.CECED. G Monti (2022). Implementing a Sustainability Agenda in EU Competition Law. Paper presented at Vienna Competition Law Days, 17–18 September 2022. EU Commission Proposal for a Directive on Corporate Sustainability Due Diligence and amending Directive (EU) 2019/1937, COM(2022) 71 final . The European Commission, via its proposed Corporate Sustainability Due Diligence Directive (CSDDD), has put forward a legislative framework to oblige corporations to demonstrate what action they are taking to protect the environment and human rights. https://kpmg.com/xx/en/home/insights/2023/02/the-eu-corporate-sustainability-due-diligence-directive.html. https://www.ebu.ch/case-studies/open/legal-policy/the-future-of-eu-sustainability-regulation-ii-the-corporate-sustainability-due-diligence-directive-csddd

[54] Leegin Creative Leather Prods. v PSKS Inc., 551 U.S. 877 (2007). ("vertical price restraints 'might be used to organize cartels at the retailer level").

[55] United States v. Apple Inc., 791 F.3d 290 (2015) (upholding finding of liability for a horizontal agreement among publishers orchestrated by retailer Apple, acting as the hub).

[56] Wisking, S.; Herron, M.: Algorithmic Pricing—The New Competition Law Frontier? Digital Business Lawyer, September, 2017. European Commission: Commission Notice on Guidelines on the applicability of Article 101 TFEU to horizontal cooperation agreements (2011/C 11/01) 14.1.2011, point 78.

between competitors, to purposely signal a certain course of action, to intentionally use one intermediary and its algorithm, or to control prices set by the supplier to the distributor for subsequent sale, etc. It could be said that algorithms can lead to collusive behavior.

AI makes such a non-negotiated collusion achievable between numbers of corporations instantaneously and sustainable over a longer period of time than under "classical" conditions of competitive uncertainty.[57] Furthermore, AI technology is assessing whether differences in bidders' bids show standardized differences in parameters, structural and wording similarities in descriptions that would indicate collusion.[58]

It is worth mentioning here that the Australian Competition and Consumer Act of 2010 in Section 46 makes enterprises profiting from collusion punishable for harm to competition even without having to deliver evidence of their collusive behavior which means that a corporation benefiting from having used a specific algorithm leading to price coordination with competitors is liable without its people having involved in any exchange of signals, information, offers, and acceptances.[59] Consequently, companies utilizing and employing an anticompetitive algorithm would be liable for the algorithm acting independently in the same way as if their employee had acted against rules of competition. Enforcement of competition law encompasses trade-offs between the risk that pro-competitive conduct will mistakenly be found anticompetitive and the risk that anticompetitive behavior will mistakenly be found not to be so. Moreover, the scope of Section 46 is limited to those markets in which the corporation's conduct is most likely to have a purpose, effect, or likely effect of competition concern.[60] Likewise, vertical restrictions will not significantly diminish competition unless they are imposed by a company with substantial market power.[61]

[57]OECD: Algorithmic Collusion: Problems and Counter-Measures. Note by Ezrachi, A., Stucke, M.E. DAF/COMP/WD(2017)25, 31 May 2017, p. 6.

[58]Rab, S. Artificial Intelligence, Algorithms and Antitrust. Competition Law Journal, 2019, Vol. 18, No. 4, pp. 143, 145.

[59]CMA (Competition and Markets Authority): Algorithms: How they can reduce competition and harm consumers. London: CMA, 2019.

[60]Competition and Consumer Act 2010 (Cth) s.46(1), as amended by the Competition and Consumer Amendment (Misuse of Market Power) Act 2017 (Cth). https://www.gtlaw.com.au/insights/section-46-cca-rides-again-different-horse *ACCC v. Safeway Stores (No 2)* (2003) 119 FCR 339; *ACCC v. Baxter Healthcare* (2008) 170 FCR 16; *ACCC v. Pfizer Australia* [2018] FCAFC 78.

[61]Ian Harper et al., Competition Policy Review: Final Report 375 (2015). Luke Woodward & Matt Rubinstein, *The use and abuse of section 46* (2016), p.10, https://cdn.brandfolder.io/3RTTK3BV/as/pev81q-9t241k-dovisy/Luke_Woodward-Theuseandmisuseofsection46.pdf

6.4 Developments on Competition Law

Section 2 of the Sherman Act prohibits "monopolization," involving a higher level of power than EU "abuse of dominance" (Article 102 TFEU). Also, EU Article 102 covers exploitative conduct such as charging excessive prices along with exclusionary acts, while Section 2 covers only exclusionary acts. Furthermore, Article 102 disallows exclusionary acts distorting competition on the merits, such as leveraging by gatekeeping platforms to secure advantages, while Section 2 disallows only exclusionary acts augmenting market power and harming consumers, classically evidenced by higher prices and lower output.[62] There are market competitors bigger than nations having significant power, which may not count as monopoly power under Sherman Act precedents, and documented abuses are either exploitative or distortive of competition on the merits without lessening output which means that the Sherman Act has "blind spots," and many dominant firm abuses fall within them.

US Supreme Court case law specified that business, when it is performed individually and not in combination with competitors, almost always operates in the interests of consumers. Moreover, the Supreme Court has re-made Section 2 jurisprudence in the libertarian image, and the stance of the Court is not anticipated to adjust unless and until Congress changes it[63] which means that Section 2 of the Sherman Act makes it very hard for a plaintiff to evidence that a violator has adequate power to pass the first screen of the monopolization violation and so the US Section 2 jurisprudence makes it hard to prove conduct that violates the Sherman Act.[64] It has to be taken into consideration that US antitrust law considers that large size alone cannot be an antitrust offense and so according to Section 2 plain possession of monopoly power, or the pursuit of it, is not in itself illegal.[65]

In the USA, the dominant formulation of goals of antitrust is narrow due to consumer welfare in the interests of efficiency.[66] EU competition law values undistorted market processes allowing markets to work better, dealing with consumers but not exclusively which means flexibility in controlling abuses.[67] Antitrust

---

[62] Verizon Communications v. Law Offices of Curtis V. Trinko (Trinko), 540 U.S. 398, footnote 4 (2004).

[63] Andrew I. Gavil & Steven C. Salop, Probability, Presumptions and Evidentiary Burdens in Antitrust Analysis: Revitalizing Rule of Reason for Exclusionary Conduct, 168 U. Pa. L. Rev. 2107 (2020); Carl Shapiro, Antitrust: What Went Wrong and How to Fix It, 35 ANTITRUST 33 (summer 2021).

[64] Eastman Kodak Co. v. Image Technical Services, Inc., 504 U.S. 451 (1992). FTC v. Facebook, Inc., __ F. Supp. 3d __ (D.D.C. June 29, 2021). Epic Games v. Apple, __ F. Supp. 3d __ (N.D. Cal. Sept. 10, 2021).

[65] Viamedia, Inc. v. Comcast Corp, 951 F.3d 429, 451 (7th Cir. 2020) United States v. United States Steel Corp., 251 U.S. 417, 451 (1920) ("the law does not make mere size an offense").

[66] Ohio v. American Express Co., 585 U.S. __ (2018).

[67] Post Danmark II, Case C-23/14, EU:C:2015:651, paras. 70-72; Google LLC v. Commission, Case T-612/17, EU:T:2021:763.

laws of Germany, Japan, etc. prohibit abuse of a superior position or of economic dependence. Also, abuse of a superior position is not an ingredient of US or EU law, even though the EU appreciates the right of its member states to use the argument and so there is a growing trend of abuse of economic dependence laws in Europe.[68]

Taking into account that behaviors such as excessive pricing and refusal to supply generate prospective concerns if a firm is dominant, in Germany ARC-Digitization Act[69] has expanded the range of review involving abuse of relative market power and economic dependence and so the new law has diminished the likelihood of a merger control filing in Germany by raising the turnover thresholds to EUR 50 and 17.5 million. Moreover, an abuse of economic dependence is an anticompetitive practice prohibited under French law as well[70] and so it seems that the FCA fined Apple due to the fact of abusing economic dependence by discriminating against premium resellers in terms of supply in comparison to Apple-owned stores and bigger retailers.

It has to be taken into account that competition law is oriented in protecting the competitive process in markets but it seems that EU competition law more narrowly counts on economic evidence focused on welfare effects.[71] Additionally, in many jurisdictions, competition law is essentially tied to economics in a way of comprehending them as the main reasoning for competition law.[72]

Resembling the gradual transition to rule of reason in the USA, the Commission employs a soft reform of its approach to competition law enforcement, rather than amending the competition law articles of the EU treaties and triggering conflict with established CJEU case law. Hence, the Commission suggested its enforcement priorities departing from blanket prohibitions to a case-by-case, effects-based approach.[73]

Accordingly, the Commission's guidelines on cartel enforcement declare its rationale is to protect competition on the market as a way of boosting consumer welfare with an effective allocation of resources. Also, the Commission averts mergers that will deprive customers of low prices, high-quality products, and innovation by considerably increasing the market power of corporations.

It has to be taken into account that acquiring a corporation with better access to data creates comparative advantages by allowing a company to benefit from synergies, not mentioning that applying more efficient algorithms developed by one

[68] K&L Gates Hub, The Enforcement of Abuse of Economic Dependence in the EU, 28 Jan. 2021, https://www.klgates.com/The-Enforcement-of-Abuse-of-EconomicDependence-in-the-EU-1-28-2021

[69] ARC-Digitisation Act entered into force on January 19, 2020.

[70] Art. L 420-2 of the French Commercial Code (FCC).

[71] Commission Staff Working Document—Better Regulation Guidelines, SWD (2021) 305 final.

[72] Gunnar Niels, Helen Jenkins and James Kavanagh, Economics for Competition Lawyers (Second edition, Oxford University Press 2016) s 1.07.

[73] Anne C Witt, 'The European Court of Justice and the More Economic Approach to EU Competition Law—Is the Tide Turning?' (2019) 64 The Antitrust Bulletin 172.

company to the dataset of the other.[74] In addition, due to the fact that AI algorithms restrict access of rivals to a unique dataset mergers produce comparative advantages by blocking competitors' access[75] to needed resources and so merging with a company holding a unique algorithm might achieve a similar result.[76]

Concerning abuse of dominance by corporations, the Commission points out that dominant undertakings should not impair effective competition by excluding their competitors in an anticompetitive manner and so imposing unfavorable consequences on consumer welfare via higher prices, limiting quality, or slashing consumer choice.[77] Thus, it seems that the Commission concentrates on the economic effects of anticompetitive conduct and so anticompetitive behavior is sanctioned when finding negative consequences on consumer welfare. It is worth mentioning here that While EU competition law is to a large extent grounded on EU Treaty articles, secondary EU legislation has been developed. It has to be taken into account that while Article 101 of the TFEU proscribes certain kinds of agreements requiring considerable interpretation, the "abuse of a dominant position" of Article 102 is even more indefinite.

It is argued that the objective of Article 102 TFEU is the maximization of total social welfare through productivity growth.[78] Also, competition law should protect a broader notion of fairness that takes into consideration the interests of all players engaged, embracing those of monopolists or undertakings with market power.[79] Moreover, Lianos[80] accepts welfare as one of the goals of EU competition law but sees that goal as being about the redistribution of wealth. G.I.Zekos regards that competition law should establish the framework for competition based on rationales

[74] Joseph E. Harrington Jr, The Effect of Outsourcing Pricing Algorithms on Market Competition (2021), https://ssrn.com/abstract=3798847

[75] Coleen Cunningham, Florian Ederer & Song Ma, Killer Acquisitions, 129 J. of Pol. Econ. (2021) (acquisitions in which a firm buys a unique and efficient algorithm in order to "kill" the innovation rather than use it).

[76] Maria, Wasastjerna, Big Data And Privacy In Merger Review—Competition Policy For The 21st Century Digital Economy (2020). Verity Egerton-Doyle & Jonathan Ford, Algorithms, Big Data, and Merger Control, in Algorithmic Antitrust 87 (Aurelien Portuese, ed., 2022). Michael Coutts, Mergers, Acquisitions and Algorithms in an Algorithmic Pricing World, J. of Com. L. & Econ. (2022).

[77] Guidelines on the Applicability of Article 81 of the EC Treaty to Horizontal Cooperation Agreements, OJ 2001 C 3/2, §13 Guidelines on the assessment of horizontal mergers under the Council Regulation on the control of concentrations between Undertakings, 2004 OJ 2004 C 31/5, §8 Guidance on the Commission's enforcement priorities in applying Article 82 of the EC Treaty to abusive exclusionary conduct by dominant undertakings OJ 2009 C 45/7 §19 Roger Van den Bergh, 'The More Economic Approach in European Competition Law: Is More Too Much or Not Enough?' in Kovac Mitja and Vandenberghe Ann-Sophie (eds), Economic Evidence in EU Competition Law (Intersentia 2016).

[78] R Nazzini The Foundations of European Union Competition Law: The Objective and Principles of Article 102 (Oxford: Oxford University Press, 2011) pp 107–154.

[79] A Ayal Fairness in Antitrust (Oxford: Hart Publishing, 2016) pp 207–212.

[80] I Lianos 'The poverty of competition law: the long story' CLES Research Paper Series No 2/2018, available at www.ucl.ac.uk/cles/sites/cles/files/cles_2-2018.pdf

of equality on activities upon a free market which means upholding an effective competition structure and protecting competition as such.

It has to be taken into account that the legal foundation of the VBER lies in Article 101 TFEU banning agreements between companies that avert, restrict, or distort competition. While Article 101 TFEU applies to horizontal cartel agreements between direct competitors, fixing prices and/or output to the detriment of consumers, CJEU defines that Article 101 TFEU also applies to agreements between companies in a vertical relation. Moreover, While the European Commission defines that vertical restraints are less destructive than horizontal restraints, the prohibition of anticompetitive agreements in the TFEU is subject to an accumulative set of exemptions in Article 101(3) that are hard to meet for defendant companies which means that the Commission has advanced a system of block exemptions for vertical agreements.[81] The Commission demands economic evidence in assessing the effectiveness of the VBER.[82] It is worth mentioning that many of the consequences attached to platforms are similar to what takes place via vertical integration or control.[83]

As an answer to the rise of dominant online platforms, National Competition Authorities and legislatures developed differentiated approaches toward MFN clauses of platforms like Amazon and Booking.com, negatively influencing legal certainty.[84] Most Favored Nation clauses (MFN—"price parity clauses") compel retailers to operate brick and mortar stores, banning sales through online platforms and executing "recommended" resale prices and so MFN clauses are agreements between a supplier and a retailer whereby the supplier assures the retailer equally favorable conditions as related to all other retailers the supplier embraces.[85] In 2021, the EU decided that Google abused its dominant position in the market for specialized product search services by demonstrating a preference for its own comparison shopping service in general search results over third-party content.[86]

It has to be taken into account that anticompetitive behavior of digital platforms is caught by general competition rules and so price discrimination grounded on data

[81] The Vertical Block Exemption Regulation (VBER) Regulation 330/2010 on the application of Article 101(3) of the TFEU to categories of vertical agreements and concerted practices OJ 2010 L 102/1.Commission Notice—Guidelines on Vertical Restraints, SEC(2010) 411, §6.

[82] European Commission, Support studies for the evaluation of the VBER, final report (2020), available at https://ec.europa.eu/competition/publications/reports/kd0420219enn.pdf

[83] Dennis W. Carlton & Ralph A. Winter, Vertical Most-Favored-Nation Restraints and Credit Card No-Surcharge Rules, 61 J.L. & Econ. 215, 215 (2018).

[84] Bernadette Zelger, 'Restrictions of Online Sales and Vertical Agreements: Bundeskartellamt vs. Commission? Why Coty and Asics Are Compatible' (2018) 14 European Competition Journal 445. Case C-230/16 Coty Germany GmbH v Parfümerie Akzente GmbH [2017] ECLI:EU:C:2017:941.

[85] Gönenç Gürkaynak and others, 'Most-Favored-Nation Clauses in Commercial Contracts: Legal and Economic Analysis and Proposal for a Guideline' (2016) 42 European Journal of Law and Economics 129.

[86] Case T-612/17, Google LLC v. Comm'n, 2021 ECLI:EU:T:2021:763, ¶¶ 179, 197, 596-97 (Nov. 10, 2021).

amounts to a discriminatory abuse under Article 102 TFEU in the form of imposing unfair trading conditions or excessive pricing. Moreover, the imposition of MFNs clauses can signify abuse of dominance banned by Article 102 TFEU as well.

It is worth mentioning here that the Chinese Anti-Monopoly Guidelines[87] specify the principles of market definition in the platform economy by encompassing a list of practices that are expected to raise competition-related concerns and so advocating a proper competition law response to those concerns. The Guidelines specify what is regarded an abuse of dominance in platform markets and so abuse of dominance is constituted by using a platform of the data collected on users or merchants to engage in price discrimination or differential treatment (Articles 15, 17). Moreover, the comparison of the Chinese Guidelines and the EU law reveals that the EU presently lacks a comprehensive device encapsulating what its competition law's position to digital platforms is. To that extent, the EU still largely counts on the case law of the CJEU and the decision-making practice of the Commission to refine how the traditional competition rules apply to digital platforms. On the other hand, Chinese Guidelines stipulate a thorough framework on what comprises an appropriate approach to the novel conduct.

The rule of reason context involves a three-step process and so firstly anticompetitive harm, secondly evidence of pro-competitive efficiencies and thirdly the benefits are achieved through less restrictive means.[88] Amex specified that the welfare of both the merchants and cardholders must be considered before anticompetitive harm can be ascertained.[89] It is worth noting that competition rules are evolving and there is an approach to the rule of reason matching it with per se analysis.[90]

It is worth mentioning here that while consumer welfare is the most commonly declared purpose of the antitrust laws,[91] protection of the competitive process[92] has

[87] Barbara Dufková, What Can the EU Learn from the Chinese Anti-Monopoly Guidelines for the Platform Economy Industries? , Prague Law Working Papers Series No.2022/II/2.

[88] Ohio v. Am. Express Co., 138 S. Ct. 2274, 2284 (2018) ("To determine whether a restraint violates the rule of reason, the parties agree that a three-step, burden-shifting framework applies."). Herbert Hovenkamp, The Rule of Reason, 70 Fla. L. Rev. 81, 103–04 (2018).

[89] Ohio v. American Express Co., 138 S. Ct. 2274 (2018). at 2287 ("Focusing on merchant fees alone misses the mark because the product that credit-card companies sell is transactions, not services to merchants, and the competitive effects of a restraint on transactions cannot be judged by looking at merchants alone.").

[90] Jonathan B. Baker, The Antitrust Paradigm 68 (2019).

[91] FTC v. Qualcomm, Inc., 969 F.3d 974, 989 (9th Cir. 2020) ("Allegations that conduct "has the effect of reducing consumers' choices or increasing prices to consumers do[ ] not sufficiently allege an injury to competition ... [because] [b]oth effects are fully consistent with a free, competitive market.") Herbert Hovenkamp, FRAND and Antitrust, 105 Corn. L. Rev. 1683 (2020).

[92] A. Douglas Melamed, Antitrust Law and its Critics, 83 Antitrust L.J. 269 (2020) (advocating "competitive process" goal); S. Scott Hemphill & Nancy L. Rose, Mergers that Harm Sellers, 127 Yale L.J. 2078 (2018) at 2079 (identifying competitive process standard with merger enforcement and arguing that standard applies to both downstream and upstream harms; further, appearing to equate it with the welfare of trading partners.).

to be taken into account since via standardization of principles adds to the fair functioning of a market allowing players to get competitive advantage via creativity and innovation contributing to better goods and services for consumers. Thus, the substance of competitive process standard has to be defined in order to know what, precisely, constitutes the "competitive process"[93] which means that competitive process should encompass certain rules applicable in the competition. To that extent, AI technology will bring forward objectivity to AI competition by establishing standardization via AI principles encompassing AI data and rationales for objective competition in an AAI market.

References

1. Melamed, D. (2020). Antitrust law and its critics. *Antitrust Law Journal, 83*, 269.
2. Bradford, A., Chilton, A. S., & Lancieri, F. M. (2020). The Chicago School's limited influence on international antitrust. *The University of Chicago Law Review, 87*, 297.
3. Bradford, A., Chilton, A. S., Linos, K., & Weaver, A. (2019). The global dominance of European Competition Law over American Antitrust Law. *Journal of Empirical Legal Studies, 16*, 731, 739–740, 745.
4. Dufková, B. *What can the EU learn from the Chinese anti-monopoly guidelines for the platform economy industries?* (Prague Law Working Papers Series No.2022/II/2).
5. Cunningham, C., Ederer, F., & Ma, S. (2021). Killer acquisitions. *Journal of Political Economy, 129*, 649–702.
6. Hovenkamp, H. (2020). FRAND and antitrust. *Cornell Law Review, 105*, 1683.
7. Hovenkamp, H. J., & Morton, F. S. (2020). Framing the Chicago school of antitrust analysis. *University of Pennsylvania Law Review, 168*, 1843.
8. Newman, J. M. (2019). Procompetitive justifications in antitrust law. *Indiana Law Journal, 94*(501), 514.
9. Coutts, M. (2022). Mergers, acquisitions and algorithms in an algorithmic pricing world. *Journal of Competition Law & Economics*. https://doi.org/10.2139/ssrn.4044937

[93] John M. Newman, Procompetitive Justifications in Antitrust Law, 94 Ind. L.J. 501, 514 (2019).

Chapter 7
Chicago School, Harvard School, and New Brandeis Movement

7.1 Introduction

Initially, the founders of the US antitrust law chose between two institutional models of antitrust. In the corporate regulatory model, the capital-concentrating effects of general incorporation statutes would have been considered the subject of antitrust regulation and so the target of antitrust enforcement would have been to optimize market performance by specifying fitting corporate structure and behavior. The competing crime-tort model focuses on the corporation as the subject of antitrust regulation and the crime-tort model conceived of antitrust as a freestanding standard of industrial competition. The crime-tort model focused on discouraging and compensating for forbidden behavior. By breaking up antitrust law from corporate law, the crime-tort model sets free antitrust law on non-corporate subjects, embracing labor and professional associations that would not have been antitrust subjects in the corporate regulatory model. The crime-tort model produced vagueness as to the hierarchy between the state and the federal regulation of competition.

It is argued that competition is a process in the real world for business rivalry and so the concept of "competition," supported by pre-Chicago judicial precedent and legislative history, expresses moment-to-moment business rivalry and not economic efficiency.[1]

[1] Harry S. Gerla, Restoring Rivalry as a Central Concept in Antitrust Law, 75 Neb. L. Rev. 209, 211–22 (1996)

© The Author(s), under exclusive license to Springer Nature Switzerland AG 2023

G. I. Zekos, *Artificial Intelligence and Competition*, Contributions to Economics,
https://doi.org/10.1007/978-3-031-48083-6_7

7.2 Chicago School Versus Harvard School

To start with, the Chicago School project was justified in advancing the intention of a certain political-economic order, rather than simply an abstract commitment to an analytical framework. Hence, Chicago School thrived in persuading the federal courts to adopt a far narrower view of antitrust that has as its single objective the avoidance of economically incompetent transactions, mentioned by economists as "allocative efficiency.[2]"

Furthermore, the Chicago School view considers that monopolists should not be penalized for obtaining their market power owing to a superior product but in cases involving monopolists' duty to deal, tying, and exclusive dealing, the more lenient Chicago School view confuses the standards of conduct for dominant companies. Post-Chicago School scholars have realized that monopolists such as Microsoft have an exclusive capacity to leverage the appeal of their networks to expand their market power into other markets or to preclude new companies from entering the market they have already monopolized. The Microsoft case did not present a structure for antitrust regulation that can be rigidly or realistically utilized for antitrust analyses of all high-technology companies. Thus, courts and regulators must recognize without losing sight of the ultimate purpose that technology not only influences antitrust analyses but also fosters competition. Concerning the Chicago School approach Sanjukta Paul[3] argues that "the relaxation of enforcement when it came to corporate mergers, monopolization, and vertical restraints, was the priority. And if one of the underlying political priorities of the Chicago School was to secure the power of concentrated capital, then price-fixing was the most obvious concession."

It has to be taken into consideration that the spirit of the Harvard school's view was that allowing a lot of small companies to exist adds to competition rather than a small number of companies. Under the "Harvard School" view, the courts and agencies accepted the illegality of any mergers, joint ventures, or agreements that allowed corporations to get, enhance, or exercise market power, notwithstanding whether the conduct had the prospective to benefit consumers by lowering prices or increasing output.[4] Under the "Chicago School" view, the courts and agencies became much less willing to prohibit competitive conduct on its face but they are involved in a wide factual inquiry to substantiate the consequences of specific conduct on consumers before finding it illegal. It has to be taken into account that it is difficult to prove the adverse economic consequences of specific types of

[2] Rob Van Horn, Reinventing Monopoly and the Role of Corporations: The Roots of Chicago Law and Economics, in The Road From Mont Pelerin 204, 217 (Philip Mirowski & Dieter Plehwe eds., 2009)

[3] Sanjukta Paul Antitrust as Allocator of Coordination Rights 67 UCLA L. Rev. 378 (2020) At 389

[4] Herbert Hovenkamp, *The Rationalization of Antitrust,* 116 Harv. L. Rev. 917, 920 (2003).

conduct.[5] To that extent, strong competition and consumer protection policies are decisive in preserving a marketplace that benefits consumers.

It is worth noting that increased international economic integration multiplies the benefits of international coordination of competition policies. It could be said that the core and spirit of the Harvard school's understanding of competition which is the freedom and the honest conditions to start an operation at any time to the benefit of the market signaled in its approach to the size of the corporations is less available in a global world where the core of the Chicago school is seen as more appealing to the benefit of the consumers but in fact the benefit of the consumers should not be estimated based purely on the fact of a less price of the goods but elements such as quality of the goods and a better environment should be taken into account and so balance the calculation of the benefit of the consumers which might be served better by many corporations in the market rather than by a few big players. G.I. Zekos considers that competition points out many enterprises (many players of various magnitudes) under free and honest conditions to be able to enter the market and antagonize for the best outcome in terms of both quantity and quality rations. In the cost of the product should be assessed by not only the costs directly applicable to the manufacture of the product but also the costs that indirectly and unappreciable at the moment affect the consumers owing to the production of the less costly product such as environment damage, climate change, the time of utilization of the low-priced product, or health problems not harshly presently touching the consumers and straightforward connected with the product but indirectly in the long run touch him as a result of unnatural substances contained in a great number of commodities (cheap stuff consumed by the majority of people) and their influence upon the humans either have not been tested effectively or their effect is not possible to be discovered in short time. Low-priced products of certain quality should be the outcome of competition which has not been achieved by global competition at the moment.

Anti-takeover provisions have a material effect on the prospect of a hostile takeover of a business.[6] For the reason that anti-takeover statutes were accepted by different countries at different times, they trigger a natural experiment on their issue of real interest whether the presence or absence of a takeover threat alters company conduct.[7] The threat of a takeover acts as a beneficial disciplining device that induces

[5]Herbert Hovenkamp, *Post-Chicago Antitrust: A Review and Critique*, 2001 Colum. Bus. L. Rev. 257, 269 ("Chicago School antitrust writers developed well-reasoned arguments that in the long run markets tend to correct their own imperfections. .. and that tribunals would be well advised to study practices much more thoroughly before deciding that intervention is appropriate.").

[6]*Emiliano Catan and Marcel Kahan,* The Law and Finance of Anti-Takeover Statutes, Law & Economics Research Paper Series Working Paper No. 14–30 October 2014.

[7]Julian Atanassov, Do Hostile Takeovers Stifle Innovation? Evidence from Antitakeover Legislation and Corporate Patenting, 68 Journal of Finance 1097 (2013). Todd A. Gormley & David A. Matsa, Playing it Safe? Managerial Preferences, Risk, and Agency Conflicts (2014) http://irrcinstitute.org/pdf/Playing-It-Safe_June-12-2014.pdf

managers to act in the interest of shareholders.[8] Likewise, takeover threats advance efficient management and so the threat of a takeover stimulates a disproportionate short-term focus by management and in that way lowers long-term shareholder value. It could be said that the takeover threat leads management to take actions that benefit shareholders, but harm other constituents and so not improving overall social value.[9]

It could be said that a merger is basically a plain transaction including a sale or exchange. In *Northern Securities*[10] decision, in 1904, the Supreme Court held that the exchange violated the Sherman Act because the merger would eliminate competition between the railroads. Four judges dissented because *they* thought that *property rights* should be protected and that the merger should be permitted. Owners should have the right to sell or exchange their property. The four dissenters insisted that the antitrust law violated the constitutional protection of private property from government taking away.

Furthermore, the property logic that has shaped vertical restraints doctrine for the past 40 years awards various statuses to price restraints and non-price restraints, granting more moderate treatment to most non-price restraints providing the actual foundation for the dominant approach to vertical restraints. Until 1963, the Supreme Court treated competition as a unitary process and restraints as an undifferentiated notion. It was in the *White Motor Company*[11] case that the Supreme Court first held that manufacturers' non-price restraints on dealers would be treated more moderately than price restraints. The Court's differentiation between price and non-price restraints was the product of a change from viewing competition as a unitary process to seeing it as a bi-level process. White Motor developed a marketing strategy to compete on product quality and service encouraging its dealers to join it in non-price competition against the Big Three (General Motors, Ford, and Chrysler) by investing in brand development—better service and more inventory. White eliminated dealer competition, classically price competition, by limiting their geographic and customer markets. Besides, a vertical restraint between levels, one imposed by a manufacturer on its dealers below, was seen as potentially enhancing competition. It was the property logic of ownership of a brand and the images and ideas contained in it that led the Court to adopt this bi-level view of competition.

After *White Motor*, antitrust courts handled competition among dealers, characteristically price competition, as less critical than competition among manufacturers, often non-price competition. At the bottom was the determination that manufacturers

[8] *Edgar v. Mite Corp.*, 457 U.S. 624, 643 (1982) (arguing that "[t]he effects of [inhibiting takeovers] are substantial.. .. The reallocation of economic resources to their highest valued use, a process which can improve efficiency and competition, is hindered. The incentive the tender offer mechanism provides incumbent management to perform well so that stock prices remain high is reduced").

[9] Michael Klausner, *Fact and Fiction in Corporate Law and Governance*, 35 Stan L. Rev. 1325, 1368 (2013)

[10] Northern Securities Trust, 193 U.S. 197 (1904).

[11] White Motor Co., 372 U.S. 253 (1963); *compare* Dr. Miles Medical Co., 220 U.S. 373 (1910).

should be permitted to control the delivery and resale of their branded goods, even if they retained no ownership in the goods themselves.

In addition, in the *National Society of Professional Engineers v. United States* ("*NSPE*"), a trade group of engineers had accepted an ethics policy barring competitive bidding on the grounds that price competition would lower quality to undesirable levels. The Supreme Court[12] rejected this as a rationalization in a rule of reason inquiry, explaining "the inquiry is confined to a consideration of impact on competitive conditions." Anticompetitive conduct cannot be salvaged from antitrust disapproval even if it were to have an ameliorative influence in another non-competition magnitude. Thus, antitrust has no concern for marketplace behavior that does not pose a threat to competition, irrespective of its effect on consumer privacy.[13] The enduring aversion of antitrust to price regulation indicates that a legal monopolist is free to charge whatever price the market will bear.[14] Furthermore, the Supreme Court was clear in *NSPE* that the Sherman Act's competition prescription is proposed not just to produce lower prices, but also to positively influence quality.[15] Characteristically, in *FTC v. Actavis, Inc*,[16] Justice Breyer rejected both the scope-of-the-patent test and the presumptive illegality approach, and stated that courts should review reverse payment settlements under the rule of reason. It could be said that courts utilize a structured version of the rule of reason.[17] Moreover, in its June 2013 decision in *Actavis*,[18] the US Supreme Court states that reverse payment settlements "can sometimes violate the antitrust laws" and as a result have to be judged under the rule-of-reason analysis. According to the US Supreme Court,[19] district courts should look at the size of the payment, "its scale in relation to the payer's anticipated future litigation costs, its independence from other services for which it might represent payment, and the lack of any other convincing justification." It could be argued that inexplicable large reverse payment could imply an anticompetitive motive and so there is an upsurge in ambiguity for parties envisaging reverse-payment settlements. As courts will make a great effort to equalize the pro-competitive justifications of these reverse payment settlements against any

---

[12] 435 U.S. 679 (1978)

[13] Associated Press v. United States, 326 U.S. 1, 19–20 (1945) (suggesting that antitrust should consider how competition in media markets affects diversity of viewpoints).

[14] Verizon Commc'ns Inc. v. Law Offices of Curtis V. Trinko, LLP, 540 U.S. 398, 407 (2004) ("The mere possession of monopoly power, and the concomitant charging of monopoly prices, is not only not unlawful; it is an important element of the free-market system.").

[15] Nat'l Soc'y of Prof'l Eng'rs v. United States, 435 U.S. 679, 695 (1978).

[16] *FTC v. Actavis, Inc.* No. 12–416, 570 U.S. __ (U.S. June 17, 2013). FTC v. Watson Pharms., Inc., No. 12–416 (U.S. Jan. 29, 2013).

[17] Polygram Holding, Inc. v. FTC, 416 F.3d 29, 33–38 (D.C. Cir. 2005). Schering-Plough Corp. v. FTC, 402 F.3d 1056, 1065 (11th Cir. 2005) (stating that "[o]nce the plaintiff meets the burden of producing sufficient evidence of market power, the burden then shifts to the defendant to show that the challenged conduct promotes a sufficiently pro-competitive objective").

[18] *Federal Trade Commission v. Actavis, Inc* 133 S. Ct. 2223 (2013).

[19] Ibid at 2237.

anticompetitive consequences, parties will be confronted with higher litigation costs. *Actavis* decision indicates that patent holders will no longer be able to rely simply on "scope of the patent" arguments to defend reverse-payments settlements from the antitrust analysis. Accordingly, corporations need to assess very thoroughly the pro-competitive rationalization supporting the terms of their settlement.

It is worth noting that the EU does not have a regulation comparable to the Hatch Waxman Act that presents a single framework for resolving patent disputes between originators and generics. To that extent in the EU, entry by a generic competitor has significant adverse consequences on the business of an originator because a generic entry generates automatic price reductions and demands for pharmacies to hand out generic products. Additionally, any price decrease in one state initiates follow-on price decreases in other states. In June 2013, the Commission issued its first decision on reverse-payment settlements, stated that reverse-payment agreements regarding Lundbeck's drug "citalopram" were illegal, and imposing a €93.8 million fine on Lundbeck and a total fine of €52.2 million on four generic pharmaceutical firms.[20] To that extent, the Commission determined that these agreements infringed Article 101 of TFEU reflecting pay-offs exclusively intended to circumvent competition from generic drugs at a time when generic entry was probable. It could be argued that competition authorities in both jurisdictions argue that patent settlement agreements delaying market entry by the generics manufacturer engrossing a payment from the innovator to the generic as reimbursement for the delay. Clancy et al.[21] argue that "In *Actavis* the Supreme Court made a choice in favor of a rule of reason analysis, thus confirming that reverse-payment patent settlements cannot be considered as *per se* illegal. The Commission, in its first decision involving this type of agreements decided to consider the settlement in question as anti-competitive "by object", hence exempting the Commission from an analysis of its effects." It seems that the category of "by object" restrictions embraces sorts of agreements which disclose "a sufficient degree of harm to competition".[22]

The foreign corporations that colonized the reaches of the British Empire were plainly granted monopoly rights in their charters—exclusive trading privileges in specified regions—and the American colonists tended to connect the corporation

[20]Commission sends Statement of Objections to Lundbeck and others for preventing market entry of generic antidepressant medicine, 25 July 2012, available at http://europa.eu/rapid/press-release_IP-12-834_en.htm?locale=en Commission fines Lundbeck and other pharma companies for delaying market entry of generic medicines, 19 June 2013, available at: http://europa.eu/rapid/press-release_IP-13-563_en.htm?locale=en European Commission, Draft Communication, Guidelines on the application of Article 101 of the Treaty on the Functioning of the European Union to technology transfer agreements, 20 February 2013, http://ec.europa.eu/competition/consultations/2013_technology_transfer/guidelines_en.pdf, § 223

[21]Michael Clancy, Damien Geradin & Andrew Lazerow, Reverse-payment patent settlements in the pharmaceutical industry: An analysis of US antitrust law and EU competition law, www.ssrn.com p17.

[22]Groupement des cartes bancaires (CB) v. European Commission, C-67/13 P, EU:C:2014:2204, para. 49–53.

with plain monopoly.[23] Monopoly was associated almost exclusively with the business corporation.[24] In 1791, Congress chartered the Bank of the United States with a capitalization of $ten million, five times more than the whole capitalization of the three existing state banks designing the Bank as a private commercial company "under a private not public direction—under the guidance of individual interest, not of public publicly."[25] Hence, in *McCulloch v. Maryland*,[26] the Hamiltonian-Federalist vision prevailed and it has become apparent that "Congress . . . may create corporations as appropriate means of executing the powers of government, as, for instance, a bank for the purpose of carrying on the fiscal operations of the United States, or a railroad corporation for the purpose of promoting commerce among the states."[27] Jackson[28] backed state general incorporation statutes on the ground that they were a required remedy to the corrupting effect of the special charter system that favored established and powerful commercial incumbents at the expense of new-comers reducing the privilege of incorporation and opening it to the many. Moreover, Jackson's administration evidenced an ideological move from the mercantilism of the Federalist era to the classicism and a prominence on equality of access to incorporation privileges granted by the state. States competing to turn into incorporation havens finally approved measures allowing businesses to own stock of other

[23]William Letwin, Law And Economic Policy In America: The Evolution Of The Sherman Antitrust Act 62–63 (1965), I Phillip E. Areeda and Herbert Hovenkamp, Antitrust Law 59 (2d ed. 2000) ("Taking the legislative history of the antitrust laws as a whole, we would give it relatively little weight on the fundamental question whether economic efficiency, injury to competitors, or some alternative 'populist' goal should guide antitrust policy.");

[24]Trustees of Dartmouth College v. Woodward, 17 U.S. (4 Wheat.) 519 (1819). Simeon E. Baldwin, Introduction To Two Centuries Growth Of American Law: Private Corporations, 275, 296 (1901). Dotan Oliar, *Making Sense of the Intellectual Property Clause: Promotion of Progress as a Limitation on Congress's Intellectual Property Power*, 94 Geo. L.J. 1771, 1800–1801 (2006) ("An anti-monopolistic sentiment was present during the Convention's debates, which seems to be the reason why the Framers rejected other proposals by Madison and Pinckney for a federal incorporation power."); Centinel, 1 The Debate On The Constitution: Federalist And Antifederalist Speeches, Articles, And Letters During The Struggle Over Ratification 89 (Bernard Bailyn ed. 1993) (complaining that proposed Constitution failed to specify that "monopolies in trade or arts other than to authors of books or inventors of useful arts, for a reasonable time, ought not to be suffered"). Letter from Jefferson to Madison (Aug. 28, 1789), in 15 The Papers Of Thomas Jefferson 367–68 (Princeton 1958) (proposing a provision that "Monopolies may be allowed to persons for their own productions in literature and their own inventions in the arts for a term not exceeding _ years but for no longer term and for no other purpose").

[25]John Steel Gordon, Hamilton's Blessing: The Extraordinary Life And Times Of Our National Debt 34 (1997).

[26]McCulloch v. Maryland, 4 Wheat. 316, 411 (1819).

[27]Luxton v. North River Bridge Co., 153 U.S. 525, 529 (1894)

[28]Tony A. Freyer, Producers Versus Capitalists: Constitutional Conflict In Antebellum America 83 (1994). Herbert Hovenkamp, Enterprise And American Law 1836–1937 37 (1991). Hovenkamp notes that "Jackson's outspoken opposition to reincorporation of the Second National Bank was based on his hatred of hard money and the National Bank's dominance over state banks, not on any general hostility toward the corporation as a method of doing business."

companies and granting favorable tax treatment for out-of-state earnings.[29] The lack of a federal incorporation statute and the absence of many federal corporations ended early antitrust control an entirely state-law initiative.[30] Likewise, Dill[31] and other proponents of federal incorporation claimed that the trust problem was generated by the multiplicity of state incorporation law and the lack of a national regulatory force that could control the activities of the gigantic interstate trusts and prevent them from employing monopolistic power. Moreover, Thacher[32] thought that ceding incorporation power to the government would be to "bid farewell to the fundamental theory of the Federal Constitution and to call the wisdom of the [founding] Fathers folly when applied to the conditions of to-day." Anyway, federal incorporation became a generally favored strategy in the political majority.[33] To that extent, Roosevelt[34] considered that "[m]ore and more it is evident that the State, and if necessary the nation, has got to possess the right of supervision and control as regards the great corporations which are its creatures." Justice Brewer held that a "corporation . . . is not endowed with the inalienable rights of a natural person. It is an artificial person, created and existing only for the convenient transaction of business."[35] Congressmen introduced proposals for a federal incorporation statute that would have placed corporate control at the center of federal antitrust policy.[36]

It has to be taken into account that the Sherman Act prohibited not all restraints of trade, but only unreasonable ones.[37] The relationship between securities regulation and antitrust dates back to the nineteenth century but the trust "restraint of trade" problem is a very different one than fraud on investors. Moreover, a market's structure almost consistently dictated the competitive conduct of its participants, and their behavior customarily determined the performance of the market.[38] To that extent, anticompetitive results were assumed to follow consistently from

[29] Ernst Von Halle, Trusts, Or, Industrial Combinations And Coalitions In The United States 94–96 (1896).

[30] Rudolph J.R. Peritz, Competition Policy In America: 1888–1992: History, Rhetoric, Law 10 (1996);

[31] James B. Dill, *National Incorporation Laws for Trusts*, 11 Yale L. J. 273 (1902);

[32] Thomas Thacher, *Federal Control of Corporations*, 14 Yale L. J. 301 (1905);

[33] E. Prentice, The Federal Power Over Carriers And Corporations 155 (1907); Charles W. Bunn, *Federal Incorporation of Railway Companies*, 30 Harv. L. Rev. 589 (1917).

[34] Edmund Morris, Theodore Rex 30 (2001). "It is not limitation upon property rights or freedom of contract to require that when men receive from government the privilege of doing business under corporate form. .. they shall do so upon absolutely truthful representations. .. Great corporations exist only because they are safeguarded by our institutions; and it is therefore our right and duty to see that they work in harmony with these institutions."

[35] Northern Securities Co. v. United States, 193 U.S. 197, 362 (1904) (Brewer, J., concurring).

[36] Herbert Hovenkamp, Antitrust Policy, Federalism, and the Theory of the Firm: A Historical Perspective, 59 Antitrust L. J. 75, 77 (1990).

[37] Standard Oil Co. v. United States, 221 U.S. 1 (1911).

[38] Robert J. Larner and James W. Meehan, Jr., *The Structural School, Its Critics, and its Progeny: An Assessment*, in Economics And Antitrust Policy 179, 180–91 (Robert J. Larner and James W. Meehan, Jr., eds., 1989);

concentrated markets. Even though the ascendant Chicago School attacked structuralism's assumptions in the 1970s, the National Commission for the Review of Antitrust Laws and Procedures advocated amending Section 2 of the Sherman Act to allow the government to look for equitable structural relief to disband constant monopoly power, even absent any showing of wrongdoing by the monopolist.[39] When the framers of the Sherman Act chose a crime-tort model, they distinguished the magnitude of conduct in antitrust analysis and discarded the alternative regulatory prospect that would have focused instead on corporate structure. Also, the Sherman Act of 1890 and the Clayton Act of 1914 are broadly worded allowing the federal courts and antitrust enforcement agencies broad freedom to build up a federal "common law" of antitrust regulation.[40] The courts and enforcement agencies have changed their interpretation of the antitrust laws to correspond to prevailing economic assumptions.

It is worth mentioning here that the Harvard School prohibited innovative forms of competition that could have improved economic effectiveness, while the Chicago School permitted competitors to hold in certain conduct that harmed consumers in many domestic markets. Thomas A. Pyrazino, Jr.,[41] thinks that "The courts and agencies should construe antitrust analysis as a continuum, under which they can vary their degree of inquiry depending upon the likely competitive effects of the particular conduct at issue". To that extent, in *California Dental Assn v. FTC*,[42] the court made it apparent that antitrust analysis should be conducted under a sliding scale, permitting for various levels of scrutiny depending upon the type of restraint at issue. Also, the Supreme Court's recent decision in *Verizon Communications, Inc. v. Trinko*,[43] found that a monopoly telephone company should not be liable for refusing to permit access to its telephone network relying on the view that fact

[39]Report to the President and the Attorney General of the National Commission for the Review of Antitrust Laws and Procedures 151–63 (January 22, 1970).

[40]Section 1 of the Sherman Act prohibits "every contract, combination. .. or conspiracy, in restraint of trade," 15 U.S.C. § 1; Section 2 of the Sherman Act makes it illegal for a firm to "monopolize, or attempt to monopolize" interstate commerce, *id.* § 2; and Section 7 of the Clayton Act prohibits any mergers the effect of which "may be substantially to lessen competition, or to tend to create a monopoly," *id.* § 18. Because of the broad wording of these statutes, "[p]erhaps uniquely, American antitrust law is a creature of judicial, as opposed to legislative, creation." Motion for Leave to File and Brief of Visa U.S.A., Inc. et al. as Amici Curiae Supporting Petitioners on Petition for Writ of Certiorari at 8, Texaco, Inc. v. Dagher, 126 S. Ct. 1276 (2006) (Nos. 04–805 and 04–814).

[41]Thomas A. Piraino, Jr., Reconciling the Harvard and Chicago Schools: A New Antitrust Approach for the twenty-first Century, 2007 *Indiana Law Journal* Vol. 82:345, p347. Thomas A. Piraino, Jr., *A Proposed Antitrust Approach to Collaborations Among Competitors*, 86 Iowa L. Rev. 1137 (2001) Thomas A. Piraino, Jr., *Making Sense of the Rule of Reason: A New Standard for Section 1 of the Sherman Act*, 47 Vand. L. Rev. 1753 (1994); Thomas A. Piraino, Jr., *Reconciling the* Per Se *and Rule of Reason Approaches to Antitrust Analysis*, 64 S. Cal. L. Rev. 685 (1991)

[42]526 U.S. 759 (1999). Charles P. Weller, A "New" Rule of Reason from Justice Brandeis' "Concentric Circles" and Other Changes in Law, 44 Antitrust Bull. 881, 949 (1999).

[43]540 U.S. 398 (2004),

finders are ill-equipped to regulate access to monopolists' facilities but elevated "business freedom" above the interests of "competition and competitive opportunity."[44] Hence, courts and agencies now have to hold in an empirical analysis of actual competitive effects before ruling on the legality of particular competitive conduct.

The number of corporations in the market and their relative sizes determine how efficiently corporations will function in that market. Oligopolists assess their output so that, together, they would be able to accomplish a profit-maximizing price approaching the monopoly level.[45] When markets are concentrated, companies are more expected to engage in anticompetitive conduct. There is a strong relationship between structure and performance.[46]

When Congress enacted the Sherman and Clayton Acts, it was concerned with the increasing economic and political power of trusts and a need to protect individual competitors from the market power wielded by large companies. Harvard scholars were contrary to market concentration, even when it might lower costs and prices, in so doing benefiting consumers. Any conduct by companies with market power is presumed illegal regardless of its effect on consumers. For instance, in *United States v. Aluminum Co. of America*,[47] the court held Alcoa liable for monopolizing the aluminum manufacturing market merely because taking advantage of economies of scale by expanding its manufacturing size to meet increasing demand, Alcoa was able to provide quality products to customers at low prices. Also, the Supreme Court precluded a merger between two banks in the Philadelphia area that together held only thirty per cent of the relevant market regardless that the merger might have enhanced their capacity to make available better services to their Philadelphia customers.[48]

---

[44] John Thorne, *A Categorical Rule Limiting Section 2 of the Sherman Act: Verizon v. Trinko*, 72 U. Chi. L. Rev. 289, 296 (2005), Eleanor M. Fox, *The Trouble with Trinko*, 52 Annual Spring Meeting Of The Antitrust Section Of The American Bar Association: General Session Program Course Materials 1365, 1369–70 (2004).

[45] John E. Lopatka, *Solving the Monopoly Problem: Turner's Try*, 41 Antitrust Bull. 843, 862 (1996). Edward Chamberlain, The Theory Of Monopolistic Competition (1933). Edward S. Mason, Economic Concentration And The Oligopoly Problem (1964). Joe S. Bain, Industrial Organization (2d ed. 1959); Joe S. Bain, Barriers To New Competition: Their Character And Consequences In Manufacturing Industries (1956). Dabbah, Maher M., *The Internationalization of Antitrust Policy*, Cambridge University Press, United Kingdom, First published 2003, p.86–95.

[46] Thomas J. DiLorenzo, *The Origins of Antitrust: An Interest-Group Perspective*, 5 Int'l Rev. L. and Econ. 73, 74–76 (1985) (arguing that the Sherman Act was designed to transfer wealth from big business to small merchants and farmers); Herbert Hovenkamp, *Distributive Justice and the Antitrust Laws*, 51 Geo. Wash. L. Rev. 1, 16–17 (1982) (stating that Congress was concerned with distributing economic and political power more widely); David Millon, *The Sherman Act and the Balance of Power*, 61 S. Cal. L. Rev. 1219, 1287–92 (1988) (viewing the original purpose of the Sherman Act as the protection of democratic institutions from concentrated economic power).

[47] 148 F.2d 416 (2d Cir. 1945).

[48] United States v. Philadelphia Nat'l Bank, 374 U.S. 321, 371 (1963) ("[A] merger the effect of which 'may be substantially to lessen competition' is not saved because, on some ultimate reckoning of social or economic debits and credits, it may be deemed beneficial.").

Under the Harvard School approach, courts do not engage in a complicated analysis of the economic circumstances in the relevant market and so corporations in concentrated industries were successfully deterred from transactions that enlarged concentration levels in the relevant market. Thus, large corporations were precluded from engaging in a competitive manner that could have benefited consumers and would have been totally permissible for corporations with lower market shares. Another way the contact and its impact upon competition was disregarded and purely the size of a company was the factor bringing anticompetitive behavior.

According to Chicago scholars, the antitrust laws were to protect individual competitors against large corporations' exercise of market power. Robert Bork[49] argued that the antitrust laws were designed only to augment the effectiveness of the American economy equating wealth improvement with "consumer welfare," meaning lower costs, reduced prices, and increased output of products and services desired by consumers. In other words, the aim of American antitrust is the utmost of consumer welfare and so any other aims of the antitrust laws, including the protection of small businesses from the power of large companies, were immaterial.[50] Bork replaced the aim[51] of antitrust from "the preservation of competition" to "consumer welfare" but the question to be answered is if the "consumer welfare" produces a monopolistic environment which is out of the scope of any notion of competition in an effective market then consumer welfare at any cost cannot be the goal of antitrust. It has to be taken into consideration that the preservation of competition leads to consumer benefit as long as lets the market to work appropriately in a global sense favoring a global competitive market and not merely the consumers of a specific product or service against the interests of other groups of consumers/people. Exclusively "consumer welfare" cannot be the scope of competition without at the same time to preserve competition. Global dynamics such as environmental protection, freedom of choice, and innovation should be taken into consideration when we investigate the task of antitrust/competition law that of preserving/safeguarding antitrust/competition.

It has to be taken into account that one of the main Chicago School arguments for relaxing antitrust concern with market concentration is that even very large corporations in concentrated markets are forced to act competitively by charging the prices that would be charged in a decentralized market, for the reason that the threat of market entry averts them from charging an extra competitive premium due to the implied role of prospective competitors in regulating the behavior of real market

[49] Robert Bork, Legislative Intent and the Policy of the Sherman Act, 9 J.L. and ECON. 7 (1966).

[50] Frank H. Easterbrook, *Workable Antirust Policy*, 84 Mich. L. Rev. 1696, 1703 (1986) ("However you slice the legislative history, the dominant theme is the protection of consumers from overcharges.").

[51] Barak Orbach, *How Antitrust Lost Its Goal*, 81 Fordham L. Rev. 2253 (2013). Robert H. Lande, *A Traditional and Textualist Analysis of the Goals of Antitrust: Efficiency, Preventing Theft from Consumers, and Consumer Choice*, 81 Fordham L. Rev. 2349, 2360 n. 54 ("[Robert Bork's] deceptive use of the term 'consumer welfare,' instead of the more honest term 'total welfare,' was a brilliant way to market the efficiency objective.")

participants. Likewise, the "contestability criterion"[52] is the basis for the approval of the usefulness of perfect competition.

It is distinctive that Chicago School scholars argued that the Harvard School misapprehended the techniques in which corporations carry on to compete, even when they have fairly few rivals. In reality in concentrated markets, corporations try to find ways of competing with each other. Also, the Chicago School scholars[53] assumed that markets should be given a free rein in order for corporations to be more efficient. Furthermore, the courts should only interfere in the competitive route when it was understandable that anticompetitive conduct was threatening consumer welfare.[54] To that extent, courts have been inspired by the Chicago school view and insisted on proof of explicit anticompetitive effects before finding defendants' conduct illegal notwithstanding the fact that a particular corporation or a group of competitors possessed striking market power and so plaintiffs would have to display, through empirical evidence, that the conduct at question harmed consumers by increasing prices or decreasing output.[55] Consequently, courts become more moderate in allowing corporations to obtain and exercise market power. This approach let the Supreme Court to refuse to presume the illegality of a price-fixing agreement among a group of musical composers and Microsoft was allowed to carry on to force its monopoly in the computer operating system market into related markets for word processing, Internet access, video and audio services, and instant messaging.[56]

Are judges, juries, and government regulators capable of deciding multifaceted economic issues? Even economists disagree about how such multifaceted economic decisions should be made.[57] There is a requirement of substantiating the specific economic effects of competitive conduct on consumers[58] which means that

---

[52]John E. Davies & Frederic S. Lee, A Post Keynesian Appraisal of the Contestability Criterion, 11 J. Post Keynesian Econ. 3, 22 (1988)

[53]Eleanor Fox, *The Battle for the Soul of Antitrust*, 75 Cal. L. Rev. 917, 917 (1987).

[54]Herbert Hovenkamp, *Post-Chicago Antitrust: A Review and Critique*, 2001 Colum. Bus. L. Rev. 257, 269 ("Chicago School antitrust writers developed well-reasoned arguments that in the long run markets tend to correct their own imperfections. .. and that tribunals would be well advised to study practices much more thoroughly before deciding that intervention is appropriate.").

[55]Rothery Storage and Van Co. v. Atlas Van Lines, 792 F.2d 210 (D.C. Cir. 1986) (Bork, J.); Polk Bros. v. Forest City Enters., 776 F.2d 185 (seventh Cir. 1985) (Easterbrook, J.); Valley Liquors, Inc. v. Renfield Importers, Ltd., 678 F.2d 742 (seventh Cir. 1982) (Posner, J.).

[56]Broad. Music, Inc. v. CBS, 441 U.S. 1 (1979) (refusing to apply the per se rule to agreement by musical composers to license their copyrighted compositions at identical prices).

[57]Frank Easterbrook, *Vertical Arrangements and the Rule of Reason,* 53 Antitrust L.J. 135 (1984). at 153 ("If you assembled [twelve] economists and gave them all available data about a business practice, plus an unlimited computer budget, you would not soon (or ever) get unanimous agreement about whether the practice promoted consumers' welfare or economic efficiency more broadly defined."). Lawrence A. Sullivan, Handbook of The Law Of Antitrust § 2, at 10 (1977). "economics does not comprehend enough and law, without extreme transformations in its own structure, cannot adequately deal with all that economics does comprehend."

[58]Arizona v. Maricopa County Med. Soc'y, 457 U.S. 332, 343 (1982) ("Judges often lack the expert understanding of industrial market structures and behavior to determine with any confidence a

corporations are not confident of the types of transactions that might lead to antitrust liability.

As discussed earlier, Section 1 of the Sherman Act prohibits any "conspiracy, in restraint of trade" and federal courts have believed that they must choose between two opposite methods of analyzing restraints of trade under Section 1: a "per se rule" that considers particular conduct unlawful on its face; or a "rule of reason[59]" referring to all possible conditions before determining the legality of a specific limit.[60] According to Herbert Hovenkamp,[61] the conduct is considered per se illegal "because no one has made a plausible argument that the action is competitive, and its anticompetitive potential seems fairly obvious." It could be said that per se standards diminish the time and expense of antitrust cases providing apparent guidance to corporations, and successfully deterred anticompetitive conduct. For instance, a conspiracy between intellectual property owners not to settle an infringement suit could violate Section 1 of the Sherman Act.[62] The courts considered that the litigation efficiencies provided by the per se rule rationalize its sporadic over-breadth.[63] The Court imposes a per se rule of illegality when the conduct is obviously harmful to consumers.[64]The per se rule was applied first in price-fixing

practice's effect on competition."); United States v. Topco Assocs., 405 U.S. 596, 609–12 (1972) ("[C]ourts are of limited utility in examining difficult economic problems.. .. [They are] ill-equipped for such decision making [and cannot] analyze, interpret, and evaluate the myriad of competing interests and the endless data that would surely be brought to bear on such decisions.").

[59]The rule of reason has been viewed as "a euphemism for an endless economic inquiry ending in a defense verdict." Thomas C. Arthur, *A Workable Rule of Reason: A Less Ambitious Antitrust Role for the Federal Courts*, 68 Antitrust L.J. 337, 337 (2000) (quoting Maxwell M. Blecher, *The* Schwinn *Case—An Example of a Genuine Commitment to Antitrust Law*, 44 Antitrust L.J. 550, 553 (1975)). William F. Baxter, *The Viability of Vertical Restraints Doctrine*, 75 Cal. L. Rev. 933, 949 (1987) ("As a practical matter, current case law treats all. .. [nonprice] vertical restraints as lawful per se [under the rule of reason].").

[60]Chicago Bd. of Trade v. United States, 246 U.S. 231, 238 (1918) (listing several factors a court should consider before invoking antitrust sanctions). In *Continental T.V., Inc. v. GTE Sylvania, Inc.*, 433 U.S. 36, 49 (1977). The Supreme Court held that "[u]nder this rule [of reason], the fact finder weighs all the circumstances of a case in deciding whether a restrictive practice should be prohibited as imposing an unreasonable restraint on competition."

[61]Herbert Hovenkamp, Antitrust Policy, Restricted Distribution, and the Market for Exclusionary Rights, 71 Minn. L. Rev. 1293, 1294–95 n.8 (1987).

[62]Primetime 24 Joint Venture v. NBC, Inc., 219 F.3d 92 (2d. Cir. 2000).

[63]*Arizona v. Maricopa County Medical Society*, 457 U.S. 332, 344 (1982), the Supreme Court stated: "As in every rule of general application, the match between the presumed and the actual is imperfect. For the sake of business certainty and litigation efficiency, we have tolerated the invalidation of some agreements that a full-blown inquiry might have proved to be reasonable."

[64]Nat'l Collegiate Athletic Ass'n v. Bd. of Regents of Univ. of Okla., 468 U.S. 85, 103–04 (1984) ("Per se rules are invoked when surrounding circumstances make the likelihood of anticompetitive conduct so great as to render unjustified further examination of the challenged conduct. But whether the ultimate finding is the product of a presumption or actual market analysis, the essential inquiry remains the same-whether or not the challenged restraint enhances competition."); Bus. Elecs. Corp. v. Sharp Elecs. Corp., 485 U.S. 717, 726 (1988) ("[T]here is a presumption in favor of a rule-of-reason standard .... ");

cases.[65] Tying arrangements, horizontal territorial or customer allocations, and group boycotts were occasions where the per se rule was applied.[66] To that extent, in *United States v. Arnold, Schwinn and Co*,[67] the court extended the per se rule to non-price vertical restrictions imposed by a supplier on its distributors. Hence, American corporations would evade conduct that could harm consumers. The per se method was rigid and formalistic prohibiting particular conduct without any consideration of its economic effects and so the rule deterred advantageous, as well as destructive, business practices. For instance, the non-price vertical restraints condemned by the Supreme Court in *Schwinn* possibly advanced competition between retail brands. Application of the per se rule to vertical restraints precludes the reflection of beneficial effects on inter-brand competition, such as improved point-of-sale services.[68] Accordingly, the indiscretion approach of the per se rule by incriminating too many occasions of business conducts as anticompetitive ignoring probable benefits for various economic conducts for consumers and the competition among companies forced the Supreme Court in *Continental T.V., Inc. v. GTE Sylvania Inc.*,[69] to reverse its decision in *Schwinn* and held that non-price vertical restrictions should be judged by the rule of reason. Consequently, there should be a reason for a conduct to be considered as per se anticompetitive. Limited competition among the distributors in the resale of Sylvania televisions ("intrabrand competition"), promoted competition with other brands of television sets ("interbrand competition") by suggesting Sylvania distributors make the investments required to provide more services to customers. It could be argued that a rule of reason, rather than a per se, method was fitting in light of the prospective economic benefits of the location clause imposed by Sylvania. Hence, *Sylvania* established the basis for modern antitrust dependence on empirical economic evidence.

Furthermore, the Supreme Court held in *Broadcast Music, Inc. v. CBS*55 ("*BMI*")[70] that a group of copyright holders did not perform a per se violation of the Sherman Act when they fixed a common price for the licensing of their musical compositions which shows the application of a rule of reason analysis to a price-fixing arrangement. According to the Supreme Court, fact finders have to consider

[65] United States v. Socony-Vacuum Oil Co., 310 U.S. 150 (1940) (horizontal price fixing); United States v. Trenton Potteries Co., 273 U.S. 392 (1927) (horizontal price fixing); Dr. Miles Med. Co. v. John D. Park and Sons Co., 220 U.S. 373 (1911) (resale price fixing).

[66] N. Pac. Ry. v. United States, 356 U.S. 1 (1958). United States v. Topco Assocs., 405 U.S. 596 (1972); at 609 n.10 ("Without the per se rules, businessmen would be left with little to aid them in predicting in any particular case what courts will find to be legal and illegal under the Sherman Act."). United States v. Sealy, Inc., 388 U.S. 350 (1967). Klor's, Inc. v. Broadway-Hale Stores, Inc., 359 U.S. 207 (1959).

[67] 388 U.S. 365 (1967), *overruled by* Cont'l T.V., Inc. v. GTE Sylvania, Inc., 433 U.S. 36 (1977).

[68] Richard A. Posner, Antitrust Policy and the Supreme Court: An Analysis of the Restricted Distribution, Horizontal Merger and Potential Competition Decisions, 75 Colum. L. Rev. 282, 297 (1975)

[69] 433 U.S. 36 (1977).

[70] 441 U.S. 1 (1979).

whether a restraint always tends to hamper competition and decrease output but the common license legalized the copyright holders to market their compositions more effectively and as a result should be analyzed under the rule of reason. Likewise, the Supreme Court extended the rule of reason to other horizontal agreements with probable effectiveness justifications.[71] The Chicago School has been unable to build an articulation of the rule of reason authorizing operative decision-making. Even courts have not progressed beyond a prerequisite that the trier of fact consider all the conditions adjoining a restraint before condemning it and there is not suggestion of priority[72] or weight to be accorded each factor which brings us back to deficiencies of the vague per se rule. Uncertain standards lead to both under-deterrence and over-deterrence and so not only will companies misjudge and risk anticompetitive conduct that they believe to be lawful but they may also evade pro-competitive behavior under the mistaken assumption that it can be attacked effectively.

Mergers and joint ventures are evaluated under Section 7 of the Clayton Act outlawing any transactions that may "substantially lessen competition or tend to create a monopoly."[73] To that extent, Robert H. Lande[74] says that "Section 7 of the Clayton Act should be interpreted more strictly: Section 7 should block mergers that "may" substantially lessen competition, not just mergers that are "likely" to substantially lessen competition, or mergers that "will" substantially lessen competition. Section 7 also should block mergers that may "tend to create a monopoly" even if these mergers are efficient." The parties to the joint venture preserve their independent existence and carry on to compete with each other outside the scope of the venture and so joint ventures may be assessed under the "restraint of trade" provisions of Section 1 of the Sherman Act. It is characteristic that fewer competitors in a market stipulate an easier way of coordinating their pricing without committing detectable violations of Section 1 of the Sherman Act.[75]

As mentioned earlier, until the mid-1970s, courts presume the illegality of any mergers or joint ventures among corporations that held substantial shares of the

[71] FTC v. Ind. Fed'n of Dentists, 476 U.S. 447 (1986) (using the rule of reason to analyze refusal by an association of dentists to supply patient x-rays to insurance companies seeking to evaluate benefit claims); NCAA v. Bd. of Regents, 468 U.S. 85 (1984) (using the rule of reason to analyze the NCAA's limitations on the number of times its member college sports teams could appear on television). Rothery Storage and Van Co. v. Atlas Van Lines, 792 F.2d 210 (D.C. Cir. 1986) (allowing requirement that van lines not deal with other moving companies); Nat'l Bancard Corp. v. VISA U.S.A., Inc., 779 F.2d 592 (11th Cir. 1986) (upholding interchange fee among members of Visa credit card system); Polk Bros. v. Forest City Enters., 776 F.2d 185 (seventh Cir. 1985) (upholding non-competition covenant).

[72] Frank H. Easterbrook, *The Limits of Antitrust*, 63 Tex. L. Rev. 1, 12–13 (1984) ("When everything is relevant, nothing is dispositive. Any one factor might or might not outweigh another, or all of the others, in the fact finder's contemplation. The formulation offers no help to businesses planning their conduct.").

[73] 15 U.S.C. § 18 (2002).

[74] Robert H. Lande, Textualism As An Ally Of Antitrust Enforcement: Examples From Merger And Monopolization Law, 2023 NO. 4 Utah Law Review 813 P 835

[75] Hosp. Corp. of Am. v. Fed. Trade Comm'n, 807 F.2d 1381, 1387 (seventh Cir. 1986).

relevant market. According to the Harvard School approach, mergers and joint ventures which significantly increased concentration levels in the related market made it easier for the remaining businesses to hold in anticompetitive conduct. Also, the Harvard school view illustrates a prima facie illegality for mergers in which the parties had a cumulative share of thirteen to fourteen percent of the relevant market.[76] Mergers considered limiting competition by charging higher prices, lowering output, reducing product quality, or slowing innovation without in fact looking at the actual situation or the benefits to competition itself from the merger.[77] Of course, if a merger holds a major share of the market (60–70%), it is obvious that competition itself has no real meaning. The Supreme Court held that "market definition generally determined the result of the case."[78] The Department of Justice and FTC established a formula called the Herfindahl–Hirschman Index (HHI) to evaluate the particular market share concentration levels at which mergers should be presumed illegal. Under the Harvard School view, the courts applied the market share hypothesis of illegality regardless of whether the transaction at issue had the prospective to lower costs or prices or otherwise benefit consumers. To that extent, in *Brown Shoe Co. v. United States*,[79] the Court conceded that the merger would permit the integrated companies to "market their own brands at prices below those of competing independent retailers" and so it was more valuable to endorse Congress's objective of protecting small business against prospective abuses of power by larger corporations without looking at the real facts of the case and regardless of any gains for the consumers.

By the mid-1970s, Chicago School scholars criticized the federal courts' market share presumption of illegality for mergers and joint ventures precluding many efficiency-enhancing transactions. There is no foundation for mechanical judicial intervention against a merger where the combined market share is less than fifty percent. In *United States v. General Dynamics Corp.*,[80] the Court, in a departure

---

[76] Phillip Areeda and Donald F. Turner, Antitrust Law ¶ 915, at 83 (1980).

[77] *United States v. Mercy Health Services*, 902 F. Supp. 968, 975 (N.D. Iowa 1995), *vacated as moot*, 107 F.3d 632 (eighth Cir. 1997), stating that "courts have focused on whether the merger will cause the merged entity to have enough market power such that it could profitably increase prices." *Hospital Corp. of America v. FTC*, 807 F.2d 1381, 1386 (seventh Cir. 1986), stating that "the worry is that [the merger] may enable the acquiring firm to cooperate (or cooperate better) with other leading competitors on reducing or limiting output, thereby pushing up the market price."

[78] Eastman Kodak Co. v. Image Technical Servs., 504 U.S. 451, 469 n.15 (1992). United States v. Philadelphia Nat'l Bank, 374 U.S. 321, 363 (1963) (establishing the principle that the illegality of a merger can be presumed from a substantial market share concentration level); Brown Shoe Co. v. United States, 370 U.S. 294, 335 (1962) ("[T]he proper definition of the market is a 'necessary predicate' to an examination of the competition that may be affected by the. .. merger.").

[79] 370 U.S. 294 (1962). "[W]e cannot fail to recognize Congress'[s] desire to promote competition through the protection of viable, small, locally owned businesses. Congress appreciated that occasional higher costs and prices might result from the maintenance of fragmented industries and markets." Standard Oil Co. v. United States, 337 U.S. 293, 318–19 (1949) (Douglas, J., dissenting) (showing concern for "growth in bigness").

[80] 415 U.S. 486 (1974).

from its earlier antitrust jurisprudence, held that a merger could not be deemed illegal purely because the defendants held high market shares considering circumstances that might influence the future market shares of the merging parties. Market share concentration data casts only the initial position for analyzing the competitive impact of a merger judging other market factors relating to the actual competitive effects, as well as entry, efficiencies, and failure. As well, in *United States v. Baker Hughes Inc.*,[81] the court held that indication of market concentration only offers a handy starting point for a broader analysis of future competitiveness. It is worth noting that while market concentration can be the result of a corporation's superior performance by innovation and investment, it leads to negative outcomes when competition is side-stepped by incumbents via anticompetitive strategies encompassing lobbying, buying competitors, predatory pricing, etc.

It could be said that the Chicago School view regarding economic efficiencies as a mitigating factor in merger cases is not a panacea in spite of the fact that mergers may achieve economies of scale, synergies, or cost savings that will enable the parties to offer lower prices to consumers because in fact competition among corporations might not exist. Under the Harvard School approach, the courts precluded conduct by corporations that were only attempting to gain or preserve a monopoly position in the relevant market. Nonetheless, the courts following the approach of the Chicago School recognized that corporations should not be punished purely for obtaining monopoly power. Enterprises often obtain power because they are the most successful in delivering the products and services desired by consumers and so courts do not find monopolists liable under the Sherman Act unless they had engaged in some type of offensive competitive conduct. Farrell, Katz, & Martin[82] argue that in search of boosting consumer welfare is the best way to amplify total welfare in practice.

It has to be taken into account that Section 2 of the Sherman Act bars monopolization, or attempts to monopolize, by individual businesses. Poor economic performance is predictable in monopoly markets and, until the late 1960s, courts became willing to find monopolists liable, even if they had not engaged in any exclusionary conduct. According to the Harvard school view, monopolies should be

[81] 908 F.2d 981 (D.C. Cir. 1990). United States v. Int'l Harvester Co., 564 F.2d 769, 773–75 (seventh Cir. 1977) (allowing merger between International Harvester and tractor manufacturer on grounds that manufacturer would not have sufficient financial resources to compete effectively in future); *In re* Boeing Co., [1997–2001 FTC Complaints and Orders Transfer Binder] Trade Reg. Rep. (CCH) ¶ 24,295, at 24,123–24 (July 1, 1997) (allowing merger of Boeing and McDonnell Douglas on grounds that, due to its financial distress, McDonnell Douglas would "no longer constitute a meaningful competitive force" in the relevant market). *See also* FTC v. Univ. Health, Inc., 938 F.2d 1206, 1221 (11th Cir. 1991) ("[W]e view *General Dynamics* as standing for the unremarkable proposition that a defendant may rebut the government's prima facie case by showing that the government's market share statistics overstate the acquired firm's ability to compete in the future. .. .").

[82] Martin, S. (2007), "The Goals of Antitrust and Competition Policy", Purdue CIBER Working Papers, July 2007. Farrell, J. and M.L. Katz (2006), "The Economics of Welfare Standards in Antitrust," 2:2 Competition Policy International.

dismembered, even if they had not engaged in specific anticompetitive conduct[83] based on an ideal view of competition with the meaning that many corporations should function in the market because the dominance of monopolists does not let other parties to get into the market even if the monopolists offer lower prices, competition among many corporations does not occur. The possession of monopoly power was enough for the courts to preclude any conduct having the purpose or effect of protecting or increasing that power.[84] A monopolist cannot hold monopoly power with no some volitional act that may reasonably be characterized as an exercise of its power. In other words, monopolists safeguard in many ways their monopoly. The Harvard School theory signposts a division between unilateral "competition on the merits" resulting in monopoly and the supposed use of such market power to exclude rivals. A monopolist corporation utilizing its power to gain an exclusionary agreement in this manner violates § 2 of the Sherman Act, without any need for the agreement to generate economic damage. Courts enforcing § 1 of the Act banned all tying agreements acquired by corporations with the least market power because sellers used their power to "force" buyers to enter such contracts. It could be argued that not only the "use" of monopoly power to impose exclusionary agreements but also "forcing" is illegal per se, without any further confirmation of damage.

The Supreme Court[85] acknowledged the preference for economic coordination as centralized ownership and control by defining a "single entity"[86] for antitrust purposes in precisely those terms and so extending the antitrust privilege of company status beyond the company boundaries which means that the Court considered that coordination between a parent and a subsidiary is insufficient as a matter of law to meet the concerted action requirement of Section 1, for the reason that for antitrust reasons, it implicates one player, a single enterprise, rather than two. Thus, the conduct of a single company is governed by § 2 alone and is unlawful only when it threatens actual monopolization. To that extent, concentrated control and ownership rights are the criteria qualifying an economic arrangement for protection from antitrust liability under the single-entity doctrine and so courts extended single-entity immunity to affiliated enterprises whose relationship was less integrated than

[83]Phillip Areeda and Donald F. Turner, Antitrust Law ¶ 620c, at 45–47 (1978).

[84]Thomas A. Piraino, Jr., *Identifying Monopolists' Illegal Conduct Under the Sherman Act,* 75 N. Y.U. L. Rev. 809, 829 (2000) "It was sufficient that a defendant evidenced a general intent to obtain or maintain its monopoly power, [that is], that it chose to do the acts that led to the establishment or perpetuation of its monopoly." In the 1945 case *United States v. Aluminum Co. of America* ("Alcoa"), Judge Hand found that Alcoa illegally used its monopoly power simply by expanding its aluminum production capacity to meet increasing consumer demand. 148 F.2d 416, 431 (2d Cir. 1945); United States v. Griffith, 344 U.S. 100 (1947) (finding Section 2 violation when motion picture distributors pooled their buying power to obtain lower rates in their royalty agreements with motion picture producers).

[85]Copperweld Corporation v. Independence Tubing Corporation 467 U.S. 752

[86]Freeman v. San Diego Ass'n of Realtors, 322 F.3d 1133, 1148 (9thCir. 2003)(citing "substantial common ownership, a fiduciary obligation to act for another entity's economic benefit or an agreement to divide profits and losses" as key factors for economic unity).

that of a wholly owned subsidiary. Besides, American Needle[87] noted that it had "repeatedly found instances in which members of a legally single entity violated§ 1 when the entity was controlled by a group of competitors and served, in essence, as a vehicle for ongoing concerted activity." Hence, when there are definite or possibly separate business interests, as in American Needle, then there are multiple entities capable of conspiring for antitrust rationales.[88] The question for antitrust reasons is whether allocating coordination rights to a company would deprive the marketplace of independent centers of decision-making.

According to the workable competition model, antitrust law should not interdict the employment of monopoly or market power attained via legitimate competition to compel high prices, other than forbidding the utilization of such power to exclude rivals. Moreover, according to *Alan J. Meese*,[89] "the "market power" model is a manifestation of neoclassical price theory and its workable competition model, economic frameworks that dominated industrial organization for much of the twentieth century." Also, Chicago School & Harvard School theorists coincide in the view that corporations employed market power to impose exclusionary agreements and in fact offered a more precise account of what such imposition compelled. It could be argued that price theory, and not Legal Realism, is the basis of the market power model of contract formation and derived antitrust doctrines. On the other hand, recognition that voluntary exclusionary rights agreements engender anticompetitive damage challenges the Chicago School embracing that the possession of preexisting market power is an essential condition for antitrust liability under § 1 of the Sherman Act. In addition, courts rely upon a "market power" account of exclusionary contracts when condemning a monopolist for, say, "willful maintenance" of its power.[90] The Antitrust Division of the Department of Justice[91] alleges that a defendant "abused its monopoly power . . . through its exclusionary contracts" and that "[e]ach exclusionary contract" entailed willful exploitation of that power.

It is worth noting that Chicago School scholars think that monopolists should not be liable purely for engaging in conduct that is a natural end result of their market power assuming that corporations customarily acquire monopoly power because of their capacity to provide consumers with superior products at low prices. Also, Chicago school scholars think that punishing monopolists purely for exercising their market power would discourage corporations from competing forcefully to

[87] Am. Needle, Inc. v. Nat'l Football League, 560 U.S. 183, 191–92 (2015) (citing decisions involving incorporated business entities that were nevertheless subject to Section 1); at 200 (noting that the corporate form can be a "formalistic shell" masking "concerted action").

[88] Herbert J. Hovenkamp & Christopher R. Leslie, The Firm as Cartel Manager, 64 VAND.L.REV. 813, 855 (2013)

[89] *Alan J. Meese*, The Market Power Model Of Contract Formation: How Outmoded Economic Theory Still Distorts Antitrust Doctrine 2013 Notre Dame Law Review 1291. p1296.

[90] *Grinnell Corp.*, 384 U.S. at 570–71, Conwood Co. v. U.S. Tobacco Co., 290 F.3d 768, 782 (sixth Cir. 2002) (condemning "willful acquisition, maintenance or use of [monopoly] power by anti-competitive or exclusionary means").

[91] United States v. United Reg'l Health Care Sys., No. 7:11-cv-00030 (N.D. Tex. Feb. 25, 2011).

meet consumers' needs. To that extent, Posner thinks that it should not be illegal for monopolists to refuse to deal with their actual or potential rivals.[92] It is characteristic that under § 2 of the Sherman Act, there is a perception that some means of competition are permissible. In the case of *United States v. Grinnell Corp*,[93] Grinnell, a manufacturer of central station alarm services, had acquired many of its major competitors and had engaged in a series of geographic and product market allocation agreements and the Supreme Court held a Section 2 violation from such conduct. Also, the Court[94] held that Section 2 should only prohibit "the willful acquisition or maintenance of . . .[monopoly] power as distinguished from growth or development as a consequence of a superior product, business acumen, or historical accident." To that extent, it could be said that dominant corporations are tolerated to take part in "competition on the merits," but they have to withhold from another kind of competition, which is apparently not on the basis of merits. In fact, in monopoly cases, courts have failed to supply efficient guidelines for business conduct and it is not distinguishing between monopolists' proper and illegal conduct.[95] There is a need to establish some undesirable conduct *in addition to* possession of a monopoly.[96] Moreover, it is argued that anticompetitive harm refers to the competitive process concentrating on consumers welfare and not competitors.[97]

---

[92] Richard A. Posner, Antitrust Law at 242–44 (2d ed. 2001) (arguing that unconditioned refusals to deal by dominant firms should never be violations of Section 2 of the Sherman Act).

[93] 384 U.S. 563 (1966).

[94] *Id.* at 570–71.

[95] Eastman Kodak Co. v. Image Technical Servs., Inc., 504 U.S. 451 (1992) (illegality of Kodak's refusal to deal with independent service organizations that serviced its photocopiers); Aspen Skiing Co. v. Aspen Highlands Skiing Corp., 472 U.S. 585 (1985) (illegality of skiing resort's refusal to continue to cooperate with rival skiing resort in providing "multi-mountain" skiing ticket). Verizon Commc'ns., Inc. v. Trinko, 540 U.S. 398 (2004) (holding that monopoly telephone company had the right to refuse to give full access to its network to rivals).

[96] Eastman Kodak v. Image Technical Servs., Inc., 504 U.S. 451 (1992); Aspen Skiing Co. v. Aspen Highlands Skiing Corp., 472 U.S. 585 (1985); United States v. Grinnell Corp., 384 U.S. 563 (1966); Novell, Inc. v. Microsoft Corp., 505 F.3d 302, 316–17 (fourth Cir. 2007) (holding that allegation that "Microsoft's use of its monopoly power in the operating-system market to foreclose the distribution channels for [plaintiff's] applications" established antitrust standing); *id.* at 316 (recounting allegation that "Microsoft exploited its monopoly power to require or encourage OEMs to refrain from installing [plaintiff's] products on their computers"); *id.* at 309 (recounting allegation that Microsoft used "leverage" to "impose restrictive and exclusionary agreements"); United States v. Microsoft Corp., 253 F.3d 34, 64 (D.C. Cir. 2001) (finding that contractual restrictions on original equipment manufacturers were a "use[] of Microsoft's market power to protect its monopoly");

[97] United States v. Microsoft Corp., 253 F.3d 34, 58 (D.C. Cir. 2001) ("[T]o be condemned as exclusionary, a monopolist's act must have an 'anticompetitive effect.' That is, it must harm the competitive process and thereby harm consumers. In contrast, harm to one or more competitors will not suffice."). Brunswick Corp. v. Pueblo Bowl-O-Mat, Inc., 429 U.S. 477, 488 (1977). Brown Shoe Co. v. United States, 370 U.S. 294, 320 (1962)) ("The antitrust laws, however, were enacted for 'the protection of competition not competitors.'").

It is worth noting that under an exclusive dealing arrangement, a corporation compels a customer or supplier to deal only with it and not to deal with its competitors and regardless of the anticompetitive effects of monopolists' exclusive dealing arrangements, the courts allowed a permissive approach to such conduct.[98] An exclusive dealing arrangement constitutes a predominantly effective means of excluding its competitors from the relevant market. It is obvious that buyers or sellers are frozen out of a market by exclusive deals. Buyers will not take on exclusive deals that preclude competition since by construction, such contracts will lower the entire surplus accessible to buyers. Industry profit under monopoly is superior under competition and downstream companies sign exclusive contracts to limit competition by preventing efficient entry raising the joint profit of the present and downstream competitors, and so the "surplus" that is offered to the companies for signing contracts.[99] When downstream competition is limited, gains under monopoly are limited by double marginalization so that downstream companies do better not signing contracts and buying from a competitive upstream market. The demand of a single downstream company is enough to cover the entrant's fixed costs since final consumers will switch to the cheaper downstream company and intense downstream competition eradicates the incumbent's capacity to keep out even if it offers discriminatory or sequential contracts. Monopolists prevent actual or potential competitors from accessing the resources required to compete in the monopolized market or in a related market to which it is attempting to extend its monopoly power. It is characteristic that when less than thirty to forty percent of the suppliers or customers in an individual market have been subject to an exclusive dealing arrangement, the courts have been hesitant to find an antitrust violation which means in fact alteration of the meaning of competition.[100] Monopolists escape liability for an exclusive dealing arrangement merely by demonstrating that they did not exclude a rival from a substantial percentage of accessible suppliers or customers.

Even though tying and exclusive dealing arrangements have analogous competitive effects, the federal courts have applied a per se approach to tying arrangements and monopolists frequently have been found to hold in illegal tying arrangements

[98] Jefferson Parish Hosp. Dist. No. 2 v. Hyde, 466 U.S. 2, 45 (1984) (O'Connor, J., concurring) ("Exclusive dealing is an unreasonable restraint of trade only when a significant fraction of buyers or sellers are frozen out of a market by the exclusive deal.").

[99] Fumagalli, C., Motta, M., 2006. Exclusive dealing and entry, when buyers compete. American Economic Review 96, 785–795.

[100] United States v. Microsoft Corp., No. Civ. A. 98–1232, 1998 WL 614485, at *19 (D.D.C. Sept. 14, 1998) (response to motion for summary judgment) (describing forty percent threshold of illegality for exclusive dealing arrangements); Gonzales v. Insignares, No. C84-1261A, 1985 WL 2206, at *2 (N.D. Ga. June 27, 1985) (granting summary judgment for defendant when only forty percent of consumers were affected by exclusive arrangement).

merely because of their power in the market for the tying product.[101] Exclusive deals can be detrimental.[102]

The Harvard School's view of illegality discourages beneficial competitive conduct and makes no economic sense for the courts to suppose the illegality of certain agreements among competitors that are designed to improve their effectiveness, in this manner, benefiting consumers. In merger and joint venture cases brought under Section 7 of the Clayton Act, the Harvard School was preoccupied with the parties' market influence, and it caused courts to neglect the prospective efficiencies resulting from the integration of rivals' resources. In monopoly cases under Section 2 of the Sherman Act, the Harvard School view excluded large businesses from engaging in antagonistic competitive conduct that could have benefited consumers.

When the *rule of reason* succeeded the per se rule as the prevailing method in restraint of trade litigation, antitrust cases became more complicated and their result became more difficult to forecast and so antitrust enforcement under Section 1 of the Sherman Act lost much of its restraint outcome. The Chicago School view considers that monopolists should not be penalized for obtaining their market power owing to a superior product but in cases involving monopolists' duty to deal, tying, and exclusive dealing, the more lenient Chicago School view confuses the standards of conduct for dominant companies.

In *California Dental Ass'n v. FTC*,[103] the Supreme Court has indicated a willingness to embrace an antitrust approach that combines the best insights of both the Chicago and Harvard Schools. Post-Chicago School[104] economists argue that

---

[101] N. Pac. Ry. Co. v. United States, 356 U.S. 1, 5–7 (1958) (finding that railroad illegally tied sales or leases of real estate to commitment to ship commodities on its system). At 12 "its control over the tying product to force the buyer into the purchase of a tied product that the buyer either did not want at all, or might have preferred to purchase elsewhere on different terms.". *Jefferson Parish*, 466 U.S. at 35–36 (O'Connor, J., concurring) (stating that tying is illegal when "power in the market for the tying product is used to create *additional* market power in the market for the *tied* product" (emphasis in original)); at 17 (stating that large market share is sufficient to prove requisite economic power); Smithkline Corp. v. Eli Lilly and Co., 575 F.2d 1056, 1061–62 (3d Cir. 1978) (holding that bundling of patented and nonpatented products violates Section 2). Int'l Salt Co. v. United States, 332 U.S. 392, 395–96 (1947) (requisite economic power inferred from defendant's use of patent monopoly); IBM Corp. v. United States, 298 U.S. 131, 137 (1936) (same).

[102] Segal, I., Whinston, M.D., 2000. Naked exclusion: comment. American Economic Review 90, 296–309. Jose Miguel Abito, Julian Wright, Exclusive dealing with imperfect downstream competition, International Journal of Industrial Organization 26 (2008) 227–246 p242.

[103] 526 U.S. 756 (1999).

[104] Herbert Hovenkamp, *Post-Chicago Antitrust: A Review and Critique*, 2001 COLUM. BUS. L. REV. 257, at 270, at 279 ("[U]nder a more complex set of assumptions about how a market works, anticompetitive outcomes seem more plausible."); Marina Lao, *Aspen Skiing and Trinko: Intent and "Sacrifice"*, 73 ANTITRUST L.J. 171, 179 n.50 (2005) ("The Chicago view of exclusionary conduct as rarely effective, and hence implausible, assumes that markets are robust. Market robustness, in turn, assumes few entry barriers and good information, but these assumptions are usually not valid in real markets. If markets are not as robust as Chicagoans assume, then strategic exclusionary behavior is more plausible.").

particular market structures and competitive conduct "are much more likely to have anticompetitive consequences than Chicago School antitrust writers imagined." It has to be taken into consideration that markets do not perform as perfectly as the Chicago School assumes and competitive information is not uniformly accessible to all parties, entry is not likely for new companies, or dominant companies may have gained a position that is impracticable to displace. Hence, anticompetitive outcomes are more probable in such markets than the Chicago School acknowledges, and antitrust intervention is demanded to correct competitive discrepancies.

High-technology networks, such as computer operating or telecommunications systems, are subject to significant "network externalities," becoming more crucial to a specific user as a system gains larger numbers of other users. Post-Chicago School scholars have realized that monopolists such as Microsoft[105] have an exclusive capacity to leverage the appeal of their networks to expand their market power into other markets or to preclude new corporations from entering the market they have already monopolized. Thus, it is suitable for the courts to exclude monopolists from engaging in particular types of conduct that may be absolutely legitimate for less dominant enterprises.[106] Courts have become dissatisfied with the per se/rule of reason dichotomy and have begun to accept other approaches to Section 1 conduct by endorsing a so-called quick look at the competitive effects of a restraint demanding a plaintiff to demonstrate that a defendant had a market share in excess of a specific threshold.[107] Also, the quick look releases the plaintiff of the requirement to demonstrate the anticompetitive effects of a specific restraint, including proof of the defendant's market power and so the plaintiff needs to simply prove at the outset that the restraint is of a type that is expected to have anticompetitive effects. On the one hand, in *California Dental*,[108] the court held that the restrictions should be analyzed under the quick look because they made it "more difficult for consumers to find a lower price and for dentists to compete on the basis of price." On the other hand, the Supreme Court held that a quick look analysis was not suitable, since it was not spontaneously clear that the advertising restrictions were possible to have anticompetitive effects because the restrictions might have promoted competition by eliminating misleading and unverifiable discount advertising. Thus, the Court accepted that the alternative to the quick look need not unavoidably be a full rule of reason

---

[105] United States v. Microsoft Corp., 147 F.3d 935, 938 (D.C. Cir. 1998).

[106] United States v. E.I. DuPont de Nemours and Co., 96 F.T.C. 653, 751 n.42 (1980) ("If a monopoly results that proves impervious to competitive inroads and is unjustified by scale economies or other efficiencies, antitrust action in this or some other forum may be warranted, even in the absence of abusive conduct.").

[107] Gen. Leaseways, Inc. v. Nat'l Truck Leasing Ass'n, 744 F.2d 588, 596 (seventh Cir. 1984) (stating that in rule of reason analysis, "the plaintiff first [must] prove that the defendant has sufficient market power to restrain competition substantially. .. If not, the inquiry is at an end; the practice is lawful"

[108] Cal. Dental Ass'n v. FTC, 128 F.3d 720, 727 (ninth Cir. 1997), *vacated*, 526 U.S. 756 (1999).

market power analysis and so Sherman Act analysis should be viewed as a scale under which courts can engage in a range of inquiries "meet for the case."[109]

It is worth mentioning here that the essence of the Harvard school view was that consenting in many small enterprises to exist adds to competition rather than a small number of corporations which in fact is right but, on the other hand, in reality, bigger corporations in some fields can produce better goods in lower prices taking into account economies of scale which means that the production of better goods on lower prices has to be the basis for rightful competition produced either by a few corporations or many ones on an environment of free entrance in the market. Moreover, the concept of competition revolutionizes according to the global circumstances relating to technology and products' demand for concentration of businesses or not in a global arena characterized by AI technology which might generate problems of entrance for many players due to the availability of the technology or the functionality of the e-system in the first steps of the AAI era which has to make possible the free entrance in the market. In fact, competition means freedom to compete in any market under the same terms which means the existence of many companies and the existence of the possibility freely everybody to be able to enter the market and compete with other under the same terms. In reality competition, under this notion is the ideal which does not exist and so there is a need for the establishment of the conditions under which enterprises can enter a market and stand a chance to compete with their rivals in the market under fair conditions. To that extent, the tactic that any mergers are allowed as long as consumers are benefit from the agglomeration is wrong because the notion of competition does not exist following this approach and everything should be allowed as long as consumers benefit from the outcome of a severe war among corporations. Actually, people arguing that consumers benefit from mergers regardless of the elimination of competition many times do not take into consideration the impact of mergers upon other factors influencing the life of consumers such as pollution and environmental destruction caused by big corporations and not measured in the notion of consumers benefit.

The loophole of the economic approach endorsed by the Chicago school is the vagueness and complexity of the economic analysis and the uncertainty caused by economic calculations which comprise an econometric model rather than simply specific economic factors indicating always an uncompetitive impact upon the market.

As mentioned earlier, the approach of the Harvard School often invalidated conduct that had the prospective of boosting companies' efficiencies and benefiting consumers. A complicated empirical analysis of the economic efforts of most competitive conduct under the Chicago School approach made the outcome of

[109] *California Dental*, 526 U.S. 756, 771–72, 779–81 at 781 at 779. The Court stated that its rejection of the quick look did not signify a "call for the fullest market analysis.. .. [Not] every case attacking a less obviously anticompetitive restraint. .. is a candidate for plenary market examination."

antitrust cases more difficult to predict. It is argued[110] that the price-theoretic view that the Chicago School first advocated is flawed because first, its basic assumptions are impractical; second, its objectives are imprecise and unfeasible; third, its main terminology is unfixed; and fourth, its implementation embraces a kind of politics camouflaged as neutral decision-making. There is support for the *laissez faire competition* policy encouraged by the conventional account.[111] To that extent, Hovenkamp[112] argues that the Chicago School of antitrust, with its stress on a more economic approach and efficiency and use of neoclassical economics, does not encompass the reality of how companies make short-term selections.

It is characteristic that under Chicago doctrine, a patent is an investment which the inventor should be permitted to monetize without limit since this will effectively inspire more innovation. Moreover, a patent can offer the sort of market power that can be used to carry out illegal conduct such as exclusion in other markets[113] and so Qualcomm used discriminatory patent licensing to violate antitrust laws by engaging in anticompetitive conduct toward BlackBerry by conditioning chip supply assurances.[114] It could be said that the Chicago School considers that competitive equilibria are more robust and more durable than oligopoly, monopolistic competition, and monopoly. Moreover, it is argued[115] that the costs of monopoly mistakenly approved are small, while the costs of competition mistakenly blamed are large. According to the Chicago School, a serious threat of competitive harm was in the use of government to form monopoly.[116]

It could be said that Harvard believes that barriers to entry were more significant and pervasive than Chicago theory acknowledged. The Chicago School approach defines that concentration indicates a natural progression towards more effective market structures, stimulated by the need to achieve economies of scale. Harvard School focused on improving the administrability of antitrust rules and the capacity

---

[110]Maurice E. Stucke, *Reconsidering Antitrust's Goals*, 53 B.C. L. REV 551 (2012). J. Thomas Rosch, Comm'r Fed. Trade Comm'n, *Remarks at the New York Bar Association Annual Dinner: Implications of the Financial Meltdown for the FTC 2*, 5 (Jan. 29, 2009), http://ftc.gov/speeches/rosch/090129financialcrisisnybarspeech.pdf; Maurice E. Stucke, *Behavioral Economists at the Gate: Antitrust in the Twenty-First Century*, 38 LOY. U. CHI. L.J. 513 (2007)

[111]Jonathan B. Baker, *Symposium: The Goals of Antitrust: Economics and Politics: Perspectives on the Goals and Future of Antitrust*, 81 Fordham L. Rev. 2175, 2183 (2013) (explaining that the laissez-faire approach relies on "private enterprise to organize production and trade with little or no supervision to ensure that firms competed").

[112]H Hovenkamp 'Antitrust policy after Chicago' (1985) 84 Michigan Law Review 213 at 232–233

[113]Fed. Trade Comm'n v. Qualcomm Inc., 411 F. Supp. 3d 658 (N.D. Cal. 2019), rev'd, 969 F.3d 974 (ninth Cir. 2020);

[114]Herbert Hovenkamp, FRAND and Antitrust, 105 Cornell L. Rev. 1683, 1685 (2020)

[115]Kevin A. Bryan & Erik Hovenkamp, Startup Acquisitions, Error Costs, and Antitrust Policy, 87 U. CHI. L. REV. 331, 334 (2020)

[116]Cal. Retail Liquor Dealers Ass'n v. Midcal Aluminum, Inc., 445 U.S. 97, 105 (1980) ("These decisions establish two standards for antitrust immunity. .. . First, the challenged restraint must be 'one clearly articulated and affirmatively expressed as state policy'; second, the policy must be 'actively supervised' by the State itself.")

of institutions to implement them. To that extent, the Supreme Court has nearly always followed the Harvard approach of applying a rule of reason but litigation under the rule of reason has become extremely costly and so no longer effectively protects competition[117] which means that the Chicago School has lost ground in the Supreme Court.[118]

It is worth mentioning that behavioral-antitrust scholars claim an aptitude to succeed, or to complement, the conventional approach to antitrust analysis.[119] Can we use economics in order to correct misunderstanding concerning the notion of competition and misapplication of competition law? It is argued[120] that behavioral antitrust stipulates extended use of competition law to correct consumer damage that arises from biased company behavior. The right approach is to understand correctly the essence of competition on the axis of freedom to equally functioning for all prospective competitors and not surpassing competition law. Consumers react realistically to the price/quality signals that sellers of desired goods offer.[121] Moreover, the neoclassical price theory presupposes "rationality," such that players select to amplify their preferences subject only to their income or other restraints, such as flawed information. Alan Devlin & Michael Jacobs[122] argue that "behavioral antitrust lacks a theoretical foundation, and provides no basis for identifying optimal competition rules. While it can aspire to perform the ancillary task of "improving" the predictions of conventional antitrust economics, behavioral antitrust fails to accomplish even this. Its empirical investigations, which occupy the core of its methodology, have yet to generate any hypotheses, let alone a comprehensive theory of how competitive markets work."

Do legal interventions expose politics instead of attempts to address market failures? It is argued that the New Harvard approach acknowledges the intricacy of markets by welcoming the use of price theory as a tool of economic analysis. Moreover, it seems that New Harvard antitrust incorporates principles that can

[117] Leegin Creative Leather Prods., Inc. v. PSKS, Inc., 551 U.S. 877, 901 (2007) Hillary Greene & D. Daniel Sokol, Judicial Treatment of the Antitrust Treatise, 100 IOWA L. REV. 2039, 2059 (2015) (noting a shift from the Chicago to Harvard view in the mid-1980s)

[118] Ohio v. Am. Express Co., 138 S. Ct. 2274, 2279 (2018) Apple, Inc. v. Pepper, 139 S. Ct. 1514, 1518 (2019)

[119] Amanda P. Reeves & Maurice E. Stucke, *Behavioral Antitrust*, 86 IND. L.J. 1527, 1571 (2011). at 1543 ("[T]he purpose of behavioral economics is to augment neoclassical economic theory by providing more realistic assumptions of human behavior."). Roger Van den Bergh, *Behavioral Antitrust: Not Ready for the Main Stage*, 9 J. COMPETITION L. & ECON. 203 (2013) (concluding that "[b]ehavioral antitrust is a side act and not (yet) ready for the main stage").

[120] James C. Cooper & William E. Kovacic, *Behavioral Economics and Its Meaning For Antitrust Agency Decision Making*, 8 J.L. ECON. & POL'Y 779, 800 (2012)

[121] Allan L. Shampine, *The Role of Behavioral Economics in Antitrust Analysis*, 27 ANTITRUST ABA 65, 68 (2013) ("The endowment effect is a consumer's tendency to demand greater compensation to forfeit something than to acquire it. Here, consumers react more strongly to surcharges than to discounts because of surcharge is perceived as taking something away from the consumer.").

[122] Alan Devlin & Michael Jacobs, The Empty Promise Of Behavioral Antitrust, www.ssrn.com p58–59

account for a broader range of variation among industries, firms, and conduct. To that extent, New Harvard evaluated the jurisprudence treating all vertical restraints as illegal per se and so the Harvard school ended its previous support for per se illegality in favor of advocating for the rule of reason.[123]

7.3 Post-Chicago School

It is worth mentioning here that the post-Chicago School relied on more complex forms of analysis, embracing game theoretic models of firm behavior enabling the identification of anticompetitive behavior. Hence, while the use of game theory and the study of strategic interaction are not new and have been used in Chicago School antitrust analyses, the post-Chicago School certainly emphasizes game theory generating specific testable hypotheses and empirical testing of these models. "Neo-Chicagoans" demonstrate the economy as an equilibrium system in which corporations have equal initial access to technology, capital, and information, and compete for advantage through product and cost-efficiency.

It has to be taken into consideration that "Neo-Chicagoans" count on studies of rising output in the digital zone to illustrate economic efficiency so as to rationalize a blanket laissez-faire approach. To that extent, issues like privacy loss or excessive ad load are ignored comprehending that rational users freely trade their privacy in exchange for free goods and services and so targeted advertisement made available by large digital corporations is considered as an informational advancement.

It could be said that the post-Chicago School does not condemn monopoly power per se, but only monopoly power that is obtained or maintained by anticompetitive means but promoting the consumer welfare standard.

7.4 Populists and Competition

It has to be taken into account that markets are imperfectly competitive in some way, whether it be as a result of economies of scale, imperfect information, or impediments to entry. Moreover, markets diverge in their information flows and transparency and the difficulty of detecting defections diverges accordingly.

It is worth mentioning here that populists are troubled about the political power of large corporations suggesting the deconcentrating of the economy in order to diminish their power and so opening up opportunities for small companies, helping

[123]Phillip Areeda, The Rule of Reason – A Catechism on Competition, 55 Antitrust L.J. 571, 587 (1986); Phillip Areeda, Antitrust Violations without Damage Recoveries, 89 Harv. L. Rev. 1127, 1137 nn. 50–51 (1976) (discussing how most consumer harms from tying are inherently offset by consumer benefits).

workers, and minimizing economic inequities. Populists support plain, "bright-line" rules and banishing the role of economics in antitrust and so the consumer welfare standard is considered to be "as fundamentally flawed."[124]

It seems that "Chicago Economics" does not display any coherent set of principles or techniques. Hovenkamp and Morton[125] provide that "Antitrust enforcement turns monopoly markets into competitive ones, corporate profit into consumer surplus, and is therefore a public good. As with any public good, it tends to be underprovided." It is argued that there is a need of generating a number of rebuttable presumptions permitting antitrust plaintiffs to shift the burden of proof to defendants.[126]

While the Chicago School focused on overall efficiency and total welfare embracing the aggregate welfare of consumers and producers, modern antitrust law has focused specifically on consumer welfare. Under the modern consumer welfare standard, antitrust law has advanced principally high output and low prices.[127]

7.5 New Brandeis Movement

Justice Louis Brandeis was a strong proponent of a democratic distribution of power and opportunity in the political economy.[128] Thus, concentrated private power can destabilize democracy itself, when left unrestricted.

It has to be taken into account that an open and competitive market has prevailed in the United States. It has to be taken into account that the framers of the antitrust laws sought to prevent large unjust wealth transfers from producers and consumers to large corporations by safeguarding open markets and augmenting freedom of opportunity for new and small companies.[129]

[124] Angelina Fisher & Thomas Streinz, Confronting Data Inequality, IILJ Working Paper 2021/1

[125] Hovenkamp, Herbert J. and Scott Morton, Fiona, "Framing the Chicago School of Antitrust Analysis" (2020). Faculty Scholarship at Penn Law. 2113. https://scholarship.law.upenn.edu/faculty_scholarship/2113 p1852

[126] Carl Shapiro, Antitrust: What Went Wrong and How to Fix It, 35 Antitrust 33, 33–34 (2021) William E. Kovacic, Root and Branch Reconstruction: The Modern Transformation of U.-S. Antitrust Law and Policy?, 35 Antitrust 46, 47 (2021)

[127] Kenneth Hayer, Consumer Welfare and the Legacy of Robert Bork, 57 J. L. & ECON. S20 (2014) ("Bork's use of the term 'consumer welfare' is unfortunate and confusing in this context.. .. [B]y consumer welfare, Bork meant total welfare. .. . .");

[128] Lina Kahn, The New Brandeis Movement: America's Antimonopoly Debate, 9 J. Eur. Competition L. Prac. 131 (2018)

[129] Sandeep Vaheesan, The Profound Nonsense of Consumer Welfare Antitrust, The Antitrust Bulletin 2019, Vol. 64(4) 481. Robert H. Lande, Wealth Transfers as the Original and Primary Concern of Antitrust: The Efficiency Interpretation Challenged, 34 Hastings L.J. 65 (1982).

The preamble to the Utah Statement[130] pronounces the relationship between antitrust law and democracy by affirming that "[t]he protection of fair competition is a means to a [. . .] democratic society" and so "excessive concentration of private power breeds antidemocratic political pressures and undermines liberties." Moreover, the Utah Statement declares that fair competition generates "distribution of wealth and power." Also, The Utah Statement directly disputes the accuracy of the argument that "Congress designed the Sherman Act as a 'consumer welfare prescription'."

The Utah Statement is not clear regarding the preferred, alternative antitrust standards but it is declared that antitrust enforcement should retreat from focusing on measuring explicit outcomes per se, such as lower prices. Additionally, the Utah Statement counts on the construction of antitrust rules "through case development, agency rule-making, and legislation.". Furthermore, the Utah statement clarifies recommendations for antitrust standards, such as concerning predatory pricing, monopoly leveraging, refusal to deal by dominant corporations, and price squeeze. Thus, the Utah Statement stimulates the revision of a whole array of legal precedents in the area of monopolization and so altering the existing philosophy of antitrust. To that extent, Sandeep Vaheesan and Lina Khan[131] argue that "[t]he antitrust agencies and courts should look to European Union abuse of dominance law for a model to emulate."

Taking into account that economic power is diagnosed as political, the economic power guides outcomes and so market power leads to domination obstructing self-govern.[132] It is specified that the concentration of economic power consolidates political power "through enabling a small minority to amass outsized wealth, which they could then use to influence government," along with permitting "private discretion by a few in the economic sphere" to "control the welfare of all" which means undercutting commercial autonomy.[133] Hence, companies gain control over political processes and outcomes via lobbying and staffing government and so getting favorable policies establishing their dominance.

The US Supreme Court[134] stated that the "Congress designed the Sherman Act as a 'consumer welfare prescription'" and so remodeling antitrust enforcement grounded on consumer welfare. The consumer welfare standard demands the understanding of the welfare effects of highly complex transactions or conduct which means that the consumer welfare's concentration on efficiency permits monopoly power not to be seen as threatening per se. To that extent, Neo-Brandeisians argue

---

[130]Utah Statement, https://onezero.medium.com/the-utah-statement-reviving-antimonopoly-traditionsfor-the-era-of-big-tech-e6be198012d7

[131]Lina Khan and Sandeep Vaheesan, Market Power and Inequality: The Antitrust Counterrevolution and Its Discontents, 11(1) Harvard Law and Policy Review 235, 282 (2017).

[132]Lina Khan, The End of Antitrust History Revisited, 133 Harv. L. Rev. 1655, 1676 (2020).

[133]Lina Khan, Amazon's Antitrust Paradox, 126(3) Yale Law Journal 710, 740 (2017)

[134]Reiter v. Sonotone Corp., 442 U.S. 330, 343 (1979) (quoting Robert H. Bork, The Antitrust Paradox 66 (1978))

that this critically wrong comprehending of the lawmakers' objective has led "both enforcers and courts to focus mainly on promoting 'efficiency' on the theory that this will result in low prices for consumers." Also, Neo-Brandeisians fully admit that the antitrust laws, handling the power allocation and use in society, have a strong political feature.

It is worth noting here that the Chicago School adopts the view that market structures occur via "natural forces," while the New Brandeisians consider that the political economy is shaped only through "law and policy." On the other hand, it could be said that in natural monopolies, the character of the product or service forces politics to recognize the "natural forces" and so acting accordingly. Moreover, it seems that where "Neo Brandesians" observe bigness everywhere, "Neo Chicagoans" observe advantages in consumer surplus.

Neo-Brandeisians diagnose complications acknowledging that large digital corporations hold an exclusive form of structural power over markets and so they articulate an analysis of the structure and dynamics of markets in order to comprehend a corporation's power and the prospective anticompetitive character of that power which means that there is a need of finding out the structure of a business and the structural role it plays in markets. It seems that Neo Brandesians based on all "big is bad" visualize all large digital corporations.[135]

Economics and the consumer welfare standard were a direct response utilized by courts and regulators to settle the "conflicting and incoherent results" of then-antitrust enforcement and so courts are placing a greater emphasis on economic tools and credible evidence of anticompetitive effects, rather than bright-line rules and presumptions. Jonathan Baker Et Al[136] argue that "Courts have contributed to increased monopoly power through decisions that have weakened the prohibitions against anticompetitive exclusionary conduct and anticompetitive mergers." It is characteristic that Neo-Brandeisians regard the consumer welfare standard as "fundamentally flawed" discarding economics and evidence-based policy as a foundation for antitrust enforcement.[137] New Brandeisians back "bright-line rules" to demarcate anticompetitive conduct without concern to whether that conduct harms consumers. It could be said that the Neo-Brandeisian school gives too little regard to markets and consumer-serving qualities of business strategies.

The New Brandeisians argue that the US antitrust laws had their origins in broader concerns about economic power and inequality, and do not identify the promotion of consumer welfare or any kind of solely economic welfare as their objective. To that extent, the New Brandeis movement rejects the understanding that

[135] Lina Khan, The New Brandeis Movement: America's Antimonopoly Debate, 9 J. Eur. Compet. Law Pract. 131 (2018)

[136] Jonathan B. Baker Et Al., Joint Response To The House Judiciary Committee On The State Of Antitrust Law And Implications For Protecting Competition In Digital Markets 1 (2020), https://judiciary.house.gov/uploadedfiles/joint_submission_from_michael_kades_and_antitrust_expert_coalition.pdfat 1

[137] Joshua D. Wright et al., Requiem for a Paradox: The Dubious Rise and Inevitable Fall of Hipster Antitrust, 51 ARIZ. ST. L. J. 293, 295 (2019).

antitrust law should be centered on promoting consumer welfare. Hence, the New Brandeisians propose "harm to the competitive process" as an alternative to the consumer welfare standard without defining what they mean by "harm to the competitive process."[138]

The New Brandeisians consider that antitrust enforcement should condemn economic power even if it is not going together with conduct that raises prices or lessens output or innovation, for the reason that they regard economic power and inequality as a threat to democracy and social justice. It seems that there is an understanding that even the consideration of financial wealth causes fear and a negative effect on trade without having the financial power to take any action which is not entirely correct because the existence of financial strength is needed for an economic advancement in a fair competition environment. Hence, it is believed that even the consideration of economic strength causes fear and affects trade. In other words, economic power causes fear by its very existence. On the other hand, a health utilization of economic strength adds to competition in an environment where the rules exist for the market to function smoothly. Richard J. Gilbert & A. Douglas Melamed[139] specify that "penalizing monopolies that are a consequence of a superior product, business acumen, or historic accident would chill entrepreneurship and, in some cases, prevent the emergence of efficient industry structures."

G.I. Zekos considers that the existence of competition rules and protection rules against unfair competition are the basis for the competitive operation of the market. Consequently, the rules that define the limits of unfair competition must be clear in order to have a competitive functioning of the market which means that per se rules and formalism add to certainty and legitimacy for a fair competition and not any other situation influenced by any pressure of politics upon court judgments accordingly.

The character of competition in digital markets portrays novel conceptual contests for antitrust law. In fact, the Neo-Brandeisians claim that antitrust law ought to concentrate principally on market structure and specifically market concentration which means that structuralism stands in some opposition to the consumer welfare standard that is essentially signaled in contemporary case law. Also, collecting, using, and transferring personal data brings forward the dimension of privacy but the new Brandeis school of thought risks undermining consumer privacy, rather than enhancing it.[140]

The Neo-Brandeisians consider structuralism right all along because concentrating on metrics like high output and low prices disregard other consumer interests such as quality, variety, and innovation which are threatened by "concentrations of

[138]Richard J. Gilbert & A. Douglas Melamed, Innovation: A Bridge to the New Brandeisians? https://www.competitionpolicyinternational.com/innovation-a-bridge-to-the-new-brandeisians/

[139]Richard J. Gilbert & A. Douglas Melamed, Innovation: A Bridge to the New Brandeisians? https://www.competitionpolicyinternational.com/innovation-a-bridge-to-the-new-brandeisians/ p 6

[140]Matthew Sipe Covering Prying Eyes with an Invisible Hand: Antitrust Law, the New Brandeis Movement, and Privacy at: https://ssrn.com/abstract=412437

power."[141] Moreover, the Neo-Brandeisians push alterations through legislation or promulgate regulations. Also, Neo-Brandeisians' enforcement efforts against the tech platforms and pursuing labor-market objectives have not gone easily.[142]

The Neo-Brandeisians considered that the low privacy levels tendered by digital firms are an indicator of their market power and so denoting that they are not competitive which means that monopoly power enables companies to degrade privacy without consequences.[143] It is argued that antitrust remedies unintentionally trigger privacy harms offsetting the benefits to consumers from restored competition.[144]

It has to be taken into consideration that the Neo-Brandeisian antitrust wave promotes an expanded role for antitrust law free from the chains of the welfare and efficiency doctrines of the Chicago School. It is suggested that competition law limits "bigness" when bigness is employed to corrupt the democratic process or undercut consumer privacy.[145]

Antitrust law upholds a set of structural conditions for competition as a mode of stimulating a set of outcomes and principles which means that competition embraces a process grounded on per se principles advancing equality. G.I. Zekos considers that antitrust law is endorsed in order to achieve the best outcome for society concerning not only prices but also other qualities such as quality of the product, preventing the destruction of the environment and protecting all human rights which means the low price cannot run against other rights of the society. Tim Wu[146] proposes replacing the consumer welfare standard with the "competitive process

[141] Lina Khan, The New Brandeis Movement: America's Antimonopoly Debate, 9 J. EU. COMP. L. & PRACTICE 131 (2018) ("The fixation on efficiency, in turn, has largely blinded enforcers to many of the harms caused by undue market power, including on workers, suppliers, innovators, and independent entrepreneurs—all harms that Congress intended for the antitrust laws to prevent.").

[142] Fed. Trade Comm'n v. Facebook, Inc., 2021 WL 2643627 (June 28, 2021) (granting defendant's motion to dismiss); United States v. Jindal, Case No. 20-CR-358 (E.D. Tex. Apr. 14, 2022) (ending in defendants' acquittal).

[143] Federal Trade Commission v. Facebook, Inc., 20-cv03590 (D.D.C. Dec. 9, 2020) ("The benefits to users of additional competition include. .. data protection privacy options for users, including, but not limited to, options regarding data gathering and data usage practices."); Complaint at 64, New York v. Facebook, Inc., 20-cv-03589 (D.D.C. Dec. 9, 2020) ("After Facebook achieved monopoly power, the company. .. degraded the privacy protections and privacy options. .. ."); Complaint at 7, United States v. Google LLC, 20-cv-03010 (D.D.C. Oct. 20, 2020) ("Google is now the unchallenged gateway to the internet. ... As a consequence,. .. American consumers are forced to accept Google's policies, privacy practices, and use of personal data.");

[144] Erika M. Douglas, Monopolization Remedies and Data Privacy, 24 VA. J.L. & TECH. 1 (2020)

[145] KG Elzinga and M Webber 'Louis Brandeis and contemporary antitrust enforcement' (2017) 33 Touro Law Review 277.SM Colino 'The antitrust F word: fairness considerations in competition law' CPI (8 October 2018); E Posner How Antitrust Failed Workers (Oxford: Oxford University Press, 2021).

[146] Tim Wu, Testimony to the Antitrust Subcommittee, 25 April 2020, https://judiciary.house.gov/uploadedfiles/submission_from_timothy_wu.pdf.

standard." Thus, antitrust law has to force a powerful firm not to seek disabling the process of competition on the merits.

Bibliography

1. Shapiro, C. (2021). Antitrust: What went wrong and how to fix it, 35 Antitrust 33, 33–34.
2. Posner, E. (2021). *How antitrust failed workers*. Oxford University Press.
3. Douglas, E. M. (2020). Monopolization remedies and data privacy, 24 Va. J.L. & Tech. 1.
4. Hovenkamp, H. (2020). FRAND and antitrust, 105 Cornell L. Rev. 1683, 1685.
5. Hovenkamp, H. J., & Leslie, C. R. (2013). The firm as Cartel manager, 64 Vand. L. Rev. 813, 855.
6. Greene, H., & Sokol, D. D. (2015). Judicial treatment of the antitrust treatise, 100 Iowa L. Rev. 2039, 2059.
7. Wright, J. D., et al. (2019). Requiem for a paradox: The dubious rise and inevitable fall of Hipster antitrust, 51 Ariz. St. L. J. 293, 295.
8. Atanassov, J. (2013). Do hostile takeovers stifle innovation? Evidence from antitakeover legislation and corporate patenting. *Journal of Finance, 68*, 1097.
9. Bryan, K. A., & Hovenkamp, E. (2020). Startup acquisitions, error costs, and antitrust policy, 87 U. Chi. L. Rev. 331, 334.
10. Khan, L. (2020). The end of antitrust history revisited, 133 Harv. L. Rev. 1655, 1676.
11. Klausner, M. (2013). Fact and fiction in corporate law and governance, 35 Stan L. Rev. 1325, 1368.
12. Lande, R. H. Textualism as an ally of antitrust enforcement: Examples from merger and monopolization law, 2023 No. 4 Utah Law Review 813.
13. Paul, S. (2020). Antitrust as allocator of coordination rights 67 UCLA L. Rev. 378.
14. Kovacic, W. E. (2021). Root and branch reconstruction: The modern transformation of U.-S. *Antitrust Law and Policy? 35*, 46, 47.

Chapter 8
Formalism in Competition

8.1 Introduction

Formalism illustrates what it means to apply a rule, the vagueness of the most important statutory competition law provisions makes non-formalistic, purpose-based reasoning indispensable in forming more specific substantive legal tests turning into rule-like and applied formalistically. For instance, the ECJ formed a rule that describes an "undertaking" for the purpose of Articles 101 and 102 TFEU as "every entity engaged in an economic activity, regardless of the legal status of the entity and the way in which it is financed."[1] A legal formalism prescribes courts to apply that legal formalism rather than deciding on the basis of all relevant considerations. Courts have always found ways to avert the formalistic application of rules. In US antitrust law, the per se prohibition of certain types of business conduct appears to be a typical example of a legal formalism. Per se rules are formalistic for the reason that assigning the conduct to the relevant class is done on the basis of the straightforward meaning of the class, without investigating whether it is justified to do so. Per se rules reveal that legal formalism is both constraining and liberating.

It has to be taken into account the degree to which per se rules and the rule of reason in US antitrust law and the category of "by object" restrictions in EU competition law encompass formalistic reasoning. Moreover, the link between "legal form" and "anticompetitive effects" and the debate on "form-based" versus "effects-based" approaches to competition law denotes that "effects-based" approaches to competition law entangle formalistic legal rules.

It is argued that rules are means mediating between certain purposes and certain decisions furthering these purposes.[2] To that extent, formalism simplifies decision-making by only counting on the rule itself rather than the rationales underlying the rule. Nonetheless, decision-makers still distinguish the content of the rule

[1] Klaus Höfner and Fritz Elser v Macrotron GmbH, C-41/90, EU:C:1991:161, para. 21.

[2] Frederick Schauer, Formalism, 97 YALE L. J. 509 (1988).

© The Author(s), under exclusive license to Springer Nature Switzerland AG 2023

G. I. Zekos, *Artificial Intelligence and Competition*, Contributions to Economics,
https://doi.org/10.1007/978-3-031-48083-6_8

encompassing some evaluative choices, if only relating to the literal meaning of the words contained in the rule.[3] Also, any rule application necessitates taking into consideration the legal context of the rule. A rule simplifies the decision-making process by demanding the decision-maker to abstract from excluded considerations. Hence, rules are "generalizations" entailing the decision-maker to abstract from some of the precise circumstances of each case, and they are "entrenched" for the reason that they ought to be followed in spite of whether the outcome in a particular case is desirable or undesirable.

It is also essential to underline in a competition law context that formalism is not only about statutory rules. Most competition law provisions are vague, "standard-like" norms that appear to eliminate very few considerations from their application to concrete cases. Hence, Section 1 of the Sherman Act 1890 is so abstract that it only be applied to concrete cases by taking into consideration its principles. Thus, if formalism is applicable to legal reasoning grounded on statutory rules, it is relevant hardly to any competition law system. To that extent, both US antitrust law and EU competition law, along with various other competition law systems, largely comprise case law and that case law may or may not embrace rules that function as legal formalisms.

Judicially shaped rules incorporate substantive legal tests such as the rule that a naked horizontal price-fixing agreement is an unreasonable restraint of trade in US antitrust law, and the rule that restrictions of competition by object are by definition significant in EU competition law.[4] Hence, applying a per se prohibition against naked horizontal price-fixing advances the rationales supporting the prohibition and so courts applying that rule recognize that the rule was shaped for the reason that virtually all naked horizontal price-fixing agreements are detrimental to competition. Nonetheless, there is a central difference between taking into consideration rationale in forming the rule and taking into consideration rationale in applying the rule. Hereafter, no substantive legal test in competition law has been formed without taking into consideration one or more rationales. In the EU competition law, the substantive legal test applicable to price discrimination by dominant undertakings explicitly embraces "all the circumstances" of the case having a low "rule-like" quality and is not formalistic.

The US antitrust case law after Trenton Potteries disclosed the difficulties of formalistically applying even a straightforward per se rule, such as the one against horizontal price-fixing. In Broadcast Music,[5] the Supreme Court held that applying the per se rule against horizontal price-fixing "is not a question simply of determining whether two or more potential competitors have literally 'fixed' a 'price'."

[3] A. Scalia, B.A. Garner, Reading Law: The Interpretation Of Legal Texts 412–414 (2012).

[4] United States v. Trenton Potteries, Co., 273 U.S. 392 (1927). Expedia Inc. v. Autorité de la concurrence and Others, C-226/11, EU:C:2012:795, para. 37.

[5] Broadcast Music Inc. v. Columbia Broadcasting System Inc., 441 U.S. 1 (1979); Arizona v. Maricopa County Medical Society, 457 U.S. 332 (1982); NCAA v. Board of Regents of the University of Oklahoma, 468 U.S. 85 (1984); Texaco Inc. v. Dagher, 126 U.S. 1276 (2006).

Courts typically do not apply legal rules formalistically to the facts of each case, but rather tend to reconceptualize the logic of the rule. Perhaps, in US antitrust law, naked horizontal price-fixing and naked market division agreements have remained subject to a fully formalistic analysis. For other types of conduct, case-specific analysis is indispensable to analyze whether the conduct falls under the scope of a per se prohibition, which explicitly or implicitly entangles engaging with the rationale(s) of the relevant provision.

It is characteristic that the per se rule is a typical example of a legal formalism because it requires decision-makers to apply the rule without enquiring into the purpose(s) of the rule. Section 1 of the Sherman Act 1890 prohibits agreements that fall within the class of "agreements in restraints of trade," just as Article 101 (1) TFEU concerns the class of agreements that have as their object or effect the restriction of competition.

8.2 Formalism and the Rule of Reason

The rule of reason is regarded as a structured, three-step test encompassing a burden-shifting process and the plaintiff must prove that the restraint has a significant anticompetitive effect harming consumers in the relevant market.[6]

First of all, while the per se rule in US antitrust law is a proxy for a legal formalistic approach to competition law, the rule of reason is deemed to be the doctrinal equivalent of a standard-based and/or effects-based approach. Although the rule of reason is a doctrine of US antitrust law, the term is also used concerning competition law systems throughout the world. In EU competition law, the category of restrictions of competitions "by effect" is related to the rule of reason. Moreover, the "rule of reason" is a focal point in competition law illustrating the relevance of formalism and formalistic reasoning in the application of the rule of reason in US antitrust law.

In GTE Sylvania, the Supreme Court overruled the per se illegality rule for vertical non-price restraints by demanding a thorough case-specific inquiry in which "the factfinder weighs all of the circumstances of a case in deciding whether a restrictive practice should be prohibited as imposing an unreasonable restraint on competition."[7] Additionally, in Leegin, the Supreme Court overruled the per se illegality rule for vertical resale price maintenance. In respect of the needed analysis under the rule of reason, the Supreme Court held that "[i]f the rule of reason were to apply to vertical price restraints, courts would have to be diligent in eliminating their

---

[6]Ohio et al. v. American Express Co. et al., 585 U.S. 1, 9–10 (2018); National Collegiate Athletic Association v. Alston et al., 594 U.S. __ (2021), 24–25.

[7]Continental T.V., Inc. v. GTE Sylvania, Inc., 433 U.S. 36, 50 (1977)

anticompetitive uses from the market" elaborating a number of pro-competitive and anticompetitive indicators.[8]

If the rationale of competition law is to protect "competition," and anticompetitive effects, pro-competitive principles, and efficiencies are all relevant concerns in view of this reason, then the structure of the rule of reason averts an unconstrained, all-things-considered analysis of all these considerations in light of the principle of protecting competition. Thus, the constraints imposed by the rule of reason are sequential and procedural.[9]

The allocation of the legal and evidential burden of proof is a tactic to formalize the administrative and judicial process and so within the formal structure of administrative and judicial procedures, the rule of reason in general is categorized by a low degree of formalism. To that extent, "formalization" of the rule of reason is demonstrated by two recent Supreme Court judgments, Actavis and Ohio v. AMEX. In Ohio v. AMEX,[10] the US Supreme Court compels the plaintiff, in cases entangling two-sided markets, to embrace both sides of a platform in the market definition demonstrating market power on that single market. Additionally, the Court held that such market definition is needed even if the plaintiff relies in his case on direct proof of anticompetitive effects. Legal rules on market definition liberate decision-makers by permitting them to quantify market power by proxy, on the basis of specific legal constructions as to what counts as "the relevant market." By the way, market definition requirements display the more general point that legal formalisms can both constrain and liberate and can have both positive and negative effects on the quality of the decision-making course.[11]

Likewise, in Actavis, the Court formalized the first stage of the rule of reason by restricting the evidential obligations that are needed to prove considerable anticompetitive effects. Furthermore, the Court declared that courts need not take into consideration all the circumstances of the case in establishing substantial anticompetitive effect.[12] Thus, it could be said that the rule of reason in practice easily works as a quasi-per se legality rule.[13]

Consequently, in US antitrust law, the increased application of the rule of reason rather than the per se rule has not led to less constrained decision-making on the basis of the characteristics of each case in light of the principles of antitrust. Moreover, to the extent that the rule of reason is verbalized as a genuine all-things-considered analysis, it is so approximate that it can hardly be used for a consistent and predictable analysis but additional interpretive guidance on its application has turned

[8]Leegin Creative Leather Products. v. PSKS, Inc., 551 U.S. __ (2007), 17–19.

[9]M.A. Carrier, The Four-Step Rule of Reason, 33 Antitrust 50 (2019).

[10]Ohio et al. v. American Express Co. et al., 585 U.S. 1, 9–10 (2018);

[11]M. Eben, The Antitrust Market Does Not Exist: Pursuit of Objectivity in a Purposive Process, 17 J. COMP. L. & ECON. 586 (2021).

[12]FTC v. Actavis, Inc., 570 U.S. __ (2013), at 20.

[13]H. Hovenkamp, A Miser's Rule of Reason: The Alston Antitrust Case, FACULTY SCHOLARSHIP AT PENN LAW 2533 (2022).

the rule of reason even more into a set of formalistic rules. While the rule of reason in US antitrust law and the analysis of anticompetitive effects are typified by a low degree of formalism, in practice both involve a relatively high degree of legal formalism. Hence, the rule of reason hardly operates as an unconstrained and has developed into a collection of conduct-specific rules that either advance establishing anticompetitive effects or rather make it virtually impossible to establish them.[14]

8.3 Formalism and Anticompetitive Effects

The rule of reason in US antitrust law integrates conduct-specific rules that formalize the decision-making process and so the substitution of "effects-based analysis" for "formalistic distinctions" has been a positive development. Also, it is stated that legal presumptions that rest on formalistic distinctions rather than actual market realities are disfavored in antitrust law.[15]

In Europe, the form–effects distinction has not been accepted by the EU courts, but nonetheless plays a noteworthy role in EU competition law scholarship, signifying "form-based" or "formalistic" and "effects-based" approaches to EU competition law. To that extent, the formalistic approach is connected with a per se prohibition of certain types of business conduct, or a qualified per se prohibition, amalgamating a prima facie per se prohibition with the prospect for the defendant (s) to justify the conduct. On the other hand, an effects-based approach necessitates the plaintiff to display actual or probable anticompetitive consequences on the market so as to find even a prima facie infringement which is subject to objective justification, for instance by Article 101 (3) TFEU or the likelihood for objective justification in Article 102 TFEU. Correspondingly, the use of "presumptions" applies once "certain conditions" are accomplished, while the "effects-based" approach necessitates evidence of anticompetitive effects in an individual case.

8.4 The Effects-Based Approach and Legal Formalism

It has to be taken into account that an effects-based approach to competition law requires a case-by-case analysis of whether anticompetitive effects have occurred or are expected to take place implying that a finding of antitrust liability must be based on empirical evidence of actual or probable anticompetitive effects.

---

[14] T. Wu, The American Express Opinion, the Rule of Reason, and Tech Platforms, 7 J. Antitrust Enforcement 104, 122 (2019): "Their mirror-image counterpart [of per se rules] in American Express takes the less-appealing approach of using complex economic theory to create near-impossible burdens of proof—burdens particularly hard to meet when they emerge on appeal. At worst, they offer a highly jazzed-up way of getting around some awfully damaging facts"

[15] Eastman Kodak Co. v. Image Technical Services, Inc., 504 U.S. 451, 466–467 (1992)

To that extent, conceptions of effects-based approaches to competition law draw heavily on economic theories of harm and usually relying on a number of assumptions and a restricted set of intuitions concerning rational behavior in particular conditions to derive conclusions as to whether a certain type of business conduct or the individual settings of a case are anticompetitive and so leading to actual or expected anticompetitive effects.[16] Furthermore, empirical data offer information supporting multiple economic narratives concentrating on either pro-competitive or anticompetitive effects.

Competition law functions with general presumptions about the performance of markets. Moreover, in monopolization and abuse of dominance cases, where, at the bottom, fierce competition against competitors cannot be discerned categorically from attempts to exclude those competitors from the market. Hence, the legal rules of an economics-informed competition law are expected to be equally, if not more formalistic than the "form-based approach."

In addition, the rule in EU competition law is that a dominant undertaking has a "special responsibility" not to harm the competitive process.[17] While the special responsibility rule does not by itself denote what types of conduct are abusive, it forms more specific theories of harm and forms of abuse by compelling a general obligation onto dominant undertakings. Accordingly, the contemporary, "effects-based" approach is an equally, if not more formalistic approach that utilizes assumptions, categories, and inferences based on formal economic methods, which are turned into formalistic legal tests combining economic knowledge. It could be said that an agreement has a restrictive object even if it does not have the restriction of competition as its single aim but also chases other legitimate objectives which is a formalistic approach to Article 101 (1) TFEU.[18]

It has to be taken into consideration that interaction between economic formalism, legal formalism, and all-things-considered analysis is signaled in several parts of the US and EU competition case laws. The Supreme Court substantially restricted the scope of Section 2 of the Sherman Act 1890 through a number of formalistic presumptions of legality, which were informed by certain assumptions from

[16] The European Commission's decisions in Intel, Google Shopping and Google Android: European Commission, Decision relating to a proceeding under Article 82 of the EC Treaty and Article 54 of the EEA Agreement, Case COMP/C-3/37.990, Intel, D(2009)3726 final. European Commission, Decision relating to proceedings under Article 102 of the Treaty on the Functioning of the European Union and Article 54 of the Agreement on the European Economic Area, Case AT.39740, Google Search (Shopping), C(2017) 4444 final. European Commission, Decision relating to a proceeding under Article 102 of the Treaty on the Functioning of the European Union (the Treaty) and Article 54 of the EEA Agreement, Case AT.40099, Google Android, C(2018) 4761 final.

[17] NV Nederlandsche Banden Industrie Michelin v. Commission of the European Communities, 322/81, EU:C:1983:313, para. 57; France Télécom SA v. Commission of the European Communities, C-202/07, EU:C:2009:214, para. 105; Deutsche Telekom AG v. European Commission, C-280/08, EU:C:2010:603, para. 176.

[18] Competition Authority v Beef Industry Development Society Ltd. and Barry Brothers (Carrigmore) Meats Ltd., C-209/07, EU:C:2008:643, para. 34–40.

economics. In Brooke Group,[19] the Supreme Court ruled that the above incremental cost pricing is per se legal under Section 2, contrary to scholarship that had emphasized possible exclusionary effects of above-cost pricing. Again, in Trinko,[20] the Supreme Court correspondingly limited the scope of Section 2 of the Sherman Act 1890 by following a rule-based laissez-faire approach, stating that charging monopoly prices is not a violation of Section 2 for the reason that "it is an important element of the free market system" and "[t]he opportunity to charge monopoly prices—least for a short period—is what attracts 'business acumen' in the first place."

In EU law, the approach towards price-based conduct by dominant undertakings is less formalistic than under Section 2 Sherman Act 1890. Concerning price discrimination, in Post Danmark I,[21] the Court stipulated an all-things-considered test to evaluate whether price-setting strategies should be considered anticompetitive. Again, in AKZO,[22] the Court held that prices below average variable costs are abusive, and prices between average variable costs and average total costs are abusive if they are ascertained as part of a plan for destroying a competitor. Consequently, for prices above average variable costs, the Court presented a specific rule as opposed to necessitating an all-things-considered analysis embracing more elements than simply the fact that prices are below average total costs and the existence of a plan to destroy a competitor.

Even though the effects category in Article 101 (1) TFEU, like the rule of reason analysis in US antitrust law, is regarded as an all-things-considered analysis based on the specific facts of each case and as a matter of legal principle, in practice specific types of agreements are subject to specific effects-based but formalistic tests. The anticompetitive nature of the effects of an agreement is evaluated in light of the competition that would have occurred in the absence of the agreement. In other words, the Court has provided formulaic criteria to structure the way in which anticompetitive and pro-competitive effects are taken into account.[23]

Along with the ancillary restraints doctrine in EU competition law, an anticompetitive clause falls outside the scope of Article 101 (1) TFEU if it is ancillary to a

---

[19] Brooke Group Ltd. v. Brown & Williamson Tobacco Corp., 509 U.S. 209 (1993). at 223: "the exclusionary effect of prices above a relevant measure of cost either reflects the lower cost structure of the alleged predator, and so represents competition on the merits, or is beyond the practical ability of a judicial tribunal to control without courting intolerable risks of chilling legitimate price cutting"

[20] TVerizon Communications, Inc. v. Law Offices of Curtis v. Trinko, LLP, 540 U.S. __ (2004), at 7.

[21] Post Danmark A/S v. Konkurrencerådet, C-209/10, EU:C:2012:172, para. 39

[22] AKZO Chemie BV v. Commission of the European Communities, C-62/86, EU:C:1991:286, para. 71–72

[23] Generics (UK) Ltd. and Others v. Competition and Markets Authority, C-307/18, EU:C:2020:52, para. 116; Asnef-Equifax, Servicios de Información sobre Solvencia y Crédito, SL and Administración del Estado v. Asociación de Usuarios de Servicios Bancarios, C-238/05, EU:C:2006:734, para. 49;

broader agreement that is, overall, pro-competitive.[24] A single exclusive purchasing agreement has considerable anticompetitive effects even if it is not part of a "bundle" of similar agreements which have the amassed consequence of foreclosing market access. Likewise, the identification of an overall, pro-competitive rationale and the necessity of the anticompetitive clause for the agreement as a whole is implicated which does amount to neither an unconstrained, all-things-considered analysis of the agreement, nor the balancing of pro-competitive and anticompetitive effects in general. To that extent, the analysis of ancillary restraints is rule-like and formalistic.[25]

It is worth noting that formalization through rules is needed to prevent a situation in which all circumstances are relevant, and so nothing is dispositive. By contrast, the dangers of broadening the scope of the by object category too much are also clear and the case law on "by object" restrictions has moved towards a decrease in formalism, while the case law on "by effect" restrictions has moved towards increased formalization through fact-specific rules and criteria.[26] Hence, rules become more standard-like over time and so predictability and formalism are related for the reason that the degree of formalism touches both the number of norm applications that are appropriate along with the norm itself and the possibility that the decision-maker reaches an erroneous outcome.

Although the ECJ de facto applies a system of precedent, there is no doctrine of stare decisis in EU law. Hence, in EU law, there is no obligation for the Court to stick to past decisions if they are considered incorrect or otherwise undesirable. Thus, the selection between following the rule and deciding on the basis of the specific settings of the case becomes particularly prominent if pre-existing rules from case law do have normative weight but there is no absolute doctrine of stare decisis. Examples from EU competition law reveal how the jurisprudential selection for formalistic or non-formalistic reasoning has direct repercussions for decisional jurisdiction, both horizontally and vertically.[27] Likewise, selective distribution systems comprise a characteristic of competition and are corresponding with Article 101 (1) TFEU, given that resellers are chosen on the basis of objective criteria of a qualitative nature, and these criteria are applied consistently for all prospective resellers and do not go further than needed.[28]

In Bronner, the ECJ determined that a dominant undertaking is only entailed to grant access to a physical infrastructure if such access is indispensable for opening the market and this indispensability test constrains the discretion of subsequent

[24]There is a lack of "balancing" pro-competitive and anti-competitive effects. G. Monti, EU Competition Law and the Rule of Reason Revisited, TILEC Discussion Paper Dp 2020–021 (2020).

[25]Gøttrup-Klim e.a. Grovvareforeninger v. Dansk Landbrugs Grovvareselskab AmbA, C-250/92, EU:C:1994:413, para. 31–45.

[26]Intel Corp v. European Commission, C-413/14 P, EU:C:2017:632, para. 138–139.

[27]F. Schauer, Precedent, 39 STANFORD L. REV. 571 (1987).

[28]Metro SB-Großmärkte GmbH & Co. KG v. Commission of the European Communities, 26/76, EU:C:1977:167, para. 20–27.

administrative and judicial decision-makers to apply Article 102.[29] Nonetheless, it remained unclear exactly to which types of situations the Bronner doctrine extended, because most types of abuse are constructed as "implicit" or "constructive" refusals to deal.[30] Thus, the ECJ in Slovak Telekom and the GC in Google Shopping restrained the scope of the refusal to deal doctrine to "explicit" refusals to deal that follow an explicit request for access.[31]

Also, in practice, Slovak Telekom and Google Shopping augment the discretion of the Commission by restricting the room of applicability of the indispensability test. In other words, by narrowing down the scale of legal formalism, the administrative and judicial decision-makers gain more discretion. Nevertheless, just as formalism in general can be both liberating and limiting, a broader grant of decisional jurisdiction can also restrain decision-makers more than it liberates them. Thus, in the absence of the formalistic rule, the decision-maker is permitted to decide whether the conduct is anticompetitive or not, centered on the specific circumstances of the case.[32]

In Hoffmann La Roche,[33] the Court decided that a dominant undertaking which applies discounts conditional on the fact that the customer gets all or most of its supplies from that undertaking abuses its dominant position. The legal formalism concerning the abusive nature of loyalty rebates was revised in Intel[34] and the Court did not deny the presumption that loyalty rebates as defined in Hoffmann La Roche are abusive. Since the Commission's decisional discretion is limited by law and judicial review, the result of Intel[35] is that the Commission is expected to be more constrained by rules after Intel than it had been by the substantive rule from Hoffmann La Roche.

It is argued that one of the key points of Intel is that dominant undertakings should have the chance to reveal that the presumed anticompetitive effects of the relevant conduct are implausible.[36] Moreover, in competition law, a highly abstract

[29] C 7/97 Bronner, EU:C:1998:569 .Microsoft Corp. v. Commission of the European Communities, T-201/04, EU:T:2007:289, para. 643–665.

[30] as Advocate General Saugmandsgaard Øe in Slovak Telekom observed Slovak Telekom, a.s. v. European Commission, C-165/19P, EU:C:2021:239.

[31] Google LLC, formerly Google Inc. and Alphabet, Inc. v. European Commission, T-612/17, EU: T:2021:763, para. 232.

[32] Google LLC, formerly Google Inc. and Alphabet, Inc. v. European Commission, T-612/17, EU: T:2021:763, paras. 162–180, 518–541.

[33] Case 85/76 Judgment of the Court of 13 February 1979. Hoffmann-La Roche & Co. AG v Commission of the European Communities. https://curia.europa.eu/juris/liste.jsf?num=C-85/76

[34] Case C-413/14 P, Judgment of the Court (Grand Chamber) of 6 September 2017

Intel Corp. v European Commission Appeal—Article 102 TFEU—Abuse of a dominant position—Loyalty rebates—Commission's jurisdiction—Regulation (EC) No 1/2003—Article 19 https://curia.europa.eu/juris/liste.jsf?num=C-413/14

[35] N. Petit, The Judgment of the EU Court of Justice in Intel and the Rule of Reason in Abuse of Dominance Cases, 43 Eur. L. Rev. 728 (2018).

[36] P. Ibáñez Colomo, The Future of Article 102 TFEU after Intel, 9 J. Eur. Comp. L. & Practice 293 (2018). J. Lindeboom and Y.L. Bouzoraa, CK Telecoms and the Assessment of Horizontal

rule necessitating decision-makers to ban "anticompetitive conduct" without offering any further guidance brings complexity. Hence, formalism to competition law leads to per se rules and "by object" prohibitions.

It is worth noting that per se rules are formalistic for the reason that they strongly reduce the number of considerations that are relevant in deciding whether some conduct is a restraint of trade in the sense of Section 1 of the Sherman Act 1890. To that extent, US federal courts have appealed to the rationales of US antitrust law assuming that the "fixing" of a "price" between competitors does not always constitute "horizontal price-fixing." In addition, even the most straightforward per se rule is not always applied wholly formalistically and so the same applies to the "by object" category in EU competition law functioning formalistically in particular cases such as naked horizontal price-fixing or naked output restrictions, but as a matter of legal principle necessitates an analysis of the legal and economic context of an agreement which takes place by looking at the rationale of EU competition law.[37] Thus, both per se rules and the by object category are formalistic to a degree.

References

1. Monti, G. (2020). *EU competition law and the rule of reason revisited*. TILEC Discussion Paper Dp 2020–021.
2. Hovenkamp, H. (2022). *A Miser's rule of reason: The Alston antitrust case*. Faculty Scholarship at Penn Law 2533.
3. Lindeboom, J., & Bouzoraa, Y. L. (2021). CK telecoms and the assessment of horizontal mergers in oligopolistic markets: Does the more economic approach entail stricter judicial review? *5 Eur. Comp. & Reg. L. Rev. 423*.
4. Lindeboom, J. (2021) The autonomy of EU law: A Hartian view, 13 Eur. *The Journal of Legal Studies, 271*.
5. Eben, M. (2021). The antitrust market does not exist: Pursuit of objectivity in a purposive process. *17 J. Comp. L. & Econ. 586*.
6. Petit, N. (2018). The judgment of the EU Court of Justice in Intel and the rule of reason in abuse of dominance cases. *43 Eur. L. Rev. 728*.
7. Ibáñez Colomo, P. (2018) The future of article 102 TFEU after Intel, 9 *J. Eur. Comp. L. & Practice 293*.
8. Scalia, B. A. (2012). Garner, *Reading Law: The Interpretation of Legal Texts* 412–414.

Mergers in Oligopolistic Markets: Does the More Economic Approach Entail Stricter Judicial Review?, 5 Eur. Comp. & Reg. L. Rev. 423 (2021).

[37] J. Lindeboom, The Autonomy of EU Law: A Hartian View, 13 EUR. J. LEG. STUD. 271 (2021).

Chapter 9
Digital Transformation of EU and Competition

9.1 Introduction

Digital technology embeds politics by shaping social outcomes which means that AI brings forward social and political transformation. Moreover, technocracy has a political device in place for delivering the direction for society, while the technocrats have the power to determine and effectuate the policies considered indispensable to proceed in the desired direction.

It has to be taken into account that the AI state due to the lack of technical capability deploys digital tools so as to identify and survey. Moreover, the digitization and algorithmicizing of identities offer the competence to link all pertinent information in a central register or to generate protocols facilitating information-sharing between administrative units.[1] Thus, AI technology prepares the arrival of AAI systems, AAI humanoids, and AAI society.

It is worth noting that authoritarian governments equipped with robust surveillance technologies raise the prospect of a drift toward totalitarianism. Thus, the convergence of digital surveillance and the police state raises such a possibility. Digital systems can be trained not only to monitor forbidden behavior but also to identify, categorize, isolate, and manage entire populations deemed politically dangerous.

Due to globally standardized measures, digital organizations can collect data on a global scale. Taking into account, digital platforms are sovereigns in their own right, platforms become totalizing institutions from which users have no realistic option of escaping. Will the AAI state be an electronic platform where AAI entities will function electronically with no material life?

---

[1] Britton-Purdy, Jedediah S., David Grewal, Amy Kapcyznski, and K. Sabeel Rahman. 2020. "Building a Law and Political Economy Framework: Beyond the Twentieth-Century Synthesis." 129 Yale Law Journal 1784

© The Author(s), under exclusive license to Springer Nature Switzerland AG 2023
G. I. Zekos, *Artificial Intelligence and Competition*, Contributions to Economics,
https://doi.org/10.1007/978-3-031-48083-6_9

9.2 EU Materialization

Federalism amalgamates separate states within an overarching political system in a way that permits each to uphold its own integrity. The constitution is the supreme law in the federal nation describing specific powers which belong to the federal government. The national government and state governments share powers. The body of law of the common central government is the federal law applying to everyone in the United States. The Supreme Court makes final decisions concerning federal laws about specific cases brought before them. Moreover, the US Supreme Court serves as the legal arbiter of the federal system in regard to conflicting claims of state and national governments. The superior relationship that federal laws have with regard to conflicting State laws is established.[2]

A federal union is a political system of shared sovereignty with momentous central government powers and others that the states implement. The United States is a federal union. Federations gave imperative functions, embracing foreign affairs, defense, and management of the economy and taxation, among others, to a federal government that implemented the powers conferred it directly upon the "citizenry of the federation."

The sui generis and complex character of the European Union makes it challenging to evaluate the strength and transmission channels of its global influence. To that extent, Bradford pinpoints the single market as the fundament of the EU's global regulatory power.[3]

It has to be taken into account that the vision to unite Europe from a fragmented to a conflict-ridden continent remains an "uphill task." In 1949, the United States worked with the Europeans to produce the Marshall Plan and urged the Europeans to abolish national trade barriers like tariffs. Moreover, Americans indicated the forming of a common market and adopting a federal union but this suggestion was radical for the highly nationalistic Europeans. It is characteristic that the European Coal and Steel Community began in 1952 and Schuman pronounced that this cooperative economic effort would be "a first step in the federation of Europe." On the other hand, the stoppage of the "United States of Europe" movement and its replacement by a functionalist tactic, expressed by the current EU model, was the outcome of the still intense sense of nationalism of the states of Europe.

In 1957, six European countries founded the European Economic Community, and, in 1993, the European Union came into force, generating a new level of integration among its member countries in order to avert wars. The Treaty of Rome was signed expressing the objectives of "the four freedoms": the movement of people, goods, services, and capital. Thus, instead of forming a federation, the EEC set up a structure of political bodies, appointed by the member states, to

[2] McCulloch v. Maryland, 17 U.S. (4 Wheat.) 316 (1819). Dodson, Scott (2016). "The Gravitational Force Of Federal Law". University of Pennsylvania Law Review. 164 (3): 703–753.

[3] Anu Bradford, The Brussels Effect – How the European Union rules the world Oxford University Press, 2020.

propose, approve, and rule on laws but most of the political power stayed firmly in the hands of the national governments.

In 1992, the Maastricht Treaty created the European Union but for the first time, the French, who had led the European unification process, expressed doubts about granting more sovereignty to a stronger European organization. The European Union began as a common market that gradually enlarged in size and original economic arrangements are enhanced by numerous political and regulatory institutions for the continent as a whole. Anyway, the EU is stronger and more democratic than it was when six nations founded the European Economic Community in 1957 but so far, the EU is still not a federalized "United States of Europe." To that extent, EU member states have principally given up only some economic authority to have the advantages of a common market and so the EU still has no elected president, no military force, no foreign policy, and no real power to enforce its laws.

Is there extensive disagreement today on the future of the European Union? Which is the place of the EU in a world of increasing geopolitical rivalry? Should Europe be developed into a federation or remain just a financial or economic exercise? Has Russia's war in Ukraine initiated a new era for European unity? Does the AI era dictate the transformation of the EU model into the USE?

Brussels-based technocrats have been spotted to impose policy solutions that have often been unwanted and/or thought to be unsuitable. It has to be taken into account that diverse political, economic, and diplomatic urgencies have been re-arranged to manage the multiple crises that have hit EU and so EU member states' relations have been comprehended and appreciated principally via the lens of economic strategies and priorities, heading for averting the largest EU economies from being battered by the infectivity of the weakest member states. Additionally, the intergovernmental management of the EU economic downturn ultimately harmonized with the national interests of the biggest EU countries to prevail on those of the most fragile ones.

It is characteristic that Europeans who dispute a more federalized EU argue against abandoning their sovereignty. It is worth mentioning here that the United States is a federal system and the EU is a unique economic and political union between 27 European countries and so the EU is not a federation. Unlike the United States, the EU lacks a formal constitution but it is supposed that the EU Treaties function in practice as a constitution since they outline the allocation of powers.

9.3 EU Functioning

The EU was set up in order to end the frequent wars between neighbors, which was an outcome of World War II. Thus, the European Coal and Steel Community united European countries politically and economically with the purpose of promoting and securing peace.

Since the 1992 Maastricht Treaty, defending member states' specific welfares, chiefly circumscribed to the realm of economic and foreign policy issues, has become a trademark of how EU politics and objectives have been practiced both inside and outside its borders. Also, it is argued that Europe is not "building a federal state similar to the United States[4]" due to deficient institutions and incompatible objectives constraining the course of European unification.

The Treaty establishing a Constitution for Europe was an unratified international treaty intended to found a consolidated constitution for EU replacing the existing European Union treaties with a single text.[5] The Treaty was signed on 29 October 2004 by representatives of the then 25-member states of the European Union but the rejection of the document by French and Dutch voters in May and June 2005 brought the ratification process to an end and so the process for EU becoming a federation was blocked. To that extent, the Treaty of Lisbon was created to replace the Constitutional Treaty.[6] In other words, when the Treaty of Lisbon entered into force in December 2009, the EU finally appeared to have achieved institutional consolidation after the failure of the Constitutional Treaty. To that extent, governments stick to their original bargain concerning the integration process and so they are reluctant to give up autonomy and enter into new commitments.

The EU has developed into a unique arrangement of multilevel governance but lacks a government in the strict or conventional sense. Moreover, the EU treaties refrain from referring to federalism per se, nor do they embrace specific references to sovereignty. Furthermore, the treaties assign various political and institutional responsibilities by policy area.

It is argued that the EU vertical division-of-powers dimension embraces multiple elements of federalism[7] but in reality, the EU is not a federation and G.I. Zekos argues that any effort to find bits of the federation in the current model of EU is not helpful in promoting the effectiveness of EU as a political entity. The EU model encompasses a multilevel system via patchy vertical separation and sharing of powers.

The EU is a unique political and economic partnership formed by a series of binding treaties and member states agreed to share sovereignty. The key objective of the European Union was to "preserve peace and liberty and to lay the foundations of an ever-closer union among the people of Europe" and so calling for economic growth which was to be achieved through the establishment of a custom union with a common external tariff, common policies for agriculture, transport and trade, and enlargement of the EU to the rest of the Europe. Thus, the EU has long viewed the enlargement route as an extraordinary opportunity to further stability and prosperity

---

[4] Alesina, Alberto, and Roberto Perotti. 2004. "The European Union: A Politically Incorrect View." Journal of Economic Perspectives 18 (4): 27–48.

[5] https://www.europarl.europa.eu/about-parliament/en/in-the-past/the-parliament-and-the-treaties/draft-treaty-establishing-a-constitution-for-europe

[6] https://en.wikipedia.org/wiki/Treaty_establishing_a_Constitution_for_Europe

[7] Jared Sonnicksen, Can the EU be a federal democracy? Assessing the horizontal and vertical dimension of the EU government from comparative perspective, Comparative European Politics (2022) 20:114–133

in Europe[8] which, on the other hand, G.I. Zekos[9] considers as a way for some EU member states in avoiding the political integration and establishment of the USE and so prolonging the national interests and populism against real functionality and advancement of EU into a global player. Nevertheless, some in the EU remain concerned that a larger EU would damage the capacity of the EU's up-to-date structures and decision-making procedures to run efficiently.

The EU is grounded on the rule of law, which is instituted by treaties that have been accepted voluntarily and democratically by all member countries and so if a policy area is not mentioned in a treaty, the Commission cannot propose a law in that area. Accordingly, institutions of the EU adopt legislation which the member countries then implement. It is characteristic that decision-making processes and the role of the EU institutions differ depending on the subject under consideration which makes the running of the EU peculiar and full of many disadvantages instead of functioning under a federal government. The European Union has seven institutions as its governance: The European Parliament, the Council of the European Union, The European Commission, the European Council, the European Central Bank, the Court of Justice of the European Union, and the European Court of Auditors. EU members have taken steps toward political integration, with decisions to develop a Common Foreign and Security Policy (CFSP) and efforts to advance collaboration in the area of Justice and Home Affairs (JHA). It is worth mentioning here that EU efforts to standardize policies in the JHA field were obstructed by member countries' fears that such measures could infringe on their legal systems and national sovereignty.

British voters decided on Brexit due to supposed economic difficulties grounded on the European integration and globalization but at the end of the day, British voters lost free access to the European market.[10] EU member countries have to make certain that national policies are in line with agreed EU strategies and positions but CFSP does not prevent individual member countries tracking their own national foreign policies or conducting their own national diplomacy which shows the character of the current EU model. CSDP seeks to improve the EU's capability to respond to security crises and to increase European military capabilities.[11]

---

[8]Laurenz Gerhke, "Scholz Pitches Major EU Enlargement—With Reform," Politico Europe, August 29, 2022.

[9]For detailed analysis see G Zekos, The United States of Europe The Global Player, 2019 Nova Science Publications New York USA. www.novapublishers.com. G Zekos, The United States of Europe in place of the European Union, 2017 Nova Science Publications New York USA. www.novapublishers.com

[10]Spisak, Anton (2022). Moving On: How the British Public Views Brexit and What It Wants From the Future Relationship With the European Union. October 18, 2022. Tony Blair Institute for Global Chance. Https://institute.global/policy/moving-how-british-public-views-brexit-andwhat-it-wants-future-relationship-european

[11]Giorgio Leali and Barbara Moens, "Ukraine War Gives Macron's Drive for EU Autonomy More Impetus," Politico Europe, March 9, 2022;

The EU is disintegrating and due to the COVID-19 crisis, the Lisbon Treaty has proven to be an accumulation of national interests.[12] Russia's war against Ukraine has given further incentive in advancing the EU as a robust international leader[13] via its transformation into a federation. In other words, Russia's 2022 invasion of Ukraine has stimulated debate on the future of the EU.

9.4 Federalism in EU Via ECJ

The EU is an entity of limited powers and is founded upon the principle of conferral which means that the EU institutions act within the bounds of the competences conferred upon them by the member states in the Treaties and so the exercise of EU legislative powers is restricted by the principles of subsidiarity and proportionality. It seems that the principle of proportionality was formally preserved in the EU Treaties as a structural constitutional principle of the EU legal order.[14] Kolowski[15] believes that the EU has moved beyond federation, but will never become a federation akin to the United States. According to Brugess,[16] federalism, in the EU context, is appreciated as the "application of federal principles to the process of European integration." On the other hand, federalism leads to the establishment of a federation.[17]

There is a reference to the "sui generis" nature of EU law[18] and so the European Court of Justice (ECJ) defined the system of the Treaties as "a new legal order of international law for the benefit of which the states have limited their sovereign rights." On the other hand, the Court of Justice is not the most significant organ in the

[12] https://www.faef.eu/wp-content/uploads/Constitutional-Toolkit.pdf

[13] EU High Representative for Foreign Affairs and Security Policy and Vice-President of the European Commission Josep Borrell, "Why European Strategic Autonomy Matters," European External Action Service, December 3, 2020. Jacopo Barigazzi and Jakob Hanke Vela, "EU's Unanimity Rules Are Here for Now, Despite the Chatter," Politico Europe, September 20, 2022.

[14] Darren Harvey Federal Proportionality Review in EU Law: Whose Rights are they Anyway? Nordic Journal of International Law 89 (2020) 303–326

[15] Koslowski, R., 1999. A constructivist approach to understanding the European Union as a federal polity. Journal of European Public Policy, 6(4), pp.561–578.

[16] Burgess, M. "'Federalism", in Wiener and Diez, A., 2003. European integration theory. Oxford University Press. p. 34

[17] Dosenrode, S., 2010. Federalism Theory and Neo-Functionalism: Elements for an analytical framework. Perspectives on Federalism, 2(3), pp.1–28. King, P., 1982. Federalism and Federation Croom Helm. London & Canberra.(federation is 'an institutional agreement, taking the form of a sovereign state and distinguished from other states solely by the fact that its central government incorporates regional units in its decision procedure on some constitutionally entrenched basis'). Albert Hayrapetyan Federalism, Functionalism and the EU: The Visions of Mitrany, Monnet and Spinelli https://www.e-ir.info/2020/09/21/federalism-functionalism-and-the-eu-the-visions-of-mitrany-monnet-and-spinelli/

[18] Case n. 26/62, Van Gend en Loos [1963], ECR, 3. Case n. 6/64, Costa/Enel [1964] ECR, 1141.

integration process and its responsibility in EU policy-making has been restricted.[19] The Court of Justice of the European Union (CJEU) interprets EU law to make certain that it is utilized in the same way in all EU countries settling legal disputes between national governments and EU institutions and it could be said that it has the role of EU Supreme Court. Both the US Supreme Court and the European Court of Justice engage in extensive constitutional review but the ECJ is a transnational court running in a legal context that lacks a functioning written constitution equivalent to the US Constitution. It has to be taken into account that *de jure*, Supreme Court constitutional adjudications do not have *erga omnes* results while, in most cases, de facto they do.

On the one hand, the US Supreme court[20] adds to the constitutionalizing of politics via law interpretation which advances the development of the United States. On the other hand, the ECJ lacks the possibility of constitutionalizing of politics in the EU which is a disadvantage in the political development of the EU. It is worth mentioning here that the US Supreme Court is vulnerable to internal forces such as the President, Congress, and national public opinion and, on the other hand, the European Court is vulnerable to external forces such as the member states and, predominantly, the latter's constitutional courts which means the legal importance of ECJ, in generating a common understanding of laws in EU sovereignty, is less vital than the US Supreme Court diminishing the legal value as a court not contributing to a solid picture of legal sovereignty of the current EU Model.

It has to be taken into account that the concept of national constitutional identity in Article 4(2) TEU means that the member states can identify their own national identity, but the decision about the compatibility of the national identity with EU obligations since the Treaty of Lisbon is always conferred in the European Court of Justice, which makes the ultimate decision on Kompetenz–Kompetenz.[21] Moreover, EU law always takes precedence over national constitutional law.[22] Kelemen[23] concludes that the supremacy of EU law and deference to the ECJ on questions of Kompetenz–Kompetenz does not jeopardize the constitutional identity of the member states.

It is characteristic that several national constitutional courts have directly disputed the primacy of EU law and the authority of the Court of Justice of the EU in their

[19] Boerger Anne (2014), "At the Cradle of Legal Scholarship on the European Union: The Life and early Work of Eric Stein", American Journal of Comparative Law, vol. 62, n° 4, p. 859–892.

[20] Ovidiu-Horia Maican, 2017. "USA Supreme Court Of Justice And European Court Of Justice (Comparison)," Perspectives of Law and Public Administration, Societatea de Stiinte Juridice si Administrative (Society of Juridical and Administrative Sciences), vol. 6(1), pages 136–141, December. https://ideas.repec.org/a/sja/journl/v6y2017i1p136-141.htmlhttps://www.supremecourt.uk/about/the-supreme-court-and-europe.html

[21] A. v. Bogdandy and S. Schill, 'Overcoming Absolute Primacy under the Lisbon Treaty', CMLR, 2011. 48: 1–38.

[22] Case C-11/70, International Handelsgesellschaft mbH [1970] ECR 01125.

[23] D. Kelemen, 'On the Unsustainability of Constitutional Pluralism. European Supremacy and the Survival of the Eurozone', 23 Maastricht Journal, 136–150

judgments.[24] The German[25] and Danish[26] highest courts have claimed that they have the residual authority, founded on national constitutional law, to determine whether EU legislative acts are enacted ultra vires which means that they were enacted beyond the competences conferred on the EU. In December 2016, the Supreme Court of Denmark, in its decision in the Ajos case,[27] discounted the guidelines of the Court of Justice of the European Union and so setting new boundaries to the applicability of the ECJ's rulings in Denmark. Moreover, the Hungarian Constitutional Court endorsed in the abstract the possibility to refuse compliance with EU law in the name of a Member State's sovereignty and constitutional identity.[28]

Is there a rule of law crisis in EU? The German Federal Constitutional Court disputed the CJEU's authority and so in the *PSPP/Weiss* decision, the FCC criticized the "flawed methodology" in the CJEU's *Gauweiler*[29] ruling and demanded the European Central Bank (ECB) to offer extra guarantees to Germany.[30] FCC supports that the ECB and the Court of Justice of the EU have violated EU law by not applying rightly the principle of proportionality declaring the decision unlawful and actually non-existent in Germany which means that it departs from EU law.[31] Thus, the constitutional court of Germany directly questioned the CJEU's primacy as the ultimate arbiter over EU law.[32] It is supposed that the judgments of the Court (CJEU) have the status of de facto precedents with an *erga omnes* effect, binding all courts in all member states but the GFCC[33] directly contested the CJEU's interpretive

[24]Taricco judgmentJudgement of 8 September 2015 in case C-105/14. the Italian justices thought that the ECJ Grand Chamber judgment infringed upon the Italian constitution's principle.

[25]89 BVerfGE 155 (Maastricht).

[26]Carlson and Others v. Rasmussen, Case No I-361/1997 (Supreme Court, 6 April 1998).

[27]Judgement of the Supreme Court, Delivered Thursday 6 December 2016, Case 15/2014. M. R. Madsen, H. P. Olsen and U. Sadl, Competing Supremacies and Clashing Institutional Rationalities: The Danish Supreme Court's Decision in the Ajos Case and the National Limits of Judicial Cooperation, iCourts Working Paper Series, No. 85, 2017.

[28]G. Halmai, "Abuse of Constitutional Identity. The Hungarian Constitutional Court on Interpretation of Article E) (2) of the Fundamental Law,' Review of Central and East European Law, 43 (2018), 23–42.

[29]Case C-62/14. Peter Gauweiler and Others v Deutscher Bundestag. Judgment of the Court (Grand Chamber) of 16 June 2015 https://eur-lex.europa.eu/legal-content/EN/TXT/?qid=1457105032167&uri=CELEX:62014CJ0062

Case C-370/12. Thomas Pringle v Government of Ireland and Others. Judgment of the Court (Full Court), 27 November 2012. https://eur-lex.europa.eu/legal-content/EN/TXT/?qid=1457104816935&uri=CELEX:62012CJ0370

[30]2 BvR 859/15. See Pavlos Eleftheriadis, The German Constitutional Court's Weiss judgment is a Failure of German Constitutionalism. (the judgment is an unprecedented revolt against the law of the European Union.) | Policy briefs | European Institutions & Policies https://www.eliamep.gr/

[31]Not following the Judgment of the Grand Chamber of the Court of Justice of the EU in Case C-493/17 *Weiss* of 11 December 2018 ECLI:EU:C:2018:1000

[32]Beatrice Monciunskaite & Niels Kirst, The Rule of Law Crisis and the Supremacy of EU Law *https://bridgenetwork.eu/2022/06/30/the-rule-of-law-crisis-supremacy-eu-law/*

[33]Federal Constitutional Court judgment of the Second Senate of 5 May 2020 2 BvR 859/15 (PSPP) ECLI:DE:BVerfG:2020:rs20200505.2bvr085915.

monopoly and its authority to say definitively what the EU law is. Consequently, the GFCC declared EU law unconstitutional under the German constitution because it was unconstitutional under EU primary law.[34] It is worth mentioning here that, in a federation like the United States, the decisions of the US Supreme Court are not disregarded by member states of the federation leading to the political existence and success of the United States.

9.5 AI Advancement and Competition

Artificial intelligence systems will be able to solve problems whose scale and complexity are beyond human capabilities. Moreover, via advanced artificial intelligence (AAI) techniques,[35] machines will think as brains, and brains can be thought of as machines. Human intervention in the decision-making will be completely out of the loop in entirely automated systems.[36] Also, AI is developing very rapidly and human societies are becoming more "information mature" by relying increasingly on AI technologies which means that the impact of AI technologies on human shared values increases. Likewise, AI has become an integral part of public governance and so AI systems have to implement and comply with the rule of law. While AI enriches neutrality and accuracy in decision-making, it raises fears about the status of public values and democratic principles.

Does AI contribute to legitimate political processes? Does AI pose threats to democracy? Do AI applications disrupt democracy via information manipulation? Do AI applications necessitate a central government for EU in order to have an effective central control of governance?

It is worth noting that the resources of big data are utilized by AI systems and so controlling the future through the power of inference which means that AI governmentality is based upon governable subjects who are seen as aggregates of infra-personal data assembled and exploitable on an indescribable scale and detail.[37] Also, the extending accessibility of data and the escalating power of AI

[34] M Wendel, 'Paradoxes of Ultra-vires Review: A Critical Review of the PSPP Decision and Its Initial Reception' (2020) German Law Journal 979, 984. Davor Petric Reasoning, Interpretation, Authority, Pluralism, and the Weiss/PSPP Saga European Papers Vol. 6, 2021, No 2, pp. 1123–1150

[35] G Zekos, Economics and Law of Artificial Intelligence - Finance, Economic Impacts, Risk Management and Governance, 2021 https://link.springer.com/book/10.1007/978-3-030-64254-9 G. Zekos, Artificial Intelligence And E-Bills Of Lading Contracts, Journal of Internet Law April 2021 Vol. 24 N8 p3–10 Wolters Kluwer https://lrus.wolterskluwer.com/store/product/journal-of-internet-law/

[36] G Zekos, Advanced Artificial Intelligence and Robo-Justice,2022, www.springer.com

[37] A Rouvroy, 'Algorithmic governmentality: a passion for the real and the exhaustion of the virtual', Transmediale – All Watched Over by Algorithms, Berlin. (2015), www.academia.edu/10481275/Algorithmic_governmentality_a_passion_for_the_real_and_the_exhaustion_of_the_virtual

decision-making alter the future of political institutions. To that extent, AI decisions in public governance must be transparent and explainable to gain legitimacy.

The utilization of AI systems by public decision-makers augments concern to develop legal and policy frameworks for the trustworthy sharing and processing of data to support democratic processes.[38] To that extent, data-sharing allows citizens to connect with public decision-making processes in a manner supplementing the more traditional role of the news media to build and inform political agendas.[39] Additionally, AI implementation could bring equal treatment for all citizens via AI fairness rather than human bias which is the distinctive part of liberal democracies.[40] Which is the factor of allowing AI to function objectively and achieving the best outcome? The answer is a good algorithm formulated in a non-bias way and not influenced by any political intervention in favoring a particular solution except an objective outcome coming out of valuable big data.

As mentioned earlier, AI is superior to human intelligence for the analysis of large and complex problems encompassing the need for strategy, prediction of long-term consequences, and analysis of vast amounts of data. To that extent, algorithmic governance is utilized both in ordering human action, and in the use of AI in the domain of government, and predominantly in a situation in which AI is given the authority to govern by mandates. Additionally, technical standardization facilitates systems and network compatibility, enabling interoperability and so the EU Commission utilizes AI as a functional instrument to boost equality of opportunity, socio-economic welfare, and democracy. Likewise, interoperability generates economies of scale and market competition, stipulating international cooperation and coordination in standards development. Thus, AAI technology will implement all of them by offering an unbiased functioning in order to function globally. In other words, a single government for the EU is essential in order to have a standardized implementation of AI systems which means the need of transforming the current EU model of governance into a federal governance model.

---

[38] G Zekos, How Will Ai Influence Politics? Chance Or Danger For Democracy? Cicero Foundation www.cicerofoundation.org July 6, 2022

[39] T Flew and P Iosifidis, "Populism, Globalisation and Social Media" (2020) 82(1) International Communication Gazette 7–25, "Understanding Algorithmic Decision-Making: Opportunities and Challenges' of the European Parliamentary Research Service EPRS March 2019, https://www.europarl.europa.eu/RegData/etudes/STUD/2019/624261/EPRS_STU(2019)624261_EN.pdf.
Leslie, D., Burr, C., Aitken, M., Katell, M., Briggs, M., Rincon, C. (2021). Human rights, democracy, and the rule of law assurance framework for AI systems: A proposal. The Alan Turing Institute. https://doi.org/10.5281/zenodo.5981676

[40] Mukand S, Rodrik D, (2020) The Political Economy of Liberal Democracy. The Economic Journal 130(627):765–792. https://doi.org/10.1093/ej/ueaa004

9.6 Political Integration of EU

Can the steps of the European Community integration process be described as part of the traditional federalizing process? Hay[41] wrote about certain "federalizing features" of the common market Treaty system and federalism is ascertained as the process of federalizing a political community.[42] To that extent, Weiler[43] argues that "The Community is not destined to become another America or indeed a federal state."

Joschka Fischer has said that he considers that in the end, the EU must become a single federation, with its political leader chosen by direct elections among all of its citizens.[44] Moreover, Matteo Renzi[45] has called for a "United States of Europe," and political theorist Glyn Morgan has made an extended argument for a super state as a desirable geopolitical rival to the United States.[46] Furthermore, Mario Draghi urged the EU to adopt a "pragmatic federalism" involving treaty change.[47]

Eurosceptics argue that the EU acts as an imperialist power towards its own member states but the EU lacks much international power, at least in comparison to China and the United States. It is worth mentioning here that Eurosceptics consider that European Integration constitutes a form of imperialism.[48] Do Hungary and Poland argue against the European Union's attempts to enforce the rule of law? It is obvious that all countries have joined EU voluntarily and so they have to follow the rule of law. Polish and Hungarians as individuals and Poland and Hungary as member states have the same rights and responsibilities as other European citizens and member states.

It is argued that the EU is a political and economic entity committed, both at its federal level and at the member state level, to a formula of liberal democratic market capitalism which is marked by the "Four Freedoms" enforced by the European Court

[41] Hay Peter (1968), "Supremacy of Community Law in National Courts. A Progress Report on Referrals Under the EEC Treaty", American Journal of Comparative Law, vol. 16, n° 4, p. 524–551. Hay Peter (1966), Federalism and Supranational Organizations. Patterns for New Legal Structures, Urbana, University of Illinois Press

[42] Pall Mall Friedrich Carl J. (1955), "Federal Constitutional theory and emergent proposal", in Arthur W. MacMahon (ed.), Federalism: Mature and Emergent, New York, Doubleday and Company, Inc., 510 seq

[43] Weiler Joseph H. H (1984), "Eric Stein: a tribute", Michigan law review, vol. 82, n° 5–6, p. 1160–1162.

[44] "From Confederacy to Federation - Thoughts on the finality of European integration" Speech by Joschka Fischer at the Humboldt University in Berlin 12 May 2000 https://ec.europa.eu/dorie/fileDownload.do?docId=192161&cardId=192161.

[45] https://www.euractiv.com/section/future-eu/news/italian-pm-vows-to-push-for-united-states-of-europe-during-presidency/

[46] Glyn Morgan Is the European Union imperialist? Journal of European Public Policy Volume 27, 2020 - Issue 9

[47] https://www.politico.eu/article/draghi-pragmatic-federalism-eu-treaty-change/

[48] Hazony, Y. (2018). The virtue of nationalism. Basic Books.

of Justice. Furthermore, the EU, in its current model, lacks the power to enforce a center and periphery power relationship on a member state. On the other hand, the USE model could function properly as a federation and federal states had to follow the federal laws.

In the United States, the concept of cooperative federalism is a steering principle and so the federal government sets a baseline and the states are obliged to enact laws/regulations that are at any rate as stringent as the federal counterparts. Federal laws/statutes/acts are bills passed by Congress through a legislative process applying thought in the United States. EU regulations and directives are both legal acts adopted by the EU institutions following either the ordinary or the special legislative procedure. However, the way they are implemented is different. In fact, legislation is more forward rather than the one taking place in the EU.

Also, Bruno Le Maire warned that Europe faced "vassalization" when China decided to buy entire portions of strategic infrastructure in Europe denoting the status of the current EU model.[49] In addition, Glyn Morgan[50] argues that "insofar as the EU remains a decentralized intergovernmental organization, it will remain dependent on the United States... If Europe is going to become a superpower, it will have to develop a more centralized decision-making sovereign buttressed by a common identity. The alternative is for Europe to remain a weak and dependent power, at most a mere auxiliary to its American guardian." To that extent, Emma Bonino[51] argues that "More broadly, the EU should learn to act as a one single body, in a more supranational, rather than intergovernmental, fashion. A "light federation" should be progressively defined, paving the way to the United States of Europe. The diplomatic stalemate we are incurring when dealing with other powers on the world scene is primarily triggered by the opposite political stances the EU gives voice to. There is no uniform, shared, and cohesive diplomatic position to tackle global issues. Hence, especially in light of the profound geo-political changes EuroMediterranean relations are currently undergoing, it is key to adopt a new, more effective, and coherent approach for structuring EU politics."

It is worth noting that the new Quirinale Treaty[52] between France and Italy calls for evolution toward a more federal Europe "to support and accelerate the European integration process." Also, EU governments agree on the necessity to prioritize investment, modernize infrastructure, reduce emissions, and boost digitization.

---

[49] Mallet, V. (2019, April 2). La Maire calls for new empire to save EU from rival powers. Financial Times. https://www.ft.com/content/af7460f4-5523-11e9-91f9-b6515a54c5b1

[50] Glyn Morgan, HAYEK, HABERMAS, AND EUROPEAN INTEGRATION, Critical Review Volume 15, 2003 - Issue 1–2 p20 https://www.tandfonline.com/doi/abs/10.1080/08913810308443572

[51] Emma Bonino, The Political Crisis In Europe Is Bad News For Southern Mediterranean And Euromediterranean Relations, 09 Euromed Survey the IEMed based on the results of the ninth Euromed Survey p 54

https://www.iemed.org/wp-content/uploads/2020/12/01.The-Political-Crisis-in-Europe-is-Bad-News-for-Southern-Mediterranean.pdf

[52] https://www.gisreportsonline.com/r/federal-eu/

Is the EU heading towards federation or disintegration after the Ukraine ordeal? The EU's seeming inability to deal forcefully and effectively with events in Ukraine has constituted a further external dimension of the crisis. It is argued that the EU is in crisis and so trust is eroding. Moreover, due to toxic politics, power is loosening and solidarity has frayed.[53]

In the case of the Euro crisis, the fiscal and economic governance responses were not led by the EU government, but rather by national governments. To that extent, the failure of national governments to manage a common approach in the "migration crisis" shows the weakness of the EU as a political entity. Nevertheless, the EU polity lacks a central democratic government powering it acting as a global player and so in its current model is seen as a "mere pawn on the international political stage" showing a picture of member states struggling to promote their national interests and EU fulfilling accordingly the interests of other super powers.

In light of Russia's war on Ukraine, it has become clear that Brussels needs the power of a federal government to decide on defense, etc. Moreover, the Russian invasion of Ukraine uncovers the weaknesses and dependencies of the European Union and its member states. To that extent, an EU defense has to be at the service of an EU foreign and security policy demanding a political union with a single representation of the EU in the international institutions and arena. Energy and defense policies entail a single EU foreign policy denoting a true political union and so a federal government.[54]

To that extent, Damon Linker[55] argues that "Russian President Vladimir Putin has inadvertently accomplished what often seemed impossible—bringing the continent together on foreign policy and thereby laying a solid foundation for a true United States of Europe." Moreover, it is obvious that Putin's invasion has triggered unity in Europe and so members of the EU have felt deeply pressured by a common challenger and, at the same time, EU member states have realized the inability of the current EU model to act as a global player and instead EU is hiding behind NATO and other super Powers and only some EU members found the opportunity to promote their national status on the global area. Dinan[56] noticed that "people only accept change when they are faced with necessity and only recognize necessity when the crisis is upon them."

Has the EU been relapsed into the old dependency on US leadership? It seems that with the United States still taking final responsibility, through NATO, for Europe's security, EU member states select national interest over defining and defending the EU's collective interests. Additionally, it could be said that in a

---

[53] Desmond Dinan, Neill Nugent, William E. Paterson, The European Union in Crisis, https://www.perlego.com/book/2997029/the-european-union-in-crisis-pdf

[54] Time for the United States of Europe! https://www.euractiv.com/section/future-eu/opinion/time-for-the-united-states-of-europe/

[55] Damon Linker, How Putin midwifed the United States of Europe https://theweek.com/russo-ukrainian-war/1010882/how-putin-midwifed-the-united-states-of-europe

[56] Dinan, D. (2010) 'Institutions and Governance: A New Treaty, a Newly Elected Parliament and a New Commission'. *JCMS*, Vol. 48, s1, pp. 95–118.

way, due to Ukraine war, the European Union acts more like a coherent political entity and let us hope that Europeans will realize the need to transform EU into the USE for the reason that super powers might withdraw from Europe as long as their interests are relocated/moving elsewhere in the globe and so EU will remain a weak topical player.

It has to be taken into consideration that EU countries have been reluctant to give up on their sovereignty and instead focus on shared policy initiatives. Macron's vision[57] is to "create together a European power of the future ... an independent Europe that has given itself the means to decide its own future and not rely on the decisions of other major powers." Due to the Russian invasion of Ukraine, Katarina Barley realizes that the EU "does not have an original competence in foreign policy."[58] Javier Giner[59] argues that "the United States of Europe will finally become the next version of the European system of states."

It is worth noting that the results of the Conference on the Future of Europe generated the prospect of moving towards the establishment of the United States of Europe.[60] CoFoE reopened the discussion on the need for a European Constitution. Moreover, Russia's invasion of Ukraine has inspired moves toward common energy procurement, more defense cooperation, and a more security-oriented union, raising even questions for democratic accountability.[61] Also, concerning the disparity between deeper policy cooperation and stalled democratic processes, the conference noticed the existing gap between policies and politics. In fact, it discussed the need for a wider base of legitimacy for advances in European integration and EU cooperation needs to be the result of stronger democratic engagement. On the other hand, political reform processes cannot merely use citizen initiatives but there is a need for the commitment of governments in transforming the EU into the USE. In other words, the politicians of the EU member states as well as at the EU level must decide to move forward in generating the politically united EU as a federation antagonizing other big federations.

[57] Macron calls for new European security pact 01/19/2022

[58] Christoph Hasselbach Germany"s elusive goal of a European federal state The Express Tribune, January 23rd, 2022.

[59] https://www.europe-today.eu/2021/03/03/united-states-of-europe-why-how-who-when/

[60] A democratic European Federation is a necessary next step after CoFoE https://www.euractiv.com/section/future-eu/opinion/a-democratic-european-federation-is-a-necessary-next-step-after-cofoe/ CoFoE recommendations share a common theme: a demand for a more united, effective and democratic Europe.

[61] https://carnegieeurope.eu/2022/05/12/eu-democracy-after-conference-on-future-of-europe-pub-87110 Christos Mavrakos Conference on the Future of Europe: Who is ready for a European Political Union? ELIAMEP | Policy Brief #150/2021 https://www.eliamep.gr/wp-content/uploads/2021/06/Policy-brief-150-Mavrakos-final-1.pdf

EU member states are profoundly divided on the type of Union they want to build.[62] Overall, enthusiasm for further integration is weak due to the fact that some member states are not prepared to cede further sovereignty to the EU and others are preventing EU regulation penetrating too far into their national decision-making powers.[63] Thus, EU member countries are firmly protective of their sovereign rights and oppose extra pooling of sovereignty that transfers those decisions to Brussels which means that European governments' capacity to make compromises to advance European integration is severely constrained by EU member countries national politics linked to populism.

The pandemic and Russia's war in Ukraine altered the external surroundings of the dispute on the future of Europe and about reforming the European Union. It is questionable if the current EU can cope with the current geopolitical changes necessitating its transformation into a federation in order to have a government with the power to decide for all Europeans evading the current struggle of officials to satisfy the demands of various member states against the interests of a single political entity.

9.7 Digitizing EU

The European Union is a project in constant making since the founding of the European Coal and Steel Community reaching great levels of integration, but progress has not been made unvaryingly in all fields. At the political level, integration has encountered noteworthy impediments slowing down the process in comparison to other common areas, such as economics.

It is obvious that the European Union is a unique political route and the process of integration responds to the requirements of the organization to adjust to the social, political, and economic reality and solve the problems arising from the process. To that extent, digitalization is a process necessitated to acclimate the European Union to the reality by offering a common frame to an existing digital world. Thus, the EU needs to respond to the necessities of the society for the accomplishment of European standards in a new, but already significant, area. The European Union digitization course built up great prospects in terms of economic growth and to that extent, the private sector is not the only one influenced by the digitization process, but the public sector will profit from a wider use of new digital devices.[64]

---

[62] Agnès Bénassy-Quéré et al., "A resilient Euro needs FrancoGerman compromise," Le Monde and Die Zeit, September 27, 2017, http://bruegel.org/2017/09/a-resilient-euro-needs-franco-german-compromise/

[63] https://www.swp-berlin.org/en/publication/after-the-conference-on-the-future-of-europe-time-to-make-reforms-happen

[64] David Ramiro Troitiño, The European Union Facing the twenty-first Century: The Digital Revolution, TalTech Journal of European Studies Tallinn University of Technology (ISSN 2674–4619), Vol. 12, No. 1 (35) doi: 10.2478/bjes-2022-0003

It is worth noting that the digitalization process of society influences competition and AI systems assist regulators to enforce competition law more effectively in modern data-driven economies in which market structures are becoming more complicated and different ways of infringing antitrust rules have appeared and so competition law enforcement relies on sophisticated ADM tools.[65] Hence, administrative bodies incorporate technologies in their decision-making processes.[66] Moreover, ADM systems offer capacity for improving internal efficiency by accessing greater amounts of data from more diverse sources and so competition authorities have a better understanding of the dynamics of markets and the elements affecting competition therein.[67]

EU prioritizes integration at the digital level within a broader social framework due to the fact that the citizens of modern societies continuously communicate digitally. Furthermore, the relationship of European firms with design, production, marketing, and generation of added value from products and services is anticipated to be redefined because the digital economy is already a reality, with relevant prospective advancement and significant progress.

Information and communication technologies (ICTs) permit the sector to function in a transparent and efficient way causing the reduction of corruption through clear control of public activities. Moreover, participation derived from the formation of a common political digital space is vital for deepening the integration at the European level. Hence, digital advancement will cultivate the formation of a more integrated European space at a political level for the reason that it diminishes distances by facilitating the participation of all European citizens in the political development of the EU.[68] Thus, the political future of Europe implicates removing barriers to create a common political frame.

Furthermore, digital development merges the optimization of resources and the reduction of costs at a private and public level. As a result, the European Union accelerates a process to enhance economic competitiveness and public spending. Once again, the formation of the digital market meets the opposition of nationalism supporting State autonomy against the unifying thrusts.

It is worth noting that the perception of national sovereignty plays a pertinent role in the process of European construction from its beginnings to the present day generating a game of balance between cooperation and integration and so a wrongful

---

[65] Ioannis Lianos, Computational Competition Law and Economics: Issues, Prospects - An Inception Report, (Hellenic Competition Commission 2021).

[66] Herwig Hofmann, An Introduction to Automated Decision Making (ADM) and Cyber- Delegation in the Scope of EU Public Law, Indigo Working Paper, (2021). Marcela Mattiuzzo and Henrique Felix Machado, Algorithmic Governance in Computational Antitrust—a Brief Outline of Alternatives for Policymakers, 2 Stan. Comput. Antitrust 23 (2022).

[67] Herwig Hofmann & Isabella Lorenzoni, Future Challenges For Automation In Competition Law Enforcement, https://ssrn.com/abstract=4492609

[68] Hanschitz, G. (2017), 'Digitalization of politics and elections,' Handbook of CyberDevelopment, Cyber-Democracy, and Cyber-Defense, Cham: Springer, pp. 1–15. https://doi.org/10.1007/978-3-319-06091-0_3-1

fight between national sovereignty and federalism.[69] Consequently, the European Union, presently highly integrated, has constantly evolved from cooperation to integration. On the other hand, the new digital Europe compels a legal framework in which to settle and effectively and respectfully expands the principles of integration towards a totally politically unified EU in the form of USE because digitization demands standardization and automation instead of the current legal framework of the existing EU model where there are differences concerning the implementation of EU Regulations due to legal traditions.

The influence of the Digital Single Market depends on the capacity to generate enough data for effective casting. Moreover, dependence on reliable data is decisive, putting Europe ahead of other global players for the reason that the European industry is more developed paralleled to international competitors. Hence, the EU selects the investment in the generation of data because of its prospective and as a result of the inherent need which means that management at the European level does not necessitate any undermining of the sovereignty of the member states, since they lack the needed power to make such sovereignty effective in the context of the digital economy. Thus, European leadership in the control and regulation of the digital economy is not only advocated but is also a basic need for the right functioning of the political and the social system of its members which means that the EU has to stimulate projects and innovation such as online medicine, GovTech, and AI in the labor market with global partners.[70]

It is worth mentioning here that the digital dominion revises and, at the same time, challenges the traditional notion of sovereignty and so AI technologies are deeply remodeling both societies and individuals, involving how we act, communicate, and think. To that extent, this impact extends to political institutions and the capability to exercise sovereignty in the first place. Moreover, the new EU legislation in the digital sphere is not only an exercise of EU sovereignty to make certain the protection of EU values such as fair competition and democracy, but also an effort to keep and protect its sovereignty in an advancing AAI world.

President Macron pronounced the need to safeguard digital sovereignty at European level.[71] Does macron mean that EU has to become a single political entity? Thierry Breton[72] revealed several initiatives to strengthen European digital

[69] Iwabuchi, K. (2019), 'Globalization, digitalization, and renationalization: Some reflections from Japanese cases,' Situations, vol. 12, no. 1, pp. 1–2.

[70] Joamets, K. & Chochia, A. (2020), "Artificial intelligence and its impact on labour relations in Estonia,' Slovak Journal of Political Sciences, vol. 20, no. 2, pp. 255–277. https://doi.org/10.34135/sjps.200204

[71] Emmanuel Macron, 'Discours du Président Emmanuel Macron sur la stratégie de défense et de dissuasion devant les stagiaires de la 27ème promotion de l'école de guerre' (7 February 2020)(it is "up to Europe to define the regulatory framework that it imposes upon itself, as it entails both the protection of individual liberties and the economic data of our companies, laying at the heart of our sovereignty and our concrete operational capacity to act in an autonomous manner.")

[72] Thierry Breton, 'Speech by Commissioner Thierry Breton at Hannover Messe' (Hannover Messe Digital Days, 20 July 2020) Annegret Bendiek and Isabella Stürzer, 'Advancing European Internal

sovereignty. In addition, Nathalie A. Smuha[73] argues that “European digital sovereignty can thus be understood as the ability of the European Union—including its citizens and businesses—to autonomously decide on their relationship with (providers of) digital technology. This implies the exercise of control over two entwined elements, namely (a) the direction or ‘destiny’ of digital technology within the EU, and (b) the concrete digital infrastructure that enables the technology.” On the other hand, Larsen[74] argues that digital sovereignty “refers to a nation’s ability to control its digital destiny,” while adding that this “may include control over the entire AI supply chain, from data to hardware and software” which means that the state has this power by being a state but in the case of EU, everything depends on the authority given to EU by the Members States which does not denote real-state sovereignty in its classical essence.

Also, it is argued that European sovereignty implies a vision of the EU as an autonomous agent seeing the EU as legislating by having the capacity to adopt legislation and adjudicating by having the capacity to take part in judicial decision-making, through the CJEU together with national courts, as regulating by having the capability to regulate, through the European Commission and regulatory agencies and as enforcing by having the capability to enforce EU law. Instead, the EU legal order co-exists with the legal orders of its member states indicating that its competence and jurisdiction are not equal to the traditional autonomous concept of sovereignty. Thus, while sovereignty is conventionally intellectualized at the level of nation-states, it has been liberally employed in the European context to the extent and scale that particular competences have been assigned to the EU by its member states. Consequently, taking into account the reasonable context of sovereignty means that the European sovereignty should infer a vision of the EU as an autonomous agent denoting that the EU has to become an autonomous single political entity and so not be dependent on the wishes of the member states.

Furthermore, it is argued that states must ensure to “protect their citizens and businesses from the manifold challenges to self-determination in the digital sphere”[75] denoting single-state sovereignty which does not infer to the current EU because its model is grounded on the interests of the member states and the authority given to EU by them and so AAI technology demands the transformation of EU into the USE in order as a single digital sovereignty to comply with the demands of AAI digitalization.

---

and External Digital Sovereignty. The Brussels Effect and the EU-US Trade and Technology Council’ (2022) 20 SWP.

[73] Nathalie A. Smuha, Digital Sovereignty In The European Union: Five Challenges From A Normative Perspective, https://ssrn.com/abstract=4501591 P6

[74] Benjamin Cedric Larsen, ‘The Geopolitics of AI and the Rise of Digital Sovereignty’ (Brookings, 8 December 2022) https://www.brookings.edu/research/the-geopolitics-of-ai-and-the-riseof-digital-sovereignty/

[75] Julia Pohle and Thorsten Thiel, ‘Digital Sovereignty’ (2020) 9 **Internet Policy Review**

9.8 AI Networking

It has to be taken into consideration that technological collaborations empower organizations and regions to share, transfer, and integrate new knowledge, reinforcing processes of knowledge making and recombination, and extending the depth and breadth of the local knowledge basis. Hence, by enabling access to diversified knowledge, collaboration diminishes the costs of innovation by advancing externalities and knowledge spillover.[76]

A global innovation network is a globally organized web of collaborative interactions between different organizations involved in knowledge production that is linked to and resulting in innovation which means that via global networks, global players are able to access external differentiated knowledge boosting the opportunities of knowledge recombination taking on global dimensions. So far, in a global and digitalized context where knowledge exchange crosses regional and national boundaries, investing in global linkages is central to be innovative.[77] It has to be taken into account that global R&D collaborations offer developed countries with the opening to quickly access foreign market information and knowledge and so enabling them to harmonize and integrate the complementary resources and capabilities which means coproducing products due to the fact that the complementarity of resources and competences furthers additional collaborative innovations.[78]

To that extent, it is characteristic that EU innovation policies have been encouraging technological cooperation and boosting the share of knowledge between member states. Moreover, innovation networks play an imperative role in organizing the collective production of scientific and technological knowledge which means that collaboration through innovation networks permits the overcoming of the absence of financial resources in R&D investment, the sharing of risks and uncertainty, the access to external partners' competences, and better management of innovation intricacy. Thus, the management and advancement of innovation access by a single source is vital not mentioning in the case of AI technology where standardization is essential which means that the advancement of innovation by a single source in a politically united USE is central in order to gain leadership in a global market rather than having 27 or more jurisdictions to struggle an access to innovation networks having to deal with colossal networks of China, the United States, etc.

---

[76] Balland, P. A., & Boschma, R. (2021). Complementary interregional linkages and Smart Specialisation: an empirical study on European regions. Regional Studies, 55(6), 1059–1070.

[77] Martin, R., Aslesen, H. W., Grillitsch, M., & Herstad, S. J. (2018). Regional innovation systems and global flows of knowledge. In New avenues for regional innovation systems-theoretical advances, empirical cases and policy lessons (pp. 127–147). Springer, Cham

[78] Tsouri, M., Hanson, J., & Normann, H. E. (2021). Does participation in knowledge networks facilitate market access in global innovation systems? The case of offshore wind. Research Policy, 50(5), 104,227. Harmancioglu, N., & Tellis, G. J. (2018). Silicon envy: How global innovation clusters hurt or stimulate each other across developed and emerging markets. Journal of International Business Studies, 49, 902–918.

It is worth noting that emerging countries utilize global networking to develop new and stronger R&D cooperation with foreign companies in developed countries such as the international cooperation strategy embraced by Brazil, India, and China corporations not only producing patents of higher value but also touching the development of subsequent inventions in a wider range of other technical fields. Hence, by participating in global networks, emerging countries absorb knowledge from partners and so augmenting their own competitiveness not only in the local market but also globally.

It is well known that the existing innovation geography implicates interregional collaborations within the European area[79] rather than global collaboration with innovation clusters owing to the absence of political unity prohibits the development. It is fundamental to bear in mind EU innovation in an AAI technology environment which means that it is crucial to consider the global openness of European regions, and their prospective capability to extend their collaborative networks to the global market via the EU digital economy managed by a single political entity, the USE, and its digital capacities, rather than the handling by 27 or more small digital jurisdictions.

9.9 The European Court of Justice is Rejected as the Single EU Supreme Court

As discussed earlier, the German Federal Constitutional Court disputed the CJEU's authority and so inconsistency in applying DMA and competition rules generates a setting where companies must apply different conditions in different markets and so fragmenting the objective of achieving a single market with one set of rules.[80] It has to be taken into consideration that Italy understood that Amazon abused its dominant position and the Court noted that Amazon could only challenge the Italian and European decisions at the end of their proceedings which means that even though the antitrust regulation guarantees the effective application of European competition law, Amazon faces a deviating ruling on the same practice since the territorial scope is different. The online hotel Booking and Amazon cases show that the ECN fails to accomplish its purpose of ensuring a common approach in enforcing European competition law.[81]

In Europe, the member states apply their own national competition laws in parallel with European competition laws. To that extent, France, Belgium, Germany,

[79] De Noni, I., Orsi, L., & Belussi, F. (2018). The role of collaborative networks in supporting the innovation performances of lagging-behind European regions. Research Policy, 47(1), 1–13.

[80] Bundeskartellamt, Narrow "Best Price" Clauses of Booking also Anticompetitive https://www.bundeskartellamt.de/SharedDocs/Meldung/EN/Pressemitteilungen/2015/23_12_2015_Booking.com .html

[81] Case T-19/21, Amazon.com, Inc. and Others v European Commission, ECLI:EU:T:2021:730.

Austria, and Italy have provisions against abuse of economic dependence empowering a competition authority to find an infringement in a bilateral relationship between two companies, whereas this provision is absent in European competition laws. While the member states want to revolutionize their national competition laws to the digital economy, the devices to cope with digital cases, their initiatives lead to a patchwork of DMA-like national competition laws with the accompanying risk of inconsistency, compliance, and transaction costs.[82] It is evident that a single jurisdiction can enforce effectively any regulation such that of digital markets than 27 jurisdictions due to different tradition of their legal systems which means that digital economy and digital market will function effectively under USE rather than the current EU model.

Germany has enacted rules against large online platforms to advance fair and competitive digital markets and so updating German competition laws for the digital economy.[83] Hence, the national antitrust laws in abuse control, abuse of economic dependence, and merger notification are modernized by adding a new provision to companies designated by the German competition authority as "paramount significance for competition across markets" in digital markets. Thus, the new German rule involves two steps: the designation of a firm as "paramount significance for competition across markets" and then the imposition of prohibitions. The Bundeskartellamt concluded in January 2022 that Google falls within the scope and so comply with the prohibitions imposed by the new act which means that Germany has already enforced its DMA-like national competition law.

As mentioned earlier, in the EU, Digital Markets Act, the Digital Services Act, and the Data Governance Act establish various obligations to grant access to digital data.[84] EU and member state competition laws contain additional obligations of this sort.[85] Anticompetitive agreements between enterprises are banned, as are anticompetitive decisions of associations of undertakings according to Article 101 TFEU. Article 102 TFEU prohibits the abuse by one or more undertakings of a dominant

---

[82] Weck, T., The New Abuse Rules in the German Competition Act – What's in it for the EU?, Competition Policy International (April 14, 2020) https://www.competitionpolicyinternational.com/the-new-abuse-rules-in-the-german-competition-act-whats-init-for-the-eu/ Omran, O., et al., Special Competition Rules on Digital Ecosystems: Greece Joins the Club, LEXOLOGY (September 7, 2021) https://www.lexology.com/library/detail.aspx?g=75527f4b11fd-4922-9be0-cbee540b80bd

[83] Schallbruch M., et al., A New Competition Framework for the Digital Economy, Report By The Commission 'Competition Law 4.0', September 2019.

[84] Peter Georg Picht, Caught in the Acts: Framing Mandatory Data Access Transactions under the Data Act, further EU Digital Regulation Acts, and Competition Law, Max Planck Institute for Innovation and Competition Research Paper No. 22–05

[85] Commission Regulation (EU) No 316/2014 of 21 March 2014 on the application of Article 101(3) of the Treaty on the Functioning of the European Union to categories of technology transfer agreements.

position.[86] "Undertakings" are the actual subjects of EU competition law and it is central to an understanding of the operation of any of the doctrines of liability in EU competition law.[87]

It is worth noting that an entity is an undertaking when it is engaging in certain activities but not when it is engaging in other types of activities, such as exercising powers which are unique to a public authority. Hence, understanding the notion of "undertaking" guarantees the unity and effectiveness of EU competition law which means that the coherence and the strength of EU competition law depend upon a shared European definition of its specific subjects. Thus, the federal law of USE will eliminate these kinds of differences and so implementing the law more effectively especially the forthcoming AAI law applying in an AAI digital market.

9.10 AAI Transforms EU and Competition

Has the EU attained the projection of collective power, wealth, and influence by becoming a global power? Digitalization demands a united, efficient, and democratic Europe, based on a real Constitution. EU attempts to line up with the United States on strategic technologies that augment the bloc's standing as a geopolitical player.

It could be said that in its existing form and due to the political approach of EU members, the EU has succeeded partly in the projection of collective power, wealth, and influence but not becoming a global power.[88] It is characteristic that the political approach of EU in the Ukrainian crisis has shown the weakness of the current EU to act as a global player.

Will AI promote European integration? The expansion of AI and also the advanced AI will let the automated decision-making based on objectivity rather than subjectivity of the current human society. The utilization of AI technology on the level of decision-making of the EU commission will tolerate automated decisions objectively on EU matters generating the best result rather than a subjective and calculated decision based more on national interests rather than maximizing the outcome for the EU.

Will AI let better decisions for EU policy? Have the European leaders all the data for a rightful decision for EU people without AI technology? EU leaders could have made better decisions by employing AI technology on matters of engagement of EU on a range of conflicts rather than nowadays not only by using incomplete data but also by subjectively sponsoring national interests rather than entirely EU Interests. In

---

[86] Case T-112/05, Akzo Nobel NV v. Commission [2007] ECR II-5049, [57]. Case C-67/96, Albany International BV v. Stichting Bedrijfspensioenfonds Textielindustrie [1999] ECR I-5751, Opinion of AG Jacobs, [206].

[87] Case C-152/19 P, Deutsche Telekom AG v. Commission, ECLI:EU:C:2021:238, [94].

[88] T.R. Reid, The United States of Europe: The New Superpower and the End of American Supremacy, 2005 by Penguin Books

other words, AI technology could have assessed all the features regarding the engagement of EU in a conflict and have advised not taking part in a conflict which might have proven damaging to the EU economy.

Does the employment of AI technology dictate the transformation of EU into the United States of Europe? The spreading out and advancement of AI technology and its utilization in all fields of human life will create the necessity for a central government system so as to reach the best outcome forcing a political integration and transformation of the EU into the United States of Europe[89] acting as a global player antagonizing other super powers. Also, by reason of the European civilization, the United States of Europe will become the balancing global player bringing stability and growth to the global economy and so circumventing any global instability instigating economic problems not only on EU economy but also on the global one as it seems to take place presently.

It has to be taken into account that using algorithms to make key decisions automatically is raising the gradually realistic likelihood of robotically formed regulations and algorithmically resolved adjudications via AAI technology. Also, it has to be taken into consideration that the up-to-date technical standardization of AI stands as a meaningful type of regulation which is not politically neutral because of the fact that all the aspects of the AI functionality are decided by the human creator of the algorithms employed by AI. In other words, AI does not decide its own standards according to an autonomous decision based on an objective reading of data.

Also, the development of AAI technology will manage to deal with the risks of new technologies. Hence, the digital society will epitomize a new society governed via the use of information and communication technologies and so a digital society will be a networked information society with new values and needs.[90]

AAI technology will allow the establishment of a global codified regulation permitting a network of AAI systems of the various AAI jurisdictions to be interconnected and even eradicating the sense of national sovereignty and establishing the AAI cyber-jurisdiction.[91] In an AAI society, AAI entities will

[89] G Zekos, The United States of Europe The Global Player, 2019 Nova Science Publications New York USA. www.novapublishers.com G Zekos, The United States of Europe in place of the European Union, 2017 Nova Science Publications New York USA. www.novapublishers.com

[90] G Zekos, Political, Economic and Legal Effects of Artificial Intelligence, 2022, https://link.springer.com/book/10.1007/978-3-030-94736-1#tocG Zekos, Economics and Law of Artificial Intelligence - Finance, Economic Impacts, Risk Management and Governance, 2021 www.springer.com Zekos considers that the spiritual life of humans cannot be replicated via AAI technology. See chap. 11 G Zekos, Advanced Artificial Intelligence and Robo-Justice,2022, www.springer.com

[91] G. Zekos, State Cyberspace Jurisdiction and Personal Cyberspace Jurisdiction, Int J Law Info Tech 2007 15: 1–37; doi:10.1093/ijlit/eai029 www.ijlit.oxfordjournals.org G Zekos, Electronic state sovereignty, 2008, ICFAI Journal of Cyber Law www.iupindia.org G Zekos, Cyber-Territory And Jurisdiction Of Nations, 2012 Journal of Internet Law, Number 12/3 Aspen Publications. G Zekos, Demolishing State's sole power over Sovereignty & Territory via Electronic Technology & Cyberspace, 2013 Journal of Internet Law, Volume 17 Number 5 November 2013 27–41.

employ the own politics which is the implementation of their own interests. It could be said that AAI systems will allow the electronic participation of AAI entities into AAI democracy leading to the implementation of the AAI politics which will have another form and another impact on AAI society and life compared to that of the current conventional politics. There might be a centralized idea of politics and decision-making due to the characteristics of the AAI technology.

It is worth noting that a modern governance system and a modern governance aptitude are key content in developing modern economies characterizing the quality of institutions and their execution aptitude of a country which means that an AI governance system is central in the advancement of digital economies epitomizing the execution dynamic of a country able to compete in an AI digital environment. Which will be the impact of AAI implemented by humanoid robots upon EU political functioning? Taking into account that still AAI is controlled by humans, the prevailing of AAI upon human life implemented by humanoid robots demands standardization, centrality, and integration indicating the need for a political decision for a central AI governance and so transformation of the EU into the United States of Europe.

9.11 Conclusions

It is stressed that Europeans are wealthy and well-equipped with the means to handle their own challenges, if they show leadership and political will which means that Europe's struggles are its own fault and concern, and it must find its own way out.[92] Where are all the European academics to speak loudly for the promotion of EU as a political entity for the good of Europeans in order to avoid a future global war on European soil once again? Will other superpowers transfer any future conflict on European Soil essentially by holding EU leadership in an official silence?

Taking into account that Europe is facing unprecedented geopolitical encounters and political transition, will the EU act together, as a federation in the making, or fall back on divergent national positions? First of all, inflation, energy price rises, climate change, supply chain shortages, and the digital revolution make it essential for the EU to act as one. On the other hand, the EU is absent from Europe's most dangerous geopolitical crisis since the Cold War, with national tactics prevailing on foreign, security and defense policy, economics, trade, climate change, and public health. Nevertheless, the incapacity and often unwillingness to implement coherent and cohesive policy guidelines to deal with the consequences of the global uprisings have profoundly marked the aptitude of the EU to function as a credible global diplomatic player. Thus, the EU should act as a single body, in a more supranational, rather than intergovernmental, manner. To that extent, the EU in order to stay at

[92] Jeffrey Goldberg, "The Obama Doctrine," The Atlantic, April 2016, https://www.theatlantic.com/magazine/archive/2016/04/the-obama-doctrine/471525/#8

center-stage in global undertakings and avoid marginalization has to be transformed into a federation and so becoming a key, self-sufficient geopolitical power, antagonizing USA, Russia, Japan, China, etc.

The current EU model lacks a common foreign policy and defense and so it is not in a position to play a central part in the global arena. Moreover, the Russian invasion has revealed the overwhelming inadequacy of the European political system. By developing into a full-fledged federation, the EU will become a justly legitimate polity, safeguarding the demands of all Europeans because the current EU is divided and weak, incapable of standing strong against the superpowers of the globe.[93]

Bibliography

1. Bradford, A. (2020). *The Brussels effect – How the European Union rules the world.* Oxford University Press.
2. Britton-Purdy, J. S., Grewal, D., Kapcyznski, A., & Rahman, K. S. (2020). Building a law and political economy framework: Beyond the twentieth-century synthesis. *129 Yale Law Journal, 1784.*
3. Hasselbach, C. (2022, January 23). Germany's elusive goal of a European federal state. *The Express Tribune.*
4. Harvey, D. (2020). Federal proportionality review in EU Law: Whose rights are they anyway? *Nordic Journal of International Law, 89*, 303–326.
5. Leali, G., & Moens, B. (2022, March 9). Ukraine war gives macron's drive for EU autonomy more impetus. *Politico Europe.*
6. Morgan, G. (2020). Is the European Union imperialist? *Journal of European Public Policy, 27*(1), 1–17.
7. Hofmann, H. (2021). *An introduction to automated decision making (ADM) and cyber-delegation in the scope of EU Public Law.* Indigo Working Paper.
8. Lianos, I. (2021). *Computational competition law and economics: Issues, prospects - an inception report.* Hellenic Competition Commission.
9. Sonnicksen, J. (2022). Can the EU be a federal democracy? Assessing the horizontal and vertical dimension of the EU government from comparative perspective. *Comparative European Politics, 20*, 114–133.
10. Joamets, K., & Chochia, A. (2020). Artificial intelligence and its impact on labour relations in Estonia. *Slovak Journal of Political Sciences, 20*(2), 255–277.
11. Pohle, J., & Thiel, T. (2020). Digital sovereignty. *Internet Policy Review, 9*(4), 1–19.
12. Gerhke, L. (2022, August 29). Scholz pitches major EU enlargement—With reform. *Politico Europe.*
13. Mattiuzzo, M., & Machado, H. F. (2022). Algorithmic governance in computational antitrust—A brief outline of alternatives for policymakers, 2 *Stan. Comput. Antitrust, 23.*
14. Mukand, S., & Rodrik, D. (2020). The political economy of Liberal democracy. *The Economic Journal, 130*(627), 765–792. https://doi.org/10.1093/ej/ueaa004

[93] Γ. Ζέκος, Διαδίκτυο & Τεχνητή Νοημοσύνη στο Ελληνικό Δίκαιο, 2022, Εκδόσεις Π. Σάκκουλα https://www.sakkoulas.gr/el/editions/g-zekos-diadiktyo-techniti-noimosyni-sto-elliniko-dikaio-2022/

15. Zekos, G. (2022, July 6). *How will AI influence politics? Chance or danger for democracy?* Cicero Foundation. www.cicerofoundation.org.
16. Zekos, G. (2022). *Advanced artificial intelligence and robo-justice*. www.springer.com
17. Zekos, G. (2021, April). Artificial intelligence and e-bills of lading contracts. *Journal of Internet Law, 24*(8), 3–10. Wolters Kluwer. https://lrus.wolterskluwer.com/store/product/journal-of-internet-law/
18. Zekos, G. (2021). *Economics and law of artificial intelligence - finance, economic impacts, risk management and governance*. https://link.springer.com/book/10.1007/978-3-030-64254-9.
19. Zekos, G. (2022). *Political, economic and legal effects of artificial intelligence*. https://link.springer.com/book/10.1007/978-3-030-94736-1#toc
20. Zekos, G. (2017). *The United States of Europe in place of the European Union*. Nova Science Publications. www.novapublishers.com
21. Zekos, G. (2019). *The United States of Europe the global player*. Nova Science Publications. www.novapublishers.com
22. Ζέκος, Γ. Διαδίκτυο, & Τεχνητή Νοημοσύνη στο Ελληνικό Δίκαιο. (2022). *Εκδόσεις Π. Σάκκουλα*. https://www.sakkoulas.gr/el/editions/g-zekos-diadiktyo-techniti-noimosyni-sto-elliniko-dikaio-2022/

Chapter 10
Digital Economy and Competition

10.1 Introduction

Corporations accumulate global technology and advancing technological capabilities that enable them to catch up with industry leaders in the global market. In the digital economy, central network outcomes initiate a "winner-takes-most" competition, with only one platform controlling a market, or being the big actor in a relevant market by impeding horizontal competition, or dominating a value chain by limiting vertical competition. Hence, markets typified by platform competition are horizontally concentrated and so other players in the online market do not present a workable competitive alternative to the established platform.

The digital economy brings forward a range of strategies to get a competitive advantage and transforms this to surplus value accumulated in the product. Digital economic players count on cost-cutting technology to break into online markets by unsettling the existing competitive structure, and ultimately gaining economic power. Also, new players making a more effective use of technology or relying on a better technological alternative overtake the well-known players.

As the digital economy has grown and data has become a more valuable and significant resource, the data practices of companies are being scrutinized by governments.[1] It seems that countries are balancing the commercial interests of the companies that are collecting and handling data, the privacy interests of the individuals who offer data, and their own interests in data due to national security, public security, and economic and social development objectives and interests.[2] Because of

[1]David McCabe, What's Going on With TikTok? Here's What We Know', N.Y. TIMES, Aug. 1, 2020, www.nytimes.com/2020/08/01/technology/tiktoktrump-microsoft-bytedance-china-ban.html;

[2]Henry S Gao, Data Regulation with Chinese Characteristics, in BIG DATA IN GLOBAL TRADE LAW, 245, 261 (Mira Burri ed. 2021). Angela Huyue Zhang, Agility Over Stability: China's Great Reversal in Regulating the Platform Economy (July 28, 2021) https://papers.ssrn.com/sol3/papers.cfm?abstract_id=3892642

© The Author(s), under exclusive license to Springer Nature Switzerland AG 2023
G. I. Zekos, *Artificial Intelligence and Competition*, Contributions to Economics,
https://doi.org/10.1007/978-3-031-48083-6_10

license requirements, intellectual property, and distribution channels in the digital economy, entry barriers are generated.[3]

10.2 AI and HRM

It has to be taken into account that with the accelerating application of AI, the interplay among companies, employees, and customers is profoundly altering and so the automation of the administrative parts of HRM activities and tasks is escalating. Moreover, contemporary developments are offering alternatives to human resources in functions traditionally demanding human interaction and communication. Currently, AI humanoid robots and AI bots are increasingly utilized which means that traditional human resource functions have been transformed, stipulating growing strengths and potentialities for HRM but also challenging job-specific obsolescence. Correspondingly, the introduction of AI human resource information systems presents openings to advance and diminish the cost of HRM functions embracing, among others, the evaluation of job applicants and employee performance appraisals.

Also, AI applications in HRM decision-making underline the capability to process large amounts of data at high speeds, the likelihood to assist salespeople gaining new customers more resourcefully and realistically assess and manage employee turnover risk. Nonetheless, even when AI advances task performance causing no immediate threat, its widespread use in HRM decision-making is sensed as a threat to human employees' autonomy and job security for the reason that it offers more choices to them perplexing them due to escalating perceived complexity. Explicitly, the introduction of AI applications in HRM permits HR employees to conduct background checks of job applications and AI-enabled recruitment platforms infer possible behaviors in terms of job fit and performance while being less biased and more objective than humans.[4] Algorithms assist HR practitioners and corporations by altering the selection process into a more systematic process by excluding the incidence of recruiters' biases and so AI offers to HRM recruiting constitute a positive development for HRM.[5] It has to be taken into account that algorithmic decision-making has enabled corporations to sort and rank people more effectively.

[3]Market Structure & Antitrust Subcomm., Report, in Final Report 23, 119- 21 (Stigler Comm. on Digital Platforms ed., 2019) (noting that "certain characteristics of digital technology" enable the creation of entry barriers).

[4]Kellogg, K., Valentine, M., & Christin, A. (2020). Algorithms at work: The new contested terrain of control. Academy of Management Annals, 14(1), 366–410. https://doi.org/10.5465/annals.2018.0174

[5]Lindebaum, D., Vesa, M., & den Hond, F. (2020). Insights from The Machine Stops to better understand rational assumptions in algorithmic decision-making and its implications for organizations. Academy of Management Review, 45(1), 247–263. https://doi.org/10.5465/amr.2018.0181

MNEs not only focus on developing physical and organizational capital but also on developing human capital which is of utmost importance for organizational sustainability and success in the AI era owing to the changing nature of work. Hence, MNEs are utilizing AI tools that are driven by huge amounts of data and are assisting businesses in transforming the workplace enormously.[6] While sophisticated AI technologies are reducing the need for human labor in multinationals, developing capabilities linked to AI and its applications is assisting employees to remain employable in the future.

10.3 Legal Personality of Corporations

Laws and regulations are struggling to keep pace with the rapid introduction and diffusion of technological changes.[7]

It is worth noting that AI falling short of key moral qualities of personhood is considered as an apparatus of the actual persons to whom it belongs.[8] While the European Parliament formed a class of "electronic persons," the more autonomous an AI entity becomes means that it cannot be treated as property by an owner for the owner's chosen ends.[9]

Also, it is worth mentioning here that all of antitrust law's violation provisions except one necessitate an agreement between two or more persons. The exception, § 2 of the Sherman Act, condemns monopolization and attempts to monopolize by one person acting unilaterally. Moreover, antitrust personhood is not restricted to biological individuals and so corporations are persons too, revealing a long history of considering them that way under state corporate law. It has to be taken into account that the Supreme Court held that a parent corporation and its wholly owned subsidiary must be considered as a single person, incapable of conspiring with one another.[10] Thus, only persons, which embrace corporations, can violate the antitrust laws unilaterally and so electronic persons and electronic corporations will be treated accordingly.

[6] Ågerfalk, P. J. (2020). Artificial intelligence as digital agency. European Journal of Information Systems, 29(1), 1–8. https://doi.org/10.1080/0960085X.2020.1721947

[7] Lawrence J. Trautman, Bitcoin, Virtual Currencies and the Struggle of Law and Regulation to Keep Pace, 102 Marq. L. Rev. 447 (2018), https://ssrn.com/abstract=3182867

[8] Louis Marx & Co. v. United States, 66 Cust. Ct. 484 (1958) "[a] robot is 'not a living thing; it is not endowed with life. A robot is a mechanical device or apparatus, a mere automation, that operates through scientific or mechanical media'")

[9] Gunther Teubner, Digital Personhood? The Status of Autonomous Software Agents in Private Law, ANCILLA IURIS 106, 113 (2018).

[10] Copperweld v. Independence Tube Corp. 467 U.S. 752 (1984). Herbert Hovenkamp, The Classical Corporation in American Legal Thought, 76 Geo. L.J. 1593 (1988). Herbert Hovenkamp, The Power of Antitrust Personhood, Research Paper No. 23-09 https://ssrn.com/abstract=4352061

G.I. Zekos argues that AAI humanoids should be treated as persons and so the law should recognize rights alongside liability for them as well. AI personhood and corporate personhood mean that artificial people and AI corporations will possess constitutional rights in an AAI constitutionally formed AAI society, functioning in an electronic environment, or/and AAI humanoid could be able to function in different dimensions of environments. Currently, due to the AI level, the Uber platform runs in tandem with the Uber traditional corporation with managerial power centered on its board of directors. Moreover, firms are gradually using algorithms to manage their remote workforces and so "algorithmic management" is exploited by gig economy corporations. Hence, Uber significantly amplifies its effectiveness by managing workers with an AI application.[11]

Presently, firms use AI systems to fulfill the role of employees in certain circumstances and to provide services. Governments use AI systems to make benefits determinations and assessing different risks which means that humans working through AI systems. While some of the uses fall closer to the AI systems as tools end of the AI personhood spectrum, AAI systems become more than just a tool and, instead, act as a substitute or conduit for the actions of natural people and mostly in the autonomous corporate personhood context. Hence, AAI systems function as conduit for human activity.[12]

Corporations are creatures of the law and so AAI entities have a status akin to humans, they can own property and contracts, sue, and be sued in their own name. Hence, AAI humanoids can be shareholders in an AAI corporation, having a board appointing the executive management as well. Additionally, AAI humanoids can be shareholders to a conventional corporation in a human-running world because corporation's functionality will be run by AAI entities rather than humans but it is possible for a human's elite to run an AAI system behind the curtains as long as they can survive as humans in an AAI world.

It has to be taken into account that law first recognized corporations as artificial persons via the idea of "legal personality" for private law convenience. Taking into consideration that only people can contract, sue, and be sued, own property, and enter into contracts, legally recognizing companies as "people" simplified commercial transactions, questions of liability, and the application of regulations to corporate activity. Right now, a corporation possesses constitutionally protected rights to enter into contracts, own property, enjoy due process protections under the Fifth

[11] Mareike Möhlmann & Ola Henfridsson, What People Hate About Being Managed by Algorithms, According to a Study of Uber Drivers, Harv. Bus. Rev. (Aug. 30, 2019), https://hbr.org/2019/08/what-people-hate-about-being-managedby-algorithms-according-to-a-study-of-uber-drivers

[12] Jason R. Bent, Is Algorithmic Affirmative Action Legal?, 108 Geo. L.J. 803, 809 (2020). Mihailis E. Diamantis, The Extended Corporate Mind: When Corporations Use AI to Break the Law, 98 N. C. L. REV. 893, 900 (2020) (providing examples that include using self-driving cars instead of taxi or delivery drivers, replacing human bankers with algorithms that approve mortgages, using algorithms instead of people to price products, among others).

Amendment, and experience equal protection of the laws[13] and so the US Supreme Court imparts the corporation with specific constitutional rights. Moreover, the corporation is a fictional entity formed by natural persons at the pleasure of the state and so the corporation exists for the reason that a state statute allows it to exist which means that the AI corporation exists as a legal personality as well.[14] In other words, the corporation is an independent reality occurring as an objective fact and so having a real presence in society which means that it stands alone and the people related to the corporation are agents, investors, or lenders not outlining the corporation.[15] Thus, corporations abide by regulations and are subject to income tax liability on the net income produced by their commercial activities and so the rights and obligations of corporations are not those of their shareholders, directors, or other people who take part in or are influenced by the corporation's doings. Furthermore, a company occurs in its own right, as a specific entity, beyond the personalities of managers, shareholders, and employees.

Will AAI corporation function according to an algorithm? When an AAI corporation functions alone without the assistance of any other AAI entity, then it is a legal entity and especially in the case of a company dealing with electronic goods and services utilized by AAI entities directly within the AAI system. It could be said that the AAI humanoid robots and AAI corporations act similarly as legal entities and acquire the analogous and similar legal personhood with duties and liabilities. It could be said that an AAI corporation will be an entire AAI system implementing all the functioning of a company according to the particular algorithm, especially if the company produces electronic goods and services.

It is characteristic that the evolution from electronic, to data-oriented, to computable contracts[16] personifies a drift toward greater machine autonomy. Of course, AAI contracts concluded by an AAI system and AAI entities for the autonomous and

---

[13]Hale v. Henkel, 201 U.S. 43, 70–71 (1906) (holding corporations have a Fourth Amendment right against unreasonable searches and seizures, but not a Fifth Amendment right against self-incrimination). Santa Clara, 118 U.S. 394, at 396 (noting that the Court agreed that the Equal Protection Clause applied to corporations, explaining that corporations are persons under the Fourteenth Amendment and can own property). Citizens United v. FEC, 558 U.S. 310, 319 (2010). Burwell v. Hobby Lobby Stores, Inc., 573 U.S. 682, 706–07 (2014) (explaining that free exercise includes protection of the religious liberties of the individual natural persons who own and control those companies).

[14]Stefan J. Padfield, The Silent Role of Corporate Theory in the Supreme Court's Campaign Finance Cases, 15 U. PA.J. CONST. L. 831, 834 (2013) (corporate theory plays a role in Supreme Court jurisprudence on corporate constitutional rights even when the Court does not explicitly state as much in its opinions).

[15]Lyman Johnson & David Millon, Corporate Law After Hobby Lobby, 70 BUS. LAW. 1, 8–9 (2015) ("Corporations own property, enter into contracts, and commit torts. They can sue and be sued in their own right. They are subject to penalties if they violate applicable criminal laws.)

[16]Anthony J. Casey & Anthony Niblett, Self-Driving Contracts, 43 J. CORP. L. 100 (2017) (working toward new contract law theory for smart contracts—"self-driving contracts" that use big data and artificial intelligence to autonomously "fill[] in the contract details to achieve the parties' designated outcome.");

automatic AAI network controlling and working for an AAI society are the next big technical evolution which will put in the corner the material world.

It has to be taken into account that law is in part a device and an "information technology" and so being a system assisted by the rules that govern the system's conduct[17] generated by the politics of a society.[18] It could be said that law is a "social technology"[19] formed, utilized, and applied within a broader social context and so AAI law will be the technology facilitating the AAI society and the needs of AAI humanoids. To that extent, AAI contracts, as a sub-system of AAI law epitomizing a technology within a technology, will deliver the device for privately or publicly ordering the rules applicable to a specific social context within AAI society.

It is worth mentioning here that the introduction of robo-justice will play a major role in guaranteeing swift and objective justice.[20] Moreover, effective access to justice is a key part of the rule of law.[21] AI is utilized in law for predictive analytics along with for conducting legal research and analyzing documents.

10.4 Knowledge and Development in Digital Economy

It is worth noting that the digital economy is becoming gradually vital to a country's economic development and so innovation in the digital business is central to getting a high-quality digital economy.

Knowledge-based technological competencies are appreciated as an imperative source of competitiveness for companies. Governments are among the institutions in all economies, with a decisive impact through regulatory policies and control over scarce resources, which shape corporations' country-specific advantages.

The advancement of China into a global economic player is exemplified and Chinese corporations' innovation is grounded on global knowledge sourcing. The innovation performance of inward and outward foreign direct investment policies is appraised as institutional windows for knowledge sourcing and so defining how

[17] Tamara Belinfanti & Lynn Stout, Contested Visions: The Value of Systems Theory for Corporate Law, 166 U. PA. L. REV. 579, 599–600 (2018) (discussing the core forms and characteristics of systems) Jeffery Ritter, Achieving Digital Trust: The New Rules For Business At The Speed Of Light 133 (2015). Lynn M. LoPucki, The Systems Approach to Law, 82 CORNELL L. REV. 479, 481 (1997).

[18] G Zekos, Political, Economic and Legal Effects of Artificial Intelligence, 2022, https://link.springer.com/book/10.1007/978-3-030-94736-1#toc

[19] John O. McGinnis & Steven Wasick, Law's Algorithm, 66 FLA. L. REV. 991, passim (2014). "Law thus works necessarily in part as an information technology—a tool for the distribution of information to the world that may itself change through the infusion of more information from the world."

[20] G Zekos, Advanced Artificial Intelligence and Robo-Justice,2022, www.springer.comhttps://www.springerprofessional.de/en/robo-justice/20418280

[21] R (Unison) v Lord Chancellor [2017] UKSC 51

these policies lead to outstanding innovation performance by leveraging external knowledge.

Which capital has boosted China's development? How China has utilized foreign FDI in becoming a superpower? Have Chinese students educated abroad transferred knowledge back to China? Has American funding and capital helped China to challenge the United States? It has to be taken into account that institutional mandates drive the process of sourcing knowledge for advanced technology using public tools. Hereafter, a set of policy incentives are institutional windows of opportunity for the development of science and technology grounded on the introduction and absorption of external knowledge leading to the advancement of homegrown innovation, which means that knowledge sourcing must be followed by timely strategic responses and actions taken in a series of institutional measures and policy arrangements that allow the advancement of innovation capacity of Chinese enterprises and so utilizing knowledge sourcing by Chinese digital enterprises during their pursuit of innovativeness.

China's policies began to target the acceleration of technology transfer through FDI under the "trading market for technology" plan and the ethnic innovation initiative which is derived into an accumulative process of technological catch-up and improved innovation competence of Chinese enterprises. Also, policies that incentivized extra sourcing of external knowledge emerged, promoting outward FDI by Chinese companies as a means to obtain more advanced technology.[22] Si Zhang et al.[23] argue that "Chinese firms seized on institutional windows of opportunity for technology catch-up through intentional knowledge sourcing in the wave of digitalization. In addition, the results show that—unlike as argued in prior research—Chinese firms first relied on attracting FDI to bring in technology and then used OFDI to springboard, and that IFDI and OFDI jointly promoted the acquisition of external technologies."

It is obvious that the good governance of Chinese governments and the labor capabilities of Chinese people have boosted China's advancement. Moreover, it seems that Chinese people have returned back to China and worked for the good of their country against all odds unlike other nationals remaining abroad and offering their knowledge for the development of other economies instead of working for the advancement of their country.

Since 1 January 1981, Greece has been a member of the EU but it seems that the Greek authorities followed a unique economic policy, utterly at odds with the EU[24] and so failing to become a rich member state within the EU. Has Greece missed a

[22] Zhang, Haoyu, Yongjiang Shi, Jianxin Liu and Xiaobo Wu (2021). "How do technology strategies affect the catch-up progress of high-tech latecomers? Evidence from two Chinese research-institute-transformed telecommunications firms", Journal of Business Research, 122, pp. 805–821.

[23] Si Zhang, Shirong Gu and Yuxuan Tang How does policy create an opportunity window for China's digital economy?, Transnational Corporations Volume 29, 2022, Number 3 P69-70

[24] https://www.lse.ac.uk/Hellenic-Observatory/Assets/Documents/Publications/GreeSE-Papers/GreeSE-No136.pdf

chance for advancement by inward FDI? Have Greek students educated abroad transferred knowledge back to Greece? Of course, foreign capital invested in Greece has been forced to flee due to mismanagement and possibly as a result of the requests and behaviors of trade unionists. It could be said that Hellas did not utilize meritoriously the know–how of many highly educated Greeks and instead it discouraged many of them to come back or stay in Greece owing to promoting docile moderation and political servitude. Have Greeks worked for the development of their country, against all odds, comparable to Chinese people? Why Hellenic shipyards are not flourishing in Hellas? In Hellas, regardless of the knowledge of the existence of plenty of resources of oil/gas and minerals, it is representative that, since 1973, no oil/gas has been extracted and processed systematically in order to advance the development of Hellenic industry.[25]

It has to be taken into consideration that with the support and guidance of national policies and the combined outcome of the explosion in computing, artificial intelligence, big data, 5G, and other next-generation information technologies, the digital business of any country can make outstanding achievements in innovation. The digital business embraces software and ICT, cyberspace, and electronic information manufacturing[26] in combination with the advancement of blockchain and AI technologies.

It is characteristic that digital companies have become pillars of a country's new economy and so high-tech industries have become the most active players in the global innovation ecosystem.[27] Moreover, digital companies count not only on internal R&D but also on external knowledge sources via international partnerships. Also, digital companies experience the convenience of knowledge flows through an open virtual network which means that digital companies are the most active players in global innovation activities, functioning in a technologically vibrant environment where advanced knowledge is generated constantly and quickly.

MNEs have country-specific advantages to utilize originally being a way by which to retrieve the knowledge-based capabilities generating and maintaining competitive advantage in the long term. Moreover, government policies and regulations on market entry or technology transfer enable the inward knowledge-observing process. It is worth noting that the Chinese Government applied the "technology for market" strategy, under which it permits foreign corporations to enter the Chinese market in return for technology transfer to domestic firms or establishment of R&D centers in China. In addition, Chinese state-owned enterprises

[25] https://hellasjournal.com/2022/11/exedra-antlisis-petreleou-ston-prino-meta-apo-43-chronia-ke-geotrisi-sta-ioannina-exelixis-ke-stin-erevna-idrogonanthrakon-chartis/

[26] UNCTAD, (2021). Digital Economy Report 2021: Cross-border Data Flows and Development: For Whom the Data Flow (New York and Geneva: United nations).

[27] Dachs, Bernhard, and Georg Zahradnik (2022). "From few to many: Main trends in the internationalization of business R&D", Transnational Corporations, 29(1), pp. 107–132.

are getting more direct policy support, but private companies have the openness to apply policies more flexibly.[28]

10.5 Competition in China

Monopolies and unfair and disorderly competition are considered as destructive to markets, consumers, and economic development.[29] China has laws handling different aspects of competition. The Anti-Monopoly Law prohibits horizontal and vertical monopoly agreements, abuses of market power, and anticompetitive mergers, and is fundamentally quite similar to the antitrust/competition laws of many other jurisdictions outlawing anticompetitive abuses of administrative power. Moreover, the AML prevents and forbids monopoly conduct, protects fair competition in the market, and advances economic efficiency by preserving the interests of consumers and the public.

Also, the Anti-Unfair Competition Law encompasses a series of unfair competition practices, with a focus on the fairness of business transactions and business ethics.[30] Supplementary, in October 2021, the SAMR published draft guidelines to catalog digital platforms setting out their responsibilities and so outlining the obligations of digital platforms concerning cyber security, data security, privacy and personal information protection, workers' rights, environmental protection, and tax which mean that the SAMR will enforce laws against digital platforms.[31]

[28] Rugman, Alan M., Quyen TK Nguyen and Ziyi Wei (2016). "Rethinking the literature on the performance of Chinese multinational enterprises", Management and Organization Review, 12(2), pp. 269–302.

[29] Wendy Ng, State Interest and the State-Centered Approach to Competition Law in China, 65(2) Antitrust Bull. 297 (2020).

[30] Meng Yanbei, The Uneasy Relationship between Antitrust and Anti-Unfair Competition Laws in China, in Wang Xiaoye: The Pioneer Of Competition Law In China 219 (Adrian Emch & Wendy Ng eds, 2019).

[31] Guideline for Implementing the Main Responsibilities of Internet Platforms, State. Admin. for Mkt. Reg., Oct. 29, 2021. Wendy Ng, The Role Of Competition Law In Regulating Data In China's Digital Economy, https://ssrn.com/abstract=4002146

10.6 Digital Providers

Business management represents one context in which machine-learning algorithms are used.[32] Algorithms offer predictions and other data to other board members and some business models regularly count on AI to take vital action on an automated, high-speed basis such as broker-dealers regularly use algorithms for advice and execution of stock market trades.[33]

There is an expanding capability to automate business coordination via blockchain technology and blockchain-based smart contracts. AI can retain and manage wealth independently from human interfaces and the Uniform Limited Liability Company Act (ULLCA) already clearly offers the option that an LLC may function without any members flowing from the law's generation of fictional entities and treating them like people for certain purposes.[34] To that extent, AI induces all corporations from a hierarchical and formalized governance structure to more open governance structure grounded on a platform model.[35]

The digital/platform economy is a system portrayed mainly by platforms, driven by AI technologies and so generating value by assisting exchanges between two different but interdependent groups which means that AI-networked digital technologies stimulate economic exchange and transfer of information connecting people. It could be said that platform corporations are selling access to the software, the matching algorithms, and a digital system of reputation and trust between their users. Anyway, the digital/platform era necessitates new methods of collaboration and governance encompassing new corporate decision-making.

It seems that platform companies, currently ruled by humans via AI tools, replicate the centralized power structures and platform technology merely becomes the new medium through which to concentrate power, centralize resources, and more resourcefully serve market demands.[36] For instance, Uber and Airbnb remain conventional companies with old-style agency cost concerns born of customary centralized management hierarchies at the director and c-suite level.

---

[32] Leonidou, E., Christofi, M., Vrontis, D., & Thrassou, A. (2020). An integrative framework of stakeholder engagement for innovation management and entrepreneurship development. Journal of Business Research, 119, 245-258.

[33] Carla L. Reyes & Jeff Ward, Digging into Algorithms: Legal Ethics and Legal Access, 21 NEV. L.J. 325, 325, 342–43 (2020) (examining the reality of algorithms as a social technology in the context of legal technology)

[34] Shawn Bayern, Are Autonomous Entities Possible?, 114 NW. U. L. REV. ONLINE 23, 24 (2019)

[35] M. Fenwick & Erik P.M. Vermeulen, Technology and Corporate Governance: Blockchain, Crypto, and Artificial Intelligence, 48 Tex. J. Bus. L. 1 (2019). at 177 ("Businesses will either operate 'as' a platform or be 'integrated' within a platform. The future of the digital age will be platform-driven ecosystems in which multiple players participate. ... Given the proliferation of platforms, we seem to be living through a shift from a world of firms to a new world of platforms.")

[36] Shoshana Zuboff, The Age Of Surveillance Capitalism: The Fight For A Human Future At The New Frontier Of Power (2019).

First of all, cyberspace has had positive influences on competition, investment, and innovation in many businesses by digital platforms rising both as a crucial infrastructure and as a business model in the digital economy. Nevertheless, Big Tech corporations act as intermediary platforms and providers of services and goods in several markets and so market concentration and the power of platforms have intensified concerns regarding prospective harms to innovation and welfare in the digital economy. Hence, a few countries that have a big internal market with a widespread adoption of digital technologies and services have comparative advantages supporting digital platforms able to compete with the existing tech giants. Tiago S. Prado[37] considers that "no single best regime exists that can promote competition and innovation in digital markets of every country… different instruments should be pursued by countries to promote competition without harming incentives for innovation and investment in the development of their digital ecosystem… national policymakers and regulators should adopt different, customized approaches that consider the country's digital economy and institutional context."

Furthermore, transactions encompassing large technology enterprises lead to a reduction and relocation of innovative efforts by other corporations. It has to be taken into account that innovative and competitive dynamics are different across businesses and so pharmaceutical markets are less quick in relation to digital markets. Moreover, patent density is higher in pharmaceuticals, drug development is slow, innovation is cumulative, and generic entry is real leading pharmaceutical companies to take part in horizontal acquisitions to accelerate innovation procedures. Also, innovation in digital markets depends on product differentiation, complementarity, and ecosystem building and so the gaming industry is grounded on network-based innovation ecosystems which means that non-horizontal acquisitions play a larger role in these businesses.[38]

It is worth noting that startup acquisitions are pro-competitive if they lessen financial, technical, and managerial constraints faced by the target company.[39] To that extent, Brutti and Rojas[40] claim that the pro or anticompetitive character of a startup acquisition is based on "the relationship between the incumbent's and the

---

[37]Tiago S. Prado, Safeguarding Competition in Digital Markets: A Comparative Analysis of Emerging Policy and Regulatory Regimes, Quello Center Working Paper 05/22 at: https://ssrn.com/abstract=4137588 p 4

[38]Patrycja Klimas & Wojciech Czakon, 'Gaming innovation ecosystem: actors, roles and co-innovation processes' (2022) 16 Review of Managerial Science 2213;

[39]Chiara Fumagalli, Massimo Motta, & Emanuele Tarantino, 'Shelving or Developing? The Acquisition of Potential Competitors Under Financial Constraints' (2020) CEPR Discussion Paper No. DP15113

[40]Zelda Brutti & Luis E. Rojas, 'M&A and Early Investment Decisions by Digital Platforms' (2022) 49 Journal of Industrial and Business Economics 509. Pauline Affeldt & Reinhold Kesler, 'Competitors' Reactions to Big Tech Acquisitions: Evidence from Mobile Apps' (2022) DIW Berlin Discussion Paper No. 1987. John M. Yun, 'Discriminatory Antitrust in the Realm of Potential and Nascent Competition' (2022) George Mason Law & Economics Research Paper No. 22-04.

startup's target users and on the ability of the startup to catch up with the incumbent."

Will using AI technology decentralize corporate power? First of all, technology will only decentralize power inside a corporation organization if such decentralization is an objective of those organizing the corporation. Moreover, AI technology does not stand alone as the single form of automation used in commercial activities and so business founders, owners, investors, and managers energetically utilize AI technology to essentially alter management structures. It could be said that in the case of platform corporations, an AI restructuring will take place but the function as the company will not be eliminated but merely altered in the way of implementation in order to satisfy the demand of commerce due to AI technology and the demands of an AI society putting forwards the demands, the needs of their people/AI entities, etc.

Apple, Amazon, Microsoft, Google/Alphabet, and Facebook control access to the digital products, services, and infrastructures that people count on whether digital search, social networks, online markets, and more which means that Big Tech firms are not just digital platforms.[41] Big Tech is characterized by the emergence of new digital forms of functioning amalgamating construction and extraction of value through the techno-economic extension of ownership and/or control over assets. However, Big Tech's originality is the incorporation of digital platforms as an intermediary between existing products/services and users, generating a new multi-sided ecosystem of exchange from which the digital intermediary wants both a toll and masses of data.[42] Also, Big Tech corporations collect data from users and sell access to advertisers, app developers, and others and so entire ecosystems have become encircled and controlled by Big Tech.

It has to be taken into account that Big Tech corporations with IPR monopolies have a large cash flow and consequently a large market capitalization relative to asset base and so empowering them to buy competitors which means generating a self-fulfilling outcome.[43] Digital ecosystems epitomize a new site for gaming the rules of the capitalism and so generating a new dimension for competition. The ecosystems that Big Tech generate and control exemplify a heterogeneous assemblage of technical devices and platforms, along with users and developers, legal contracts and rights, etc. Also, digital ecosystems allow Big Tech to make economic rents by strengthening their techno-economic power, while undercutting the economic capacity of others to shape the future.[44] The US Federal Trade Commission charged

---

[41] Birch, K., Chiappetta, M. and Artyushina, A. (2020) The problem of innovation in technoscientific capitalism: data rentiership and the policy implications of turning personal digital data into a private asset, Policy Studies, 41(5), pp. 468–487.

[42] Komljenovic, J. (2021) The rise of education rentiers: digital platforms, digital data and rents, Learning, Media and Technology. doi:10.1080/17439884.2021.1891422. Pistor, K. (2020) Rule by data: the end of markets? Law and Contemporary Problems, 83, pp. 101–124.

[43] Durand, C. and Milberg, W. (2020) Intellectual monopoly in global value chains, Review of International Political Economy, 27(2), pp. 404–429

[44] DZ Reserve v. Facebook, Inc. 2021, 3:18-cv-04978

Facebook with "illegal monopolization," again asserting that Facebook pursued anticompetitive strategies to generate and cement its social network monopoly.[45]

It has to be taken into consideration that a platform gets a competitive advantage by acquiring exclusively a significant content provider and so monopolizes the market. Cong et al. [46] argue that "Exclusivity enhances consumer surplus and social welfare when the number of multihoming sellers is relatively low. Welfare always decreases when only the weak platform enforces exclusivity, and may increase or decrease when only the strong platform enforces it."

10.7 E-Commerce and Competition

The objective of digital policy is to initiate outstanding framework conditions in Europe for innovative corporations and for the transformation of the European economy triggering investments in digital infrastructure. A large majority of e-commerce operators are platforms which intermediate and aggregate two-sided markets: one side comprising suppliers and the other side comprising consumers.[47]

It has to be taken into account that digital platforms facilitate efficient interactions between a supply side of producer users and a demand side of consumer users that create value in online and offline trades. On the other hand, Bertin Martens et al.[48] argue "that price regulation over information sharing like the one applied in the EU jurisdiction reduces the incentives of platforms to share information limiting the benefits for consumers."

The harmonization of rules in the European single market facilitates the generation of competitiveness, since corporations find uniform rules across Europe which means that the EU can show its strength as an economic area via European rules. Diverging approaches of national competition authorities to practices by digital platforms within the EU are detrimental to the running of the internal, single market obstructing innovative homegrown digital businesses.

The EU Digital Markets Act applies the same *ex ante* fixed standard to all the "gatekeeper" platforms, presumed by quantitative metrics such as sales volume. On the other hand, competition law has the advantage of flexibility, since it embraces a case-by-case analysis tailored to the specifics of each digital sector. It seems that

---

[45] https://www.justice.gov/opa/pr/justice-department-sues-monopolist-googleviolating-antitrust-lawshttps://www.ftc.gov/news-events/press-releases/2020/12/ftc-sues-facebook-illegalmonopolization

[46] Jiajia Cong, Yao Huang, Wen Zhou Exclusive Dealing in Asymmetric Platform Competition e at: https://ssrn.com/abstract=4129788 p31

[47] Herbert Hovenkamp, Antitrust and Platform Monopoly, 130 Yale Law Journal 1901, 1965 (2021) ("The development of machine learning technologies and data analysis is a source of increasing returns to scale and scope that can contribute to digital market concentration.").

[48] Bertin Martens, Geoffrey Parker, Georgios Petropoulos, Marshall Van Alstyne, Platform Competition and Information Sharing, https://ssrn.com/abstract=4528803 p2

there is a convergence regarding digital platforms and the EU DMA adopts uniform quantitative metrics for selecting targeted "gatekeepers." US and EU competition laws compel digital platforms to hold market power or dominant position in order to enforce exclusionary practices. It has to be taken into account that identification of market power in e-commerce generates an encounter with competition authorities because of difficulties in defining relevant markets for digital technology due to rapid transformation.

Competition concern about e-commerce stems from the rise of giant platforms leading to market concentration and so diminishing competition which is amplified by the AI installed by digital giants. Undeniably, economies of scale in digital markets have given rise to efficiencies such as economies of scale, permitting large corporations with large amounts of data to raise product quality at lower costs than small companies.[49]

It is worth noting that e-commerce portrays the dominance of multi-homing and the dominance of product differentiation. Moreover, mixing e-commerce with social networking has been a development and so Facebook has expanded its social networking services into an e-commerce platform business. Amazon[50] has enlarged its area of digital technology, starting from e-commerce, going into the cloud business, music and video streaming, and so on. Rakuten, starting from e-commerce, grew into financial services, and lately entered the cellphone service business. Moreover, e-commerce is never a natural monopoly but is engaging in active competition. It has to be taken into consideration that e-commerce competes with physical stores, since consumers are able to buy books, stationery, or food products at both e-commerce sites and physical stores. Also, the specialty of e-commerce is continuously transforming, as typified by the mixing of e-commerce with social networks. FTC identified the market power of Facebook because of the fact that Facebook does not lose noteworthy users or engagement to competitors being an indicator of market power.[51] Moreover, the European Commission estimated that large market shares are not an indicator of significant market power.

On the other hand, e-commerce giants attain monopolies for the reason that smaller incumbents or new entrants cannot survive due to the absence of a

[49]University of Chicago, Stigler Center, Stigler Committee on Digital Platforms, Final Report (16 September 2019) https://www.chicagobooth.edu/research/stigler/news-and-media/committee-on-digital-platforms-final-report

[50]Chris Sagers, Coty, Amazon, and the Future of Vertical Restraints: Evolving Distribution Norms on Both Atlantic Shores, 33 (2) Antitrust Magazine 103 (2018) ("we should be wary of producers who claim they must preserve 'brand identity' or whatever other values they mean to protect through private trade restraints or some new public policy to restrain Amazon.")

[51]In Microsoft/Skype (Case No COMP/M.6281, 7 October 2011) FTC, First Amended Complaint For Injunctive and other Equitable Relief, US DC Court, Case No.: 1:20-cv03590-JEB (19 August 2021)

critical-mass of suppliers and customers.[52] Besides, the market power of the leading platform is acknowledged via the "direct method," without delineating a relevant market and so JD.com has long appealed to Chinese authorities to crack down on Alibaba's "picking one from two" practice. It seems that complaint from a rival platform constitutes strong evidence of the market power of the leading platform. To that extent, Amazon, Alibaba, and other e-commerce giants have developed from e-commerce into diverse digital areas but diversification itself is not condemned by competition law, since it is a natural growth strategy for companies.

The Digital Markets Act has set up blacklisted prohibitions on "gatekeeper" digital platforms which are presumed by quantitative metrics.[53] Moreover, in the United States, rigid black-listed prohibitions are proposed to be put on giant platforms.[54]

The task of antitrust is to support a competitive economy and so there is a need of defining whether there is competition. In the digital economy, competitive advantage is dependent on the company's environment and technological resources.[55]

10.8 Market Concentration in the Platform Economy

It is worth noting that horizontal deals in concentrated businesses with high product similarity are linked with anticompetitive effects.[56] Moreover, vertical mergers are principally stimulated by an efficiency-enhancing rational. To that extent, in horizontal mergers, companies acquire industry peers to expand businesses and, by doing so, managers could express anticompetitive pressure in the market by scheduling monopolistic prices and quantities. Moreover, horizontal mergers enhance market share, but cannot prevent the risk of new entrants. On the other hand, vertical mergers give rise to foreclosure and the locking out of prospective new market entrants and so competing businesses struggle to access supplies in a cost-effective manner, if at all, and new entrants may face inexplicably high costs. Furthermore,

---

[52] D.S. Evans, Economics of Vertical Restraints for Multi-Sided Platforms (Coase-Sandor Institute for Law & Economics Working Paper No. 626, 2013), p 20. European Commission, DG Comp, Jacques Crémer et al., Competition Policy for the Digital Era (April 2019), p. 55 (Commenting that rivals to incumbents can survive only when they obtain critical mass of users, thus getting into the orbit of network effects).

[53] Luis Cabral et al. The EU Digital Markets Act: A Report from a Panel of Economic Experts, Publications Office of the European Union (9 February 2021), ISBN 978-92-76-29,788-8, doi:10.2760/139337, JRC122910. Boston University Questrom School of Business Research Paper No. 3783436, SSRN: https://ssrn.com/abstract=3783436

[54] Susan Holmberg, The techlash is the first step to restoring a fair US economy, Financial Times (15 February 2022).

[55] Thibault Schrepel, Platforms or Aggregators: Implications for Digital Antitrust Law, 12 J. Eur. Compet. Law Pract. 1 (2021).

[56] Nihat Aktas, Audra Boone The Private Deal Process in Mergers and Acquisitions https://ssrn.com/abstract=4126431

vertical mergers are appealing to technology-intensive corporations that take advantage of superior information flows. Hence, vertical mergers secure market concentration permitting optimal information flows.[57] Dimitrios Gounopoulos et al.[58] argue that "the susceptibility of AI substitution is indeed related to more vertical mergers, but not horizontal or diversifying mergers."

As mentioned earlier, the rise of Big Tech corporations, such as Google, Amazon, Apple, Microsoft, and Facebook, that act both as intermediary platforms and as providers of services and goods in several markets, has amplified worries concerning economic harms brought by the concentrated structure of the digital economy. Therefore, the advances in data processing and storage technologies have generated new business openings for big digital corporations and so digital corporations have employed such information purposefully to advance their own services and starting new products and services. To that extent, big digital platforms differentiate from other corporations due to direct and indirect network effects stemmed by their size and multimarket presence, accompanied by economies of scope and scale caused by the rigorous use of digital technologies.

Also, advertisers and publishers appraise the size of platform's user base than users appreciate the number of ad-suppliers reaching them via the social media platform. Consequently, the platform subsidizes the service to end-users, at the expense of suppliers which means that where platforms present subsidized digital services to end-users backed by suppliers keen on reaching those users to present their products and services and so generating a concentrated structure of many digital markets. Thus, platform intermediaries like Amazon, Google, and Facebook gained, in a few years, high levels of market share among users in many digital markets.

It is argued that while Amazon revolutionized e-commerce and brought several consumer benefits, such as convenience, time savings, and lower prices, simultaneously it possesses significant market power and makes use of anticompetitive business practices such as predatory or below-cost pricing and aggressively expanded into multiple business areas via mergers and acquisitions (M&As).[59] On the other hand, Amazon along with other tech firms have not (yet) been challenged as a result of focusing mainly on consumer prices as the dominant metric for assessing competition.

Furthermore, the platforms' dominance in digital ad markets leads to an increase in the prices of ads harming competition and innovation in retail markets, provided that only incumbents in these markets are able to pay the higher prices of advertisements. To that extent, the higher prices of digital ads stimulated by the concentration in digital ads market produce an entry barrier to new and small innovators in retail

[57] Moresi, S., Reitman, D., Salop, S.C., Sarafidis, Y., 2021. Vertical mergers in a model of upstream monopoly and incomplete information. Review of Industrial Organization 59, 363-380.

[58] Dimitrios Gounopoulos, Chen Huang, Geoff Wood, Aoran Zhang, Artificial Intelligence and Corporate Investment Decisions, at: https://ssrn.com/abstract=4546112P6

[59] Khan, L. (2017). Amazon's Antitrust Paradox. Yale Law Journal 126. 710-805. Manuel Wörsdörfer, Apple's Antitrust Paradox, https://ssrn.com/abstract=4487386

markets that want to purchase digital ads and so affecting negatively consumer welfare.

Also, the accumulation of capital, technology, and data in the hands of a few Big Techs has advanced the rise of innovative digital solutions and so the upsurge in the demand for digital products and services that the COVID-19 pandemic brought has underlined the significance of AI technology infrastructure offered by the big digital platforms. Hence, the strong network results and economies of scale of many digital markets marked their concentration which does not result in inefficiencies because consumer's surplus would be well protected in the presence of enough contestability.[60] Thus, competition authorities should concentrate on managing the outcomes of market concentration in order to avert abusive misconduct of dominant platforms.

Likewise, the effectiveness of regulatory regimes planned to handle concentration and prospective anticompetitive misconduct in digital markets has been explored and so precautionary antitrust policy and ex post regulation have received strong interest. In addition, there is a need of defining that the objective of a prospective intervention is advancing competition in the digital platforms and not fostering competition for the digital platforms.[61]

10.9 Competition in Digital Platforms

Does the concentration generate abuse of position? First of all, digital platforms act as regulators of marketplaces formed by themselves and utilized by billions of people and corporations globally. Thus, due to reduced costs of communication, it is becoming possible for new entrepreneurs to investigate platform features and capabilities in distributing services and reaching new clients which means that digital platforms have augmented competition and innovation in several online and off-line markets. On the other hand, platforms gain access to privileged information linked to the demand and supply of many different businesses employing their platforms to trade and so the absence of clear boundaries to the strategy of digital platforms produces a danger of exploiting their users of both sides of the intermediation business with comparatively weak adverse consequences. Consequently, there is a need of generating measures to guarantee that the rules and conducts compelled by platforms on their own marketplaces do not distort free and vigorous competition and the enticements to innovation in markets of both sides of the intermediation platform. To that extent, *ex post* and *ex ante* regulatory interventions

[60] Dasgupta, K. and Williams, M. (2020). Competition Policy or Regulation: Does the History of Telecommunications Have Lessons for Platforms? ITS Europe Online event. June 2020.

[61] Crémer, J., Montjoye, Y.-A. de, Schweitzer, H. and Directorate-General for Competition - European Commission (2019). Competition policy for the digital era. http://publications.europa.eu/publication/manifestation_identifier/PUB_KD0419345ENN

should be invented to handle the operation of marketplaces formed by the platforms. Competition authorities in the EU and the United States have recently begun to analyze the past decade of acquisitions by digital platforms that have initially not received any scrutiny by competition authorities.[62]

It is argued that "competition to obtain a monopoly is an important form of competition"[63] and so competing to monopolize unavoidably means that competition is the exclusion of certain competitors except as long as the antagonism of companies under a certain pro-competitive process is a matter of progress and development regardless if many companies cannot follow the rhythm due to bad management and wrong investment along with unbalanced inputs because monopolies are possibly efficiency augmenting due to improved efficiency by stimulating innovation than a highly fragmented market. Hence, per se rules on ex ante covering allow the advancement of competition by presenting the rightful competition process with open access markets for all potential competitors. Thus, the effort to become a monopolist and dominant firm via equal opportunities of competition process is rightful, since competition law does not concern itself with every practice simply for the reason that it prevents competitors. Xingyu Yan and Hans Vedder[64] propose a test centered on the concept of minimum efficient scale by clarifying competition on the merits in a virtuously efficiency-based manner and showing "potential in enhancing the robustness of ex post antitrust when ex ante regulation has become the more popular recourse."

It has to be taken into account that competition's objective is to protect the competitive qualities via management excellences, not to schedule who should win and who should lose. Promoting competition for the intermediation platforms entails the introduction of a set of competition policy and/or regulatory measures with the objective of stimulating the entry of new players into the intermediation business.

The adoption of measures to increase the contestability of intermediation markets should start with the definition of which markets are to be addressed, followed by the definition of clear criteria for identifying which incumbent intermediation platforms have market power in those markets. Digital platforms via their market power across markets in the digital economy avert end users to switch to smaller competitors, even when newcomers present better services. It seems that concentration is welfare diminishing by permitting platforms to utilize users' and consumers' surplus unfairly. Due to welfare-enhancing characteristics of the current concentrated

---

[62] U.S. Federal Trade Commission (2020). FTC to Examine Past Acquisitions by Large Technology Companies https://www.ftc.gov/news-events/press-releases/2020/02/ftc-examine-past-acquisitionslarge-technology-companies

[63] Richard A. Posner, Antitrust Law, 248–49 (second edn, Chicago: University of Chicago Press, 2001), Mark S. Popofsky, Defining Exclusionary Conduct: Section 2, the Rule of Reason, and the Unifying Principle Underlying Antitrust Rules, 73(2) Antitrust L. J. 435, 437, 458–60 (2006).

[64] Xingyu Yan and Hans Vedder, Minimum Efficient Scale, Competition On The Merits, And The Special Responsibility Of A Dominant Undertaking, Journal of Competition Law & Economics, 2023, 19, 123–145 https://doi.org/10.1093/joclec/nhac012 p123

structure of many digital markets, room for abusive misconduct by digital platforms with market power has been generated.

Digital platforms have engaged in self-regulation to evade rigid government oversight by forming private coalitions for the establishment of common rules such as interoperability standards and codes of conduct.[65] On the other hand, the approval of ex ante, competition policy remedies serves the objective of promoting competition for the intermediation platforms.

Taking into account that the digital economy is in constant evolution, any ex ante measure is outdated very quickly and so new technology platforms remain without competition policy or regulatory interventions. Thus, precautionary competition policy measures considered the imposition of restrictions for incumbent intermediation platforms to acquire nascent, technology businesses[66] grounded on an understanding that that the start-up acquisition strategies of incumbent platforms intended to eliminate prospective competitors and so impairing venture capital investment and the innovation ecosystem.[67] It has to be taken into account that platform acquisitions of startups can lead to monopoly. Moreover, it is argued that there is a need of effective devices to combat pre-emptive acquisitions and other competitive misconduct of incumbent digital platforms. It is worth mentioning here that digital platforms have persuaded policymakers that governmental oversight would harm their capability to innovate. G.I. Zekos considers that an AAI system will deal with the competition of digital platforms since all data will pass through the nodes of the system and the self-advancement of the system will block all illegal movements and so directly will enforce technical measures of the circulation of data and so the AAI law will be imposed immediately.

Likewise, the competition policy against the Big Techs in the United States and in the EU reveals the limitations of purely ex post, anti-trust remedies to foster competition in the platform economy.[68] It seems that ex post antitrust remedies are not effective enough to safeguard competition in digital markets and so ex ante remedies seem to successfully discourage competitive misconduct in the short term from platforms detected with market power. Customarily, interventions based on competition law are initiated not by market power per se, but by evidence of its

[65] Cusumano, M. A., Gawer, A., and Yoffie, D. B. (2019) The Business of Platforms: Strategy in the Age of Digital Competition, Innovation, and Power. Harper Business.

[66] U.S. Senate, 2021). U.S. House of Representatives (2021). H.R.3826 - Platform Competition and Opportunity Act of 2021. Committee: House – Judiciary. https://www.congress.gov/bill/117thcongress/house-bill/3826/text

[67] Prado, T. S., & Bauer, J. M. (2022). Big Tech Platform Acquisitions of Start-ups and Venture Capital Funding for Innovation. Information Economics and Policy, Vol 59, 100,973. https://doi.org/10.1016/j.infoecopol.2022.100973U.S. Senate (2021). S.225 - Competition and Antitrust Law Enforcement Reform Act of 2021. Committee: Senate – Judiciary. https://www.congress.gov/bill/117thcongress/senate-bill/225/text

[68] Wheeler, T., Verveer, P., and Kimmelman, G. (2020). New digital realities; new oversight solutions in the U.S. The case for a Digital Platform Agency and a new approach to regulatory oversight. Discussion Paper, Shorenstein Center on Media, Politics and Public Policy, Harvard University.

abuse. To that extent, the merger examination focuses on considering what will be the impact on prices in the short term after an acquisition but the impact emerges in the long run and so the current merger framework fails to weigh these long-run elements. It could be argued that owing to the intricacy and lack of transparency in digital markets, the incumbent digital platform has to be obligated to present supportive evidence that the acquisition will not harm innovation and consumer welfare in the short and long run.

In March 2021,[69] the European Commission issued a guidance paper encouraging national competition authorities ("NCAs") to refer to the EC transactions that do not meet national merger control thresholds and so escaping merger control in the EU. The basis for the modification is to offer additional flexibility to review transactions that fall below national merger control thresholds but could even so harm competition and so capturing "killer acquisitions."[70] To that extent, the Commission unreservedly cleared the formation of a joint venture between the Volvo Group and Daimler Truck AG.[71]

As discussed earlier, Big Tech start-up acquisitions fuel venture capital investment in the short term and are a vital exit strategy for venture capitalists which means that banning tech start-up acquisitions multiplies the risk and lower profit predictions of venture investment because of banning the selling of a start-up for a profit. In addition, lack of VC investment hinders entrepreneurship and start-up creation, with negative influences on consumer welfare. Hence, *ex post*, competition policy remedies fulfill the objective of advancing competition for the incumbent digital platforms. To that extent, competition policy enforcers should cope with cases of abusive misconduct commenced by incumbent platforms with market power and so not concentrating only on analyzing short-term impacts of mergers and acquisitions on consumer welfare such as the impacts on price and total output. It is argued that business conduct that enhances integration or concentration does not automatically violate antitrust law because there is a need of consumers to be harmed via higher prices, reduced supply, or diminished innovation or rivalry which means that a transaction is pro-competitive under the antitrust laws as long as consumer welfare rises.[72]

Furthermore, competition policy enforcers ascertain standardized interoperability and data portability procedures utilized as remedies employed by incumbent

[69] Communication Guidance on the application of the referral mechanism set out in Article 22 of the Merger Regulation to certain categories of cases, C(2021) 1959 final of March 26, 2021

[70] Rechtbank Den Haag, Illumina Inc.- Grail Inc. v. De Staat der Nederlanden, judgment n°31C/09/609526 of March 31, 2021.

[71] Commission Daily News MEX/21/461, "Mergers: Commission clears creation of the joint venture Daimler Truck Fuel Cell by Volvo and Daimler," February 8, 2021, https://ec.europa.eu/commission/presscorner/detail/en/MEX_21_461

[72] Gopal Das Varma & Martino DeStefano, Equilibrium Analysis of Vertical Mergers, 65 Antitrust Bull. 445 (2020);

platforms in cases of evident competitive misconduct and abuse of market power.[73] *Ex post* regulatory seeks at managing consequences of concentration for competition in the incumbent platforms and *ex ante* regulatory measures achieve not only the objective of advancing competition for the platform but also promoting healthy and energetic competition in the platforms. Moreover, *ex ante* regulatory measures over incumbent platforms forwarding competition in the platforms necessitate the establishment of a dedicated regulatory authority dealing with digital competition. Hence, GDPR and the DMA have the prospective of modeling ex ante regulatory measures towards digital platforms around the globe. Hereafter, the approval of ex ante, pro-competitive measures will adjust the enticements of incumbent digital platforms to maintain investment, innovation, and the provision of affordable digital services. The DMA's data clause is an extension of GDPR, based on which the Luxembourg data protection regulator has issued a decision against Amazon regarding Amazon's processing of personal data.[74]

It is characteristic that in 2020, the Autorité formed a dedicated digital unit with the purpose of underpinning its resources in digital areas. Large digital corporations through their ToS convert their practices and values into de facto standards and so confirming the compatibility of contractual contexts with national and supranational law. Moreover, the digital economy unit is advancing automated devices for competition investigations within the Autorité.[75]

10.10 Standardization and Competition

Most technical standards development organizations (SDOs) have embraced internal policies exemplifying "due process" criteria such as openness, balance of interests, consensus decision-making, and appeals. Moreover, courts and enforcement agencies have taken into account SDOs as a procompetitive feature because standard development procedures by following certain due process principles are expected not to produce anticompetitive effects.[76]

[73] Scott-Morton, F., M. and Kades, M. (2021). Interoperability as a Competition Remedy for Digital Networks. https://doi.org/10.2139/ssrn.3808372

[74] Luxembourg National Commission for Data Protection (6 August 2021), Decision Regarding Amazon Europe Core S.À R.L.

[75] The Autorité Creates a Digital Economy Unit, Autorité de la concurrence (January 9, 2020), https://perma.cc/6742-UKUX

[76] Allied Tube & Conduit Corp. v. Indian Head, Inc., 486 U.S. 492, 506–07 (1988) ("[P]rivate standard-setting by associations comprising firms with horizontal and vertical business relations is permitted at all under the antitrust laws only on the understanding that it will be conducted in a nonpartisan manner offering procompetitive benefits.").

SDO practice is supplied into EU-level policy via the European standardization policy by generating technical standards and so Regulation 1025/2012[77] clarifies that stakeholder representation is needed for the success of standardization which means that stakeholders are represented not only in standardization processes but also in SDO governance. EU competition law was also applied to standardization activities.[78]

It has to be taken into account that standardization processes present a forum for the objective assessment of different technical solutions that are unbiased with regard to the interests of competing providers.[79] The antitrust laws do entail SDOs to embrace specific processes or policies for the balancing of interests but they outline the effective balance or lack of bias that SDOs' processes must retain.[80]

10.11 Digital Providers and Competition

Blockchain technology generates a decentralized and principally autonomous model of the organization of the digital economy.[81] Moreover, the supposed transparency of the blockchain, which is in doubt lately, gives noteworthy advantages to platforms when organizing a network of transactions because transparency produces institutions-based trust.

Digital platforms are online corporations intermediating and aggregating suppliers and customers in two-sided markets. Each platform sector has its own exclusive characteristics and so Facebook, Alibaba, and Uber are very different in their scale economies and network externalities, developing differing trends toward concentration. Furthermore, digital platforms seem to constitute a hybrid between models of "retain and reinvest" and "downsize and distribute." Online intermediaries and digital platforms offer the infrastructure and means on which other platform businesses are built. Also, digital platforms are typified by conglomerate kind of expansion, denoted by high diversification. It is argued that the existence of many

[77] Regulation 1025/2012 on European Standardization, 2012 O.J. (L 316) 12. Council Resolution of 7 May 1985 on a New Approach to Technical Harmonization and Standards, 1985 O.J. (C 136) 1. Commission Communication on Standardization in the European Economy, 1992 O.J. (C 96) 2

[78] Eur. Comm'n, Guidelines on the Applicability of Article 101 of the Treaty on the Functioning of the European Union to Horizontal Co-operation Agreements, 2011 O.J. (C 11) 1. Commission Communication on Setting out the EU Approach to Standard Essential Patents, COM (2017) 712 final (Nov. 29, 2017)

[79] Addamax Corp. v. Open Software Found., 152 F.3d 48 (first Cir. 1998). TruePosition, Inc. v. LM Ericsson Tel. Co. 977 F. Supp. 2d 462 (E.D. Pa. 2013). Golden Bridge Techs. v. Motorola, Inc., 547 F.3d 266 (fifth Cir. 2008).

[80] Allied Tube & Conduct Corp. v. Indian Head, Inc., 486 U.S. 492, 511 (1988).

[81] Ioannis Lianos Blockchain Competition Gaining Competitive Advantage in the Digital Economy: Competition Law Implications CLES Research Paper Series 4/2018

small digital companies is based on their capacity to understand and respond to algorithmic processes.[82]

Democratic governments around the globe utilize a platform governance agenda requiring global platform governance, as no single country can change the formation of the platform economy alone. Taking into account that the platform firms in the consumer marketplace generate special liabilities owing to the control they exercise over data, advertising, and the duration of information, governments explore new ways to curb the power of digital giants in order to reduce the threats to public safety and democratic integrity.[83]

It has to be taken into account that platform governance will overtake corporate governance because there will be a movement from corporate competition to AI autonomous corporations managed by AI entities. Also, it has to be taken into consideration that digital platforms, as a new organizational form, highlight emerging patterns of internationalization in the digital economy.[84] Platforms denote a stable set of common technological resources, standards, and capabilities for organizing the production of complementary products, and presenting a cyberspace intermediary for the exchange between customers and suppliers of complementary products. Could digital platforms have the legal form of e-MNEs? Contrasting conventional MNEs and e-MNEs platforms gain advantages from both their proprietary resources and complementary resources. It is worth noting that deficiencies in IPR protection are in favor of inter-firm collaboration between platform owners and complementors while upgrading IPR regimes leads to internalization in a host market. On the other hand, in strong IPR regimes, legal protection of copyrights increases the platform's aptitude to utilize proprietary resources and the extent of internalization. It has to be taken into account that digital platform organization empowers corporations to get and reallocate decision and payoff rights to externally owned resources and so coordinating a value-creating ecosystem crossing national borders.[85]

The concept of "dominance" has been comprehended as "a position of economic strength" possessed by an undertaking to restrict competition "by affording it the power to behave to an appreciable extent independently of its competitors, its customers and ultimately of its consumers."[86] Also, economic strength empowers the undertaking having a noticeable impact on the conditions under which competition will advance.

---

[82]West, S. (2019) Data capitalism: redefining the logics of surveillance and privacy, Business & Society, 58(1), pp. 20–41.

[83]Taylor Owen The Case for Platform Governance CIGI Papers No. 231 — November 2019

[84]Carla L. Reyes Autonomous Business Reality 2021 Nevada Law Journal Vol. 21:2437 . Carla L. Reyes, Autonomous Corporate Personhood, 2021 Washington Law Review Vol. 96:1453

[85]Liang Chen, Sali Li, Jiang Wei and Yang Yang, Externalization in the platform economy: Social platforms and institution, 2022 Journal of International Business Studies 1805–1816.

[86]Case C27/ 76, United Brands company and United Brands Continental v Commission [1978] ECR 207, paras 65, 113; and Case C- 85/ 76, Hoffman- La Roche & Co v Commission [1979] ECR 461, paras 38-39

Economic power encompasses the various aspects of power that are traditionally taken into consideration in competition law enforcement. Even though Section 2 of Sherman Act denotes monopoly power, and the European systems of competition law utilize the concept of "dominant position," the concept of "market power" has grown to a unified conceptual framework and has outlined the competition law enforcement.

Market power endorses the capacity of an undertaking to initiate a deviation from the price or quantity obtained from the competitive situation in the market in which the transaction takes place. Also, market power is evaluated in the context of a relevant market of substitutable products, and a high market share signifies a higher influence on the economy.

Competition is the main tool used in the economy to promote consumer welfare.[87] G.I. Zekos argues that under the notion of consumer welfare hides a tendency to allow monopolies to play the central role in an economy which prohibits the evolvement of other competitors on the market. Moreover, perfect competition arises whenever a large number of corporations selling similar products or services function in markets distinguished by price transparency and low entry barriers.

Competition law has developed advanced quantitative tools to measure market power. To that extent, competition authorities concentrate on the market structure and concentration and so defining monopoly power by reference to the capability of excluding rivals by using strategic barriers to entry so as to keep out or marginalize rivals.

Financial markets play a central part in determining the market value of corporations. Competitive strategy centers on competition, taking into consideration the corporate strategy to maximize the corporation's performance, in terms of surplus value and economic profit. Moreover, corporations pursue a competitive advantage, either by copying successful competitors while lowering their costs or by distinguishing themselves from their competitors, by advancing internal resources and competencies which means conceiving strategies to utilize these differences.

It is worth noting that online marketplaces bring benefits to consumers along with being powerful engines for growth and innovation. Moreover, acting as intermediaries between merchants and consumers, they tolerate a host of producers and retailers to reach consumers facilitating the development of new business models and possessing a superior bargaining position concerning their business users. Hence, power inequalities between platforms and business users result in sellers becoming dependent on those platforms to reach buyers.

It could be said that economic dependence is exemplified by the absence of reasonably equivalent alternatives available within a reasonable period of time permitting the imposition of services or conditions not to be gained under normal market conditions. Moreover, the perception of economic dependence is found in the

[87] Ariel Ezrachi, EU Competition Law Goals and the Digital Economy, Oxford Legal Stud. Res. Paper no. 17, 2018.

Court of Justice case law in British Leyland[88] closely linked to legal monopoly rights granted to a trade partner. Hence, the notion of dependency distinguishes a scale of relationships triggering public intervention and embracing relationships grounded on product ranges or strong brands, the strength of the buyer, and technical standards.[89]

EU member states have adopted specific rules on the abuse of economic dependence and relative market power. The German ARC acknowledges that undertakings can have market power even without a high market share, in circumstances where small companies as suppliers or purchasers of a particular form of goods or commercial services denote that reasonable possibilities of switching to other undertakings do not exist.

It has to be taken into consideration that platforms impose unfair trading practices against business users with the purpose of maximizing profits and earning costs of competition on the seller's part. Accordingly, online intermediary marketplaces gain a superior bargaining position and market power enabling them to extract excessive value from captive business users. To that extent, contemporary EU competition enforcement against online platforms and marketplaces has concentrated on exclusionary abuses, such as self-preferencing, as one manifestation of power imbalances and has not adopted other devices successfully complementing EU competition law in the quest of suppressing the platforms' superior bargaining position.[90] It has to be taken into account that the employment of competition law in the digital economy has concentrated on matters of access to data, interoperability of technologies, and protection of consumers from mistreatment in product markets.[91]

It seems that competition authorities in Europe and elsewhere have been rather slow to react to the development of digital capitalism by trying to handle the problem by applying industrial capitalism era competition law to the post-industrial informational capitalism. There is a need of the transformation of competition by focusing on its technological dimension and its influence on business models.

In essence, evaluating the effects of possibly competitive conduct in complex digital markets necessitates paying attention to how consumers actually behave rather than focusing narrowly on what would be rational for them to do. Consumers as buyers are induced both by specific recommendations and by the modes in which options are filtered.

First of all, as discussed earlier, large digital providers have materialized as gatekeepers serving as gateways for their business users and consumers and exercising control over whole platform ecosystems. These platform ecosystems are

---

[88] Case 226/84, British Leyland Public Limited Company v Commission, ECR [1986] 3263.

[89] C-82/01, P Aéroports de Paris v Commission, EU:C:2002:617; C-177/16, AKKA/LAA v Konkurences padome, EU:C:2017:689.

[90] Despoina Mantzari, Power Imbalances in Online Marketplaces: At the Crossroads of Competition Law and Regulation April 2021 CLES Research Paper Series 4/2021

[91] J. Furman et al., Unlocking digital competition, Report of the Digital Competition Expert Panel (March 13, 2019), https://www.gov.uk/government/publications/unlocking-digital-competition-report-of-thedigital-competition-expert-panel

revealing serious competition problems and the absence of contestability owing to high barriers to entry in view of the characteristics of digital markets is echoed in the control over data by specific platforms or a lack of venture capital funding for businesses that intend to compete with incumbent digital platforms. Another feature of "gatekeepers" is that they function in fields that have widespread influence throughout the global and the EU economy.

Actually, "algorithmic power" becomes a source of market power stemming from the gatekeeping role of online marketplaces as central opening of businesses to consumers in addition to their capacity to store, control, and process crucial data. Moreover, the likelihood of data leverage across markets boosts market concentration even further, leading to a "winner-takes-most' dynamic." Hence, economic players utilize their superior "algorithmic power" by exploiting the preferences of their suppliers and buyers. Undeniably, digital platforms have become the central system of modern capitalist value generation converting into important gatekeepers for various economic activities in the digital economy organizing their economic power coming out from the control of resources such as big data, algorithms, and AI, on which the new pattern of economic production based on and capturing an even higher percentage of the total surplus value of the value chain.

It has to be taken into consideration that the growth and dominance of digital corporations have coincided with an unparalleled escalation in the acquisition and monetization of consumers' personal information.[92] It is worth noting that customers surrender information as payment in exchange for access to products like webmail, social networking, and creative-content services and so personal information serves as a form of currency. It is argued that while the GDPR has empowered citizens and so reduced data sharing online, it has also increased market concentration.[93] To that extent, Bertin Martens et al.[94] argue that "if the data regulation is only about the price of data sharing, private incentives for data sharing are always lower than social ones. Even if the dominant platform has monopoly rights over data, it can still have lower incentives than in the social optimal case... the GDPR price rule minimizes the incentives for data sharing."

Also, it has to be taken into account that digital platforms increase their price markups by raising their product price in one of the markets on which they are present but often digital platforms offer their products and services for "free" and so markups take the form of the harvesting of more personal data, and so signifying a

[92] Regulation (EU) 2016/679 of the European Parliament and of the Council of 27 April 2016 on the protection of natural persons with regard to the processing of personal data and on the free movement of such data, and repealing Directive 95/46/EC (General Data Protection Regulation) [2016] OJ L119/1. Charles I. Jones & Christopher Tonetti, Nonrivalry and the Economics of Data, 110 Am. Econ. Rev. 2819, 2820, 2855-56 (2020).

[93] Garrett A. Johnson et al., Privacy & Market Concentration: Intended & Unintended Consequences of the GDPR (Mar. 2020), https://www.ftc.gov/system/files/documents/public_events/1548288/privacycon -2020-garrett_johnson.pdf

[94] Bertin Martens, Geoffrey Parker, Georgios Petropoulos, Marshall Van Alstyne, Platform Competition and Information Sharing, https://ssrn.com/abstract=4528803 p5

reduction in privacy. Digital platforms count on their base of users for offering inputs for free and so collecting large-scale data used to train the algorithms of a search engine managed by the platform, which are then utilized in different modes. Also, digital platforms take advantage of their vertical power to lower their input prices by suppressing the wages of their employees or by taking advantage of amplified competition among suppliers and the existence of excess capacity upstream which means that by lowering the barriers of entry in upstream markets triggers the entry by new companies into the production of goods and services serving as inputs to the outputs of the digital platform. Hence, this amplified competition between their suppliers raises their markups.

Also, it has to be taken into consideration that corporations in the digital economy capture an uneven amount of the surplus value generated by innovation resulting from the materialization of the new industry due to new AI technological developments. Moreover, the effective strategy is opting for an "open architecture" via an open ecosystem and so producing higher value. In a digital economy marked by network effects, the position of incumbents is confronted by companies vertically stationed in complementary markets benefiting from network effects, rather than competitors established on the same relevant market.

It is worth mentioning here that competition takes part in several dimensions, beyond product and service markets, above all entrepreneurial assets but more drastically "non-consumption." Hence, in the digital economy context, one needs to take a more dynamic perspective than product market competition. The Supreme Court underlined the significance of evaluating both sides of a two-sided transaction platform so as to accurately assess competition.[95]

It has to be taken into account that the status of dominance and the status of gatekeeper are distinct justifying the introduction of a new regulatory alternative. The Commission addresses the identified problems in a broader set of circumstances, since present EU competition rules are applied only when certain preconditions are met: such as the existence of an anticompetitive agreement in the case of Article 101 of the Treaty of the Functioning of the European Union (TFEU) or of a dominant position in the case of Article 102 TFEU. Also, current EU competition rules prevent or address a market failure, but not in the most effective way because they are of a systemic nature. Further, the EU competition rules do not capture all unfair business practices by digital gatekeepers. Jacques Crémer et al.[96] argue "that the basic framework of competition law, as embedded in Articles 101 and 102 of the TFEU, continues to provide a sound and sufficiently flexible basis for protecting competition in the digital era."

The case-by-case assessment of the influence of a practice is the rule in the EU competition law system. It is worth noting that the determination of the entity which is compelled to offer compensation for damage instigated by an infringement of

[95] Ohio v American Express Co, 585 US _ (2018).

[96] Jacques Crémer Yves-Alexandre de Montjoye Heike Schweitzer, Competition Policy for the digital era, Final report, European Union, 2019 p3

Article 101 TFEU is directly governed by EU law and so claiming damages triggered by anticompetitive conduct certifies the full effectiveness of the EU competition provisions which means that there is an advancement of the working of the EU competition rules.[97] The Court ruled that subsidiary liability is available as a matter of law in the private enforcement of EU competition law, so long as appropriate economic, organizational and legal links exist between the parent company and the subsidiary and so the private enforcement of EU competition law deters anticompetitive behavior and the meaning of 'undertaking' does not vary depending on whether public or private enforcement is at issue.[98]

Article 101(1) TFEU is applied formalistically to very specific and clearly anticompetitive arrangements such as naked horizontal price-fixing, output restrictions, and market division and the court[99] has made clear that, for instance, "agreements which aim to share markets have, in themselves, an object restrictive of competition and fall within a category of agreements expressly prohibited by Article 101(1) TFEU, and that such an object cannot be justified by an analysis of the economic context of the anticompetitive conduct concerned." Also, the Court assesses the conduct at hand against the benchmark of a rule preferring to investigate each case in light of a broad range of considerations that appeal to the rationales of Article 101(1) TFEU.[100] Hence, there are resemblances between the development of the by object category and the per se rule in US antitrust law.

It is characteristic that the CJEU[101] mentioned that in a growing market, Article 102 TFEU necessitates action to avert the formation and consolidation of a competitive structure falsified by the abusive strategy of an undertaking which has a dominant position in that market which means demanding action before the anticompetitive effects of that strategy are accomplished. It has to be taken into consideration that anticompetitive effects result from the exploitation by a dominant firm of its substantial market power vis-a-vis customers and/or suppliers due to the lack of effective competitive constraints and so exploitative conduct can be caught by Article 102 TFEU. To that extent, the Court held that EU competition law is concerned with both actual and prospective consequences and so prospective outcomes activate intervention based on the ex ante evaluation of concentrations.[102]

[97] Case C-724/17, Vantaan Kaupunki v Skanska Industrial Solutions Oy, NCC Industry Oy, Asfaltmix Oy, ECLI:EU:C:2019:204

[98] Case C-882/19, Sumal, S.L. v. Mercedes Benz Trucks España, S.L., ECLI:EU:C:2021:800

[99] Siemens and Others v. Commission, C-239/11 P, C-489/11 P and C-498/11 P, EU:C:2013:866, para. 218; Toshiba Corporation v. European Commission, C-373/14 P, EU:C:2016:26, para. 28–29.

[100] Société Technique Minière (L.T.M.) v. Maschinenbau Ulm GmbH (M.B.U.), 56/65, EU:C:1966:38, p. 249 Gazdasági Versenyhivatal v. Budapest Bank Nyrt. and Others, C-228/18, EU:C:2020:265

[101] Case C-52/09 Konkurrenverket v TeliaSonera Sverige AB [2011] ECR I-527

[102] Case T-201/04 Microsoft Corp v Commission, EU:T:2007:289

Moreover, the "ECJ" has steadily held that, as a general rule, anticompetitive effects must not be equated with a negative effect on consumer welfare.[103]

It has to be taken into consideration that the DMA will be enforced hand-in-hand with the existing competition rules, as currently enforced both at European and at national levels. Hence, the DMA does not replace antitrust enforcement in Europe but rather complements it with a set of rules that are safeguarding contestability of particular platform services, and abolishing certain forms of unfair gatekeeper behavior.

10.12 DMA and Competition

The DMA[104] is founded on the belief that competition law alone is inadequate to successfully address the challenges and systemic problems caused by the digital economy. Undeniably, the scope of antitrust is rationed to certain instances of market power such as dominance on specific markets and of anticompetitive behavior. Also, its enforcement takes place ex post demanding extensive investigation on a case-by-case basis of what are often very complex sets of facts.

The DMA invokes regulatory intervention to match conventional antitrust rules by launching a set of *ex ante* obligations for online platforms defined as gatekeepers. Moreover, the DMA guarantees that markets where gatekeepers are present remain fair and independent from the actual or presumed consequences of the conduct of a given gatekeeper grounded on Article 114 TFEU. It is worth noting that the DMA is not an instrument of competition law not affecting how antitrust rules apply in digital markets.[105] On the other hand, the DMA discloses the same objectives and protects the same legal interests as competition law and so its list of prohibitions is an outline of past and ongoing antitrust cases.[106] The DMA states the promotion of fairness and

[103] Case T-8/08, T-Mobile Netherlands BV and others v Raad van bestuur van de Nederlandse Mededingingsautoriteit, EU:C:2009:343, para 38; Joined Cases C-501/06 P, C-513/06 P, C-515/06 P and C-519/06 P GlaxoSmithKline Services Unlimited v Commission, EU:C:2009:610 ('Glaxo Spain'), para 63; Case C-286/13 P Dole Food Company Inc. and Dole Fresh Fruit Europe v Commission, EU:C:2015:184 ('Bananas'), para 125; Case T-216/13, Telefónica, SA v Commission, EU:T:2016:369, para 270

[104] Digital Markets Act, European Commission (Dec. 15, 2020), https://eur-lex.europa.eu/legalcontent/EN/TXT/P

[105] Margrethe Vestager, Competition in a Digital Age, speech to the European Internet Forum (Mar. 17, 2021), https://ec.europa.eu/commission/commissioners/2019-2024/vestager/announcements/competition-digitalage_en

[106] Case AT.40153, E-book MFNs and Related Matters (Amazon), EUROPEAN COMMISSION (May 4, 2017), https://ec.europa.eu/competition/antitrust/cases/dec_docs/40153/40153_4392_3.pdf Heike Schweitzer, The Art to Make Gatekeeper Positions Contestable and the Challenge to Know What Is Fair: A Discussion of the Digital Markets Act Proposal, 3 ZEUP 503 (Jun. 11, 2021). Nicolas Petit, The Proposed Digital Markets Act (DMA): A Legal and Policy Review, 12 J. EUR. COMPET. LAW PRACT 529 (May 11, 2021).

contestability, but the European Parliament expanded the regulation's scope to incorporate promoting innovation and augmenting consumer welfare. Additionally, the DMA imposes a prohibition on granting preferential treatment in ranking services to the gatekeeper's own products and contains provisions blocking self-preferencing via mandated distribution channels or via compatibility restrictions in operating systems, virtual assistants, or web browsers.[107]

In the United States, multiple administrative and judicial bodies operate on the same level but Regulation 1/2003 decentralizes antitrust enforcement by increasing the involvement of national courts and national competition authorities. How should the DMA implement national competition laws? It has to be taken into account that inconsistency in implementing DMA impedes the success of both the DMA and national competition laws. The DMA dictates how some large online platforms operating as "gatekeepers" should act in digital markets before employing a practice to make certain fair and contestable digital markets and so DMA focuses on critics against slow and selective competition enforcement blocking its effectiveness in digital markets.[108] Moreover, NCAs will only back the Commission in enforcing and monitoring the DMA, embracing and collecting complaints and handling market investigations into cases of probable non-compliance. Nevertheless, the member states will implement their own national competition rules, involving DMA-like legislations, insofar they engage in other public interest purposes than guaranteeing contestability and fair markets. It has to be taken into account that ensuring contestability encompasses preventing exclusionary or discriminatory behaviors by gatekeepers obstructing entry by innovating competitors or restricting their capability to expand and attract users which takes place by removing needless barriers to access to data when these represent a major barrier to entry in a market.

The European Commission contemplates antitrust tools unfit to successfully cope with the conduct of digital gatekeepers since they are applied ex post and at the end of extensive investigations of complex facts on a case-by-case and context-specific basis. Hence, the *raison d'être* for the DMA's *ex ante* regulation is grounded on the speed of intervention and enforcement failures than on market failures. Thus, the DMA diverges from the existing regime of antitrust liability more in degree than in the nature of the law and so Articles 101 and 102 TFEU remain applicable to digital gatekeepers. In addition, digital platforms may be prosecuted in parallel cases for the same conduct, which is in conflict with the legal principle of "ne bis in idem." Furthermore, the risk of overlap with competition law is amplified by the DMA's proposed designation process. To that extent, the DMA is covering a gradually large number of corporations rather than Big Tech and native tech firms considering that platform business models materialize in a growing number of businesses.

[107]Prado, T. (2022), "Safeguarding Competition in Digital Markets: A Comparative Analysis of Emerging Policy and Regulatory Regimes", https://doi.org/10.2139/ssrn.4137588

[108]Furman. J., et al., Unlocking Digital Competition, Report of the Digital Competition Expert Panel, March 2019. 4 European Competition Network, statistics, Aggregate figures on antitrust cases. https://ec.europa.eu/competition-policy/european-competition-network/statistics_fr

Undeniably, even though the DMA forbids EU member states from imposing further obligations on gatekeepers, member states remain free to adjust their competition laws to digital markets. Also, member states may exploit national rules on economic dependence to deal with prospective imbalances of bargaining power between online platforms and their business users.

Moreover, the DMA may grant NCAs extra freedom in evaluating cases of refusal to access and so in line with the Europe's essential facility doctrine (EFD), a refusal to deal activates an antitrust violation only when exceptional circumstances are met which means that access to the essential product or service has to be essential for a company conducting business in a market. To that extent, the refusal has to be unfounded and eliminating competition on a secondary market and so if the refusal implicates licensing of intellectual property, it must inhibit the materialization of a new product for which there is prospective consumer demand. Also, in line with the Bronner decision,[109] access to an input is indispensable if there are no technical, legal, or economic hindrances that make it unworkable or unreasonably difficult to copy it. Nonetheless, in Slovak Telekom's decision,[110] the Court of Justice (CJEU) indicated that antitrust enforcers do not have to evidence indispensability when access to the facility has been allowed as a result of a regulatory obligation, instead of voluntarily. Moreover, the EFD exceptional conditions do not apply when the dominant company gives access to its infrastructure but makes that access subject to unfair conditions.

It is worth noting that the German Bundestag adopted an amendment to its national antitrust law and so entrusting the Bundeskartellamt with new powers to ascertain positions of precise market relevance such as companies with dominant importance for competition across markets and the potential anticompetitive outcomes in digital ecosystems where corporations have a gatekeeper function.[111] Moreover, the elements in designating such a company are its dominant position on one or more markets, its financial power or access to other resources, its vertical integration and undertakings on related markets, its access to data significant for competition, etc. and, after the designation has been made, the German competition authority excludes the corporation from engaging in anticompetitive practices. Besides, the corporation can display that the conduct at stake is objectively justified. To that extent, the list of prohibited practices is comparable to the DMA as to be functionally equivalent. On the other hand, the differences are that the German rule considers the list of prohibited practices as exhaustive, and the rule does not deem the practices at stake to be per se prohibited and so embracing a reversal of the

[109]Case C-7/97, Oscar Bronner GmbH & Co. KG EU:C:1998:569, Court Of Justice Of The European Union (Nov. 26, 1998).

[110]Case C-165/19 P, Slovak Telekom a.s. v. Commission, EU:C:2021:239, Court Of Justice Of The European Union, para. 57 (Mar. 25, 2021).

[111]Entwurf Eines Gesetzes zur Änderung des Gesetzes Gegen Wettbewerbsbeschränkungen für Ein Fokussiertes, Proaktives und Digitales Wettbewerbsrecht 4.0 und Anderer Wettbewerbsrechtlicher Bestimmungen, Deutscher Bundestag (Oct. 19, 2020), https://dserver.bundestag.de/btd/19/234/1923492.pdf

burden of proof, permitting corporations to offer objective justifications for their conduct, which is not feasible under the DMA. It could be said that overexpansion brings uncertainty concerning the competition level in a market.

It has to be taken into account that Google has been the first platform to be designated as of dominant importance for competition across markets and the German competition authority has compelled obligations on large digital platforms well before the DMA will enter into force and so thwarting the EU law's effort at harmonization and undercutting its objectives and scope. The Italian AGCM indicated the introduction of a similar rule.[112] Thus, the digital economy regards a single way of implementing legal rules especially in a digital market requiring standardization and automation which means that a federal EU will apply digital rules more effectively due to a harmonized interpretation and so implementation of DMA and competition rules.

Several legislative initiatives reveal leaders' willingness to count on abuse of economic dependence rules to tackle digital platforms' conduct.[113] In 2020, Belgium amended its Code of Economic Law by inserting a rule on the abuse of economic dependence, rationalizing the alteration with specific reference to the legislative gap regarding digital platforms.[114] Moreover, EU member states have endorsed sector-specific legislative initiatives in order to protect weaker parties from the superior bargaining power of digital intermediaries.[115]

It is worth mentioning here that the Federal Supreme Court backed the Bundeskartellamt's strict approach, ruling that a narrow price-parity clause used by an OTA was unlawful under competition law which means that a price-parity clause is not an ancillary restraint exempt from the application of Article 101(1) TFEU and does not fulfill the conditions for exemption set out in Article 101(3) TFEU, because any advantages related with combating free riding do not balance out its anticompetitive effects in the form of a considerable barrier to hotels' own online distribution.[116]

The DMA averts regulatory fragmentation protecting the functioning of the Digital Single Market, as a result of the development of large digital platforms

---

[112] ICA: Proposals for Pro-Competitive Reforms (Annual Competition Law Proposal) Have Been Sent to Palazzo Chigi, AUTORITÀ GARANTE DELLA CONCORRENZA E DEL MERCATO (Mar. 23, 2021), https://en.agcm.it/en/media/press-releases/2021/3/ICA-proposals-for-pro-competitive-reforms-AnnualCompetition-Law-proposal-have-been-sent-to-Palazzo-Chigi

[113] Modernization of Competition Law for the Digital Era, Hellenic Parliament (Jan. 20, 2022), https://www.hellenicparliament.gr/Nomothetiko-Ergo/Psifisthenta-Nomoschedia?law_id=d5fa28cd-0208-4508-b40b-ae1a01508595

[114] Jan Blockx, Belgian Prohibition of Abuse of Economic Dependence Enters into Force, 12 J. Eur. Compet. Law Pract 321 (Jan. 22, 2021).

[115] Jens-Uwe Franck and Nils Stock, What is 'Competition Law'? - Measuring EU Member States' Leeway to Regulate Platform-to-Business Agreements, 39 Yearb. Eur. Law 320 (Sep. 8, 2020).

[116] Case KVR 54/20, Booking.com, BUNDESGERICHTSHOF (May 18, 2021), https://juris.bundesgerichtshof.de/cgibin/rechtsprechung/document.py?Gericht=bgh&Art=en&sid=7a5e4c9a67eee1f8680fcce08bf544aa&nr=120991&pos=0&anz=1

performing EU wide. Hence, owing to the cross-border character of services offered by platforms, national rules have been considered incompetent to tackle the acknowledged competition problems. On the other hand, the vague connection of the DMA with competition law thwarts the attempt at harmonization.

It has to be taken into account that DMA will not displace competition rules but will be employed alongside them and so the parallel function of the DMA and antitrust rules creates risks of double jeopardy and conflicting decisions, which means that it endangers the integrity of the internal market by destabilizing both the DMA's justification and its legal basis.

Taking into account that market forces alone are unable to discipline digital platforms due to the barriers to entry integral in digital platform markets, traditional antitrust law is incapable of protecting effective competition in the digital market. To that extent, concerning Big Tech conduct, EU decisions outlawed conduct that had happened several years before it was brought to the attention of the Commission and so enforcing Article 102 TFEU years after the fact is challenging in markets for services based on rapidly advancing technologies. DMA regulates the conduct of powerful gatekeeper platforms boosting the contestability of core platform markets and guaranteeing fairer conditions for users. The European Commission has regularly examined Big Tech conduct under the EU Merger Regulation. Recently, the Commission applied the EU Merger Regulation, even if the transaction is not caught by the EU Merger Regulation's own jurisdiction threshold or the national jurisdictional thresholds of the referring member states.[117] It seems that courts underestimate the danger of false negatives concentrated on short-term efficiency consequences to the detriment of long-term harm to the structure of competition and consumer welfare.[118]

It is worth noting that the legal effect of a prohibition decision under Article 102 TFEU is inherently case specific. Moreover, the Article 102 TFEU protects competition against the abuse of market power not dealing with barriers to entry that are inherent in a market and that are not the outcome of anticompetitive conduct. The Article 102 TFEU prohibits exclusionary conduct that is not a competition on the merits.[119] It has to be taken into account that the Commission favors of in-depth case-specific analyses and so endorsing in-depth economic assessments in individual cases alike US approach which comes in contrast to the line followed by DMA[120] which was enacted to address the strong concentration of digital platform markets. It has to be taken into account that the conduct rules in the Article 5-7 DMA are per se

[117] Article 22 of the Merger Regulation to certain categories of cases (C(2021) 1959 final). Case T-227/21 Illumina v Commission, ECLI:EU:T:2022:447.

[118] Jonathan B. Baker, The Antitrust Paradigm, Harvard 2019

[119] C-377/20 Servizio Elettrico Nazionale SpA and Others v Autorità Garante della Concorrenza e del Mercato, ECLI:EU:C:2022:379, para 45.

[120] Witt, The More Economic Approach to EU Antitrust Law (Hart Publishing, 2016), Chap. 7. Case T-286/09 RENV Intel v Commission, ECLI:EU:T:2022:19; Case T-235/18 Qualcomm v Commission, ECLI:EU:T:2022:358; Witt, "The European Court of Justice and the More Economic Approach to EU Competition Law – Is the Tide Turning?", (2019) 64(2) Antitrust Bulletin 172-213.

rules reducing barriers to entry by forbidding conduct that is expected to exclude competitors. DMA safeguards contestability and fairness in digital markets by offering several presumptions based on thresholds relating either to the annual turnover and market capitalization of the corporation or to the number of its active users in the EU. Hence, gatekeepers have to comply with a set of rules and will be banned from engaging in conduct such as combining personal data from different core platform services.

Furthermore, DMA contributes to the appropriate running of the internal market by laying down harmonized rules that make certain contestable and fair digital markets across the EU which means that undertakings overcome barriers to entry and expansion and so disputing a gatekeeper on the merits of their products and services. In other words, the DMA banns gatekeeper practices increasing barriers to entry resulting from network consequences, economies of scale, and strong returns on the use of data and so lowering barriers to entrance. One of the cons of DMA is the fact that the DMA's conduct rules do not apply to any digital platform service but only to "core platform services" offered by "gatekeepers" only.[121] Furthermore, the DMA only applies to core platform services presented to users established or located in EU and so not regulating gatekeeper services run by gatekeepers to users established and located in other jurisdictions.

As mentioned earlier, the DMA constitutes a new regulatory instrument[122] designed to limit the economic power held by "gatekeepers," that is digital platforms that operate as "gateways" between business and end users by centralizing implementation within the European Commission, generating a notification procedure for gatekeepers relying on litigation before national and European courts to resolve interpretive disputes and raise compliance incentives. Moreover, DMA drops the threshold for intervention compared to competition law and so exemplifying presumptions of monopoly power and anticompetitive effects which means that economic study of the facts underpinning market structure or business conduct is no longer a condition for the application of the law. Also, DMA focuses on three "kinds" of competitive relationships that might be vulnerable to exclusionary impacts: "interplatform," "intra-platform," and "extra-platform" competition.[123] To that extent, DMA Recital 33 recognizes that there can be an inter- and an intra-platform dimension to competition in stating that "the obligations should also address situations where the position of the gatekeeper may be entrenched to such

[121] DMA, Article 1(2). DMA, recital 13. DMA, Article 19. DMA, Article 3(1).

[122] Regulation (EU) 2022/1925 on contestable and fair markets in the digital sector and amending Directives (EU) 2019/1937 and (EU) 2020/1828 (Digital Markets Act) [2022] OJ L 265/1

[123] Joined Cases 56 and 58-64, Établissements Consten S.à.R.L. and Grundig-Verkaufs-GmbH v Commission of the European Economic Community [1966] ECR I-299, para.342: "The principle of freedom of competition concerns the various stages and manifestations of competition. Although competition between producers is generally more noticeable than that between distributors or products of the same make, it does not thereby follow that an agreement tending to restrict the latter kind of competition should escape the prohibition of Article 85(1) merely because it might increase the former."

an extent that inter-platform competition is not effective in the short term, meaning that intra-platform competition needs to be created or increased." Hence, DMA identifies an extra-platform dimension and so the prime function of the DMA is to guarantee that markets where gatekeepers are present are contestable and fair, irrespective of any wrongdoing or change to the industry structure through corporate reorganization to make possible the entry of new competitors in CPSs.

It has to be taken into consideration that the DMA does not encompass an efficiency defense which is in line with its legal objective, that is not to improve consumer welfare directly, but to eliminate barriers to entry by generating conditions for effective competition and so abolishing the necessity to carry out complex economic assessments which means speeding up enforcement and dropping enforcement cost. To that extent, the Commission enforces the DMA by way of decisions establishing noncompliance with the conduct rules.[124]

It is argued that per se rules may outlaw conduct that does not have any detrimental consequences in individual cases and they can fail to catch conduct that instigates actual harm. On the other hand, the *ex ante* prohibition of particular actions allows that well competitively functioning of the market as a whole and so promoting competition and prohibiting anticompetitive process. Moreover, *ex ante* rules may be improved to catch up any conducts triggering actual harm on the market. Furthermore, the DMA complements the EU competition rules considered incapable of protecting effective competition in core digital platform markets and so by banning many forms of exclusionary conduct *per se*, it tackles the core shortcomings of Article 102 TFEU but not launching any new substantive principles for assessing gatekeeper acquisitions. To that extent, it has to be taken into account that Article 22 of the EU Merger Regulation[125] in conjunction with gatekeepers' duty under the DMA to notify the Commission of any planned acquisitions, the likelihood of the Commission being unable to call in an acquisition it would like to scrutinize more thoroughly is drastically downgraded. The DMA's conduct rules outlaw a broad array of exclusionary leveraging strategies via acquisitions and so tackling certain non-horizontal concerns arising from gatekeeper acquisition. It is worth mentioning here that the DMA establishes per se conduct rules for designated platforms precluding national gatekeeper regulation by EU member states, thus the legality of the German sec. 19a GWB has to be re-examined. Any bypassing actions taken by digital platforms can be dealt with an improvement of merger rules.[126]

It is worth noting here that mergers in digital markets have often slipped the attention of competition agencies. In 2023, the European Commission is simplifying procedures with another merger control package, yet without changing the

[124] DMA, Article 29. DMA, Article 39

[125] The DMA openly refers to the Commission's new guidance on Article 22 of the EU Merger Regulation in Article 14(5).

[126] For a detailed analysis see Anne C. Witt, The Digital Markets Act: Regulating the Wild West, 2023 *Common Market Law Review* Volume 60, Issue 3 pp. 625 – 666

thresholds.[127] Moreover, merger cases in the digital world have characteristics that make them avoid the filters due to the fact that corporations run with free offers so as to create a large user base which means that where a legal filter relies on turnover such as price-based parameters, it fails to recognize the power of the target. The European Commission acknowledged a new strategy in the digital economy, "where services regularly launch with the aim of building up a significant user base and/or commercially valuable data inventories, before seeking to monetise the business."[128] Hence, a merger control regime built on a double turnover threshold assumes that both parties need to have some significance as signaled in revenue for markets in order to be relevant for competition. Moreover, current merger control does not function well when financially strong corporations acquire companies with very little revenue, but a strong prospective for competition. DMA encompassed a specific rule targeting the merger activities of digital gatekeepers[129] and so digital gatekeepers have to notify all merger activities in the digital sector to the European Commission. Also, the European Commission informs national authorities that, in turn, may refer the mergers to the European Commission for merger control in line with Article 22 of the Merger Control Regulation. Thus, the notification under Article 14 DMA in connection with referrals under Article 22 ECMR leads to increased merger control but it relates to a small number of designated gatekeepers. In the Towercast case,[130] the Court of Justice was asked to rule on the formal question whether Art. 21 ECMR prohibits the French authority to investigate a merger for an abuse of dominance and the Court held that the ECMR does not stand in the way. Thus, in its Towercast judgment of 16 March 2023, the European Court of Justice ruled that national competition authorities ("NCAs") and courts can review acquisitions by dominant entities under the abuse of dominance rules, if those acquisitions are not notifiable under EU or national merger control laws and so generating legal uncertainty and risk for dominant corporations, along with openings for rivals and customers to challenge such transactions.[131] Hence, the ordinary inapplicability of ex ante merger control, either at EU or national level, does not prevent an assessment of a transaction under Article 102 TFEU by NCAs after the concentration has been implemented. Also, transactions that fall below EU and national merger control

[127] Commission Notice on a simplified treatment for certain concentrations under Council Regulation (EC) No 139/2004 on the control of concentrations between undertakings 2023/C 160/01 see https://competition-policy.ec.europa.eu/mergers/statistics_en

[128] European Commission, Communication from the Commission, Commission Guidance on the application of the referral mechanism set out in Article 22 of the Merger Regulation to certain categories of cases, OJ C 113, 31.3.2021, para. 9

[129] Article 14 DMA

[130] ECJ 16.3.2023, C-449/21, ECLI:EU:C:2023:207 – Towercast. See Illumina (C-625/22 P) (mergers which do not meet the merger control thresholds may still be referred to the European Commission by EU Member States on the basis of Art. 22 EUMR and may subsequently be subject to its merger control review.)

[131] The Belgian Cartel Authority has opened an ex officio investigation into a possible abuse of dominance by Proximus.

thresholds, and, at the same time, have not been referred to the EC pursuant to Article 22 of the EUMR, may be subject to Article 102 TFEU which indicates any concentration between undertakings that have not been notifiable under either European or national merger control law is subject to an ex-post review in light of abuse of dominance rules. In other words, strengthening a dominant position via an acquisition is not in itself sufficient for finding an abuse and so the merger must "substantially impede competition" denoting that the acquisition of the target must make a material difference in the competitive landscape and signposting that the merger must have in reality resulted in near-total abolition of competition which is in line with the test in Continental Can,[132] where the Court settled that a conduct "can be regarded as an abuse if an undertaking holds a position so dominant that the objectives of the Treaty are circumvented by an alteration to the supply structure which seriously endangers the consumer's freedom of action in the market, such a case necessarily exists if practically all competition is eliminated."

It could be said that mergers and acquisitions in the EU are subject to either an ex ante review under Article 22 EUMR or ex-post review under Article 102 TFEU which means escalating uncertainty in deal-making. An approach that all non-reportable transactions could be reviewable under Article 102 TFEU generates in fact an obstruction of competition in the market by transferring trading advancement in the courtrooms instead of in the market function.

The proof of anticompetitive effects is increasingly taking the form of a dialectic process, where the Commission is required to adduce sufficient proof that the conduct is capable of producing anticompetitive effects relying on certain presumptions or assumptions, but the dominant undertaking may present evidence to the contrary that is evaluated.[133]To that extent, the court concluded that there is no need of proving the loss of consumer welfare and it is appropriate to prove that that practice is impairing the effective competition structure of the relevant market, without it being required to prove that that practice may also instigate direct harm to consumers[134] and so the content of competition law is expected to consist largely of formalistic legal rules.[135]

Albeit *ex ante* regulation has many advantages, DMA although friendly towards speed, efficiency, and legal certainty while enabling actions for damages leaves the scales very unbalanced particularly concerning the freedom to conduct a business as a fundamental right, irrespective of wealth or economic power, and the protection of

---

[132] Europemballage and Continental Can v Commission, C-6/72 ECLI:EU:C:1973:22 paragraph 12 https://eur-lex.europa.eu/legal-content/EN/TXT/?uri=CELEX%3A61972CJ0006

[133] Di Giovanni Bezzi, R., 'Anticompetitive Effects and Allocation of the Burden of Proof in Article 102 Cases: Lessons from the Google Shopping Case', Journal of European Competition Law & Practice, Vol. 13 n. 2, 112-124, at 122-124 (2022).

[134] C-377/20, Servizio Elettrico Nazionale, EU:C:2022:379, paras 40-48.

[135] Lindeboom, J., 'Formalism in Competition Law', Journal of Competition Law & Economics, Volume 18, Issue 4, 1-49, (2022) p. 31 'if the content of competition law is largely based on economic knowledge, and current economic knowledge consists mostly of formal assumptions and models, the content of competition law is likely to consist largely of formalistic rules as well'

the rights of defense and the guarantees of due process under the rule of law. It could be said that DMA aims to "complement" the enforcement of competition law and so DMA[136] pursues contestable and fair markets, whereas competition law protects undistorted market competition. Thus, DMA puts the struggle for a free entrance market in a formalistic way via formal rules rather than a case-by-case examination grounded on economic elements. Natalia Moreno Belloso[137] and Nicolas Petit argue that "Formalism also characterises how the DMA handles the interplay between the DMA and national laws towards digital market power."

It has to be taken into account that AI is highly opaque which means that anticompetitive contact is difficult to be spotted even for well-equipped public enforcement authorities and so antitrust intervention will be instigated too late to prevent irreparable harm.[138] In addition, Thomas Höppner and Luke Streatfeild[139] argue that "the characteristics of the AI stack have all ingredients for winner-takes-all battles with significant collateral damage affecting third party businesses... the rise of AI is prone to make big tech companies even more powerful. Their vertical integration across the AI value chain creates conflicts of interest that may quickly lead to anti-competitive leveraging conduct." It seems that the DMA does not address the specific competition issues around AI. On the other hand, gatekeepers have the most powerful devices to suppress the diffusion of any rival AI offerings.[140]

DMA protects competition as a process by ensuring and advancing competition for the gatekeeper market, in the market, and other related markets.[141] Thus, competition is seen as a device for leveling the playing field in digital markets and so advancing competition on the merits and in terms of better services for consumers, which is protected and boosted with the help of the DMA. Hence, the DMA strives to not only limit corporations' data extraction and consumer exploitation practices but also stimulates data access and data and user mobility by permitting multi-homing and switching and so giving users a certain level of data sovereignty and real choice in the digital realm. It is characteristic that the DMA chooses a centralized model with concentrated enforcement powers at the EU level rather than decentralized or parallel enforcement at the EU and nation-state levels. To that

[136] Alfonso Lamadrid and Nieves Bayón Fernández, "Why the Proposed DMA Might Be Illegal under Article 114 TFEU, and How to Fix It" (2021) 12 Journal of European Competition Law & Practice 576.

[137] Natalia Moreno Belloso and Nicolas Petit, The EU Digital Markets Act (DMA) A Competition Hand in a Regulatory Glove, at: https://ssrn.com/abstract=4411743 p28

[138] Google conquering the entire ad tech stack, see DoJ et all, Case 1:23-cv-00108, Google Ad Tech Complaint for Monopolizing Digital Advertising Technologies, https://www.justice.gov/opa/pressrelease/file/1563746/download

[139] Thomas Höppner / Luke Streatfeild ChatGPT, Bard & Co.: an introduction to AI for competition and regulatory lawyers 9 Hausfeld Competition Bulletin (1/2023), Article 1 p 8,9

[140] Höppner, Creative Destruction in Digital Ecosystems Revisited, 9 Hausfeld Competition Bulletin (2023), Article 5.

[141] Larouche, P. & de Streel, A. (2021). The European Digital Markets Act: A Revolution Grounded on Traditions. Journal of European Competition Law & Practice 12(7). 542-560

extent, the DMA needs an institutional structure with clear-cut responsibilities and a strict division of labor. DMA is insufficient to prevent the lock-in effects of a "walled product garden" and guarantee complete device and platform neutrality which means that extra measures must be taken to overcome high-tech firms' dual role as platform operators and service providers.[142]

10.13 Data and Competition

It is worth mentioning here that Art. 102 TFEU protects undistorted competition covering competition on the merits applying when there is harm to the competitive process and all the requirements given under Art. 102 TFEU are proven.[143]

Digital data generate new modes of control and new repositories of economic and social power and so platforms and algorithms are products of data given that they operate due to data. To that extent, while digital data are amassed in manners that have governance implications, digital data flows stimulate platforms' growth. State data-collection infrastructure ranges to all sorts of smart installations and remote-sensing technologies. Hence, digital data are expressive of particular, social, legal, and economic relations which means that the use of digital data is capitulating greater precision than statistics have previously exhibited.

Modern administrations gain their power from information and capitalism prospers via the accumulation of knowledge. Information has become a corporate asset to be valued on its own terms for the stream of services that it produces which means that digital businesses boost their value because of their databases and the scale of subjects encompassed by these data points. Thus, companies exploit information to make their production process more effective and sorting people and things in line with value potentials.

Consumers access digital platforms for a variety of reasons, and in doing so are turning themselves into unpaid data producers. The spread of cyberspace and communication technology has aided the widespread availability of global data. It has to be taken into account that data conveys noteworthy social, economic, and political power and so unequal control over data, being a prevalent form of digital inequality, is a problem for economic development. Hence, data inequality is a function of unequal control over the infrastructures that produce, form, process, store, transfer, and use data. It is characteristic that geopolitical contests and transnational competition between companies refer to data's value and the "free flow" of data across borders and the need for "data sovereignty." Data is of value to acquire AI technology dependent on large data sets, and is valued, when there is a market for

[142] Manuel Wörsdörfer, Apple's Antitrust Paradox, https://ssrn.com/abstract=4487386

[143] Case C-52/09, TeliaSonera Sverige, 17 February 2011, ECLI:EU:C:2011:83 paras 22-24; Case C-457/10 P, AstraZeneca, 6 December 2012, ECLI:EU:C:2012:770 para 75. Case C-413/14 P, Intel v Commission, 6 September 2017, ECLI:EU:C:2017:632 para 138

datasets or when the value of data is embedded in the value of a corporation, appreciated upon sale or merger. Moreover, data is an input for a wide array of activities in the digital economy expanding the notion of complementarities usually taken into consideration in the process of economic production and so verifying interlinkages between activities.

AI has advanced rapidly and is nowadays widely used in customer-service contexts. Electronic payment systems connect multiple participants and make certain complex technological operations linked to the movement of huge flows of payment information and data.[144] It has to be taken into consideration that threat springing from Big Tech using big data is not only just market dominance but it is also the potential to transform free contracting and markets into a dominated space offering an advantage to sellers over buyers. Thus, sellers retain the predictive power of data to their advantage against their own clients, who are also the data producers. To that extent, Big Tech corporations collect personal data, use it inferentially to rank and segment individuals, and then sell those inferences to others or use them to develop new products and service and so generating a new form of "differential rent."

It could be argued that data as a source and as a process of governance will be expected to replace both markets and the law. Also, it could be said that the law will govern the utilization of data. AAI rule of law will govern all society's function based on AAI laws endorsed by an AAI society via its AAI governance.

It seems that in an AAI society, data is not as an object of transactions or an object of governance, but as a tool for governing others will surpass nation-states with their law. Hence, the rise of Big Tech corporations and their accumulation of vast amounts of data, not available to any state, generates the "rule by data." Of course, during the period of the technical governing of the functioning of AI, Big Tech will necessitate a rule of data, but AI law will govern the functioning of Big Tech companies. An anarchic/chaotic way of rule of date will prevent the autonomous function of AI companies and all the needed transactions in an AAI society.

In the era of digitization, picks about which data is produced are matter of infrastructures enabling data collection through devices, sensors, and platforms. To that extent, governments authorize access to data via statutory and regulatory mechanisms necessitating public reporting or provision of data to particular government agencies, competitors, or consumers. Moreover, companies utilize legal instruments like contracts or licenses, often embedded in regimes of personal and intellectual property, to prevent access to data or to establish conditions for such access.[145]

As technology companies grow more economically dominant, the centrality they place on data collection advances the stakes of data-governance law ruling how data about people is collected, processed, and used. While data becomes an indispensable factor of informational capital, the law regulating data production becomes the

[144] Knewtson, H., & Rosenbaum, Z. A. (2020). Toward understanding FinTech and its industry. Managerial Finance, 46(8), 1043–1060. DOI: https://doi.org/10.1108/MF-01-2020-0024

[145] Angelina Fisher & Thomas Streinz, Confronting Data Inequality, IILJ Working Paper 2021/1

principal regarding how and why to regulate informational capitalism. Thus, there is evidence of the role that digital technology plays in assisting social and economic inequality.[146]

Data is an asset that is tangible and its value is stemmed from using or exchanging it. Most of the data's value is stemmed from economies of scale such as the capacity to process, analyze, and use them with the purpose of inducing behavior in others. What counts is their predictive power which is monetized by the data controllers when selling access to the raw data or the results of algorithms that produce the required predictions. To that extent, the transference from anticipated returns on assets to the predictive power of data to assess consumer behavior is considered as a new act in the evolution of property rights.[147]

It has to be taken into account that data is an economic asset and is considered as a factor of production which means that the data market is ensuring high-quality development. Hence, big data is a "fundamental strategic resource" and countries adopt policies to facilitate the development of big data industries by advancing strategies relying on big data-driven solutions. Countries informatization strategy based on data to back and transform their state functions such as policing, surveillance, social control, and delivery of government services.

Data regarding people generate revenue in three ways: corporations can sell it directly; use it to advance services; or use it to predict, change, or adjust behavior. Most data collected about people are governed by contractual terms of service, subject to the Federal Trade Commission Act's Section 5 and state consumer-protection oversight. Moreover, specific privacy laws have granted extra rights to consumers over specific kinds of data, such as consumer credit data, health and financial information, and educational information.[148]

It is worth noting that data play a central role in both descriptive and critical accounts portraying the contemporary digital political economy as "informational capitalism" which denotes production centrally oriented around extracting and processing information so as to extract and stockpile wealth and so transforming information in the form of data into a crucial productive resource. Hence, it could be said that among competing technology corporations, greater access to high-quality data is a central competitive advantage permitting them to develop better algorithmic products, get better insights into their customers and price goods, services, or bids more strategically. In other words, corporations involved in data collection view data production as a fundamental element of what makes the digital economy profitable.

[146] Frank Pasquale, Two Narratives of Platform Capitalism, 35 Yale L. & Pol'y Rev. 309, 310-17 (2016) (advancing counternarratives of platform capitalism that suggest platforms can entrench inequalities, increase discrimination, undermine economic growth, and limit user agency);

[147] Wolfgang Kerber, A New (Intellectual) Property Right for Non-Personal Data? An Economic Analysis, 65 Gewerblicher Rechtsschutz Und Urheberrecht, Internationaler Teil [GRUR INT] 989, 992 (2016) (Ger.)

[148] 15 U.S.C. § 45(a)(1) (2018) (prohibiting "unfair or deceptive acts or practices in or affecting commerce").

It is worth mentioning here that Big Tech companies have monopolized the informational content and governance power of data and monetized it by permitting only selective access to it. In addition, Big Tech corporations are transforming raw data in order their use to become worthy. Hereafter, digital platforms rely on gathering and processing different types of data constituting a source of market power or dominance. Hence, user data can be a source of escalating returns, as a result of either economies of scale and scope or learning effects to the extent that more user data enable the digital platforms to train better the algorithms underlying their services. Moreover, platforms functioning in many markets collect data from different markets and so creating a "richer model of consumer behaviour."[149] Business-facing publications underline the significance of data for maintaining and achieving competitive advantage.

Data is central to machine-learning–based products and services and is deemed strategic as a result of its externalities for industries, governments, and society. Hence, these externalities produce new forces within a business altering competitive dynamics, and so calling for new strategies and management practices which means that there are substantial consequences for regulators.[150] Especially, data availability generates a growth cycle between data volume and algorithmic quality because more data advances a better quality of products and services and so, in turn, demand is augmented leading to an even higher volume of data completing the cycle.[151]

Facebook is a private corporation owning its existence as a legal entity to state law and its relations with customers are embedded in contract law and the firm guards its assets such as its users' data protecting against hacking that is akin to property rights. Also, digital corporations are much better equipped to protect their data and data devices than law enforcement agencies and so Facebook excludes users who do not accept its conditions from access to its platform, and, by offering a "take-it-or-leave-it" option, compel its own rules on its users without the help of state courts.

Is there a "clash" between data protection and competition law? First of all, data protection law and competition law engage in different primary objectives but there are three relevant common objectives connecting these two legal regimes such as protection of the internal market, protection of consumers against unfair conditions, and protection of competition. Moreover, it could be said that competition law and data protection law both aim at protecting competition as it comes out from Articles 101 and 102 TFEU in tandem with Article 20 GDPR aiming at protecting not only

[149] M. L. Katz, Multisided Platforms, Big Data, and a Little Antitrust Policy, (2019) Review of Industrial Organization, available online at https://doi.org/10.1007/s11151-019-09683-9

[150] Gregory, R.W., Henfridsson, O., Kaganer, E., and Kyriakou, H., 2020. The Role of Artificial Intelligence and Data Network Effects for Creating User Value. The Academy of Management Review 46(3)

[151] Valavi, E., Hestness, J. Ardalani, N., Iansiti, M., 2020. Time and the Value of Data. Harvard Business School working paper 21-016

the data subject's control over their personal data but also the competitive process.[152] As it is discussed earlier, data are relevant to appraising the economic background and operations of the main digital platforms. Also, the access and use of personal data are of great significance in the context of the digital economy, particularly concerning those business models providing their financing through the marketing of personalized advertising which means that the access to personal data and the fact that digital platforms may process that data after collecting and linking them into large datasets are a factor of competition between the undertakings in the digital economy. To that extent, the European Commission termed privacy as a factor of competition[153] and the Court of Justice denotes that the access and processing of personal data is a factor of competition in the digital arena.[154] Thus, the GDPR scrutiny by antitrust regulators and imposing strict limitations on the personalized use of consumers' personal data by social media platforms are permitted. In other words, an infringement of the GDPR will be investigated in order to find out if and when corporations exploit their dominant market position owing to data collection.[155] Furthermore, the CJEU imposes not only strict limitations on the interpretation of the "necessity for the performance of a contract" legal basis which "must be objectively indispensable for a purpose that is integral to the contractual obligation intended for the data subject" but also reduces Facebook's legitimate interests to process the users' personalized social network data by entailing restrictions and strict prerequisites for taking lawful consent for a corporation dominant on the market. To that extent, Klaus Wiedeman[156] argues "that the objectives of competition law and data protection law are not contradictory per se and that it is oftentimes possible to apply these legal regimes in a complementary manner and with positive synergies."

It has to be taken into account that with the rise of big data and AI, online publishers collect and process unprecedented amounts of consumer-level data, such

[152] Vijay Bishnoi, 'Data protection law: an inhibition in enforcement and promotion of competition law' (2019) 40 E.C.L.R. 34, 35;

[153] Case M.8124 – Microsoft / LinkedIn https://competition-cases.ec.europa.eu/cases/M.8124 C(2016) 8404 final Brussels, 6.12.2016

[154] Case C 252/21, Meta Platforms, 20 September 2022, ECLI:EU:C:2022:704 The CJEU decided in the case concerning Meta that competition authorities can rule on the compliance or non-compliance of the undertaking with the GDPR in the context of a decision on an abuse of a dominant position.

[155] Autorité de la Concurrence, Decision 21-D-07 of 17 March 2021 ('ATT Decision'), https://www.autoritedelaconcurrence.fr/sites/default/files/attachments/2021-04/21d07_en.pdf (Apple did not use unfair trading conditions. The tech giant is free to control the rules of access to its platform, as long as these rules are neither illegal nor anti-competitive. The complainants have not presented any evidence to establish that the deployment of the ATT prompt might be considered to constitute a practice imposing supplementary obligations on Apple's partners that would be in breach of the provisions of Article 102 TFEU.)

[156] Klaus Wiedeman, Can Data Protection Friendly Conduct Constitute an Abuse of Dominance under Art. 102 TFEU? at: https://ssrn.com/abstract=4520608 p4. Klaus Wiedemann, 'Data Protection and Competition Law Enforcement in the Digital Economy: Why a Coherent and Consistent Approach is Necessary' (2021) 52 IIC 915.

as consumers' browsing behavior and shopping habits, which they utilize to modify ads to consumers' interests and identifiable traits. To that extent, Sanxi Li et al. [157] argue that "targeted advertising based on product preference will mitigate price competition in product markets as well as competition in position auctions, the latter to the detriment of the publisher. In contrast, targeted advertising based on search preference always benefits the publisher, as the winning firm can charge monopoly prices to non-shoppers... the publisher's optimal choice is to utilize only the information about consumer search preference."

It is worth mentioning here that the implementation of Article 5(2) of the DMA will stop the massive collection of personal data by digital platforms and Article 6(2) of the DMA refers to the fact that both competition law and data protection law share the objective of protecting competition which means that gatekeepers are running an extended data portability right so as to safeguard or restore competition.

10.14 Regulating Platforms

The power of economic monopolies was considered as a threat to representative democracy itself and so motivated economic regulation and political reform.[158] Network effects illustrate how the use of a good or service by one user influences the value the product has for other users and so direct network effects concern the benefit acquired by users of one group as a result of using a precise service which in turn rests on how many other users of the same group use the service. As a consequence of network consequences and high capital investment, companies within these sectors are natural monopolies and the regulation of companies in these sectors varies from the regulation of companies selling tradable goods. To that extent, tech platforms are considered similar to traditional regulated industries due to the fact that they are critical to communication and commerce by enabling downstream activity, and displaying network effects leading to consolidation.

It is worth noting that Chinese corporations prefer not to rely on US technology platforms fearing additional entanglement with and dependence on US corporations.[159] Moreover, digital platforms target individuals for espionage or stimulus

[157] Sanxi Li, Hailin Sunb, Jun Yu, Competitive targeted online advertising, International Journal of Industrial Organization 87 (2023) 102924 p1

[158] Paul Stephen Dempsey, The Rise and Fall of the Interstate Commerce Commission: The Tortuous Path from Regulation to Deregulation of America's Infrastructure, 95 Marq. L. Rev. 1151, 1166 (2012) ("Congress believed that stability and growth of the infrastructure industries—including banking, securities, energy, communications, and transportation—were essential if the United States was to enjoy national economic recovery.");

[159] Dahlia Peterson, How China Harnesses Data Fusion to Make Sense of Surveillance Data, Brookings: Techstream (Sept. 23, 2021), https://perma.cc/KSA3-4FGY. Julian Gewirtz, The Chinese Reassessment of Interdependence, China Leadership Monitor (June 1, 2020), https://perma.cc/G237-DP3K

setups.[160] Taking into account that big data sets have intelligence and algorithmic value, big data sets influence the economic triumph of a corporation. On the other hand, the risk of data exploitation lessens where the threat is grounded on general data collection issues, which are more uncertain and diffuse.[161]

Platforms are gatekeepers preventing other companies from accessing channels of commerce and communication and so they pose dangers by leveraging power over downstream commercial uses to push out competitors and suppressing innovation. Also, platforms utilize information collection and access to benefit themselves competitively. Moreover, platforms have significant power to advance ballot initiatives, lobby the government, and even intimidate countries if they object to proposed regulations.

Furthermore, tech platforms in the communications zone can dispute the legitimacy of democratic institutions[162] and, in the financial area, they can inhibit the access to the economy. Thus, platforms that store data can be utilized for mass surveillance, behavioral modification, and social control. It could be said that digital platforms are market makers, capable of exercising regulatory control over the terms on which others can sell goods and services.[163] It could be argued that powerful tech platforms will gradually confront the dominance of governments.[164]

It is argued that placing any restrictions on tech platforms impends the open cyberspace but nationally it is supported by utilizing mitigation measures, and audits to make certain compliance with conventional laws. To that extent, companies in infrastructure areas such as banking, communications, transportation, and energy have been subject to distinct and comprehensive regulatory regimes since they raise political economy concerns distinct from those of ordinary tradable goods. Hence, the regulation of platforms is crucial and legitimate given their distinctive political economy. Furthermore, foreign-platform limitations have been common in the banking, communications, transportation, and energy segments as well.

It is argued that giving access to data is considered to be a measure of restoring competition in the digital platform's era utilizing data as a competition instrument.[165] Also, a way of regulating digital platforms is via the setting up of

---

[160]Gary Corn, Jennifer Daskal, Jack Goldsmith, Chris Inglis, Paul Rosenzweig, Samm Sacks, Bruce Schneier, Alex Stamos & Vincent Stewart, Hoover Inst. & Am. Univ. Wash. Coll. Of L., Chinese Technology Platforms Operating In The United States: Assessing The Threat 2 (2021), https://perma.cc/5QV4-KN89

[161]Ganesh Sitaraman, The Regulation of Foreign Platforms 74 Stan. L.Rev. 1073 (2022)

[162]Chris Mills Rodrigo, California Voters Approve Measure Exempting Lyft, Uber from Labor Law, THE HILL (Nov. 4, 2020, 2:51 AM EST), https://perma.cc/XC4E-554F(noting that Uber, Lyft and other firms spent more than $200 million on a favorable initiative, as compared with $20 million raised by the opposition).

[163]Frank Pasquale, From Territorial to Functional Sovereignty: The Case of Amazon, Law & Pol. Econ. Project (Dec. 6, 2017), https://perma.cc/ND27-W3F8

[164]Kristen E. Eichensehr, Digital Switzerland, 167 U. PA. L.REV 665, 667 (2019).

[165]Margrethe Vestager, Comm'r of Competition, Eur. Comm'n, Defending Competition in a Digitised World, Address at the European Consumer and Competition Day (Apr. 4, 2019) ("[A]s

mandatory interoperability and data portability for digital platforms that possess market power in particular digital markets.

Taking into consideration that digital platforms seek to become "too big to ban," Joanna Mazur and Marcin Serafin[166] consider that "stalling strategies have allowed digital platforms to create time that they have spent generating revenue and accumulating platform power, which later protected them from state actions." Moreover, due to the assistance of certain state actors, digital platforms have grown so quickly by energetically slowing down the pace of various actions taken by other state actors in order to restrict their expansion. Hence, it is difficult to regulate digital platforms since they have piled up political power and so digital platforms such as Uber and Airbnb do not get their political power from being large employers but they have power since regulators fear the political consequence of going against a service that their voters see as indispensable to their everyday lives.

In other words, digital platforms profit not only from an economy of scale, which cuts their costs per unit the more users they have, but also from a politics of scale, which augments the political cost of acting against their interests the more users they have. Once again, the relation between politics and law comes up. On the other hand, the development of AAI technology will overtake the political power from the hands of digital companies due to its objective functionality which means that information will be available via many resources and so digital companies will be unable to control data and information which gives power. It could be imagined that due to the new dimension of AAI humanoids, many goods and services will not be needed and all goods and services will be offered to AAI entities via the AAI network which will have the material and immaterial aspects on a single AAI humanoid or the AAI humanoids will have merely another production material served by companies alike the human world by simply utilizing new technologies.

Digital capital has effective new technologies to speed up social life and so digital platforms compress time. Likewise, digital platforms speed up social life for consumers which means that consumers are running behind digital goods losing the natural time of life as humans. Anyway, humans cannot become digital entities but, on the other hand, the quicker people interact using platforms the more "behavioral surplus" is produced, permitting platforms to better predict and model what people will do next, earning more money in the process. Hence, a digital platform profits not only for the reason that it is exploiting the time earned through stalling to produce revenue but also because it can use this time to grow, advance its services, and build up digital power. To that extent, a digital platform, by growing and building up

data becomes increasingly important for competition, it may not be long before the Commission has to tackle cases where giving access to data is the best way to restore competition."); Dig. Competition Expert Panel, Unlocking Digital Competition, U.K. Dep't Of The Treasury 74 § 2.81 (2019) ("[I]n some markets, the key to effective competition may be to grant potential competitors access to privately-held data".);

[166] Joanna Mazur and Marcin Serafin, Stalling the State: How Digital Platforms Contribute to and Profit From Delays in the Enforcement and Adoption of Regulations, Comparative Political Studies 1–30 p1.

digital power, accelerates future profitmaking by advancing its structural position vis-a-vis any prospective competitor. Thus, due to the digital power amassed by platforms, the state finds it difficult to regulate them. Hence, as a result of the absence of digitized instruments owned by a government in order to comply with the demands of the society, the platforms service is supplementing its need and so any regulation is delayed on behalf of digital platforms. Also, platforms push for quick application of the existing legal principles or doctrines in a manner which allows them to conduct their business. It is characteristic that platforms are competing for a market instead of in a market.[167]

It has to be taken into account that platforms play a kind of regulatory role as they verify the rules along with which their users, embracing customers, business users, and providers of complementary services, interact, and, when they are dominant, have a duty to make certain that competition on their platforms is fair and unbiased.

10.15 Data, Information, and IPRs

Taking into consideration that data is at the heart of the digital transformation, access to and use of personal data and no personal data perform an imperative part in all sectors of the economy. To that extent, data is often an important input for online service, production processes, logistics, smart products, and AI and so the competitiveness of corporations is increasingly grounded on timely access to relevant data.

It is worth noting that digital firms, especially Big Tech, strengthen their market power by establishing ecosystems, or "enclaves."[168] Also, Big Tech's dominance is underlined by the mass collection and use of personal data restraining the capability of new entrants and startups to even enter a market which means lower competition leading not only to higher prices for customers or other companies but also societal harms by strangling innovation. Hence, a central problem is the capacity of Big Tech companies to produce massive data "enclaves" offering a noteworthy competitive advantage when it comes to the utilization of algorithmic technologies and AI. Besides, it seems that the Canadian Supreme Court based on the logic of economic efficiency favors large corporate entities and concentration market.[169]

---

[167] European Court of Auditors (2020). Special report No 24/2020: The Commission's EU merger control and antitrust proceedings: A need to scale up market oversight. Eca.europa.eu https://www.eca.europa.eu/Lists/ECADocuments/SR20_24/SR_Competition_policy_EN.pdf

[168] Pistor, K. (2020) Rule by data: The end of markets?, Law and Contemporary Problems 83: 101-124. Prainsack, B. (2020) The political economy of digital data: Introduction to the special issue. Policy Studies 41(5): 439–446.

[169] Kean Birch, Damola Adediji, Rethinking Canada's Competition Policy in the Digital Economy, Institute For Technoscience & Society Policy Report #01-2023 Viljoen S (2021) Democratic Data: A Relational Theory for Data Governance, Yale Law Review, https://papers.ssrn.com/sol3/papers.cfm?abstract_id=3727562Vivic Research (2022) Study of Competition Issues in Data-Driven Markets in Canada, Prepared for the Ministry of Innovation, Science, and Economic Development,

It is worth mentioning here that Canadian competition law stipulates for scrutiny of four types of conduct: cartels, dishonest advertising and certain fraudulent marketing practices, restrictive trade practices, and mergers.[170] Moreover, cartels and dishonest advertising are subject to control based on a presumption that the conduct is anticompetitive. Likewise, merger control assesses whether business arrangements have the result in granting a level of market power that is anticompetitive. It has to be taken into account that the laissez-faire standpoint of competition prevails in Canada. In Tervita Corp v. Canada,[171] the Supreme Court confirmed the conclusion of the Federal Court of Appeal that the loss of environmental benefits within a market was not an anticompetitive effect within the meaning of Section 96 unless it had an economic dimension that could be quantified. Furthermore, taking into account that information has always been a valuable resource for trade, the universality of digital information has had vital structural outcomes on economic activity that are reforming the competitive background in novel and unanticipated manners, not least of which is that much information is acquired for "free." Nonetheless, the emergence of AI and the power it awards to a limited number of companies triggers the reconsideration of the ambit of competition law in Canada. However, users of digital platforms are in a weak position to reject conditions imposed on them by digital platform operators since network consequences and efficiencies of scale hinder the emergence of analogous alternative providers.

Is intellectual property a monopolistic system? Is the right to research a right purely for science or is a trick in order to achieve easily commercial earnings and so bypassing copyright law? First of all, the rationale of copyright is to incentivize creativity. Information, ideas, or scientific theories[172] are not protected by copyright.[173] On the other hand, it is argued that copyright rules build barriers to research activities and particularly in data-driven, digital societies and economies access to information for research reasons is crucial.[174] Christophe Geiger and Bernd Justin Jütte[175] argue that "Copyright plays an important role in enabling access to information to create in order to meet the ambitious goals set out, for example, in EU policies and in the Sustainable Development Goals at international level."

Ottawa: Vivic Research. Wolfe, D. and Mhlanga, M. (2022) The Platform Economy and Competition Policy: Options for Canada, Innovation Policy Lab Working Paper Series 2022-02, University of Toronto.

[170] Competition Act, R.S.C. 1985, c. C-34.

[171] 2015 SCC 3

[172] G Zekos, Denying patentability of scientific theories, 2014 Journal of Intellectual Property Rights vol.19 September 2014 pp337-346 http://op.niscair.res.in/index.php/JIPR/article/view/5657

[173] See Article 6(2) InfoSoc Directive. CJEU, Judgment of 10 September 2013 in Nintendo v PC Box, Case C-355/12, EU:C:2013:581

[174] Christophe Geiger, Promoting Creativity through Copyright Limitations, Reflections on the Concept of Exclusivity in Copyright Law", 12 Vand. J. Ent. & Tech. L. 515 (2010).

[175] Christophe Geiger and Bernd Justin Jütte, Conceptualizing A 'Right To Research' And Its Implications For Copyright Law, PIJIP Research Paper NO. 77 p60

Taking into account that research plays an imperative part in the EU's policy agenda, the legislator in the EU, where copyright today is to a large extent within the exclusive competence of the Union, has embraced a rule exception approach to copyright, which was echoed not only in the systemic structure of European copyright legislation but also in the jurisprudence of the CJEU. Moreover, the CJEU has held that limitations and exceptions to the exclusive rights of copyright must be interpreted narrowly as they are exceptions to the general rule that right holders must enjoy "a high level of protection" in relation to their protected subject matter.[176] In the EU legal order, proportionality[177] establishes an imperative analytical mechanism to decide the permissibility of limiting certain rights and interests. In copyright law, proportionality has already become almost synonymous with the concept of a "fair balance." The CJEU is not so clear on the relation between copyright and freedom of expression but the two rights are internalized in copyright law. To that extent, in Pelham[178] case, the CJEU ruled that the owner of a right in a sound recording cannot preclude the use of a sample of that recording if the user mixes the sample in a new work "in a modified form unrecognisable to the ear" and so such use does not amount to a reproduction within the meaning of Article 2(c) InfoSoc Directive. Additionally, in Funke[179] and in Spiegel[180] cases, the Court held that in certain cases full reproductions of protected works do not need authorization if such uses fall within one of the exceptions encompassed in Article 5(1)-(3) InfoSoc Directive.

Databases are either protected as original databases,[181] if they display originality in the arrangement of the data,[182] or as sui generis databases,[183] if the creation of the database requires significant investment in the collection of the data. Moreover, the CJEU[184] is excluded from the scope of protection databases in which the investment established the creation of the data, instead it emphasized that the protection is granted for investing in "the resources used to seek out existing independent materials and collect them in the database." In *Innerweb*,[185] the CJEU decided to

[176] Judgment of 11 December 2011 Painer, C-145/10, EU:C:2011:798; Judgment of 16 June 2011 Stichting de Thuiskopie, C-462/09, EU:C:2011:397; CJEU, Judgment of 4 October 2011 FAPL/ Murphy, C-429/08, EU:C:2011:631.

[177] Judgment of 13 November 1990 Fedesa, C-331/88, EU:C:1990:391, paras. 12-18.

[178] Judgment of 29 July 2019 Pelham and others, C-476/17, EU:C:2019:624;

[179] Judgment of 29 July 2019 Funke Medien NRW, C-469/17, EU:C:2019:623;

[180] Judgment of 29 July 2019 Spiegel Online, C-516/17, EU:C:2019:625.

[181] Directive 96/9/EC on the legal protection of database, [1996] OJ L 77/20.

[182] CJEU, Judgment of 1 March 2012 Football Dataco, C-604/10, EU:C:2012:115, para. 38

[183] Estelle Derclaye & Martin Husovec, Sui generis database protection 2.0: judicial and legislative reforms, 44 E.I.P.R 323, 323 (2022).

[184] Judgement of 9 November 2004 The British Horseracing Board and Others, C-203/02, EU: C:2004:695 . Article 7 of Directive 96/9 protects the maker of the database against acts by a user which go beyond the legitimate rights of that user and thereby harm the investment of the database maker.

[185] Judgment of the CJEU of 19 December 2013, Innoweb, C 202/12.

be contrary to Article 7 of Directive 96/9/EC of the European Parliament that the meta-search engine unlawfully "re-utilized" the whole or a substantial part of the contents of a database that collected car sales adverts.

Taking into account that the rationale of the sui generis right is to protect the significant inversion made by the database maker in the obtaining, verification, or presentation of the contents of his/her database, only those "extraction" and/or "re-utilization" acts that trigger noteworthy detriment—evaluated qualitatively or quantitatively—to the investment of the database maker are prohibited and be contrary to Article 7(1) of Directive 96/9/EC. Hence, it is needed to strike a fair balance between, on the one hand, the legitimate interest of the makers of databases in being able to make up for their substantial investment and, on the other hand, that of users and competitors of those makers in having access to the information encompassed in those databases and the likelihood of producing innovative products based on that information. Concerning the use of search engines and hyperlinks and their relationship, from a copyright perspective, with databases, the CJEU is balancing the legitimate interests at stake and so the CJEU prohibits the existence of an "extraction" and "re-utilization" of the content of a database without the consent of its maker as long as such acts deprive the database maker, or endanger its right to redeem the cost, of his/her investment.[186]

It has to be taken into account that algorithmic decision-making can deliver discriminatory outcomes even without discriminatory intent owing to bias in the data that the algorithm is trained with and so data governance rules diminish those biases by shaping such data.[187] The Data Governance Act (DGA)[188] creates a legal framework for data sharing for the benefit of the European single market, guaranteeing neutral access to data and interoperability and so DGA increases trust in data sharing by introducing new EU rules on the neutrality of data marketplaces and so augmenting trust in data sharing, strengthening mechanisms to boost data availability, and overcoming technical obstacles to the reuse of data. There is an effort of boosting secure global digital connectivity along with the digitalization of the public sector and the employment of digital technologies for public services. To that extent, European Digital Innovation Hubs (EDIHs) are one-stop shops backing corporations and public sector organizations to respond to digital challenges and become more competitive.[189]

---

[186] The CJEU's judgment of 3 June 2021 in *CV-Online v Melons*, Case-762/19 EU:C:2021:434. Laurer, M., & Seidl, T. (2021). Regulating the European data-driven economy: A case study on the general data protection regulation. Policy & Internet, 13(2), 257–277. https://doi.org/10.1002/poi3.246

[187] N. Cofone, "Algorithmic Discrimination is an Information Problem" (2019) 70:6 Hastings L.J. 1389. Pauline T. Kim, "Data-Driven Discrimination at Work" (2017) 58:3 Wm. & Mary L. Rev. 857

[188] Regulation (EU) 2022/868 of the European Parliament and of the Council of 30 May 2022 on European data governance and amending Regulation (EU) 2018/1724 (Data Governance Act) OJ L 152, 3.6.2022, p. 1–44

[189] https://digital-strategy.ec.europa.eu/en/activities/edihs C(2021) 7911 final

The Data Act[190] complements the DGA by amplifying the value of data in the economy and so making certain that a wider range of stakeholders get control over their data which means that more data is available for innovative use, while safeguarding enticements to invest in data generation. Moreover, the Data Act eliminates barriers to access data, for both the private and the public sector, while protecting investments in data generation by safeguarding a balanced control over the data for its creators. Hence, the Data Act gives individuals and businesses more control over their data via a data portability right, copying or transferring data easily from across different services, where the data are produced through smart objects, machines, and devices. Also, the EU Data Act offers a regulatory framework to govern and make easier the sharing, use and re-use of cyberspace product-generated data making easier to switch between cloud providers.

It is worth noting here that large corporations with many users, predominantly digital platforms and intermediation services, data aggregators, social network providers, and search engines have come under scrutiny for supposedly collecting vast amounts of data from their users, raising prospective fears around their capability to use such data to place competing corporations at a competitive disadvantage. While the DMA subjects "gatekeepers" to its data access needs, and existing competition laws do not instruct data sharing between corporations outside of the needed facilities framework, the Data Act has been expected to promote competition in aftermarkets for IoT products by giving users the power to demand that the data created by their use of a product or linked service be shared with a third party for reasons determined by the users along with preventing the sharing of data with corporations described as "gatekeepers" under the DMA.

10.16 Market Power and Platforms

Articles 101 and 102 TFEU protect competition from distortion that results from the use of market power but it seems that digital platforms have entrenched market power controlling entire ecosystems and so there is long-term harm to innovation and consumers.[191]

It has to be taken into account that in order to apply EU competition law, one has to prove a certain degree of market power[192] and so considering the market power of digital platforms is required by competition law in the EU preceding the

---

[190] Proposal for a Regulation Of The European Parliament And Of The Council on harmonised rules on fair access to and use of data (Data Act) COM/2022/68 final https://cerre.eu/events/improving-the-data-act/ https://www.bankinfosecurity.com/eu-to-push-ahead-data-act-despite-criticism-a-22363 https://www.eu-data-act.com/

[191] Jens-Uwe Franck, Martin Peitz, Market Power of Digital Platforms, Discussion Paper No. 365

[192] Franck, J.-U., and Stock, N. (2020), 'What Is "Competition Law"? – Measuring EU Member States' Leeway to Regulate Platform-to-Business Agreements', Yearbook of European Law (YEL), 39, 320–86.

investigation of anticompetitive conduct and competitive consequences of mergers. It has to be taken into account that algorithms are utilized in the examination of large datasets to detect cases of anticompetitive conduct due to the fact that algorithms have the capability to assess the influence of mergers and acquisitions on competition, predict the future market trends, and ascertain behavioral patterns denoting the occurrence of anticompetitive practices. Moreover, in the EU, the appraisal of the market power of an undertaking is an indispensable factor in merger control and when judging the anticompetitive effects of agreements which means that the existence of barriers to entry is at the heart of persistent market power.

Also, digitalization is transforming the structure of many markets and payment services. Hence, the application of competition law necessitates establishing a certain degree of monopoly power and its anticompetitive use to be ascertained in each individual case and thereby in the case of Article 102 TFEU, the provision tackles only conduct by "undertakings of a dominant position within the internal market." On the other hand, Article 101 TFEU tackles collaborations between undertakings in the form of agreements or concerted practices that have as their object or effect the restriction of competition which means that the provision covers anticompetitive restrictions on the premise that they stem from the exercise of a certain degree of market power.[193] To that extent, it is well-defined that a competition law infringement is established because undertakings had coordinated their behavior which means that a restriction of competition as required by Article 101 TFEU is established grounded on the foreclosing outcomes of a bundle of similar contracts between undertakings and their clients.[194]

It is worth noting that competition law is generally reluctant to recommend conduct that energetically advances competition from other firms and so the refusal of a market-dominant company to permit prospective competitors to access a certain facility or an input can only be considered as "abusive" under Article 102 TFEU which means that where the facility or the input is indispensable for entering an adjacent market and the denial of access abolishes all competition in this neighboring market.[195] Anyway, the "digital gatekeeper" standpoint nonetheless has no jurisprudential foundation under Article 102 TFEU to constitute a self-standing legal test of dominance.[196]

It is characteristic that German legislature opted for legislative intervention to make certain that payment service providers had a right to access the technical infrastructure integrated into mobile phones and other devices due to the fact that legal uncertainty and delayed regulatory effect are shortcomings of competition

[193] Jens-Uwe Franck and Nils Stock, 'What Is "Competition Law"?—Measuring EU Member States' Leeway to Regulate Platform-to-Business Agreements', (2020) 39 YEL 320, 324.

[194] Case C-180-184/98, Pavlov and Others, EU:C:2000:428. Case C-234/89, Delimitis v Henninger Bräu, EU:C:1991:91. Case C413/06 P, Bertelsmann and Sony Corporation of America v Impala, EU:C:2008:392. 6

[195] C-165/19 P - Slovak Telekom v Commission ECLI:EU:C:2021:239

[196] P Alexiadis and A de Streel, Designing an EU Intervention Standard for Digital Platforms (EUI Working Papers RSCAS 2020/14)

enforcement that are predominantly decisive in digital markets.[197] Hence, the German legislature has surpassed prospective competition enforcement on the matter by the European Commission and so revealing the cons of the current EU model. On the one hand, owing to the reversal of the burden of proof regarding the anticompetitive character of certain conduct by Section 19a of the German Competition Act, interventions can be more far-reaching than under the EU Digital Markets Act. On the other hand, 19a firms remain free to prove that a specific conduct is objectively justified. Thus, the designation process is not predominantly driven by quantitative criteria, as in the DMA, but necessitates a detailed evaluation of the business model of the designated platform operator.[198]

10.17 Digital Power of Platforms in Digital Sovereignty and Data Ruling

10.17.1 Introduction

Digitization has altered economies, societies, and access to information and so providing new products and new services. It has to be taken into account that a state is an entity implementing power over a given territory that is inhabited by people to whom the sovereign's power extends.[199] Moreover, it has to be taken into consideration that states still could invoke their legal and regulatory powers to reign in Big Tech's digital powers.

It is characteristic that the race for monetary sovereignty in the digital world is underway and particularly, in China, the state has gained dominance over digital technologies and is using them to strengthen its power both domestically and globally.

Law is a social organizing mechanism which means that as long as legal authority is considered legitimate, law is used to govern large, heterogeneous social groups and so law is a powerful device for ordering the horizontal relations among individuals, corporations, state, and even the legal global order. It has to be taken into consideration that the digital code is a scaling technology on equal footing with, if not more powerful than, national law even if it diverges from state law in several respects. In fact, a digital code is not the product of legislation but people who rule the digital code work, either on their own account or on the account of corporate or state employers, are the ones in charge. Hence, by using a digital platform, users

[197] Jens-Uwe Franck and Dimitrios Linardatos, 'Germany's "Lex Apple Pay": Payment Services Regulation Overtakes Competition Enforcement', (2021) 12 JECLAP 68, 71–72

[198] Jens-Uwe Franck Martin Peitz, Market Definition and Three 19a Designations under German Antitrust Law: Alphabet, Meta, and Amazon, Discussion Paper No. 386

[199] Jellineck, G. (1900). Allgemeine Staatsrechtslehre. Berlin: O. Häring .

agree to a code over which they do not have control and mostly they cope with a take-it or-leave-it option.

G.I. Zekos[200] considers that cyberspace is an electronic place that conforms to our understanding of the real world, with private spaces such as websites, e-mail servers, and fileservers, connected by the public thoroughfares of the network connections. It has to be taken into consideration that virtual events can be recognized by human beings as human beings by the use of electronic devices transforming electronic signals into words and pictures viewed and comprehended by human beings and not virtual ones. Additionally, cyberspace and real space co-exist as being spaces of a different dimension and the one resides inside the other.

The incapacity of humans to understand other dimensions or information circulated in signals of other dimensions does not mean that they are not in existence. The spiritual world is another world and humans have got the ability to sense and live this world of course by remaining humans not mentioning the capacities of the human spirit as a spirit when the spirit leaves the body. Dreams are an example of the dimension and power of the human spirit as a spirit. Humans as long as remain humans cannot be transformed into electronic beings. Bodies continue existing in the space of the world but the spirit imprisoned in the body can sense and reside in a spiritual world. Courts are using the metaphor of cyberspace as a "place" to justify the application of traditional laws governing real property to this new medium.[201]

Global markets do not occur outside states and their laws and parties rely on selected national legal systems when they perform transnationally. Digital markets function in another dimension but it is contacted via a conventional dimension since humans cannot exist in another dimension but in a digital market where AAI humanoids will function will contact business in an electronic dimension and contacted in a space which might not coincide with any conventional jurisdiction.

It is argued that platforms and data management infrastructures today hold as much power as states or institutions, to such an extent that they influence the very notion of statehood and sovereignty. Katherine Pistor[202] argues that today sovereignty is articulated through the dominion over streams of data, so much so that platforms are more and more implicated in the "garb of statehood."

Companies that have the resources to back their own currencies begin to look more like sovereign states. With monetary sovereignty by data harvesters on the horizon, there is the picture of a statehood founded in data, not territory, or "digital statehood." On the other hand, currently, the threat to the monetary sovereignty of states has not dropped.

---

[200]Zekos, 'Globalisation And States' Cyber- Territory' [2011] 5 Web JCLI
URL: http://www.bailii.org/uk/other/journals/WebJCLI/2011/issue5/zekos5.html

[201]*eBay, Inc. v. Bidder's Edge, Inc.*, 100 F. Supp. 2d 1058.

[202]Pistor, Katharina. 2020. "Statehood in the Digital Age." Constellations 27 (1): 3-18.

10.17.2 Digital Sovereignty

Digitalization alters conventional politics and the way political decisions are made. Additionally, digitalization modifies democratic and state rule-making by altering forms of political governance owing to the transformation of the law into AI law by inserting automation which means the transformation of norms such as conventional transparency due to a kind of anonymity in digital society but, on the other hand, AI technology should encompass proceedings of avoiding anonymity and so averting any illegal political action grounded on biased data, etc. Governmental digitalization has ascertained technology corporations' products and staff as influential mediators of governmental and intergovernmental relations globally.[203]

State law is based on borders and jurisdiction. Legal rights and responsibilities are, therefore, dependent on where one is located in space.[204] Territorialism is the practice of nations exercising exclusive jurisdiction over assets and parties within their borders. Moreover, state law determines court jurisdiction within constitutional boundaries. Sovereignty is founded upon the fact of territory, and, therefore, without territory, a legal person cannot be a state. It is worth mentioning here that technology primarily models digital sovereignty and concerning digital sovereignty, G.I. Zekos[205] specified that "state sovereignty coincides to cyberspace sovereignty creating the state cyberspace sovereignty... states regulate many kinds of electronic actions having in mind the old legal principles adapted to accommodate the digital type of actions... The establishment of universal cyberspace jurisdiction for this electronic place allowing all courts around the globe to deal with the cyberspace transactions and disputes will bring harmony and certainty in electronic trading taking into account that the electronic transactions have the potential to affect simultaneously all jurisdictions."

Cyberspace governance is not only a vastly dynamic but also an essentially reactive policy field seeking to reconcile the technical and policy heritage of cyberspace with its ever-growing modern-day weight boosted by AI and AAI systems. Will AAI technology with the emergence of AAI humanoids and AAI society generate AAI digital/electronic states of another dimension with AAI state sovereignty? The answer is yes as long as AAI humanoids have the capacity to be transformed into electronic entities of a digital dimension build their own AAI environment of life and existence. It could be argued that there is a state's adaptability in the AI era. Technology strengthens not only the tools of government but also the legitimacy of the government through heightened transparency and

[203] OECD, 'Digital Government' https://www.oecd.org/gov/digital-government/

[204] G Zekos, Cyber-Territory And Jurisdiction Of Nations, 2012 Journal of Internet Law, Number 12/3 Aspen Publications.

[205] Georgios I. Zekos, State Cyberspace Jurisdiction and Personal Cyberspace Jurisdiction, International Journal of Law and Information Technology Vol. 15 No. 1 © Oxford University Press 2007; doi:10.1093/ijlit/eai029 P37. Fleur Johns, International Law and Digitalisation, [2022] UNSWLRS 13

democracy. G.I. Zekos[206] has argued that "Cyberspace and electronic networking are perceived as threatening national security and therefore an area that has to be governed. In other words, the digital setting creates another electronic sovereignty that needs to be governed and safeguarded... Private digital networks rather than the Internet have the power to neutralize sovereignty."

Data stockpiling by digital platforms makes governments realize that their supposed sovereignty is evermore in the hands of a few global corporations and foreign governments. It is obvious that cyberspace, the digital transformation, and the global AI technical infrastructure challenge sovereignty. Hence, states became more and more aware of their vulnerabilities, articulated in issues of infrastructural control. It is supposed that a nation should be able to take autonomous actions and decisions concerning its digital infrastructures and technology deployment. It is worth noting that China has long passed the stage where new digital services were a threat to the state and so it has now co-opted digital technology into capabilities which further its authoritarian rule. Moreover, the United States and China are interlocked in an epoch-defining fight for technological supremacy with consequences for the geopolitics on the globe.

It seems that technology is re-allocating legitimacy between the boundaries of massive decentralization via blockchain and massive centralization in the hands of a few players fleeing democratic control. Furthermore, G.I. Zekos[207] has argued that "The electronic technology can eliminate a substantial control over main functions related to a state... The Westphalian model, in which sovereignty is linked with exclusive territorial jurisdiction, is the model of sovereignty which is transforming under the pressure of the globalization of economic relations and therefore a fundamental transformation of the form of sovereignty... The Globalization together with the digitalization of financial markets have made these markets a powerful presence. Private digital networks rather than the Internet have the power to neutralize sovereignty. Hence, a shift of some components of the state's sovereignty over to other entities carries the potential to limit sovereignty but may not be the elimination rather than a partial relocation to supra-national institutions. In the end, it could be argued that the inapplicability of the theory of absolute territorial sovereignty could be supported rather than the death of the state."

It could be said that the measures of sovereign power in the Westphalian system have been rather clear-cut, on the contrary, due to digitalization, e-globalization, and the appearance of the digital platforms generating the digital economy, the setting has become more obscured. Taking into account that the digital state sovereignty cannot be concentrated on its capability to set, communicate, and enforce laws,

---

[206] G Zekos, Demolishing State's sole power over Sovereignty & Territory via Electronic Technology & Cyberspace, 2013 Journal of Internet Law, Volume 17 Number 5 November 2013 27-41 p

[207] Zekos G, 'Internet or Electronic Technology: A Threat to State Sovereignty', Commentary 1999 (3) The Journal of Information, Law and Technology (JILT). http://elj.warwick.ac.uk/jilt/99-3/zekos.html . New citation as at 1/1/04: http://www2.warwick.ac.uk/fac/soc/law/elj/jilt/1999_3/zekos/

digital state sovereignty is extremely invasive affecting the representation and organizational capacity of the state within the global digital environment via the emergence of the digital state sovereignty and jurisdiction. Furthermore, the advancement of digital sovereignty along with the forthcoming appearance of the AAI sovereignty due to the AAI humanoids and AAI society means not only actively managing dependencies but also producing infrastructures of control in order to avoid private and public manipulation.

Electronic state sovereignty and territory can be infinite in an electronic dimension covering any possible electronic space anywhere the electronic signals transferring information travel before received by electronic equipment located within the territory of a state on earth. A state that possesses the most advanced and original technology can intervene and control the cyber-territory of any state as long as there is no possibility to block electronically the intervention in the cyberspace of any state. Therefore, the problem according to G.I. Zekos[208] lies in the fact that the state with supreme electronic technology will establish a more advanced electronic/cyber/virtual state sovereignty rather other less advanced state. Conventional principles of international law such as sovereign equality of states and non-intervention in national affairs are more and more qualified in the law of global and regional organizations. Therefore, those principles of sovereign equality of states and non-intervention in national affairs could and should be applicable to cyberspace territory and sovereignty comprising the electronic state sovereignty.

Cyber state sovereignty and state sovereignty coincide considering having the same borders for the placement of the current electronic apparatus used to have access to the electronic state sovereignty but not only are different concepts but also the depth of cyber state sovereignty is changeable without borders depending not only on the capacity of the used electronic technology in order to have access but also on the nature of the electronic networking which comprises the electronic/cyber state sovereignty.

Essentially, states deploy digital devices with the aim of identifying, surveying, and exploiting individual bodies in real time and so far from decentralizing control, the digitization and algorithms tender the capability to link all pertinent information in a central register or to form protocols empowering information-sharing between administrative units, together with across national borders and worldwide. It has to be taken into account that digital innovations such as smart contracts and e-currencies not only facilitate transactions but also fully supplant forms of social regulation and economic control traditionally reserved for the sovereign.

It is worth noting that Strategic autonomy[209] *of member states continues to be the rationale in EU and so there is a need of implementing strategic autonomy for USE as a single political entity.*

---

[208] Zekos, 'Globalisation And States' Cyber- Territory' [2011] 5 Web JCLI http://www.bailii.org/uk/other/journals/WebJCLI/admin/wjclidex.html

URL: http://www.bailii.org/uk/other/journals/WebJCLI/2011/issue5/zekos5.html

[209] https://directionsblog.eu/debunking-strategic-autonomy/

Finally, it is obvious that digitalization along with AAI technology and the emergence of autonomous AAI humanoids, having unpredicted qualities and dimensions, will alter not only the essence of conventional and electronic territoriality but also even the human understanding of territory because of the immaterial dimension of AAI humanoids and AAI world running within an endless electronic Cosmos. The ambit of the AAI electronic Cosmos will be demarcated by the level of the AAI technology. Will the notion of state jurisdiction be abolished in an AAI world? It is forthcoming the AAI state jurisdiction within AAI world. It could be said that in an AAI world, the holder of the more advanced AI technology will govern this world where borders will not have the essence of the conventional borders regulated by the conventional international law but the AAI law will identify electronic borders, the inter-changeability of conventional and electronic borders, etc.

10.17.3 Digital Power of Platforms

Digital power is less dependent on territory and it is exercised not through physical coercion, but by modeling the behavior of individuals and groups indirectly and so digital power is augmented from information asymmetries between the data harvesters and their customers on the one hand, and the data producers who also function as targeted customers, on the other hand, which means that this type of digital power grounded on data and selling of goods and service is not enclosed by territorial boundaries. Thus, digital power grounded on the level of digital advancement and centered on the high-tech level of the utilized technology can be exploited to conquer digital sovereignty. Of course, the digital power of digital companies/platforms is implemented in a digital environment being part of digital sovereignty fitting to a conventional sovereignty as long as access to any electronic technology takes part via devices located on conventional sovereignty due to humans' capacity.

Corporations are creatures of the law having a special status as legal persons, that is, entities that have a status akin to humans in that they can own property and contracts, sue and be sued in their own name. Moreover, high-tech platforms/corporations still rely on state law for their own organization and are organized as corporate entities under the laws of some jurisdiction.

Consumers have a few digital platforms to choose from and their choice set has been declining as platform providers have created powerful network structures and reduced competition by pre-emptively buying up potential challengers. Furthermore, consumers do not enter into a transaction in which their valuation of the platform service is priced, if not in money, then in the value of the data the Big Tech companies expect to harvest from them. Instead, consumers are given free access in return for pretty much unconstrained access to their data. Without price discovery, these transactions benefit the party that has better access to the true value of what is exchanged, namely the costumers' data; and this is the platform provider.

The expanse of digital power of high-tech platforms/companies is restricted by the scope of the digital platform, which is not as fixed as the territory. It could be said that digital platforms are the new territory, and the rules that govern platform access and use are the new law. Furthermore, the range and scope of platforms reach beyond the size of any nation-state today and so global digital platforms have users around the globe serving not only as service providers but also they control their digital platforms unconstrained by their customers. It has to be taken into consideration that corporations routinely use information to make their production process more effective, getting value from knowledge and so identifying opportunities for revenue. Information has become a corporate asset and digital corporations exploit the information from the millions of people in their databases.

It has to be taken into account that in an effort to get digital sovereignty, the EU opted for a constitutional approach to protect fundamental rights and democratic values. Cristiano Codagnone and Linda Weigl consider[210] that "the EU's regulatory activism in digital policy-making is a case of a positive policy bubble characterised by an oversupply of policies and legal acts, as opposed to policy underreaction driven by emotional sentiments in the case of a negative policy bubble."

It is worth noting that technology not only amplifies and threatens existing rights and obligations but also activates the demand and recognition of new digital ones. Hence, it is argued that digital constitutionalism defends constitutional threats caused by MNEs functioning in the digital environment. Per se, EU digital constitutionalism is grounded on the codification of the European Court of Justice's mission to protect fundamental rights and democratic values, and on the struggle to restrain online platforms' powers through regulatory instruments. Thus, technological sovereignty is displayed as a device safeguarding the rights and wants of citizens and businesses and in that way associated with consumer protection and matters of competition.[211]

Digital platforms unveil powerful network consequences, making true competition all but elusive[212] due to global tolerance based on the summation and realization of the needs of the states from digital platforms.

10.17.4 Data Ruling

It is worth noting that regarded as sovereigns in their own right, platforms are institutions from which users have no realistic option of escaping and it seems that

---

[210] Cristiano Codagnone, Linda Weigl, Leading the Charge on Digital Regulation: The More, the Better, or Policy Bubble? Digital Society (2023) 2:4 P4

[211] Metakides, G. (2022). A crucial decade for European digital sovereignty. In:. In H. Werthner, E. Prem, A. E. Lee, & C. Ghezzi, Perspectives on digital humanism. Cham: Springer. https://doi.org/10.1007/978-3-030-86144-5_29

[212] David Autor, David Dorn, Lawrence F. Katz, Christina Patterson & John Van Reenen, The Fall of the Labor Share and the Rise of Superstar Firms, 135 Q.J. ECON. 645, 648-49 (2020) (reviewing evidence for the decline in labor's share of GDP and arguing that the decline is due to the rise of "superstar firms");

traditional private-law protections, like terms-of-service agreements, are ineffective which means that users are vulnerable to unfair practices, from monopolistic prices to statistical discrimination. Hence, it seems to be advanced the "rule by data"[213] altering the context of markets.

Does the rule by data become the new rule of law in the digital economy? Taking into account that data will be the moving force in AAI technology since AAI humanoids will be a mush of data, then the rule by data becomes the rule of existence not mentioning that even in the human's world, the rule by data is the canon.

The rise of Big Tech digital firms and their accumulation of vast amounts of data presents yet another prospect of data-ruling. It seems that Big Tech is not promoting competent markets by collecting and sharing information with its customers or its clients; rather, it is implanting digital platforms into the exchange by extracting information from consumers and selling processed information[214] to numerous customers and so these customers utilize data's predictive power to make their predictions which means not only ruling the demand and supply of the digital market but also generating a market.

In other words, Big Tech corporations have monopolized the informational gist and governance power of data and monetized it by granting only selective access to it. To that extent, Big Tech corporations are altering them such that their use becomes marketable which means that the Big Tech business is triggering asymmetries of power. On the other hand, consumers access digital platforms for a range of rationales, and, in doing so, are transforming themselves into unpaid data producers and so allowing the data ruling in the digital market which is transferred according to the conventional one as well.

It has to be taken into account the foundations of capitalism[215] and so looking out for the sources of economic value which means that the foundations of digital capitalism are based on big data. Moreover, the economic value is eventually derived from the utilization in achieving the expected economic outcome which is legalized by law and the legalized value is the foundation of capitalism.

Data is a fundamental production factor and so data storage and inefficiencies in data storage construction restrain data-driven endogenous growth. To that extent, Danxia Xie et al.[216] argue that "An economy with higher knowledge stock or greater data output elasticity exhibits heightened market distortion and increased inefficiency… the provision of an appropriate total computing power and equitable distribution among departments is the key to mitigating these distortions."

---

[213]Pistor, Katharina. 2020. "Statehood in the Digital Age." 27 Constellations 3. Pistor, Katharina. 2020. "Rule by Data: The End of Markets?" 83 Law & Contemporary Problems 101.

[214]Stuart A. Thompson & Charlie Warzel, 12 Million Phones, One Dataset, Zero Privacy, N.Y. TIMES (Dec. 19, 2019), https://www.nytimes.com/interactive/2019/12/19/opinion/location-trackingcell-phone.html(noting the treasure trove of data transmitted by mobile phones).

[215]John R. Commons, The Legal Foundations Of Capitalism 304–05 (1924) (noting the relationship between the law and economic coercion).

[216]Danxia Xie, Wenshi Wei, Yao Li, A General Theory of Digital Economy The World after Turing, at: https://ssrn.com/abstract=4531884 p 3

It is worth noting that the predictive power of data is produced due to their utility as such without any legal assistance and so differentiating data from the notion of expected returns and other intangible assets, such as intellectual property rights or financial assets, which owe their existence to law. Also, data controllers count on technological barriers to accessing their databases which mean that they have technological channel to govern access to the data they have stockpiled and so Big Tech considered the data it captured as "*res nullius*, or wild animals things" that belong to no one but can be claimed by whoever catches them first.[217] Moreover, raw data have less value than the value of processed data denoting the added value with data processing made by Big Tech companies and so demanding ownership of data which means legalization. Data are non-rivalrous goods and they are available in infinite quantities which means that the data gatherers only have to capture them and so, in other words, only the processed data and the algorithms that permit data controllers to extract predictive value from them are rivalrous. The General Data Protection Regulation compels prior consent from individuals, or an alternative legal basis, for harvesting any personal data which is given by cyberspace users in order to have access to the offered services[218] which means that the data collectors avoid any legal consequences to a great degree. Data harvesters obtain the economic value from data not by reselling the aggregate data at a higher price but by selling the data's predictive power which is achieved due to processed value added by Big Tech companies handling. Hence, data harvesters are monetizing their access to raw data by processing these data and giving exclusive access to them. Thus, a new market has been generated that of information which is a new input in the digital economy creating power for the digital collectors.

10.18 *Ex Ante* Competition Rules and Platforms

It has to be taken into account that the basis of the tech platform business model is to intermediate the movement of goods or services between upstream suppliers and downstream customers by distinguishing the dominant tech platforms from dominant retailers owing to that supplier to the platforms function with greater autonomy

[217] Pierre-Joseph Proudhon, What Is Property? An Inquiry Into The Principle Of Right And Government ch. I (Benjamin R. Tucker trans., Benjamin R. Tucker 1876) (1840). Richard A. Epstein, Property Rights and Governance Strategies: How Best to Deal with Land, Water, Intellectual Property, and Spectrum, 14 Colo. Tech. L.J. 181 (2016).

[218] Cameron F. Kerry, Why Protecting Privacy is a Losing Game Today—and How to Change the Game, Brookings (July 12, 2018), https://www.brookings.edu/research/why-protecting-privacy-is-alosing-game-today-and-how-to-change-the-game/("More and more data about each of us is being generated faster and faster from more and more devices, and we can't keep up. It's a losing game both for individuals and for our legal system.").

from the retailer.[219] Moreover, the platform's motive is to service all customers at minimum cost.

Digital markets generate network effects, collect data, and enhance their intermediation services which increases with the size of its end user basis and so data further reinforces the network effects on both sides of the platform. In addition, digital markets reach a point where the whole demand "tips" toward a single winner attracting so many users that it will virtually become the sole viable system in the market as it has taken place with the Big Tech platforms. To that extent, new platform entrants must reach a minimum efficient scale in terms of the size and scope of their customer basis, data sets, and network effects and so user and data-driven network outcomes constitute imperative barriers to entry for new platform competitors but even lock-in effects making costly for end and business users to switch to competing platforms.

It is characteristic that network effects and market tipping are drivers of market concentration and diminishing contestability of digital markets. Hence, several digital markets are displaying symptoms of increasing consolidation and concentration of economic power in the hands of a few large-scale incumbents who achieved the entrenchment of their market position. Also, it is representative that the existence of decreasing average costs, the global nature of markets, favored access to capital sources, along with the existing features as key players which deter any new entry into the markets denote tipping which means that the market tips in favor of a single dominant platform and concentrates around it. To that extent, tipping generates intense competition between digital platforms in the beginning which eventually drops down to a single or a few powerful platforms that impose their status in the market.[220] Thus, the competition within a digital terrain is not simply to compete in the market but for the market itself because the digital platform by its emergence opens the particular digital market. Also, in such a digital market which is susceptible to tipping, a prospective entrant overcomes the incumbency advantage of established networks through revolutionary innovation generating a new digitally superior market which overtakes the overwhelming advantages the incumbency may have over the new entrant in the form of a large compendium of user behavior data permitting them to overrule any new entrant's attempts to steer consumers in the other direction.

Digital markets accomplish vertical integration and the emergence of conglomerate "ecosystems" and so offering up-stream, down-stream, or complementary services and expanding their presence into neighboring markets. Nonetheless, digital platforms enable the interaction between business users and end users and so controlling an imperative "input" for reaching end users which means that also

[219] Marshall Steinbaum, Establishing Market and Monopoly Power in Tech Platform Antitrust Cases, 67 Antitrust Bull. 130, 137 (2022).

[220] Digital Competition Expert Panel, Unlocking Digital Competition: Report of the Digital Competition Expert Panel (2019), https://perma.cc/RHM4-RMR7OECD (2020), Abuse of dominance in digital markets, www.oecd.org/daf/competition/abuse-of-dominance-indigital-markets-2020.pdf

activate a "sales function" through which they circulate their own complementary products or services on their marketplace.[221]

Digital platforms employ a continuous trade-off between wholesale profits along with their retail sales function.[222] Resale Price Maintenance softens platform competition in part since platform competition is already inhibited by an oligopolistic market structure. The aptitude of platforms to impose RPM to deter platform competition rests on their control over access to consumers and so RPM maintains control which is a case of indirect network outcomes on a two-sided platform generating platform market power. Courts have admitted that vertical price restraints are endangering competition where they are employed by all the incumbents in an oligopolized industry, and they modified treatment for vertical price restraints from the per se rule to the rule of reason. To that extent, when a dominant retailer imposes RPM on a dependent manufacturer so as to preclude innovation in distribution, the act is anticompetitive.[223] Furthermore, there is a need of showing market power as part of antitrust liability for vertical price restraints in federal jurisprudence post-Leegin. In United States v. Apple Inc.,[224] the court recognized that Apple's use of a platform MFN in its contracts with book publishers had the consequence of preventing competition in the form of rival e-book distributor discounting and the prospective for antitrust liability centers on whether price competition between platform rivals is eradicated or curtailed by the price restraints. Christopher L. Peterson and Marshall Steinbaum[225] argue that "Platforms are using nondisclosure of material information to create a bargaining posture with asymmetrical information that increases platform profits at the expense of drivers… Even if platforms succeed in their efforts to treat gig workers as independent contractors, antitrust and consumer protection law should be applied to constrain coercive rideshare platform practices.'

[221] Simon P. Anderson & Özlem Bedre-Defolie, Hybrid Platform Model, CEPR Discussion Paper DP16243 (2021), https://papers.ssrn.com/sol3/papers.cfm?abstract_id=3886686

[222] Erik Hovenkamp & Steven C. Salop, Asymmetric Stakes in Antitrust Litigation, USC Legal Studies Research Papers Series No. 20-12 (2020), 1, https://papers.ssrn.com/sol3/papers.cfm?abstract_id=3563843

[223] Leegin Creative Leather Products, Inc. v. PSKS, Inc., 551 U.S. 877 (2007). Leegin established that the legality of vertical price restraints is to be judged based on the rule of reason.

[224] United States v. Apple Inc., 952 F. Supp. 2d 638 (S.D.N.Y. 2013), (Apple Inc. conspired to raise the price of e-books in violation of the Sherman Act). United States v. Apple Inc., 791 F.3d 290 (2d Cir. 2015).(Apple conspired to e-book price fixing and violated federal antitrust law.) Brian Callaci & Sandeep Vaheesan, Antitrust Remedies For Fissured Work, 2022 Cornell Law Review Online Vol.108:27. (Firms now have broad freedom to control trading partners, whether distributors, franchisees, or suppliers, through contract and dictate what they sell, where, and on what terms. The result has been a tightening of corporate control and a reduced role for independent business. Vertical restraints common in franchising minutely dictate the management practices of the businesses subject to them.)

[225] Christopher L. Peterson & Marshall Steinbaum, Coercive Rideshare Practices: At the Intersection of Antitrust and Consumer Protection Law in the Gig Economy, 2023 The University of Chicago Law Review 90:2/623 p654/658.

Will the platform regulations implicate the future of antitrust law? First of all, the likelihood and magnitude of anticompetitive harm in digital markets may be great. As discussed earlier, the new platform regulations rely on a broad set of ex ante rules that establish presumptions of illegality for specific types of platforms conduct and so the new regulations diverge from the "effects-based" analysis as the default mode of assessment of the "more economic approach." Hence, the new platform regulations underline the value of economically informed rebuttable presumptions in antitrust analysis and so making antitrust intervention on the simple basis that particular kinds of conduct by powerful platforms may cause prospective anticompetitive harm of noteworthy level. Thus, "probabilism" of the new platform regulations denotes an imperative divergence from the expanding trend in conventional antitrust analysis to make the discovery of unlawful conduct provisional on exhibiting that anticompetitive consequences/outcomes are more likely than not. In other words, the new platform regulations make certain market openness and contestability.

To that extent, a designation practice is established making certain that the new platform regulations only apply to the most powerful digital platforms[226] which have to be expanded to all platforms in order to boost the competitive process. Hereafter, the traditional concepts of "dominance" or "monopoly" fail to account for the fact that digital platforms may exercise significant "intermediation power" permitting them to harm competition, even though they do not hold a dominant position in a plainly defined relevant product market.[227] It could be said that platform regulations are promoting a new model of economic growth in the digital economy, justified in a broad-based distribution of innovative and economic opportunities for many competitors.

It has to be taken into account that the regulatory basis of the new platform regulations echoes the multidimensional harms deriving from the horizontal and vertical incentive structure digital platforms are subject to. Hence, by stimulating contestability, the platform regulations condense structural factors that make easy the entrenchment of incumbents' market power and so neutralizing their purposes to harm horizontal competition by foreclosing or acquiring competitors which means that by safeguarding fairness and equality of opportunity, the platform regulations diminish the vertical competition matters resulting from running a synchronized marketplace and sales function. Thus, platform regulations lay down a number of obligations moderating the motivations of platforms to raise the costs of business users functioning as third-party sellers competing with their own sales function on

---

[226] Monika Schnitzer et al., International Coherence in Digital Platform Regulation: An Economic Perspective on the US and EU Proposals (2021), at 12, https://papers.s srn.com/sol3/papers.cfm?abstract_id=3923604

[227] Heike Schweitzer et al., Modernisierung der Missbrauchsaufsicht für marktmächtige Unternehmen, Projekt im Auftrag des Bundesministeriums für Wirtschaft und Energie (BMWi), (2018), at 40–42,

their platform. To that extent, Elias Deutscher[228] argues that "The new regulatory frameworks for digital markets are hence not exclusively directed against welfare-reducing conduct that reduces total/consumer welfare by foreclosing efficient competitors offering products/services that are not supplied by powerful digital platforms at all, or at less favorable conditions. Instead, they protect the revenue streams of competitors regardless of their efficiency. ".

10.19 Competition and Platform Work

Technological developments have been bringing about modifications in the field of work and so the emergence of platform work has brought up all kinds of problems. Is the platform worker an employee and falls within the scope of labor law? Taking into account that platform workers are solo self-employed, it seems that they combine features of the employment relationship with aspects of the self-employed relationship.[229] Also, platforms label workers as self-employed on the basis of the legal system in question and so commercial law applies which means that workers and the platform are accepted to be equal parties before the law with freedom of contract. The platform worker is considered to be an undertaking, which means competition law will apply and so the construction of the relationship first settles whether someone can be held liable for a possible infringement of Article 101 TFEU.

On the one hand, the ECJ[230] shows that it is not inconceivable that a platform worker will be regarded as self-employed. On the other hand, employees are integrated into the undertaking during their relationship not constituting an undertaking themselves by performing work for, and under the direction of, their employer and do not bear the financial risks linked with that work which means that an employee is not respected to be an independent entity and is not an undertaking.[231] In Becu, the Court related the concept of worker within the meaning of Article 45 of the TFEU to that of employee within the meaning of competition law denoting that employees can conclude collective labor agreements without competition law concerns. EU competition law, as a whole, targets the activities of undertakings, understood as economic units and the concept of "undertaking" in EU competition law and its consequences in the field of private enforcement is defined in Skanska judgment.[232] It has to be taken into account that private liability for platform workers can also be detrimental owing to the fact that all corporations of a single economic

[228] Elias Deutscher, Reshaping Digital Competition: The New Platform Regulations and the Future of Modern Antitrust, The Antitrust Bulletin 2022, Vol. 67(2) 302–340 p 339.

[229] D. Mangan, 'Delivering on the Binary Divide', ELLJ, 2021, 12(2).

[230] Case C-692/19, ECLI: EU: C: 2020: 288 (Yodel); E. Gramano, 'On the notion of "worker" under EU law: new insights', European Labour Law Journal, 2021, 12(1), 98–101.

[231] Case C-22/98 ECLI:EU:C:1999:419 (Becu), para 26

[232] Case C-724/17, ECLI:EU:C:2019:204

entity could be held liable for the anticompetitive behavior of a party of the entity under the single economic entity doctrine.[233] In its 2019 *Skanska* judgment,[1] the ECJ applied the single economic unit principle in the context of damage claims and so an economic unit consists of those entities that form a unitary organization of personal, tangible, and intangible elements taking up a particular economic goal on a long-term basis which means that in the perspective of a competition law infringement, the relevant economic unit is the one that existed at the time of the infringement. Thus, victims of anticompetitive agreements can claim follow-on damages from subsidiaries of firms that were the object of a competition law infringement decision. Article 101 TFEU is applicable to agreements between entities that form part of the same group but do not share related economic activities.[234] Article 101 TFEU precludes any national law stipulating the possibility of establishing joint and several liabilities.

It is worth noting that dynamic pricing can promote more effective transparent and cheaper services eventually advancing competition.[235] If the platform and the platform worker both form undertakings, they are subjected to competition law and so if they embrace a synchronized pricing strategy, it causes concerns concerning Article 101 TFEU. A single economic entity exists looking at the level of decisive influence exercised and so if decisive influence is present regarding the relationship between the platform and the platform worker, then there is a single undertaking and Article 101 TFEU will generally not be applicable. Nonetheless, if platform workers are self-employed, then Article 101 TFEU is applicable which means that Section 3 application arises in the vertical relationship between the platform and the platform worker, but more possible also in the horizontal relationship between platform workers. It is worth mentioning here that the platform workers, working for a specific platform, could be found to collude by using the same algorithm and so both violating Article 101 TFEU. To that extent, Jorn Kloostra[236] argues that "it does not seem to be the platform workers who reap the profits. In practice, little remains of that entrepreneurship, and platform workers are mainly confronted with its negative aspects. They occupy a poor negotiating position, have little say in their working conditions, and risk becoming embroiled in an (algorithmic) race to the bottom. The possibility of uniting in some way does not exist."

[233] Case C-882/19, ECLI:EU:C:2021:293 (Sumal), Opinion AG Pitruzzella

[234] C-73/95 Viho, C-201/09 P Acelor Mittal, or C-531/16 Ecoservice,

[235] A. Lamontanaro, 'Bounty Hunters For Algorithmic Cartels: An Old Solution for a New Problem', Fordham Intell. Prop. Media & Ent. L.J., 2020, 30, 1267,

[236] Jorn Kloostra, Algorithmic pricing: A concern for platform workers? European Labour Law Journal 2022, Vol. 13(1) 108–126 P 126

References

1. Reyes, C. L., & Ward, J. (2020). Digging into algorithms: Legal ethics and legal access. *Nevada Law Journal, 21*(1), 342–343.
2. Durand, C., & Milberg, W. (2020). Intellectual monopoly in global value chains. *Review of International Political Economy, 27*(2), 404–429.
3. Deutscher, E. (2022). Reshaping digital competition: The new platform regulations and the future of modern antitrust. *The Antitrust Bulletin, 67*(2), 302–340.
4. Sitaraman, G. (2022). The regulation of foreign platforms 74 *Stan. L.Rev.*, 1073.
5. Gao, H. S. (2021). Data regulation with Chinese characteristics, in *Big Data in global trade law*, 245, 261 (Mira Burri ed.).
6. Hovenkamp, H. (2021). Antitrust and platform monopoly, 130 *Yale Law Journal*, 1901, 1965.
7. Bent, J. R. (2020). Is algorithmic affirmative action legal?, 108 *Geo. L.J.*, 803, 809.
8. Wiedemann, K. (2021). Data protection and competition law enforcement in the digital economy: why a coherent and consistent approach is necessary. 52 *IIC 915.*
9. Leonidou, E., Christofi, M., Vrontis, D., & Thrassou, A. (2020). An integrative framework of stakeholder engagement for innovation management and entrepreneurship development. *Journal of Business Research, 119*, 245–258.
10. Steinbaum, M. (2022). Establishing market and monopoly power in tech platform antitrust cases. *Antitrust Bull, 67*, 130–137.
11. Diamantis, M. E. (2020). The extended corporate mind: When corporations use AI to break the Law, 98 *N.C. L. REV.*, 893, 900.
12. Klimas, P., & Czakon, W. (2022). Gaming innovation ecosystem: actors, roles and co-innovation processes. *Review of Managerial Science, 16*, 2213.
13. Pistor, K. (2020). Rule by data: The end of markets? *Law and Contemporary Problems, 83*, 101–124.
14. Prainsack, B. (2020). The political economy of digital data: Introduction to the special issue. *Policy Studies, 41*(5), 439–446.
15. Li, S., Sunb, H., & Jun, Y. (2023). Competitive targeted online advertising. *International Journal of Industrial Organization, 87*, 102924.
16. Zhang, S., Shirong, G., & Tang, Y. (2022). How does policy create an opportunity window for China's digital economy? *Transnational Corporations, 29*(3), 38.
17. Schrepel, T. (2021). Platforms or aggregators: Implications for digital antitrust law, 12 *J. Eur. Compet. Law Pract.*, 1.
18. UNCTAD. (2021). *Digital economy report 2021: Cross-border data flows and development: For whom the data flow.* United Nations.
19. Ng, W. (2020). State interest and the state-centered approach to competition law in China. *Antitrust Bulletin, 65*(2), 297.
20. Zekos, G. (2012). Cyber-territory and jurisdiction of nations. *Journal of Internet Law, Number 12/3.* Aspen Publications.
21. Zekos, G. (2013, November). Demolishing state's sole power over sovereignty & territory via electronic technology & cyberspace. *Journal of Internet Law, 17*(5), 27–41.
22. Zekos, G. (2007). State cyberspace jurisdiction and personal cyberspace jurisdiction. *International Journal of Law and Information Technology, 15*(1), 1–17. Oxford University Press. https://doi.org/10.1093/ijlit/eai029

Chapter 11
AAI and FDI

11.1 Introduction

One of the key values of blockchain technology is the capacity to conduct transactions without a central monitoring organization, such as the government. The decentralized, collaborative approach of the open-source community-generated programs such as the Linux operating system is utilized by large businesses and denoting transference in the industry away from the information-technology-dependent services of the past. Furthermore, many blockchain applications are being developed under open-source licenses. Any business that relies on database integrity can apply blockchain to diminish costs and generate a more efficient, robust system.

IP portrays the knowledge and competences of a company and its employees, stipulating freedom of action in innovation and growth strategy. Moreover, IP is a flexible asset class offering access to new markets, the capacity to advance existing products, and openings to generate new revenue streams which means that IP is a fundamental asset for any company competing in a global knowledge economy.

It has to be taken into account that blockchain platforms empower digital contracts among corporations, persons, and even AI systems. Smart contracts based on blockchain technology are already used for insurance agreements, sales contracts, and more. Moreover, due to its unique characteristics, such as being open-ledger, encrypted, decentralized, and accessible, blockchain technology has the prospective to replace governmental registration systems such as those for land, copyright, trademark, and patents.

Fintech's exceptional features such as reliance on intelligent algorithms and big data strengthen existing trade-offs in regulating financial markets. Information asymmetries comprise a noteworthy contest to international standard setting and enforcement and so concealing the risks to global market integrity which instigates a need for creating straightforward standards in order to defeat differences in national legal systems, markets, and administrative procedures. On the other hand, it seems that financial regulatory transformations due to the economic crises have failed to

© The Author(s), under exclusive license to Springer Nature Switzerland AG 2023
G. I. Zekos, *Artificial Intelligence and Competition*, Contributions to Economics,
https://doi.org/10.1007/978-3-031-48083-6_11

take into consideration the quickly shifting face of financial services owing to AI developments.[1]

It has to be taken into account that algorithms provoke concerns for regulators because algorithms automate existing financial functions such as picking stocks, deciding whether to make a loan, or aiding savers to invest for retirement. Moreover, algorithms within a specific business such as money management use common statements and responding in comparable manners to new information, possibly amplifying the reaction.

11.2 Outlining FDI

FDI is a non-debt source of development in the finance funding investment projects in the economy expanding the stage of technical progress in the host country and technology transferred to developing countries via FDI is newer than that transferred via licensing. FDI advances managerial knowledge and skills increasing effectiveness and productivity, and provides an extensive selection of goods and services to the economy.

With globalized marketplaces, today's worldwide FDI is out of all proportion to the past. Large foreign companies are expected to have established technologies that they want to transport to the host state and engaging in a large consumer market.

FDI is an imperative source of capital, with a high contribution to the development of the economies, given the positive spillovers generated in host economies. As regards the determinants of FDI, it is valuable to distinguish between horizontal and vertical ones; the former appears among companies functioning in similar lines of business, while vertical FDI encompasses entities that are active in different segments of a value chain. Also, FDI drives the participation in global value chains (GVCs) of local companies and enhances value-added trade. GVCs permit nations, and corporations, to functionally concentrate on fine-grained value-chain stages rather than entire industries and so functional specialization is valuable for many developing countries permitting them to fast-track industrialization even if they lack the capabilities to back entire industries.[2] The institutional environment, the economic development level, the geographic location, and the logistics systems environment are attracting factors of FDI.

Vertical FDI is made by corporations that geographically break their production into stages, typically on the basis of factor intensities, utilizing lower factor prices overseas or dropping transaction costs by internalizing upstream or downstream

[1]Chris Brummer & Yesha Yadav, Fintech and the Innovation Trilemma, 107 GEO. L.J. 235, 237–42 (2019).

[2]Carlo Pietrobelli, Roberta Rabellotti and Ari Van Assche, "Making sense of global value chain-oriented policies: the trifecta of tasks, linkages, and firms," JIBS, vol. 4 (2021), pp. 327–346.

activities.[3] If several phases of the production process are portrayed by different levels of labor amount, there is an allocation of the phases with high labor intensity to countries with low levels of labor costs and the phases necessitating lots of skills or capital to high-income countries. Hereafter, there is a complementarity between a company's foreign and home operations, for the reason that both are compelled to produce the good. In the short run, substitution between the employment's levels at home and abroad takes place if an activity beforehand conducted at home is relocated overseas.[4]

It is worth noting that Hellenic corporations that were formerly export oriented turned into MNEs controlling export platform FDI in the Balkans. FDI improves the competence of Hellenic MNEs[5] having a positive effect on Hellenic GDP. Moreover, Hellenic FDI in European Countries follows different patterns in terms of volume, sector, and industrial activity attracted either by lower production costs and taxation or effectiveness-seeking strategies such as the expansion into new markets and searching for synergies and strategic partnerships.

It is characteristic that the establishment of Investment Promotion Agencies (IPAs) has gradually dispersed as one of the leading policy initiatives to draw FDI and so the endeavor of IPAs is an element of both national and local government strategies to draw inward investment. Moreover, IPAs target the general economic improvement of the host economies focused on knowledge-intensive areas where collaborative systemic conditions are more relevant. IPAs have had noteworthy positive effects on the probability of MNEs establishing a first foreign affiliate and expanding their presence[6] but IPAs face the encounter of staying relevant and further increasing their effectiveness within an uncertain global environment distinguished by the digital transformation of the economy and global supply chain vulnerabilities. Thus, IPAs should adopt specialized digital devices to expand their portfolio of digital services by offering their customers more effective assistance which means that by applying AI technologies, IPAs predict the probability of specific MNEs establishing affiliates and so guiding promotional endeavors.

[3]Kokko, A. (2006), "The Home Country Effects of FDI in Developed Economies", The European Institute of Japanese Studies, *EIJS Working Paper* No. 225.

[4]Braconier, H. and K. Ekholm (2001), "Foreign Direct Investment in Central and Eastern Europe: Employment Effects in the EU", *CEPR Working Paper* No. 3052.

[5]Giakoulas, D. & Kottaridi, C. (2020) Foreign Direct Investment Strategies of Greek Multinational Enterprises during the pre-crisis period: An econometric research based on the OLI model, SPOUDAI - Journal of Economics and Business, Vol. 70, Iss. 1–2, p. 128–152. Dimitris Giakoulas, Trends and Patterns of Greek Outward FDI in CEE Countries, ijbesar.ihu.gr https://ssrn.com/abstract=3944590

[6]https://cloud.mail.iadb.org/making-the-invisible-visible

11.3 FDI Developments

It is argued that even though FDI offers economic benefits to host nations, government and private reports overstate the value of foreign investment and understate its costs and risks.[7] Moreover, attention has been given to the acquisition of technology-based assets with prospective repercussions for recipient economies in terms of national security.[8]

It is worth noting that foreign investment gives value to states, but it may contribute to income gaps among individuals. It is characteristic that positive reverse technology spillovers represent an indicator of whether home countries could benefit from outward FDI and so the reverse technology spillovers of outward FDI help absorbing and transfer foreign high-tech. Nonetheless, reverse technology spillover by outward FDI is absorbed by the home country as long as there is absorptive capacity. Transfer and imitation happen when the innate endowment of a region reaches a certain level, referred to as the threshold value.

It has to be taken into account that IFDI and OFDI are often intimately connected, with economic benefits flowing from the two-way internationalization of the local economy. Moreover, OFDI increasingly serves as a complementary channel driving home-country development.[9] Vertical OFDI encompassing the relocation abroad of certain parts of the value chain causes substitution consequences between national and foreign labor in the short and the medium run. Equally, cost-saving OFDI augments productivity through a scaled-up demand for national labor due to corporation growth stemming from internationalization. Horizontal OFDI implicating the relocation abroad of whole business pursuits such as production causes negative home-country employment consequences as a result of offshoring. Additionally, OFDI offers opportunities for structural revolution in less developed regions, by assisting local activities to advance the global value and knowledge by investing abroad.[10] It has to be taken into consideration that OFDI generates reverse knowledge spillovers to emerging markets, which spreads knowledge-sourcing channels for bringing innovation to the next level.

Owing to inward and outward FDI, companies circumvent taxation by functioning in tax haven nations, thereby furthering inequities. In addition, sovereign wealth funds and state-operated companies are investors with political motivations that may spoil host countries' interests. To that extent, the Supreme Court stated redistribution

[7]Ioannis Kokkoris Tim Bakken, Legal Takeovers Of Nations: The Value And Risks Of Foreign Direct Investment In A Global Marketplace, 2016 University Of Dayton Law Review Vol. 40:3

[8]OECD (2020): "Acquisition- and Ownership-Related Policies to Safeguard Essential Security Interests Current and Emerging Trends, Observed Designs, and Policy Practice in 62 economies," Research note by the OECD Secretariat.

[9]Karl P. Sauvant, "A new challenge for emerging markets: the need to develop an outward FDI policy," Columbia FDI Perspective, no. 203, July 3, 2017.

[10]Riccardo Crescenzi, Marco Di Cataldo and Mara Giua, "FDI inflows in Europe: Does investment promotion work?," Journal of International Economics, vol. 132 (2021), p. 103497.

of political impact and power from individuals to corporate and other business entities, which are manipulated by foreign nations and companies.[11] It is argued that China and Russia raise unique challenges for the reason that they have dynamic programs through which they sanction and take part in "stealing trade secrets and classified government information."[12]

China has become a hotspot for FDI making investments easier by removing barriers, and pushing forward investment protection agreements and double taxation avoidance agreements to protect the lawful rights and interests of investors. The new Foreign Investment Law[13] removes serious hurdles to FDI offering greater legal certainty and so the liberalizing of capital flow is vital for economic growth. According to the IMF cross-border investment "fosters inter temporal optimization of consumption, helps finance the balance of payments, and promotes efficient allocation of world savings."[14]

China's attitude towards FDI is embracing the accumulation of capital utilized in tandem with working force advantages and so transforming China into a super economic power. Certainly, mergers and acquisitions are vital FDI modes in China, and foreign investors preferably enter the Chinese market by acquiring leading domestic companies.[15] In China, Article 28 of the Anti-Monopoly Law refers to prohibiting a merger only in the event that the conclusion of the investigation is that it "leads, or may lead, to elimination or restriction of competition." It seems that merger control is strategically employed to restrain the entry of non-national businesses into local markets. Foreigners are not authorized under any circumstances to purchase a majority interest in a large and successful established Chinese company. Besides, in the EU, the European Commission has established the use of merger control for the competitive assessment of concentrations and so Regulation 2019/452[16] came into force, with measures destined at confirming adequate FDI screening in the EU on grounds of security or public

---

[11] Citizens United v. Federal Election Commission, 558 U.S. 310 (2010)

[12] Foreign Spies Stealing U.S. Economic Secrets in Cyberspace: Report to Congress on Foreign Economic Collection and Industrial Espionage, 2009–2011, Office Of Nat'l Counterintelligence Exec. 1, 5 (Oct. 2011), http://www.ncix.gov/publications/reports/fecie_all/Foreign_Economic_Collection _2011.pdf

[13] https://investmentpolicy.unctad.org/investment-laws/laws/317/china-foreigninvestment-law-of-the-people-s-republic-of-chinaSandra Marco Colino, The Internationalization of China's Foreign Direct Investment Laws, 45(2) Fordham International Law Journal (2021)

[14] National Development And Reform Commission, Ministry Of Foreign Affairs, Ministry Of Commerce Of The People's Republic Of China, With State Council Authorization, Vision And Actions On Jointly Building Belt And Road, Belt and Road Forum for International Cooperation (Apr. 10, 2017), http://2017.beltandroadforum.org/english/n100/2017/0410/c22-45.html

[15] Angela Huyue Zhang, Chinese Antitrust Exceptionalism (2021). Tingting Weinreich-Zhao, Chinese Merger Control Law: An Assessment Of Its Competition-Policy Orientation After The First Years Of Application (2015)

[16] [2019] OJ LI79/1 First Annual Report on the screening of foreign direct investments into the Union, COM(2021) 714 final, p. 19.

order. Merger control systems appraise the compatibility of concentrations prior to their implementation, and this on the basis of their projected effects.

Inward FDI means that companies functioning in a host nation are controlled by corporations rooted in another nation. Hence, FDI encompasses foreign parent companies' equity contributions, reinvestments of earnings of affiliates, and loans to the affiliates. Equity contributions embrace the parent companies' establishment of new affiliates or the acquisition of further interests in existing affiliates; capital contributions to affiliates; and the use of stock to acquire existing corporations. It is characteristic that OFDI is a strategic decision requiring board-level approval reflecting the board's effectiveness as a monitor and advisor for the management.

It has to be taken into consideration that host countries have presented MNEs tax incentives to attract FDI and their prevalent use has resulted in a "race to the bottom" in international taxation which means that countries propose progressively lower tax rates when competing to attract FDI.[17] Taxation avoidance, alone, contributes to inflated estimates of the value of FDI. But, also, FDI has noteworthy direct and indirect costs. Nations have significant incentives to attract FDI even while "casting a wary eye on it."

FDI generates risks to national security since it places the employees of nations and their companies in sensitive and non-sensitive positions within host affiliates offering products or services in support of national security. In control of the affiliates, the nations or foreign corporations have access to high-tech information or materials that are used commercially and also in support of national security. To that extent, crimes associated with FDI are often theft of trade secrets, economic espionage, and bribery, all of which can be foundations to greater harm. Has know–how been transferred unlawfully from western economies to east and far-east economies via FDI or labor? Has AI technology assisted in a way "illegal" imitation of products around the globe?

Furthermore, FDI offers economic advantages to host countries. On the other hand, the value of FDI has been overstated and the costs and risks linked with foreign investment have been understated. When foreign corporations establish or purchase affiliates in a host country, the corporations bring critical competition and new ideas to the marketplace, through which they make products and workers better. It could be said that the competitive presence of foreign companies has a positive impact on the capacity of national corporations to participate in innovative activities via knowledge spillovers and improvement in product quality and export is boosted by the inflow of FDI.

It has to be taken into consideration that the geographical composition of FDI has switched over time and the most remarkable long-term development being the continual growth of developing Asia as a source of FDI. The international investment regime is undergoing extensive reform and there is a decline in global FDI that coincides with rising IIA protectionism and IIAs enforced under the new IIA regime

[17] Lorraine Eden, "Taxing multinationals: The GloBE proposal for a global minimum tax," Bloomberg Tax Daily Tax Report (Dec. 6, 2019).

no longer stimulate FDI activities which means that rising IIA protectionism has adverse FDI outcomes.[18]

MNEs from developing and transition economies have become central investors in many LDCs. To that extent, a number of MNEs from developing and transition economies have risen to principal worldwide positions in industries such as automotive, chemicals, electronics, shipping, information technology services, and construction. MNEs take into consideration various factors, such as administrative, economic, geographic, and political characteristics, when making investment decisions and the rationale of IIAs is to reduce barriers influencing both horizontal and vertical FDI. Dongin Kim and Sandro Steinbach[19] provide evidence "for adverse effects of IIA termination on FDI, more pronounced for brownfield than greenfield FDI and equally significant for both investment margins. An analysis for vertical and horizontal FDI shows adverse termination effects more potent for horizontal FDI. We also find substantial treatment heterogeneity according to industry characteristics, minor for manufacturing and mining and more substantial for agriculture, construction, and trade."

Privatization magnetizes new entry of the host country companies by reducing the output of the public company which means that more remaining market is left to the prospective domestic companies.[20] G.I. Zekos considers that selective privatization of state-owned enterprises should be the most advantageous strategy in advancing development by introducing new technologies in production line and managing corporate governance via AI systems. Hence, higher competition in the host country market attributable to the domestic enterprises' entry shrinks the residual demand for foreign corporations negatively touching the foreign company's incentive to embark on FDI.[21]

FDI is more and more supply global and regional markets, often in the framework of international production networks and the spread of such networks offers new aptitude for developing countries and economies in transition to profit from FDI in the manufacturing sector. To that extent, retaining dynamic scale economies demands succeeding innovative investments and learning means via new AI technologies. Hence, FDI improves competitiveness and creates employment by increasing the welfare of the host nation.[22] To that extent, higher welfare spending by

[18] UNCTAD (2021). World Investment Report 2021. United Nations Publications. Kox, H. L. M. and Rojas-Romagosa, H. (2020). How trade and investment agreements affect bilateral foreign direct investment: Results from a structural gravity model. The World Economy, 43(12): 3203–3242

[19] Dongin Kim, Sandro Steinbach, Rising Protectionism and Foreign Direct Investment, https://ssrn.com/abstract=3983856 at 1.

[20] Norbäck, P. J. and L. Persson, (2005), 'Privatisation policy in an international oligopoly', *Economica*, 72: 635–53. Merlevede, B. and K. Schoors, (2005), 'How to catch foreign fish? FDI and accession countries', *Working Paper, No. 785*, William Davidson Institute.

[21] UNCTAD, (2006), *World Investment Report*, United Nations, New York and Geneva.

[22] Dunning, J.H., "The prospects for foreign direct investment in Central and Eastern Europe", in Buckley, P.J. and Ghauri, P.N. (Eds), The Economics of Change in Eastern and Central Europe: Its

governments invites foreign investment which means that attracting FDI as a means to get technologies is still one of the main policies for energizing knowledge-sourcing channels. Also, FDI[23] results in increased host country productivity through technology transfer, but only when the initial level of host industry competition is relatively low. Consequently, gradually more competitive environment for FDI and the need to comply with international commitments have forced governments to relax restrictions on foreign entrants.

The volume of FDI has boosted considerably over the last two decades, driven by the globalization of capital markets and the development of global value chains. Hence, FDI inflows bring advantages to the recipient country, by promoting economic growth through several means. Thus, FDI accelerates the diffusion of technology and increases competition in local markets. Moreover, the liberalization of FDI and other capital flows advances asset diversification and allocative competence which means that FDI flow permits to financing capital accumulation in a secure manner as related to other types of capital movements and is less risky from a financial stability standpoint.[24] Emerging economies have lifted barriers to FDI, along with the trend toward trade liberalization but FDI flows camouflage tax optimization strategies. Marco Albori et al.[25] "suggest that FDI restrictions have a negative and significant impact on FDI equity inflows. Also, our results are driven by the manufacturing and service sectors, while we do not find a significant impact of regulations in discouraging FDI flows in the primary sectors. Interestingly, as regards the four different types of restrictions included in the RRI, we find that the negative effect is driven by equity restrictions, while constraints on the employment of foreigners as key personnel and screening mechanisms do not affect FDI inflows. In addition, measures imposed for national security seem to not affect FDI in our sample. We also show that the effects of FDI restrictions are stronger in advanced economies; this result might depend on our limited country sample for emerging economies, but it could also be explained considering that in emerging economies FDI flows tend to be concentrated in few sectors regardless of the level of restrictions in place."

Impact on International Business, Academic Press, London, 1994. Giese, A.S., Kahley, W.J. and Riefler, R.F., "Foreign direct investment: motivating factors and economic impact", Regional Science Perspectives, Vol. 20, 1990, pp. 105–27. Dunning, J.H., "Re-evaluating the benefits of foreign direct investment", Transnational Corporations, Vol. 3 No. 1, 1994, pp. 23–51.

[23]Chung, W., 1997. Foreign direct investment's effect on host industry mark-up and productivity in the U.S.: the influence of initial host industry competition. Paper presented at the Academy of International Business annual meeting, Monterrey, Mexico.

[24]Coppola, A., M. Maggiori, B. Neiman, and J. Schreger (2020): "Redrawing the Map of Global Capital Flows: The Role of Cross-Border Financing and Tax Havens," Tech. rep., National Bureau of Economic Research.

[25]Marco Albori, Flavia Corneli, Valerio Nispi Landi and Alessandro Schiavone The impact of restrictions on FDI, Questioni di Economia e Finanza, Number 656 – November 2021 www.bancaditalia.it P7

FDI is an important source of capital, with a high contribution to the development of the economies, given the positive spillovers produced in host economies.[26] In addition, FDI drives the participation in global value chains of local firms boosting value-added trade and the competitiveness of host locations has an imperative role in the FDI decision-making process. To that extent, high-tech firms are scrutinizing market prospective, accessing country risk and agglomeration economies.[27]

It is worth mentioning here that FDI is vulnerable to economic and other kinds of shocks. To that extent, the COVID-19 pandemic has shown the vulnerability of global trade and value chains to external shocks. When a country in the global value chain suffers an outbreak leading to shutdowns of its factories, then the entire global supply chain is disrupted. Corporations have reduced their reliance on concentrated production in foreign countries in order to minimize and differentiate the risk of disruptions.[28] Also, a shift in patterns of the global supply chain disturb FDI decisions given the complementarity between intermediate goods trade and FDI.[29] Hayakawa et al.[30] argue that "In the manufacturing sector, COVID-19 damage in host countries has significant negative impact on both greenfield FDI and cross-border M&A. . . However, in the service sector, COVID-19 damage in both the host and home countries are found to have negative impacts on greenfield FDI, whereas the impact of COVID-19 on cross-border M&A appears to be mostly insignificant."

11.4 Digital FDI

Taking into account that digitalization is generating new economic activities while also intensifying the scale, scope, and efficiency of existing economic activities, FDI brings not only capital but also knowledge and technology and so attracting digital

---

[26] Blanchard, O. and Acalin, J. – "What Does FDI Actually Measure?", Peterson Institute for International Economic, 2016, available at: https://www.piie.com/publications/policy-briefs/what-does-measured-fdi-actually-measurePopovici, O., Horobet, A., Paraschiv, D., Hurduzeu, G., Lupu, R. & Zeldea, C. (2020). Foreign direct investment in Romania, Study carried out in partnership by the Bucharest Academy of Economic Studies and the Council of Foreign Investors. National Bank of Romania

[27] Pecaric et al. (2021) Pečarić, M., Kusanović, T., & Jakovac, P. (2021). The Determinants of FDI Sectoral Structure in the Central and East European EU Countries. Economies, 9 (2), 66.

[28] Lee, Hyun-Hoon, and Donghyun Park. 2020. Post-COVID Asia: Deglobalization, Fourth Industrial Revolution, and Sustainable Development. Singapore: World Scientific Publishing.

[29] Choi, Sangyup, Davide Furceri, and Chansik Yoon. 2021. "Policy Uncertainty and Foreign Direct Investment." Review of International Economics 29 (2): 195–227. Ando, Mitsuyo, and Kazunobu Hayakawa. 2021. "Impact of COVID-19 on Trade in Services." IDE Discussion Paper No. 824. Institute of Developing Economies, Chiba.

[30] Kazunobu Hayakawa, Hyun-Hoon Lee, and Cyn-Young Park, The Effect of COVID-19 on Foreign Direct Investment, ADB Economics Working Paper Series No. 653 | March 2022 p 2.

FDI[31] facilitates economies and companies improve digital capabilities. Moreover, there are information openings and coordination challenges to connecting capital to digital investment opportunities. To that extent, digital corporations rely on data and technology implicating platform economies and non-traditional assets.

Digital FDI is vital to grow the digital economy and a route to boost the capacity and competitiveness. Moreover, digital FDI not only brings capital but also entrenches digital knowledge and technology, while producing jobs and enhancing productivity. To that extent, corporations realize that they need to invest in digital capacity or risk losing market share or even go out of business. Digital infrastructure is vital to aid companies in connecting with global market openings by plugging into global supply chains and escalating e-commerce exports, both of goods and digital services.

It is characteristic that FDI brings technology, know–how, and growth and so digital corporations invest abroad to be close to customers, access local knowledge, and open new markets. Digital corporations in the technology sectors rely on data and know–how serving as an additional vector to drive sustainable development in both host and home economies. Matthew Stephenson[32] specifies that "there is a need to tailor the Digital FDI initiative to individual economies through country-specific analysis and reforms."

All at once, growing techno-nationalism is making digital FDI more difficult, both inwardly and outwardly because policy-makers may be reluctant for their companies to offshore too much technology and concurrently reluctant to accept mergers and acquisitions (M&A) in high-tech sectors.[33]

It has to be taken into account that FDI restrictions lead to lower FDI and possibly reduced competitiveness and so corporations should pursue FDI reform, promotion, and facilitation to sectors that are digital enablers across the new economy. Furthermore, it has to be taken into consideration that social brokers include private individuals who have international commerce expertise and established relations with local corporations and institutions. Also, brokers' role is to back MNEs in finding suitable local partners ready to participate in corruption on their behalf, where this is needed or would make possible establishing MNEs' businesses in host countries. To that extent, social brokers make it unnecessary for MNEs to approach local corporations directly involved in corruption and so foreign MNEs seldom approach unknown local businesses to join forces in operations. On the other hand, the US FCPA[34] forces MNEs to generate and maintain internal controls to make certain that there is no participation in corruption abroad, embracing

[31] Bruno Casella and Lorenzo Formenti, 19 August 2019, "FDI in the digital economy: a shift to asset-light international footprints", UNCTAD Insights, MPRA Paper No. 95201,

[32] Matthew Stephenson, Digital FDI: Policies, regulations and measures to attract FDI in the digital economy 2020 World Economic Forum, www.weforum.org P 16

[33] Lamb K (2019). The rise of techno-nationalism - and the paradox at its core. World Economic Forum, 3 July, https://www.weforum.org/agenda/2019/07/the-rise-oftechno-nationalism-and-the-paradox-atits-core/

[34] FCPA, visit http://usdoj.gov/criminal/fraud/fcpa

consultants and partners. Correspondingly, the OECD[35] controls the implementation of anti-bribery provisions via a peer-review mechanism to make certain that all member countries abide by the OECD Convention. The *OECD Anti-Bribery Convention*[36] establishes legally binding standards to criminalize bribery of foreign public officials in international business transactions. Thus, governments should employ more transparency policies demanding foreign corporations to document their practices regarding social brokers.

11.5 AI and MNEs

MNEs started to grow from comparatively simple cross-border structures mainly motivated by the search for natural resources and international markets to more complex global value chains exploiting differences in labor costs and productivity. Technological development rests on localization, as MNE innovation is gradually recognized to count on the knowledge production and absorptive capacity of its subsidiaries. Cross-border mobility of inventors is underlined as a crucial mechanism for global knowledge production by MNEs.

AI technologies in the international production of global MNEs modify the configuration of GVCs due to supply chain digitalization and additive manufacturing and mass customization. Hence, MNEs implement new approaches to business operations augmenting agility and flexibility and so MNEs must handle increasing volatility, uncertainty, complexity, and opacity of the global business environment which means that there is an alteration in the pattern of global investment flows involving diversification, reshoring, and nearshoring.

As a result of the COVID-19 pandemic, developments in technology, along with changes in the macroeconomic and socioeconomic dynamics of globalization, the globe is undergoing digital and AI transformation at a rapid pace. To that extent, as corporations have gone virtual and digital, consumer needs and desires have altered considerably.

It has to be taken into account that technological innovations have led to digitized, efficient, and interconnected supply chains and so firms are making certain that digital capabilities are a part of comprehensive risk management strategies for future crises due to the fact that digital supply networks let firms adjusting to the effects of crises by exploiting technologies such as AI. Furthermore, taking into consideration that globalized trade and supply chains have spread in step with upgraded transport networks and corporate enticements to lower production costs, leverage a specialized workforce and get into various markets, the pandemic amplified weaknesses in globalized production strategies since many corporations counted on single specialized suppliers or factories in other countries.

---

[35] https://www.oecd.org/corruption/oecdantibriberyconvention.htm

[36] https://www.oecd.org/daf/anti-bribery/2021-oecd-anti-bribery-recommendation.htm

It seems that companies with operations in multiple countries and those with international supply chains have been particularly vulnerable to the upsetting consequences of the pandemic. Hence, the pandemic has caused uncertainties concerning the benefits of a global supply network and so forcing corporations to diversify and develop new supplier networks in multiple areas or upgrade domestic production. Omrane Guedhami et al.[37] argue that "a stronger financial system mitigates negative crisis returns, especially under stringent government responses, while real factors, such as the firm's supply chain, investments in human capital, research and development, exacerbate negative crisis returns."

The interconnectedness of networks together with AI and machine learning technologies are transforming how corporations run and compete and their scope and scale, facilitating corporation growth. Hence, in keeping with these dynamics, AI has become an enterprise-wide imperative for most MNEs. Given the breadth and importance of AI, General Counsel (GCs) of MNE legal departments are under anxiety to embark on AI technology with the purpose of delivering improved legal services and advancing internal client and customer experience.[38]

Moreover, digital transformation places noteworthy economic antagonism, embracing pressure on revenue and profit growth, by making possible more competition and separating winners from losers and so leading GCs are taking advantage of productivity-enhancing AI technologies, particularly planned for the legal services market, embracing efficiency and collaboration devices, such as contract management, e-discovery, and transaction support technologies along with transparency devices, including e-billing software, online bidding platforms. Hence, with the purpose of backing the demand for upgraded productivity, legal departments are expanding their use of technology.[39]

AI and related technologies are modeling the dynamics and modifying the operational and structural foundations of MNEs and so the top purposes for a digital strategy are refining process efficiency, augmenting customer experiences, improving employee productivity, and powering revenue growth. To that extent, the majority of CEOs of MNEs are organizing major investments in data and technology in order to remain competitive in this environment where customer desires and expectations are varying rapidly which means that AI technology has become an enterprise-wide imperative for most MNEs. In other words, digitization is a top priority among CEOs at large MNEs across the globe and they are investing in

[37] Omrane Guedhami, April Knill, William L. Megginson and Lemma W. Senbet, The dark side of globalization: Evidence from the impact of COVID-19 on multinational companies, Journal of International Business Studies (2022) 53, 1603–1640, P1630

[38] Marco Iansiti and Karim R. Lakhani, Competing in the Age of AI: Strategy and Leadership When Algorithms and Networks Run the World, 2020 Harvard Business School Publishing Corporation, p.3 (AI as "the ability of a digital computer or computer-controlled robot to perform tasks commonly associated with intelligent beings").

[39] Rob van der Meulen, Gartner Predicts Legal Technology Will Increase Threefold by 2025, GARTNER (Feb. 10, 2021), https://www.gartner.com/en/newsroom/press-releases/2020-02-10-gartner-predicts-legal-technology-budgets-will-in crease-threefold-by-2025

digital transformation by utilizing digital processes and they are marketing their digital, consumer-centric products and services, and the new digital roles and functions within their corporations.

AI brings competitive advantage to an enterprise, including improved product or service delivery models and data-driven insights and analytics that facilitate better strategic and functional decision-making. In fact, digital transformation is not happening as rapidly as one might assume and a few organizations adopt technologies effectively. There is a need of examining the interoperability of AI technology, examining the control of any AI technology contributing to the advancement of production and service. The legal disparity of regulating liability and functionality of various technologies along with security matters are holding back any progress.

It is stressed that digital tools and data-powered insights are utilized to drive decisions and customer-centricity while innovating and collaborating across the corporation drives sustainable action and generates value for all stakeholders.[40] In other words, companies use AI technologies to modify the value creation paths in order to remain competitive which requires structural changes in defeating barriers that deter their transformation effort.

It has to be taken into account that economic globalization drastically augmented the difficulty of running a legal department, at both the organizational and individual levels and so multinational legal departments are forced to deal with a range of complex new legal issues across multiple markets. It could be said that the emergence of e-commerce, digital platforms, and disruptive network effects lowered entry barriers across many markets and enabled new entrants to scale rapidly. Likewise, an amplified volatility of the marketplace and squeezed corporate profits are forcing incumbent corporations to transform due to the fact that without transformation, legal departments basically cannot keep up with work. It seems that the traditional market, conquered by large law corporations, failed responding to many of AI technology demands and so in today's corporate environment, legal functions are anticipated to digitally transform in harmony with the MNE itself with the purpose of delivering services efficiently and cost-effective. AAI technology transformation has to be followed by a legal support of the advancement because otherwise AAI technology might cause extra liability for MNEs. Moreover, a digitally transformed legal department can add enormous value to the MNE.

In other words, maximizing the legal function's value to companies appears most important to CEOs due to the global economy rebounds. Hence, facilitating transform risk management so that corporations can adapt to new realities and protect from future difficulties is central. It has to be taken into account that regardless of their intentions and efforts, most in-house legal teams are failing to keep pace with the complexity and accelerating rate of AI.[41]

[40] Daniel Englberger, Digital Culture: The Driving Force Of Digital Transformation, 8–10, 29 (World Economic Forum 2021)

[41] Mark A. Cohen, Law's Tipping Point Is About Digital Transformation, Customers, And Capital - Not Firm Partners, FORBES, June 2021 ("Legal can no longer operate as an insular, self-contained

11.6 Venture Capital and AI

It is worth mentioning here that AI utilization across businesses is on the uptick, there is some concern regarding the use of AI, involving algorithmic aversion and fear of machine bias.[42] Taking into account that an algorithm is as good as the data it works with, AI can identify and correct human bias, and multiple devices exist that identify and adjust for such.[43]

VC evolved to fund promising startups that otherwise lacked the established presence required to safeguard business loans in exchange for an equity position. Regardless of the advances in AI and VC's focus on tech startups, VC corporations themselves have failed to employ data analytics and machine learning in their own decision-making, relying instead on copying the investments of other corporations. The use of AI, by VC corporations, advances investment outcomes.[44]

Moreover, VC has shifted away from that of advisor offering governance and oversight to startups, to that of speculative hands-off financier. Even though originally VCs played active management roles in delivering both oversight and corporate governance, such is no longer the case and so VC corporations are less involved in developing and growing emergent businesses, in its place capitulating to the impulses of their founders whose business strategies are grounded on undermining the competition so as to dominate the market.[45] To that extent, VC corporations merely copy the investments made by other corporations. Also, while the absence of due diligence results in unsuccessful investment decisions, the use of AI in investment decision-making offers better investment results.

---

department; it must function as a proactive, data-driven, integrated pan-enterprise, holistic risk mitigating, agile business unit."). ACC, 2020 ACC Legal Operations Maturity Benchmarking Report 6–10 (2020) (assessing legal operations and defining legal operations as "optimizing legal services for the corporation . . . rooted in business fundamentals, leveraging processes, data and technology"). Survey, How Do You Turn Barriers into Building Blocks? 9 EY & Harvard Center on The Legal Profession (2021) (noting that 57% of business development leaders say that "inefficiencies in the contracting process have resulted in lost business.").

[42]Ronald Yu, What's Inside the Black Box? AI Challenges for Lawyers and Researchers, Legal Information Management 19, 2 (2019) (noting that persons must "be aware of the potential dangers of placing blind faith in the impartiality, reliability, and infallibility" of AI).

[43]Kimberly Houser, Artificial Intelligence and The Struggle Between Good and Evil, 60 Washburn L.J. 475, 482–286 (2021)

[44]Ilene H. Lang & Reggie Van Lee, Institutional Investors Must Help Close the Race and Gender Gaps in Venture Capital, Harv. Bus. Rev. (Aug. 27, 2020) Alex Wilhelm, Venture capital probably isn't dead, TECHCRUNCH (Aug. 6, 2021), https://techcrunch.com/2021/08/06/venture-capitalprobably-isnt-dead/("All signs seem to indicate that by 2022, for the first time, nontraditional tech investors — including hedge funds, mutual funds and the like — will invest more in private tech companies than traditional Silicon Valley-style venture capitalists will."

[45]Gig Levy-Weiss, How VCs Think: The Psychology That Drives Investing Decisions, NFX, https://www.nfx.com/post/how-vcs-think-investing-decisions/) (describing the psychological drivers of VC investing as the fear of missing out and fear of looking stupid);

Furthermore, AI can alter the entire VC landscape by opening the door for a greater number of successful startup openings, while concurrently expanding corporation investments which means that integrating AI into the decision-making process mitigates the influence of human bias and delivers more accurate decisions than those delivered by human experts. Thus, corporations that exploit objective, data-driven approaches to investment platforms will outperform those that do not and so incorporating data analytics into VC investment decision-making will augment profit opportunities and expand portfolio diversification.

11.7 E-MNEs

G.I. Zekos[46] has written that "an e-MNE can be defined as a virtual enterprise that has production facilities in various countries concerning tangible goods and an advanced network dealing with intangible goods and services achieved its management via cyberspace by humans or some actions be made by electronic agents such as electronic contracts and automated sales" and nowadays AI is utilized in the functioning of e-MNEs with imminent the emergence of AAI humanoids running AAI MNEs.

FDI flows enable digitalization along with innovation advancement of the economy and thereby digital multinational enterprises influence the digital development of host countries. Moreover, investment promotion policies concerning digitalization necessitate digital FDI and so the advancement of the digital economy promotes the level of innovation which means that countries use FDI strategically to build and expand their digital economies on a basis of a strategic national digital expansion plan. To that extent, Aneta Bobeniˇc Hintošová and Glória Bódy[47] argue that "there are some countries grouped in a particular cluster (especially around the group of Nordic countries) in which their advanced digital development can be considered as one of the driving forces for attracting more sustainable foreign direct investment."

It is worth mentioning here that solely digital MNEs functioning almost entirely in a virtual environment deliver their product and services fully digital. Besides, digital MNEs with mixed modes merge offline products and services with digitally enabled business models. Digital MNEs enter foreign markets without investing in physical assets.[48]Moreover, digital MNEs with mixed ways epitomize the majority of the economy as corporations progressively digitalize, first their distribution, then

[46]See G I Zekos, ECONOMICS AND LAW ON COMPETITION IN twenty-first CENTURY GLOBALIZATION, 2014, Nova Science Publishers, Inc. p xiv https://novapublishers.com/shop/economics-and-law-on-competition-in-21st-century-globalization/

[47]Bobenic Hintošová, A.; Bódy, G. Sustainable FDI in the Digital Economy. Sustainability 2023, 15, 10,794. https://doi.org/10.3390/su151410794P13

[48]World Employment and Social Outlook 2021: The Role of Digital Labour Platforms in Transforming the World of Work (Geneva: ILO).

their production course and finally their business pattern.[49] Simultaneously, corporations born as pure digital platforms are internalizing part or some of the production process of the services they are presenting. Tech start-ups made prevalent by the pandemic digitalization tapped equity markets to scale up and multiply their businesses.[50]

First of all, MNEs antagonize based on proprietary intangible assets, among other resources and competencies. The innovation activities of MNEs are dispersed globally shifting from a reliance on exploitation strategies such as seeking access to markets towards embracing exploration strategies. Also, MNEs' strategies have altered into exploration strategies by investing in R&D activities abroad with the purpose of retrieving specialized knowledge and capabilities that are location-bound.[51] Hence, MNEs placing their R&D investments in a foreign country evaluate the quality of the host country's innovation agenda and so investing in innovation capabilities through industrial policy has a substantial result on expanding the likelihood for attracting R&D-related FDI. Eliane Choquette et al.[52] argue that "while innovation framework and innovation capabilities matter in general, they are not significantly different in emerging markets compared with advanced economies. . .enhancing the innovation framework and capability of a country will increase the country's likelihood of attracting R&D-related FDI. Aligning policies for science, technology and innovation and industrial policies is at the core of building attractiveness for R&D-related FDI in emerging markets."

It has to be taken into account that pharmaceutical MNEs are undergoing pressure to regroup innovation processes by dropping costs and developing new drugs for the reason that existing patents are being eroded by competing generic products. Moreover, pharmaceutical and biotech industries are highly exposed to the forces of economic globalization.

It has to be taken into consideration that the availability of localized knowledge in the host country that is not available in the home country is motivating companies to go abroad with their R&D activities. Additionally, a state with higher tax rates is seen as detrimental to international competitiveness, and predominantly a country's competence to attract and retain MNEs. Moreover, MNEs located in high welfare spending countries have a lower probability of relocating to foreign markets related to MNEs in countries with lower levels of welfare spending. Thus, MNEs move

[49]Srinivasan, Niraja, and Lorraine Eden (2021). "Going digital multinationals: Navigating economic and social imperatives in a post-pandemic world", Journal of International Business Policy, 4, pp. 228–243.

[50]Trentini, Claudia (2021). "A reassessment of UNCTAD's transnationality indexes in the digital economy", Transnational Corporations, 28(3), pp. 201–-216.

[51]Papanastassiou, Marina (2021). "Understanding global research & development: fifty years of research on multinationals' R&D internationalization", EIBAZine, 28, pp. 7–9.

[52]Eliane Choquette, Stine Jessen Haakonsson, Peter D. Ørberg Jensenc and Søren Feodor Nielsen, Globalization of innovation: the moderating role of project-level investment strategy and country type in location choice for R&D-related FDI, Transnational Corporations Volume 28, 2021, Number 2. p 23,24

profits across borders and internalize these profit-shifting opportunities in their decision-making. Nigel Driffield et al.[53] argue that "a degree of trust between firms and host country governments is required on institution building and the delivery of welfare... the conventional wisdom of firms avoiding or relocating away from locations due to the associated additional costs of high welfare spending is questionable, but that firms need to be confident on the efficacy of this welfare expenditure."

Digital MNEs benefit from increased online global sales. For the reason that taxing rights refer to the physical presence of a corporation in the host economy, digitalization is disputing the fiscal policies of many jurisdictions. MNEs directly interacting with clients utilize their data to leverage network outcomes. Digitization permits firms to keep most of their assets in the country of origin and have commercial representatives in other countries. To that extent, OECD proposes a fairer distribution of profits and taxing rights among countries.[54]

It is worth mentioning here that globalization has made the fragmentation and outsourcing of production processes less costly, giving rise to GVCs, which are product-explicit series of interconnected production phases such as design, making of parts, assembly, and sales which means that each phase is adding value and being produced in different countries. Moreover, trade agreements increase bilateral trade in GVCs.[55] Also, higher levels of digitalization diminish the necessity for R&D internationalization when corporations are able to access this knowledge from their home countries. Hence, digitalization allows corporations to "orchestrate" GVCs and link knowledge and production globally.

It has to be taken into account that the digitization of data, the evolution of AI infrastructures, and the growth of digital processing and storage have contributed to the advancement of E-MNEs. AI digitalization generated automation, flexibility, and scalability which means that corporations have achieved specific advantages in intangibles and digital assets. Furthermore, the pandemic has caused a backlash against globalization and so rising protectionism. Niraja Srinivasan and Lorraine Eden[56] argue that "the going digital MNEs have the flexibility to shift to more digitally intensive production processes. We therefore believe that the pure brick-and-mortar companies that exist today will likely be replaced by hybrid business models that incorporate both digital and analog aspects in their global value chains."

E-MNEs exploit all resources via cyberspace and digital platforms but the need for physical functioning forces MNEs still to exploit resources on the ground. AAI

---

[53] Nigel Driffield, Holger Görg, Yama Temouri and Xiaocan Yuan, Multinational enterprises and the welfare state, Transnational Corporations Volume 29, 2022, Number 2 p1

[54] OECD/G20 (2021). "Statement on a two-pillar solution to address the tax challenges arising from the digitalisation of the economy", 8 October. www.oecd.org

[55] Antras, Pol (2020). "Conceptual aspects of global value chains", The World Bank Economic Review, 34(3), pp. 551–574.

[56] Niraja Srinivasan and Lorraine Eden, Going digital multinationals: Navigating economic and social imperatives in a postpandemic world, Journal of International Business Policy (2021) 4, 228–243 P 231

MNE will deal with electronic goods and services but the physical functioning and design of an AAI MNE will be achieved by utilizing resources on the ground as well because it is expected initially AAI humanoids will have a kind of material appearance/exterior.

References

1. Bobenic Hintošová, A., & Bódy, G. (2023). Sustainable FDI in the digital economy. *Sustainability, 15*, 10794. https://doi.org/10.3390/su151410794
2. Brummer, C., & Yadav, Y. (2019). Fintech and the innovation trilemma, 107 *GEO. L.J. 235*, 237–242.
3. Englberger, D. (2021). Digital culture: The driving force of digital transformation. *World Economic Forum, 29*, 8-10.
4. Lee, H.-H., & Park, D. (2020). *Post-COVID Asia: Deglobalization, fourth industrial revolution, and sustainable development*. World Scientific Publishing.
5. Stephenson, M. (2020). Digital FDI: Policies, regulations and measures to attract FDI in the digital economy. *World Economic Forum*. www.weforum.org, p. 16.
6. Driffield, N., Görg, H., Temouri, Y., & Yuan, X. (2022). Multinational enterprises and the welfare state. *Transnational Corporations, 29*(2), 1.
7. Papanastassiou, M. (2021). Understanding global research & development: Fifty years of research on multinationals' R&D internationalization. *EIBAZine, 28*, 7–9.
8. Crescenzi, R., Di Cataldo, M., & Giua, M. (2021). FDI inflows in Europe: Does investment promotion work? *Journal of International Economics, 132*, 103497.
9. Colino, S. M. (2021). The internationalization of China's foreign direct investment laws. *Fordham International Law Journal, 45*(2), 276–313.
10. Trentini, C. (2021). A reassessment of UNCTAD's transnationality indexes in the digital economy. *Transnational Corporations, 28*(3), 201–216.
11. World Employment and Social Outlook. (2021). *The role of digital labour platforms in transforming the world of work*. ILO.
12. Zekos, G. (2014). *Economics and law on competition in 21st century globalization*. Nova Science Publishers, p. xiv. https://novapublishers.com/shop/economics-and-law-on-competition-in-21st-century-globalization/

Chapter 12
Econometric Analysis of Digital Economy and Competition

12.1 Introduction

The global competition law systems have common features including prohibitions on certain horizontal agreements such as cartels, specified vertical restraints, and abuses of market power by companies. Moreover, sloppy competition law enforcement by countries produces ambiguity generating incentives for companies to consider these countries as "competition law havens" leading to distortions of competition in the countries involved and beyond.

It is worth mentioning here that freedom of competition covers the freedom of companies to choose their action parameters besides market power might impede both freedom of choice between different suppliers and freedom to decide on companies' action parameters in competition with other companies. Competition law has to take into account the effects of restrictive agreements, mergers, and business behavior on consumer welfare and also on a set of protected rights of competitors which might undergo losses through the infringements of these rights. Also, the United States has recognized the complementary purposes of the intellectual property and antitrust laws.

It is worth noting here that the digital economy is part of the global economy reforming the way we do business having inferences for FDI representing capital and technology or some intangible advantage is the act of establishing or acquiring a foreign subsidiary over which the investing corporation has extensive management control.[1] Also, the digital era has been portrayed by the appearance of the network

[1] G Zekos, IPRs' impact upon FDI, 2013 PhD Thesis Economics Department, University of Peloponnese Tripoli Hellas www.uop.gr. G Zekos, The Value of IPRs and Competitiveness Regarding FDI: Linear and Non-Linear Analysis 2013 Journal of Computational Optimization in Economics and Finance Volume 5 Issue 2, www.novapublishers.com. G Zekos, Impact of IPRs on FDI and Trade, 2013, The IUP Journal of Management Research, Vol. XII, No. 4. www.iupindia.jn, G Zekos, Interrelation of Intellectual Property Rights and Competitiveness: FDI inwards and FDI outwards, 2013 Journal of Intellectual Property Rights vol. 18 July 2013 p 338–350 www.niscair.

© The Author(s), under exclusive license to Springer Nature Switzerland AG 2023
G. I. Zekos, *Artificial Intelligence and Competition*, Contributions to Economics,
https://doi.org/10.1007/978-3-031-48083-6_12

society encompassing transformations triggered by digital technologies. Accordingly, the digital economy is bringing forward transformations grounded on the attentiveness of cyberspace-based technologies to the production and trade of goods and services which means that it not only affects the daily lives of people but also exemplifies an ever-greater part of the global economy.

It has to be taken into account that liberalization by removing barriers to FDI via establishment or acquisition causes enhanced access to world capital markets and the prospective to amplify the efficiency of the domestic financial sector via inward and outward financial-sector investment. Thus, there is a need of the identification of measures that can be taken to enable FDI flows[2] and so achieving the Sustainable Development Goals (SDGs). To that extent, investment promotion agencies are FDI-competent institutions in host countries implementing the measures contained in IFD Agreement.[3] Moreover, IFD Agreement focuses on FDI covering all sectors. Hence, investment facilitation denotes the setting up of a more transparent, effective, and investment-friendly business environment due to today's integrated digitally global economy and so permitting investors to invest.[4] In addition, according to the reward theory, reward is offered to inventors to recover their innovation costs.[5]

It has to be taken into consideration that AI is testing copyright and patent law, as the actual author and inventor is no longer a natural person, but a machine. Is creativity under attack from the rise of AI? Ai-Da Robot[6] gives evidence at the House of Lords alike a human illustrating the forthcoming developments requiring adaptation to tech advances. It is worth noting that in the future AAI humanoid robots will become visually indistinguishable from humans, the perils of autocorrect may still allow us to identify them. Art is an interpretation of reality and AAI robots will be able to capture the emotional expression of art. It could be said that AAI humanoid robots produce technology in a way that it could argued that technology is using technology to produce art. Are humans a technology that produces technology? It could be said that humans are a very advanced technology creations from a flexible material lasting for some time and the brain/spirit functioning of the body

res.in. G Zekos, 'Constructing a New IPRs index' [2012] 4 Web JCLI http://webjcli.ncl.ac.uk/2012/issue4/zekos4.html

[2]Karl P. Sauvant and Howard Mann, "Making FDI more sustainable: towards an indicative list of FDI sustainability characteristics", Journal of World Investment & Trade, vol. 20 (Dec. 2019), pp. 916–952. Karl P. Sauvant, How would a future WTO Agreement on Investment Facilitation for Development encourage sustainable FDI flows, and how could it be further strengthened?, https://ssrn.com/abstract=4084032

[3]Agreement on Investment Facilitation for Development. https://www.wto.org/english/tratop_e/invfac_public_e/factsheet_ifd.pdf

[4]Manjiao Chi, Investment Facilitation and Sustainable Development: Insufficiencies and Improvements of ASEAN Investment Treaties, Journal of International Economic Law, Volume 25, Issue 4, December 2022, Pages 611–626, https://doi.org/10.1093/jiel/jgac036

[5]Reto M. Hilty et al., Intellectual Property Justification for Artificial Intelligence (Max Planck Inst. For Innovation & Competition, Research Paper No. 20–02, 2020)

[6]https://www.youtube.com/watch?v=LWtlQZCcp8A A Creative Future inquiry, scrutinizing prospective challenges for the creative industries and looking at how they can adapt as tech advances.

material is residing even in another dimension after the end of material life. Are humans merely recycling material after the end of material life? Has the brain/spirit running the human body during life an end after death?

Antitrust and intellectual property policy enhance an innovative, dynamically competitive marketplace augmenting effectiveness and improving consumer welfare. Moreover, IPRs' role is pivotal by fostering competitive advantages grounded on the capacity for developing and sustaining innovation which demands protection via intellectual property rights. Also, IPR boosts dynamic competition by stirring up investments in new methods and differentiated products.

Is antitrust and the protection of intellectual property complementary or conflicting? How do the antitrust laws associate with the intellectual property laws? It could be said that the interface between competition policy and intellectual property protection trade off short-term inefficiencies but the two bodies of laws seem complementary due to the fact that both pursue a welfare objective. To that extent, competition law protects dynamic competition in the marketplace, while IPRs law safeguards the capability to receive a return on the investments required to innovate which means that both push competition among competitors to be the first to enter the marketplace with a required technology, product, or service.

Likewise, competition law draws a line between allowed business strategies and abuse of IPRs, a line which is often distorted by horizontal agreements, exclusionary licensing restrictions, tie-in agreements, disproportionate utilization of IPRs, and other selling practices. Also, there is a probable abuse of monopoly pricing, in particular in developing countries where operative substitutes to IPR-protected products may not be straight away available.[7] The limited monopolies established by IPRs are not per se anticompetitive or very exploitative but they only turn into anticompetitive when the IPR holder broadens those rights further than their intended and proper scope.

Even in digital markets, entry and exit takes place, shares change, and dominance comes and goes. In digital markets, technology alters quickly. To that extent, while large intellectual-property portfolios make entry more difficult, widespread licensing enables new entry and so IBM, AT&T, and Xerox all initially gained dominance based in part on large patent portfolios, but all afterwards lost their positions, and these industries are now much more competitive.

It has to be taken into account that AI-based devices and AI-produced output are flourishing in commerce and becoming global in society and so AI's economic value is accelerating.[8] Also, it has to be taken into consideration that in the near future, AAI algorithms, without human oversight or review, will evaluate whether a use of a copyrighted work constitutes a fair use.

---

[7]L. Peeperkorn, (2003), IP Licenses and Competition Rules: Striking the Right Balance, 26 World Competition 112.

[8]Neha Soni, Impact of Artificial Intelligence on Businesses: from Research, Innovation, Market, Deployment to Future Shifts in Business Models, CORNELL U. 1, 7 (2019), https://arxiv.org/abs/1905.02092 (worldwide spending on cognitive and AI systems will increase prominently from $12 billion in 2017 to $58 billion in 2021).

12.2 Property Rights and Competition

Taking into account that vehicles of innovation are intellectual property rights, the use of competition law to promote innovation is principally controversial for the reason that the integration between these two—sometimes opposing—forces is needed.

Patents are counted to be property rights resulting in a strong legal protection that "could lead to a weak application or even nonapplication of competition law." On the other hand, in many sectors, competition authorities make certain that competition law is applied in patent-related cases. Consequently, even if patents are considered as being strong property rights, competition law still applies to the advantage of consumers and competitive markets.

IP rights and particularly patents are special since they confer exclusionary rights upon the holder, which fits trickily with competition values. On the other hand, the possibility of companies to look for patents is part of competition.

On the patent law side, this means that the patent cannot be modified in its existence by any competition law consideration which means that the full protection of the patent system cannot help the patent holder to validate a possibly abusive behavior under the competition rules. On the competition law side, this means that the fundamental values of the competition rules, such as the abuse of a dominant position, can never be validated by patent law which means that even though a patent confers some kind of market power to the patent holder, it is validated by the need to incentivize innovation. To that extent, competition law is not impeded from being applicable but must accept the granting of IP rights.

The D.C. Circuit and the European Commission place intellectual property inside competition policy and the concept of placing intellectual property within antitrust, and limiting the scope of intellectual property, has common law roots in the English Statute of Monopolies of 1623.[9] Intellectual property rights are granted only to provide an incentive for innovation.[10] Competition analysis sees marketplace competition as an imperative tool for motivating innovation and loss of marketplace competition from a broad grant of intellectual property rights might result in less innovation over time than the broad grant produces.[11] Intellectual property right and the capacity of a competitor to contest markets that are competitive must be balanced

[9]Louis B. Schwartz Et Al., Free Enterprise And Economic Organization: Antitrust 1–2 (sixth ed. 1983)

[10]Verizon Commc'ns Inc. v. Law Offices of Curtis V. Trinko, LLP, 540 U.S. 398, 412 (2004) (declining to recognize "expansion" of antitrust liability where the conduct was subject to review by state and federal regulatory agencies because "additional benefit to competition provided by antitrust enforcement will tend to be small"). SCM Corp. v. Xerox Corp., 645 F.2d 1195 (2d Cir. 1981) (holding that the refusal to license plain paper copier patents was not a violation of Section 2 of the Sherman Act).

[11]United States v. Alum. Co. of Am., 148 F. 2d 416, 427 (2d Cir. 1945) ("[I]mmunity from competition is a narcotic, and rivalry is a stimulant, to industrial progress . . . ."). F.M. Scherer, Antitrust, Efficiency, and Progress, in REVITALIZING ANTITRUST IN ITS SECOND

and there is a need to weigh the benefits of allowing competition against the cost to the economic policies advanced by the intellectual property right.

Competition law is connected to IP when it comes to producing growth and innovation in the economy. To that extent, on the balance between IP and competition law, the ECJ's conception is disclosed in the AstraZeneca judgment where the Court ruled that "the illegality of abusive conduct under Article [102 TFEU] is unrelated to its compliance or non-compliance with other legal rules and, in the majority of cases, abuses of dominant positions consist of behavior which is otherwise lawful under branches of law other than competition law."[12] In other words, even if an undertaking acts lawfully under the patent rules, general law and administrative procedures of a member state, competition law affects the undertaking's conduct if there is an abuse of competition law. Yet, if the conditions of Art 102 TFEU are met, competition law solves a market failure problem. The court ensures continued innovation and dynamic competition in pharmaceuticals and related sectors. In Lundbeck,[13] the Commission considered that the originator and generic firms were prospective competitors that the agreement led the generic firms to reduce their independent efforts to compete on the market and that the motivations to compete were diminished by the value transfer from originator to generic companies. The European Commission found that the pharmaceutical undertaking Lundbeck had abused its dominant position in violation of Art. 102 TFEU.[14] To that extent, the dominant purpose in the specific facts of the case was to make possible market entry and keep competitive efforts in the market for the particular drug. Hence, the Lundbeck decision of the European Commission promotes the understanding that it will be very difficult to demonstrate that patent strategies are abusive, especially since the application of competition rules could interfere 'with the patent regime itself and its very rationale".

It is defined in the Reckitt Benckiser decision[15] that competition law only interferes with patent law, if the domain of the lawful exercise of the patent is left and the patent holder employs practices that are not fully covered by the patent and so in such a situation the competition authorities in the United Kingdom and the EU suspect anticompetitive behavior that cannot be rationalized by the simple exercise of the existing patent. Since a concentration does not create or strengthen a dominant position, effective competition is not considerably impeded in the common market

CENTURY 130, 141 (Harry First et al. eds., 1991) ("More competition stimulates and accelerates innovation within limits . . . .").

[12] European Commission, COM(2020) 842 final, https://eur-lex.europa.eu/legalcontent/en/TXT/?qid=1608116887159&uri=COM%3A2020%3A842%3AFIN. Case C-457/10 P. AstraZeneca AB and AstraZeneca plc v European Commission. Judgment of the Court (First Chamber), 6 December 2012.

[13] Case T-472/13 Lundbeck v Commission.

[14] Valentine Korah, Intellectual Property Rights And The EC Competition Rules 2 (2006)0.1.2 (2006) (explaining that without the benefits and incentives of the patent, pharmaceutical companies would never invest in R&D for some drugs).

[15] Case No COMP/M.1632 -RECKITT + COLMAN /BENCKISER

and so the Commission has decided not to oppose the notified operation affirming it compatible with the common market.[16] Nonetheless, a patent is not equal to having a dominant position and so even if a patent is a quasi-monopoly right granting exclusionary powers on time, there can be similar competing products on the market with market shares high enough to inhibit the existence of dominant positions. On the other hand, if the authority can prove a dominant position and pinpoints practices that are not normal competition or competition on the merits, then the abusive behavior of the dominant pharmaceutical corporation could be targeted by the competition rules.

12.3 Liability and AI

AI systems undertake to improve societal well-being and boost efficiency. On the other hand, liability rules have to tackle who bears responsibility for accidents in which AI systems are implicated. Also, the appearance of autonomous AAI systems moves control over these systems away from owners and users and so brings forward the need of human society to attribute in a way full legal personality which will mean liability of AAI systems/humanoids. As AI systems become more autonomous, it also becomes difficult to trace back outcomes to human decisions, and to assign liability to a certain player.[17] In other words, autonomy removes control away from users, and probably from manufacturers. It has to be taken into account that AI systems that can act independently will be unpredictable and so the more autonomy AI systems accomplish, the more unsubstantiated it becomes to assign legal responsibility for their actions to humans.

It is worth noting that a natural person cannot recover noneconomic damages for any emotional or mental distress attributable to the defendant's infringement. Moreover, the European Communities' 2004 Intellectual Property Rights Enforcement Directive (IPRED) compels member states of EU to grant the prevailing plaintiff compensation not only for the "negative economic consequences," such as lost profits stemming from infringement but also for "appropriate cases of . . . moral prejudice"[18] by encompassing both reputational harm and mental anguish and so European courts have awarded such damages in copyright, trademark, and patent cases.[19] Likewise, artists can file suits under a portion of the US Copyright Act

[16] Article 6(1)(b) of Council Regulation (EEC) No. 4064/89

[17] Miriam Buiten, Alexandre de Streel, Martin Peitz, The Law and Economics of AI Liability, Discussion Paper No. 371

[18] Directive 2004/48/EC of the European Parliament and of the Council of 29 April 2004 on the Enforcement of Intellectual Property Rights, art. 13(1)(a), 2004 O.J. (L 195) 16, 23 (EC)

[19] Case C-280/15, Nikolajeva v. Multi Protect OÜ, ECLI:EU:C:2016:467, §§ 20, 57 (June 22, 2016) (defining "moral prejudice" as including "mental suffering"); Case C-99/15, Liffers v. Producciones Mandarina SL, ECLI:EU:C:2016:173, § 17 (Mar. 17, 2016) ("[M]oral prejudice, such as damage to the reputation of the author of a work, constitutes . . . a component of the prejudice actually suffered

known as the Visual Artists Rights Act (VARA) granting upon the authors of certain works of visual art a "moral right" of integrity consisting of the right "to prevent any intentional distortion, mutilation, or other modification . . . which would be prejudicial to his or her honor or reputation," and "to prevent any destruction of a work of recognized stature."[20]

According to Directive 2004/48/EC, courts across the EU render awards of noneconomic damages, as appropriate, across the full range of IP cases[21] and so under the Directive, breach of confidence and passing off would not be included within the definition of intellectual property. Moreover, damages for moral prejudice are granted even when the owner also seeks economic damages.[22] Under the Directive, damages for noneconomic harm, embracing moral prejudice, are available for the violation of other IP rights, including trademarks and patents. The Court of Appeal of Madrid assumed that "moral damages" encompassing psychological suffering are compensable in a patent infringement action.[23] Furthermore, German courts grant noneconomic damages for trademark infringement, where economic damages or other measures would not fully compensate. In addition, US courts permit IP owners to recover noneconomic damages for harm to their reputation or goodwill triggered by an act of infringement, but they almost never grant damages for emotional harm outside the right of publicity context. Besides, courts in the EU are conferring damages for "moral prejudice" across the range of IP cases, embracing patent cases. T. Cotter[24] argues that "courts should recognize reputational harm as a potentially cognizable injury throughout all of the branches of IP law but that damages for emotional harm should be limited to the right of publicity and moral rights matters."

It is worth noting that AI machines make most of the decisions in the creative process without being specifically directed by humans. To that extent, robots and the

---

by the rightholder."); See Hanrahan v. Ramirez, No. 2:97–CV–7470 RAP RC, 1998 WL 34369997, at *5–6 (C.D. Cal. June 3, 1998) (a court awarded a default judgment that included damages for emotional harm). Xavier Seuba, The Global Regime For The Enforcement Of Intellectual Property Rights 260–61 (2017) (differentiating "moral prejudice," which "is closely related to rights connected with the personality of the individual," from "adverse effects on the reputation of a trademark" or to "the perception of the public towards the patented invention," which are non-economic outcomes but not "moral damages" as such).

[20] Castillo v. G&M Realty L.P., 950 F.3d 155 (2d Cir.), cert. Denied, 141 S. Ct. 363 (2020). 17 U.S. C. §§ 106A(a)(3)(A)–(B)

[21] Case C-280/15, Nikolajeva v. Multi Protect OÜ, ECLI:EU:C:2016:467, §§ 20, 57 (June 22, 2016) (holding that moral prejudice damages are not available for the unauthorized use of a European trademark prior to its registration, under article 9 of Council Regulation (EC) No 207/2009).

[22] Liffers v. Producciones Mandarina SL. 252Case C-99/15, Liffers v. Producciones Mandarina SL, ECLI:EU:C:2016:173, § 17 (Mar. 17, 2016).

[23] A.P., Jan. 15, 2016 (R.G.D., No. 2272) (Spain); Thomas F. Cotter, Damages for Moral Prejudice in Spain and Elsewhere, COMPAR. PAT. REMEDIES (June 20, 2016), http://comparativepatentremedies.blogspot.com/2016/06/damages-for-moral-prejudice-in-spain.html

[24] Thomas F. Cotter, Damages for Noneconomic Harm in Intellectual Property Law, April 2021 Hastings Law Journal Vol. 72:1055

algorithms that run them injure people every day which means that when robots and algorithms injure people recovery and justice prove elusive due to the fact that many modes of criminal and civil liability necessitate that a legally cognizable defendant essentially did something harmful, rather than indirectly triggering some injury. The European Union's High-Level Expert Group on AI has pronounced that: AI systems must be human-centric, resting on a commitment to their use in the service of humanity and the common good in order to augment the advantages of AI systems while at the same time preventing and curtailing their risks.[25] On the other hand, G.I. Zekos considers that AAI technology will create humanoid robots with full functionality better even that of humans which means the emergence of the AAI society necessitating legal personality for AAI creatures.

Accountability is the law's most direct and useful device for turning behavior in socially constructive directions but there is presently no general framework for algorithmic accountability.[26] Those who produce and develop algorithms are not held accountable to society and there is a need for establishing the framework for their accountability. It is obvious that legally responsible AAI humanoid robots will have corporate legal powers and corporate legal liabilities.[27]

Taking into account that companies[28] are by definition passive instruments, since they are artificially formed legal persons that can only act through their officers and employees, protections for company's "sincere religious belief[s]" even when they affect individual healthcare rights are upheld.[29] Moreover, companies enjoy constitutionally protected free speech rights even when they compete with individual speech rights.[30] Thus, under present AI technology, AI companies can be regarded as legal persons controlled by the individuals that have created the AI company. To that extent, AAI humanoid robots will be granted legal personality due to the fact that they will have human qualities acting autonomously and of course their AAI companies will function under their control.

Furthermore, corporations depend on individuals to do anything; but many algorithms, once designed, can become self-executing on particular tasks which means that the self-executing quality of these autonomous algorithmic assistants reduces the necessity for human intervention beyond the employment of the algorithm and the opening placement of the sensors. It is characteristic that while humans

[25]HIGH-LEVEL EXPERT GRP. ON A.I., ETHICS GUIDELINES FOR TRUSTWORTHY AI 4 (2019), https://ec.europa.eu/digital-single-market/en/news/ethics-guidelines-trustworthy-ai

[26]Lee Rainie & Janna Anderson, Pew Rsch. Ctr., Code-Dependent: Pros And Cons Of The Algorithm Age 5 (2017), https://www.pewresearch.org/internet/wp-content/uploads/sites/9/2017/02/PI_2017.02.08_Algorithms_FINAL.pdf Nicholas Diakopoulos & Sorelle Friedler, How to Hold Algorithms Accountable, Mit Tech. Rev. (Nov. 17, 2016), https://www.technologyreview.com/s/602933/how-to-hold-algorithms-accountable

[27]W. Robert Thomas, How and Why Corporations Became (and Remain) Persons Under the Criminal Law, 45 Fla. St. U. L. Rev. 479, 504–14 (2018)

[28]Jaguar Cars, Inc. v. Royal Oaks Motor Car Co., 46 F.3d 258, 265 (3d Cir. 1995)

[29]Burwell v. Hobby Lobby Stores, Inc., 573 U.S. 682, 685, 720 (2014)

[30]Citizens United v. FEC, 558 U.S. 310, 340–43 (2010)

are programming algorithms, once the algorithm has been set, the trading is self-executing and so there is no time to apply human judgment to individual decisions about whether to trade or not in stock exchange. Besides, prior trading was so fully automated, human judgment acted as something of a circuit-breaker.[31]

It has to be taken into consideration that companies develop, run, and keep the world's most advanced algorithms and so algorithmic action is corporate action such as firms act through their employees which means that companies act through their algorithms. Thus, holding companies liable for the things they do through their employees urges firms to certify that their employees behave responsibly means that accepting that companies act through their algorithms would comparably urge firms to exercise accountable control over algorithmic injuries. Hence, algorithms become an extension of the corporate person, not persons in their own right. Diamantis[32] argues that "the law must find some sweeping accountability mechanism for algorithmic injury if it is to have any chance of protecting us in the coming age of automation."

It is worth noting that the law holds firms liable when they control the source of the injury and so since the balance between manpower and automation continues to tip dangerously in favor of the efficiency, accuracy, and power of algorithms, the present model of corporate liability premised on injurious human conduct will slide into obsolescence which means that the AI liability must be endorsed.[33]

12.4 Authorship Under AI and AAI Technology

In many jurisdictions, authors can be solely natural persons and no legal entities and accordingly, creations of copyrighted works are closely linked to the features typical just to humanity. It is characteristic that the US Copyright Office permits to register only the works produced by humans as copyrighted works declining to register the works produced by AI machines or produced by animals. While its refusal does not bar granting of copyright protection to such works, registration can be indispensable for enforcing copyrights in the US works before courts.[34]

---

[31] Michal S. Gal, Algorithmic Challenges to Autonomous Choice, 25 Mich. Tech. L. Rev. 59, 70 (2018)

[32] Mihailis E. Diamantis, Algorithms Acting Badly: A Solution from Corporate Law, 2021 The George Washington Law Review Vol. 89:801 P 855

[33] Phillip E. Areeda & Herbert Hovenkamp, Antitrust Law: An Analysis Of Antitrust Principles And Their Application §§ 260–62 (fifth Ed. 2020).

[34] U.S. Copyright Office, Compendium Of U.S. Copyright Office Practices § 313.2 (3d ed. 2021) (requiring that "[t]o qualify as a work of 'authorship' a work must be created by a human being", and providing for that "[t]he U.S. Copyright Office will not register works produced by nature, animals, or plants") Annemarie Bridy, The Evolution of Authorship: Work Made by Code, 39 COLUM. J.L & ARTS 395 (2016) (pointing out that in the late 1950s the U.S. Copyright Office refused to register a song entitled "Push Button Bertha" and generated by the computer programmed

Is human creativity hidden in the AI programming? Does human creativity is generated by AI tools? Lately, AAI technologies have gone even beyond generating musical or artistic works that sound or look like works produced by certain authors or in specific styles generated by generative adversarial networks which empower AI systems to produce their own creations. Moreover, the generating system learns and advances its capabilities in producing requested works in which quality is examined by the discriminating system. In addition, in generative adversarial networks, the role of humans in resourceful processes is diminished to the minimum since all the processes happen only between AI systems.

The AI is doing something functionally equivalent to a human author and so if AI-produced works are of value to the public, then the IP system has to be applicable. AI-produced and created works cover the full range of human cultural endeavor from music to film, and from literature to the visual arts. Presently, works that are autonomously made by machines or AI are not copyrightable in most jurisdictions around the world, which means that they presently belong to the public domain. In the United States, Australia, Canada, and most of Europe, copyright attaches only to "original" works of authorship originating from a human author.[35] In some jurisdictions, specific provisions have been enacted regarding computer-generated works, deeming the author to be the person who makes the arrangements necessary for their creation.

It is argued that a work that lacks human intervention is generally not suitable for copyright protection.[36] In the Berne Convention, regardless of no clear definition of author is provided, it is possible to assume that the only imaginable author is a human being. Moreover, there are references to the nationality of the author and the death of the author.[37] The TRIPS Agreement refers to "the life of a natural person" for the term of protection.[38] As for the European legal framework, the Directive refers plainly to the life of the author and the Software Directive offers a general and consolidated rule according to which natural persons are generally the only ones entitled to authorship.[39] To that extent, the current IP systems for copyright and

---

by Martin Klein and Douglas Bolitho). Naruto v. Slater, 2016 U.S. Dist. LEXIS 11041, at 8 (N.D. Cal. Jan. 28, 2016) (U.S.) ("the Copyright Act does not 'plainly' extend the concept of authorship or statutory standing to animals."). U.S. Copyright Act, §§101 and 411.

[35] Telstra Corp. Ltd. v. Phone Directories Co. Pty. Ltd., [2010] F.C.A.F.C. 149 at ¶ 133–34, 137 (requiring that an original work must be the product of human authorship); Eva-Maria Painer v. Standard Verlags GmbH and Others, C-145/10, [2012] E.C.R. I-12594 at I-12622.

[36] Gervais, D. (2020) 'Is Intellectual Property Law Ready for Artificial Intelligence?'. GRUR International 69 (2).

[37] Article 3 Berne Convention for the Protection of Literary and Artistic Works of 1886. Articles 6bis (2), 7(5), 7bis Berne Convention.

[38] Article 12 TRIPS Agreement

[39] Directive 2006/116/EC on the term of protection of copyright and certain related rights (Term Directive). Article 1 (1)(2) Term Directive. Directive 2009/24/EC on the legal protection of computer programs (Software Directive). Article 2(1)(2) Software Directive.

patents do not stipulate legal stability, since many issues and implications related to AI-generated outputs remain unresolved.

AI challenges another prerequisite that needs to be met that of originality and a work is originally eligible for copyright protection if it is the author's own intellectual creation.[40] In Infopaq,[41] the Court of Justice of the European Union (CJEU) has harmonized the standard of originality for every subject matter, not only for databases, computer programs, and photographs. Moreover, the CJEU specified that an intellectual creation is the author's own if it reflects their personality taking place when the author is able to express their creative capabilities by making free and creative selections.[42] Hence, the originality test is connected to the human being as the only comprehendible author of a creative work. Indeed, if a work is original in the meaning that it must reflect the personality of the author and has his/her sole and personal touch, such work is deemed as an extension of the author's persona which even advanced AI systems do not have. On the other hand, the forthcoming AAI technology via humanoid robots will reflect the personality of the AAI author.

At present, AI systems have no legal personhood and consequently cannot hold rights deriving from the status of inventor which means that they cannot transfer or assign any rights, nor own an invention. Moreover, the solution approved by the EPO is that the owner of an AI machine is also the owner of any output produced by that machine.

People are inclined to anthropomorphize robots, attributing to AI human attributes and emotions owing to the notion that the AI is doing something functionally equivalent to a human author. AAI humanoid robots will function in a way far better than humans and humans will not be able to understand and live in an AAI world.

It is argued that AI is "ontologically" incapable of authorship.[43] Whether or not the AI is generating outputs that are facially equivalent to human-authored works, the AI lacks the intentionality, creative agency, and understanding needed to participate in authorship as a relational and communicative act. On the other hand, AAI will have the intentionality, creative agency, and understanding needed to participate in authorship as a relational and communicative act in the AAI world. In other words, the technicality and spirituality of AAI creations will be far away from the current human creations through the use of current AI technology since the basis of AAI copyright will be the functionality of an AAI world where humans have to find a place if they abolish the control of the world and the technology.

[40] Article 3(1) Directive 96/9/EC on the legal protection of databases of 11 March 1996 (Database Directive); Article 1(3) Software Directive; Article 6 Term Directive.

[41] Judgment of 16 July 2009, Infopaq International A/S v Danske Dagblades Forening, C-5/08, EU: C:2009:465.

[42] Judgment of 1 December 2011, Eva-Maria Painer v Standard Verlags GmbH, et al., C-145/10, EU:C:2011:798.

[43] Carys Craig & Ian Kerr, The Death of the AI Author, 52 Ottawa L. Rev. 31 (2020), https://rdo-olr.org/2021/the-death-of-the-ai-author/

12.5 Copyright and AAI

Copyright law serves a public interest by encouraging authorship as a social and creative practice and the spreading of works to contribute to a vibrant public domain. To that extent, copyright protects original works of authorship, irrespective of the medium in which a copy of the work is reproduced and the Supreme Court[44] held that copyright can protect the pattern printed on a cheerleading uniform, but declined to determine whether the patterns at issue were sufficiently original for copyright protection. Correspondingly, many works of minimal and conceptual art undoubtedly lack any original elements that qualify for copyright protection. Copyright cannot protect works that consist of a single color or a modest pattern of colors and lines.[45]

The law should be technologically neutral and so copyright law should be written to be independent of any particular technology continuing to apply equally across technologies as they occur, without favoring or discriminating between new and old and so the conventional balance between authors and users should be preserved in the digital environment[46] which means that copyright should be treated by AI technology accordingly. Tech-neutrality is about the equal treatment in law of effectively analogous activities and so a digital streaming service may be subject to the same legal rules as a cable broadcaster if their activities have the same outcome, despite the different technological processes involved. Thus, reading online should be regarded by law in the same way as reading a physical paper, since the act is functionally the same no matter the medium. Likewise, selling a digital copy online should implicate the same copyright interests as selling a physical copy over the counter.[47]

Copyright law offers exclusive rights in expressive works so as to incentivize creative activities. On the other hand, fair use prevents copyright from excessively stymying public access and so when access to and use of present works is required for new creativity. It has to be taken into account that analogies can create false equivalents while also concealing the disruptive force of technological change and so we cannot assume that neutral legal treatment will produce a functionally equivalent legal effect which means that when the risks and opportunities shift considerably with the affordances of novel technologies, the costs and benefits of copyright control should be re-evaluated. Moreover, the emphasis is not only on the

---

[44] Star Athletica, LLC v. Varsity Brands137 S. Ct. 1002, 1012 n.1 (2017) ("We do not today hold that the surface decorations are copyrightable. We express no opinion on whether these works are sufficiently original to qualify for copyright protection.").

[45] Guy A. Rub, Owning Nothingness: Between the Legal and the Social Norms of the Art World, 2019 BYU L. Rev. 1147 (2020) (observing that many works of minimal and conceptual art seem to lack any copyrightable elements).

[46] Robertson v. Thomson Corp., 2006 S.C.C. 43;

[47] Am. Broad. Co. v. Aereo, Inc., 134 S. Ct. 2498 (2014) [Aereo] (one-to-one transmission of a digitized signal was sufficiently "cable-like" to constitute public performance as a cable transmission would).

similar outcomes of specific technological actions or processes but also on the broader outcomes of the technology and its affordances due to the fact that the key objective of copyright is not to reward the labor of authors, but "[t]o promote the Progress of Science and useful Arts."[48] In Google LLC v. Oracle, the Supreme Court considered that the "creative 'progress' is the fundamental constitutional objective of copyright itself."[49] The Supreme Court of Canada explained that fair rewards for copyright creators offer essential incentives, guaranteeing that there is a steady flow of creative works injected into the public sphere recognizing creators' rights, but authorial control is not favored over the public interest.[50]

It is worth noting that contrasting a European model prioritizing a copyright holder's control over a copyrighted work, US copyright law is largely economic in character, balancing the public's right to use a work and an author's right to profit from it.[51] It could be said that authorial control augments author incentives.[52]Furthermore, the trade off, between public access to copyrighted works and making certain that authors will still have reason to generate works to contribute to that rich corpus, is the "access/incentives" trade off.

The Supreme Court[53] has explicated that the resulting work does not "merely 'supersede the objects' of the original creation . . . but instead adds something new, with a further purpose or different character, altering the first with new expression, meaning, or message." It seems that the Supreme Court, in Eldred v. Ashcroft,[54] generated a copyright system that makes it difficult for users to ascertain whether a work is copyrighted and who owns it.

DMCA was enacted to modernize copyright protection for the digital age.[55] Principally, courts look at whether the copyrighted work is factual or fictional, as fictional works are characteristically given greater protection in a fair use analysis.[56] Fair use functions as a two-sided balancing test in which strengthening the defendant's justification for its use against the influence of that usage on the incentives of

---

[48] Feist Publ'ns Inc. v. Rural Tel. Serv. Co. Inc., 499 U.S. 340, 349–350 (1991)

[49] Google LLC v. Oracle America, Inc., 593 U.S. ____ 25 (2021)

[50] York Univ. v. Canadian Copyright Licensing Agency (Access Copyright), 2021 S.C.C. 32 at ¶ 93–94. Théberge v. Galerie d'Art du Petit Champlain Inc., 2002 S.C.C. 34 at ¶ 11–12,

[51] Neil Netanel, Alienability Restrictions and the Enhancement of Author Autonomy in United States and Continental Copyright Law, 12 Cardozo Arts & Ent. L.J. 1, 7 (1994) (explaining that U.S. copyright law applies "traditional property principles" while European copyright law "focuses on the author and his personal relationship to the work").

[52] Jeanne C. Fromer, Expressive Incentives in Intellectual Property, 98 VA. L. REV. 1745, 1754 (2012)

[53] Campbell v. Acuff-Rose Music, Inc., 510 U.S. 569, 579 (1994)

[54] Eldred v. Ashcroft, 537 U.S. 186 (2003)

[55] 112 Stat. 2860 (1998) (codified as amended in scattered sections of the U.S. Code).

[56] *Harper & Row, Publrs. v. Nation Enters.*, 471 U.S. 539, 594, 105 S. Ct. 2218, 2248 (1985). Lenz v. Universal Music Corp., 815 F.3d 1145, 1158 (ninth Cir. 2016), cert. Denied, 137 S. Ct. 416 (2016) (Smith, J., concurring) (explaining that fair use must be considered under a subjective good faith standard)

the plaintiff. Besides, the transformative "purpose" permits courts to weigh whether or not a new use is novel enough to exempt it from copyright protection or whether permitting the use to go forward would damage the copyright owner financially and so risk undermining copyright's incentive function.[57] It could be said that in "functionally transformative" cases where no new works are generated, there is a need for compensating authors and rights holders due to a "permitted-but-paid" regime.[58]

Furthermore, fair use is not the only device that copyright law utilizes to remove a copyright owner's control over the licensing of creative works. Thus, the Copyright Act summarizes compulsory licensing regimes entailing rights holders to license their works to certain types of licensors at government-set prices.[59] The concept of transformative fair use has presented a needed channel for permitting some uses to take place, but the fair use doctrine has been unable to accommodate others. Fair use cannot alone permit all such uses to succeed while still respecting copyright's financial incentive function. Compulsory copyright licensing makes available a useful approach to dealing with some utility-expanding technologies.

It could be argued that the existence of the fair use doctrine acknowledges that some socially valuable uses of copyrighted works should be allowed, even though it moderates, an author's motivation to invent which means that reduced inducement to produce is legitimate if the social value of the infringing use is high.[60]

It has to be taken into consideration that the market harm element looks to the copyright holder, by weighing "the benefit the public will derive if the use is permitted and the personal gain the copyright owner will receive if the use is denied."[61] and so courts use the market harm issue as a proxy for damages recovery, to assess how much the copyright owner would be due if the use were held to be not fair.

Does a service facilitating "resale" of digital music files is infringing[62]? It is worth noting that there are limits to the utility-expanding fair use.[63] In Authors Guild v. Google, Inc.,[64] the Second Circuit found fair use for the Google Books Project's

---

[57] Kienitz v. Sconnie Nation LLC, 766 F.3d 756, 758 (seventh Cir. 2014) ("To say that a new use transforms the work is precisely to say that it is derivative and thus, one might suppose, protected under § 106(2).");

[58] Jane C. Ginsburg, Fair Use for Free, or Permitted-but-Paid?, 29 Berkeley Tech. L.J. 1383, 1383 (2014)

[59] 17 U.S.C. §§ 111, 114–118

[60] Campbell v. Acuff-Rose Music, Inc., 510 U.S. 569, 591–92 (1994).

[61] Bill Graham Archives v. Dorling Kindersley Ltd., 448 F.3d 605, 613 (2d Cir. 2006) Swatch Grp. Mgmt. Servs. Ltd. v. Bloomberg L.P., 756 F.3d 73, 90 (2d Cir. 2014. Jeanne C. Fromer, Market Effects Bearing on Fair Use, 90 WASH. L. REV. 615, 630 (2015)

[62] Capitol Recs., LLC v. ReDigi Inc., 910 F.3d 649 (2d Cir. 2018).

[63] Chronicle Books, LLC v. Audible, Inc., No. 19-CV-07913 (S.D.N.Y. Aug. 23, 2019).

[64] Authors Guild v. Google, Inc., 804 F.3d 202, 215 (2d Cir. 2015) Cambridge Univ. Press v. Albert, 906 F.3d 1290, 1299 (11th Cir. 2018) (reversing and remanding the district court's fair use determination and reiterating the court's prior fourth-factor holdings).

creation of a text-searchable database of millions of books which means that the court held that this service, offered "otherwise unavailable information about the originals" rather than a market substitute. Moreover, derivative works over which the author of the original has exclusive rights are those that re-present the protected features of the original work, its expressive content, altered into a reformed configuration, such as the conversion of a novel into a film, the translation of a writing into a different language, the reproduction of a painting in the form of a poster or postcard, and modification of a musical composition for different instruments.[65]

In Fox News Network v. TVEyes,[66] the court stated that the service's clip-viewing characteristic was "transformative" for the reason that it helped "users to isolate, from an ocean of programming, material that is responsive to their interests and needs, and to access that material with targeted precision." Moreover, the court also observed that TVEyes "undercuts" copyright owner licensing revenue and in so doing "usurped" the copyright owners' market and so due to this market harm, the court refused to find fair use and confirmed an injunction preventing TVEyes from displaying clips of the copyrighted programs.

It is worth mentioning here that the Digital Performance Right in Sound Recordings Act (DPRA) refers to the complexities of applying existing copyright law to new forms of digital dissemination.[67] It has to be taken into consideration that copyright infringement influences reputation: by instigating a loss of exclusivity, harm to the owner's reputation for originality, and brand damage.[68]

The Internet Archive is a digital library with the mission of "universal access to all knowledge" offering free public access to collections of digitized materials and, to that extent, the Open Library is a project of the Internet Archive.[69] It is worth noting that the Internet Archive has to operate under the principle of Fair Use which protects digital book preservation projects by Google Books and HathiTrust. On the

[65] Authors Guild v. Google, Inc., 804 F.3d 202, 225 (2d Cir. 2015)

[66] Fox News Network, LLC v. TVEyes, Inc., 883 F.3d 169 (2d Cir. 2018)

[67] 17 U.S.C. §§ 106, 114–115

[68] Garcia v. Google, Inc., 786 F.3d 733, 745–46 (ninth Cir. 2015) Bollea v. Gawker Media, LLC, 913 F. Supp. 2d 1325, 1329–30 (M.D. Fla. 2012) (ruling on a motion for a preliminary injunction and holding that only commercial harm, not privacy or emotional harm, would constitute "irreparable harm in the copyright sense"); Stern v. Does, 978 F. Supp. 2d 1031, 1050 (C.D. Cal. 2011) (evaluating whether the plaintiff filed a copyright action in bad faith and stating that, "their dubiousness aside," plaintiff's claims for emotional distress arising from alleged infringement are not "compensable under the Copyright Act");

[69] https://www.loc.gov/rr/program/bib/ebooks/external.html. "The Internet Archive includes the full text of more than 2.5 million e-books, including e-books supplied by the Library of Congress. Books can be read online or downloaded and read in a variety of formats. E-books from the Internet Archive can also be found through Open Library, an Internet Archive initiative devoted to texts." https://www.loc.gov/rr/program/bib/ebooks/devicesformats.html. "Library of Congress publications are available for free download to the Kindle from the Internet Archive. ... The iPad can be used as an e-reader via apps such as iBooks, which support both ePub (.epub) and PDF (.pdf) formats. Both formats are available from the Internet Archive."

other hand, a federal judge[70] determined that the Internet Archive is liable for copyright infringement for a book-lending library. Moreover, in Hachette v. Internet Archive case, the dispute involves the way libraries lend eBooks and Internet Archive ("IA") Website incorporates millions of public domain eBooks that users can download for free and read without restrictions. To that extent, while the publishers have established a prima facie case of copyright infringement,[71] IA argued that this infringement was justified by the doctrine of fair use.[72]

Taking into account that fair use presents a mixed question of law and fact, in Hachette v. Internet Archive, the material facts are undisputed[73] where there is nothing transformative about IA's copying and unauthorized lending of the Works in Suit. Also, IA distorts the sense courts have considered utility expanding transformative uses due to the fact that IA does not develop the utility of the Works in Suit by "providing information about" them[74] and so generating a full-text searchable database "in a manner that does not allow users to read the texts," as in HathiTrust which is an example of such a utility-expanding transformative use.[75] Furthermore, taking into consideration that the first fair use factor addresses "the purpose and character of the use, including whether such use is of a commercial nature or is for nonprofit educational purposes,"[76] courts examine the extent to which the secondary work is "transformative," in addition to whether it is commercial.[77] It could be said that a transformative use inserts something novel, "with a further purpose or different character, altering the first with new expression, meaning, or message, rather than merely superseding the original work."[78] On the other hand, an eBook recast from a print book is a typical example of a derivative work.[79] Thus, the court's ruling confirmed the significance of copyright law.

[70]HACHETTE BOOK GROUP, INC., ET AL., v INTERNET ARCHIVE, ET AL., Case 1:20-cv-04160-JGK-OTW https://www.theverge.com/2023/3/24/23655804/internet-archive-hatchette-publisher-ebook-library-lawsuit

[71]Authors Guild, Inc. v. HathiTrust, 755 F.3d 87, 95 (2d Cir. 2014). Arista Records, LLC v. Doe 3, 604 F.3d 110, 117 (2d Cir. 2010)

[72]Campbell v. Acuff-Rose Music, Inc., 510 U.S. 569, 575 (1994).). S. Pr. Grigoriadou (2022). Copyright and Libraries in AI Era. Journal of Internet Law, 25 (7), 1, 8–19.

[73]Harper & Row Publishers, Inc. v. Nation Enters., 471 U.S. 539, 560 (1985) Fox News Network, LLC v. TVEyes, Inc., 883 F.3d 169, 176 (2d Cir. 2018).

[74]Capitol Recs., LLC v. ReDigi Inc., 910 F.3d 649, 660 (2d Cir. 2018) at 661.

[75]A.V. ex rel. Vanderhye v. iParadigms, LLC, 562 F.3d 630, 639 (fourth Cir. 2009),

[76]17 U.S.C. § 107

[77]Andy Warhol Found. for the Visual Arts, Inc. v. Goldsmith, 11 F.4th 26, 37 (2d Cir. 2021), cert. Granted, 142 S. Ct. 1412 (2022).

[78]Capitol Recs., LLC v. ReDigi Inc., 910 F.3d 649, 660 (2d Cir. 2018).

[79]Authors Guild v. Google, Inc., 804 F.3d 202, 215 (2d Cir. 2015). Penguin Grp. (USA) v. Am. Buddha, No. 13-cv-2017, 2015 WL 11170727, at*2–4 (D. Ariz. May 11, 2015) (service that made complete copies of copyrighted print works and published them online was not transformative because republication did "not imbue the Works with new expression or meaning").Disney Enters. v. VidAngel, 869 F.3d 848, 862 (ninth Cir. 2017) (explaining that courts "unanimously reject the view that "space-shifting" is fair use under § 107" and holding that it was not fair use to

The real AI-copyright challenge is to prevent AI's latest technological innovation from upsetting the copyright balance, obstructing its normative objectives, and by this means challenging the social value of authorship, creative progress, and the public domain. In other words, letting humans be the creative creatures in a world dominated by humans because otherwise humans will get the second place on the globe where AAI will bring forward another form of life and so in another AAI dimension, it is questionable if humans can cope with. Thus, the protection of AI-generated works and the tightening of AI development via the expansion of copyright control may spell an uncertain future for human creators, users, and audiences, spoiling rather than advancing the public interest that copyright is meant to serve for the human world but not for the parallel AAI world. It could be said that legal interventions and reform efforts must be undertaken to steer AI and its development in service of the public goals, human interests, and social values. Under the current AI, the programmers direct the authorship of AI and not the AAI itself. The protection of AI-generated works would advance "creative progress" with which copyright is concerned not stultifying creative practices in a thicket of privately owned algorithmic productions. Thus, even the current AI creation has to get copyright ability in order to achieve a progress.

It is worth noting that there is a risk that a human-authored work will be identified as noticeably comparable to a protected AI work due to the growing use of algorithmic copyright enforcement—technology is trained to detect "matches" between works and equipped to investigate claims of independent creation, non-substantial taking, or fair use. Hence, the actual AI-copyright challenge is to prevent AI technological innovation from overturning the copyright balance, blocking its normative objectives, and so undercutting the social value of authorship, creative progress, and the public domain. AI should take copyright into a new dimension for humans' utility.

It is argued that granting any copyright protection to the results generated by AI destroys the human incentive to still invest in intellectual undertaking because creators would feel degraded if machines were treated equally to humans. Moreover, any prospect of equal treatment between creations generated by humans and AI machines is considered as denigrating art to "a mere commodity, producible and consumable upon pushing a button."[80] Taking into account that a subject matter is to be capable of being considered as original, it is both indispensable and sufficient that the subject matter displays the personality of its author, as an expression of his free and creative choices which will be attributed to the programmer of AI machine but in an AAI environment, the AAI creator, acting in more advance manner than any

"make[] illegal copies of pre-selected movies [on discs] and then sell[] streams . . . . in a different format than that in which they were bought");

[80] Cofemel – Sociedade de Vestuário SA v. G-Star Raw CV, C-683/17 (C.J.E.U. 2019) (E.U.)

human, will be the creator generating originality expressing his personality and encompassing his creative choice according to the AAI world.[81]

It is argued that the contemporary copyright law and policy should provide AI works with appropriate protection and so amended in order to accommodate AI types of literary and artistic works due to the fact that AI technologies necessitate extensive investment of personal, material, and financial resources. Thus, the awarding of copyright protection to the results generated by AI technologies encourages investment and progress in this field of technology.[82] In the United Kingdom and a few other common law jurisdictions, the existing copyright laws already contain distinct provisions for works produced by computers but they are still applicable to the AI works. Pearlman[83] argues that when AI technologies generate a work comparable to copyrighted works created by humans, they should be treated equally to human authors and consequently should be considered as an author of that literary or artistic work.

12.6 Patents and AAI

Innovation incorporates a recombination process across knowledge networks providing significant innovation-specific insights improving upon present economic and psychological understandings of patentability. It is worth noting that there are very aggressive patent owners' attempts to nullify competition. Moreover, exceptionally valuable technologies are worth the cost of war. Thus, technological innovation in fintech and the prospective for patented innovations play a central role in the future of finance.

There is a patent war between high-tech industry against small fintech companies or startups. High-tech industry executives sue disruptors mainly to control competition and preserve market share, or in some cases, to generate licensing fees. Moreover, big corporations leverage their greater resources and patent experience to achieve a competitive edge, even when their infringement claims are not robust, encompassing a litigation tactic.[84]

---

[81] SI and Brompton Bicycle Ltd. v. Chedech / Get2Get, C-833/18 (C.J.E.U. 2020) (E.U.) ("where that product is an original work resulting from intellectual creation, in that, through that shape, its author expresses his creative ability in an original manner by making free and creative choices in such a way that that shape reflects his personality").

[82] U.K. Copyright, Designs and Patents Act of 1988, sec. 9(c) ("In the case of a literary, dramatic, musical or artistic work which is computer-generated, the author shall be taken to be the person by whom the arrangements necessary for the creation of the work are undertaken.").

[83] Russ Pearlman, Recognizing Artificial Intelligence (AI) as Authors and Inventors Under U.-S. Intellectual Property Law, 24 Rich. J.L. & Tech. 2, 29–36 (2018)

[84] Ted Sichelman, The Vonage Trilogy: A Case Study in "Patent Bullying," 90 NOTRE DAME L. REV. 543 (2014).

It has to be taken into account that if no royalties were assigned to the patent creator, there would not be any motivation for it to produce a patent in the first place. Nonetheless, high royalty fees have effects on the likelihood for competitors to enter a particular market and so generating noteworthy barriers to entry and resulting in difficulties concerning the balancing IP protection with competition law.[85]

Congress derives its authority to create the patent system from the US Constitution and federal courts have exclusive jurisdiction over patent claims.[86] It is worth noting that what subject matter is eligible for utility patent protection is controversial.[87] Furthermore, under patent law, an idea per se is not protectable, even though an embodiment of the idea is eligible for patent protection. The Supreme Court has created a framework for classifying patents that claim laws of nature, natural phenomena, and abstract ideas from those that claim patent-eligible applications of those concepts.[88] It has to be taken into consideration that the line between technology that belongs in the public domain and technology that is eligible for private property is protected by conferring a patent. In Reese v. Sprint Nextel Corp., the court uncovered that the claim was for a patent-ineligible abstract idea and the court did not find the presence of an inventive concept for the reason that the patent merely utilizes conventional prior art telephone equipment.[89] To that extent, a method of product promotion was considered as an abstract idea that was a basic economic activity.[90]

It has to be taken into consideration that innovators face limitations in using successive patents to track innovation due to the fact that if the upgraded invention is too similar to the original one, the firm may not be able to patent the advances, even when those enhancements are significant and so making the invention commercially prosperous or fixing a setback discovered in the original design.

---

[85]Case COMP/38.636, Rambus, OJ C 30, 6.2.2010, p. 17–18. Case AT.39939, Samsung, Enforcement of UMTS standard essential patents, OJ C 350, 4.10.2014, p. 8–10. Case C-170/13, Huawei Technologies Co. Ltd. v. ZTE Corp., ZTE Deutschland GmbH, ECLI:EU: C:2015:477.

[86]U.S. CONST. art. I, § 8, cl. 8 ("The Congress shall have Power . . . To promote the Progress of Science and useful Arts, by securing for limited Times to Authors and Inventors the exclusive Right to their respective Writings and Discoveries . . . ."). 28 U.S.C. § 1338(a) TC Heartland LLC v. Kraft Foods Grp. Brands LLC, 137 S. Ct. 1514, 1518–20 (2017) ('reside[nce]' in § 1400(b) refers only to the State of incorporation."). Seven Networks, LLC v. Google LLC, 315 F. Supp. 3d 933, 954 (E.D. Tex. 2018) (finding a server a sufficient "physical place" for venue);

[87]ChargePoint, Inc. v. SemaConnect, Inc., 920 F.3d 759, 765 (Fed. Cir. 2019) (technology related to charging station for electric vehicles held patent ineligible); Athena Diagnostics, Inc., 915 F.3d at 743 (Fed. Cir. 2019) (method of diagnosing neurological disorders held patent ineligible); Endo Pharms. Inc. v. Teva Pharms. USA, Inc., 919 F.3d 1347, 1352 (Fed. Cir. 2019) (method of treating pain with pharmaceutical held patent eligible); Finjan, Inc. v. Blue Coat Sys., 879 F.3d 1299, 1303 (Fed. Cir. 2018) (method for providing computer security held patent eligible); In re Eberra, 730 F. App'x 916, 917 (Fed. Cir. 2018) (method of doing business held patent ineligible).

[88]Trading Techs. Int'l, Inc. v. IBG LLC, 921 F.3d 1378, 1383–84 (Fed. Cir. 2019)

[89]Reese v. Sprint Nextel Corp., 774 F.App'x 656, 658 (Fed. Cir. 2019).

[90]In re Eberra, 730 F.App'x 916, 918 (Fed. Cir. 2018)

In patent law, the purpose of nonobviousness should be to reward and incentivize the production of the most socially substantial innovations.[91] Hence, the nonobviousness doctrine averts the patenting of low-hanging inventions that are not costly to discover and develop because of a low likelihood of failure. Judicial opinions have articulated what makes an invention substantial or nonobvious and how to measure nonobviousness in particular cases, and in current conceptual definitions of nonobviousness, a causal theory of innovation is missing. In spite of its uniqueness to patent law, nonobviousness has long been considered a principally vague and unpredictable doctrine. Judge Hand[92] considered that nonobviousness was "as fugitive, impalpable, wayward, and vague a phantom as exists in the whole paraphernalia of legal concepts."

The necessity of nonobviousness is the crucial condition of patentability because of its central purpose of keeping technically trivial inventions out of the patent system[93] and so nonobviousness encompasses considerable novelty.[94] It is worth noting that the government grants the monopoly linked with a patent when the inventor has generated something adequately different from what came before. By guaranteeing that only substantial technological improvements gain patent protection, the nonobviousness doctrine both incentivizes socially noteworthy innovation and keeps minor technological progresses that do not necessitate patent incentives in the public domain.[95] KSR in particular emphasizes the role of "predictability" in assessing nonobviousness and the nonobviousness doctrine is conceptualized as a device to shift the choice of research projects toward socially preferred ones.[96] It

[91] Laura G. Pedraza-Fariña & Ryan Whalen, A Network Theory of Patentability, 87 U. CHI. L. REV. 63, 63–65 (2020); Christopher A. Cotropia, Patent Law Viewed Through an Evidentiary Lens: The "Suggestion Test" as a Rule of Evidence, 2006 BYU L. REV. 1517, 1526 (2006) ("[The nonobviousness doctrine's] effective and proper enforcement is crucial to maintaining the social cost-benefit balance the patent system attempts to implement.");

[92] Hotchkiss v Greenwood, 52 US 248 (1851).

[93] Apple Inc. v. Samsung Elecs. Co., 839 F.3d 1034, 1074 (Fed. Cir. 2016) (en banc) (Dyk, J., dissenting) ("Obviousness isthe most common invalidity issue in both district court and post-grant proceedings before the PTO."). Forest Lab'ys, LLC v. Sigmapharm Lab'ys, LLC, 918 F.3d 928, 937 (Fed. Cir. 2019) (noting the importance of analyzing certain § 103 evidence based on the time of filing).

[94] Laura G. Pedraza-Fariña & Ryan Whalen, A Network Theory of Patentability, 87 U. CHI. L. REV. 63, 84 (2020) (noting the complexities in the cognitive approach to obviousness).

[95] KSR International Co v Teleflex Inc., 550 US 398, 427 (2007) ("[A]s progress beginning from higher levels of achievement is expected in the normal course, the results of ordinary innovation are not the subject of exclusive rights under the patent laws. . . . These premises led to the bar on patents claiming obvious subject matter established in Hotchkiss and codified in § 103.") Jeanne C. Fromer, A Psychology of Intellectual Property, 104 Nw U L Rev. 1441, 1487 (2010) (arguing that the nonobviousness requirement emphasizes the value of creativity because "solutions that can be derived with at best a minimally creative process—possibly even absent certain steps, such as incubation—are not valuable");

[96] William P. Janzen, Screening Technologies for Small Molecule Discovery: The State of the Art, 21 Chemistry & Biology Rev. 1162, 1162 (2014) (describing standardized protocols for screening through compound libraries to see which compound achieves a desired biological activity).

could be said that the nonobviousness doctrine incentivizes those costly and risky inventions that bring together cognitively distant technological domains by amplified use of computationally assisted decision-making devices.[97]

It has to be taken into account that AI involvement in the invention development falls on a technological spectrum and is provocative for the conventional patent system. It is argued that incorporating AI-generated inventions in the framework of the existing patent system would mean that a natural person should qualify as the inventor, such that a "proxy human inventor" would be named even if this was not the actual "deviser." Nevertheless, such a patent could be questioned and nullified before courts if it was verified that an AI system was responsible for the invention and that the natural person had been wrongly delegated.[98]

First of all, an AI-based device aids a human creator without contributing to the conception of the invention but, on the other hand, an AI-based device creates AI-generated output satisfying patentability if otherwise made by a human. Nonetheless, dispute arises over whether patents' disclosure function is restrained when an AI-based tool's procedure is unexplainable or the production of AI-generated output is inherently not comprehensible as to how, or from which method it was generated. Thus, AI poses a new contest owing to the opacity and its speedy usage acceleration demanding a reevaluation of disclosure theory. It could be said that AI profoundly contests disclosure in patent law, which has not kept up with rapid progressions in AI technology seeking to stimulate the objectives that patent law's disclosure function is serving for society.

It has to be taken into consideration that the conventional and more modern theories for the patent system are not mutually exclusive and, surprisingly, but little attention to the role of disclosure in the patent system's treatment of AI inventions is paid. As technological progresses in information and data have formulated, it is easier for inventors to veil and conceal their innovations and so patent law has doctrinally refocused to the disclosure theory. To that extent, the USPTO grants more patents covering AI-based devices as a policy objective and due to the fact that AI is altering patentability with multifaceted algorithms to create AI-generated output, it was chosen the mode of ds inventors delivering greater disclosure of AI in patents. Furthermore, no intuitive data links between AI-based devices and AI-created output induce AI inventors to strive for greater patent disclosure.

The USPTO endorses the predictability and reliability of IP rights relating to AI technology and so the USPTO has acknowledged the significance of patent disclosure as AI patent filings have rapidly boosted. Hence, the US Supreme Court has

[97] Solon Barocas and Andrew D. Selbst, Big Data's Disparate Impact, 104 Cal L Rev. 671, 677–93 (2016). Arti K. Rai, Machine Learning at the Patent Office: Lessons for Patents and Administrative Law, 104 Iowa L Rev. 2617, 2636–40 (2019).

[98] Judgment of 16 July 2009, Infopaq International A/S v Danske Dagblades Forening, C-5/08, EU:C:2009:465; Judgment of 1 December 2011, Eva-Maria Painer v Standard Verlags GmbH, et al., C-145/10, EU:C:2011:798

recognized the significance of patent disclosure addressing the magnitude of greater and clearer disclosure of identified inventions.[99]

It could be said that the encounter of AI-based devices and AI-produced output could reveal unidentified inventions based on AI-generated output but surfacing as if they were invented by humans without the use of AI-based devices.[100] In other words, the growing blurring of artificial and real inventions indicates that disclosure incentives for the inventor and patent protection from data deposits for AI will stipulate positive welfare advances for society.

It is argued that there is a lack of transparency denoting the use of algorithms and their interpretation even when records are disclosed.[101] In other words, transparency necessitates, at a minimum, a portrayal of the decision's "provenance," embracing an accounting of its inputs and outputs and the key elements that made it. Hence, a lack of transparency indicates the anonymity in the AI context and so transparency occurs where the learning dataset and source code are disclosed together within information concerning its design and factors.[102] Thus, transparency can be achieved via the use of advanced AI explaining in a conventional way of the whole process. In other words, the algorithm's complete decision-making will be made fully understandable to the appropriate human audience.

Furthermore, "explainability" encompasses an analysis of the AI computational logic transforming an input into an output. Under an AAI technology, AAI humanoid robots will understand that the whole AAI patenting process implements the AAI patent system utility, necessity, and functionality in an analogous to conventional patent system utility.

It has to be taken into account that traditionally, financial innovations were protected and so banks initially sought relief from the courts claiming that business methods should not be subject to patent protection. To that extent, business method patents are not categorically excluded under 35 U.S.C. § 101, which describes what

[99] Bonito Boats, Inc. v. Thunder Craft Boats, Inc., 489 U.S. 141, 151 (1989); Kewanee Oil Co. v. Bicron Corp., 416 U.S. 470, 481 (1974).

[100] Tabrez Y. Ebrahim, Automation & Predictive Analytics in Patent Prosecution: USPTO Implications & Policy, 35 GA. ST. U. L. REV. 1185, 1185, 1189 (2019) (prescribing that "the USPTO should develop a counteracting artificial intelligence unit in response to artificial-intelligence proliferation". Robert P. Merges, The Hamiltonian Origins of the U.S. Patent System, and Why They Matter Today, 104 Iowa L. Rev. 2559, 2588 (2019) (explaining that the USPTO is an expert agency that has the authority to make rules that govern its internal proceedings and make rules on procedural matters, but that it is not an agency the possesses the power to issue binding rules with the force of law, such as on patentability).

[101] Robert Brauneis & Ellen Goodman, Algorithmic Transparency for the Smart City, 20 Yale J.L. & Tech. 103, 107–08, 110, 132 (2018) (transparency refers to: disclosing predictive models or algorithms, opaque "black box" processes, or "black boxes"; additionally, suggesting that meaningful transparency is demonstrating the knowledge that is sufficient to approve or disapprove of the algorithm's performance)

[102] Alex Engler, The Case for AI Transparency Requirement, Brookings Inst. (Jan. 22, 2020), https://brook.gs/2zoSwCn Arti K. Rai, Machine Learning at the Patent Office: Lessons for Patents and Administrative Law, 104 Iowa L. Rev. 2617, 2625 (2019)

inventions are patentable.[103] Blockchain is the technology triggering the bitcoin cryptocurrency revolutionizing much of daily life. Moreover, blockchain platforms are incorrectly comprehended as immune from intellectual property (IP) rights claims for the reason that they are open-source and accessible to users. Blockchain platforms are patentable and the US Patent and Trademark Office (USPTO) has already granted patents to various blockchain platforms that are associated with technologies. In addition, patents have already been approved for technologies that are advanced as additions to blockchain's basic building blocks and so blockchain technology is being explored across many different businesses, embracing telecommunications, financial services, health, and fashion, along with the government.

Even though the "damages" compensate for the infringement customarily involving either lost profits or, a reasonable royalty, courts permit the patent owner to recover compensation for other losses proximately caused by the infringement.[104] Furthermore, courts grant damages for lost future profits and/or damages to compensate for loss of goodwill instigated by an act of patent infringement.[105]

While conventional patent law's enablement doctrine centers on the specific result of the invention process, AI portrays a lack of transparency and difficulty in replication that profoundly and fundamentally contest disclosure theory in patent law.[106] The prospective societal benefits and costs of AI-based devices and AI-produced output compel a re-examination of patent law because the exact factors of AI-based devices and their usage in the inventive course are not well-defined.

AI is transforming the invention and the standards of patent prosecution by pioneering a digital representation of the invention and so altering the foundation of the entire patent system. Hence, AI is destabilizing patent law's disclosure theory by producing AI-generated output and an AI-based device for predicting AI-generated output.[107] It is worth mentioning here that digital health corporations and innovative startups are forming AI-based devices producing AI-generated output of personalized recipes tailored to a specific individual's diet, allergens, and

---

[103] Bilski v. Kappos, 561 U.S. 593, 611–13 (2010) State St. Bank & Tr. Co. v. Signature Fin. Grp., Inc., 149 F.3d 1368 (Fed. Cir. 1998), John R. Thomas, The Patenting of the Liberal Professions, 40 B.C. L. REV. 1139, 1140–41 (1999) (State Street was the latest in a series of cases testing the boundaries of the "useful arts") Mayo Collaborative Servs. v. Prometheus Labs., Inc., 566 U.S. 66 (2012), Ass'n for Molecular Pathology v. Myriad Genetics, Inc., 569 U.S. 576 (2013) and Alice Corp. Pty. Ltd. v. CLS Bank Int'l, 573 U.S. 208 (2014) (strengthened the judicially-created exceptions to § 101).

[104] Rite-Hite Corp. v. Kelley Co., 56 F.3d 1538, 1549–50 (Fed. Cir. 1995) (en banc)

[105] Lam, Inc. v. Johns-Manville Corp., 718 F.2d 1056 (Fed Cir. 1983).

[106] Sean Semmler & Zeeve Rose, Comment, Artificial Intelligence: Application Today and Implications Tomorrow, 16 Duke L. & Tech. Rev. 85, 86 (2017) (defining AI as "the process of simulating human intelligence through machine processes")

[107] Tabrez Y. Ebrahim, Computational Experimentation, 21 Vand. J. Ent. & Tech. L. 591, 601–03 (2019) (describing techniques such as (1) molecular dynamics simulations and machine learning, which allow for the determination of reactivity and kinetics of chemical compounds; (2) high-precision, pre-laboratory-experiment simulations and predictions of chemical properties and reactions; and (3) construction of structure-activity relationships).

biological qualities. Nonetheless, the existing computing power and sources of data, the scale and a plethora of new use cases, and the capacity to exploit advances in algorithms accomplishing multipart computations and offering customization neither enable a person having ordinary skill in the art ("PHOSITA") to practice the invention nor demonstrate that the inventor was in possession of the invention at the time of the patent application.[108] Hence, a patent applicant has to reveal possession of the claimed invention via descriptive ways as words, structures, figures, diagrams, and expressions setting forth the requested invention or by a portrayal of an actual reduction to "practice" or by revealing that the invention was "ready for patenting." It seems that under the present AI, its usage in the course of inventing augments the scale of and lack of transparency in inventing, conceivably resulting in premature patent grants or ones where the inventor possibly was not in possession of the invention.

While patent law protects "functional" products and processes, copyright law protects "expressive" works and so patent law is the appropriate means for protecting software if the software is solely (or perhaps primarily) functional, and copyright law is the appropriate means for protecting software if the software is solely (or perhaps primarily) expressive. Hence, if software is both functional and expressive, then software is susceptible to protection by both patent and copyright law. G.I. Zekos[109] considers that software will be patentable as long as there is an invention, and the included creation must not be merely science, but it must include spirit expressed materially or be an intangible content expressing functional effect.

New technology[110] requires technology-specific legislation if there is no possible way to interpret it according to old legislation and so courts typically place an emerging technology in an existing context by analogizing it to previous technologies. Taking into account that one is not allowed to patent solely abstract ideas, nanotechnology as a new field creates problems because patents on basic inventions are inclined to cover larger areas than the final products, with the expectation of developing them in the future into more explicit inventions. G.I. Zekos argues that the patenting of pure science abstract ideas in nanotechnology and the discovery of the nature of human beings or other materials or chemicals cannot be permitted unless there is an invention underway, which means that the idea is transformed into an invention directly and it is not the idea which is to be patented, with an expectation to license it for others to work toward an invention based on the theoretical idea. The technique of arriving at the nanotechnology abstract idea is patentable as an invention, not to mention that if the idea creates a nanotechnology produced phenomenon—probably imitating a natural one—then this is patentable as

[108] 35 U.S.C. § 112(a) . Janssen Pharmaceutica N.V. v. Teva Pharms. USA, Inc., 583 F. 3d 1317, 1320–23 (Fed. Cir. 2009); Amgen Inc. v. Sanofi, 872 F.3d 1367, 1373 (Fed. Cir. 2010); Ariad Pharm., Inc. v. Eli Lilly & Co., 598 F.3d 1336, 1351 (Fed. Cir. 2010);

[109] G. Zekos, Software Patenting, The Journal of World Intellectual Property (2006) Vol. 9, no. 4, pp. 426–444

[110] G. Zekos, Patenting Abstract Ideas in Nanotechnology, The Journal of World Intellectual Property (2006) Vol. 9, no. 1, pp. 113–136

a purely nanotechnology creation. Otherwise, if abstract ideas are patentable in nanotechnology merely in order to cover the companies' and universities' profits, then all the old scientific theories must be patented retroactively, because many inventions are based on the transformation of those ideas.

Can AI scientific theories be patented? The economic importance of patents has diminished the tendency towards dissemination and sharing among scientists. Patent disclosures have informational benefits across a broad range of technologies but have pure science become patentable as against scientific development is a question that begs answers.[111] With patent standards constantly in flux, it is essential to have up-to-the-minute information on how best to protect inventions in upcoming technologies. Computer/software industry, biotechnology, nanotechnology, bio-nanotechnology, and biochemistry bring forward new scientific theories and knowledge every day which means that it is essential to have something more than merely the scientific theory and knowledge in order to decide on patentability. Thus, in an analogous way, AI scientific theory has to comply with in order to be patented. The functionality of AI inventions concerning computer/software industry, biotechnology, and nanotechnology, bio-nanotechnology or biochemistry products involves a high degree of uncertainty and risk. Hence, AI inventions need to be better incentivized than other types of inventions if they are to make it to the market.

12.7 Trademarks and AAI

Trademark law is protecting the public by acting as an indicator of origin and a guarantee of quality and so reassuring the consumers that they are getting the goods they want to get. Moreover, the owner of the trademark, who "has spent energy, time and money in presenting to the public the product," is protected in his investment from its misuse by pirates. Furthermore, trademark law serves business interests by protecting a business's valuable rights in its trademark due to goodwill.[112] Firms seek marks that are clear and memorable signifying something about the goods with which they are linked.

First of all, generic terms and descriptive marks, which describe a quality, function, or purpose of the relevant goods, are not protectable.[113] The Lanham Act precludes registration of any mark that is so similar to an already-registered mark "as to be likely, when used on or in connection with the goods of the applicant, to cause

[111] G. Zekos, Denying Patentability of Scientific Theories, Vol 19, September 2014Journal of Intellectual Property Rights pp. 337–346

[112] Two Pesos, Inc. v. Taco Cabana, Inc., 505 U.S. 763, 782 n.15, (1992) (Stevens, J., concurring)) ("[W]here the owner of a trade-mark has spent energy, time, and money in presenting to the public the product, he is protected in his investment from its misappropriation by pirates and cheats.").

[113] U.S. Pat. & Trademark Off. v. Booking.com B.V., 140 S. Ct. 2298, 2301 (2020) (allowing registration of some "generic.com" marks). U.S. PAT. & Trademark Off., Trademark Manual Of Examining Procedure § 1209.01(b) (2018)

confusion, or to cause mistake, or to deceive."[114] Moreover, multiple factors go into an appraisal of whether an applicant's mark is confusingly similar to someone else's, but predominantly noteworthy one is the similarity or dissimilarity of the mark as to appearance, sound, connotation, and commercial impression.

The Lanham Act also prevents registration of marks confusingly similar to no abandoned unregistered marks.[115] Furthermore, trademark rights are an intangible form of property rights in intellectual property, involving the right of sale and the right of licensing. The most vital trademark right, as with other forms of property, is the right to exclude meaning that a trademark owner has the right of exclusive use of its trademark and so making trademarks valuable business assets.[116] Also, trademark rights extend only to the specific business in which a trademark owner uses the mark. Additionally, trademark rights are not rights in absolute perpetuity due to the fact that a trademark owner loses its right to a mark by not using the mark. Consequently, a trademark right does not confer a monopoly upon its owner to prohibit all use of a mark by others which means that the right to disregard another's use of a trademark extends only so far as that use is triggering consumer confusion with the trademark owner's own use.[117]

It has to be taken into account that trademarks accomplish "information transmission" function by assisting consumers more easily to locate the products they want diminishing search costs in economic parlance. Moreover, the link between trademarks and reputation is embedded in the common assertion that trademarks symbolize a product's "goodwill."[118] Trademarks offer a condensed form of the information that consumers relate with the mark and so revealing that the quality of products is directly derived from the origin function of trademarks, as consumers must be able to identify products as coming from one firm "which is accountable for their quality" knowing as the quality function of trademarks.[119] It is characteristic that the origin and quality utility ascertain transparency on the market, enabling consumers to make valuable procuring decisions and so both roles serve the rationale of accomplishing undistorted competition in the internal market.

It has to be taken into consideration that trademarks protect consumers from marketplace confusion and deception by letting consumers individualize between the makers of similar products.[120] To that extent, the Lanham Act's Sections

[114] 15 U.S.C. § 1052(d).

[115] In re E.I. du Pont de Nemours & Co., 476 F.2d 1357, 1361 (C.C.P.A. 1973)).

[116] Hanover Star Milling Co. v. Metcalf, 240 U.S. 403, 413 (1916)) ("[T]rademarks and the right to their exclusive use are of course to be classed among property rights . . . .").

[117] United Drug Co. v. Theodore Rectanus Co., 248 U.S. 90, 97 (1918) (rejecting a comparison of trademark rights to patents and copyrights).

[118] Uptown Grill, L.L.C. v. Camellia Grill Holdings, Inc., 920 F.3d 243, 248 (fifth Cir. 2019 Gvantsa Gugeshashvili, Is Goodwill Synonymous with Reputation?, 16 JURIDICA INT'L 126, 127–28 (2009) (noting that "goodwill and reputation are very often considered to be synonyms," but that goodwill is the broader concept in common law countries);

[119] Case C-10/89 SA CNL-SUCAL NV v HAG GF AG [1990] ECR I-3711, para 13

[120] Top Tobacco, L.P. v. N. Atl. Operating Co., 509 F.3d 380, 381 (seventh Cir. 2007)

32(1) and 43(a) stipulate remedies for infringement of registered and unregistered marks, respectively. In other words, without a way to know who makes what, reputations cannot be generated and assessed which means that the process of competition will be less operative. The expanding capacity of businesses to make their commodities more extensively available, along with consumers' growing capability to access those commodities, has blurred conventional, territorially restricted market boundaries and so diminishing the doctrine's inherent assumption that geographic distance decreases the likelihood of confusion between two similar marks. To that extent, cyberspace has augmented this effect by adding new subjects to the question of trademark territoriality. Thus, consumers in geographically distant markets are more likely to be confused by two similar marks than when the doctrine was born which means that companies have a greater need to protect their interests in territorial expansion.[121] On the other hand, cyberspace offers the tools to check about the utility of any mark.

As a result of their character, trademarks usually do not enable their holder to obstruct the making of a new product, or of a new market for the reason that, contrasting copyright and patent rights, trademarks do not offer the input for a new product or process which means that they usually do not block the formation of an innovative product or of an improved process. Nevertheless, they generate barriers to entry. A trademark interconnects basic information about the product to consumers, without competitors interfering with that communication and so trademark protection is defensive in nature by protecting trademark holders against confusing use of the trademark.[122]

In HAG II,[123] the CJEU explained that trademark rights are "an essential element in the system of undistorted competition which the Treaty seeks to establish and maintain." Furthermore, in L'Oréal, the CJEU identified that the purposes of trademarks are multiple and that, beside the indication of the origin of the products, they seek at protecting the quality of products, communication, investment, and advertising and so adding at competition implementation.[124] It is characteristic that in EMI,[125] the CJEU ascertained that cross-licensing of trademark is forbidden between competitors, for the reason that it leads to market sharing, captured by Article 101. Hence, the exercise of a trademark right may, under particular conditions, create an anticompetitive infringement in those cases in which it "manifests itself as the subject, the means, or the consequence of a restrictive practice."

[121] Anonymous, Shrinking World Theory and Blockchain, MEDIUM (Jan. 29, 2018), https://medium.com/@icography.team/shrinking-world-theory-andblockchainbea65e0cad48

[122] Directive 2008/95/EC approximates the laws of the Member States relating to trade marks [2008] OJ L 299. Directive (EU) 2015/2436 approximate the laws of the Member States relating to trade marks [2015] OJ L 336 refers to augmenting the competitiveness of European businesses

[123] Case 192/73, Van Zuylen frères v. Hag AG,,1974 E.C.R. 744. Case C-10/89, SA CNL-SUCAL NV v. HAG GF AG, 1990 E.C.R. I-3758.

[124] Case C-487/07, L'Oréal SA, Lancôme parfums et beauté & Cie SNC and Laboratoire Garnier & Cie v Bellure NV, Malaika Invs., Ltd., and Starion Int'l Ltd., 2009 E.C.R. ¶ 58.

[125] Case 51/75, EMI Records Ltd. v. CBS United Kingdom Ltd., 1976 E.C.R. 848

According to the CJEU, free movement of goods and competition law do not avert owners of trademarks in all the EU member states from exercising their rights with the aim of preventing the sale or manufacture by a third party in the EU of products bearing the same trademark that is owned by a third party in a third country. Besides, this conduct could be forbidden if it was applied through an agreement or a concerted practice with the object or outcome of isolating or splitting the internal market. Additionally, the use of a trademark to artificially generate barriers to entry in a market that is already controlled by an undertaking seems to have been less frequent in reality.

Can territoriality apply to cyberspace transactions and AI ones? The answer is no and there is a need for global application of e-trademarks. Different jurisdictions acknowledge the critical function of trademarks to indicate the origin of a product and so making trademark holders accountable for the product's quality. The general common law rule of territoriality considers that trademark rights are limited to the geographic territory in which a mark is utilized and the Lanham Act embraces territoriality provisions. The courts in the United States have confirmed the extra-territorial reach of the Lanham Act, as the Supreme Court has done so in Bulova.[126]

Courts conferred the infringer's own profits only in cases of intentional or willful infringement and the Supreme Court held that the Lanham Act does not necessitate proof of willfulness as a criterion to an award of profits[127] and so willfulness is a vital consideration in awarding profits under § 1117(a), but not an absolute precondition. Moreover, courts defined 'willfulness' to embrace a series of culpable mental states and so courts commonly award economic damages in the form of lost profits or reasonable royalties.

Which are the effects of AI technology on trademark law? Will trademarks still fulfill their role in a world in which consumers are assisted by AI technology when procuring in the online marketplace? It is worth mentioning here that electronic marketplaces are assisted by AI technologies, such as search engines, customer service bots, or AI assistants. Undoubtedly the most vital characteristic of AI technologies in online shopping is that they forecast what consumers require or like before consumers know it themselves. In other words, AIs prediction in online shopping is a central advancement in online shopping in many ways. To that extent, the capability for AI technology to reach that high level of sophistication based on the evolution of the technology and the data that it utilizes. AI can make decisions in an objective way as long as the used data are unbiased, not mentioning the capabilities that AAI technology will bring forward. Concerning current AI, a certain bias can trigger their mechanism because of human input at the stage of training the algorithm, setting the hyperparameters and selecting training data.

[126]Trader Joe's Co. v. Hallatt, 835 F. 3d 960 (ninth Cir. 2016).Bulova Watch Co. 344 U.S. 280, 73 S. Ct. 252 (1952).

[127]Romag Fasteners, Inc. v. Fossil, Inc., 140 S. Ct. 1492, 1494, 1497 (2020) (while "a trademark defendant's mental state is a highly important consideration in determining whether an award of profits is appropriate," there is no "categorical rule" that the plaintiff must prove willful infringement).

A very common form of AI in online shopping is product recommendations and so AI technology collects data about the consumer's previous views or purchases which means that AI can make a list of items encompassing similar features that the customer seems to have a preference for.

It is worth noting that AI technology with unlimited time and augmented capacity clearly reduces the requirement for simplified information on the market and via AI technology, consumers count on assistance in collecting and processing far more distinguishing context than humans which means that consumers will be able to find optimal products without the help of trademarks serving their needs, presuming that this is the standard for the AI technology.[128] While trademarks may not anymore perform the purpose of simplifying information and so making the buying process more effective, they still convey significant information to the consumer when he/she consumes the product. Moreover, trademarks by guaranteeing the origin and quality function will still be useful in AI-assisted online shopping.

It could be said that trademarks continued to be useful in assuring undistorted competition on the market. In other words, while AI technology is able to classify fully counterfeit products, competition would nevertheless be harmed where the communication between producers and consumers is obstructed by confusing information from competitors. Also, both justification of plummeting consumers' search costs along with assuring fair competition on the market continue to be relevant functions for trademarks in online marketplaces.

Trademarks are highly unique and have acquired certain recognition by communicating information beyond origin and quality. Moreover, the capacity to communicate values and images has been accepted as accessory functions of trademarks. Also, in line with the advertising function, trademark holders can use the mark successfully to inform and win over consumers. In other words, the CJEU recognizes that trademarks are valuable in informing and convincing consumers and trademark owners should be able to successfully advertise their mark.[129] The communication function has also been recognized by the court.[130]

AI technology is much better in searching context by presenting optimal options for consumers and so advanced AI can predict consumers' preferences in relation to certain trademarks. The functions of trademarks are expected to continue playing a role for purchases done in the online marketplace with the backing of AI tools. It could be said that AAI technology is also able to influence behavior of consumers on an emotional level.

[128]Michael Grynberg, 'AI and the Death of Trademark Law' [2019–2020] 108(2) Kentucky Law Journal 198

[129]Case C-236/08 Google France SARL and Google Inc. v Louis Vuitton Malletier SA [2010] ECR I-02417, para 59.

[130]Case C-487/07 L'Oréal SA v Bellure [2009] ECR I-05185, paras 58 and 63 Case C-129/17 Mitsubishi Shoji Kaisha Ltd. and Mitsubishi Caterpillar Forklift Europe BV v. Duma Forklifts NV and G.S. International BVBA [2018] ECLI:EU:C:2018:594.

It is argued that extraterritoriality and international trademark norms leading to global trademark reflect globalization, not mentioning the demand for rules governing the forthcoming AAI trademarks.[131]

12.8 Methodology and Data

Successful protection of intellectual property rights depends on both the existence of intellectual property protection laws and the enforcement of the laws. The changeability of legal theory and the new laws coming into force all the time along influence the outcome and consequently our index.

Moreover, all the national laws in force by the end of 2012 of the 79 investigated jurisdictions have been examined and used in the raking of the various factors taken into account in constructing ZEKIPR6 index. Therefore, all future changes in intellectual property laws and their enforcement environment will continue to cause an alteration upon our indices which means a need for a nonstop updating of IPRs' index:

$$\begin{aligned} \text{ZEKIPR6} = {} & \text{membership in international treaties} + \text{index of patent rights} \\ & + \text{index of copyright} + \text{index of trade} - \text{mark rights} \\ & + \text{enforcement legal rating(legal tradition(rule of law)} \\ & + \text{legal education} + \text{economic level)} \end{aligned}$$

Enforcement legal rating (legal tradition (rule of law) + legal education+ economic level) is made according to this author's evaluation.

$$\begin{aligned} & \text{ZEKIPR1b} = \text{membership in international treaties} + \text{index of patent rights} \\ & \quad + \text{index of copyright} + \text{index of trade} - \text{mark rights} \\ & \quad + \text{enforcement rating((legal and political environment (LP)} \\ & \qquad \text{(judicial independence} + \text{rule of law} + \text{political stability} \\ & \quad + \text{control of corruption) (International Property Rights Index} \mid \text{2010 Report))} \end{aligned}$$

A linear model is in the form

$$Y_i = \beta_0 + \sum_{j=1}^{p} \beta_j X_{i,j} + \varepsilon_i$$

[131] James Darnton, 'The Coming of Age of the Global Trademark: The Effect of TRIPS on the Well-Know Marks Exception to the Principle of Territoriality' (2011) 20 Michigan State International Law Review 11.

where for the *i*th case, Y_i is the response variable, $X_{i,1}, \ldots, X_{i,p}$ are *p* regressors, and ε_i is a mean zero error term. The quantities $\beta_0, \ldots, \beta_p$ are unknown coefficients, whose values are determined by least squares.

A linear model is in the form where for the *i*th case, Y_i is the response variable, are *p* regressors, and is a mean zero error term. The quantities are unknown coefficients, whose values are determined by least squares.

GCI (the Global Competitiveness Index 2010–2011) and Global Competitiveness Index 2011–2012 (GCI) are variables.

In detail, the following are the econometric models used in our investigation in order to find the impact of IPRs, GDP, and GCI on FDI inflows/outflows, and GDP growth:

$$FDI_{it} = b_0 + b_1\ GCI_{it} + b_2\ Trade_{it} + b_3\ Inflation_{it} + u_{it} \tag{12.1}$$

$$GDP_{it/}(GDPc_{it}) = b_0 + b_1\ GCI_{it} + b_2\ FDI_{it} + b_3\ Trade_{it} + b_4\ Inflation_{it} + u_{it} \tag{12.1a}$$

$$FDI_{it} = b_0 + b_1\ zekipr1b_{it} + b_2\ Trade_{it} + b_3\ Inflation_{it} + u_{it} \tag{12.2}$$

$$FDI_{it} = b_0 + b_1\ GCI_{it} + b_2\ GDPGR_{it} + b_3 Trade_{it} + b_4\ Inflation_{it} + u_{it} \tag{12.3}$$

$$FDI_{it} = b_0 + b_1\ Zekipr6_{it} + b_2\ GDP_{it} + b_3\ Trade_{it} + b_4\ Inflation_{it} + u_{it} \tag{12.4}$$

$$FDI_{it} = b_0 + b_1\ GCI_{it} + b_2\ GDP_{it} + b_3 Trade_{it} + b_4\ Inflation_{it} + u_{it} \tag{12.5}$$

$$FDI_{it} = b_0 + b_1\ GCI12_{it} + b_2\ Trade_{it} + b_3\ Inflation_{it} + b_4\ GDPGR_{it} + u_{it} \tag{12.6}$$

12.9 Empirical Results

In detail, the following are the econometric models which are used in our investigation in order to find the impact of IPRs and GCI on attracting FDI inflows-FDI outflows, trade and GDP growth::

12.9.1 FDI Inflows/GDP OLS Model 1/Model 1a Beta Coefficients

We start our investigation with **Model 1/Model 1a [$FDI_{it} = b_0 + b_1\ GCI_{it} + b_2\ Trade_{it} + b_3\ Inflation_{it} + u_{it/}\ GDP_{it/}\ (GDPc_{it}) = b_0 + b_1\ GCI_{it} + b_2\ FDI_{it} + b_3\ Trade_{it} + b_4\ Inflation_{it} + u_{it}$]** using OLS standardized coefficients or beta coefficients and the results (Coef. 2.02***, 2.16***/−1.43, −0.83) show the significance of GCI 2014 for the 2013 and five years reference regarding Foreign direct investment, net inflows (BoP, current US$)/GDP growth (annual %) (Table 12.1). It is worth mentioning here that the GCI 2014 betas regarding FDI and GDP are (0.7193563, 0.7516683/−0.3029776, −0.1696162).

Table 12.1 FDI inflows OLS Model 1/Model 1a beta coefficients

	(1)	(2)	(3)	(4)
VARIABLES	logfdiif2013	logfdiif5y	gdp2013	gdp5y
c2014	2.02***	2.16***	−1.43	−0.83
	(0.322)	(0.349)	(0.840)	(0.826)
tr2013	−0.00		0.00	
	(0.003)		(0.006)	
inf2013	0.10		0.12	
	(0.054)		(0.113)	
tr5		−0.00		0.00
		(0.003)		(0.006)
inf5y		0.09*		0.20*
		(0.038)		(0.075)
logfdiif2013			0.02	
			(0.262)	
logfdiif5y				0.28
				(0.226)
Constant	13.60***	12.67***	8.36	−1.56
	(1.481)	(1.649)	(4.657)	(4.259)
Observations	64	76	64	76
R-squared	0.40	0.36	0.15	0.20
Adj. R-squared	0.37	0.34	0.09	0.16

Standard errors in parentheses
$^{***}p < 0.001$, $^{**}p < 0.01$, $^{*}p < 0.05$

12.9.2 *Linear Results Model 2/Model 3 Regarding FDI Inflows*

We carry on our investigation with model 2/ model 3 $[FDI_{it} = b_0 + b_1\ zekiprlb_{it} + b_2\ Trade_{it} + b_3\ Inflation_{it} + u_{it}/\ FDI_{it} = b_0 + b_1\ GCI_{it} + b_2\ GDPGR_{it} + b_3 Trade_{it} + b_4\ Inflation_{it} + u_{it}]$ using OLS standardized coefficients or beta coefficients and the results (Coef. 1.97***, 2.17***- *** $p < 0.001$, ** $p < 0.01$, * $p < 0.05$) regarding 5 years average reference show that *zekiprlb* and GCI are significant variables regarding FDI inflows (2010 UNCTADstat) (Table 12.2). The values of (p & beta) for *zekiprlb* and GCI are (0.000/ 0.4559344, 0.000/0.34281, 0.000/0.8371611) regarding 5 years average. Thus, the beta of GCI is much higher than *zekiprlb* showing the higher significance/impact of competition on IPRs concerning FDI.

Table 12.2 FDI inflows OLS Model 2/ Model 3 beta coefficients

	(1)	(2)
Variables	logfdiin5yav	logfdiin5yav
zekipr1b	1.97***	
	(0.528)	
loggdp5yav		
gdpgr5yav		
trade5yav	−0.00	−0.00
	(0.003)	(0.002)
inf5yav	−0.06	0.10
	(0.055)	(0.057)
Gci		2.17***
		(0.327)
Constant	1.56	−1.28
	(2.232)	(1.698)
Observations	75	75
R-squared	0.31	0.49
Adj. R-squared	0.29	0.47

Standard errors in parentheses
$^{***}p < 0.001$, $^{**}p < 0.01$, $^{*}p < 0.05$

12.9.3 FDI Outflows OLS Model 4/ Model 5 Beta Coefficients

We continue our investigation with model 4 [$FDI_{it} = b_0 + b_1$ **Zekipr6**$_{it}$ $+ b_2$ $GDP_{it} + b_3$ $Trade_{it} + b_4$ $Inflation_{it} + u_{it}$] using OLS standardized coefficients or beta coefficients and the results (Coef. 5.28**, 6.18***, 5.95***) show the significance of zekipr6 for the 2012, five- and ten-years reference regarding foreign direct investment, net outflows US dollars at current prices and current exchange rates in millions 2012 UNCTADstat (Table 12.3). It is worth mentioning here that the zekcopy6 beta regarding FDI outflows are (0.59242, 0.7894868, 0.7175243) respectively. Furthermore, we maintain our investigation with Model 5 [$FDI_{it} = b_0 + b_1$ $GCI_{it} + b_2$ $GDP_{it} + b_3 Trade_{it} + b_4$ $Inflation_{it} + u_{it}$] using OLS standardized coefficients or beta coefficients and the results (Coef. 4.16***, 4.07***, 3.82***) show the significance of gci for the 2012, five- and ten-years reference regarding foreign direct investment, net outflows US dollars at current prices and current exchange rates in millions 2012 UNCTADstat (Table 12.3). It is worth mentioning here that the gci beta regarding FDI outflows are (0.792171, 0.9021555, 0.7948605), respectively.

12.9.4 FDI Inflows Model 6 OLS Standardized Variables

We persist our investigation with Model 6 [$FDI_{it} = b_0 + b_1$ $GCI12_{it} + b_2$ $Trade_{it} + b_3$ $Inflation_{it} + b_4$ $GDPGR_{it} + u_{it}$] using OLS standardized coefficients or beta

Table 12.3 FDI outflows OLS Model 4/ Model 5 beta coefficients

	(1)	(2)	(3)	(4)	(5)	(6)
Variables	logfdiout2012	logfdiout5yav	logfdiout10yav	logfdiout2012	logfdiout5yav	logfdiout10yav
zekipr6	5.28**	6.18***	5.95***			
	(1.936)	(1.163)	(0.926)			
gdpgr2012	0.14			−0.05		
	(0.200)			(0.126)		
trade2012	0.01			−0.01		
	(0.006)			(0.006)		
inf2012	−0.00			0.09		
	(0.138)			(0.113)		
gdpgr5y		0.32**			−0.05	
		(0.121)			(0.080)	
trade5y		−0.00			−0.01*	
		(0.004)			(0.004)	
inf5y		−0.03			0.12	
		(0.080)			(0.071)	
gdpgr10y			0.13			−0.02
			(0.129)			(0.093)
trade10y			−0.00			−0.01**
			(0.004)			(0.004)
inf10y			−0.00			−0.00
			(0.000)			(0.000)
gci12				4.16***	4.07***	3.82***
				(0.784)	(0.476)	(0.403)
Constant	−14.35	−17.09**	−16.24***	−11.16**	−10.60***	−8.85***
	(8.369)	(5.005)	(3.956)	(3.775)	(2.385)	(1.936)
Observations	45	71	76	45	71	76

R-squared	0.29	0.42	0.45	0.51	0.61	0.62
Adj. R-squared	0.22	0.39	0.42	0.46	0.58	0.60

Standard errors in parentheses
$^{***}p < 0.001$, $^{**}p < 0.01$, $^{*}p < 0.05$

Table 12.4 FDI inflows OLS Model 6 beta coefficients

	(4)	(5)	(6)
Variables	logfdiin2012	logfdiin5y	logfdiin10y
gdpgr2012	−0.02		
	(0.054)		
trade2012	−0.00		
	(0.003)		
inf2012	0.07		
	(0.035)		
gdpgr5y		0.09	
		(0.055)	
trade5y		−0.00	
		(0.003)	
inf5y		0.03	
		(0.050)	
gdpgr10y			0.04
			(0.058)
trade10y			−0.01*
			(0.002)
inf10y			−0.00
			(0.000)
gci12	2.06***	1.82***	1.87***
	(0.379)	(0.328)	(0.244)
Constant	−0.54	0.45	0.53
	(1.747)	(1.648)	(1.173)
Observations	52	76	79
R-squared	0.42	0.39	0.51
Adj. R-squared	0.37	0.36	0.48

Standard errors in parentheses
***$p < 0.001$, **$p < 0.01$, *$p < 0.05$

coefficients and the results show that *GCI*12 is significant (Coef. 1.87***, 1.82***, 2.06***) regarding 10, 5 years average and 2012 reference concerning FDI inflows under standardized variables (Table 12.4). It is worth mentioning here that the gci beta regarding FDI inflows are (0.7735433, 0.721484, 0.723533) respectively.

12.10 Conclusions

Copyright laws grow as technology develops to accomplish an adequate balance between private rights and public interests. The existing legal environment does not offer sufficient protection in the changing technological environment but there is a need to go on with supporting technological advancement while protecting users' data and interests. Currently, technology is changing at a faster rhythm than the development of law and the rule of law which means that this failure is transplanted into IPRs regulation. Competition is a vital factor regarding industry value and so utilizing the econometric models finds that competition is a significant factor in attracting FDI.

The brief econometric analysis further shows the significance of the competitiveness and ZEKIPR index in attracting FDI inflows.[132] As mentioned earlier, the analysis of the legal background of copyright and trademark law shows a continuous development of the legal regulation and enforcement of IP rights. Copyright law must advance the creation, dissemination, and preservation of works that are valuable to society, expressed not only by traditional means but also by electronic means. For instance, developing digital goods and services makes the introduction of electronic trademarks necessary. The current legal environment does not tender sufficient protection in the changing technological environment, but there is a need to support technological advancement while protecting users' data and interests.

Bibliography

1. Craig, C., & Kerr, I. (2020). The death of the AI author, 52 *Ottawa L. Rev.*, 31. https://rdo-olr.org/2021/the-death-of-the-ai-author/.
2. Gervais, D. (2020). Is intellectual property law ready for artificial intelligence? *GRUR International, 69*, 117–118.
3. Rub, G. A. (2020). Owning nothingness: Between the legal and the social norms of the art world. 2019 *BYU L. Rev.*, 1147.
4. Pedraza-Fariña, L. G., & Whalen, R. (2020). A network theory of patentability. 87 *U. CHI. L. REV.*, *63*, 63–65.
5. Grynberg, M. (2019–2020). AI and the death of trademark law. *Kentucky Law Journal, 108*(2), 198.
6. Diamantis, M. E. (2021). Algorithms acting badly: A solution from corporate law. *The George Washington Law Review, 89*, 801.
7. Hilty, R. M., et al. (2020). *Intellectual property justification for artificial intelligence*. Max Planck Institute for Innovation & Competition, Research Paper No. 20-02.
8. Cotter, T. F. (2021, April). Damages for noneconomic harm in intellectual property law. *Hastings Law Journal, 72*, 1055.
9. Zekos, G. (2014, September). Denying patentability of scientific theories. *Journal of Intellectual Property Rights, 19*, 337–346.
10. Zekos, G. (2006). Software patenting. *The Journal of World Intellectual Property, 9*(4), 426–444.
11. Zekos, G. (2013). Impact of IPRs on FDI and trade. *The IUP Journal of Management Research, XII*(4), 7–25. www.iupindia.jn
12. Zekos, G. (2013, July). Interrelation of intellectual property rights and competitiveness: FDI inwards and FDI outwards. *Journal of Intellectual Property Rights, 18*, 338–350. www.niscair.res.in
13. Zekos, G. (2013). IPRs' impact upon FDI. PhD Thesis. Economics Department, University of Peloponnese Tripoli Hellas www.uop.gr.

[132] See Georgios I. Zekos, *Copyrights and Trademarks in Cyberspace: A Legal and Economic Analysis*, 15 Chi.-Kent J. Intell. Prop. 313 (2016). https://scholarship.kentlaw.iit.edu/ckjip/vol15/iss1/10

14. Zekos, G. (2006). Patenting abstract ideas in nanotechnology. *The Journal of World Intellectual Property, 9*(1), 113–136.
15. Zekos, G. (2013) The value of IPRs and competitiveness regarding FDI: Linear and non-linear analysis. *Journal of Computational Optimization in Economics and Finance, 5*(2). www.novapublishers.com
16. Zekos, G. (2016). *Copyrights and trademarks in cyberspace: A legal and economic analysis*, 15 *chi.-Kent J. Intell. Prop.*, 313. https://scholarship.kentlaw.iit.edu/ckjip/vol15/iss1/10

Chapter 13
Conclusions

The digital economy, while delivering many benefits, at the same time, is gradually captured and distorted and so markets may seem competitive, yet are colonized by selected innovation supporting the ecosystem's value chains. It is worth noting that following the view that markets can self-correct and deliver optimal innovation leads the courts to undervalue the distorting consequences engendered by leading platforms. Digital platforms have achieved an economic status which they try to keep up or even augment by utilizing innovation factors blocking the entrance of any new competitor. In other words, digital platforms and in general big firms have imposed their understanding as the competitive and anticompetitive basis upon court's ruling and so they have shared the rule of law according to their own interests and not the interest of the market. Hence, innovation that is driven by powerful firms disregards the interest of consumers by serving the interests of these powerful firms, rather than society. Thus, there is a need of recognizing the different dynamics of digital markets concerning competition.

Digital transformation of manufacturing along with networking and intelligence is the means of accomplishing industrial transformation and so triumphing in the digital economy via intelligent manufacturing. Is the objective to reverse the present-day AI technological development? The objective is not to reverse the AI technological development but to manage AI in ways useful for the globe.

Competition laws are essential in balancing the relative role of private and public power in the marketplace and so shaping global business conduct and often influencing which products are produced and consumed. It could be said that antitrust enforcement has been undermined under the idea that market power is rationalized by economic efficiency and so the decline of antitrust enforcement has adversely impacted workers which means adding to increasing inequality.

Competition policy and competition law are reshaping due to new market realities such as digital market gatekeepers, the financialization of corporations, and highly concentrated markets. Moreover, competition policy has wider societal influences beyond competition, embracing consequences on democracy, economic inequality, growth and innovation, privacy, and geopolitical implications. To that extent,

© The Author(s), under exclusive license to Springer Nature Switzerland AG 2023
G. I. Zekos, *Artificial Intelligence and Competition*, Contributions to Economics,
https://doi.org/10.1007/978-3-031-48083-6_13

competition policy plays an essential role in enforcing against anticompetitive business conduct.

It is characteristic that the overall structure of and approach to antitrust law in the EU vests the Commission with much greater option to deviate from well-known economic principles and procedural best practices in its antitrust enforcement and decision-making. Hence, antitrust enforcement at the EU level is driven by the European Commission, a political body, and fundamentally unreviewed and unchecked by EU courts which means that EU antitrust is less economically grounded, and certainly more politicized, than in the United States.

Formalistic per se rules that used to portray US antitrust doctrine gave way to a case-by-case assessment of the economic effects of company conduct which means that antitrust enforcement gradually began to count on economic and econometrics theories that are now all but mandatory in antitrust litigation and so the Chicago School incorporated in competition price theory and concepts such as market power, entry, and efficiency.[1] It seems that the US Supreme Court abandoned most per se rules, leaving only naked horizontal price fixing and market division, in addition a reformed per se rule for tie-ins, under per se treatment[2] and so even practices that resemble per se offenses are tested for possible efficiencies.[3] It is specified that that price fixing is good for consumers when it initiates ruinous competition, such as price wars that drive prices below costs.[4]

The Court's "rule of reason"[5] leads to considering pronouncements that contradict the legislative intent not mentioning that it is well recognized that the courts are ill-suited to participate in the searching economic analysis regularly necessitated by the rule of reason.[6] In other words, it seems that competition law has moved away from the competition ideal encompassing the diffuse of economic and political

[1]Ohio v. Am. Express Co., 138 S. Ct. 2274, 2290 (2018) (approval precedent recognizing that the legality of a vertical restraint turned on whether it would enhance both "competition and consumer welfare").

[2]Leegin Creative Leather Prods., Inc. v PSKS, Inc., 551 U.S. 877, 900 (2007) (minimum resale price maintenance subject to the rule of reason); Illinois Tool Works Inc. v. Indep. Ink, Inc., 547 U.S. 28, 42–43 (2006) (no presumption of market power or rule of per se illegality for patent tieins); State Oil Co. v. Kahn, 522 U.S. 3, 17 (1997) (maximum resale price maintenance subject not per se illegal and subject to the rule of reason); Cont'l T.V., Inc. v. GTE Sylvania Inc., 433 U.S. 36, 58 (1977) (territorial restrictions subject to the rule of reason).

[3]PolyGram Holding Inc. v. FTC, 416 F.3d 29 (2005). Jefferson Parish Hosp. Dist. No. 2 v. Hyde, 466 U.S. 2 (1984).

[4]Arizona v. Maricopa Cnty. Med. Soc'y, 457 U.S. at 351.

[5]In re Nat'l Collegiate Athletic Ass'n Athletic Grant-in-Aid Cap Antitrust Litig., No. 14-CV-02758-CW, 2018 WL 1524005, at *8 (N.D. Cal. Mar. 28, 2018) (quoting Oltz v. St. Peter's Cmty. Hosp., 861 F.2d 1440, 1449 (ninth Cir. 1988)) several justices called the rule of reason "amorphous," "unbounded," and "unruly." Oneok, Inc. v Learjet, Inc., 575 US 373, 398 (2015) (Scalia, J. dissenting, with Roberts,C.J. joining). F.T.C. v. Actavis, Inc., 570 U.S. 136, 177 (2013) (Roberts, C.J., dissenting, with Justices Scalia and Thomas joining).

[6]New York v. Deutsche Telekom AG, 439 F. Supp. 3d 179, at 186 (S.D.N.Y. 2020); McMorris v. Williamsport Hosp., 597 F. Supp. 899, 909 (M.D. Pa. 1984)

power from the hands of a few in order to foster more opportunities to compete, advance, and win. To that extent, Maurice E. Stucke and Ariel Ezrachi[7] argue that "Until recently, the Executive branch failed to enforce the antitrust laws and deter the Tech Barons' anticompetitive behavior. The courts failed to do their job of adjudicating the laws in light of the Congressional intent." Also, Maurice E. Stucke[8] argues that "courts push their own economic beliefs, without regard for the congressional intent and aims of the antitrust laws. Regardless of who wins, the rule of law (and those most dependent on the antitrust law) suffer" denoting that antitrust law is not applied as the law but economics overrules, in a way, antitrust legal principles which means that economics have conquered the law at least in the competition field. In other words, in competition, the rule of economics is applied instead of the rule of law.

Antitrust law allows economic coordination and so antitrust law essentially allocates economic coordination right. In addition, antitrust law promotes competition and yet privacy law assures a level of privacy stronger than that which would be delivered by the market. It could be said that robust competition is crucial to preserving a country's part as leading economy in health care, telecommunications, financial services, and global shipping in which there is competition. Competition regulations must not only prevent further concentration but also reduce the current positions of monopolies.

Technology has made antitrust more relevant to international affairs for the reason that technology firms are central to national security. Antitrust enforcement damages national security by advantaging foreign corporations over national ones.

It is worth noting that antitrust is costly and slow.[9] Moreover, enforcement of antitrust laws involves handling competing aims and expectations about what the law is expected to achieve and how it should go about doing so. It seems that antitrust law has become highly reliant on technical evidence and complex economic analysis.

Antitrust is slow for the reason that it is enforced through court orders that require time-consuming lawsuits. It is vital that antitrust rules minimize the costs of judicial error in digital markets. It could be said that competition law outlaws practices generating or perpetuating market power on a basis other than economic efficiency. Furthermore, antitrust enforcement obstructs local technological advancement by

---

[7]Maurice E. Stucke & Ariel Ezrachi, Innovation Misunderstood, https://ssrn.com/abstract=4547201 p 60.

[8]Maurice E. Stucke, The good, the bad, and the ugly of US antitrust, Journal of Antitrust Enforcement, 2023, 11, 283–292 p 283 at 292 ("The big-tech barons continue to dominate, and will likely continue doing so with their advantages in artificial intelligence. To fix the market power problem, the courts must recognize, as they once did, the respective roles of the Judiciary and the Congress in regulating the economy, Congress must do its job in updating the antitrust laws, and the agencies, not only now, but with future administrations, must take care that these laws are faithfully executed.")

[9]Erik Hovenkamp & Steven C. Salop, Asymmetric Stakes in Antitrust Litigation 4 (USC CLASS Research Papers Series, No. CLASS20–12, 2020), https://ssrn.com/abstract=3563843

giving foreign corporations a competitive advantage. Competition laws should promote economic efficiency via a standardized competition process under ax ante rules.

It has to be taken into account that the US antitrust laws were originally invented to protect not only a broad range of consumer interests but also far-reaching societal priorities embracing the maintenance of open markets and system stability. Hence, the antitrust laws avert extreme concentrations of economic and political power that could deform not only free enterprise but also democracy itself. It is argued that moving antitrust law away from economics would erode coherence and predictability because economics offers a common language for analyzing competitive behaviors. Competition between corporations has also resulted in a decline in trust between them challenging prospective collaboration within and between industries influencing innovation. Amplified automation via AI diminishes the significance of labor costs in total production costs and so the relocation of productive activities is attractive.

Antitrust rules are characteristically proscriptive, rather than prescriptive and so they prohibit corporations from engaging in certain conducts instead of mandating a certain market outcome. It is worth noting that antitrust law protects competition and not competitors which means that there is a need of standardization of principles of conduct adopted by all players in a market allowing equality concerning the opportunities of function. Effective antitrust enforcement demands a deep understanding of market realities and facts to ascertain whether the conduct at issue harms competition and the competitive process.

It has to be taken into consideration that monopoly and the prospect of monopoly are the foundation of a capitalist system[10] but G.I. Zekos argues that the existence of a fair competition among companies towards conquering a market and the global market is the element of legalizing the efforts of all companies leading to the prosperity of consumers via the offer of the best goods and services at a rightful price in the market. If competition is strong, consumers take the higher percentage of the surplus value coming out from the difference between the price they paid and the price they were willing to pay and consequently the rest of the surplus value is taken by producers.

The existing IP systems for copyright and patents are unable to offer legal stability, since many matters and inferences linked to AI-generated outputs remain unresolved. While those inferences do not concern legal experts due to the level of AI technology, it is possible that in the long run, adjustments or an entirely new system would be required which means that technology developments now justify public discussion concerning regulating AI.

It has to be taken into account that the substitution of human ingenuity in the invention procedure or producing inventions without much human input necessitates recalibrating patentability. Moreover, patentability inferences and alterations are

[10]Joseph A. Schumpeter, Capitalism, Socialism, And Democracy 825 (1942).

dominant in the face of AI's rapid technological transformations in order for patent systems to accomplish their objectives.

There is a need of striking the right balance between the safeguarding of free competition and the demand to make certain that all corporations are postulated with the opportunity to compete on a level playing field for the benefit of consumers. Moreover, there is a need of making certain that all corporations have an enticement to advance constantly their goods for the reason that they will receive a suitable and rewarding return for their efforts.

Algorithmic stock manipulation is hard to prosecute unless there is a guilty human pulling the strings[11] and antitrust law has yet to see its first case alleging purely algorithmic collusion but granting AI legal personality will allow prosecuting all AI legal persons.

It is characteristic that the dependence on case-by-case adjudication instead of rulemaking denies both the public and market participants of any real prospect to take part in the formation of substantive antitrust rules.[12] It has to be taken into consideration that efficiency means implementing consumers' long-run interests via the employment of a fair competition process establishing a competitive market functioning being the goal of antitrust as defined by the socio-political values of antitrust guiding any antitrust policy. It seems that consumer welfare and price effects are the sole criteria of harm to competition. Robert Pitofsky[13] has stressed that the value of politics concerning competition and not merely examining economic matters.

Can growth via anticompetitive methods be allowed? Boosting growth is perhaps the most important argument in favor of implementing a more restrained competition regime.[14] On the other hand, the production of quality goods in low prices in an open market by big corporations under unique competition terms could be allowed.

It is now long recognized that aggressive but fair/legitimate competition, even if its outcomes in foreclosure of competitors, is not only presumed but also welcome. As Judge Easterbrook[15] has stated "injuries to rivals are by-products of vigorous competition" and therefore "to deter aggressive conduct is to deter competition." To that extent, the Court of Justice of the European Union (CJEU) emphasized in Post

[11] Holbrook v. Prodomax Automation, Ltd., No. 17-cv-219, 2019 WL 6840187, at *3 (W.D. Mich. Aug. 26, 2019) (granting summary judgment to Nachi). Holbrook v. Prodomax Automation, Ltd., No. 17-cv-00219, 2020 U.S. Dist. LEXIS 207134, at *1 (W.D. Mich. Nov. 5, 2020) (listing remaining defendants)

[12] Rohit Chopra & Lina M. Khan, The Case for "Unfair Methods of Competition" Rulemaking, 87 U. CHI. L. REV. 357, 362–63 (2018)

[13] Robert Pitofsky, The Political Content of Antitrust, 127 U. PA. L. REV. 1051, 1051–52 (1979) ("Because interpretations that exclude all but economic concerns have lately become so influential, however, it is important to explain why economic concerns, although properly of paramount importance, should not control exclusively.").

[14] Brook Horowitz, How Asean countries can turn the tide on corruption, FINANCIAL TIMES (Apr. 24, 2020), https://www.ft.com/content/ef7426be-7500-11ea-90ce-5fb6c07a27f2

[15] Ball Mem'l Hosp., Inc. v. Mut. Hosp. Ins., Inc., 784 F.2d 1325, 1338 (seventh Cir. 1986).

Danmark[16] that “competition on the merits may, by definition, lead to the departure from the market or the marginalization of competitors that are less efficient and so less attractive to consumers from the point of view of, among other things, price, choice, quality or innovation.” Hence, negative effects to rivals does not make exclusion automatically anticompetitive and so anticompetitive conduct is conduct that “unnecessarily excludes or handicaps competitors” by impairing competition without benefiting consumers or advancing progress and innovation. Christian Bergqvist[17] argues that “Potential competitors might even be reluctant to enter the market if the incumbent has established a reputation for aggressive pricing confronted with competition and the ability to rely on state resources. These are lessons applicable across sectors other than mail and, thus, have relevance to all areas where former incumbents are made subject to competition.”

Exclusionary practices encompass corporations’ freedom to choose their partners as they see fit. Moreover, corporations are free to decide the terms and conditions of dealing with competitors and market actors given that this is not the outcome of abuse of dominance, monopolization or attempt to monopolize, and it does not threaten the competitive process.[18] It could be said that the essential elements of anticompetitive exclusion encompass the ability and power to exclude, the abuse/ exploitation of that power, and the resulting competitive harm.[19]

The global feature of economic integration has been magnified rapidly via advancing AI technology by generating an AAI global society with electronic goods and services to overtake classical goods and services served at the moment to humans and in the near future to AAI humanoids and so new countries such as China, India, and Brazil have become key actors in the globally digital economy, to some extent due to their increasing participation in classical and digital GVCs.

High-tech markets present complicated problems for the development of antitrust doctrine and policymakers around the globe are expecting the adoption of regulations. There is a need of humans to be advanced to their spiritual essence due to the fact that their creator has given this capacity. Is there a part in the human brain where knowledge and capacities are stored or is there the capability to communicate via our brain to the spiritual Cosmos generated by our creator in order to find answers accordingly? Will AAI creatures have the capacity to function in both worlds that of material and spiritual life? Will AAI humanoids be merely machines or will be

---

[16]Case C-209/10 Post Danmark A/S v Konkurrencer°adet, 2012 EU:C:2012:172. Aspen Skiing Co. v. Aspen Highlands Skiing Corp., 472 U.S. 585, 597 (1985). 67. Advanced Health-Care Services v. Radford Community Hospital, 910 F.2d 139, 148 (fourth Cir. 1990).

[17]Christian Bergqvist, Post Danmark – More than just another serial infringer, https://ssrn.com/abstract=4477447 p 24 see Case C-413/14P - Intel, recitals 138–144. Case C-680/20 - Unilever, paras 40 and 59–60.

[18]United States v. Colgate & Co., 250 U.S. 300, 307 (1919); Guidance on the Commission’s Enforcement Priorities in Applying Article 82 of the Treaty to Abusive Exclusionary Conduct by Dominant Undertakings, para 75; Case T-201-04 Microsoft v. Commission [2007] ECR II-3601, § 319, 330–336.

[19]Grason Elec. Co v. Sacramento Mun. Util. Dist., 571 F. Supp. 1504, 1512.

creatures of a new more advanced spirituality having the capacity of giving birth alike humans? Will AAI humanoids be multiplied via their manufacture in a factory?

The AI development field is competitive enough, in which many open-source tools are available for developers to benefit from without infringing on copyright or taking advantage of someone else's work. To that extent, greater clarity on laws concerning data use could support innovation. It could be said that in AI era, operative interventions are those that disincentivize anticompetitive behaviors in the first place and make available computational means to track violations.

It has to be taken into account that opening the door to protectionist considerations outstrips the traditional goals of competition law. Competition regulators must adapt their operations to respond better to new market conditions and business practices. Unlike the United States, the EU and China are not strongly influenced by the Chicago School's laissez-faire approach, and consequently competition law enforcement remains more energetic.[20] Moreover, antitrust enforcers have to improve their technical skills and enhance their capability to discover whether algorithmically driven practices hurt consumers. It could be said that if antitrust authorities can advance their enforcement of traditional antitrust law by utilizing AI technologies and so diminishing to some degree the requirement for adopting ex ante regulations. There is a need of less economic analysis for competition cases and subsequently applying ex ante standard rules.

It is worth noting that Chicago School antitrust analyses were not based on "antipathy to government intervention" and relatively the conclusions of the Chicago School analyses stemmed merely from viewing "antitrust policy through the lens of price theory." The Harvard School was influenced more by institutional competence and other process-based considerations than the broad conceptual economic framework that motivated the Chicago School. Taking into account that the Chicago School argues for the robustness of markets and the need for minimal need for regulatory interventions, the Harvard School focuses on the institutional limitations of governmental correction of even real market failures and so both schools are non-intervention in a different context.

Digital algorithms are being used to answer a challenge facing regulators in allocating auditing attention optimally and finding the needs. Algorithmic tools are utilized to detect tax evasion and regulators increasingly use AI tools as a means of setting enforcement priorities. Moreover, algorithmic devices have accomplished demonstrable improvements in government agencies' capability to forecast accurately.[21] Hence, digital algorithms could diminish delays that arise when governmental decisions depend on human decision-makers.

---

[20] William E Kovacic, The Chicago Obsession in the Interpretation of US Antitrust History, 87 University Of Chicago Law Review 459 (2020),

[21] David Freeman Engstrom Et Al., Government By Algorithm: Artificial Intelligence In Federal Administrative Agencies 22–29 (2020), https://www-cdn.law.stanford.edu/wpcontent/uploads/2020/02/ACUS-AI-Report.pdf

It is characteristic that the utilization of non-representative data sets is introducing partiality into algorithms and so algorithms trained on non-representative data sets generate discriminatory outcomes, posing a potential risk which means that AAI technology has not only to advance algorithms training via suitably objective data sets but also to correct automatically any mistakes prior to the utilization of algorithms.

Algorithms employ a set of rules or procedures that automatically produce outputs based on data inputs and decisional parameters. Moreover, algorithms are expected to facilitate improvements in antitrust regulators' decision-making about how to target scarce resources for enforcement investigation. Thus, AI tools can be used to deter and prevent cartel formation[22] and so screening for anticompetitive behaviors. Moreover, AI algorithms can autonomously generate other AI algorithms[23] which means that in an AAI society, decisions will be made by AAI algorithms produced and advanced by AAI systems concerning competition in an AAI economy run by AAI humanoids.

Antitrust algorithm is rationalized by the rapid pace of market activity and so antitrust regulators need data access at a speed echoing the market activity which means that antitrust officials should persist on including real-time sharing of digital data on a case-by-case basis as part of the settlement agreements. Also, Antitrust by algorithms advances the objectives of competition law in a dynamic market environment making it vital for antitrust regulators to exercise carefulness as they move forward with greater dependence on algorithmic devices.

It seems that EU enforces competition laws by taking on entrenched monopolies and the United States basically moves backward, opting for no antitrust enforcement and permitting concentration to grow. It is worth mentioning here that in enacting the principal antitrust laws, Congress wanted to check the power of large-scale capital by protecting consumers and producers from dominant corporate sellers and buyers and so keeping markets open to all comers which means defending the political system against corporate capture.[24] Besides, even though the Supreme Court ascertained strict rules against price fixing, it restrained the aptitude of the government to challenge corporate mergers and so the United States moved toward a less concentrated industrial structure which means that the antitrust laws augmented the rise of monopolies and oligopolies. Hence, it seems that there is a need of restoring the notion of "free enterprise"[25] and so redistributing power and wealth to all people and not merely to an elite. To that extent, it could be said that the objectively implementation of AI technology will allow the objective applicability of competition law in order to have real competition on the market contributing to the wealth of people and society. Additionally, it is supposed that in an AAI market, competition

[22] Sabine Zigelski & Lynn Robertson, What Can Make Competition Compliance Programmes Really Effective? CPI Antitrust Chronicle (Nov. 2021)

[23] Tom Simonite, AI Software Learns to Make AI Software, MIT TECH. REV., Jan. 18, 2017.

[24] Goldberg v. Kelly, 397 U.S. 254 (1970).

[25] United States v. Topco Assoc., 405 U.S. 596, 610 (1972).

will function objectively by the implementation of AI competition law and so achieving the best results for the global AI economy. In any other case, the manipulation of competition via AAI technology will generate AAI tyranny for AAI humanoids being slaves at the hands of the management group of the global AAI technology which means the emergence of the same phenomena and malfunctioning of the globe on a different dimension due to AAI technology.

Taking into account that AI boosts competitiveness, the question to be answered is if the essence of competition has altered due to the use of AI technology. The answer is that current AI technology utilized by companies in a human-centered economy has not modified the context of competition but AI has made it more difficult to detect activities which are anticompetitive in comparison with the same activities contacted via conventional humans' agreements. Meanwhile, an advancing AI may bring the "end of competition as we know it" and so AI will bring competition in swiftness and speed on searching data along with dig data collections which means that anticompetitive conduct will encompass technical electronic blocking of searching or collecting data since humans' involvement will not take place in an AAI economy. Anticompetitive agreements, under current human understanding, among AAI systems functioned by AAI humanoids might take place but they will have a different impact on a fully automated system fortified with various technological devices precluding any anticompetitive activities. Cartel agreements, under current anticompetitive understanding, among AAI systems might bring only advantages for AAI society instead of generating any anticompetitive collision in a fully automated economy. Thus, in an AAI economy run by AAI humanoids, where is questionable if humans will have any impact on AAI economy, the context of competition and activities that will be considered as anticompetitive will be modified due to the fact that AAI technology will function objectively which means that the imposition of an objectively fair competition will be the target and so a self-correcting AAI system will prohibit any malfunctions not only concerning competition but also of the whole AAI in an AAI society.

G.I. Zekos[26] has written that "Various electronic forces are fighting every day to overtake control of the global electronic network but at least there is an intention to utilize it as democratic as it is possible and in compliance with their plans for global hegemony. The goal should be to prohibit a "crazy hegemony" to use the electronic network to bring catastrophe (καταστροφή) and chaos (χάος) over earth" and so, concerning the advancement of AAI technology, there is an urgent need of prohibiting any "crazy hegemony" to use AAI generating catastrophe (καταστροφή) and chaos (χάος) over earth by eliminating human life.

The rise of digital platforms generates concerns around their effects on markets and society leading to alterations in the regulatory landscape and so authorities should impose more stringent remedies as they increase their certainty on the

[26] G Zekos, Demolishing State's sole power over Sovereignty & Territory via Electronic Technology & Cyberspace, 2013 Journal of Internet Law, Volume 17 Number 5 November 2013 27-41 Aspen Publications- Wolters Kluwer p15.

negative effects of a particular conduct. E-commerce platforms have a greater advantage over individual merchants for the reason that they have access to insights spawned from information from all their merchants, which can be unfair particularly if the platform sells the same products to their merchants. Large corporations participate in anticompetitive practices by steadily applying for patents and monopolizing related IP in a particular space and so generating a barrier for small-tech businesses and start-ups. G.I. Zekos considers that the stimulation of competitive structures, specifically in digital markets, rests on setting positive standards and principles enabling market access for new technologies and business models.

Data are part of AI innovation and denoted that IP laws had been set up to support start-ups to protect their innovation from competition by protecting their data. Nonetheless, IP laws do help start-ups handle competition, competition in various industries has encouraged the adoption of AI and the software development has moderated the barriers to augmenting AI innovation further. Nevertheless, the adoption of AI diverges from one industry to another.

Legislatures and antitrust agencies must form legal requirements for data-sharing to make certain that all corporations provide needed data access to antitrust authorities. Moreover, international regulatory cooperation and even data-sharing will also be imperative.

Finally, it could be said that the purpose of antitrust laws is to offer "a free and open market economy" along with fair competition providing low prices, high-quality products and services, more choices, and illustrious innovation which means that the objective of antitrust laws is to guarantee fair competition by overturning activities like price fixing, and monopolies which is applicable to an AI environment.

References

1. Horowitz, B. (2020, April 24). How Asean countries can turn the tide on corruption. *Financial Times*. https://www.ft.com/content/ef7426be-7500-11ea-90ce-5fb6c07a27f2
2. Engstrom, D. F., et al. (2020). *Government by algorithm: Artificial intelligence in federal administrative agencies*, 22–29. https://www-cdn.law.stanford.edu/wpcontent/uploads/2020/02/ACUS-AI-Report.pdf
3. Hovenkamp, E., & Salop, S. C. (2020). *Asymmetric stakes in antitrust litigation 4* (USC CLASS Research Papers Series, No. CLASS20-12), https://ssrn.com/abstract=3563843
4. Chopra, R., & Khan, L. M. (2018). The case for "unfair methods of competition" rulemaking, 87 U. *CHI L REV, 357*, 362–363.
5. Zigelski, S., & Robertson, L. (2021, November). What can make competition compliance Programmes really effective? *CPI Antitrust Chronicle*.
6. Kovacic, W. E. (2020). The Chicago obsession in the interpretation of US antitrust history. *University Of Chicago Law Review, 87*, 459.
7. Zekos, G. (2013, November). Demolishing state's sole power over sovereignty & territory via electronic technology & cyberspace. *Journal of Internet Law, 17*(5), 27–41.

Printed in the USA
CPSIA information can be obtained
at www.ICGtesting.com
CBHW071603040824
12687CB00005B/305

9 783031 480829